T0338217

Machine Learning and Big Data with kdb+/q

Founded in 1807, John Wiley & Sons is the oldest independent publishing company in the United States. With offices in North America, Europe, Australia and Asia, Wiley is globally committed to developing and marketing print and electronic products and services for our customers' professional and personal knowledge and understanding.

The Wiley Finance series contains books written specifically for finance and investment professionals as well as sophisticated individual investors and their financial advisors. Book topics range from portfolio management to e-commerce, risk management, financial engineering, valuation and financial instrument analysis, as well as much more.

For a list of available titles, visit our Web site at www.WileyFinance.com.

Machine Learning and Big Data with kdb+/q

JAN NOVOTNY
PAUL A. BILOKON
ARIS GALIOTOS
FRÉDÉRIC DÉLÈZE

WILEY

This edition first published 2020

Registered office
John Wiley & Sons Ltd, The Atrium, Southern Gate, Chichester, West Sussex, PO19 8SQ, United Kingdom

For details of our global editorial offices, for customer services and for information about how to apply for permission to reuse the copyright material in this book please see our website at www.wiley.com.

Library of Congress Cataloging-in-Publication Data is Available:

ISBN 978-1-119-40475-0 (hardback)
ISBN 978-1-119-40474-3 (ePDF)
ISBN 978-1-119-40473-6 (epub)

Cover Design: Wiley
Cover Image: © Hanna Begayeva/Shutterstock

Set in 10/12pt STIXTwoText by SPi Global, Chennai, India

Printed in Great Britain by TJ International Ltd, Padstow, Cornwall, UK

10 9 8 7 6 5 4 3 2 1

J.N.: To Andrea and Evelina

P.A.B.: To Oleksandr (Alex) and Nataliya Bilokon

A.G.: To those who seek elegance

F.D.: To Victor

Contents

Preface

HISTORY OF kdb+ AND q

kdb+ and q are intellectual descendants of an older programming language, APL. The acronym "APL" stands for "A Programming Language", the name of a book (Iverson, 1962) written by the Canadian computer scientist Kenneth (Ken) Eugene Iverson (1920–2004). Iverson worked on automatic data processing during his years at Harvard (1955–1960), when he found that the conventional mathematical notation wasn't well suited to the task. He proceeded to develop his own notation, borrowing ideas from linear algebra, tensor analysis, and operators à la Oliver Heaviside. This notation was further elaborated at IBM, where Iverson worked alongside Adin Falkoff (1921–2010) from 1960 until 1980. The collaboration between Iverson and Falkoff would span nearly two decades.

The two main ideas behind APL are the efficient-notation idea (Montalbano, 1982) and the stored-program idea. The stored-program idea, which dates back to John von Neumann (1903–1957), see von Neumann (1945), and amounts to being able to store (and process) code as data, has been taken a step further in languages such as q, where function names evaluate to their source code. The efficient-notation idea, the idea that developing a concise and expressive syntax is critical to solving complex iterative problems correctly and efficiently, was pioneered by Iverson. In the preface of Iverson (1962) he defines a programming language in the following terms:

> Applied mathematics is largely concerned with the design and analysis of explicit procedures for calculating the exact or approximate values of various functions. Such explicit procedures are called algorithms or programs. Because an effective notation for the description of programs exhibits considerable syntactic structure, it is called a programming language.

Later, in 1979, Iverson would give a Turing Award Lecture with the title *Notation as a Tool of Thought* (Iverson, 1979). Iverson's notation was effective as it was simple. It relied on simple rules of precedence based on right-to-left evaluation. The fundamental data structure in APL is a multidimensional array. Languages such as APL and its progenitors are sometimes referred to as array, vector, or multidimensional programming languages because they implicitly generalise scalar operations to higher-dimensional objects.

Iverson's notation was known as "Iverson's notation" within IBM until the name "APL" was suggested by Falkoff. After the publication of *A Programming Language* in 1962, the notation was used to describe the IBM System/360 computer.

Iverson and Falkoff then focused on the implementation of the programming language. An implementation on System/360 was made available at IBM in 1966 and released to the outside world in 1968.

In 1980, Iverson moved to I. P. Sharp Associates (IPSA), a Canadian software firm based in Calgary. There he was joined by Roger K. W. Hui (b. 1953) and Arthur Whitney (b. 1957). The three of them continued to work on APL, adding new ideas to the programming language. Hui, whose family emigrated to Canada from Hong Kong in 1966, was first exposed to APL at the University of Alberta. Whitney had a background in pure mathematics and had worked with APL at the University of Toronto and Stanford. He met Iverson for the first time well before he joined IPSA, at the age of 11, in 1969. Iverson had been his father's friend at Harvard. Whitney's family then lived in Alberta but would visit Iverson in his house in Mount Kisco. There Iverson introduced Whitney to programming and APL.

In 1988, Whitney joined Morgan Stanley, where he helped develop A+, an APL-like programming language with a smaller set of primitive functions optimised for fast processing of large volumes of time series data. Unlike APL, A+ allowed functions to have up to nine formal parameters, used semicolons to separate statements (so a single statement could be split into multiple lines), used the last statement of a function as its result, and introduced the so-called dependencies which functioned as global variables. The programming language is now available online, http://www.aplusdev.org/. Programmers can also download the `kapl` font, which includes the special characters used by APL and A+.

One summer weekend in 1989, Whitney visited Iverson at Kiln Farm and produced – "'on one page and in one afternoon'" Hui (1992) – an interpreter fragment on the AT&T 3B1 computer. Hui studied this fragment and on its basis developed an interpreter for another APL variant, J. Unlike APL and A+, J used the ASCII character set. It included advanced features, such as support for parallel MIMD operations. Whitney's original fragment appears under the name *Incunabulum* in an appendix in Hui's book, see Hui (1992)[1]. Other ideas by Whitney found their way into J: orienting primitives on the leading axis, using prefix rather than suffix for agreement, and total array ordering (Hui, 2006, 1995). Ken Iverson, his son, Eric Iverson, and Hui all ended up working in a company called Jsoftware in the 1990s–2000s.

Whitney left Morgan Stanley in 1993 and co-founded Kx Systems with Janet Lustgarten, where he developed another APL variant, called `k`. On its basis he developed a columnar in-memory time series database called `kdb`. Kx Systems was under an exclusive agreement with UBS. It expired in 1996 and `k` and `kdb` became generally available. `ksql` was added in 1998 as a layer on top of `k`. Some developers regard it as part of the `k` language. `ksql` includes SQL-like constructs, such as `select`.

`kdb+` was released in June 2003. This was more or less a total rewrite of `kdb` for 64-bit systems based on the 4th version of `k` and `q`, a macro language layer (or a query language, hence the name) on top of `k`, defined in terms of `k`. Both `q` and `k` compile to the same byte code that is executed in the `kdb+` byte interpreter. For example, `type` in `q`

[1]It is also available online: http://code.jsoftware.com/wiki/Essays/Incunabulum.

is the equivalent of `@:` in `k`. `q` is much more readable than `k` and most `kdb+` developers write their code in `q`, not `k`.

The `q` programming language contains its own table query syntax called `q-sql`, which in some ways resembles the traditional SQL.

MOTIVATION FOR THIS BOOK

`q` and `kdb+` stand in a special ground between – as well as overlapping – the purely technical world of software engineering and the world of data science. On the one hand, they can be used for building data services which communicate with each other, whether this is simply to expose a time series database – something `q` excels at – or a chain of Complex Event Processing (CEP) engines calculating analytics and signals in real-time. On the other hand, q's fast execution on vectorised time series enables its application to data science, hypothesis testing, research, pattern recognition, and general statistical and machine learning, these being the fields more traditionally focused on by quantitative analysts.

In practice, the distinction between the two worlds can become blurry: they are both very interconnected. An idea cannot be validated without rigorous and fast[2] statistical analysis and backtesting, where the algorithms and their parameters are well understood, avoiding black-box solutions. It is then natural to expand our model validation code into the actual production predictive analytics. This is facilitated by the reliability, resilience, scalability, and durability of `kdb+`.

q's *notation as a tool of thought and expression* enables it to succeed at both these tasks; its roots, traceable from `APL` and lambda calculus (Church, 1941), its vector language, the fast columnar database, and its query language make `q` a unique all-in-one tool.

Although previously notorious as a language which "cannot be googled" due to its short name and lack of documentation, `q` and `kdb+` are nowadays well-documented from the programming language and infrastructural perspectives, with some excellent sources of material both on https://code.kx.com/ and in books, such as Borror (2015); Psaris (2015).

Moreover, `kdb+` is widely used in the market as a time series database combined with real-time analytics, whereas a lot of the data science, statistical and machine learning (ML) work is done outside of `q`, by extracting data into, or interfacing with, Python or R.

The aim of this book is to demonstrate that a lot of the power of `q` can be harnessed to deal with a large part of everyday data analysis, from data retrieval and data operations – specifically on very large data sets – to performing a range of statistical analysis with a few lines of code.

We then move on to illustrate how we can quickly and productively apply ML algorithms on the data without having to ever leave our `q` instance, or necessarily trouble

[2]The word "fast" here is used both in the sense of computational performance and rapid development, enabling the prototyping of ideas and rapid iteration of changes.

with interfacing with other tools, thus staying close to the data and to our data mapping logic. The raw power of kdb+, its ability to quickly (both in terms of computational speed and rapid rate of development) process, make inferences, and build apps on vast amounts of data using only a few CPU cores, coupled with its mathematical and algebraic design, is still astonishing and deserving of praise.

We hope this book helps provide the tools for someone with a basic grasp of programming, mathematics and statistics to quickly build software which can help them focus on the decision at hand, without worrying about spending too much time on building all the plumbing.

q lends itself well to fast, result-driven and iterative programming, which is the holy grail of every data-driven business: when trying to rapidly assess decisions, we build only what is needed now and attempt to make it easy to generalise later.

q's functional approach, which treats functions as data, usually enables us to answer non-trivial questions with only a few lines of code. Later on, if and when time to invest in scalability becomes available, the code can be generalised or rewritten. Ideas on how the latter is best achieved and tips on how the danger of "read-only" code can be mitigated are covered in this book.

We have found the concise and general nature of q's syntax, when combined with modular code, results in clean and precise implementations. The resultant codebase is much shorter when compared to most other programming languages. q developers find it easier to focus on a few lines of code and scan the whole function in one go, rather than scrolling up and down across hundreds of lines of code.

At the same time, in q's terse world, it is sometimes easy to forget that clarity is paramount for maintainable code. With that in mind, we advocate that a balance between brevity and verbose naming of functions and variables, combined with high code modularity, can lead to code which is easy to share, modify and evolve.

Although we believe the current literature is comprehensive at covering the technical aspects of the language and database themselves, there is still room for covering the data science and ML aspects of q and approaching the language from a quantitative developer's point of view, yet still stressing the importance of engineering in the way we build, develop and maintain our systems.

We therefore believe this book will benefit quantitative analysts, quantitative developers and traders alike, software engineers, data scientists, statistical and machine learning professionals and students, and anyone with an interest in "big data" analysis and, more generally, fast time series databases and functional programming.

The book provides a fresh perspective on how to approach machine learning problems outside of the mainstream paradigm and simultaneously achieve high productivity, accompanied with the joy of discovering and defining one's own paths, learning a functional programming language which has become the de facto time series processing tool in the financial domain, and enabling one "to boldly go where no one has gone before".

CODE STRUCTURE

An inherent part of this book is the significant body of q code. Our objective is to introduce various machine learning methods and illustrate their algorithms and features through a q implementation. By building the implementations of a large number of machine learning algorithms and numerical methods in the form of stand-alone functions, we believe the reader will get an opportunity to both appreciate the nuances of each algorithm and, at the same time, acquire, improve on and challenge their q programming skills. In this sense, we believe that the reader can not only utilise the provided code in their every day work, but also expand on it.

The objective of this book is to provide educational material, to show and encourage our readers to code on their own and learn the principles of machine learning and q through implementation and interactively running and building the code while studying the concept illustrated. We have therefore chosen a slight bias towards clarity of code rather than building a fully optimised production system, which should enable someone new to q to follow the code flow and appreciate the main concepts of both the algorithm and the language itself.

We encourage readers to play – we use the word "play" rather than work – with the functions in order to increase their learning experience and become more fluent in q. For that reason, we have created a github repository available at https://github.com/hanssmail/quantQ/, where we plan to keep the functions and examples created within this book. We encourage readers to participate in contributing to the repository, extend and improve the codebase and implement more machine learning methods.

STRUCTURE OF THE BOOK

We organise the text into four parts. In the first part, we introduce the principles of the q programming language. Although this is not an exhaustive deep dive into kdb+ and all its database features, no prior knowledge of the language itself is expected and the fundamental concepts covered enable us to proceed with the more advanced sections.

In the second part, we focus on the necessary tools required for us to efficiently work with large data sets, and we cover joins, parallelisation, data cleaning operations, and parse trees. Some of these concepts may be at first compelling, yet appreciation of them increases the flexibility of the language syntax, and speeds up calculations tremendously. The section concludes with a set of practical working examples from the financial domain.

In the third part, we present elements of data science. We start with a basic overview of statistics, a first port of call when facing a new data set. We then present one of the most powerful techniques of data science, linear regression. We further extend the concepts of linear regression into a time series domain, where we implement ARIMA models and Granger causality framework. This section also covers complex numbers, Fourier transforms, Eigensystem calculations, and outlier detection techniques. Finally, we show how to simulate time series data for economic research.

The fourth section of the book focuses on machine learning methods. We start with formulating basic principles, before discussing bias-variance trade-off and its remedy: regularisation. In particular, we present two ways of the linear regression regularisation – Ridge regression and the Lasso regression. Further, we discuss several supervised machine learning methods: the nearest neighbours principles – in particular, three different methods for employing the nearest neighbours, neural networks, and tree-based methods – AdaBoost with decision stumps, decision trees, and random forests. We continue with unsupervised machine learning methods, namely the Apriori algorithm, an algorithm initially developed for exploring shopping patterns. We move on to Foundations of Artifical Intelligence and define the multi-arm bandit problem and extend the notions of exploration and exploitation into a Monte Carlo Tree Search algorithm, which is an advanced logic behind many decision engines. We illustrate it on the game engine for the tic-tac-toe game and discuss its links to Alpha Go. Finally, we show some leading findings from econophysics. Last but not least, we conclude the book by encouraging readers to use the programming language beyond the daily workflow and perform some algorithmic art.

PREREQUISITES

We aim to keep the prose of the book such that we fully explain all the presented topics and, at the same time, introduce readers to the intricacies of the q language. It is worth noting that we tacitly assume some relevant prerequisite knowledge. Firstly, we implicitly expect that our readers already have some programming experience. We do not expect prior experience with q, though. Secondly, we assume our readers have a working knowledge of algebra, basic calculus and probability theory. These two ingredients are sufficient to enjoy our book.

About the Authors

Jan Novotny

Jan is an eFX quant trader at Deutsche Bank. Before his current role, he was a front office quant at HSBC in the electronic FX markets. Before joining HSBC team, he was working in the Centre for Econometric Analysis on the high-frequency time series econometric models analysing the dynamics of multivariate price jumps. Prior to that, he worked on several research projects at Manchester Business School, CERGE-EI, and Czech Academy of Sciences. He was a visiting lecturer at Cass Business School, Warwick Business School, Politecnico di Milano and New York University in Prague. Jan co-authored a number of papers in peer-reviewed journals in finance and physics, contributed to several books, and has presented at numerous conferences and workshops all over the world. He holds his PhD from CERGE-EI, Charles University in Prague. During his PhD studies, he co-founded a start-up, Quantum Finance CZ. He is a machine learning enthusiast and explores kdb+/q for this purpose. He spends his free time with his family and supporting various educational projects for universities and higher schools.

Paul A. Bilokon

Paul is CEO and founder of Thalesians Ltd and an expert in electronic and algorithmic trading across multiple asset classes, having helped build such businesses at Deutsche Bank and Citigroup. Before focusing on electronic trading, Paul worked on derivatives and has served in quantitative roles at Nomura, Lehman Brothers, and Morgan Stanley. Paul has been educated at Christ Church College, Oxford, and Imperial College. Apart from mathematical and computational finance, his academic interests include machine learning and mathematical logic.

Aris Galiotos

Aris is currently the global technical lead for the eFX kdb+ team at HSBC, where he helps architect, develop and support a big data installation capturing and processing billions of real-time records per day. Before that, he was the APAC head of the Equities Data and Analytics team at Citi, where he implemented pre- and post-trade analytics, alerts and real-time signals for the algorithmic trading team. Before moving to Hong Kong, he worked as a consultant for various investment banks and financial institutions in London, New York and Toronto. He came across kdb, k and q in the mid-2000s, was astonished by the speed, elegance, simplicity of the language and direct user support, and never looked back. Aris holds an MSc in Financial Mathematics with Distinction from the University of Edinburgh, after completing a degree in Mathematics at the University of Patras, Greece. An avid traveller, outside of the financial domain and his interest in statistics and machine learning, he has supported non-profit organisations in raising awareness around community development work, responsible tourism, and exploring opportunities of using technology to link people to educational and environmental support causes. In his spare time, he enjoys hiking and the outdoors, as well as a perpetual attempt to play the piano.

Frédéric Délèze

Frédéric is an independent algorithm trader and consultant. He has been playing several roles in quantitative finance for the last 15 years. As a quantitative trader, he designed and implemented automated trading strategies for hedge funds. As a financial engineer and risk manager, he developed quantitative models for market and counterparty credit risks for several investment banks and financial software companies. He also consulted for clearing houses to optimise margin requirements. He has been extensively using kdb+/q for various front office projects. Frédéric is the co-author of several peer-reviewed articles in market microstructure, asset pricing and econophysics. He holds an MSc in Computer Science from the Swiss Federal Institute of Technology Lausanne (EPFL), an MSc in Banking and Finance from HEC Lausanne and a PhD in Finance from Hanken School of Economics in Helsinki, Finland.

PART One

Language Fundamentals

CHAPTER 1

Fundamentals of the q Programming Language

This chapter starts our journey to programming with q. It aims to equip the reader with the basic concepts and ideas needed to code in q. In the subsequent chapters, we will delve deeper into the detail of the language and its features. We will always consider their applications to practical tasks as the primary motivation for our book.

1.1 THE (NOT SO VERY) FIRST STEPS IN q

We start with the assumption that the reader already has a working installation of kdb+ on his or her computer. Hence the *not so very* in this section's title. If the reader is fortunate enough, kdb+ has already been installed by the system administrator. Otherwise, the best strategy is to follow the instructions under "Download" on http://kx.com/.

kdb+ is available for industry-standard 32- and 64-bit architectures (including AMD Opteron, Intel Xeon, and Sun) running Linux, Windows or Solaris. As of the time of writing, Kx Systems offer a limited version of kdb+/q for non-commercial use. "Commercial use" is defined as any use for the user's or any third party's financial gain or other economic benefits, whether this is production use or beta testing. However, developing a proof-of-concept application, even in a commercial setting, is not regarded as commercial use. The non-commercial version can also be used for academic research. It is also fully suitable for exploration of the language as presented in this book. This book does not dwell on the nuances of running kdb+ on different architectures and operating systems.

The maximum amount of memory available to a 32-bit application is around 4 GB. This limits the applicability of the 32-bit version of kdb+. The 64-bit version can be used to implement large (multi-TB) in-memory databases that are common in high-frequency trading and big data applications.

To start kdb+, open your favourite shell, change the current directory to the one that contains the kdb+ executable (usually named q or q.exe), and launch that executable by typing in q. This executable is the q programming language interpreter – the face of the kdb+ system as seen by the user. By default, it is installed in one of the following directories:

```
// main linux/mac directory with ~ being home
    ~/q
// linux executables
    ~/q/l32
// mac executables
    ~/q/m32
// main windows directory
    c:\q
// windows executables
    c:\q\w32
```

For the 64-bit version, “32” in the path is replaced with “64”.

We recommend that the reader will install kdb+ in the default directory. If this is not possible, one can customise the installation using the environment variables (QHOME, QINIT, etc.). In the sequel, we assume that kdb+ is installed in the default directory.

Once kdb+ is running, we will see the prompt

```
q)
```

This prompt indicates that the q interpreter is awaiting our first commands. From now on, we shall assume that we are always in an open q session and therefore shall omit the prompt q) from our listings.

Let us experiment with the q language by typing in the expression

```
1+1
```

We shall see the output

```
2
```

We have just evaluated our first q expression!

Any introduction to a programming language requires the presence of a “hello world” example. We create a script file, named helloWorld.q in the directory from which we have launched our q session. The file contains the following line:

```
show "hello world!"
```

From the q session, we launch the script with system command \l:

```
\l helloWorld.q
```

which produces the output:

```
"hello world!"
```

The system command \l loads the file helloWorld.q, which applies the show function to its argument, the string "hello world!". The show function outputs its argument to the console.

To close the q session, we enter at the prompt the system command

```
\\
```

You may have noticed that the system commands, which control the q environment, all start with a backslash "\". The quit system command, \\, is no exception. Alternatively, we may evaluate the `exit` function

```
exit 0
```

where the integer argument passed to `exit` (in this case, 0) will be set as the exit status of the q interpreter process. The convention is to use `0` for the normal exit status and integers larger than zero to signal errors. Alternatively, pressing `Ctrl+d` will do the same job as either \\ or `exit`.

Having had our first glimpse of the q programming language in action, let us introduce its basic elements.

1.2 ATOMS AND LISTS

The most basic element of the q programming language is the atom, the smallest irreducible element of the language. An atom may be an integer, boolean or floating point variable, a function, or a date. We distinguish atoms by their types. We can find out the type of the number 2 using the command `type`:

```
type 2
```

```
-7h
```

the negative sign is used to distinguish atoms from lists. A negative type number, such as `-7h` in our case, indicates atoms, whereas a positive type number (or zero) is reserved for vectors, since q is by design a vector language. `-7h` tells us that 2 is an atom of long type, as indicated by the number 7. The extra letter, `h`, actually says that number −7, which indicates the *type of 2*, is itself a short integer.

So the `type` function always returns a short integer. Yes, q decides the default format of number 2 for its user, in this case, a long integer. We may, however, change it and define number 2 as a short integer, which will only require a quarter of memory space compared to a long integer, by appending the suffix "h" to the literal 2:

```
type 2h
```

```
-5h
```

which corresponds to short type, the result of `type` equal to −5 stands for the short integer.

A float can be defined as:

```
type 2f
```

```
-9h
```

or

```
type 2.0
```

```
-9h
```

where the number 9 stands for the float type.

If we define a list of atoms, the `type` of such a list does not express the type of all individual elements, but the type of a list as a whole. The list thus has a special place in q on its own, which is not surprising since q is a vector language. Let us find out the type of a list consisting of 2 and 3:

```
type (2;3)
```

```
7h
```

The result of `type` changed the sign from negative to positive. We conclude that the provided object is a list – positive sign – and all the entries are of the same type – long integer. The list itself is treated as one object.

What if we want to construct a list which contains only one element? The function `enlist` does the job for us:

```
type 2
```

```
-7h
```

while the single element list reads

```
enlist 2
```

```
,2
```

which suggests the output is a list. We can confirm this using

```
type enlist 2
```

```
7h
```

We may achieve the same result with

```
2,()
```

```
,2
```

where `()` plays the role of an empty list.

q enables one to define a list containing elements of mixed types. The type number of such a list is 0h:

```
type (2; 2h; 3; 2.0)
```

```
0h
```

By default, this is also the type of an empty list:

```
type ()
```

```
0h
```

An empty list can be explicitly cast to a different type using a type cast:

```
type `short$()
```

```
5h
```

In our example

```
2,()
```

type coercion still ensures that the result is a list of type float.

Mixed lists may also contain other lists as their elements:

```
type (2; 1; (1; 2; 3))
```

```
0h
```

If we want to see the type of each elements of a list, we can run

```
type each (2;3)
```

giving the expected output

```
-7 -7h
```

```
type each (2; 2h; 3; 2.0)
```

```
-7 -5 -7 -9h
```

We will devote more space in the subsequent sections to explain adverbs, such as `each`, which are fundamental for efficient programming in `q`.

Table 1.1 summarises all data types in `q`. By calling `type` on an object, we obtain one of the following types. The `number` column summarises the output of the `type` as printed out by `q`, which is a short integer. Let us proceed to introduce all types formally.

Recall a positive type is a list, a negative type is an individual atom. And a list of atoms of different types is typed `0h` as we can see from

```
type (2h;2f)
```

```
0h
```

Types 1 to 19 correspond to primitive types, i.e. simple data objects. There are two special "values" for some of the primitive types: the null/missing, and the infinity. Let us look at nulls, or missing values, which are typed entities without a value. Nulls can exist as

TABLE 1.1 The list of all types in kdb/q+ when using type

name	character	size	number	format	null	infinity
boolean	b	1	1	0b		
guid	g	16	2		0Ng	
byte	x	1	4	0x00		
short	h	2	5	0h	0Nh	0Wh
int	i	4	6	0i	0Ni	0Wi
long	j	8	7	0 or 0j	0Nj or 0N	0W or 0Wj
real	e	4	8	0e	0Ne	0We
float	f	8	9	0.0 or 0f	0Nf or 0n	0w
char	c	1	10	"a"	" "	
symbol	s		11	`abc	`	
timestamp	p	8	12	2010.01.01D00:01:00.000	0Np	0Wp
month	m	4	13	2010.10m	0Nm	0Wm
date	d	4	14	2010.10.10	0Nd	0Wd
datetime	z	8	15	dateTtime	0Nz	0Wz
timespan	n	8	16	00:00:00.000000000	0Nn	0Wn
minute	u	4	17	00:00	0Nu	0Wu
second	v	4	18	00:00:00	0Nv	0Wv
time	t	4	19	00:00:00.000	0Nt	0Wt
enumerations			20-76			
unused			77			
mapped list of lists t			78-96			
nested sym enumeration			97			
table			98			
dictionary			99			
lambda			100			
unary primitive			101			
binary primitive			102			
ternary operator			103			
projection			104			
composition			105			
f'			106			
f/			107			
f\			108			
f:			109			
f/:			110			
f\:			111			
dynamic load			112			

elements of a vector or list. The general format of a null is `0N?` where `?` is the character entry from Table 1.1.

We can check whether a value is null using the `null` function. This function returns an atom of type boolean, one that can take on the value `0b` (false) or `1b` (true):

```
null 3h
```

```
0b
```

```
null 0Nh
```

```
1b
```

There are a few exceptions among the primitive types: the boolean and byte types do not have a null at all, whereas char and symbol have null values " " and `` ` ``, respectively, reflecting their non-numeric format. Besides, for a null float, we may use the shorter notation `0n` instead of `0Nf`, and for a null long we may use the shorter notation `0N` instead of `0Nj`.

```
type 0Nj
```

```
-7h
```

while

```
type 0Nf
```

```
-9h
```

as well as

```
type 0n
```

```
-9h
```

The code is case sensitive, which we can see from

```
type 0N
```

```
-7h
```

The result of basic arithmetic operations involving a null is usually a null itself:

```
0Nj+2
```

```
0N
```

Nulls follow type promotion:

```
0Nj+2.0
```

```
0n
```

```
type 0Nj+2.0
```

```
-9h
```

similar to

```
type 1j+2.0
```

```
-9h
```

In terms of ordering, nulls have the smallest numerical value as can be seen when using `<,>,<=,>=,=`

```
0Nj<-1000
```

```
1b
```

saying it is true that `0Nj` is smaller than a given number `-1000`. This is an illustration. For proof that the null has the lowest numerical value, we need infinities. This is the second special "value" that we have introduced above.

The infinity is generally represented by `0W?`, where ? is the character from Table 1.1. The concept is in line with what we saw for null types, except for the guid type, which does not have infinity. A float infinity is denoted using lower case, where `0Wf` is the same as `0w`, while `0W` is the same as `0Wj`. Since temporal variables are internally stored as some numeric value, nulls/missing values and infinities are well defined for them, too.

One more thing regarding infinities: they are only well-behaved for floats, where infinity behaves in a proper mathematical sense. Let us illustrate the difference as follows:

```
0W+1
```

```
0N
```

```
0W+2
```

```
-0W
```

```
0W+3
```

```
-9223372036854775806j
```

Long infinity is the largest possible long number. If such a number is incremented by one, we obtain the null long, which, as we have pointed out above, is the smallest long number. Adding two to the long infinity, we obtain the negative long infinity. Adding three to the long infinity, we obtain the next smallest long after the negative long infinity.

On the other hand, the floating point infinities (i.e. the float and real infinities) are well-behaved infinities as we can see from an analogous exercise:

```
0w+1f
```

```
0w
```

```
0w+2f
```

```
0w
```

```
0w=(0w-3f)
```

```
1b
```

Only the floating point infinities demonstrate arithmetic behaviour consistent with the notion of infinity in mathematics.

1.2.1 Casting Types

The casting, i.e. explicit conversion, of types in q is done through the dollar function with the infix notation `"newType"$variable`, where `newType` is a character representation of the new type for the `variable`. The conversion works as intuition suggests:

```
type 1
```

```
-7h
```

while the converted version

```
type "f"$1
```

has the type of

```
-9h
```

An alternative syntax is `` `newType$variable``, where `newType` is a name representation of the new type for the `variable`:

```
type `float$1
```

```
-9h
```

The character representation is more in the spirit of q to use concise code. For illustration, let us consider type casting for temporal variables:

```
now:2099.01.01D01:02:03.456789000;
type now
```

```
-12h
```

The conversion of the variable now can be directly seen in the output:

```
"j"$now
```

```
3124227723456789000
```

```
"t"$now
```

```
01:02:03.456
```

```
"d"$now
```

```
2099.01.01
```

```
"m"$now
```

```
2099.01m
```

```
"u"$now
```

```
01:02
```

```
"v"$now
```

```
01:02:03
```

```
"n"$now
```

```
0D01:02:03.456789000
```

We encourage the reader to experiment with the casting of various data types on her or his own. We will focus on a special type of conversion which is quite frequent in empirical work: converting a string (i.e. a character vector) into a particular type. The data we work with may come from various sources and may be available in text format.

In order to analyse the data, it will need to be converted into the appropriate data types. Let us illustrate this with `"1.1"`, which is meant to be a float:

```
"f"$"1.1"
```

```
49 46 49f
```

This may be a surprise at first. If we think of the string as an array of individual characters and the conversion as done element-wise, i.e. element-by-element, we realise that the first number 49 is an ASCII representation of the character `"1"`, while the second number 46 is an ASCII representation of the character `"."`.

In order to cast a string into a single float number, we have to use upper case:

```
"F"$"1.1"
```

```
1.1f
```

The conversion is done using the syntax `"NEWTYPE"$variable`, where `NEWTYPE` is a capitalised character representation of the new type for the `variable`. We can see that

```
"J"$"1.1"
```

```
0Nj
```

as we cannot convert it into an integer. This works for other types as well:

```
"D"$"2017.01.01"
```

```
2017.01.01
```

while an improper use of casting gives:

```
"d"$"2017.01.01"
```

```
2000.02.20 2000.02.18 2000.02.19 2000.02.25 2000.02.16 2000.02.18
    ↪ 2000.02.19 2000.02.16 2000.02.18 2000.02.19
```

The reason why the latter casting "works", i.e. does not raise an error, is that the underlying numeric type behind `"d"` is an integer. The casting is thus done character by character, where the dot, for example, gives

```
"d"$"."
```

```
2000.02.16
```

Let us finish this section with conversion to string and symbol. First, the conversion to string is achieved by using the function `string`, which takes one argument, and the function's result is that argument converted to a string. Let us see `string`'s application in the following examples:

```
string 123.45
```

```
"123.45"
```

The double quotes mean the output is a string. Analogously, we can convert other types like dates, times, etc.

```
string 2017.01.01
```

```
"2017.01.01"
```

The conversion to a symbol, on the other hand, is done using the following notation:

```
`$"123"
```

```
`123
```

We can only convert a string into a symbol. Symbols play a special role in `kdb+` in large tables, and we will cover them in the subsequent sections. For now, they can be described as internalised strings or a string pool which efficiently stores strings internally for fast lookups.

1.3 BASIC LANGUAGE CONSTRUCTS

In the previous paragraphs, we have reviewed some of the basic building blocks for data. In order to build a complex program, we have to learn more operators and language syntax. The syntactic rules of `q` are derived from `k` and do not bear much similarity to standard programming languages such as `C`, `Python`, or `Java`. Indeed, `q` belongs to a different language family.

1.3.1 Assigning, Equality and Matching

The basic element of any program is variables. To assign a value to a variable, the usual = is represented by the assignment operator `:`. It works as follows:

```
a:1.0
```

We confirm that the variable `a` is now equal to 1.0 as:

```
a
```

```
1.0
```

Conveniently, the assignment operator also returns the result of the expression which is assigned. We can, therefore, continue processing:

```
2+a:1.0
```

```
3f
```

In this example, the variable `a` ends up having the value `1f`, whereas the overall result of the expression is `3f`.

Thus we can chain multiple assignments:

```
b:a:1.0
```

It is worth repeating that `q` is case sensitive. Many languages carry some conventions on which types of variables would be lower case and which would be upper case. In `q`, there are no such conventions, partly since few standard libraries exist; however, it is common to use single-letter variables and functions. This is convenient if we want to fit complex functions into a single line – one could argue that solutions to a large number of problems can fit into a single line in `q`. In this book, we follow the *camelCase* convention. This allows us to give intuitive names to building blocks of code and indicate the role of each variable and function by its name.

We should avoid the use of underscore (`_`) in names, as it is an operator in `q`. Another character to avoid is a dot, (`.`), which defines the context or namespace. Finally, `q` contains a limited number of operators and reserved words. We should avoid using them and be especially careful not to define them as table column names accidentally. A common mistake is to name a column `value`, which is a reserved word. In addition, as we will see in the next chapter dedicated to functions, `x`, `y`, and `z` play a special role as default arguments to a function.

Another useful syntactic rule to follow is using the semicolon, `;`. A semicolon denotes the end of a statement. Therefore, the following throws an error, as variable `b` is not defined:

```
b:1 b
```

```
'b
```

yet the following works:

```
b:1; b
```

```
1f
```

For clarity, we encourage putting each statement on a separate line:

```
b:1;
```

and

```
b
```

```
1f
```

Semicolons are *required* when we want to separate statements inside functions. In integrated development environments (IDEs), the use of semicolons allows us to run blocks of code.

We have already seen that the assignment operator, `:`, allows us to assign values to variables. We can check whether the values of the variables are the same using the equality operator, (`=`):

```
a1:1;a2:2;a1=a2
```

```
0b
```

where we have used the semicolon to fit the example into a single, dense, line. The usage is straightforward when comparing two atoms: we get either `1b` if both atoms are the same, or `0b` if not.

The inequality operator is `<>` and works as expected:

```
a1<>a2
```

```
1b
```

The equality operator is overloaded for lists: if two lists of the same length are provided, the equality operator performs comparison element-wise, and the result is a list of booleans:

```
1 2 3=1 2 4
```

```
110b
```

If a list and an atom are provided, each element of the list is compared against the atom, and the result is again a list of booleans:

```
1 2 3=2
```

```
010b
```

If two lists of different length are provided, the operation is not well defined, and we get a `'length` error, suggesting that unequal lists were provided:

```
1 2 3=1 2
```

```
'length
```

If we want to check whether two lists are an exact match (same length and all respective elements are equal), we use the operator (`~`), which will compare the lists (or any two variables) as a whole:

```
1 2 3~1 2 3
```

```
1b
```

```
1 2 3~1 2
```

```
0b
```

1.3.2 Arithmetic Operations and Right-to-Left Evaluation: Introduction to q Philosophy

Before we dive into the world of big data analytics and machine learning, we should at least be confident that we know how to sum up or multiply two numbers. Feeling courageous, we attempt to do both:

```
10*100+1000
```

```
11000
```

Wait! The answer should be 2000 under the usual mathematical conventions. q thinks otherwise, though. In its quest for efficiency, speed and less program noise – aka "We Don't Need No Stinkin' Brackets" (Borror, 2015) – q follows a simple parsing rule: Expressions are evaluated right-to-left, and all operators have the same priority. This may look bizarre to a newbie but results in simplicity, since there is only one rule. One may disagree with this decision, but nothing can be done about it. It also makes the parsing of statements simpler and faster. As a result, the following two expressions yield different results:

```
v:1 2 3
neg[v]+3
```

```
2 1 0
```

```
neg v+3
```

```
-4 -5 -6
```

Our initial example can be written as:

```
1000+10*100
```

```
2000
```

We have explicitly stated that we want to first evaluate 10*100 and then add 1000. Even though such decomposition may seem obvious, thinking in terms of the operator precedence commonly used in other programming languages, such as Python, Java, and C++ may result in trivial but hard to detect errors until our brains get used to the q way.

We could have achieved the desired result of 2000 by using brackets in our initial example:

```
(10*100)+1000
```

The motivation for no precedence of operators and using a strict right-to-left evaluation stems from the fact that operator precedence requires to evaluate the full expression to determine the evaluation tree step by step. This is avoided in q and thus the evaluation may proceed as the expression is being read letter by letter. This was also demonstrated in an earlier example with the assignment of a variable and subsequent addition, all in the same statement.

The right-to-left evaluation is one of the biggest sources of misunderstanding and errors during the early stages of coding in q. The difficulty is further pronounced as the same lack of priorities holds for functions. We thus encourage readers who are starting with q to pay extra attention even to the most simple expressions until they get the right-to-left evaluation under their skin. So we will illustrate this concept with another example:

```
2 xexp 2
```

```
4
```

which is as expected. However, when we want to add 1 to the result of the evaluation above, we cannot write:

```
2 xexp 2 + 1
```

as this results in

```
8
```

rather than 5. The solution to this problem is to either use brackets:

```
(2 xexp 2) + 1
```

```
5
```

or

```
1 + 2 xexp 2
```

```
5
```

Finally, in order to divide two numbers in q, we use %

```
5%2
```

```
2.5
```

For now, we should keep in mind that / does something entirely different in q.

1.4 BASIC OPERATORS

There is a number of useful basic operators, or *verbs*, defined in q. These native symbol operators are in fact functions, which are heavily overloaded based on their argument. They form the basics of the programming language and offer powerful functionality for data analysis – familiarity with these and their variations will be required to read and write q.

Random numbers/find/conditional

The symbol ? generates a vector of random numbers. The command to do so is:

```
10?5
```

```
1 2 0 3 4 2 1 4 3 1
```

The previous display generates 10 integers from 0 … 4. Since q is derived from C, indexing starts at 0.

In order to generate random floats, we simply replace the integer on the right with a float:

```
10?5.0
```

```
4.096725 2.802929 2.239135 2.933982 1.828879 2.121043 1.233712 3.857119
    ↪ 4.44315 0.2670197
```

where numbers are generated from the range [0, 5.0]. This basic functionality thus allows us to generate uniformly distributed random numbers. Random numbers following any other distribution function have to be derived from the uniform distribution.

We can also generate a random array from any specified list. For example, to generate a random word from a list of letters, we type:

```
10?"abcdefg"
```

```
"gfdafbcade"
```

The domain can also be a list of symbols:

```
10?`a`b`c`d`e`f`g
```

```
`a`g`b`c`a`a`e`e`a`b
```

If we want to sample without replacement, the first argument needs to be negative. This will guarantee uniqueness of resultant elements:

```
-5?10
```

```
1 9 0 3 4
```

Attempting to generate more numbers than the number of unique instances will give us an error:

```
-10?5
```

```
'length
```

The unique random number generator also works on any list of unique values:

```
-4?`a`b`c`d`e`f`g
```

```
`a`g`b`c
```

However, the unique random number generator does not work when the second argument is a float:

```
-2?2.0
```

```
'type
```

The random number generator uses a seed which can be set using the –S start-up flag or seen by typing:

```
\S
```

```
-314159
```

The seed does not change during the call of the random number generator. If we want to set another seed, we specify an argument to \S which is a non-zero integer.

The function ? further serves as an operator to find an element within a vector. In such a case, the first argument is the list to search through and the second argument is an element to find:

```
arr:1 2 3 4 5 6;
arr?3
```

```
2
```

The function will exit upon finding the first occurrence of the element:

```
arr2:1 2 3 3 3 3;
arr2?3
```

```
2
```

If the element to be found is not present in the list, the query returns an index equal to `1+count[arr]`:

```
arr?7
```

```
6
```

Finally, ? allows us to replace elements of one array by elements of another array according to a boolean list:

```
inp1:1 2 3 4 5;
inp2:10 20 30 40 50;
booleanSwitch:01010b;
?[booleanSwitch;inp1;inp2]
```

```
10 2 30 4 50
```

where we have generated the output by choosing all values in `inp1` where `booleanSwitch` is true and values from `inp2` where `booleanSwitch` is false. All three arrays have to have the same length. The boolean vector can be generated by any logical expression; for example, we may produce a vector which always takes the maximum value of two vectors:

```
inp1:1 30 2 6 5;
inp2:10 20 30 40 50;
?[ inp1 > inp2 ;inp1;inp2]
```

```
10 30 30 40 50
```

Note that a more optimal way to do the above is using the built-in `or (|)` function

```
inp1:1 30 2 6 5;
inp2:10 20 30 40 50;
inp1|inp2
```

```
10 30 30 40 50
```

xbar

The function `xbar` rounds each element of the vector on the right down to the nearest multiple of the number on the left.

```
5 xbar 2 -1 3.5 10 13 21
```

```
0 -5 0 10 10 20f
```

But also:

```
0D00:00:05 xbar 2099D01:00:05.1 2099D01:00:06.5 2099D01:00:20.1
```

```
2099D01:00:05.000000000 2099D01:00:05.000000000 2099D01:00:20.000000000
```

The latter being a very convenient way to *bucket* a time vector into 5-second buckets.

Fill

The symbol ^ fills the null elements of an array by a specified value.

```
0^1 2 3 0N 5 6 0N 8
```

```
1 2 3 0 5 6 0 8
```

where the element on the left-hand side of ^ is the value used to replace any `null` in the array on the right-hand side of ^. Fill will promote the value when replacing nulls for each type. Thus, for floats, we may use:

```
10^1.0 2.0 3.0 0n 5.0 6.0 0n 8.0
```

```
1 2 3 10 5 6 10 8f
```

In addition, the argument on the left can be a vector of the same length as the vector on the right. In this case, the null symbols are not replaced by a single value but by the corresponding value from the vector on the left:

```
(10 20 30 40 50 60 70 80)^1.0 2.0 3.0 0n 5.0 6.0 0n 8.0
```

```
1 2 3 40 5 6 70 8f
```

Take/reshape

The symbol # creates a list from the data provided on the right-hand side of # with a dimension specified on the left-hand side. The basic specification is such that the left-hand side argument is an integer and the right-hand side argument is a vector. # takes the first elements of the vector, as specified by the first argument:

```
3#1 2 3 4 5 6
```

```
1 2 3
```

If the first argument is negative, # takes the specified number of elements from the *end* of the vector:

```
-3#1 2 3 4 5 6
```

```
4 5 6
```

If the provided vector is shorter than the length demanded by the integer, the array itself will be repeated:

```
13#1 2 3 4 5 6
```

```
1 2 3 4 5 6 1 2 3 4 5 6 1
```

thus, the output has always the length specified by the argument.

The symbol # can also reshape the array. If the left-hand side argument is a two-dimensional array, the output is a matrix with dimensions specified by the arguments formed of an array on the right-hand side, where the vector itself may be repeated:

```
3 3#1 2 3 4 5 6
```

```
(1 2 3;4 5 6;1 2 3)
```

Drop/cut

The (_) function drops a subset from a vector. It removes the elements either from the start or the end. In order to drop elements from the start, the first argument is a positive integer denoting the number of elements to drop while the second argument on the right is a list from which the elements are dropped:

```
3_0 1 2 3 4 5 6 7 8 9
```

```
3 4 5 6 7 8 9
```

In order to drop elements from the end, the left-hand side argument of _ is a negative integer denoting the number of elements to drop:

```
-3_0 1 2 3 4 5 6 7 8 9
```

```
0 1 2 3 4 5 6
```

The drop command can be used to drop a particular element from a list. In this case, the argument on the left is the list from which to drop an element while the argument on the right is an integer denoting the position at which the drop is performed:

```
0 1 2 3 4 5 6 7 8 9_3
```

```
0 1 2 4 5 6 7 8 9
```

We have to keep in mind that q starts vector indexing at zero.

We can combine the drop operator with the find operator ? described above. Given the provided list and a certain element, which may be in the list, we may want to keep the part of the list from the first occurrence of the element onwards. Let us illustrate this:

```
array:0 1 2 3 4 5 6 7 8 9;
element:4;
(array?element)_array
```

```
4 5 6 7 8 9
```

The find operation `(array?element)` identifies the position of the first occurrence of `element` in `array`. The drop command is then used to remove the part of the list to the left of the `element`. Alternatively, we may remove elements from the right.

In order to remove the element itself, we swap the order of arguments in the drop command:

```
array _ (array?element)
```

```
0 1 2 3 5 6 7 8 9
```

Finally, if the element is not in the list, the command does nothing as the find operation returns an index equal to the count of the array plus 1:

```
array _ (array?999)
```

```
0 1 2 4 3 5 6 7 8 9
```

The function (_) also cuts the list into partitions, which are specified by the list of indices. The provided indices denote the start of each partition. The cut is used as:

```
0 3 6_ 1 2 3 4 5 6 7 8 9
```

giving as the output the list of partitions, each being an individual list:

```
1 2 3
4 5 6
7 8 9
```

This is as requested: the first partition starts at index 0, the second starts at index 3, i.e. a 4th element of the list, and, finally, the last partition is the rest of the list from index 6 onwards. If the first index specified is different from zero, we obtain the following:

```
1 3 6_ 1 2 3 4 5 6 7 8 9
```

```
2 3
4 5 6
7 8 9
```

Also, the cut always returns a partition in the form of a list:

```
2 3 6 9_ 1 2 3 4 5 6 7 8 9
```

```
,3
4 5 6
7 8 9
`long$()
```

where the first partition is a one-element list while the last partition is an empty list. The command thus always returns the number of partitions which were requested and if the index reaches beyond the length of the array, an empty list is returned.

Max/reverse

The symbol | goes through the provided list element by element and returns the maximum compared to the provided number. It can be used as follows:

```
4|0 1 2 3 4 5 6 7 8 9
```

```
4 4 4 4 4 5 6 7 8 9
```

which is as expected: every element of the vector on the right of the max operator is checked against the number on the left, and the maximum value is returned.

The left-hand side argument can be also a list of the same length as the list to be iterated through. In such a case, the max operator is applied *pairwise*, element by element on both lists:

```
0 10 2 30 4 50 6 70 8 90|0 1 2 3 4 5 6 7 8 9
```

```
0 10 2 30 4 50 6 70 8 90
```

If lists of unequal length are provided, an error is returned:

```
1 1|0 1 2 3 4 5 6 7 8 9
```

```
'length
```

If the max operator is applied on a boolean vector, it acts as boolean "or", which returns `0b` when both arguments are of type `0b`, otherwise it returns `1b`. In particular:

```
1100b | 1010b
```

```
1110b
```

The (|) operator can be used to reverse the ordering of the list. In such a case, a single argument is provided:

```
(|) 0 1 2 3 4 5 6 7 8 9
```

```
9 8 7 6 5 4 3 2 1 0
```

The operator works on any type; in particular, it can be used to reverse the letters in a word:

```
(|) "hello"
```

```
"olleh"
```

q prefers to keep the valence constant for a given operator (but overload for a given valence), so the above can also just be written as

```
reverse "hello"
```

```
"olleh"
```

Min/where

The symbol (&) goes through the provided list element by element and returns the minimum compared to the provided number, analogously to the | operator. The min operator works as follows:

```
4&0 1 2 3 4 5 6 7 8 9
```

```
0 1 2 3 4 4 4 4 4 4
```

which works as expected: every element of the array on the right-hand side of the min operator is checked against the number on the left-hand side of the operator and the minimum value is returned.

The left-hand side argument can be also a list of the same length as the list to be iterated through. Similar to the max operator, the min operator is applied element by element on both lists:

```
0 10 -2 30 -4 50 -6 70 -8 90&0 1 2 3 4 5 6 7 8 9
```

```
0 1 -2 3 -4 5 -6 7 -8 9
```

When lists of unequal length are provided, the error `'length` is returned.

Analogously to the max operator, when min operator is applied on a boolean vector it acts as a boolean "and", which returns `1b` when both arguments are true, `1b`, otherwise it returns false `0b`:

```
1100b & 1010b
```

```
1000b
```

Finally, the `where` operator takes a single argument of a boolean list:

```
where 0101b
```

```
1 3
```

which returns the indices of all elements which can be interpreted as true, i.e. non-zero.

More generally, `where` applied to a vector of integers (or a dictionary with integer values) can be defined as a function returning the number of occurrences of those integers according to the integer values:

```
where `a`b`c`d!til 4
```

```
`b`c`c`d`d`d
```

The argument on the left in the above example is a *dictionary*, which will be introduced in the next chapter.

Join

The symbol , is used to join two lists:

```
(0 1 2 3 4), (5 6 7 8 9)
```

```
01 2 3 5 6 7 8 9
```

The join operator can join lists of any type:

```
(0 1 2 3 4), `a, "hello"
```

```
((0 1 2 3 4);`a;"hello")
```

Print to console

The symbol ! has important functionalities which will be reviewed later. The particular function involving ! is:

```
0N!3
```

```
3
```

which prints the argument on the right-hand side to console in an unformatted form but also allows q to use the argument further down the statement for subsequent operations on the left. In particular, when using the q prompt, we can use `0N!` as control prints:

```
1+0N!1 +0N!1+0N!1
```

```
1
2
3
4
```

This is useful to track the evaluation of a complicated statement – such functionality, however, does not work when using IDEs.

Separator

We saw that the symbol ; denotes the end of a statement. However, when surrounded by brackets, it acts as a separator for elements within a list:

```
(1;2;3;4)
```

```
1 2 3 4
```

or nested lists:

```
(1;2;(1;2);4)
```

```
1
2
1 2
4
```

As we will see in the next chapter, the symbol ; also separates arguments when defining a function. Finally – as we saw previously – it separates statements:

```
a:1;b:2;a+b
```

```
3
```

We may easily write complicated commands within one line. If a separator is used to separate statements, the statements are evaluated one by one from the left, but within a statement, the right-to-left priority is used. q does not consider the end of a line (newline operator) as the end of a statement so one statement can also be written in multiple lines for better clarity. For reducing clutter in our code, we should also keep separate statements in separate lines.

Quit

The symbol \\ is not a symbol per se but plays an important role. When entered in the q session, it will terminate the session.

Index

The "at" sign, @, is known as "apply" and can be used to apply a monadic (one-argument) function to its argument. Since q is a functional language, indexing is a function, too, and we can use apply to index a vector to a list of indices. The following forms are all equivalent:

```
max[1 2 3]
max 1 2 3
max@1 2 3
```

```
x:1 2 3
x[0 1]
x 0 1
x@0 1
```

Precedence/list

`()` is primarily used to define the precedence execution since q evaluates expressions from right to left. When using brackets, the evaluation is commanded to start from the innermost bracket pair and move outwards:

```
((1+2)*(3+4))
```

```
28
```

and contrast this to the unbracketed form of the expression

```
1+2*3+4
```

```
15
```

The usage of brackets is very convenient as we can get the precedence order as required; however, it brings some overhead and in some cases can create more "noisy" code. The `()` can be used to form lists and create nested lists:

```
((((1;2);3);4);5)
```

```
((1 2;3);4)
5
```

which is a nested list of lists. In the topmost layer, the list contains nested list `(((1;2);3);4)` and atom `5`. `()` is also used to create tables, as we will see in the next chapter.

We saw earlier that `enlist` is a compelling function which constructs a list out of its input. The opposite operation of 'flattening' a list (or 'razing' it) is achieved by `raze`:

```
raze ((((1;2);3);4);5)
```

```
(1 2;3)
4
5
```

Block

The square brackets, `[]`, form a block of code which can be useful inside conditional expressions:

```
[a:1;b:2;a+b]
```

```
3
```

`[]` does not change evaluation precedence of statements but rather forms a sub-statement, which is evaluated as a block of code.

The brackets [] have two other functions in q: First, they denote the argument of the function, and, second, they form special multi-valence functions. Both functionalities will be described in Chapter 3.

Assign/amend

The symbol : is the assignment operator as we previously saw. The existing value assigned to a variable can be amended either by explicitly stating the operation:

```
a:1;
a:a+1;
a
```

```
2
```

or by using the short notation of

```
a:1;
a+:1;
a
```

```
2
```

This can be applied to other arithmetic operations like +, *, %, :

```
a:2;
a*:2;
a
```

```
4
```

Further, the same works if we want to amend the list by joining it with another list:

```
a:(1;2);
a,:(3;4);
a
```

```
1 2 3 4
```

Colon : also provides the "return" functionality within functions.

Identity

The symbol :: stands for the identity function, which returns its argument:

```
(::) 1
```

```
1
```

The identity is useful whenever we need to use a function, which outputs the arguments. We shall cover a use case for this in later chapters when we cover table joins.

The symbol :: stands for the identify function, but also denotes nil (generic null), global amend, and view. This functionality will be revealed through examples in the subsequent sections, when we will cover q in more detail.

1.5 DIFFERENCE BETWEEN STRINGS AND SYMBOLS

In q, we have two similar types, the string and the symbol, which seemingly do the same job. Imagine we have a database, which contains a timestamp, price and also the name of the asset the price belongs to, e.g. IBM, INTEL, AAPL. We may store the asset names as strings; however, we end up having a large number of repeated values, which will be consuming memory. We may prevent wasting memory by replacing the names by short integers, for example, and keep a separate lookup table to recover the map between short integers and names, in the form of a dictionary:

```
nameToShortMap:`IBM`INTC`AAPL!(1 2 3h);
```

This is not a very convenient way to work with data and in particular to share our work with others. In order to avoid such a troublesome approach, q uses the concept of symbols, which are internalised strings. Such strings are kept in memory only once, i.e. each distinct value is kept in memory once, and references to the original string are internally used. Under the surface, q maintains a pool of strings used as symbols and every usage of a symbol points to the value in this table.

The notion of symbols thus clearly suggests that whenever we need to use strings repeatedly, symbols are the type of choice. As the pool of strings is maintained in memory, we should constrain the use of symbols to domains with repeated values to avoid blowing up the memory. If we need unique and complicated names, we should stick to characters, i.e. strings. Alternatively, if we need to use unique identifiers, like trade IDs, we should use the guid type.

Another advantage of using symbols is that the comparison is much faster since we do not need to check every character, but merely the reference to that string. For instance, queries like

```
where name=`IBM
```

or

```
where name in `IBM`INTC
```

significantly improve the speed and simplicity of evaluation compared to using character vectors.

1.5.1 Enumeration

The q language allows us to go one step further when working with symbols and create enumerated lists. This should be a familiar concept from other languages (q *does* contain various features we are used to in "common" programming languages). The enumerated list of symbols form a new type – enumerations have a type range of short integers – and restrict the values within the existing domain. Any changes to the new type in terms of appending or changing the values are restricted to the provided list.

Let us create an enumerated list out of our three names of assets used above:

```
assetNames:`IBM`INTC`AAPL;
```

and a list of names within our hypothetical analysis involving multiple occurrences of the vector of assetNames:

```
name:`IBM`INTC`IBM`INTC`AAPL`IBM`IBM`INTC`AAPL`IBM`INTC`INTC`AAPL`IBM`AAPL;
type name
```

```
11h
```

We now "cast", i.e. enumerate the list of symbols against the domain of values:

```
name2:`assetNames$name;
type name2
```

```
20h
```

as expected from Table 1.1; enumerated types take values from 20h to 76h so the actual outcome will depend on what was already enumerated within the q session.

We can see what name2 looks like:

```
name2
```

```
`assetNames$`IBM`INTC`IBM`INTC`AAPL`IBM`IBM`INTC`AAPL`IBM`INTC`INTC`AAPL`
    ↪ IBM`AAPL
```

Let us try to append a value into the list name2 which is within the specified type, and one which is not;

```
name2,:`IBM
```

i.e. no problem, the new item was added. In contrast,

```
name2,:`C
```

```
'cast
```

and thus the specified type restricts us to the list of values within an enumerated list. We cannot add `C into our analysis unless we specify a new item into assetNames.

If we try a slightly different version of the previous command

```
name2:name2,`C
```

we do not obtain any error message and the command will go through without any issue. Why? Let us investigate:

```
type name2
```

```
11h
```

q has recast name2 back into a non-enumerated symbol type. This is because in the first case we amended name2 *in-place*, i.e. by reference, and the new value was missing from our enumeration. In the second example, q un-enumerated the result of name2,`C since `C was not an element of the enumeration domain.

1.6 MATRICES AND BASIC LINEAR ALGEBRA IN q

Matrices are represented in q as nested lists, specifically a list of columns, where the elements of the outer list are the rows of the matrix:

```
a: (2.4 -0.7 20.4; 5.7 9.8 -2.3)
```

which represents the matrix

$$\begin{pmatrix} 2.4 & -0.7 & 20.4 \\ 5.7 & 9.8 & -2.3 \end{pmatrix}.$$

One can use the dyadic take function # to create such lists of lists:

```
c: 2 3 # 2.4 -0.7 20.4 5.7 9.8 -2.3
```

The match function ~ can be used to check for matrix equality:

```
a ~ c
```

```
1b
```

or

```
b: (2.4 10.8 2.6; 1.2 3.1 0.8);
a ~ b
```

```
0b
```

Function `flip` can be used to transpose a matrix. We encourage readers to write an example. Functions + and – operate element-wise, so can be used to add and subtract matrices:

```
a + b
```

```
(4.8 10.1 23;6.9 12.9 -1.5)
```

```
a - b
```

```
(0 -11.5 17.8;4.5 6.7 -3.1)
```

```
a - c
```

```
(0 0 0f;0 0 0f)
```

There are several ways to reference an element of a matrix. With the dot verb and using the fact that the matrix is also a binary function (the @ verb cannot index more than one dimension):

```
a . 1 2
```

```
-2.3
```

```
.[a; 1 2]
```

```
-2.3
```

We can access the relevant row of the matrix, then index within that row:

```
a[1][2]
```

```
-2.3
```

Finally, we can use the fact that the matrix is also a binary function:

```
a[1;2]
```

```
-2.3
```

However, only this latter method can be used to mutate an element:

```
a[1;2]: -3.2;
a
```

```
(2.4 -0.7 20.4;5.7 9.8 -3.2)
```

We can access the entire row…

```
a[1]
```

```
5.7 9.8 -3.2
```

…or column of a matrix:

```
a[;1]
```

```
-0.7 9.8
```

and mutate them:

```
a[;1]: 1.4 -8.9;
a
```

```
(2.4 1.4 20.4;5.7 -8.9 -3.2)
```

Here we have *elided* the very top index of a matrix: a[;1] retrieves the items with index 1 from each item of the nested list a.

The @ verb can also be used to index rows of the matrix:

```
@[a; 1]
```

```
5.7 -8.9 -3.2
```

Matrices of compatible shapes can be multiplied using the matrix multiplication verb mmu. Thus to multiply a by a transpose of b

```
d: a mmu flip b;
d
```

```
(73.92 23.54;-90.76 -23.31)
```

The inverse of a nonsingular matrix can be computed using inv:

```
inv d
```

```
(-0.05638399 -0.05694034;0.2195372 0.1788033)
```

Note that for mmu and inv to work the matrix must have floating point entries. Thus the following will work:

```
(3 5 7f; 6 4 7f) mmu (3 2f; 12 2f; 5 2f)
```

whereas

```
(3 5 7; 6 4 7) mmu (3 2; 12 2; 5 2)
```

will fail with error 'length.

Dot product is supported through the $ operator:

```
a[0]$b[0]
```

```
51.24
```

We have demonstrated that we can implement basic linear algebra calculations within q in a very straightforward way. The provided commands can be extended by readers into more complex functions and solve more advanced problems.

1.7 LAUNCHING THE SESSION: ADDITIONAL OPTIONS

Let us conclude this section with an overview of various startup flags we can use when starting our q session:

```
> q <additional options>
```

where a number of useful <additional options> is specified below.

Block writing

The option -b prevents the user, or the client launched by the user, to write into memory. If we launch a session with this option, any client which connects to this session cannot write anything into any existing variable or create a new one. It returns `'noupdate` error when any attempt to write is made:

```
a:1
```

```
'noupdate
```

In Chapter 5 we will see another way to replicate read-only mode dynamically when desired, by using the `reval` function.

Console dimension

The option `-c rows columns` sets the console size in terms of rows and columns. The default setup is `-c 25 80`. In the case when `q` is invoked through the HTTP protocol, the dimension of the display can be set by using the capital "C", i.e. `-C rows columns`.

Error trap

The option `-e B` with `B` being binary variable sets the error trapping in the console. The error trapping is crucial for code debugging, which we will cover in Chapter 5.

Garbage collection

The option `-g b` sets the garbage collection mode. `q` has two memory modes: the deferred mode, `-g 0`, and the immediate mode, `-g 1`. The default is the deferred mode, where the memory is returned to the operating system when `q` is instructed to do so by running `.Q.gc` function or when memory allocation fails. The immediate mode is returning the memory to the operating system when it is not referenced any more. The trade-off is that immediate mode allows for more continuous memory management but comes with some overhead.

On the other hand, the deferred mode gives us control over when it happens. Notice that running `.Q.gc[]` explicitly also attempts to coalesce diced memory blocks and can, therefore, be more expensive – but also return more memory – when run, especially in a process with a very fragmented heap, which usually happens when there are many nested lists created. Depending on the trade-off between required memory to be freed and performance-critical code, we may want to choose the appropriate tool for the appropriate scenario. For example, we would usually not add frequent calls to `.Q.gc` on a time-sensitive complex event processing (CEP) process, but may do so during a quiet period or after persisting data to disk, say, once a day. Note that q *always returns unreference memory to the heap*, so the `g` flag or explicitly running `.Q.gc` are useful when wanting to *return memory back to the OS*, recommended when having multiple `q` processes or other applications competing for the same memory on a server.

Logs

The option `-l` sets the logging of the session. The log can be enabled by setting:

```
>q fileName -l
```

This option will create a file `fileName.log`, which stores the messages for any queries which change the state of the data. This option is useful to prevent the loss of data when the server crashes.

Time offset

The option `-o N` sets the offset of the internal time from GMT. The variable `N` denotes hours, if $|N| < 23$, otherwise it represents minutes. Thus, the shift by one hour forward can be expressed as:

```
> q -o -1
```

This is useful when working in different time zones and `q` is used to store the data, for example.

Port

The option `-p N` sets the port for the session. This option is needed if we want to connect to the session remotely, or if we use GUI to code in `q`. The variable `N` is the port number. It is convenient to use large values, e.g. the following option would conveniently set the port number to 6000:

```
> q -p 6000
```

The variable `N` can be negative, in which case the port will be set for a multi-threaded mode.

Display precision

The option `-P N` sets the number of decimals of the float type displayed by the terminal and when exporting data to text, such as `csv` format. The variable `N` is the integer denoting the number of decimals.

Quiet start

The option `-q` suppresses the announcement at the start-up, and the user can start coding without a single word being heard off from the `q` terminal.

Parallel executions

`q` can execute code in parallel on multiple slave threads or processes. The option `-s N` sets the environment for parallel execution, with `N` being positive or negative integer. In Chapter 8 we will cover the required setup.

Timeout

The option `-T N` sets the timeout for queries. The variable `N` is in seconds. The timeout works such that if the query lasts more than `N` seconds, the query is interrupted unfinished and the session ends up with an error. The default is no timeout, `-T 0`. The timeout option is useful when there are limited resources and the administrator has to prevent long queries.

User restrictions

The option `-u X` sets the user restrictions for the given session. The main objective is to limit the users who connect to the session remotely, e.g. through the GUI, which we will cover later, or over the network. The first option is `-u 1`, which prevents users from launching any system command. In particular, this prevents any remotely connected user to quit the session (recall the command \\).

The second option is to launch session with `-u fileName`, where "fileName" is a file to the username and password. The file can be located in the main q directory – in such a case the name of the file is provided – or anywhere else – in such a case the path has to be added. The file itself can contain, for example, the following line:

```
userName:password
```

In order to access the session remotely, the provided `userName` and `password` has to be specified. When this option is set, the user does not have access above the directory where the session started. This prevents access into other parts of the system. Such a restriction can be levied when we use a capital letter in the option `-U fileName`. In such a case, the user who knows the login details gets the full access to the other parts of the system.

Workspace limit

The option `-w N` sets the workspace limit for the session. The provided number, `N`, is in MB.

Day of the week

The option `-W N` sets the start of the week. The week by default starts on Monday, which corresponds to $N = 2$. This can be overridden by setting a different value to `N`.

Date format

The option `-z B` with `B` being binary variable sets the format of a date. Namely, the (default) option `-z 0` sets the US style for the date "MM/DD/YYYY", while the option `-z 1` sets the European style for the date "DD/MM/YYYY".

1.8 SUMMARY AND HOW-TO'S

In this final section we provide a refresher of basic operations on vectors and present common how-to's:

Create a vector of natural numbers

```
N:10
v:1+til N
```

Access the first, last, first *n*, and last *n* elements of a vector

```
first v
last v
n:5
n#v
neg[n]#v
```

Drop *n* elements from the start or end of a vector

```
n _v
neg[n]_v
```

Update multiple elements of a vector

```
v[0 9]:0N  / updates with null integer
```

Update multiple elements of a vector where a specific condition occurs

```
v[where 0=v mod 2]:0  / update the values with no remainder after dividing
    ↪ by 2, with zero
```

Sample *n* float numbers uniformly between −5 and 5

```
r:-5+n?10f
```

Update the first element of all records of a matrix or a 2-dimensional list

```
r:-5+n?10f
m:2 2#r
m[;0]:1f
```

CHAPTER 2

Dictionaries and Tables: The q Fundamentals

The fundamental data structure in q is the list. We shall refer to homogeneous lists as `vectors` and reserve the term `lists` for those of `type 0h`. From the first chapter, we recall that these are empty untyped lists or lists of lists. Two other fundamental data structures are dictionaries and tables. Dictionaries in q are simply maps. They are very general and hence very powerful. Tables are where our data will reside and the data structures we will run our q queries on. q supports its own rich query language which builds on top of the functional fundamentals to allow for `insert`, `upsert`, `select`, `update` and `delete` operations.

In this chapter we will introduce dictionaries and tables and show how, from three fundamental concepts, we can construct all q data structures; something that in itself reveals the elegant design and close relationship between everything in q.

2.1 DICTIONARY

A `dictionary` in q is a map of two `lists`. The operator which maps the keys to the values is `!`. A dictionary is therefore defined as:

```
keys!values
```

The most common use case is a key-value pair of a symbol vector – as keys – and their corresponding numeric values:

```
mydict:`a`b`c!1 2 3
```

We index the dictionary using the same notation we used to index vectors; we just replace integer indices with its keys:

```
mydict[`b]
```

```
2
```

The following statements are all equivalent. We need to be extra careful with right-to-left parsing when omitting the square brackets, if the below is written in the context of a larger statement with more operations on the right:

```
mydict[`b]
mydict `b
mydict@`b
```

The first line represents the version we will use when other statements follow on the right.

To access the key and value vectors of the dictionary, we use the intuitive:

```
key mydict
```

```
`a`b`c
```

```
value mydict
```

```
1 2 3
```

The keys and values can be anything, as long as they are lists of the same count, so there is a functional mapping to be defined. The following are therefore also dictionaries:

```
d1:"abc"!97 98 99i;
d1
```

```
a| 97
b| 98
c| 99
```

```
d2:`a`b`c!("alpha";"beta";"gamma");
d2
```

```
a| "alpha"
b| "beta"
c| "gamma"
```

```
d3:("alpha";"beta";"gamma")!`a`b`c;
```

```
vector:1 2 3!10 20 3;
```

In the last example, we will recognise our common vectors; we have just chosen to start indexing at 1 instead of zero. So vectors can be thought of as dictionaries with an integer domain as their key.

Similar to vectors, indexing dictionaries outside their domain does not result in an error, but returns the null element:

```
d1 "d"
```

```
0Ni
```

```
d2`d
```

```
""
```

```
vector 4
```

```
0N
```

Even the following is a dictionary:

```
m1:(1 2 3f;4 5 6f);
m2:(10 20f;30 40f);
(m1;m2)!(count m1;count m2)
```

```
1 2 3 4 5 6| 2
10 20 30 40| 2
```

therefore:

```
matdict:(m1;m2)!(count m1;count m2);
matdict (10 20f;30 40f)
```

```
2
```

More specifically, dictionaries in q define what is known as an algebraic map which is a *partial function*. It is worth mentioning this since uniqueness of key is not guaranteed in q:

```
isThisAllowed: `a`b`a`a!til 4
isThisAllowed`a
```

```
0
```

The values of repeated entries for a key cannot be accessed.

The type of a dictionary is 99h as can be seen from:

```
type dict
```

2.2 TABLE

A table is defined using the following syntax:

```
t:([] sym:`a`b`c; time:0D00:00 0D00:01 0D00:02; price:10 20 30f)
```

This is effectively a list of columns with their names assigned, separated by semi-colons. The square brackets at the start denote the table's primary keys, which in this case are none.

Note that even for a non-keyed table, the [] are required since the following syntax would simply end up creating a list of three `vectors` and assign them to corresponding variables as a side effect:

```
l:( sym:`a`b`c; time:0D00:00 0D00:01 0D00:02; price:10 20 30f)
l
```

```
a                       b                       c
0D00:00:00.000000000 0D00:01:00.000000000 0D00:02:00.000000000
10                      20                      30
```

```
sym   / sym now exists as a global variable which was not our intention
```

```
`a`b`c
```

We can now view our table:

```
t
```

```
sym time                 price
------------------------------
a   0D00:00:00.000000000 10
b   0D00:01:00.000000000 20
c   0D00:02:00.000000000 30
```

its columns

```
cols t
```

```
`sym`time`price
```

its keys

```
keys t
```

```
`symbol$()
```

and its count

```
count t
```

```
3
```

We insert into a table by passing in the table name as a *reference*, which is achieved by passing in the table name as a `symbol`:

```
`t insert ([]sym:enlist `a;time:enlist 0D00:03;price:enlist 15f)
```

```
,3
```

Working with tables is done using `q-sql` syntax. Querying the table is intuitive:

```
select sym,time from t
```

```
sym time
------------------------
a   0D00:00:00.000000000
b   0D00:01:00.000000000
c   0D00:02:00.000000000
a   0D00:03:00.000000000
```

where `select ... from ...` allows us to extract any columns of the table into a subtable.

Further, we may update the content of the existing table by either modifying the existing column or adding a new one:

```
update size:100 200 300 400 from t
```

```
sym time                 price size
-----------------------------------
a   0D00:00:00.000000000 10    100
b   0D00:01:00.000000000 20    200
c   0D00:02:00.000000000 30    300
a   0D00:03:00.000000000 15    400
```

Using the same `select` paradigm, we can obtain aggregate summary statistics of the table using functions applied on the entire columns:

```
select avg price from t
```

```
price
-----
18.75
```

We can calculate aggregate statistics and group as follows:

```
select avg price by sym from t
```

```
sym| price
---| -----
a  | 12.5
b  | 20
c  | 30
```

Notice the two nice side effects of the by clause which come for free: the resultant table is keyed by symbol (denoting uniqueness) and also sorted by its key.

We confirm the presence of a primary key:

```
keys select avg price by sym from t
```

```
,`sym
```

We constrain our query using the where function, familiar to us from Chapter 1:

```
select avg price by sym from t where time>=0D00:02
```

```
sym| price
---| -----
a  | 15
c  | 30
```

Multiple where clauses are joined by ,:

```
select from t where sym=`a,price>10
```

```
sym time                 price
------------------------------
a   0D00:03:00.000000000 15
```

Note that right-to-left evaluation does not apply within a q-sql statement. So this is the exception to the golden rule. The where clauses are applied from left to right and are *cascading*: they are applied in order, so the first one reduces the data set to a subset before the second constraint is applied and so on. We should, therefore, make sure that the constraint which reduces our data set by the most significant amount is applied first.

We encourage the reader to create sample tables and assess the impact of the order of conditional clauses on the speed of evaluation. In practical problems, there may be a vast difference in execution time, and proper assessment of conditional clauses is a typical way of improving the code.

To define a table with primary keys, we just need to include the key columns within the [] in its definition:

```
kt:([sym:`a`b`c]name:`alpha`beta`gamma);
kt
```

```
sym| name
---| -----
a  | alpha
b  | beta
c  | gamma
```

Let us further illustrate how we can delete a column from a table:

```
ks:([sym:`a`b`c] name:`alpha`beta`gamma; name2:`a`b`c)
delete name from ks
```

```
sym| name2
---| -----
a  | a
b  | b
c  | c
```

The `delete` function can be used to selectively delete some observations based on a conditional clause:

```
delete from ks where name=`alpha
```

```
sym| name  name2
---| -----------
b  | beta  b
c  | gamma c
```

What if we wanted to directly extract a column as a `list` instead of creating a subtable? We can replace `select` with `exec`:

```
exec name from ks
```

```
`alpha`beta`gamma
```

If we extract more than one column using `exec`, the outcome will be a dictionary indexed by the column names:

```
exec name, name2 from ks
```

```
name | alpha beta gamma
name2| a     b    c
```

Finally, the type of a table is 98h as can be seen from:

```
type t
```

Another useful function for working with tables is `meta`. The argument of the function is a table and the function returns another table, where every row of the table corresponds to a column of the original table with information about its type (`t`), foreign key (`f`), and attribute (`a`) corresponding to being sorted (`` `s ``), unique (`` `u ``), partitioned (`` `p ``) or true index (`` `g ``).

The following is an example of a table without any foreign keys or attributes assigned to any of its string columns:

```
meta ks
```

```
c    | t f a
-----| -----
sym  | s
name | s
name2| s
```

2.3 THE TRUTH ABOUT TABLES

Dictionaries and Tables in q are related. We saw that they have different data types (99h and 98h respectively), but how different are they?

The answer is not that much. A dictionary which maps a vector of symbol keys to a list of vectors would appear similar to a collection of columns, which is what a table is:

```
d:`sym`time`price!(`a`b`c;0D00:00 0D00:01 0D00:02;10 20 30f)
d
```

```
sym  | a                    b                    c
time | 0D00:00:00.000000000 0D00:01:00.000000000 0D00:02:00.000000000
price| 10                   20                   30
```

A reminder of what the table t we defined earlier looks like in the q console:

```
t:([] sym:`a`b`c; time:0D00:00 0D00:01 0D00:02; price:10 20 30f)
t
```

```
sym time                 price
------------------------------
a   0D00:00:00.000000000 10
b   0D00:01:00.000000000 20
c   0D00:02:00.000000000 30
```

If only we could flip (transpose) d by 90 degrees, the two would look exactly the same! In Chapter 1 we saw that flip is used to transpose matrices, which were defined as n lists of vectors with count n. Let's try to apply flip to a dictionary:

```
flip d
```

```
sym time                 price
------------------------------
a   0D00:00:00.000000000 10
b   0D00:01:00.000000000 20
c   0D00:02:00.000000000 30
```

d and t now do indeed look exactly the same. Are they? We find out by using the match function ~:

```
t~flip d
```

```
1b
```

So q tables are simply the flip or their corresponding dictionaries. This is very powerful since – apart from providing a different syntax for table creation – it gives us a convenient way to create a table out of a dictionary and vice versa, on the fly.

Let us take a moment to reflect. d – being a q dictionary – is a map of symbol names to vectors and q is a vector language, famous for being the language of a columnar database. Surely tables cannot be the transposition of columnar maps into plain old collections of records? Rest assured they are not. A q table is still a dictionary at heart. Internally t and d are the same and "all" that happens is that indexing is allowed in a transposed way, to enable us to index a table more familiarly, i.e. indexing on records first.

Let's look at indexing and basic operations on a dictionary and a table side by side:

```
d`sym
```

```
`a`b`c
```

```
t[0 1]
```

```
sym time                 price
------------------------------
a   0D00:00:00.000000000 10
b   0D00:01:00.000000000 20
```

```
d[`sym;0 1]
```

```
`a`b
```

```
t[0 1;`sym]
```

```
`a`b
```

Here q is just tricking us into believing they are the transposition of each other. In fact, a table and a q dictionary both have the efficiency and speed that comes from mapping names to vectors stored in contiguous memory.

Upon further investigation, q does convince us that this is indeed the case, by allowing us to do the following as well on t, as if it was a dictionary:

```
t[`sym]
```

```
`a`b`c
```

```
t `sym`price
```

```
a  b  c
10 20 30
```

Transposing a table also gives us a dictionary:

```
d~flip t
```

```
1b
```

Also, applying `flip` twice results in identity operation:

```
d~flip flip d
```

```
1b
```

```
t~flip flip t
```

```
1b
```

2.4 KEYED TABLES ARE DICTIONARIES

We just saw that tables and dictionaries are in essence the same thing under the hood, which is very efficient as well as plain handy. They appear to be different to allow us to work with both tables and maps as separate entities and have different data types.

We will now attempt to create a new construct, using both tables and dictionaries. One may ask: What would happen if we created a map of a table to another table? Let us try it:

```
kt:([]sym:`a`b`c) ! ([]name:`alpha`beta`gamma)
```

```
sym| name
---| -----
a  | alpha
b  | beta
c  | gamma
```

This looks identical to the keyed table example we gave at the start of this chapter. It is:

```
( ([]sym:`a`b`c) ! ([]name:`alpha`beta`gamma) ) ~ ([sym:`a`b`c] name:`alpha
    ↪ `beta`gamma)
```

```
1b
```

```
keys kt
```

```
,`sym
```

So a table with primary keys (aka a keyed table) is a dictionary. Not related to one, or almost identical to one like a flat table, but a *bona fide* dictionary. We know that since we defined it to be one, but we can also confirm it once again:

```
type kt
```

```
99h
```

This is yet another elegant implementation by q. Keeping things simple and generic, a primary key is simply a map (a 'partial function') of its primary keys to its values. It just happens that the primary keys and values are tables with the same length:

```
key kt
```

```
sym
---
a
b
c
```

```
value kt
```

```
name
-----
alpha
beta
gamma
```

Tables can have multiple columns, so a keyed table with a composite key is merely a dictionary whose key is a table with more than one columns. For clarity, we should stick to the standard table definition syntax when declaring flat and keyed tables. However, knowing that a table is a flip of a dictionary and a keyed table is a dictionary itself, will allow us to make full use of the power of q as we will see next.

2.5 FROM A VECTOR LANGUAGE TO AN ALGEBRAIC LANGUAGE

Up to now, we have seen that q is a vector language. Its native functions apply to vectors and result in either a vector or a scalar. In the most recent sections we also saw two new data structures which build upon vectors, the q dictionary and table. We just saw that keyed tables are also dictionaries themselves. These data structures combine vectors and the concept of mapping to give us a comprehensive set of data structures from which we can build mappings and a time-series database combined with the power of a functional language like q. In this section, we will see how the concepts we saw with vectors can be applied naturally on dictionaries and tables.

All the native operations around lookups, finding and indexing which we saw in Chapter 1 can be applied to dictionaries and tables, too. Recall table t:

```
t
```

```
sym time                 price
------------------------------
a   0D00:00:00.000000000 10
b   0D00:01:00.000000000 20
c   0D00:02:00.000000000 30
```

In the previous section we indexed the table on a vector of indices and got a subtable. What if we index it on a single index:

```
t[0]
```

```
sym  | `a
time | 0D00:00:00.000000000
price| 10f
```

The result is a dictionary. So tables can be thought of as transposed dictionaries but *also* as a list of dictionaries. The following vector functions also apply to tables:

```
first t
sym  | `a
time | 0D00:00:00.000000000
price| 10f
```

```
last t
sym  | `c
time | 0D00:02:00.000000000
price| 30f
```

Recall the _ (drop) function:

```
-2_ t
```

```
sym time                 price
------------------------------
a   0D00:00:00.000000000 10
```

? (find) also works. We use dictionaries as elements to find:

```
t? `sym`time`price!(`c;0D00:02:00.000000000;30f)
```

```
2
```

Just like when using ? with vectors, we can also search for lists: in this case, the list is a list of dictionaries, i.e., a table:

```
t? ([]sym:`c`c;time:0D00:02:00.000000000 0D00:02:00.000000000;price:30 40f)
```

```
2 3
```

Due to the interchangeability of indices in tables, we can do things like:

```
t[0]`sym`time
```

```
`a
0D00:00:00.000000000
```

or,

```
t[`sym`time]0
```

```
`a`b`c
```

We can also run this command, which extracts the sub-set of columns with a given row index:

```
`sym`time#t 0
```

```
sym | `a
time| 0D00:00:00.000000000
```

or just extract columns:

```
`sym`time#t
```

```
sym time
------------------------
a   0D00:00:00.000000000
b   0D00:01:00.000000000
c   0D00:02:00.000000000
```

The `# (take)` function is, therefore, naturally extended to dictionaries and tables. So apart from just taking the first `n` elements of a vector, it can select a subdomain of keys of a dictionary or columns of a table. In fact it can also apply to a superdomain of a dictionary's keys:

```
`sym`price`somecol#t 0
```

```
sym    | `a
price  | 10f
somecol| `
```

Now let's extend the above concepts to key `tables`. Remember, key `tables` in `q` are `dictionaries`! Let's use previously defined `kt` and the following happen naturally:

```
kt[ ([]sym:`a`c) ]
```

```
name
-----
alpha
gamma
```

```
kt ? ([]name:`alpha`zeta)
```

```
sym
---
a
`
```

```
kt enlist[`sym]!enlist `a
```

```
name| alpha
```

```
kt ([]sym:`a`c`d)
```

```
name
-----
alpha
gamma
`
```

```
([]sym:`a`c`d)#kt
```

```
sym| name
---| -----
a  | alpha
c  | gamma
d  |
```

The last statement allows us to create new entries into our table by providing a superdomain of values! q naturally fills the values of those new entries with `null` for that column's data type. This is indeed powerful. For example, a very useful use case is to build a full-time series from a sparsely sampled population. Recall:

```
t
```

```
sym time                 price
------------------------------
a   0D00:00:00.000000000 10
b   0D00:01:00.000000000 20
c   0D00:02:00.000000000 30
```

Let's aggregate the price by 30-second intervals. According to the definition of `xbar`, q will group by rounding down to the nearest value which divides the existing time vector:

```
select avg price by 0D00:00:30 xbar time from t
```

```
time                | price
--------------------| -----
0D00:00:00.000000000| 10
0D00:01:00.000000000| 20
0D00:02:00.000000000| 30
```

In this example, that's simply the values themselves. What if we wanted to force the 30-second granularity? We start by creating this granular time series:

```
([]time:`timespan$0D00:00 + 30* 1e09 * til 5)
```

```
time
--------------------
0D00:00:00.000000000
0D00:00:30.000000000
0D00:01:00.000000000
0D00:01:30.000000000
0D00:02:00.000000000
```

We now `take` this superdomain from the keyed `table` on the right:

```
([]time:`timespan$0D00:00 + 30* 1e09 * til 5)#select avg price by 0D00
    ↪ :00:30 xbar time from t
```

```
time                | price
--------------------| -----
0D00:00:00.000000000| 10
0D00:00:30.000000000|
0D00:01:00.000000000| 20
0D00:01:30.000000000|
0D00:02:00.000000000| 30
```

We have just resampled the time series. Not using some fancy function but just working with native operators and understanding the underlying `q` data structures. Clearly, `q` is *more* than just a vector language. Its primitives naturally extend, and we can achieve powerful algebraic calculations simply by using its native operators.

CHAPTER 3

Functions

q defines the following function types:

- operators and primitive functions
- q-SQL functions, as described in the previous chapter, e.g. select, update, upsert, insert
- user-defined functions
- derived functions, with the use of *adverbs*.

All predefined q functions can be used in both infix or prefix notations, whereas user-defined functions must be called using a prefix notation. For example, the predefined dyadic operator (function) + can be written as follows:

```
5 + 7 // infix notation
+[5;7] // prefix notation
(+) . 5 7 // apply notation
```

A q function is delimited with open and closed curly brackets { and }. The optional arguments of the function are defined in square brackets separated with semicolon, i.e. `[arg1;arg2;...;argn]` declared at the beginning of the function. Function parameters `x`, `y` and `z` are implicitly defined. Functions can have a name with the assignment operator : as for variables.

A function returning the square of a number is defined as:

```
{x*x}
```

Hence,

```
{x*x} 5f
```

returns

```
25f
```

Alternatively, we can write:

```
{x*x}[5f]
```

to get the same output. Using the square brackets explicitly may be required when the call to function is used within longer expressions due to the *right-to-left* evaluation and is generally a good practice for code clarity.

It can be applied to a list of variables of several types:

```
{x*x} 5 6 7 8f
```

returns the square of the floating numbers 5, 6, 7 and 8.

```
{x*x} 5 6 7 8i
```

returns the square of integers 5, 6, 7 and 8.

The function `compute` below has three arguments, `a`, `n` and `theta`, and returns the output of the equation $a * \cos(n * \theta)$:

```
compute:{[a;n;theta]a*cos n*theta}
```

Hence,

```
compute[5;3.5;1.57]
```

returns

```
3.525666
```

Functions can be nested:

```
a:{[x;w]v:{[x;w]3*w+x};v[x;2*w]-4f}
```

The function `a` returns `v - 4f`, where `v` is a nested function returning `3(w+x)`. Hence,

```
a[4f;3f]
```

first calls the `v` function:

```
v[4f;2*3f]
```

and subtracts `4f`, i.e.

```
v[4f;2*3f]-4f = (3*6f+4f) - 4f = 30f - 4f
```

which will result in following output when executed:

```
26f
```

Functions and variables defined within a function are local. They are created and exist in the scope of the function. Therefore, in the example above, the scope inside the `v` function has no visibility to the local variables or the arguments of the `a` function. Global variables are declared with a double `::` symbol:

```
a:4;
f:{[b]a::6;a+b};
f[7]
```

```
13
```

with a being updated accordingly:

```
a
```

returns

```
6
```

The variable a defined within the function f is global.

Multivalent functions can be projected by specifying only part of the parameters of the functions while keeping the remaining arguments. Projection is related to currying in functional programming. A function of n parameters is equivalent to a function of the first parameter that returns the function of the n-1 remaining parameters.

A monadic function – frequently referred as unary function – g can be a projection of a dyadic function – or binary function – f by fixing only its first argument:

```
f:{x+y};
g:f[4;]; // projection on f where x takes the value 4: {x+y}[4;]
```

Hence

```
g[5]
```

returns

```
20
```

3.1 NAMESPACE

A namespace is a context within which a name resolves to a unique value. Functions and variables are defined in a namespace as follows:

```
.namespaceName.variableName
```

Hence, the variable *x* and function *f* defined in namespace1 and namespace2 have different values:

```
.namespace1.x:4f;
.namespace1.f:{5+x};
.namespace2.x:5;
.namespace2.f:{1f+log x};
```

We can call function f from the two different contexts as follows:

```
.namespace2.f[.namespace1.x] // returns 1f+log 4f
```

```
2.386294
```

and

```
.namespace1.f[.namespace1.x] // returns 5+4f
```

```
9f
```

3.1.0.1 .quantQ. Namespace

In this book, we use one root namespace under which all functions and variables are defined. The namespace is called .quantQ. It allows us to easily recognise the functions we have defined and relate them to the text in this book. Each area of focus – usually corresponding to a chapter – will also have its dedicated sub-namespace, which will be directly under .quantQ. and contain all relevant functions. This helps us naturally group different concepts and also makes it easier to search for specific functions across different sections of the book. For example, all functions relating to complex numbers and their usage in discrete Fourier transform (15) are under the .quantQ.complex.* namespace. We can, therefore, search for a function by interrogating the functions under that namespace:

```
\f .quantQ.complex
```

```
`conjugate`dft`dft1k`dftTab`dftTs`div`exp`fractal`log`mandelbrot`mandelbrot
    ↪ _`multi`norm`polar..
```

and the relevant code will be found under the eponymous file complex.q. Using a consistent namespace also prevents us from naming conflicts and accidentally overriding existing functions one may have.

Besides, the code used in this book follows a certain philosophy, for instance using comments within functions which may make the code longer than necessary, but helps present the function implementations in the book text.

3.2 THE SIX ADVERBS

kdb+ has nouns, verbs and adverbs. Functions and data objects are nouns. Verbs are syntactic sugar introduced to improve the readability of the language. They allow for infix notation to reduce the number of square brackets and parentheses in expressions. Arithmetic and logical operators or dyadic functions written in infix notation are verbs. Hence, the verb * in:

```
4*5
```

reads right-to-left as "multiply 5 by 4" and can also be written as

```
*[4;5]
```

Adverbs are higher-order functions that modify the behaviour of functions applied to lists. They return derived functions, known as derivatives.

3.2.1 Each

The "each" adverb comes in several forms. each modifies monadic functions, i.e. functions with valence of one. The more general each-both, denoted ' modifies dyadic – or more generally, polyadic – functions provided that all arguments have equal length. Each-left and each-right, denoted by \: and /:, respectively, are two other forms of each for dyadic functions. A combination of each-left and each-right provides the cross product.

3.2.1.1 Each

The each adverb modifies a monadic function so that it applies to each item in a list rather than to the list as a whole. Hence, the adverb each in the following code applies the monadic function reverse to each single element of the nested list.

```
reverse each ((`a`b`c);(`d`e`f))
```

```
c b a
f e d
```

Without introducing the verb each, the two sublists would be inverted:

```
reverse ((`a`b`c);(`d`e`f))
```

returns

```
d e f
a b c
```

3.2.1.2 Each-left \:

The each-left adverb `\:` modifies a dyadic function so that it applies the second argument on each item of the first argument. In other words, `x f \: y` applies `f` between `y` and items of `x`. The following expression:

```
(4 5 6f) { x-y xexp 2 }\:(5 6 7f)
```

applies the dyadic function `x-y xexp 2` with the second argument `y:(5 6 7f)` on each of the first argument `x:(4 5 6f)`:

4 - 5 xexp 2   4 - 6 xexp 2   4 - 7 xexp 2
5 - 5 xexp 2   5 - 6 xexp 2   5 - 7 xexp 2
6 - 5 xexp 2   6 - 6 xexp 2   6 - 7 xexp 2
namely:

```
-21 -32 -45
-20 -31 -44
-19 -30 -43
```

Note the above can alternatively be written using a combination of a *projection* and the unary each in one call:

```
{ x-y xexp 2 }[;5 6 7f]each 4 5 6f
```

```
-21 -32 -45
-20 -31 -44
-19 -30 -43
```

The outer product between two vectors $u \otimes v = uv^T$ can be written as:

```
.quantQ.outer:{x *\:y}
```

where we have defined the function within the book's namespace.

3.2.1.3 Each-right /:

The each-right adverb /: modifies a dyadic function so that it applies the first argument to each item of the second argument. Applying the each-right adverb to the same x-y xexp 2 function and the same arguments:

```
(4 5 6f) { x-y xexp 2 }/:(5 6 7f)
```

returns:

```
-21 -20 -19
-32 -31 -30
-45 -44 -43
```

Moreover, similarly to the each-left case, this can alternatively be written as

```
{ x-y xexp 2 }[4 5 6f;]each (5 6 7f)
```

```
-21 -20 -19
-32 -31 -30
-45 -44 -43
```

The identity matrix can be built with each-left or each-right adverbs as follows:

```
.quantQ.identity:{[n] `float$(til n)=/:til n}
```

It checks whether each element of `til n` namely `0,1, 2, ..., n-1` is equal to each element of `til n` on the right-hand side.

```
.quantQ.identity[4]
```

returns:

```
1 0 0 0
0 1 0 0
0 0 1 0
0 0 0 1
```

3.2.1.4 Cross Product /: \:

The cross product or Cartesian product is the composition of an each-right with an each-left. It pairs each item on the left with each item on the right:

```
(4 5 6f) { x-y xexp 2 }/:\:(5 6 7f)
```

It is equivalent to:

```
(4 {x -y xexp 2}\:(5 6 7f); 5 {x -y xexp 2}\:(5 6 7f); 6 {x -y xexp 2}\:(5
    ↪ 6 7f))
```

and returns:

```
-21 -32 -45
-20 -31 -44
-19 -30 -43
```

The built-in operator `cross` computes the Cartesian product between two objects. For lists, `x cross y` is equivalent to `raze x,/:\:y`.

```
(4 5 6f) cross (5 6 7f)
```

returns

```
4 5
4 6
4 7
5 5
5 6
5 7
6 5
6 6
6 7
```

3.2.1.5 Each-both '

The more general each-both `'` adverb modifies dyadic functions and verbs to apply to the items of lists instead of the lists themselves. The cardinality of both lists must be the same. The expression:

```
(`a;`b;`c),'(4;5;6)
```

applies the each-both adverb `'` to the dyadic function `,` on the two lists ``(`a;`b;`c)`` and `(4;5;6)` resulting:

```
`a 4
`b 5
`c 6
```

Note that the cardinality of both lists must be the same, otherwise a `'length` error is returned:

```
(`a`b),'(`a`b`c)
```

returns the error message:

```
'length
```

The each-both adverb can be used to add columns to tables as tables are the list of records. Given two tables:

```
tbl1:([]c1:`a`b`c);
tbl2:([]c2:(1f;2f;3f));
```

```
tbl1,'tbl2
```

joins the column of `tbl1` with the column of `tbl2`:

```
c1 c2
-----
a  1
b  2
c  3
```

The adverb `'` can be applied to user-defined functions:

```
(4 5 6f) {x*y}'(5 6 7f)
```

The code applies the adverb `'` on the function `x*y` with arguments `(4 5 6f)` and `(5 6 7f)`. In this trivial example, it is equivalent to calling the dyadic function `x*y` on the two lists `((4 5 6f);(5 6 7f))` with the dot notation:

```
{x*y} . ((4 5 6f);(5 6 7f))
```

```
20 30 42f
```

Note that in many cases, the native q functions will be sufficient on a pair of lists, without having to apply the `each` or each-both `'` adverbs.

For example, the dot product between two vectors,

$$\begin{bmatrix} a_1 \\ a_2 \\ \dots \\ a_n \end{bmatrix} \cdot \begin{bmatrix} b_1 \\ b_2 \\ \dots \\ b_n \end{bmatrix} = a_1 b_1 + a_2 b_2 + \dots + a_n b_n \ , \tag{3.1}$$

need not to be defined as:

```
x:1 2 3f
y:3 4 5f
sum x * ' y
```

```
26f
```

since the native multiplication operator already applies on two vectors, as we have seen. So the above can be simplified to

```
sum x * y
```

```
26f
```

Moreover, for dot product, there is a built-in – and more computationally efficient – function, as we saw in Chapter 1:

```
x$y
```

```
26f
```

A more complex example, which better illustrates a case where we can use each-both, is when we have a more complicated calculation, and therefore makes sense to be applied over each element of the two lists in a pairwise manner. This is usually the case when we are dealing with mixed lists, i.e. lists of vectors:

```
n:10000;
t:([] a: -2.5 + (n#3) ?\: 5f; b: n?10);
```

Note above the use of each-left in calling the random number generator ? to construct a mixed list, i.e. a *nested vector* for table `t`:

```
a                                  b
------------------------------------
-1.011575  0.3837389  0.1888203    7
-0.4294275 -0.1388864 0.01773961   0
0.6903965  -0.7769351 -2.282934    3
-2.174598  2.101333   -2.306228    0
1.372702   1.740763   -0.03952036 5
-1.452881  -2.420917  0.139957     1
-2.138477  -2.430328  -2.169646    4
0.351389   -1.361123  0.8741012    5
0.2354421  -1.820678  -2.128178    9
2.232667   -0.3603936 -1.423614    8
0.4742755  -2.097245  0.8341878    5
1.872449   -2.141622  -2.093962    5
-1.538976  -0.1160515 -2.275455    5
-0.3917162 1.803389   -0.3954578   1
..
```

Here we have a table where column `a` is a *nested* column, so each entry in `a` is a vector.

We now create an example `calc` function which takes two arguments; the first argument applies to a vector, whereas the second is a scalar. Example of the two inputs, a vector and a scalar, could be the first record in our table `t`, e.g. `-1.011575 0.3837389 0.1888203` and 7.

Let's assume our function `calc` is also piecewise, thus evaluates differently based on a condition:

```
calc: { $[ all 0 <  x; x xexp reciprocal y; x xexp y] }
```

and

```
calc[-1.011575  0.3837389  0.1888203 ;7]
```

```
-1.083894 0.001225324 8.557379e-06
```

How to pass this function across all entries (records) of table t?

```
r: update c: calc'[a;b] from t;
r
```

```
a                                    b c
----------------------------------------------------------------------------
-1.011575  0.3837389  0.1888203   7 -1.083891     0.001225322   8.557395e-06
-0.4294275 -0.1388864 0.01773961  0 1             1             1
0.6903965  -0.7769351 -2.282934   3 0.3290757     -0.4689798    -11.89817
-2.174598  2.101333   -2.306228   0 1             1             1
1.372702   1.740763   -0.03952036 5 4.873953      15.98447      -9.640612e-08
-1.452881  -2.420917  0.139957    1 -1.452881     -2.420917     0.139957
-2.138477  -2.430328  -2.169646   4 20.9131       34.88666      22.15929
0.351389   -1.361123  0.8741012   5 0.005357236   -4.671822     0.51028
0.2354421  -1.820678  -2.128178   9 2.223088e-06  -219.8357     -895.5123
2.232667   -0.3603936 -1.423614   8 617.4354      0.0002845877  16.87085
0.4742755  -2.097245  0.8341878   5 0.02399682    -40.57386     0.4039422
1.872449   -2.141622  -2.093962   5 23.01705      -45.05198     -40.25724
-1.538976  -0.1160515 -2.275455   5 -8.632939     -2.105007e-05 -61.00157
-0.3917162 1.803389   -0.3954578  1 -0.3917162    1.803389      -0.3954578
..
```

What would happen to the call above if column b was also a nested column?

3.2.2 Each-prior ':

The each-prior adverb ': performs a dyadic operation on each item of a list with its predecessor. Let us consider an example:

```
4 {x-y xexp 2}': (5 6 7f)
```

which applies the function x-y xexp 2 with initial value 4 between each item of the list 5 6 7f and its predecessor. Hence, the expression is equivalent to:

```
(5 - 4 xexp 2; 6 - 5 xexp 2; 7 - 6 xexp 2)
```

and returns:

```
-11 -19 -29f
```

The monadic version of the each-prior adverb does not choose an initial value:

```
({x-y xexp 2}':)(5 6 7f)
```

It is equivalent to:

```
(5f-0n xexp 2; 6f-5f xexp 2; 7f - 6f xexp 2)
```

and returns:

```
0n -19 -29
```

3.2.3 Compose (')

The composition of a multivalent function `f[a;b;c;...]` with a monadic function `g[x]`, expressed mathematically as $g \circ f$, is defined as `'[g;f]`. For example:

```
f:{[a;b;c;d]a+(2*b)+(3*c)+4*d};
g:{log x};
d:('[g;f]);
d[5;6;7;8]
```

computes $log(5 + (2 * 6) + (3 * 7) + 4 * 8) = log(70)$, which is returned:

```
4.248495
```

3.2.4 Over and Fold /

The over adverb / modifies a dyadic function to accumulate the results over a list. Let us denote $y_i, i \in \mathbb{N}_+^*$ the ith element of a list y of length n. The expression `x f/ y` recursively applies the function `f` on `x` and each element of `y`, i.e., computes expression $f[f[...f[f[x;y_0];y_1];...y_{n-2}];y_{n-1}]$.

The expression:

```
4f {x-y xexp 2}/(5 6 7f)
```

is equivalent to:

```
(((4f-5f xexp 2)-6f xexp 2)-7f xexp 2)
```

and returns:

```
-106f
```

The over adverb / can also be applied to monadic functions without specifying an accumulator `x`. The expression `(f/) y` on the list `y` computes nested functions $f[...f[y_0]...y_{n-1}]$. Hence, the expression

```
({x-y xexp 2}/)(5 6 7f)
```

computes:

```
(5f-6f xexp 2)-7f xexp 2
```

and returns:

```
-80f
```

In prefix forms, the two previous expressions are written as follows:

```
({x-y xexp 2}/)[4f;(5 6 7f)]
({x-y xexp 2}/)[(5 6 7f)]
```

The over adverb is often called fold when the function has more than two arguments. The expression `f/[x;y;z]` computes expression $f[f[...f[f[x;y_0;z_0];y_1;z_1];...y_{n-2};z_{n-2}];y_{n-1};z_{n-1}]$.

```
({z+x-y xexp 2}/)[1 3f; 4 5f; 2f]
```

computes

```
( 2f + (2f+1f-4f xexp 2) - 5f xexp 2;  2f + (2f+3-4f xexp 2) - 5f xexp 2)
```

and returns:

```
-36 -34f
```

The adverb fold can also be thought of in a *map-reduce* context, where we fold , i.e. *reduce*, the result. A very useful built-in implementation of this is the function `raze`, which folds the input list into a single element:

```
raze (1 2 3;4 5 6)
```

```
1 2 3 4 5 6
```

Examining the implementation of `raze` reveals that it is the comma-join with the adverb fold:

```
raze
```

```
,/
```

and

```
(,/) (1 2 3;4 5 6)
```

```
1 2 3 4 5 6
```

3.2.5 Scan

The scan adverb behaves as the over adverb except that intermediary results are shown after each accumulation. Hence, `x f\ y` iteratively computes expression $f[f[...f[f[x;y_0];y_1];...y_{n-2}];y_{n-1}]$ and displays each intermediary result $(x;f[x;y_0];f[f[x;y_0];y_1],...,f[f[...f[f[x;y_0];y_1];...y_{n-2}];y_{n-1}])$.

We saw in our previous example that

```
({x-y xexp 2}/)(5 6 7f)
```

only returns the final result of the computation, i.e. `(5f - 6f xexp 2)-7f xexp 2`

```
-80f
```

while

```
({x-y xexp 2}\)(5 6 7f)
```

shows the intermediary results:

```
5 -31 -80f
```

where `5f` is the first item of the `x` variable, `-31f = 5f - 6f xexp 2` and `-80f = (5f - 6f xexp 2) - 7f xexp 2`.

3.2.5.1 EMA: The Exponential Moving Average

Let's see how scan can be applied to compute this very common iterative function for which we want the intermediate results of the time series. Given a vector $x_0, x_1, ..., x_i, ..., x_n$ and a weight λ, the EMA at point i is defined as:

$$EMA_i(\lambda) = x_{i-1} \times (1 - \lambda) + EMA_{i-1} \times \lambda,$$

where $EMA_0 = x_0$.

Thus, given the vector `10 20 30`, and a λ of `0.2`, the EMA at each point will be

```
10                        / x[0]
( 10 * 0.8 ) + 20 * 0.2    / ( x[0] * (1 - lambda) ) + x[1] * lambda
```

```
12f
```

```
( 12 * 0.8 ) + 30 * 0.2    / ( x[1] * (1 - lambda) ) + x[2] * lambda
```

```
15.6
```

We can therefore use `scan` to implement the above iteratively:

```
.quantQ.stats.expma1:{[lambda;vector]
    / lambda -- memory
    / vector -- data
    {[x;y;z] (x*y)+z}\[ first vector; 1 - lambda; vector * lambda]
 };
```

and

```
.quantQ.stats.expma1[0.2;10 20 30]
```

```
10 12 15.6
```

Note that, since version 3.1, q has an optimisation which simplifies

```
{{z+y*x}\[x;y;z]}
```

to

```
{x y\z}
```

and our function can thus be written as

```
.quantQ.stats.expma:{[lambda;vector]
    // lambda -- memory
    // vector -- data
    :(first vector)(1-lambda)\vector*lambda;
 };
```

q has a built-in function for the EMA, namely ema, which takes two arguments as per our implementation above, and has the equivalent definition.

Nonetheless, our derivation of this function using scan has hopefully illustrated how we can write optimal iterative code using adverbs and will be of use to us in other data analytics we will encounter later on; one example being the implementation of consecutive runs, as we shall see in Chapter 11.

3.2.6 Converge

The over / and scan \ adverbs recursively apply a function to each item of a list. They can also be used to iterate over a list until convergence or until a loop is detected.

3.2.6.1 Converge-repeat

The recursive pattern

```
x f/ y
```

applies the function f x times with initial value y.

If x is a boolean function to indicate a condition on recursive iteration, the expression is equivalent to a while loop:

```
x:y; / initial condition
while[x;f]
```

The following expression recursively applies the function x*x-1 2 times on the list (2 4 3 2 5f)

```
2 {x*x-1}/(2 4 3 2 5f)
```

and returns:

```
2 132 30 2 380f
```

It is equivalent to applying the result of the first iteration:

```
1{x*x-1}/(2 4 3 2 5f)
```

```
2 12 6 2 20f
```

to the function x*x-1.

```
1{x*x-1}/2 12 6 2 20f
```

The following expression recursively applies the function x*x starting with the value 2 until the condition x<20 is fulfilled:

```
{x<20}{x*x}/2
```

and returns:

```
256
```

The function x*x is first applied on 2. As the result 4 is less than 20, the iteration continues and produces 16. As 16 < 20 the function is applied and returns 256. The recursion terminates as 256 > 20 and the final result 256 is returned.

The expression is equivalent to while loop:

```
x:2;
while[x<20;x:x*x];
```

3.2.6.2 Converge-iterate

The converge-iterate pattern is similar to the converge-repeat pattern described in the previous section but using the scan adverb to display all intermediary results. Hence, the previous example applied using the scan \ adverb

```
2 {x*x-1}\(2 4 3 2 5f)
```

returns each intermediary results of the recursive iteration:

```
2 4   3  2 5
2 12  6  2 20
2 132 30 2 380
```

The first line displays the input parameters, the second line the result of the first iteration and the third line the final result.

Given the random generator function rand which returns a random number between 0 and x, the expression:

```
{0.7<x} rand\10f
```

written in prefix format as:

```
rand\[{0.7<x};10f]
```

repeatedly calls rand with parameter 10f until the condition 0.7<x is not satisfied.

```
10 7.263142 6.694028 1.211308 0.7794329 0.2265884
```

When converge only takes a single argument, it will iterate until it converges to a value. Convergence means repeated items (for non-float datatypes) or equality within float tolerance. Each output of an iteration is the input of the next call.

Let us look at two examples, one with integer convergence and one with float. We set f to be a function which always adds 1 to the result of the rand call. The output of this call will be the input of the next iteration, so we add 1 to guarantee that we always sample from a non-zero number.

```
f: { 1+rand x };
```

and

```
f\[5]
```

repeatedly calls f with parameter $f[x_i - 1]$, and $x_0 = 5$, until two consecutive values repeat, giving:

```
5 4 3
```

Passing in a float, we will observe convergence within a tolerance:

```
rand\[1e-18]
```

```
1e-18 2.580512e-19 2.228634e-19 1.703674e-19 1.495538e-19 9.947239e-20
    ↪ 1.440335e-20...
```

In q, float tolerance for two numbers x and y is defined as the ϵ, for which $(x - y) < \epsilon \times \max(x, y)$.

3.3 APPLY

The verbs @ and . apply a multivariate mapping to a list of arguments, written in prefix or infix form. Sections 3.3.1 and 3.3.2 describe the differences between the two notations.

3.3.1 @ (apply)

The verb @ is used to apply a monadic function f on indices I of a list L with the syntax: @[L;I;f]. The following expression applies the function cosine on the first and third elements of the list; the second element 1.570796 being left unchanged:

```
@[(0.7853982; 1.570796; 3.141592654);0 2;cos]
```

It returns cos 0.7853982; 1.570796; cos 3.141592654:

```
0.7071068 1.570796 -1
```

When applied to dyadic function, @[L;I;f;a] applies a dyadic function f on the I-th elements of a list L with second argument a. Example:

```
@[1 2 3 4f; 0 2; {x+2*y}; 6 7f]
```

applies the function x+2*y on the first and third elements of 1 2 3 4f, namely 1 and 3 and the second argument 6 7f. The values of L=1 2 3 4f for all elements not in 0 2 are returned, i.e. L@1= 2f and L@3 = 4f. The expression computes 1+2*6f 2 3+2*7f 4f:

```
13 2 17 4f
```

3.3.2 . (apply)

A function of arity N applied to a list x of size N is executed with the . verb as .[f;x] or f . x. Example:

```
{[a;b;c;d]a+2*b+3*c-d} . (4;5;3;7)
```

is equivalent to:

```
{[a;b;c;d]a+2*b+3*c-d}[4;5;3;7]
```

and returns:

```
-10 // 4+2*5+3*(3-7)
```

Monadic functions can be applied as:

```
{x*x} . enlist 5
{x*x}@5
{x*x} 5
{x*x}[5]
```

When applied to lists, the verb . indexes a list at depth:

```
L:((`a;4);(`c;5);(`d;7;(8;6;9f)));
L . 2 2 2
```

and returns:

```
9f
```

Elided indices with . are called with the identity item ::. Take the following matrix as an example:

```
M:(1 2 3f;4 5 6f)
M
```

```
1 2 3
4 5 6
```

```
M . (::;1)  / written in prefix notation as .[ M; (::;1) ]
```

returns:

```
2 5f
```

Equivalent notation is:

```
M[::;1]
```

or – since in prefix notation indices can be elided:

```
M[;1]
```

The verb . can also be applied to dictionaries:

```
d:`a`b`c!((4f;5f;6f);3;`t);
```

Then, we can run:

```
d . (`a;1) / returns the 2nd element of d`a namely 5f
```

```
5f
```

Analogously, we can run:

```
d . (`a;::)
```

returns:

```
4 5 6f
```

It should be obvious that the following are equivalent:

```
d . (`a;::)
d . enlist `a
d[`a]
```

Tables being the transpose of dictionaries, the following two expressions applied on table `tbl` are equivalent:

```
tbl:([]a:`a`b`c;b:1 2 3f;c:5 8 9i);
tbl . (2;`c) / returns the 3rd element of column c, namely 9i
(flip tbl) . (`c;2)
```

`.[L;I;f]` applies the monadic atomic function `f` to the `I` in-depth sub-domain of `L` and returns a new list `L`. The expression `.[`L;I;f]` modifies the existing list `L` (call by reference).

```
L:((`a;4);(`c;5);(`d;7;(8;6;9f)));
.[L;2 2;log]
```

returns a new list `L` where each element of `.[L;2 2]` is replaced with `log .L[;2 2]`:

```
(`a;4)
(`c;5)
(`d;7;2.079442 1.791759 2.197225)
```

Similarly, `.[L;I;f;a]` applies the dyadic function `f` to the `I` in-depth sub-domain of `L` and the list `a` and returns a new list `L`.

```
L:((`a;4);(`c;5);(`d;7;(8;6;9f)));
.[L;2 2;{x+2*y};1 2 3f]
```

creates a new list `L` where all elements of `.L[2 2]` are replaced with the result of the function `x+2*y` called with all elements of `.[L;2 2]` and `1 2 3f` i.e., `8f+2*1f 6+2*2f 9f+2*3f`:

```
(`a;4)
(`c;5)
(`d;7;10 10 15f)
```

3.4 PROTECTED EVALUATIONS

The concept of try-catch, or protected evaluation, is implemented with the same `@` and `.` verbs as for the apply functions covered previously. The trap function has the syntax `@[f;arg;err]` where `f` is a monadic function and `arg` its argument or `.[g;args;err]` when `g` is a multivalent function and `args` its argument list. The expression `err` is executed if the evaluation of `f` or `g` fails.

Let us consider an example:

```
f:{@[sqrt;x;`err]}
```

The function `f` executes the square root of variable `x`. If it fails, the symbol `` `err `` is returned. Let us see a number of examples:

```
f 9f
```

```
3f
```

```
f -3f
```

```
0n
```

```
f "Q"
```

```
9f
```

as the ASCII of `"Q"` is 81, and, finally,

```
f `a
```

```
`err
```

Further, the example of a protected evaluation for dyadic functions reads:

```
mult:{.[*;(x;y);`err]}
```

where the function `mult` multiplies `x` and `y`. If the multiplication fails, the symbol `` `err `` is returned. Namely:

```
mult[4;5]
```

```
20
```

```
mult[4;"toto"]
```

```
`err
```

The `err` expression can be a function whose first argument will be the error as a string:

```
mult:{.[*;(x;y);{ "Error is: ",x}]}
```

```
mult[4;"toto"]
```

```
"Error is: type"
```

3.5 VECTOR OPERATIONS

Until now, we have covered a number of native q functions and shown how to define our own. In this section, we will present a few more native functions which cover basic time series operations. We split the functions into two classes: aggregators and uniform functions.

3.5.1 Aggregators

3.5.1.1 Simple Aggregators

The first class are our basic aggregators: `min, max, avg, med, var, dev`

```
min 3 1 4 1 6 7 4 3 8 9 1 2f     / minimum
```

```
1f
```

```
max 3 1 4 1 6 7 4 3 8 9 1 2f     / maximum
```

```
9f
```

```
avg 3 1 4 1 6 7 4 3 8 9 1 2f     / average
```

```
4.083333
```

```
med 3 1 4 1 6 7 4 3 8 9 1 2f     / median
```

```
3.5
```

```
var 3 1 4 1 6 7 4 3 8 9 1 2f     / variance
```

```
7.243056
```

```
dev 3 1 4 1 6 7 4 3 8 9 1 2f    / standard deviation
```

```
2.691293
```

Note the unbiased estimator counterparts for sample variance and sample deviation:

```
svar 3 1 4 1 6 7 4 3 8 9 1 2f    / sample variance
```

```
7.901515
```

```
sdev 3 1 4 1 6 7 4 3 8 9 1 2f    / sample deviation
```

```
2.810963
```

3.5.1.2 Weighted Aggregators

Under the same class of aggregator functions, we have the weighted aggregators. Weights for a list are provided as another input argument. Namely, the functions take two arguments: the first argument is a list of length `N` with weights `(w1;w2;...;wN)`, and the second argument is a list of length `N` for which the core function is calculated.

The weights are internally normalised, i.e. `w:w%sum w`, and then the core function is applied on the list `x*w`.

- `wsum` – The function is applied on a list and returns the weighted sum, `sum`, over weighted list.
- `wavg` – The function is applied on a list and returns the weighted average, `avg`, over weighted list.

Example

```
wavg[1 2 3 1 1 1 12; 2 4 5 2 4 2 7]
```

returns

```
5.571429
```

The outcome of aggregate functions is a scalar value.

3.5.2 Uniform Functions

3.5.2.1 Running Functions

Another class is our "running" functions. Each function takes as argument a vector `x1;x2;x3;x4;...;xN` and iteratively applies the core function on the sub-vectors `enlist x1,(x1;x2),(x1;x2;x3)`, etc.

- `mins` – The function is applied on a vector and returns the running minimum, `min`.
- `maxs` – The function is applied on a vector and returns the running maximum, `max`.
- `sums` – The function is applied on a vector and returns the running sum, `sum`.

Example

```
maxs 3 1 4 1 6 7 4 3 8 9 1 2f
```

returns:

```
3 3 4 4 6 7 7 7 8 9 9 9f
```

The outcome is thus a vector of the same length.

3.5.2.2 Window Functions

The last class of functions focuses on calculating a "running" function over a moving window of fixed length. Unlike the previous case, in which the current value was the running total, the functions listed below forget observations which are too far from current observation and only focus on a fixed window.

Each function takes two arguments: the first argument is an integer `k` representing memory and the second argument is a vector `x1;x2;x3;x4;...;xN`, which is used to iteratively apply the calculation of the core function. Namely, the core function is applied on vectors of length `k`. For the first `k-1` elements, the list is truncated as there is no full memory. The first iterations are therefore applied on: `enlist x1`, `(x1;x2)`, `(x1;x2;x3)`, and once the full memory is available, the memory steps in and sub-vectors look as: `(x2;x3;...;x(k+1))` etc.

- `mavg` – The function is applied on a vector and returns the running average, `avg`, over a sub-vector of fixed length.
- `mdev` – The function is applied on a vector and returns the running standard deviation, `dev`, over a sub-vector of fixed length.
- `mcount` – The function is applied on a vector and returns running a counter of non-missing elements, `count`, over a sub-vector of fixed length.
- `mmax` – The function is applied on a vector and returns the running maximum, `max`, over a sub-vector of fixed length.
- `mmin` – The function is applied on a vector and returns the running minimum, `min`, over a sub-vector of fixed length.
- `msum` – The function is applied on a vector and returns the running sum, `sum`, over a sub-vector of fixed length.

```
mmax[3; 3 1 4 1 6 7 4 3 3 3 8 9 1 2f]
```

```
3 3 4 4 6 7 7 7 4 3 8 9 9 9f
```

and using infix notation

```
3 mcount 3 3 4 4 6 7 7 7 4 3 8 9 0n 9 9f
```

```
1 2 3 3 3 3 3 3 3 3 3 3 2 2 2
```

The outcome is thus a vector of the same length as the input. The two classes of "running" functions are also called *uniform*, since the output is equal in length to the input. In Chapter 11, we will see more applications of the moving-window functions when illustrating the calculation of a *moving VWAP*.

As a rule of thumb, when a native function is provided, use it. It will be optimised and more computationally efficient than a user-defined one. It also saves time. To illustrate this, given two vectors `x` and `y` of same length, `x wsum y` is faster than `sum x*y`. Time it!

3.6 CONVENTION FOR USER-DEFINED FUNCTIONS

We close this chapter by summarising the conventions we use for functions defined in this book. When defining a function, we try to avoid one-liners in order to make the logic more transparent and easier to read. For the sake of clarity, we also tend to name the function arguments, instead of using the defaults `x,y,z`. A few exceptions to this are one-liner utility functions which are not part of the main algorithm or concept being discussed.

We also explain every input argument in comments within a function. Although placement of descriptions for functions and their parameters tends to be done through annotations above the body of the function, for the sake of simplicity when sharing code snippets and due to the body of a function being visible in some GUIs – see Chapter 4 – we tend to keep this information inside the function definition.

We prefer descriptive variable names in order to capture their meaning and improve readability of the code. For larger algorithms, we split the functions into small functions since with modularity comes clarity.

CHAPTER 4

Editors and Other Tools

We are already equipped with enough knowledge to work with q. We have so far seen how to invoke the console. In this chapter, we focus on editors and tools we can use to work with q more efficiently. We intend to briefly introduce various tools and let the reader decide which tool to use for his or her work. Further, we aim to rebut popular but wrong belief that one has to give up on graphics tools when working with q.

In particular, we briefly remind the reader of the importance of the console as a tool for rapid development, and then focus on Jupyterq Notebook, IntelliJ, qStudio, and Q Insight Pad. The information presented in this chapter is valid as of the time of writing the book. It is likely that new or significantly improved editors will appear in the meantime and the information below becomes obsolete. Our main argument, though, should still hold: q is an extremely flexible language and a lot of the necessary tools that a user needs for software development and data science already exist and are adequate for obtaining insights into the data and for the flexible experimentation, research and expansion of their code.

4.1 CONSOLE

The console is a starting point for readers who have been following our book since the beginning. We have also discussed some useful options we can use when we invoke q. It is essential that our reader is familiar with the usage of the console since its interpreter makes starting with an idea very quick. It is available in every operating system and thus provides a universal way to run and type q. In production systems, accessing a q service through the console is also one of the most efficient ways to deal with a potential issue and understand what is going on, assuming admin access is given. Figure 4.1 shows an example of the console output for a number of commands.

Further, the console will come very useful when we need to debug the code. The enhanced q functionality to provide debugging output is reported in the console but not in GUIs (unless we have access to console from the GUI interface).

Using the console as a means of accessing q is very fast. The console can also handle cases when we either intentionally or by mistake return a large table or data set. The output of the table in the console is truncated, and we thus avoid lengthy data transfer which will happen when accessing through a GUI or IDE.

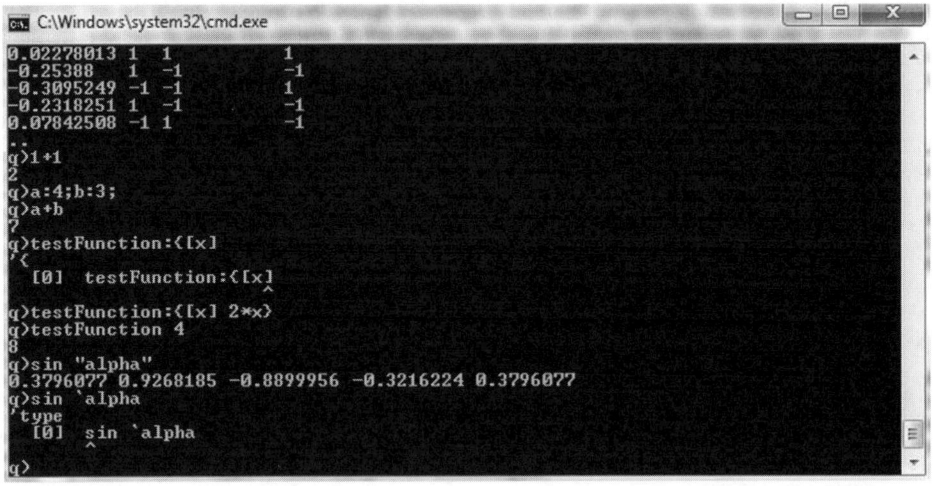

```
C:\Windows\system32\cmd.exe
0.02278013 1  1          1
-0.25388   1  -1         -1
-0.3095249 -1 -1         1
-0.2318251 1  -1         -1
0.07842508 -1 1          -1
..
q)1+1
2
q)a:4;b:3;
q)a+b
7
q)testFunction:{[x]
'{
  [0]  testFunction:{[x]
                      ^
q)testFunction:{[x] 2*x}
q)testFunction 4
8
q)sin "alpha"
0.3796077 0.9268185 -0.8899956 -0.3216224 0.3796077
q)sin `alpha
'type
  [0]  sin `alpha
       ^
q)
```

FIGURE 4.1 Console output

On the other hand, the console has limitations when dealing with large projects. For instance, working on this book within the console only would make the work much more complicated. The console itself by default does not allow syntax highlighting. One has to use further tools to achieve that. One way is to use external text editors with enabled highlighting, save the code into a script and then invoke the script from command line. One such popular editor is `vim`.

4.2 JUPYTER NOTEBOOK

The Jupyter Notebook is an open-source web application, jup (a). It supports more than 40 programming languages, including Python, R and `q`. The Jupyter Notebook allows us to create interactive documents. Such documents can contain well-edited text as well as live and executable code and allow for a wide range of visualisations, which enhance the message conveyed. Notebooks can also be easily shared, either as a file through source control software like `git`, or directly in the same way we share a link to any web page.

The Jupyter Notebook is nowadays heavily used by the machine learning and data science community. It can be used for various projects from modelling, simulations, or data visualisations, among others. The notebooks are, in particular, widespread among the Python community. It is easy to integrate systems like Spark or Apache to enhance Python performance, as well as accessing libraries like tensorflow, which are in the spotlight of the machine learning community.

Another appealing feature is that the text presented within the notebooks can contain LaTex commands. The notebooks can compile it, and text can thus nicely visualise even the most complicated mathematical formulas. Lastly, it is relevant to stress that when the Jupyter Notebook is invoked, it launches its `q` kernel. The user does not have to care about the `q` process itself much. The console is fully hidden from the user.

The Jupyter Notebook now contains support for q and the kernel can be accessed at jup (b). It brings functionalities like syntax highlighting, code completion, inline loading of scripts, and mainly the inline display of charts created through embedPy and matplotlib. It is the aforementioned library, embedPy, which allows integration of Python to q. Figure 4.2 shows an example of code run through jupyterq and is an example usage of the notebook in conjunction with matplotlib.

One slight disadvantage which may be encountered when using jupyterq is its speed. In q, we can achieve an amazing speed of execution even on large data sets without needing to install further libraries. In some cases, Jupyterq can be a performance bottleneck, and tasks like data exploration would be affected, compared to other tools. The advantage of the notebook is in sharing code and data extracts with people, as well as the extra plotting libraries. The following tools we shall cover may be more adapted to development and data exploration in q and offer some basic plotting, too. Depending on one's use case, i.e. whether one needs to navigate through much

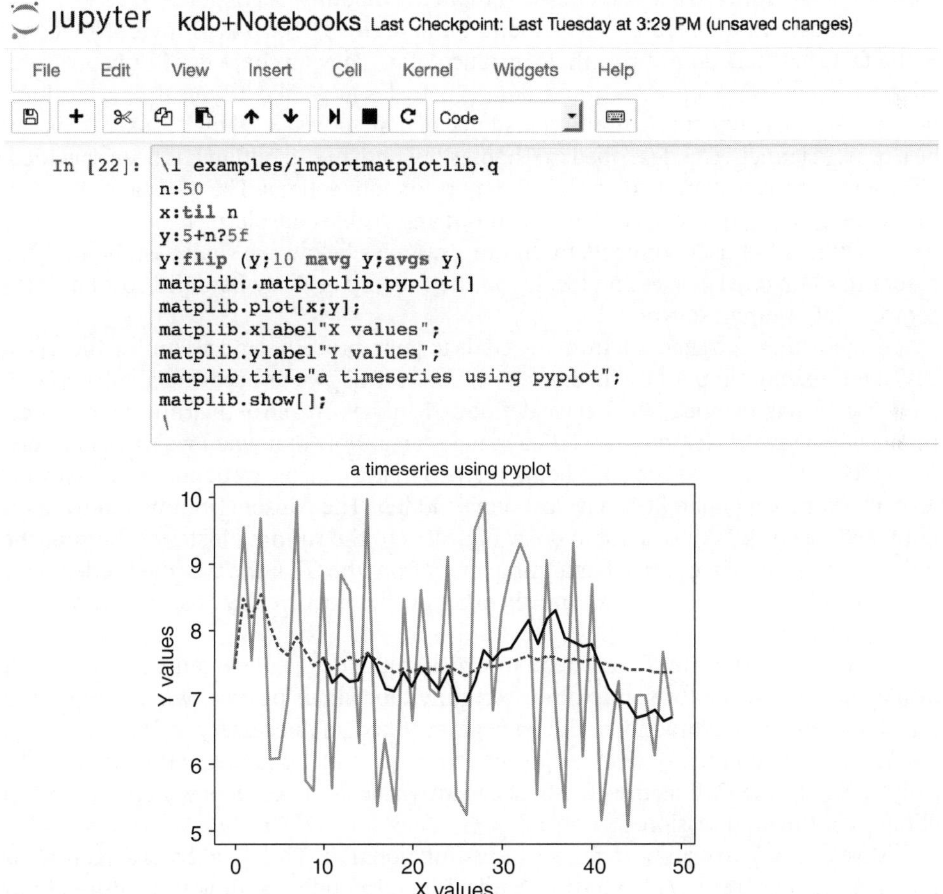

FIGURE 4.2 Jupyterq Chart window

code and investigate the data in detail – in which case a heavy lifting IDE is more appropriate – or wants to share data snippets easily, different tools in this list can be deployed appropriately.

In order to install Jupyter Notebook and the jupyterq extension, please follow the corresponding web links. Once both programs are installed, the reader can use the tool immediately and enjoy its power. This assumes that Python is installed on the computer and the reader has appropriate access rights to run `pip` or `conda`.

4.3 GUIs

Let us present two GUIs to work with `q`: `qStudio`, and `Q Insight Pad`. Both programs are just examples of the GUIs which are available to readers. They have been chosen as examples and to encourage exploration of what is on offer nowadays. Both GUIs have some common features which we will describe before proceeding with GUI-specific comments and hints to get readers using them as smoothly as possible.

The most common feature, which differentiates the GUIs to the Jupyter Notebook, is the fact that they do not run their instance of `q`. They are here to offer better visualisation when working with `q` and data. Their design – like a typical data explorer program – is to connect to a running instance of `q` already started by the user. This can be a process launched as described in Chapter 1, where the `-p` option has been specified, i.e. the process is 'listening' on a specified port for connections. The `q` instance can run in the foreground, in the background without any visible console, or it can be a remote process which the user connects to. In our examples below, we shall assume that the reader has launched a `q` session locally on their laptop or PC, where the port has been set to `-p 5000` upon startup.

Establishing a connection from the GUIs to our `q` process – and assuming the q process administrator applies no further restrictions – will give us access to all objects created within that instance. Thus, if we define `a:1` in the console of the running instance, then `a` will be available from the GUI, and vice versa. Note that when we run some code from GUI, we do not see the code being retyped in the console by default unless lower-level client message handlers have been overridden. The console from which we have launched `q` serves as one possible point of access to the running instance, but not the only one. Further, if we run a demanding query from the GUI, the console is effectively blocked and does not allow us to run any other query concurrently or submit any query into the queue.

It may seem that we do not need to work on the q console when we have a GUI available. This is true for some minor scripting. For larger projects when we need to create more complex functions, the console may become necessary as it allows us to debug the code efficiently. The output of erroneous functions or queries may not be fully visible in the GUI as the GUI is necessarily a separate process which is merely a client to our main `q` session.

Most GUIs have support for plotting functionality. This is a crucial feature as having in hand some simple plotting can facilitate in understanding the nature of our data, identify patterns or detect errors. Besides, GUIs also provide an easy interface to export tables into common external formats. This can be useful when the processed data has to be incorporated in a presentation or a document. The GUI clients, in general, cannot form interactive documents as is the case of the Jupyter Notebook. On the other hand, they provide much faster access to data and response to commands, as well as offer a grid presentation of tables which is more comfortable for the human eye to process.

4.3.1 qStudio

The first GUI we present is `qStudio`, which can be accessed through qst. This GUI is available for `Windows`, `Mac`, and `Linux` environments and is written in Java. Its functionality includes syntax highlighting, code completion, ability to query servers and then explore the objects defined on the server, advanced charting functionalities, and a tool set for importing large files. In addition it integrates with:

- `qUnit` – a light framework to run unit tests.
- `qDoc` – a generator for `html` documentation.

`qStudio` is a licensed product, and some of the functionalities like editing the database through GUI are part of the Pro version. Please refer to the product web page for more details.

Let us focus on the Default Layout organisation of the workbench as is shown in Figure 4.3. The workbench has eight different types of windows. They are grouped into three blocks. Users can rearrange the workspace as they like. We describe each of the windows:

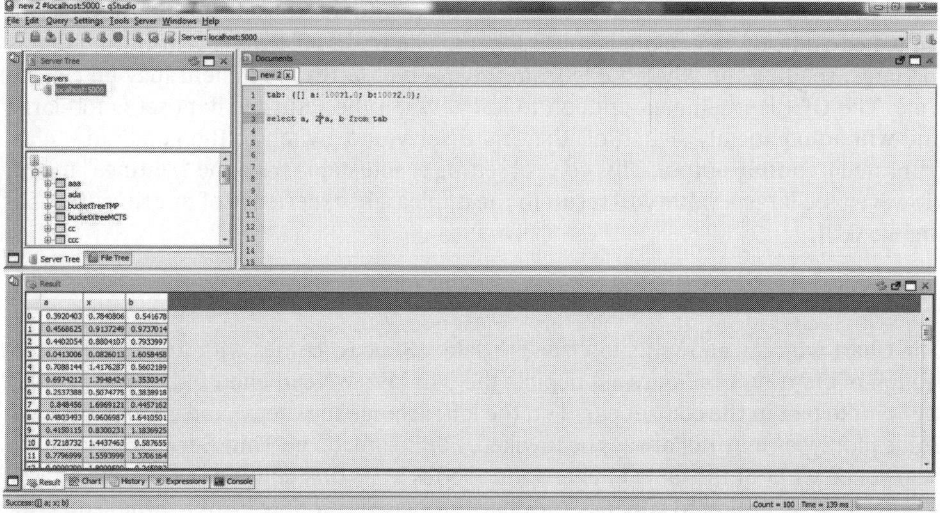

FIGURE 4.3 qStudio default layout

Server Tree

The most important window is the Server Tree window. By default it is empty – the user will have to set up a connection to `q` instance. Right-clicking on "Servers" and "Add Server..." will open the window where one has to populate the Host (enter `localhost` if the process is running on your local machine like in our current example) and Port to `5000` as we have set up an instance with this port number. If any other server setup is used, this has to be populated accordingly.

This window also contains a list of all the objects defined on the server. The main namespace, `.`, contains all global objects; in our case, the first item is table `aaa`. We can explore the properties of the table by clicking through the object.

File Tree

The File Tree window allows us to explore the files in a given directory. It provides a local version of a file manager, which is useful for navigating through the scripts we work with.

Documents

The second main window is called Documents. This window allows us to open files with scripts or notes. All the code we edit and test is run through a file opened in this window. We can run the entire file, a selected block of code, or execute a specified line. Under menu option "Query" we can see the shortcuts for each of these options.

Result

The third block of windows in the default layout visualises the output of our executed code. Tables are formatted as a grid, and in contrast to the console output they are not truncated and can be explored in full length. The trade-off here is that if the table is too large, sending the whole table from the q server to the GUI client may take some time. The GUI is intelligent enough to know when the returned data set is too large and will automatically switch off the grid display and switch to the good old – alas, truncated – console output. This control setting is adjustable from the "Settings" menu. However, too large a value will result in the unpleasant experience of freezing or crashing the GUI.

Chart

The Chart window allows us to visualise data. `qStudio` comes with an extensive collection of chart types. Figure 4.4 depicts the window. We can choose the type of chart we want to plot in the control panel on the left, arrange the theme and change the title. Some plot types may not always be invoked. For instance, the Time Series chart cannot be invoked without the table having a time series as its first column.

There is an option to enhance the charting visualisation by invoking the "sqlDashboard". This is a separate pop-up window which brings even more graphics options. See Figure 4.5 for example. The control is quite intuitive, and we encourage the reader to explore all available types.

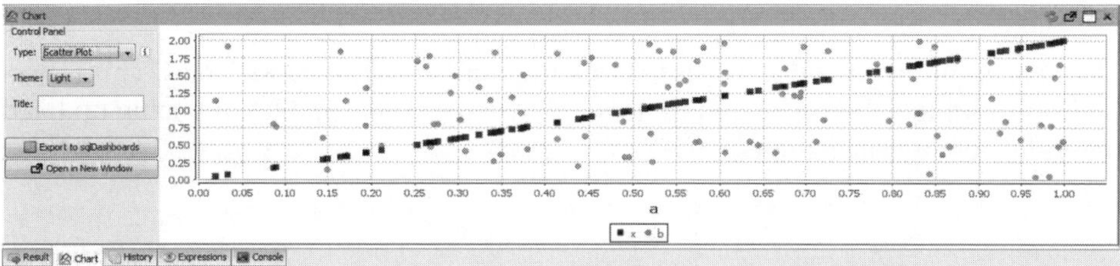

FIGURE 4.4 `qStudio` Chart window

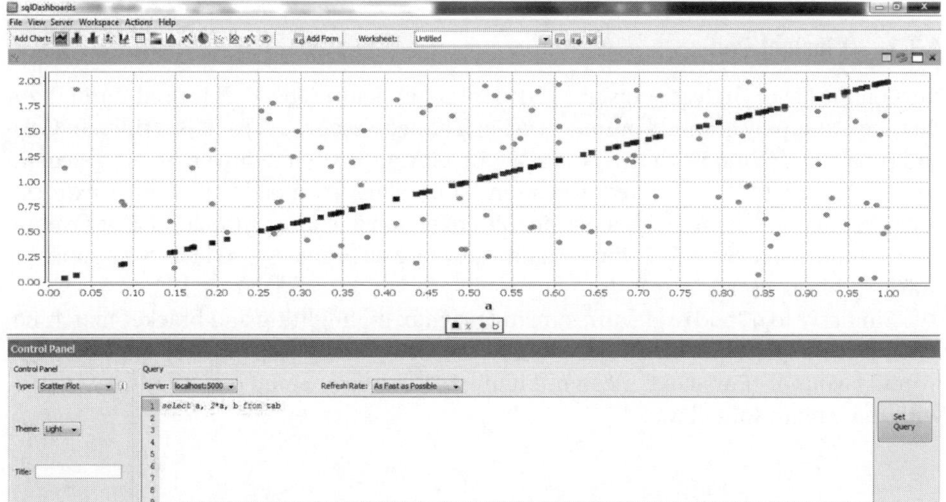

FIGURE 4.5 `qStudio` sqlDashboard window

History

The History window can be seen in Figure 4.6. The left-hand side of the window presents the list of queries run, a summary of their output and status of the calls. We can use this table to re-run commands easily. This is a useful functionality which allows going through queries we have run and revised them.

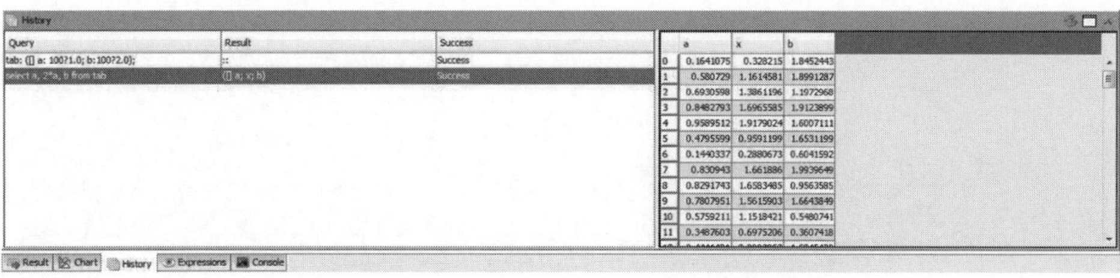

	a	x	b
0	0.1641075	0.328215	1.8452443
1	0.580729	1.1614581	1.8991287
2	0.6930598	1.3861196	1.1972968
3	0.8482793	1.6965585	1.9123899
4	0.9589512	1.9179024	1.6007111
5	0.4795599	0.9591199	1.6531199
6	0.1440337	0.2880673	0.6041592
7	0.830943	1.661886	1.9939649
8	0.8291743	1.6583485	0.9563585
9	0.7807951	1.5615903	1.6643849
10	0.5759211	1.1518421	0.5480741
11	0.3487603	0.6975206	0.3607418

FIGURE 4.6 `qStudio` History window

Expressions

The Expressions window allows us to track the values of selected variables. This is useful if we need to debug code and understand whether the variables are being updated according to our expectations.

Console

This corresponds to a q console style of output. This view can be useful in seeing errors in functions and understanding why the error occurred.

4.3.2 Q Insight Pad

Next on the list of GUIs is Q Insight Pad, or qPad for short. This GUI is used throughout this book to supply graphics output. qPad can be accessed from qpa. It is written in C++ and runs under Windows only. It is a fast, efficient, and rather lightweight GUI. Its main advantages are it is free (but requires a semi-annual re-download as its licence expires), user-friendly, and comes with a reasonable collection of charting functionality. Overall, a very comprehensive GUI whose main drawback is probably the lack of support for Mac and Linux users.

Similarly to qStudio, features include syntax highlighting and bracket matching, namespace explorer, a variable hierarchy inspector and a dependency explorer. The overall layout of qPad can be seen in Figure 4.7. The basic setup is similar to qStudio, with three main split views.

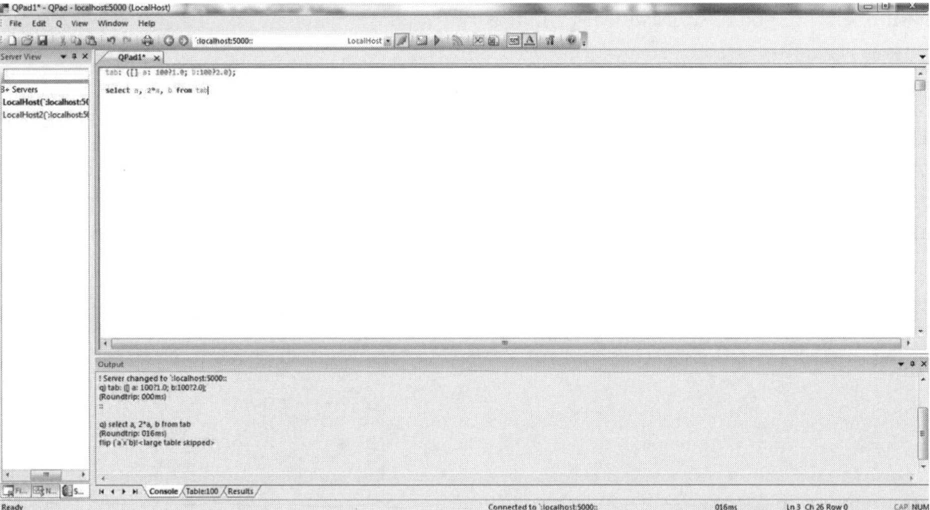

FIGURE 4.7 qPad layout

Server View

Intuitively, right-clicking and choosing "Add..." will bring up a window where we can set up the connection to our running instance of `q`. We enter the same pair of values as seen earlier for Host and Port: `localhost` and `5000`, and pick a Name of our choice. Login and Password are left empty if the server is not secured. We can set up as many servers as we wish and switch between them accordingly.

File View

The File view allows us to browse through the file structure and unsurprisingly acts as a file manager.

Namespace Explorer

We can use this view to browse all variables defined on the running q server. We can browse through objects by their type, i.e. Table or Function, among others, or by the namespace they belong to. It is worth noting that when we click on the selected object, we can see where that object is used under the "Used in function" view. This is very useful when we want to understand variable references in our code and explore any unintentional override in a more complex program.

Script View

The upper right-hand side of the default view shows all the open files and scripts, each accessible through a coloured tab. In this part, we work with queries we want to run and define functions and variables. Under the "Q" menu we can browse the shortcuts used to run the entire file, a selected code block or a given line. There is also an option to access a debugger.

Other menu options available are the "Chart grid" which brings up a window for plots, as depicted in Figure 4.8. The window allows us to choose which column of the table to be plotted is the x-axis and the colours of the columns being plotted, as well as the plotting style. There are several options to choose from, which fortunately include the Line and Circle chart types. The latter allows us to view the scatter plots which are useful in visualising the outcome of the agent-based model and machine learning outcomes resulting from the k-Nearest Neighbours algorithm. Formatting of figures within qPad is not very advanced, and thus for presentation purposes, some final touch in external programmes will probably be needed – exporting to Excel is supported ("Open in Excel"). For the book, we stick to the raw qPad output most of the time.

We have noticed performance degradation for long scripts when code highlighting is kept switched on, and we recommend toggling this value through the "Syntax Highlighting" menu.

Console

The lower right-hand side part of the default view contains three more windows. Console simulates the output of the q console itself but is not fully equivalent.

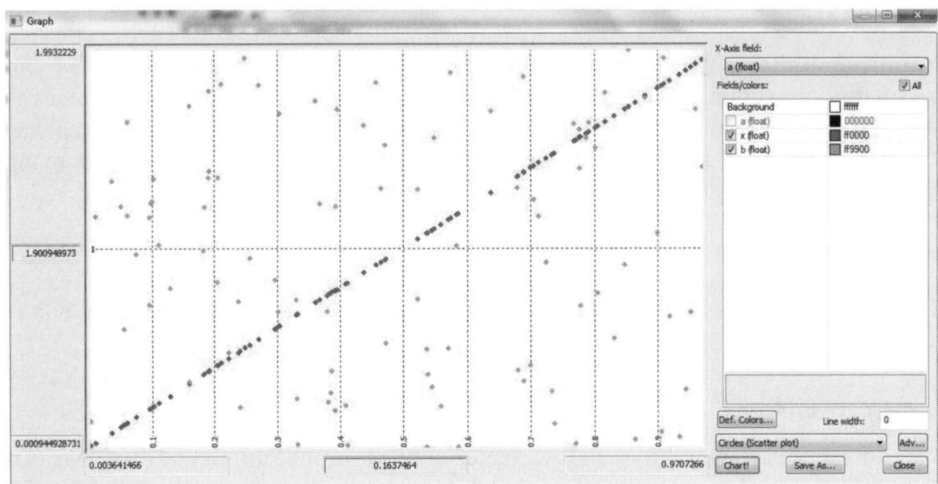

FIGURE 4.8 qPad Chart grid

Table

This is the standard Table viewer. The table is not truncated and we see it fully.

Results

The Results window returns the outcome of the latest executed code. When the outcome is a table, the results are delegated to the Table view.

4.4 IDEs: INTELLIJ IDEA

We finish this section by referring to one of the most popular kinds of Integrated Development Environment (IDE) software – and one most prominent in the Java development community – `IntelliJ` IDEA, available at https://www.jetbrains.com/idea/. This is a full-blown software development kit with very fast indexing, so that searching for function definitions and usage dependencies is straightforward and efficient. This aspect becomes essential when trying to navigate a codebase in large-scale projects, especially if it involves multiple people updating the code.

`IntelliJ` supports a `q` plugin which comes with a lot of features, highlighted in Figure 4.9. Given the plethora of plugins, we recommend this tool when involved in more severe and automated software development where we want to potentially make a small change to a codebase with multiple dependencies and commit and release the code in a fast, frequent and iterative manner. The all-in-one nature of `IntelliJ` makes it a strong candidate for this use case.

Another plugin supported by `IntelliJ`, is StudioForKDB+, which is a separate Studio for running code and visualisation of tables in itself – similar to `qPad`. Figure 4.10 shows a typical setup of `IntelliJ`, where on the left we can see the project

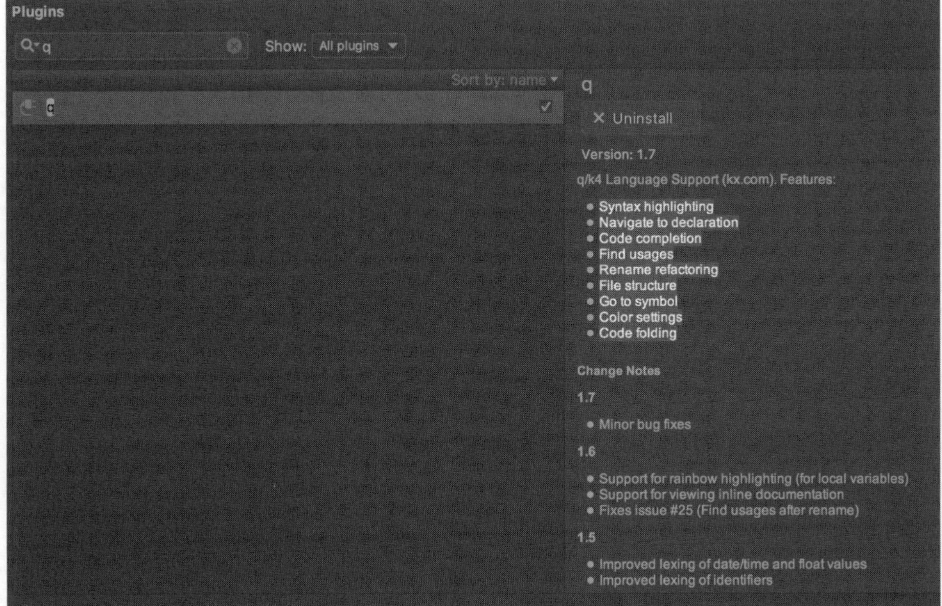

FIGURE 4.9 The `IntelliJ q` plugin window

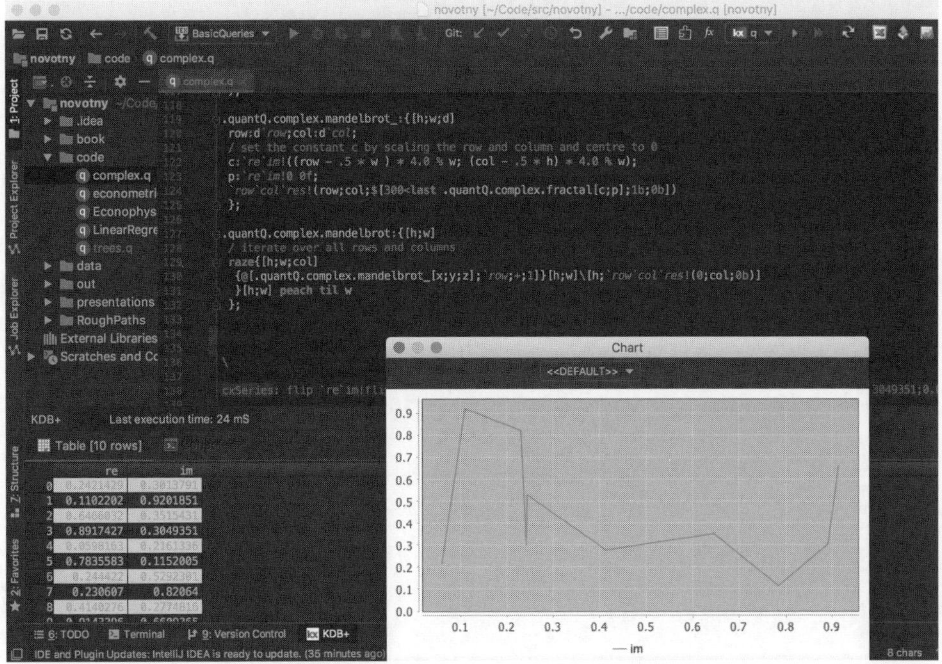

FIGURE 4.10 `IntelliJ` q development setup

navigation pane and the q code on the right, along with syntax highlighting. At the bottom, an output of executed code and a chart are shown, both of which are parts of the StudioForKDB+ plugin.

4.5 CONCLUSION

We encourage our readers to explore the space of available GUIs and development environments since an appropriate choice for the given type of work will improve productivity.

In our experience, we have found that for large-scale software development with fast integration and testing, one would probably lean towards IntelliJ due to its advanced and speedy search features, code highlighting/smart completion, shortcuts and integration with Git and the excellent q plugin. In contrast, when the majority of our time is spent on data analysis, querying, visualisation and prototyping, we would make use of tools like qPad, qStudio, StudioForKDB+ or JupyterQ. The choice is up to the user. For the rest of the book, we shall use qPad due to its simplicity and speed in presenting and visualising our data.

CHAPTER 5

Debugging q Code

The provided information is valid for version 3.5 and later. The functionality has been tested using version 3.6, but principles will likely remain the same for later versions. In the first part of this chapter, we make a brief overview of the native errors we may encounter when using incorrect syntax. We then focus on how to debug the code when encountering errors and move on to advise on how we can structure our codebase better, and debugging tools available for execution trace and dynamic debugging. The key message is to de-myth the claim that it is not possible to properly debug q code, given the improvements in tooling around debugging introduced in version 3. All in all, though, writing code which has fewer bugs, as well as the ability to detect their location quickly, will highly depend on how modular the overall code structure is: small functions, with distinct – and noticeable – responsibilities will generally lead to more maintainable code. More tips on how to design your application and structure your code will be seen in Chapter 9.

5.1 INTRODUCTION TO MAKING IT WRONG: ERRORS

One of the common reasons heard among quants against using the q language is the limited ability to debug the code, especially when compared to conventional programming languages and their IDEs. Ask any Java developer about his or her opinion of q and this argument will be almost surely mentioned among the top three arguments (given one gets beyond a blind "no"). Indeed, the debugging tools are in the case of q relatively limited. However, q and java are fundamentally different languages. q being interpreted has a much more interactive programming environment, so a lot of the development is a mixture of running small snippets of code dynamically on some sample (test or real) data and then building out from that. In other words, the ability to go through the code step by step and monitor what the code is doing is innate to the language itself. What we shall focus on is two main pain points: the first is avoiding simple syntax errors when initially writing our code in our IDE and, secondly, interpreting the generally obscure and short q errors and how we can make these more verbose while our code increases in complexity.

5.1.1 Syntax Errors

We make a brief note on this since it can be puzzling – or merely a waste of time – to figure out where a missed bracket or semicolon is when writing a few q statements which go beyond the trivial. In that sense, mainstream languages do an excellent job at this, with java practically "spelling out" the syntax or variable names to the developer's delight. Of course, this is not so much a feature of the language itself, rather than that of advanced IDEs, such as IntelliJ. Recently, support for q in this area has grown, and the IntelliJ q plugin mentioned in the previous chapter now supports a full range of syntax highlighting, variable name autocompletion and error highlights for most cases of incorrect syntax, the latter continuously improving with each release. The usual fast shortcuts for function definition and usages are also there, making searching and navigating your codebase as it grows much more productive, which arguably means that a large q codebase is very easy to index and navigate – especially since "large" in q usually means a few hundred to few thousand lines of code, instead of tens or hundreds of thousands of code in most other languages.

As mentioned, due to the very interactive nature of the language, even when using an IDE such as IntelliJ or a GUI such as QPad, one finds oneself frequently interacting with the q console directly and this is still the "go-to" place once we're past the simple syntax errors and our code breaks mid-execution.

5.1.2 Runtime Errors

In this section, we review the debugging options available. The two reasons we need to debug the code are if it breaks with an exception or if the output of the function is not as expected, the latter case being rather common as the computer does what we tell it to do, not what we think we told it to do.

First of all, let us define what "breaks" means. An interruption to the normal flow of execution, an error signal, or what is known in layman terms as an "exception" is denoted in q with the rather laconic single ' quote ', usually followed by a – naturally – laconic explanation of the error. A break will result in a q script exiting with an error due to its inability to load, or a function call within a process being interrupted due to an error.

Let us start with the ubiquitous case of the code-breaking with an exception thrown. The following function definition,

```
wrongFunction:{[x;y]
    add: x + y;
    addmore: add + 50;
    z+3
 };
```

when called, results in

```
wrongFunction[1;2]
```

```
'z
[1]  /path/to/my/code.q:13: wrongFunction:
addmore: add + 50;
z+3
^
```

or just z in the studio. This output means that we attempted to use variable z, which is not defined. In this case, we may go through the code and find the variable z and correct it. More frequently, though, we encounter one of the native q errors. Below we present what we perceive as the most frequently encountered errors, with some tips on what causes them and how they can be avoided. The full list of errors is available at https://github.com/prodrive11/log4q.

5.1.2.1 The Type Error

The following code

```
two:2;
two xexp 3
```

works as intended as we pass variable two by value; however, if we call variable two by reference, i.e.

```
variable: `two;
variable xexp 3
```

we get the following output:

```
'type
```

This is one of many native errors. In this case, the error means that we have called the function xexp with the wrong type of input.

The type error is probably the most common, and it usually occurs when

- one of the arguments of the function is of the wrong type, as in the example above. Other such examples are

```
10 + `abc      / one cannot add a symbol to an integer
```

```
til "abc"      / attempting to create a sequence of integer numbers from 0
    ↪ to "abc"
```

```
til 1.5        / attempting to create a sequence of integer numbers from 0
    ↪ to 1.5
```

```
`a#1 2 3       / take element `a from the integer vector 1 2 3
```

- q is strongly typed. Although a variable can be reassigned from anything to anything, partially updating values of a variable to a different type results in a 'type error; this includes datatypes which are normally promoted during arithmetic operations.

Therefore:

```
prices:101 101.5 101.3
```

```
prices+10   / works due to not amending prices variable itself: addition
    ↪ simply promotes an int to a float
```

```
111 111.5 111.3
```

but

```
prices,:10
```

```
    'type
    [0]  prices,:10
    ^
```

```
prices[0 1]:10
```

```
    'type
    [0]  prices[0 1]:10
    ^
```

Similarly for columns of a table, since these are simply vectors after all:

```
t:([] time:3#.z.p)
```

```
t
```

```
time
-----------------------------
2019.01.28D10:33:45.887149000
2019.01.28D10:33:45.887149000
2019.01.28D10:33:45.887149000
```

```
`t insert ([]time:2#11:00:00.0)
```

```
'type
[0]  `t insert ([]time:2#11:00:00.0)
^
```

- when we forget to end a line with a semicolon, we may accidentally merge two statements which were meant to be processed independently, resulting in a `type` error.

Due to the commonality of this error and the dynamic/interpreted nature of q, two ways of minimising these errors are:

- type checks for function arguments
- logging to trace the values of a variable as passed into a function

There are some good open-source logging libraries available for q, notably `log4.q` from https://github.com/prodrive11/log4q.

The following code illustrates this:

```
.quantQ.myspace.myfunc:{[prices;newprices]
    // prices -- vector of prices
    // newprices -- vector of new prices
    if[ type[ prices ] <> type newprices ;
        '"Price types are incompatible!"
      ];
    newprices: newprices where newprices > 0;
    :prices,newprices;
 };
```

which gives us

```
.quantQ.myspace.myfunc[1 2 3f;10 20]
```

```
'Price types are incompatible!
[0]  .quantQ.myspace.myfunc[1 2 3f;10 20]
^
```

```
.quantQ.myspace.myfunc[1 2 3f;10 20f]
```

```
1 2 3 10 20f
```

```
.quantQ.myspace.myfunc[1 2 3f;10 0f]
```

```
1 2 3 10f
```

Note in the example above, how we have used the single quote ' within our type-checking if statement to produce our exception. Thus we can use ' followed by a string of text to return an error of our own choice which replaces the generic 'type error. Alternatively, we could have returned from the function or taken some corrective action, such as an attempt to cast the data or ignore the new data.

The same function, when making use of the log4q library, could be written as

```
.quantQ.myspace.myfunc:{[prices;newprices]
    // prices -- vector of prices
    // newprices -- vector of new prices
    if[ type[ prices ] <> type newprices ;
     `..ERROR("Price types are incompatible! prices is of type %1 vs
        ↪ newprices which is %2";(type prices;type newprices));
     `..INFO"Ignoring new prices";
     : prices];  / return original prices
    newprices: newprices where newprices > 0;
    :prices,newprices;
 };
```

```
.quantQ.myspace.myfunc[1 2 3f;10 20]
```

```
ERROR [2019.01.28D11:07:41.572440000] Price types are incompatible! prices
    ↪ is of type 9h vs newprices which is 7h
INFO [2019.01.28D11:07:41.572614000] Ignoring new prices
1 2 3f
```

5.1.2.2 Other Errors

'length – Another "popular" one. This error appears when we perform an operation on two objects which have incompatible lengths:

```
1 2 + 1 2 3
```

```
'length
[0]  1 2 + 1 2 3
^
```

```
t1:([]a:1 2 3);
t2:([]a:10 20);
t1+t2
```

```
'length
[0]  t1+t2
^
```

whereas

```
t2:([]a:10 20 30)
t1+t2
```

```
a
--
11
22
33
```

`'mismatch` – When two tables are being joined with an upsert (or a comma-join), and the columns between the two tables differ

```
t1:([]a:1 2;b:3 4)
t2:([]c:10 20 30)
t1,t2
```

```
'mismatch
[0]  t1,t2
^
```

```
t1 upsert t2
```

```
'mismatch
[0]  t1 upsert t2
^
```

`'constants` – We have declared too many constants, more than 96. This may frequently happen when we use long functions and define many variables and/or constants. This is q's way of telling us to refactor our code, i.e. be more modular: keep your functions small and with well-defined responsibilities.

`'domain` – This error occurs when we evaluate function outside of the natural domain; for example, we want to create an increasing sequence of integers starting at `0` and running to a negative number.

`'from` – This error appears when we use one of the sql commands and forget (or misspell) the statement `from` or omit the table name.

`'noupdate` – This is error can be encountered when we work on a server which has protection against writing or updating globals. This is frequently the case within a working environment, where the database is protected against write access, i.e. the historical data cannot be changed by intention or by mistake.

`'nyi` – "not yet implemented". One usually gets this when the command looks meaningful but `q` is not able to execute it. If we try to do what we have intended to do in a slightly different way, we may usually find a working command.

`'os` – Operating system error. One may encounter this if the underlying system os command produces an error during its execution. For example, if we need to copy the files from a different server, we may use: `system"wget:http://sourceOfOurData/data.csv ."` Such an evaluation may proceed properly; however, we still get this error.

`'params` – This error is encountered when a function with more than eight parameters is constructed. The natural remedy to this error is to wrap parameters into a dictionary and pass the parameters through the dictionary. This approach is chosen throughout this book. It gives us flexibility in terms of the dimension of parameters.

This approach is also optimal when we construct iterations of functions for various machine learning algorithms.

'rank – We have used invalid rank or valence. Encountered when calling a function with more arguments than it expects. For example, calling wrongFunctio[1;2;3] defined above would produce this error.

'stop – When forceably interrupting execution using Ctrl+C or the "stop" button in qPad.

'wsfull – We have run out of virtual memory, or we have started q with the -w option and the latest operation requested more memory than available. The remedy to this error is to either allow the process to request more memory, buy more memory, or optimise the query in order to operate with smaller memory blocks. This error may also suggest some memory leakage in our code, i.e. storing temporary states or creating too many nested lists.

5.2 DEBUGGING THE CODE

Let's review what tools are available when we use the command line. Using the wrongFunction example:

```
wrongFunction[1;2]
```

```
'z
[1]  /path/to/my/code.q:13: wrongFunction:
addmore: add + 50;
z+3
^
}
q))
```

The first line of the output above is the unknown variable returned as an error, i.e. prepended by a single quote 'z. The second line will output the file containing the function, and the line where this function is defined, along with its name. The third line is showing us the last two lines of the function before the failure, with the caret sign pointing to the offending statement.

The error here is that the variable z is not defined and its name is therefore returned as an exception.

We notice that the q command prompt has an extra bracket: this denotes that execution is suspended at the current level of the call stack, which is the execution of wrongFunction. We therefore have access to the *scope* of this function and can access its arguments and local variables. An important internal function which will help us in further investigation is .z.s, which is the *self-reference* function:

```
q)).z.s
```

```
{[x;y]
add: x + y;
addmore: add + 50;
z+3
}
```

This will show us the full body of the function, which is useful for multi-statement functions, since we can then visualise the statement which failed and its place in the function body.

Evaluating the function by calling `value` on it presents us with a plethora of meta information, and we can parse this to create a dictionary of very useful debugging information:

```
`args`locals`globals`constants`name`path!{x[1 2 3],enlist[4_ -5_x],2#-4#x}
    ↪ value[.z.s]
```

```
args     | `x`y
locals   | `add`addmore
globals  | ``z
constants| 50 3
name     | "..wrongFunction"
path     | "/path/to/my/code.q"
```

We add this function as a utility under our namespace in case it comes in handy later on. We pass in the function we want to inspect as an argument since we will need to pass in the self-reference of the failing function, and not of the utility function itself:

```
.quantQ.debug.meta:{[func]
    // func -- function to inspect
    :`args`locals`globals`constants`name`path!{x[1 2 3],enlist[4_ -5_x
        ↪ ],2#-4#x} value[func];
 };
```

Two other useful internal variables which get populated during the suspension of execution are

- `.z.ex` the failed operator
- `.z.ey` its arguments

Note in our example above the failure is the reference to the variable z itself, but if we replaced the failed code with something like `` `a + 3``, we would then see the failed primitive and its arguments are:

```
q)).z.ex
+
q)).z.ey
`a
3
```

While in debugging mode, we have three options to proceed with:

- `'`
- `:`
- `\`

The single-quote `'` will move up the call stack and into the scope of the parent function. The colon `:` will allow us to return an appropriate value from the current scope and resume execution, e.g. in the example above we can return 2:

```
q)):2
```

giving the output:

```
q)5
```

The error was within the execution of z+3 and the command : was applied within that line. Once we corrected the value of z, the function finished the evaluation without any error.

Single escape \ will exit the debugger. Each extra bracket ')' should be escaped with a single \ followed by the return key. Please note that double escape \\ will exit the whole session, so be careful!

5.3 DEBUGGING SERVER-SIDE

It is not always possible to debug directly on the console. When using an IDE to connect to a remote server, or our local process connects to a remote q process, we may need to deal with our function failing while executing server-side.

One way to facilitate investigation here is following the guidelines we gave earlier in this chapter around safety checks using if statements and detailed logging. Another tool we have is the ability to trap execution and return the details when these fail. We define a utility function which uses the .Q.trp internal function which traps execution and returns the error and the full stack trace.

```
.quantQ.debug.trap:{ [func;args]
 .Q.trp[{value enlist[x],y}[func];args;{(x;.Q.sbt y)}]
 };
```

To illustrate the concept, assume we have a remote server which is listening to port 5000, and we do not have access to its console or logs (e.g. it could be administered by another user or running on a remote host).

We open a connection handle h to this server and run our function with its arguments passed in as a list[1]:

```
h:hopen `:localhost:5000
h (wrongFunction;1;2)
```

```
'type
[0]  h (wrongFunction;1;2)
^
```

The server returns the error 'type as expected. However, we are unsure where this occurred, and we wish to get more debug information. Stepping through the code or using the meta utility is not going to help us here since the function was run on a different process and we do not have access to the scope like previously.

[1]Execution of a function and its arguments as a list of (func;arg1;arg2;...) is generic way of evaluating code in q, as we will see in Chapter 10. In this example here, the execution of the function happens remotely by sending the list prepended with the connection handle h.

Using the `trap` utility we can trap the error and return a list of the error and the backtrace, both as strings:

```
q)result: h (.quantQ.debug.trap;wrongFunction;1 2)
```

```
q)first result
```

```
"type"
```

```
q)-1 last result;
```

```
[3]
addmore: add + 50;
`a+3
^
}
[2]  {value enlist[x],y}
^
[1]  (.Q.trp)

[0]  { [func;args]
.Q.trp[{value enlist[x],y}[func];args;{(x;.Q.sbt y)}]
^
}
```

We used standard out operator `-1` in front of the last stack trace string to format it. We now have a visual picture of the steps which led to the failure and the offending line of code.

We conclude that there are sufficient debugging options for us to pinpoint where an error occurs in q. Moreover, in a modular design with small functions, finding the incorrect statement should be straightforward. With the assistance of logging of function parameters passed in during nested calls, we can then focus on understanding the source of the offensive values.

PART Two

Data Operations

CHAPTER 6

Splayed and Partitioned Tables

6.1 INTRODUCTION

Neither the kdb+ instance, nor the q code, live in isolation. In a kdb+tick setup, the data may be captured straight into a kdb+ instance. In other cases, we may obtain the data as flat files from an external source and choose to use q to process them. It is clear why we may make this choice: the database is an excellent environment for dealing with large volumes of, more often than not, high-frequency data and q is a powerful tool for analysing this type of data.

kdb+'s efficiency extends to dealing with files: while we could use, for example, Python or R, to preprocess the flat files before exporting the data to a kdb+ instance, we will have to take a performance hit compared to kdb+'s native methods for reading files. It is true that Python and R offer richer toolkits for dealing with file system objects. It is the simplicity and speed that speak in favour of kdb+.

However, there are situations when we may still choose an external tool to preprocess the data. We may choose to apply Python's regular expressions and library functions. Alternatively, we may need to unzip or otherwise decompress the files before reading them from kdb+. We may need to call some shell commands. Luckily we can do all this without leaving the kdb+ process. kdb+ offers us tools for calling shell commands and external programs from q scripts.

In this chapter we shall discuss kdb+'s concepts of splayed and partitioned tables and also show how to load and save data directly using q. Both types of tables, especially the partitioned tables, are useful for representing large data sets. Such data sets occur in applications often referred to collectively as big data. One of the areas where we encounter big data in finance is high-frequency trading. Even if our goal is merely intraday, rather than high-frequency, trading, chances are we would still be dealing with input data captured at millisecond, or even higher frequency.

We shall use the following (rather contrived) example of a kdb+ table where each row represents a trade in a futures contract. The value in the code column identifies that contract, the date and time columns give the dates and times of the trades as reported by the exchange, the price column contains the trade prices per contract and the volume column contains the numbers of contracts traded. The name of the mktflag column stands for "market flag", which distinguishes the pit trades (in which case the value in the column is `P) from the electronic trades (in which case the value is `E). In our table, which represents a hypothetical subsample from some large data set, all the trades are electronic trades. The `comments` column contains arbitrary comments on the data rows as strings – not as `symbol`s. In practice, the specific comments in our example ("NYMEX/CME Group trade", "Transaction represents a trade in two contract months in the same class") would be implemented as `symbol` or numeric flags rather than as strings. We chose to use the string data type to demonstrate its use in a table.

```
trades : ([] code:`symbol$(); date:`date$(); time:`time$(); price:`float$()
    ↪ ; volume:`short$(); mktflag:`symbol$(); comments:());
`trades upsert (
    (`CLM16; 2016.04.07; 10:20:00.329; 38.3  ; 4h; `E; "NYMEX/CME Group
        ↪ trade");
    (`GCM16; 2016.04.07; 12:00:00.055; 1239.7; 6h; `E; "");
    (`GCM16; 2016.04.07; 12:37:02.106; 1240.5; 1h; `E; "");
    (`CLM16; 2016.04.07; 13:00:00.128; 38.04 ; 3h; `E; "NYMEX/CME Group
        ↪ trade");
    (`VXK16; 2016.04.07; 13:22:05.617; 18.85 ; 5h; `E; "");
    (`GCM16; 2016.04.07; 14:35:01.241; 1241.2; 1h; `E; "");
    (`GCM16; 2016.04.08; 10:13:01.048; 1240f ; 3h; `E; "");
    (`VXK16; 2016.04.08; 11:34:53.417; 18.53 ; 1h; `E; "Transaction
        ↪ represents a trade in two contract months in the same class");
    (`CLM16; 2016.04.08; 12:00:00.227; 40.61 ; 3h; `E; "NYMEX/CME Group
        ↪ trade");
    (`VXK16; 2016.04.08; 12:44:00.684; 18.44 ; 2h; `E; "Transaction
        ↪ represents a trade in two contract months in the same class");
    (`VXK16; 2016.04.08; 12:45:33.130; 18.49 ; 1h; `E; "Transaction
        ↪ represents a trade in two contract months in the same class");
    (`CLM16; 2016.04.08; 15:20:02.000; 40.78 ; 3h; `E; "NYMEX/CME Group
        ↪ trade");
    (`CLM16; 2016.04.11; 11:00:00.105; 41.43 ; 2h; `E; "NYMEX/CME Group
        ↪ trade");
    (`VXK16; 2016.04.11; 14:00:00.829; 18.35 ; 1h; `E; "");
    (`VXK16; 2016.04.11; 15:14:58.775; 19.05 ; 2h; `E; "");
    (`GCM16; 2016.04.11; 16:00:00.044; 1257.9; 1h; `E; "");
    (`GCM16; 2016.04.11; 16:28:34.311; 1258.7; 1h; `E; "")
 )
```

6.2 SAVING A TABLE AS A SINGLE BINARY FILE

Before we proceed with the commands, it facilitates to use an environmental variable, e.g. KDB_DATA which points to an on-disk directory of our preference. All the data we shall save will reside under it. Using an environmental variable means that we can share this as part of our profile and use it across various q sessions. This could be something like `C:/data/` on Windows or `/Users/myname/data` on linux/macOS.

We retrieve its value:

```
`datadir set getenv`KDB_DATA
datadir
```

```
`:C:/data/db
```

We can use the following command to save this table as a binary file.

```
`:tradesfile set trades
```

The resulting file will have 965 bytes on Windows and will reside in the current directory, which you can check with `\\cd`; by default this will be the directory containing the `q.exe` executable. To save it in a different directory, i.e. what we have specified as `datadir`, we could use something like this:

```
(`$":",datadir,"/tradesfile") set trades
```

The brackets are needed, as

```
`$":",datadir,"/tradesfile" set trades
```

is interpreted by `q`, from right to left, as

```
`$(":",datadir,"/tradesfile" set trades)
```

which isn't what we want. In the case of success the return is the file path as a `symbol`:

```
`:C:/data/tradesfile
```

We can then load the table from a file either using `get`, in which case we can specify the new table name (by assigning to a variable with that name the result of `get`):

```
trades1 : get `$":",datadir,"/tradesfile"
```

or using `load`, in which case the loaded table will be assigned to a new variable, that variable's name matching the name of the file, in this particular case, `tradesfile`:

```
load `$":",datadir,"/tradesfile"
```

Finally, we note that in the examples above, a file descriptor – an indicator to a file or input/output resource – is denoted by a symbol whose first character is the colon punctuation `:`. Another way to construct the file descriptor if we are already dealing with a symbol file path, is using the `hsym` function:

```
path:`$datadir
```

```
path
```

```
`/path/to/file
```

```
hsym path
```

```
`:/path/to/file
```

6.3 SPLAYED TABLES

Instead of saving the table as a single binary file, we could save it splayed, i.e. so that each column is saved in a separate binary file. This is particularly useful for medium-sized tables (up to 100 million rows) with many columns. Queries often then refer – or *should* refer in order to be optimised – to a small subset of such a table's columns. Storing the columns in separate files allows kdb+ to save time by loading only some of them. To achieve this, we would normally call `set` with a directory path, rather than a file path, as its first argument. However, the following will fail with `'type`:

```
hsym[ `$datadir,"/tradesdir/" ] set trades
```

`set` will disallow us to splay the table `trades` since it contains unenumerated columns of type `symbol`.[1] We can remove those columns and save the table in one line with

```
hsym[ `$datadir,"/tradesdir/" ]  set `code`mktflag _ trades
```

Notice the trailing "/" in the directory path. As a result of running this, the directory `tradesdir` will be created under `datadir`. It will contain files with names `.d`, `comments`, `comments\#`, `date`, `price`, `time`, and `volume`.

We couldn't save the original trades table because the columns of type `symbol`, namely `code` and `mktflag`, weren't enumerated.

We shall now show how to enumerate them. Before proceeding, delete the directory `tradesdir` with all its contents, in case you created that directory by following the steps outlined above, so that we start with a clean slate. To enumerate the `symbol` columns in trades, we use `.Q.en`:

```
tradesdir: hsym `$datadir,"/tradesdir/";
tradesenum: .Q.en[tradesdir; trades];
```

This will create the directory `tradesdir` with a single binary file in it, named sym. That file enumerates the values found in the columns of type `symbol`, namely `` `CLM16``, `` `CLM16``, `` `VXK16``, and `` `E``.

Once this is done, we run

```
tradesdir set tradesenum
```

The directory now contains the files with names `.d`, `code`, `comments`, `comments\#`, `date`, `mktflag`, `price`, `sym`, `time`, `volume`. Notice that this time, with the `symbol` columns enumerated, we were able to save the columns of type `symbol` successfully.

Note that, unlike the above command,

```
tradesdir set trades
```

will fail with 'type, as before.

[1]The same error would be thrown if the table were keyed. We would need to remove the key with `() xkey trades` before saving the table.

Let us now take a look at the individual files in the directory `tradesdir`. The files `date`, `price`, `time`, and `volume` contain the serialisations of the columns with the corresponding names. Notice that you can serialise the columns individually. The command

```
hsym[ `$datadir,"/myprice" ] set trades[`price]
```

will create a file `myprice`, whose contents are identical to those of `tradesdir/price`. Recall that `trades[`price]` is a list of type float:

```
trades[`price]
```

```
38.3 1239.7 1240.5 38.04 18.85 1241.2 1240 18.53 40.61 18.44 18.49 40.78
    ↪ 41.43 18.35 19.05 1257.9 1258.7
```

```
type trades[`price]
```

```
9h
```

When we run

```
hsym[ `$datadir,"/mycols" ] set cols trades
```

We obtain a file, `mycols`, whose contents match those of `tradesdir/.d`. Thus `.d` is the serialisation of the list of column names (as `symbols`) in the table.

However, when we run

```
hsym[ `$datadir,"/mycode" ] set trades[`code]
```

we obtain the file `mycode`, whose contents differ from those of `tradesdir/code`. This is because all the `symbols` in the enumerated table are stored in `tradesdir/sym`, whereas `tradesdir/code` contains indices of the `symbols` within `tradesdir/sym`. We *will* reproduce `tradesdir/code` by running

```
hsym[ `$datadir,"/mycode" ]set tradesenum[`code]
```

This underlines the difference between `trades` and `tradesenum`: `.Q.en` returns a copy of the table with the `symbol` columns enumerated. We can distinguish between the columns that have been enumerated and those that haven't as follows:

```
type trades[`code]
```

```
11h
```

```
type tradesenum[`code]
```

```
21h
```

although the results of meta trades and meta tradesenum look identical.

Similarly to tradesdir/code, the file tradesdir/mktflag contains serialised enumerated strings containing indices of the actual strings within tradesdir/sym. Each distinct text string, corresponding to each distinct symbol value, is stored in tradesdir/sym once. Using the terminology from Java, symbols are interned.

The column comments, whose type is string (rather than symbol), was serialised by set to two files: tradesdir/comments and tradesdir/comments\#. The latter, comments\#, contains the actual text found in the strings. Unlike the serialisations of the enumerated symbol columns, where distinct values are stored only once, comments\# contains repeats. If you open this file in a binary file viewer, you will see that "NYMEX/CME Group trade", for example, occurs multiple times. Using the terminology from Java, serialised strings are not interned, whereas serialised symbols are. The file tradesdir/comments indexes into tradesdir/comments\#.

To load a splayed table from a directory, we can use load:

```
load first ` vs tradesdir
```

This will assign the loaded table to the variable name that matches the name of the directory, tradesdir. (In hindsight, we should have named the directory trades rather than tradesdir.)

Now note how we did not directly use the value of tradesdir to load the directory. When loading the splayed table directory, we need to omit the final /. We do that by using the "vector from scalar" operator vs, which has a handy use of splitting the scalar filepath into the first part and the last \. Exactly what we wanted!

Finally, we can create two useful functions which will allow us to create and append the splayed table in the future. First, we start with the function to create a splayed table. The function needs three inputs: the path on the drive where to store the file(s), the variable along which we splay the table, and the table itself. The function is defined as:

```
.quantQ.io.saveSplayedTab:{[tabPath;pvar;table]
    // tabPath -- path where to store the table
    // pvar -- variable to sort and index on for fast querying
    // table -- name of the table to save
    :@[;pvar;`p#] pvar xasc (` sv (tabPath;`;table;`)) set .Q.en[tabPath]
        ↪ get table;
 };
```

The single line of this function essentially carries out the following operations in order: access the global table reference, enumerate the table, save it to disk and then apply the parted attribute on pvar column after sorting the table by that column.

To use this function, we may run, for instance, the following command:

```
.quantQ.io.saveSplayedTab[hsym `$datadir,"/sdb";`code;`trades]
```

Besides, we may need to update the table in the future. For this purpose, we create a function which updates the existing splayed table by adding new data. The function needs four inputs: three are the same as for .quantQ.io.saveSplayedTab, and the additional input is the new table we want to append to the existing splayed table. The function is defined as:

```
.quantQ.io.appendSplayedTab:{[tabPath;pvar;table;table2Add]
    // tabPath -- path where to store the table
    // pvar -- variable to sort and index on for fast querying
    // table -- name of the saved table
    // table2Add -- table to append
    :@[;pvar;`p#] pvar xasc (` sv (tabPath;`;table;`)) upsert .Q.en[tabPath]
        ↪ table2Add;
 };
```

The last variable is the name of the table passed into our function and thus is called without backtick (in other words, it is not passed in as a global variable reference). The example of using such a function is as follows:

```
.quantQ.io.appendSplayedTab[hsym `$datadir,"/sdb";`code;`trades;newTrades]
```

Although we have demonstrated two functions for saving a table and then appending more data to it, we note that the two functions are almost identical apart from the difference in the use of `set` for the initial save vs `upsert` for the append. `upsert` will create a table if it does not exist and can, therefore, encapsulate both operations and we can use .quantQ.io.appendSplayedTab for both examples above.

6.4 PARTITIONED TABLES

In addition to splaying a table, we may partition it: for each distinct value *v* of a column that defines the partition, a distinct directory will be created, where the binary files with serialised columns will be stored, but including only those rows with value *v* in the partition column. The standard `.Q.dpft` function performs the partitioning. The name of that function stands for its four parameters: *d*irectory, *p*artition, sort *f*ield, and *t*able name. To store the `trades` table, we can execute the following code:

```
mydbdir: hsym `$datadir,"/mydb";
{
    `trd set select from trades where date=x;
    .Q.dpft[mydbdir;x;`code;`trd];
    delete trd from `.;
 } each distinct trades[`date]
```

We will thus call `.Q.dpft` once for each of the distinct values in the `date` table, resulting in the following calls:

```
.Q.dpft[mydbdir; 2016.04.07; `code; `trd1];
.Q.dpft[mydbdir; 2016.04.08; `code; `trd2];
.Q.dpft[mydbdir; 2016.04.11; `code; `trd3];
```

where `` `trd1`trd2`trd3 `` are, respectively, the names of the three tables by selecting from trades the rows where date has one of the values, respectively, 2016.04.07, 2016.04.08, 2016.04.11:

```
select from trades where date=2016.04.07;
select from trades where date=2016.04.08;
select from trades where date=2016.04.11;
```

We could *not* implement our calls as follows

```
.Q.dpft[mydbdir; 2016.04.07; `code; select from trades where date
    ↪ =2016.04.07];
.Q.dpft[mydbdir; 2016.04.08; `code; select from trades where date
    ↪ =2016.04.08];
.Q.dpft[mydbdir; 2016.04.11; `code; select from trades where date
    ↪ =2016.04.11];
```

because of the type of the last argument to .Q.dpft: it expects, as its fourth argument, the table *name*, i.e. a global variable reference, not the actual table. The table is always saved to disc in a directory with that same name. This is why we create the temporary table, trd, with the date we will write to a variable in the global namespace (`` `. ``) using `` `trd set... `` rather than, for example, trd :. The latter would create the variable trd in the local scope of our anonymous function defined in the {...} block. We wouldn't be able to reference that variable as `` `trd ``. At the end of our local function we delete the temporary table from the global namespace:

```
delete trd from `.;
```

The following directory structure will be obtained by evaluating .Q.dpft example above:

- C:/data/mydb
    - 2016.04.07
        - trd
            - .d
            - code
            - comments
            - comments\#
            - date
            - mktflag
            - price
            - time
            - volume
    - 2016.04.08
        - trd
            - .d
            - ⋮
            - volume

```
    - 2016.04.11
        - trd
            - .d
            - ⋮
            - volume
    - sym
```

In the directory that we have specified to `.Q.dpft`, we have one subdirectory per each partition (`2016.04.07`, `2016.04.08`, and `2016.04.11`). Inside those directories, we have a subdirectory whose name is that of the table that we provided to `.Q.dpft` as an argument: `trd`. Inside `trd`, we have the same files as we encountered when splaying tables, with the exception of `sym`, which now resides two levels above. As before, the file `sym` enumerates the columns of type `symbol`. Notice that we didn't have to call `.Q.en` explicitly this time: `.Q.dpft` did this for us.

We can add another table to the `mydb` directory. Suppose that we have the following (again, highly contrived) table of quotes:

LISTING 6.1 **An example quotes table**

```
quotes : ([] code:`symbol$(); date:`date$(); time:`time$(); bidprice:`float$(); bidsize:`short$(); askprice:`float$(); asksize:`short$(); mktflag:`symbol$());
`quotes upsert (
    (`CLM16; 2016.04.07; 10:15:00.010; 38.34 ; 86h; 38.35 ; 3h ; `E);
    (`GCM16; 2016.04.07; 11:02:16.663; 1241.4; 22h; 1241.5; 1h ; `E);
    (`CLM16; 2016.04.07; 12:05:00.303; 38.12 ; 7h ; 38.13 ; 13h; `E);
    (`CLM16; 2016.04.07; 12:22:00.486; 38.11 ; 16h; 38.12 ; 8h ; `E);
    (`GCM16; 2016.04.07; 13:00:00.205; 1238.6; 8h ; 1238.7; 7h ; `E);
    (`CLM16; 2016.04.07; 15:00:00.051; 38.52 ; 9h ; 38.53 ; 18h; `E);
    (`GCM16; 2016.04.07; 15:20:02.224; 1240.9; 6h ; 1241f ; 1h ; `E);
    (`CLM16; 2016.04.08; 10:53:00.002; 40.83 ; 6h ; 40.84 ; 66h; `E);
    (`CLM16; 2016.04.08; 13:56:30.070; 40.54 ; 38h; 40.56 ; 58h; `E);
    (`CLM16; 2016.04.08; 15:20:02.000; 40.77 ; 26h; 40.79 ; 44h; `E);
    (`CLM16; 2016.04.08; 15:21:43.786; 40.76 ; 3h ; 40.77 ; 28h; `E)
)
```

We run the following code

```
{
    `qt set select from quotes where date=x;
    .Q.dpft[mydbdir;x;`code;`qt];
    delete qt from `.;
 } each distinct quotes[`date]
```

and obtain the following directory structure:

```
- C:/data/mydb
    - 2016.04.07
        - trd
```

```
        -.d
        -code
        -comments
        -comments\#
        -date
        -mktflag
        -price
        -time
        -volume
      -qt
        -.d
        -askprice
        -asksize
        -bidprice
        -bidsize
        -code
        -date
        -mktflag
        -time
   -2016.04.08
      -trd
        -.d
        -⋮
        -volume
      -qt
        -.d
        -⋮
        -time
   -2016.04.11
      -trd
        -.d
        -⋮
        -volume
   -sym
```

To load partitioned tables into kdb+, you must pass the name of the directory that contains them as a command line parameter to the q executable (we killed the already opened q instance first before restarting it in this manner):

```
C:\q\w32>q "C:\data\mydb"
```

However, we are in for a surprise:

```
\v
```

```
`date`sym`trd
```

What's the matter? It turns out that, while `trd` has the partitions `2016.04.07`, `2016.04.08`, and `2016.04.11`, `qt` had only `2016.04.07` and `2016.04.08`. Each table in `mydb` must have exactly the same partitions. We remedy things by recreating `quotes` (by running Listing 6.1) and then storing `quotes` as `qt` using

```
{
    `qt set select from quotes where date=x;
    .Q.dpft[mydbdir;x;`code;`qt];
    delete qt from `.;
} each 2016.04.07 2016.04.08 2016.04.11
```

On quitting kdb+ and then restarting it with

```
C:\q\w32>q "C:\data\mydb"
```

we see that now both `trd` and `qt` are present:

```
\v
```

```
`date`qt`sym`trd
```

We can examine the tables by running

```
select from trd
```

and

```
select from qt
```

Check (by running `\cd`) that the current directory is

```
"C:\\data\\mydb"
```

Notice that if we change it, say, with

```
\cd C:/q/w32
```

our partitioned tables stop "working":

```
select from trd
```

```
'./2016.04.07/trd/code: The system cannot find the path specified.
```

Changing the current directory in the presence of partitioned tables wasn't a good move. We fix things by changing it back:

```
\cd C:/data/mydb
```

Notice that two other variables are present in the restarted `kdb+` instance: `date`, containing the list of the partitions:

```
2016.04.07 2016.04.08 2016.04.11
```

and `sym`, containing the list of enumerated symbols:

```
`CLM16`GCM16`VXK16`E
```

Now let us suppose we want to append the following rows to the

```
morequotes : ([] code:`symbol$(); date:`date$(); time:`time$(); bidprice:`
    ↪ float$(); bidsize:`short$(); askprice:`float$(); asksize:`short$();
    ↪ mktflag:`symbol$());
.[`morequotes; (); ,; (
    (`GCM16; 2016.04.07; 15:23:21.147; 1241.2; 4h;  1241.3; 1h; `E);
    (`GCM16; 2016.04.07; 15:33:04.535; 1241.7; 17h; 1241.6; 2h; `E)
)]
```

Naïvely, we attempt to run

```
qt : morequotes;
.Q.dpft[mydbdir; 2016.04.07; `code; `qt];
delete qt from `.;
```

On restarting the kdb+ instance (we have to do this because we replaced qt with our temporary table; we wrote to qt image on disc but the in-memory representation is not updated) with

```
C:\q\w32>q "C:\data\mydb"
```

we find that we did not append to the 2016.04.07 partition of qt but replaced it:

```
select from qt
```

```
date       code  time         bidprice bidsize askprice asksize mktflag
-----------------------------------------------------------------------
2016.04.07 GCM16 15:23:21.147 1241.2   4       1241.3   1       E
2016.04.07 GCM16 15:33:04.535 1241.7   17      1241.6   2       E
2016.04.08 CLM16 10:53:00.002 40.83    6       40.84    66      E
2016.04.08 CLM16 13:56:30.070 40.54    38      40.56    58      E
2016.04.08 CLM16 15:20:02.000 40.77    26      40.79    44      E
2016.04.08 CLM16 15:21:43.786 40.76    3       40.77    28      E
```

This exposes a limitation of .Q.dpft: since it does not allow us to append to a partition but overwrites it, it requires the entire partition to be in memory for it to be written to a partitioned table. For some very large partitions this is infeasible: they simply won't fit in memory. To append to a partition on disc, we need a modified version of .Q.dpft.

By looking into the terse depths of the k implementation of dpft in q.k we realise that this is a projection of .Q.dpfts, where the s argument allows us to specify which file name to enumerate against (default is `sym). We attempt to add another parameter to this function, o, which is the operation we wish to perform: assignment (:) or upsert (,):

```
k).quantQ.io.dpftsAppend:{[d;p;f;t;s;o]
    if[~&/.Q.qm'r:+.Q.enxs[$;d;;s]`. . `\:t;'`unmappable];
    {[d;t;o;x]@[d;x;o;t x]}[d:.Q.par[d;p;t];r;o;]'[!r];
    @[d;`.d;:;f,r@&~f=r:!r];
    @[.q.xasc[f] d;f;`p#];
 t};
```

We can test it by recreating the quotes table (by running Listing 6.1), writing it to disc with our new function now and passing in the assignment (set) operator as the last argument

```
{
    `qt set select from quotes where date=x;
    .quantQ.io.dpftsAppend[mydbdir;x;`code;`qt;`sym;:];
    delete qt from `.;
} each 2016.04.07 2016.04.08 2016.04.11
```

then appending morequotes with

```
qt : morequotes;
.quantQ.io.dpftsAppend[mydbdir;2016.04.07;`code;`qt;`sym;,];
delete qt from `.;
```

This time we have achieved our goal of appending to a partition in qt: after restarting again with

```
C:\q\w32>q "C:\data\mydb"
```

we check that we have indeed appended to a partition on disc:

```
select from qt
```

```
date       code  time         bidprice bidsize askprice asksize mktflag
-----------------------------------------------------------------------
2016.04.07 CLM16 10:15:00.010 38.34    86      38.35    3       E
2016.04.07 CLM16 12:05:00.303 38.12    7       38.13    13      E
2016.04.07 CLM16 12:22:00.486 38.11    16      38.12    8       E
2016.04.07 CLM16 15:00:00.051 38.52    9       38.53    18      E
2016.04.07 GCM16 11:02:16.663 1241.4   22      1241.5   1       E
2016.04.07 GCM16 13:00:00.205 1238.6   8       1238.7   7       E
2016.04.07 GCM16 15:20:02.224 1240.9   6       1241     1       E
2016.04.07 GCM16 15:23:21.147 1241.2   4       1241.3   1       E
2016.04.07 GCM16 15:33:04.535 1241.7   17      1241.6   2       E
2016.04.08 CLM16 10:53:00.002 40.83    6       40.84    66      E
2016.04.08 CLM16 13:56:30.070 40.54    38      40.56    58      E
2016.04.08 CLM16 15:20:02.000 40.77    26      40.79    44      E
2016.04.08 CLM16 15:21:43.786 40.76    3       40.77    28      E
```

We have, therefore, been able to append last data to disk in a more efficient way – the last line of our tailored dpftsAppend function will sort (on-disk) the data by the parted field – in this case, `code and assign the `p (parted) attribute to it.

6.5 CONCLUSION

In this section we have shown how to save tables to disk in 3 ways:

- binary files: suitable for "small" (thousands or up to a few million records) tables, such as static data.
- splayed tables: suitable for "medium" size tables, or tables which are very wide, i.e. have a large number of columns.

- partitioned tables: suitable for "large" time series tables which span multiple dates, months, or years. This is the main way to save "big data" tables, and we have shown how to save but also append to these tables in a memory-efficient way.

One challenge that is found when starting to build huge data sets with many partitioned tables is how to maintain them when, for example, we have a schema change, and we need to normalise or backfill a new column or change its datatype.

CHAPTER 7

Joins

As we saw in Chapter 2, tables and dictionaries stand as giants at the top of the q datatype hierarchy. The language thus offers different types of join functions, which allow us to combine the tables, or dictionaries, into composite ones. Take, for example, combining two time series, such as a table with market orders and a table with limit orders, which are frequently provided by exchanges as two different data sets. The analysis, however, requires to have them both combined to form a model of price movements. We have to be equipped with the proper tools to be able to do such operations smoothly and efficiently.

7.1 COMMA OPERATOR

We have already covered the join operator , – the comma. Let us recall how it works on lists:

```
a: 1 2 3 4;
b: 5 6 7 8;
a,b
```

```
1 2 3 4 5 6 7 8
```

Comma-join can be used to join tables as well. This type of join is very "vanilla" and puts restrictions on the tables to be joined. Let us illustrate the usage of unkeyed tables first. We define two tables of the same structure and join them with the comma operator:

```
t1: ([] a: 1 2 3; b: 10 20 30);
t2: ([] a: 4 5 6; b: 40 50 60);
t1,t2
```

```
a b
----
1 10
2 20
3 30
4 40
5 50
6 60
```

Since both of the tables are of the same type, the type of the output table is as expected:

```
meta t1,t2
```

```
c| t f a
-| -----
a| j
b| j
```

We now introduce another table which differs from table `t2` in the type of column `b`:

```
t3: ([] a: 1 2 3; b: `10`20`30);
```

and join it with the table `t1`:

```
t1,t3
```

```
a b
----
1 10
2 20
3 30
4 `40
5 `50
6 `60
```

The output table is well defined; however, column `b` contains variables of mixed types – this can be seen from the unspecified type of column `b`:

```
meta t1,t3
```

```
c| t f a
-| -----
a| j
b|
```

We need to be cautious here: mixing two different types is allowed since we can always join two lists and comma-join simply appends different sets of lists to the end of the first table. However, this may cause issues later on when, for example, trying to save the table to disk and getting a `'type` error due to the mixed and unenumerated nature of that column. In many cases, we do not expect the list to be mixed, and this may be due to a bug which went unnoticed.

The `upsert` function is less forgiving here:

```
t1 upsert t3
```

Type checks on a column ensure that they need to be conformant types and the operation above will return a `'type` error. We, therefore, advise caution on the usage of comma-join and prefer the safer `upsert` function.

Both , and upsert verbs work well on tables which have the same columns. If we define another table, t4, which has different structure compared to table t1, i.e. it does not have matching columns, the join will fail:

```
t4: ([] a: 4 5 6; b: 40 50 60; c: 400 500 600);
t1,t4
```

```
'mismatch
```

The join fails, and the prompt shows that tables cannot be matched due to column mismatch. The same will happen with upsert. Both , and upsert verbs thus require a perfect match in the columns for tables which are to be joined. The same is true for keyed tables:

```
t5: ([a: 4 5 6]; b: 40 50 60);
t1,t5
```

```
'type
```

The key in one of the tables is causing the type error as keyed and unkeyed tables are different types. We can, however, use the comma operator on two keyed tables:

```
t6: ([ a: 4 5]; b: 40 50);
t5,t6
```

```
a|  b
-| --
1| 10
2| 20
3| 30
4| 40
5| 50
```

The join operator correctly joins two keyed tables and will also check for types when the tables are keyed:

```
(`a xkey t1),`a xkey t3
```

```
'type
```

Note xkey function takes explicit column names (or an empty list for no keys) to key a table based on the argument on the left.

The comma-join operator can also be used to join tables sideways:

```
t7: ([]c: 100 200 300; d: 1000 2000 3000);
t1,'t7
```

```
a b  c   d
-------------
1 10 100 1000
2 20 200 2000
3 30 300 3000
```

We note that , was accompanied by the each-both adverb, which makes the join work row by row. Both columns are required to have the same number of rows. The following command will thus fail due to the unequal length of the tables to be joined:

```
t1,'t7[ til 2 ]
```

```
'length
```

The join with each-both adverb works even when the two tables to be merged have the same names of columns. In such a case, the values in the table on the right will replace the values on the left for common columns:

```
t8: ([] c: 1 2 3; b: 1000 2000 3000);
t1,'t8
```

```
a b    c
--------
1 1000 1
2 2000 2
3 3000 3
```

Finally, the join with each-both adverb can be used on keyed tables as well. If two tables have the same column as a key, then a sideways join will work on common keys since we recall that key tables are dictionaries:

```
t9: ([a: 1 2 3]; c: 1000 2000 3000);
(`a xkey t1),'t9
```

```
a| b  c
-| -------
1| 10 1000
2| 20 2000
3| 30 3000
```

and

```
(`a xkey t1),'2#t9
```

```
a| b  c
-| -------
1| 10 1000
2| 20 2000
3| 30
```

This concludes the joins of tables using the , operator. The comma-join is entirely restricted in its use and does not allow a lot of the desired flexibility we may require when working with tables. For example, if we need to perform an each-both join of two tables, i.e. ,', where the tables are of the same length, and we want to perform join only when a particular column matches, a somewhat cumbersome piece code would have to be written. Since a table is fundamental datatype within the kdb+/q framework, it comes without surprise that comma operator is not the only option we have to perform joins.

q is thus equipped with eight additional commands to perform particular types of joins. In the following section, we cover these commands one by one.

7.2 JOIN FUNCTIONS

The dedicated join functions are: `ij`, `ej`, `lj`, `upsert`, `uj`, `pj`, `aj`, `asof`, `wj`. They altogether provide a powerful suite of join operations, which naturally incorporates within a table-driven framework.

7.2.1 ij

`ij`, or "inner" join, joins two tables on the key columns of the second table. Thus, the table on the right must be a keyed table, and the keys of that table have to be contained in the table on the left. As a result, the combined table contains each row from the left table, with matching values from the columns of the right table:

```
t10: ([] a: 1 2 3; b: 10 20 30;c: 100 200 300);
t11: ([a:1 2 4] c:-100 0N -400; d:-1000 -2000 -4000);
t10 ij t11
```

```
a b  c    d
---------------
1 10 -100 -1000
2 20      -2000
```

The output contains only two rows, the rows which are matched based on the values of `a` from table `t11`. The output is an unkeyed table. Finally, the provided example also illustrates the role of missing/null entries in the table, which replace the not null values during the `ij`, as can be seen from the null values in column `c`.

The inner join works in the case when table is keyed by more than one column as well:

```
t12: ([a:1 2 4; b:10 0N 0N] c:-100 0N -400; d:-1000 -2000 -4000);
t10 ij t12
```

```
a b  c    d
---------------
1 10 -100 -1000
```

If the table on the left does not contain all the key columns of the other table, an error is returned:

```
t13: ([a:1 2 4; bb:10 0N 0N] c:-100 0N -400; d:-1000 -2000 -4000);
t10 ij t13
```

```
   'bb
   [0]  t10 ij t13
   ^
```

The error 'bb denotes that this symbol is unknown and cannot be found during the ij call, which expected a bb column to be present in t10.

In an IDE, for example in qPad, we will get the following error, which gives us more hints on what is wrong with our command:

```
ERROR: 'bb
(attempt to use variable bb without defining/assigning first (or user-
    ↪ defined signal))
```

7.2.2 ej

ej, or "equi" join, joins two tables on the list of columns which are provided as an additional argument of the join. As a result, the operation returns all rows with common entries for the specified column(s). The equi join works as follows:

```
t14: ([] a:1 2 4 2; c:-100 0N -400 10; d:-1000 -2000 -4000 -500);
ej[ `a; t10; t14]
```

```
a b  c    d
---------------
1 10 -100 -1000
2 20      -2000
2 20 10   -500
```

The equi join ignores the presence of keys:

```
ej[ `a; t10; t11]
```

```
a b  c    d
---------------
1 10 -100 -1000
2 20            -2000
```

```
ej[ `a`b; t10; t12]
```

```
a b  c    d
---------------
1 10 -100 -1000
```

7.2.3 lj

lj, or "left" join, joins two tables on the key columns of the second table. Thus, the right-hand side table must be a keyed table, where keys of that table have to be contained in the left-hand side table. A left join differs from an inner join in the way it treats the entries in the left table which are not matched by the other table. The result of the left join operation is a combined table, which contains each row from the left-hand side table and updates from the right-hand side if the keys are matched, or, nulls when the rows are not matched.

We use the tables defined in the inner join section to show the difference between the two verbs:

```
t10 lj t11
```

```
a b  c    d
---------------
1 10 -100 -1000
2 20      -2000
3 30 300
```

The left join output table contains all rows of table `t10`. The first two rows have a matching entry in table `t11`. In such a case, entries are updated in the same way as we have experienced in the case of an inner join. The last row – the entry with `a=1` – does not have a matching entry in `t11` and thus was omitted in the inner join. In the left join, on the other hand, the row is inserted without any modification, and the missing values populate all distinct columns from the table `t11`.

Remark: The left join verb can be constructed using the comma functionality using the each left adverb, or `,\:`. This can be proved by:

```
(t10 ,\: t11) ~ lj[t10;t11]
```

```
1b
```

In other words, `lj`, and `,\:` are almost identical, but `lj` is a bit more general since it will still work if the table on the left is keyed.

7.2.4 pj

`pj`, or "plus" join, works like a "left" join, but instead of replacing values, it adds them:

```
t10 pj t11
```

```
a b  c   d
--------------
1 10 0   -1000
2 20 200 -2000
3 30 300 0
```

Let us further denote that missing entries are filled with zeros. The columns which are supposed to be summed together have to be of the same type. If there is a mismatch between types, a `type` error is returned:

```
t10 pj update c:"s"$c from t11
```

```
'type
```

The type error does not occur for columns which can be promoted, like integer vs floats:

```
t10 pj update c:"f"$c from t11
```

```
a b  c   d
--------------
1 10 0   -1000
2 20 200 -2000
3 30 300 0
```

The contents of the `c` column get converted into `float`. The similar conversion is performed even for mixing the numeric and time formats – as we recall that underlying format under the time formats is either integer or float:

```
t10 pj update c:"z"$c from t1
```

```
a b  c                       d
--------------------------------
1 10 2000.01.01T00:00:00.000 -1
2 20 2000.07.19T00:00:00.000 -2
3 30 2000.10.27T00:00:00.000 0
```

7.2.5 upsert

The `upsert` function is used to add entries into an existing table. The upserting of new entries assumes that two tables have an identical structure or the table on the right-hand side has a subset of columns of the table on the left. The operation works in two modes: For keyed tables, `upsert` will update the matching entries and add (append) those who are not matched:

```
t15: ([a: 4 7]; b: 400 700);
t5 upsert t15
```

```
a| b
-| ---
4| 400
5| 50
6| 60
7| 700
```

The second mode is for unkeyed tables, where new entries are always added at the end of the table:

```
(0!t5) upsert 0!t15
```

```
a b
-----
4 40
5 50
6 60
4 400
7 700
```

We have used the same tables as in the previous example while we have removed keys to tables with the `0!` function (`0!` reads as 'key the first 0 columns of the table'). The order of entries in the two tables is preserved.

When we try to add two tables with non-matching structure, the `'mismatch` error is returned:

```
(0!t5) upsert update x:1 from 0!t15
```

```
'mismatch
```

If the table is passed by reference, the table is updated:

```
`t5 upsert t15
```

The output of the adding can be recovered by inspecting the content of the referenced table:

```
t5
```

```
a| b
-| ---
4| 400
5| 50
6| 60
7| 700
```

7.2.6 uj

The "union" join is a generalisation of the comma-join (`,`) and `upsert` functions. Its purpose is to provide both a sideways join, as well as an `insert` or `upsert` functionality, when two table schemas do not necessarily match.

Let us take, for example , tables `t5` and `t15`.

```
t5
```

```
a| b
-| --
4| 40
5| 50
6| 60
```

```
t15
```

```
a| b
-| ---
4| 400
7| 700
```

We just saw that we can join these tables using `upsert`. If, however, we changed the schema of one of the tables and attempted to do the same operation:

```
update c:`A`B from `t15
```

```
t5 upsert t15
```

```
'mismatch
[0]  t5 upsert t15
^
```

we will get the above `mismatch` error since the shapes of the two tables do not conform anymore.

To create the union of the two tables, we rely on `uj`:

```
t5 uj t15
```

```
a| b   c
-| -----
4| 400 A
5| 50
6| 60
7| 700 B
```

We now have a union where the missing values are left with null.

An important caveat to `uj`: Although the function will also work on *unkeyed* tables, we *strongly recommend against using it* in these cases. The reason is that `uj` internally uses an append (`,`), which is not *in-place* (as opposed to the `upsert` function), and therefore any types of columns can be appended to each other.

To illustrate this, let's unkey tables `t5` and `t15`, and change the datatype of column b on `t5` from a `` `long`` to a `` `symbol``:

```
t5:() xkey t5;
t15:() xkey t15;
update b:`40`50`60 from `t5;
meta t5
```

```
c| t f a
-| -----
a| j
b| s
```

```
meta t15
```

```
c| t f a
-| -----
a| j
b| j
c| s
```

The join is allowed now, yet we end up with a mixed column b:

```
t5 uj t15
```

```
a b   c
-------
4 `40
5 `50
6 `60
4 400 A
7 700 B
```

This is allowed, since what the underlying code is effectively doing is just:

```
`40`50`60,400 700
```

```
`40
`50
`60
400
700
```

Yet this would be highly undesirable if the column b in t5 was accidentally or unintentionally created as a symbol further upstream. We would rather the code failed.

This is indeed the case, when the two tables are keyed, as they were originally:

```
t5:`a xkey t5
t15:`a xkey t15
t5 uj t15
```

```
'type
[0]  t5 uj t15
```

Debugging an error further down in our code whose origin is this mixed list behaviour can be very time-consuming and hard to track.

We therefore recommend avoidance of uj, unless both tables are keyed. Use upsert or comma-join instead.

7.2.7 aj

aj, or "as-of" join, is the first of the three functions which provide as-of joining functionality in kdb+/q. These functions allow us to align two time series tables with different time samplings. The as-of join accepts two tables and a list of column names. For every row of the first table, it returns the values of the second table at the "as-of" index, i.e. the index "as-of" the value of the time series column. Let us illustrate the concept of aj in the following example:

```
at1: ([] t: 0 5 7; a: 10 20 30; b: 1000 2000 3000);
at2: ([] t:(1+til 10); b:100*(1+til 10)  ; c:10000*(1+til 10));
```

where we have created two tables: table `at1` is the one which drives the times at which we want to know the last valid observations, which can be found in the other table `at2`. The notion of last valid is derived based on the variable `t` – we have started with one variable only in the initial case. The as-of join is then performed as:

```
aj[ `t; at1; at2]
```

giving the output:

```
t a  b    c
--------------
0 10 1000
5 20 500  50000
7 30 700  70000
```

The first row of `at1` has $t = 0$, for which there is no "last valid" value in the other table `at2`. The output is a table, which has the same number of rows as the table `at1`. It contains all the columns of table `at1` as well as all the columns from the other table `at2`. This simple example illustrates the difference in join behaviour vs what we saw till now. First, column `a` is present in table `at1` only and thus as such, it is present in the output fully unchanged. Second, column b is present in both tables, taking different values in each of them. The output contains only one corresponding column in the output, where the values are mixed from both tables. If there is no last valid value from the look-up table, as is the case for the first observation, the value from `at1` is used, otherwise, the last valid value from `at2` is used. Third, the column `c` is taken from the table `at2` fully, where the first row is missing as there is no value in `at2` prior to $t = 0$ and there is no default value in `at1`.

The ordering of the rows in table `at1` does not matter. Let us change the order of the table `at1`, perform the as-of join and compare it with the original join, having the outputs (and outputs only) sorted by the index `t`:

```
aj[ `t; at1; at2] ~ `t xasc aj[ `t; at1[1 2 0]; at2]
```

```
1b
```

What *is* required in terms of sorting is that the second table is sorted by the last column specified in the first argument (`` `t `` in our example). The reason for this is due to the lookup algorithm being used in an `aj` being `binary search`. Also, note that the common columns in both tables have to be of the same type.

Let us further illustrate that more than one column may be provided for the last-valid concept. The order of the columns specified *matters*: all columns specified *prior to the last column* are used for the exact join. The last column is used as an approximate lookup using binary search, which allows us to align two differently sampled time series.

The additional columns may correspond to the symbol name, traded venue or any further characteristics. The `aj` operation thus allows us to provide as-of join functionality for all the different symbols in the table. Let us create two additional model tables with extra column `sym`:

```
at3: ([] t: 0 5 7 1 2 6; sym:(3#`a),(3#`b); a: 10 20 30 40 50 60);
at4: ([] t:raze 2#enlist(1+til 10); sym:(10#`a),(10#`b); b:(100*(1+til 10))
    ↪ ,10000*(1+til 10));
```

where the column `t` plays a role of the time index and the column `sym` takes a role of the symbol for an exact match. The as-of join with both the time index and the symbol is written as follows:

```
aj[ `sym`t; at3; at4]
```

```
t sym a  b
--------------
0 a   10
5 a   20 500
7 a   30 700
1 b   40 10000
5 b   50 50000
6 b   60 60000
```

which, for every time index and symbol, i.e. every row from `at3`, finds corresponding last valid value in `at4`.

Let us keep in mind that *the ordering should be such that the left-most specified column(s) should be grouping the observations into categories while the right-most column is the actual time index, given there are significantly more timestamps relative to groups of observations*, the case which is present in most of the high-frequency analysis. Thus the command `aj[ `sym`t; at3; at4]` is preferred to `aj[ `t`sym; at3; at4]`.

To illustrate the usage of binary search in buckets – and the retrieval of the last valid record – we delete the exact matches of the time column t from at4:

```
at4: delete from at4 where t in at3`t;
at4
```

```
t  sym b
-------------
3  a   300
4  a   400
8  a   800
9  a   900
10 a   1000
3  b   30000
4  b   40000
8  b   80000
9  b   90000
10 b   100000
```

```
aj[ `sym`t; at3; at4]
```

```
t sym a  b
--------------
0 a   10
5 a   20 400
7 a   30 400
1 b   40
2 b   50
6 b   60 40000
```

Further, to enhance the speed over the large tables, it is recommended that for the in-memory lookup table on the right, the symbol `sym` is grouped, i.e. `` `g#sym``, and within the `sym`, the time index has to be sorted. On the other hand, for on-disk tables, the symbol `sym` should be partitioned with `` `p#sym`` and the time index should be sorted within the `sym`. The virtual partitions should be fully avoided.

7.2.8 aj0

This is a modified version of `aj`, which replaces the time index column from the table on the right. Let us first change the tables `at3` and `at4` such that the time indices in both of them do not overlap:

```
at5: update t:t+0.1 from at3;
at6: update "f"$t from at4;
```

and `aj` returns the time index `t` as taken from `at5`:

```
aj[ `sym`t; at5; at6]
```

```
t   sym a  b
----------------
0.1 a   10
5.1 a   20 500
7.1 a   30 700
1.1 b   40 10000
5.1 b   50 50000
6.1 b   60 60000
```

whereas, `aj0` gives the actual times from the look-up table:

```
aj0[ `sym`t; at5; at6]
```

```
t   sym a  b
----------------
0.1 a   10
5   a   20 500
7   a   30 700
1   b   40 10000
5   b   50 50000
6   b   60 60000
```

The exception is the first row, which corresponds to the case where no "last valid" observation was found and thus the time from table `at5` was used.

7.2.8.1 The Next Valid Join

Empirical analysis requires from time to time using the tangent concept of the "next valid" value. This may arise, for example, when we analyse the outcome of an action or when exploring the predictive features of the model at hand. In such a case, we may need to find the next valid quote as of a given time series. Fortunately, it is easy to derive such functionality from the functions we know.

Let us consider two sets of data, each containing information about trades – indicator of either buy or sell as well as the timestamp when the trade took place – for one asset traded at two distinct venues. Such an example corresponds to the stock traded at different exchanges, contract for differences (CDF) or currency pair traded at different electronic communication networks (ECNs). The working hypothesis we want to (dis)prove is causality between trades among the data sets, namely that the buy/sell trade in one data set is Granger-causing the buy/sell trade in the other data set.

We create two sample data sets. For simplicity, we create data such that there is no underlying law between the two data sets and any causality found would be a pure random coincidence. The first data set contains 100 observations while the second one contains 10,000 data points:

```
dataSet1: ([] time: asc "t"$-100?"j"$23:59:59.999; trade1:100?(-1 1));
dataSet2: ([] time: asc "t"$-10000?"j"$23:59:59.999; trade2:10000?(-1 1));
```

The data looks as follows:

```
dataSet1
```

```
time         trade1
-------------------
00:01:25.332 1
00:21:24.796 -1
00:38:39.521 1
00:40:41.670 -1
00:48:08.048 1
00:57:47.067 1
01:08:00.945 1
01:16:06.996 1
01:18:04.594 -1
01:41:35.331 1
01:44:34.553 1
01:53:15.027 1
01:56:57.413 1
02:01:13.658 1
02:01:32.603 1
02:03:46.211 1
02:14:19.599 1
02:48:20.645 1
02:55:22.645 1
03:01:31.152 -1
..
```

and similarly for `dataSet2`.

We shall try to reverse sort the data as the next valid join is equal to the last valid concept in inverse time. We can achieve this by doing exactly that: we revert the time such that time series $\ldots t_1 > t_2 > t_3 \ldots$ will turn into $\ldots t_1 < t_2 < t_3 \ldots$. Such operation can be done by multiplying the time by -1. This is possible as the underlying type behind timestamp variables is either float or integer:

```
exampleTime:12:34:56.789;
"j"$exampleTime
```

```
45296789j
```

while

```
exampleTime:12:34:56.789;
(neg exampleTime; "j"$neg exampleTime)
```

```
(-12:34:56.789;-45296789j)
```

The multiplication by -1 is achieved by applying the neg function. The negative time is then sorted in ascending order. We can thus achieve the "next valid" join using the following construction:

```
dataSetCombined: aj[ `time;
                      ( `time xasc update neg time from dataSet1 );
                      ( `time xasc update neg time from dataSet2 ) ];
dataSetCombined: `time xasc update neg time from dataSetCombined;
dataSetCombined
```

```
time         trade1 trade2
--------------------------
00:16:31.025 -1     1
00:42:09.536 -1     1
00:44:37.591 -1     1
00:53:31.660 1      1
01:11:57.854 -1     -1
01:26:29.905 1      1
01:53:42.097 -1     -1
02:24:40.646 1      -1
03:13:22.778 -1     -1
03:13:29.907 1      1
03:22:49.917 -1     1
04:07:07.595 1      1
04:22:50.962 1      -1
04:35:02.468 -1     -1
04:42:08.234 -1     1
..
```

In the previous insert, we have inverted the sign of the timestamp column `time` after join and further sorted the table. The result is a table which has the same number of rows as `dataSet1` and contains the next valid trade from `dataSet2`.

We will now show a second – and a more efficient – way to achieve the same result. We recall that `aj` will return the values of the lookup table as-of the time of the first table, i.e. the "last valid" observation. In order to get the "next valid" observation, we can shift forward the lookup values of the second table in order to receive the next value when we perform the `aj`. This can be written as:

```
dataSetCombined: aj[ `time; dataSet1; update next trade2 from dataSet2]
```

And the result is the same (and faster) as in the previous method.

To finish testing our hypothesis about trades at `dataSet1` Granger-causing trades at `dataSet2`, we can test the simplified Granger causality by running the correlation between `trade1` and `trade2` variables as those variables are properly linked, i.e. entry in `trade2` is the successor of entry in `trade1` within the same row. Besides, the Granger causality is based on a linear regression model and in the case of two variables, the problem is equivalent to finding a significant correlation coefficient.

We implement the Granger causality test for trades by first calculating the correlation coefficient between the two columns `trade1` and `trade2`:

```
correlation: exec trade1 cor trade2 from dataSetCombined
```

```
0.1828601
```

and, second, assessing the statistical significance of the estimated coefficient. In other words, we want to determine whether the estimated number is statistically significant from zero or not. This can be done by calculating the t-statistic of the estimate:

$$t = \rho \cdot \sqrt{\frac{N-2}{1-\rho^2}}, \tag{7.1}$$

where N is number of observations and ρ is the estimated correlation coefficient, `correlation`. The t-statistic reads:

```
.quantQ.join.tStatsCorr:{[rho;N]
    // rho -- correlation
    // N -- size of sample
    :rho*sqrt[(N-2)%1-rho*rho];
 };
```

and applied on our data set:

```
.quantQ.join.tStatsCorr[ correlation; count dataSetCombined]
```

```
1.841269
```

The corresponding p-value allows us to conclude that the correlation coefficient is not statistically significant from zero and thus there is no Granger causality link between trades – see Chapter 14 for a notion of the Granger causality. This corresponds to the data generating process, where both data sets were independent.

7.2.9 asof

The `asof` verb has similar functionality to `aj` but also supports the typical "noun verb noun" mode. The right-hand side argument is a dictionary or table, where the last key or column plays a role of the reference time for which we want to find last valid observation from the table which is on the left. If the dictionary/table has more than one key/column, the last one is considered to be time while the remaining ones play the role of the grouping column (e.g. `sym`) demonstrated in the `aj` verb.

Let us recall two tables from the previous section:

```
at5
```

```
t   sym a
----------
0.1 a   10
5.1 a   20
7.1 a   30
1.1 b   40
5.1 b   50
6.1 b   60
```

and

```
at6
```

```
t  sym b
-------------
3  a   300
4  a   400
8  a   800
9  a   900
10 a   1000
3  b   30000
4  b   40000
8  b   80000
9  b   90000
10 b   100000
```

Let us try and look up the values of `at6` as of the values of the `t` column in `at5`. First

```
select t from at5
```

```
t
---
0.1
5.1
7.1
1.1
2.1
6.1
```

and then

```
at6 asof select t from at5
```

```
sym b
-------

a   400
a   400


a   400
```

The output has the same number of rows as is the length of the values in the input table on the right. Further, the output contains all columns from at6 except the column which plays the role of the time index upon which the join is considered.

The previous query is equivalent to the following using aj and stripping the unnecessary columns :

```
select sym, b from aj[`t;select t from at5;at6]
```

```
sym b
-------

a   400
a   400


a   400
```

The verb accepts a dictionary as an argument:

```
at6 asof first select t from at5 where a=60
```

```
sym| `a
b  | 400
```

The following example shows the use of asof when the lookup is done on multiple columns:

```
at6 asof select sym,t from at5
```

```
b
-----

400
400


40000
```

The same output is achieved using aj:

```
select b from aj[`sym`t;at5;at6]
```

7.2.10 wj

`wj` is the last of the three "as-of" join functions provided in `q` and stands for a "window" join. The window join aggregates data from the lookup table over a window applying a specified function and joins the result with another table. The window join is defined as a function of four arguments. The first argument specifies the windows over which the aggregation takes place. The second argument is the list with names of the columns which are used for joining just like in `aj`: group column(s) followed by a sorted field, which is typically a time column. The third argument is a table which provides our data to join on. The last argument is a list of the lookup table to perform the aggregation on, followed by pairs of aggregator functions and the corresponding column to aggregate on.

An example helps to illustrate the case explained in the previous paragraph. We use the generated tables `dataSet1` and `dataSet2` and aim to aggregate data from trade2 over a window around the times in trade1.

```
dataSet1:([] time: asc "t"$-100?"j"$23:59:59.999; trade1:100?(-1 1));
dataSet2:([] time: asc "t"$-10000?"j"$23:59:59.999; trade2:10000?(-1 1));
```

For every realised trade in `dataSet1`, we aim to aggregate the data from the table `dataSet2` over a window starting 1 minute prior to the trade and ending at the time of the trade. Thus, we have to create a time series of paired time windows, one pair per each row in `dataSet1`:

```
window: 0 00:01:00 +\: exec time from dataSet1;
window
```

```
00:07:45.384 00:08:36.733 00:27:49.443 00:57:51.937 01:13:56.903
    ↪ 01:32:50.189..
00:08:45.384 00:09:36.733 00:28:49.443 00:58:51.937 01:14:56.903
    ↪ 01:33:50.189..
```

The aggregation functions we want to apply are:

- Counting the number of `trades2` within a window.
- Average value of the number of `trades2` within a window.
- Asymmetry between positive and negative trades.
- List of all trades within a window.

The first two bullet points can be achieved using the native `count` and `avg` functions. The asymmetry is implemented as follows:

```
.quantQ.join.asymmetry:{[x]
    :sum[ x = 1 ] % count x;
 };
```

which calculates the following quantity:

$$asymmetry = \frac{\sum_i 1_{(type=1)}}{\sum_i} \tag{7.2}$$

In order to obtain the list of all trades, we use the identity function :: which, in this case, will return all the inputs in the corresponding window.

The window join can then be executed as follows:

```
wjTab: wj[ window; `time; dataSet1;
         ( dataSet2;
          (count; `trade2 ); ( avg; `trade2 ); ( .quantQ.join.asymmetry ; `
             ↪ trade2 ); ( ::; `trade2 ) ) ];
wjTab
```

```
time         trade1 trade2 trade2     trade2    trade2
------------------------------------------------------------------------------
00:16:31.025 -1     7      0.7142857   0.8571429 1 1 -1 1 1 1 1
00:42:09.536 -1     11     0.09090909  0.5454545 1 1 -1 1 1 -1 -1 1 1 -1 -1
00:44:37.591 -1     10     0.6         0.8       1 1 -1 1 1 1 1 1 1 -1
00:53:31.660 1      9      0.5555556   0.7777778 1 1 1 -1 -1 1 1 1 1
01:11:57.854 -1     10     -0.2        0.4       1 -1 -1 -1 -1 1 1 -1 1 -1
01:26:29.905 1      3      0.3333333   0.6666667 1 1 -1
01:53:42.097 -1     9      -0.3333333  0.3333333 1 -1 -1 -1 -1 -1 -1 1 1
02:24:40.646 1      10     0           0.5       1 -1 1 -1 1 -1 -1 1 -1 1
03:13:22.778 -1     11     -0.09090909 0.4545455 -1 -1 1 1 1 1 -1 -1 -1 -1 1
03:13:29.907 1      10     0           0.5       -1 1 1 1 1 -1 -1 -1 -1 1
03:22:49.917 -1     9      -0.3333333  0.3333333 -1 1 -1 -1 -1 -1 -1 1 1
04:07:07.595 1      7      0.4285714   0.7142857 1 1 -1 1 1 1 -1
04:22:50.962 1      4      -1          0         -1 -1 -1 -1
04:35:02.468 -1     10     0.2         0.6       -1 -1 1 1 1 1 -1 1 -1 1
04:42:08.234 -1     7      0.4285714   0.7142857 1 1 -1 1 -1 1 1
..
```

For the sake of clarity, the output should have properly named columns, which can be achieved by:

```
`time`trade1`trade2count`trade2avg`trade2asym`trade2list xcol wjTab
```

```
time         trade1 trade2count trade2avg  trade2asym trade2list
-----------------------------------------------------------------------------
00:16:31.025 -1     7           0.7142857  0.8571429  1 1 -1 1 1 1 1
00:42:09.536 -1     11          0.09090909 0.5454545  1 1 -1 1 1 -1 -1 1 1 -1 -1
00:44:37.591 -1     10          0.6        0.8        1 1 -1 1 1 1 1 1 1 -1
```

Note that `wj` aggregates data over the time window including the *prevailing value as-of the start of each window*. There is another version of the "window join" function, `wj1`, which aggregates values over the strict closed window $[t_{init}; t_{end}]$. So including the observation before the beginning of the window can be avoided by using `wj1`. If there is no observation within the window, `wj1` returns an empty list. On the other hand, `wj` always returns a list with at least one observation – except the beginning of the data set.

Let us demonstrate this difference of the two window join functions using an aggregation which returns the first two times for each of the values in the aggregation windows.

```
resWJ: select timeWJ:time from wj[ window; `time; dataSet1; ( dataSet2; (
    ↪ {2#x}; `time ) ) ];
resWJ1: select timeWJ1:time from wj1[ window; `time; dataSet1; ( dataSet2;
    ↪ ( {2#x}; `time ) ) ];
```

and we join the two outcomes:

```
resWJ,'resWJ1
```

As expected, the second time in the aggregated window of `resWJ` matches the first time in the aggregated window of `resWJ1`:

```
timeWJ                    timeWJ1
---------------------------------------------------
00:16:04.541 00:16:31.458 00:16:31.458 00:16:53.304
00:42:04.669 00:42:20.409 00:42:20.409 00:42:21.177
00:44:32.102 00:44:38.511 00:44:38.511 00:44:51.036
00:52:56.289 00:53:35.451 00:53:35.451 00:53:36.342
01:11:51.877 01:12:03.518 01:12:03.518 01:12:03.665
01:26:13.297 01:27:02.906 01:27:02.906 01:27:08.944
01:53:12.688 01:53:44.424 01:53:44.424 01:53:48.625
02:24:37.333 02:24:40.737 02:24:40.737 02:25:06.555
03:13:16.520 03:13:24.917 03:13:24.917 03:13:30.552
03:13:24.917 03:13:30.552 03:13:30.552 03:13:36.945
03:22:44.808 03:23:24.780 03:23:24.780 03:23:24.916
04:07:06.239 04:07:40.210 04:07:40.210 04:07:41.584
04:22:40.879 04:22:56.412 04:22:56.412 04:23:21.883
04:34:41.816 04:35:04.211 04:35:04.211 04:35:13.811
04:42:06.116 04:42:20.370 04:42:20.370 04:42:22.475
..
```

Just like `aj`, a window join can be used with more than one column to join on, i.e. besides the time column, the `sym` and/or other columns can be specified. In such a case, the symbols should be used with a parted attribute, i.e. we ought to apply `` `p#sym ``.

Let us add the symbol attribute into the `dataSet1` and `dataSet2` tables, without assigning any attribute to the symbol:

```
dataSet1: update sym: 100?(`sym1`sym2`sym3) from dataSet1;
dataSet2: update sym: 10000?(`sym1`sym2`sym3) from dataSet2;
```

and list a few lines of the updated table:

```
dataSet1
```

```
time         trade1 sym
-----------------------
00:16:31.025 -1     sym2
00:42:09.536 -1     sym2
00:44:37.591 -1     sym2
..
```

We attempt a window join by specifying `` `sym `` as a grouping column:

```
wjTabSym: wj[ window; `time`sym; dataSet1;
          ( dataSet2;
            ( count; `trade2 ); ( avg; `trade2 ); ( .quantQ.join.asymmetry
                ↪ ; `trade2 );( ::; `trade2 ) ) ]
```

which gives us a type error:

```
'type
[0]  wjTabSym:wj[window;`time`sym;dataSet1;(dataSet2;(count;`trade2);(avg;`
    ↪ trade2);(.quantQ.join.asymmetry;`trade2);(::;`trade2))]
^
```

The correct query is:

```
wjTabSym: wj[ window; `sym`time; dataSet1;
          ( dataSet2;
            ( count; `trade2 ); ( avg; `trade2 ); ( .quantQ.join.asymmetry
                ↪ ; `trade2 ) ; ( ::; `trade2 ) ) ];
`time`trade1`sym`trade2count`trade2avg`trade2asym`trade2list xcol wjTabSym
```

```
q)wjTabSym
time         trade1 sym  trade2 trade2      trade2    trade2
--------------------------------------------------------------------------------
00:16:31.025 -1     sym2 9      0.3333333   0.6666667 -1 -1 1 1 -1 1 1 1 1
00:42:09.536 -1     sym2 13     0.07692308  0.5384615 1 -1 1 1 -1 1 1 -1 -1 1 1 -1 -1
00:44:37.591 -1     sym2 7      0.7142857   0.8571429 1 1 -1 1 1 1 1
00:53:31.660 1      sym1 3      1           1         1 1 1
01:11:57.854 -1     sym3 11     -0.09090909 0.4545455 1 1 -1 -1 -1 -1 1 1 -1 1 -1
01:26:29.905 1      sym1 1      1           1         ,1
..
```

If we inspect the outcome, this construction does not provide the correct answer. The first intuition can come from the fact that `trade2count` provides numbers comparable to the case without any symbol. In the case with symbols, on the other hand, the join should be restricted on a subset of data.

The reason why the window join does not work rests in the fact that it should be used on the `` `p#sym `` lookup table only. In order to obtain the correct window join with symbols, we have first to assign attributes to the symbol column. We create new variables for the sake of clarity:

```
dataSet1p: dataSet1;
dataSet2p: update `p#sym from `sym`time xasc dataSet2;
windowp: 0 00:01:00 +\: exec time from dataSet1;
```

The attributes can be verified by using `meta` verb:

```
meta dataSet2p
```

```
c     | t f a
------| -----
time  | t
trade1| j
sym   | s   p
```

The correct form of the window join can be then obtained by using the new set of properly parted variables:

```
wjTabSymp: wj[ windowp; `sym`time; dataSet1p;
          ( dataSet2p;
          ( count; `trade2 ); ( avg; `trade2 ); ( .quantQ.join.asymmetry
             ↪  ; `trade2 ) ; ( ::; `trade2 ) ) ];
`time`trade1`sym`trade2count`trade2avg`trade2asym`trade2list xcol wjTabSymp
```

```
time         trade1 sym  trade2count trade2avg  trade2asym trade2list
----------------------------------------------------------------------
00:53:31.660 1      sym1 4           0          0.5        -1 1 -1 1
01:26:29.905 1      sym1 4           0          0.5        -1 1 1 -1
01:53:42.097 -1     sym1 5           0.2        0.6        1 -1 1 1 -1
03:13:29.907 1      sym1 3           1          1          1 1 1
04:07:07.595 1      sym1 5           -0.2       0.4        1 -1 -1 -1 1
04:35:02.468 -1     sym1 1           1          1          ,1
..
```

7.3 ADVANCED EXAMPLE: RUNNING TWAP

Let us illustrate the usage of joins with an example on a running TWAP. A running TWAP is a function, which at every tick calculates a time-weighted average of a specified variable, usually price. We encounter such functions when calculating various benchmarks or averaging out high-frequency fluctuations. Further, the TWAP is a well-known execution strategy, which targets the execution price equal or better to the time-weighted average over the execution window.

Let us proceed with the definition of a TWAP: The data consists of a time series:

$$\ldots, x_{i-3}, x_{i-2}, x_{i-1}, x_i, x_{i+1}, x_{i+2}, x_{i+3}, \ldots,$$

which are indexed by the time index

$$\ldots, t_{i-3}, t_{i-2}, t_{i-1}, t_i, t_{i+1}, t_{i+2}, t_{i+3}, \ldots.$$

Further, let us specify the window ΔT, over which the average is calculated. The TWAP is then defined as:

$$TWAP_{i;\Delta T} = \sum_{j\geq 0} \frac{(\max(t_{i-j}, t_i - \Delta T) - \max(t_{i-j-1}, t_i - \Delta T))}{\Delta T} x_{i-j-1}, \tag{7.3}$$

where the sum runs over all current and past observations, and the role of max function is to assure that average is taken over the observations with $t \in [T_i - \Delta T, t_i]$ with all observations outside the window having a zero weight in the sum.

The previous display provides a TWAP defined as of point i, which is among the observations x's. In order to calculate the TWAP as of any time point, we can add a synthetic point into the time series. Such a point will have the time index intended to be the starting point of the TWAP and value being equal to the last valid observation. This formulation is not general in a mathematical sense but fits well in our applied approach when dealing with data within kdb+/q.

For a running TWAP we want to calculate the TWAP function as of every point in the time series. Given the time series $\ldots, x_{i-1}, x_i, x_{i+1}, \ldots$, the time series $\ldots, TWAP_{i-1;DeltaT}, TWAP_{i;DeltaT}, TWAP_{i+1;DeltaT}, \ldots$ is calculated. The q implementation assumes that we are equipped with a table comprising the time index `time` being some numeric time format, and a list of values `val` denoted above as x. Let us generate such data as:

```
data:([] time: asc "t"$-1000?"j"$23:59:59.999; val:neg[1.0]+2*1000?1.0);
data
```

```
time         val
------------------------
00:00:56.288 -0.1565722
00:01:53.448 -0.6747727
00:02:17.170 0.7495029
00:05:43.126 -0.2460277
00:10:46.012 -0.596541
00:12:44.052 0.2867985
00:13:42.235 -0.03617312
00:17:18.491 0.6755229
00:20:10.539 -0.6531074
00:20:44.277 -0.884231
..
```

We have generated data uniformly fluctuating randomly in the interval $[-1, 1]$. This data has a zero mean, and time-weighted average over a long enough window would converge towards the mean. The average, in this case, will serve as a filter, which removes the random noise around zero.

Next, let us define the window over which we calculate the TWAP. We set it to 10 minutes:

```
winTWAP:00:10:00;
```

We first calculate the approximate TWAP by using a `wj` as implemented in the following algorithm:

- Aggregate the table `data` using the window join `wj` where:
  - Variable `time`: Apply `deltas` verb for each aggregated window while removing the first element of the list.
  - Variable `val`: Apply `::` identity verb while removing the last element of the list.
- Having the aggregated table, apply the `wavg` on the two aggregated lists row by row to get the weighted average.
- Report the output.

The algorithm described in the previous display is executed as follows. First, create list of windows:

```
winForJoin: (neg winTWAP;00:00:00) +\:(exec time from data);
```

then, create table with extra variables for join:

```
dataForJoin:select time, timeWin:time, valWin:val from data;
```

perform aggregation with two lambdas for `time` and `val` variables, respectively:

```
dataJoin: wj[ winForJoin; `time; data;
          ((select time, timeWin:time, valWin:val from data);
           ( {1_deltas[x]}; `timeWin ); ( {-1_x}; `valWin ) ) ];
```

and present results:

```
dataJoin
```

```
time         val        timeWin                                         ..
------------------------------------------------------------------------..
00:00:56.288 -0.1565722 `time$()                                        ..
00:01:53.448 -0.6747727 ,00:00:57.160                                   ..
00:02:17.170 0.7495029  00:00:57.160 00:00:23.722                       ..
00:05:43.126 -0.2460277 00:00:57.160 00:00:23.722 00:03:25.956          ..
00:10:46.012 -0.596541  00:00:57.160 00:00:23.722 00:03:25.956
    ↪ 00:05:02.886 ..
..
```

The output table `dataJoin` is large and does not fit on the page. Having this table at hand, we can perform the weighted average of `valWin` using the `timeWin` as weights. This can be achieved easily:

```
dataJoin: update twapApp: timeWin wavg' valWin from dataJoin;
select time, val, twapApp from dataJoin
```

```
time         val        twapApp
-----------------------------------
00:00:56.288 -0.1565722
00:01:53.448 -0.6747727 -0.1565722
00:02:17.170 0.7495029  -0.3085559
00:05:43.126 -0.2460277 0.4511536
00:10:46.012 -0.596541  0.09307683
..
```

The output contains the column `twapApp`, which denotes the approximate TWAP according to the prescribed algorithm.

We have started this exercise by claiming that the TWAP serves as a filter with mean zero. Let us demonstrate this by calculating the first two moments of `val` and `valWin`, respectively:

```
(exec meanVal: avg val, sdVal: dev val from dataJoin),
(exec meanValTWAP: avg twapApp, sdValTWAP: dev twapApp from dataJoin)
```

```
meanVal     | -0.03710814
sdVal       | 0.5721622
meanValTWAP| -0.02660895
sdValTWAP   | 0.2616772
```

The output clearly shows that the mean of the approximate TWAP is around zero. The same is true for the original values `val` as well. The standard deviation is, on the other hand, smaller for the approximate TWAP, being approximately half the value of the original time series. Thus, the TWAP smears out the randomness in `val`.

The provided algorithm looks to be working well, and thus we should answer the question why we call this algorithm the "approximate" TWAP. The reason lies in the fact that the window over which we average the observations is always longer or equal to the specified value `winForJoin`. This comes from the verb `wj`, which takes all the values in the window AND the last valid value before the beginning of the window. The weighted average takes the unequal length of the true window into consideration, and weights sum up always to one.

The TWAP thus starts before the beginning of the window. Let us sum up `timeVal` for each row to see how long the window is:

```
dataJoin: update timeWinLength: sum each timeWin from dataJoin;
select time, timeWinLength from dataJoin
```

```
time         timeWinLength
--------------------------
00:00:56.288 00:00:00.000
00:01:53.448 00:00:57.160
00:02:17.170 00:01:20.882
00:05:43.126 00:04:46.838
00:10:46.012 00:09:49.724
00:12:44.052 00:10:26.882
00:13:42.235 00:11:25.065
00:17:18.491 00:11:35.365
00:20:10.539 00:14:27.413
00:20:44.277 00:15:01.151
..
```

The column `timeWinLength`, which summarises the length of each window, starts exceeding the prescribed window of `00:10:00` once we have enough observations in the window starting at `i>5`. The inequality of the window is pronounced for sparse data, where the window length is comparable or smaller to the frequency of the data. For high-frequency data, where updates are at millisecond frequency, and the window is on the time scale of seconds, the approximate TWAP works well. If the window gets shorter, say to tens of milliseconds, the approximate TWAP does not work well. Thus, we present the algorithm for the exact TWAP.

We calculate the TWAP using the following algorithm:

- Aggregate the table `data` using the window join `wj` where:
  - Variable `time`: Apply `::` identity verb for each aggregated window.
  - Variable `val`: Apply `::` identity verb while removing the last element of the list.

- Remove the first observation of each aggregated list of `time` and replace it by the beginning of each window.
- Apply deltas on the augmented `time` lists and remove the first element of the list.
- Having the aggregated table with `val` and the augmented list of `time`, apply the `wavg` on the two aggregated lists row by row to get the exact time-weighted average.
- Report the output.

The implementation of the algorithm reads:

```
// window join of val and time
dataJoin: wj[ winForJoin; `time; dataJoin;
            ( (select time, timeWin2:time, valWin2:val from data);
             ( {1_x}; `timeWin2 ); ( {-1_x}; `valWin2 ) ) ];
// append the beginning of the window to the aggregated time lists
dataJoin: update timeWin2: ( first[winForJoin],' timeWin2 ) from dataJoin;
// apply lambda with deltas and remove first observation
dataJoin: update timeWin2: {1_ deltas x} each timeWin2 from dataJoin;
// twap
dataJoin: update twap: timeWin2 wavg' valWin2 from dataJoin;
// illustrate the result...
select time, twapApp, twap from dataJoin
```

```
time         twapApp     twap
-----------------------------------
00:00:56.288
00:01:53.448 -0.1565722  -0.1565722
00:02:17.170 -0.3085559  -0.1770601
00:05:43.126 0.4511536   0.1339592
00:10:46.012 0.09307683  0.08880117
00:12:44.052 0.0150436   -0.01786262
00:13:42.235 0.03812392  -0.06273184
00:17:18.491 -0.1956813  -0.1876791
00:20:10.539 -0.02288131 0.07657245
00:20:44.277 -0.04647621 0.05368237
..
```

The output table in the previous display shows the approximate TWAP `twapApp` as well as the exact TWAP `twap`. Both variables show substantial differences with frequently changing sign. In terms of the first two moments, however, the two types of the TWAP are close to each other:

```
(exec meanVal: avg val, sdVal: dev val from dataJoin),
(exec meanValTWAP: avg twapApp, sdValTWAP: dev twapApp from dataJoin),
(exec meanTWAP: avg twap, sdTWAP: dev twap from dataJoin)
```

```
meanVal     | -0.03710814
sdVal       | 0.5721622
meanValTWAP | -0.02660895
sdValTWAP   | 0.2616772
meanTWAP    | -0.03319108
sdTWAP      | 0.2638219
```

Let us accompany the analysis of two TWAP types by investigating the regression between them:

```
exec twapApp cor twap from dataJoin
```

```
0.9507798f
```

The two TWAPs are highly correlated, and thus the seeming difference between them drawn from few values was incorrect.

Finally, let us calculate the length of the time deltas used in the weighted average:

```
dataJoin: update timeWinLengthExact: sum each timeWin2 from dataJoin;
select time, timeWinLengthExact from dataJoin
```

```
time         timeWinLengthExact
-------------------------------
00:00:56.288 00:00:00.000
00:01:53.448 00:10:00.000
00:02:17.170 00:10:00.000
00:05:43.126 00:10:00.000
00:10:46.012 00:10:00.000
..
```

The length of the windows is for every row except the first equal to the prescribed value of `00:10:00`. This example concludes our section on the window join. We encourage the reader to play with the `wj` function and adjust the algorithm for a TWAP which is calculated at random lists of points.

CHAPTER 8

Parallelisation

By default, a q instance is single-threaded and aims to use only one core. Aside from interrupts to the main loop to run timer jobs or check external client requests, once a function is called, the entire calculation is sequential, and there is no competition for resources as everything runs in a single queue. We may override this default behaviour and enable concurrent processing on multiple CPU cores, by setting a number of slave threads using the command-line argument:

```
>q -s N
```

which launches the q process with N slaves. In order to check the number of slaves from within a process, we may run

```
\s
```

which returns, in the case of $N = 5$:

```
5i
```

From within the process, we may check the number of slaves using the above command, as well as redefine the number of slaves from within the process using `\s N`, as long as N is less than the number of slaves set in the command-line. If we have launched a single-threaded process, we cannot add more slaves dynamically. For reference, the number of cores available on the server where q is running can be found as:

```
.z.c
```

```
8i
```

Each slave is a single thread, which can be invoked from the master process. It has its own memory management, and we can assign to each slave a memory limit using the `-w MEMORY` option with `MEMORY` being the amount of heap for each slave in Mbs.

In order to achieve maximum utilisation of resources – whether running our program on our laptop or a big server – we need to be cognisant of the total available resources on our machine and how they may interfere with each other. We should, therefore, consider setting the number of slaves to something less than the number of cores when running very CPU-demanding tasks in parallel and adjust it according to the remaining activity on the server.

When the slave instances are specified – and calculation is parallelised – global variables are copied into each slave thread. When the process within a slave thread finishes, the output is copied back to the master process. This is important to keep in mind. When we aim for parallelisation, we should remember that copying a large amount of data from the main thread to the slaves and back can become a costly overhead. We should therefore minimise the unnecessary transfer of large data between threads and focus on sending small data sets which require cpu-intensive operations.

Moreover, only the main thread can update global variables; the individual slave processes do not have write access to them. q also allows us to use parallelisation across processes rather than threads, which we will briefly discuss towards the end of this chapter. We first focus on parallelisation by using threads within a single instance.

8.1 PARALLEL VECTOR OPERATIONS

Since q is a powerful vector language, parallelisation is mainly focused on parallel execution on chunks of large data vectors. For illustration, let us consider a hypothetical function, `getDailySpread`, which takes as an argument a list of values for a date and returns the average spread for a given date (of a certain instrument). We are interested in the daily time series over a list of dates, `timeseriesForDates`. The single-threaded version of this query reads

```
getDailySpread each timeseriesForDates
```

which applies the function `getDailySpread` sequentially on the list time series data for each of the dates, i.e. `timeseriesForDates` is a list of vectors and returns the vector of daily spreads. By using slaves, we may use the parallel version of `each` and run:

```
getDailySpread peach timeseriesForDates
```

`peach` is an analogue to `each`, but able to process the function on each element concurrently across threads. We may use `peach` even when we have not specified any slaves as it defaults to `each` in such a case. Let us recall that `getDailySpread` cannot contain any functionality which would save data into global variables. If this were the case, the call would result in a `'noupdate` error.

The parallelisation proceeds in the following way: each of the first *N* elements of the list is assigned to the *N* slave threads configured, and the operation, in this case, `getDailySpread`, is executed in parallel.

If `count[ timeseriesForDates ] > N`, then once all slaves have returned the first *N* elements, the operation will repeat itself by assigning the remaining elements of the list to slaves again in one go, and so on. In other words, this operation will consist of `ceiling count[x] % N` sequential blocks, each of which will spawn `min[(N;numOfRemainingTasks)]` tasks to the *N* threads.

The operation described can be seen in the example below: First, launch the instance as

```
$ q -s 3
```

and then execute

```
timeseriesForDates: { 10000000 ? 10f } each til 5;
getDailySpread: { 0N!( .z.n; count x ); avg x };
\t r: getDailySpread each timeseriesForDates
```

```
(0D15:23:08.109042000;10000000)
(0D15:23:08.122165000;10000000)
(0D15:23:08.133187000;10000000)
(0D15:23:08.144300000;10000000)
(0D15:23:08.156924000;10000000)
57
```

```
\t pr: getDailySpread peach timeseriesForDates
```

```
(0D15:23:15.051134000;10000000)
(0D15:23:15.051123000;10000000)
(0D15:23:15.051174000;10000000)
(0D15:23:15.066006000;10000000)
(0D15:23:15.068296000;10000000)
27
```

```
r~pr
```

```
1b
```

The thread assignment described in the previous paragraph may on occasion be suboptimal: the different items in the list may be computationally different, and slaves may receive an overall computationally imbalanced list of tasks. For example, having $N = 5$ and `timeseriesForDates` starting on Monday and going over the working days only, market activity on Wednesdays may be on average significantly lower as opposed to other days. Thus, thread No. 2 will get assigned the lightest tasks computationally, which results in No. 2 finishing much earlier than other slaves. It is the responsibility of the user to know the data and think whether uniformly distributing the data for parallelisation makes sense or not, depending on the use case.

In addition to `peach`, there is another option, which allows for a different – and uniform – parallelisation, coming from `.Q` namespace, the function `.Q.fc`, which cuts the vector and executes the function over chunks in parallel. The parallelisation works by splitting a list homogeneously, assigning the function and each sub-vector to a thread for computation and then finally razing (flattening) the results.

Let's slightly modify the previous example to be a single long vector of data values and compare the single-threaded approach to a multithreaded, using `.Q.fc`:

```
timeseries: raze timeseriesForDates
avg timeseries
```

```
5.00002
```

```
.Q.fc[ avg; timeseries]
```

```
5.000607 4.999674 4.99978
```

So here we see that calling `.Q.fc` has split the vector into `N = 3` lists (equal to the slave threads we have) and returned the application of the `avg` function to those 3 sub-vectors. So calling `.Q.fc` in this example is similar to a map-reduce paradigm and we need to therefore reapply the `avg` function here to get the final result:

```
avg .Q.fc[ avg; timeseries]
```

```
5.00002
```

Let us now time the two calls; this reveals that using threads is not always optimal.

```
\t avg timeseries
```

```
58
```

```
\t avg .Q.fc[ avg; timeseries]
```

```
110
```

The reason for this is that the overhead of splitting the vector and serialising back and forth between threads is not justified here, especially since the above computation is relatively simple: an average function which is already natively optimised by q to work on large vectors.

Replace the above with a computationally heavier function and the benefits of parallelisation begin to emerge:

```
heavyFunc: { sqrt[x] xexp 2.3 }
```

```
\t r:heavyFunc 1000000#timeseries
```

```
37
```

```
\t fr:.Q.fc[ heavyFunc; 1000000#timeseries]
```

```
18
```

```
r~fr
```

```
1b
```

and `.Q.fc` has also ensured that our data was uniformly split and therefore equal resources were used across our thread pool.

The above illustrates that parallelisation itself carries a trade-off between parallel execution and the overhead needed to set the parallel execution. This is true for both `peach` and `.Q.fc`. We should aim in parallelising only computationally heavy tasks as `q` itself is powerful enough to handle simple vector tasks in a single thread.

In later chapters we will provide more examples of parallelisation when solving practical ML problems.

8.2 PARALLELISATION OVER PROCESSES

There is an alternative to threads for parallelisation in a `kdb+/q` framework, which we are going to motivate briefly: the parallelisation across processes. This means that instead of specifying a list of single-threaded slaves, we specify a list of processes over which the computation can be parallelised. This is achieved by running `-s` with negative integer argument:

```
>q -s -N
```

which allows our instance to connect to other `q` process with `N` threads, each one linked to process from a list of ports specified by a function `.z.pd`, which itself returns unique integers, each representing a handle to a slave `q` process. The parallelisation over processes is specified by the minus sign in front of `N`.

In this case, the data have to be already present on each of the processes or passed as arguments of the function. There is no implicit memory management for parallelisation across processes unless those are started using the `-w flag`. In this setup, one ought to be careful in terms of data size being transferred, or required memory, which may significantly increase the overhead.

The parallelisation over processes is useful for partitioned databases with `.Q.MAP[]` which keeps the partitions mapped to memory to prevent overhead when the historical database is being repeatedly called with `select`. Besides, we may use this option to distribute a heavy computation across different servers, which may offer us more processing cores than available to us locally, in a grid-like fashion. In such a case, the data and memory have to be managed appropriately, for example, a copy of the underlying data being stored on each server with only a relatively small output being transferred.

8.3 MAP-REDUCE

For partitioned tables, `q` has another property which makes parallelisation more useful. Let us assume that we have built our historical database as a partitioned table over dates as we demonstrated in Chapter 6. Our goal is to calculate the average spread over a list of dates for table `qt`:

```
select avgSpread: avg .5 * bidprice + askprice from qt where date in
    ↪ 2016.04.07 2016.04.08
```

In order to calculate the average, q will first apply a partial sum operation for each date partition and also count the number of elements in each date. So by running function avg, q recognises that this operation is run over a partitioned table and employs the map-reduce paradigm. This means that the average is calculated in two steps. First, the number of elements and sum of values for each date is obtained and recorded (map). Then, the sum of sums is divided by the sum of counts (reduce) and the average is returned.

Semantically, the above query can be approximated as follows:

```
map: select cnt: sum not null .5 * bidprice + askprice, avgSpread: sum  .5
    ↪ * bidprice + askprice
      by date from qt where date in 2016.04.07 2016.04.08
reduce: select avgSpread: sum[ avgSpread ] % sum cnt from map
```

This optimisation is done automatically in the first query above and has two benefits:

- Memory: it is more efficient since each on-disk partition directory is reduced to a single number, instead of reading all values for all dates into memory first and then averaging – the latter being memory inefficient.
- CPU: the above operation is independent for each directory on disk and therefore multiple dates can be mapped in parallel using slaves. q will automatically do this when a query spanning multiple dates is run, and slaves are specified.

Knowledge of the above also motivates us to have a well-thought-out partitioning scheme which suits our data needs.

We note that the functions which have built-in map reduction implemented are: count, avg, cor, scor, var, svar, dev, sdev, cov, scov, first, last, max, min, prd, sum, wavg, wsum and distinct. It is important to mention that q will only recognise these functions and apply map-reduce on these. Functions outside of this domain will return the result applied individually to each date partition. As an example, observe this oddity:

```
select last bidsize,sum deltas bidsize from qt where code=`CLM16
```

```
bidsize bidsize1
----------------
3       12
```

We would expect bidsize and bidsize1 to be the same number, since summing up the differences of a vector should give us the last value of that vector. However, removing the sum from the query reveals that map-reduce did not work exactly as expected, since (as at the time of writing) deltas is not a function which is supported:

```
select date, bidsize, dbidsize: deltas bidsize from qt where code=`CLM16
```

```
date       bidsize dbidsize
---------------------------
2016.04.07 86      86
2016.04.07 7       -79
2016.04.07 16      9
2016.04.07 9       -7
2016.04.08 6       6
2016.04.08 38      32
2016.04.08 26      -12
2016.04.08 3       -23
```

We can see that the first value of `dbidsize` on the `2016.04.08` partition is incorrect. This is simply because `deltas` has been applied to each partition independently. So the benefits of parallelisation are still here, yet the result is wrong.

A workaround for this is to amend q's bootstrap file `q.k` to support the function we desire. This requires adding the appropriate map-reduction functions of our choice under the `.Q.a*` variables. A good way to do this is by overriding the values in our bootstrap script (or `q.q`) file, since `q.k` itself is part of the `q` distribution and changes from version to version. We leave this as an exercise for the reader.

Alternatively, we can compute the correct deltas above in two – memory inefficient – steps:

```
map: select bidsize by date from qt where code=`CLM16;
map
```

```
map
date      | bidsize
----------| ----------
2016.04.07| 86 7  16 9
2016.04.08| 6  38 26 3
```

```
reduce: select date, bidsize, dbidsize: deltas bidsize from ungroup map;
reduce
```

```
date       bidsize dbidsize
---------------------------
2016.04.07 86      86
2016.04.07 7       -79
2016.04.07 16      9
2016.04.07 9       -7
2016.04.08 6       -3
2016.04.08 38      32
2016.04.08 26      -12
2016.04.08 3       -23
```

Which gives us the correct result:

```
select last bidsize,sum deltas bidsize from reduce
```

```
bidsize bidsize1
----------------
3       3
```

Finally, note that q will also not be able to identify the map-reduce functions when they are inside a lambda:

```
select distinct code from qt where code=`CLM16
```

```
code
-----
CLM16
```

but

```
select {distinct x} code from qt where code=`CLM16
```

```
code
-----
CLM16
CLM16
```

and

```
select distinct {distinct x} code from qt where code=`CLM16
```

```
code
-----
CLM16
```

8.4 ADVANCED TOPIC: PARALLEL FILE/DIRECTORY ACCESS

We have stated in the previous sections that slaves cannot write into global variables. This means that a slave cannot write to a global variable. What we *can* do though, is to update an on-disk partitioned table in parallel since – as we have previously seen – partitioned table is, in fact, a directory structure, where each table is a directory, and every column a file under that. Besides, there is a common enumeration file sitting at the top-level directory above the table name, so we should be careful about updates to that file and variable which can happen in parallel. Luckily, when updating the enumeration file on disk, q will lock that common enumeration file, which means that we can update partitioned tables for different dates (and therefore different directories on disk), in parallel. However, enumerating columns against an on-disk enumeration file will also update a global variable with the same name (usually named `sym`).

We, therefore, need a variation to the previously introduced dpftsAppend function from our `.quantQ.io` namespace, in which we first enumerate the new data and only parallelise the part which updates the on-disk table's columns and attribute sorting. We can then parallelise this on-disk operation across dates:

```
k).quantQ.io.dpftAppendNew:{[d;p;f;t;o;n]
    // d -- directory of hdb
    // p -- partition field value (.e.g. a date or an integer)
    // f -- field to sort and apply `p attribute on
```

```
    // t -- reference to on-disk partition table name
    // o -- operation: append (,) or assign (:)
    // n -- new data table to append - data, not a reference, and already
        ↪ enumerated
    {[d;t;o;x]@[d;x;o;t x]}[d:.Q.par[d;p;t];r;o;]'[!r:+n];
    @[d;`.d;:;f,r@&~f=r:!r];
    @[.q.xasc[f] d;f;`p#];
    :t;
 };
```

Here we use the k language and invoke it by using k).

We now enumerate our new data and iterate over dates calling .quantQ.io .dpftAppendNew in parallel using peach:

```
new: enlist `code`time`price`volume`mktflag`comments ! ( `NEW; .z.t; 1f; 1h
    ↪ ; `E; "");
enumNew: .Q.en[`:.;new];
{ [ new; dt] .quantQ.io.dpftsAppendNew[ `:.; dt; `code; `trd; ,; new] }[
    ↪ enumNew; ] peach date
```

```
`trd`trd`trd
```

Reloading the hdb we can see that the new values have been appended:

```
\l .
trd
```

```
date       code  time         price  volume mktflag comments
--------------------------------------------------------------------------
2016.04.07 CLM16 10:20:00.329 38.3   4      E       "NYMEX/CME Group trade"
2016.04.07 CLM16 13:00:00.128 38.04  3      E       "NYMEX/CME Group trade"
2016.04.07 GCM16 12:00:00.055 1239.7 6      E       ""
2016.04.07 GCM16 12:37:02.106 1240.5 1      E       ""
2016.04.07 GCM16 14:35:01.241 1241.2 1      E       ""
2016.04.07 NEW   06:07:56.054 1      1      E       ""
2016.04.07 VXK16 13:22:05.617 18.85  5      E       ""
2016.04.08 CLM16 12:00:00.227 40.61  3      E       "NYMEX/CME Group trade"
2016.04.08 CLM16 15:20:02.000 40.78  3      E       "NYMEX/CME Group trade"
2016.04.08 GCM16 10:13:01.048 1240   3      E       ""
2016.04.08 NEW   06:07:56.069 1      1      E       ""
2016.04.08 VXK16 11:34:53.417 18.53  1      E       "Transaction represents
    ↪  a trade in two contract months in the same class"
2016.04.08 VXK16 12:44:00.684 18.44  2      E       "Transaction represents
    ↪  a trade in two contract months in the same class"
2016.04.08 VXK16 12:45:33.130 18.49  1      E       "Transaction represents
    ↪  a trade in two contract months in the same class"
2016.04.11 CLM16 11:00:00.105 41.43  2      E       "NYMEX/CME Group trade"
2016.04.11 GCM16 16:00:00.044 1257.9 1      E       ""
2016.04.11 GCM16 16:28:34.311 1258.7 1      E       ""
2016.04.11 NEW   06:07:56.085 1      1      E       ""
2016.04.11 VXK16 14:00:00.829 18.35  1      E       ""
2016.04.11 VXK16 15:14:58.775 19.05  2      E       ""
```

To generalise, as long as we do not update in-memory variables in parallel, or try to concurrently write to the same files – which are not the enumeration file – at the same time, we can make use of peach in the same way we did when we read data.

Observe also how we can use peach in a trivial hdb read case when looping over historical dates:

```
{ s:.z.n; select from trd where date=x; ( s; .z.n ) } each date
```

```
0D06:43:42.961368000 0D06:43:42.961899000
0D06:43:42.961901000 0D06:43:42.962418000
0D06:43:42.962420000 0D06:43:42.962885000
```

whereas

```
{ s:.z.n; select from trd where date=x; ( s; .z.n ) } peach date
```

```
0D06:43:46.912248000 0D06:43:46.912930000
0D06:43:46.912229000 0D06:43:46.913000000
0D06:43:46.912230000 0D06:43:46.913009000
```

This concludes our introduction to the parallelisation features within q. The example implementations for each of the use cases mentioned in this chapter can be extended and tailored to a specific computational task. Further occurrences of peach will be seen in Part IV, Machine Learning, where an algorithm may benefit from executing chunks of the logic in parallel.

CHAPTER 9

Data Cleaning and Filtering

We shall briefly cover some practices and rules around data filtering and ways to extract the data we want from a table and a historical partitioned database.

9.1 PREDICATE FILTERING

9.1.1 The Where Clause

The `where` function is the q king of filters; we were first introduced to it in Chapter 1. It acts as a natural filter on a vector:

```
price:100000?10f;
price where price > 5f
```

```
5.615679 9.027819 6.233409 6.471146 8.091551 6.04611 5.45438 9.955497
    ↪ 8.851822 6.443215 9.732086 8.000355 9.900114 9.643722 7.929776
    ↪ 5.052403 5.779..
```

It is also our constraint filter in a `select` statement:

```
table: ([] sym: count[ price ] ? `a`b; price );
select from table where price > 5f
```

```
sym price
------------
b   5.615679
a   9.027819
b   6.233409
b   6.471146
a   8.091551
..
```

We recall from Chapter 2 that we separate multiple constraints using a `','` and these are applied from *left to right*, an exception to the usual q parsing. Note that for multiple `where` clauses, the filtering is *cascading*, i.e. the second filter is applied after the initial filter has already reduced our data set. This is a built-in optimisation in q:

```
\t:100 select from table where price > 5f, sym = `a
```

```
161
```

```
\t:100 select from table where sym = `a, price > 5f
```

```
164
```

Now in the above example, there is not much difference in switching the sym and price constraints, given that they both cut the data roughly in half.

However, a good optimisation for an in-memory table is to apply the grouping attribute `g to a frequently constrained field, usually the symbol or sym column. We do that and see the query time cut in half *when placing the attribute field first in the constraint*:

```
update `g#sym from `table
```

```
`table
```

```
meta table
c    | t f a
-----| -----
sym  | s   g
price| f
```

```
\t:100 select from table where sym = `a, price > 5f
```

```
80
```

This is not efficient when we now place the attributed field last:

```
\t:100 select from table where price > 5f, sym = `a
```

```
199
```

For partitioned databases on-disk, the `g attribute is of no benefit and replaced by `p, which stores the breakpoints between the changes of the values in that field and therefore requires that field to be sorted. We saw the application of the `p attribute in our implementation of the .quantQ.io. functions in Chapter 6.

To summarise:

- Since the where clause is cascading, we should always filter *first* on the field which will reduce our dataset the most.
- The exception to the above is when having a field with an attribute (usually `g in memory tables and `p on disk). We should start with that filter first.

- The exception to the above is when dealing with an hdb, in which case we *always* filter on the partition column (usually `date`) first, and then follow with attributed fields such as `sym`.

Omitting the 3rd rule above on a multi-year, trillion-row database usually results in a window of opportunity for a quick coffee while waiting for the processing to be over. If you have already had your coffee for the day, remember always to do `select... from table where date [in/=/within],...`.

9.1.2 Aggregation Filtering

Another way we can filter data is by using an identity function approach:

$$I_A = \begin{cases} 1, & \text{if } x \in A \\ 0, & \text{if } x \notin A \end{cases}. \tag{9.1}$$

We can use the `wsum` and `wavg` functions here to aggregate values for one field based on whether another field belongs to a set or not. This becomes particularly handy when we want to perform a query which returns aggregations over different sets. In the example below, we simultaneously calculate the average price for each symbol across all the records (`aprice` column) while also calculating the average price for large volume deals (`apriceLarge`):

```
select aprice: avg price, apriceLarge: ( size > 50 ) wavg price by sym from
    ↪ table
```

```
sym| aprice   apriceLarge
---| --------------------
a  | 4.996432 4.992332
b  | 4.978759 4.994488
```

9.2 DATA CLEANING, NORMALISING AND APIs

In an ideal world, we would all like to work with the cleanest data possible. Anyone who has ever worked with real data, though, knows that this is often a pipe dream. Many times we capture data which either is not clean, as it is given by upstream systems or vendors, or does not suit the schema and design we would like.

We attempt to summarise some general guidelines around data cleaning and how to approach this from a design point of view, which, based on our experience, has been most beneficial. Our guidelines here are really common sense, but we believe it is good to articulate them. They tend to follow a priority rule, a bit like an if-else-if statement.

1. If you have a well-defined problem and can get *or* clean the data upstream to your processing program, do it.
2. When this is not possible, or we want to subscribe to everything so we can better understand the data, or perhaps transform it in different ways, then use functional APIs (Application Programming Interfaces) to approach accessing the data.

3. When performance on our raw data becomes a consideration – even when we optimise our historical queries and have a robust database schema – consider a separate database with cleaned or aggregate data.
4. Usually you should use an API even if it is a simple abstraction. The abstraction means that the schema storage method or feed source can always change without impacting your data usage.

To elaborate on points 2 and 4 above, instead of writing complicated `select` statements with explicit column names or `where` clauses which may change over time, and then building a ton of dependencies on your data processing/ml algorithms, simply write a function whose implementation can change over time, but its call always has the input/output you expect based on your use case and specification. An excellent way to allow some flexibility on the input and output of the API, while our needs expand and we do not want to refactor/rewrite all our dependent code, is to use a `q` dictionary as input and output. Dictionaries can always have keys added to them. This is the approach we follow throughout this book. In many cases, we present implementations of a particular function where we aim to preserve the same form of input/output and add the keys into the dictionary whenever needed.

A final point in terms of design is the following: *Keep your filter code and data accessors separate from the calculation and analysis logic. Combining the two mingles different concepts and causes both confusion and also maintenance headaches when the codebase grows or is shared with others.*

CHAPTER 10

Parse Trees

Parse trees are an essential internal construct of the q language. They are a nested list – or collection – of functions and their arguments, which can be executed when desired and are expressed in the form of `(func;arg1;arg2;...)`. They reflect the λ-calculus philosophy of q. Every argument of such a function may be a function itself and any q query can be expressed as a series of nested functions. Those functions – the nested queries – can be evaluated whenever they are called, and they can be overloaded, reacting differently based on the types of their arguments. The parse tree thus represents an internal functional representation within the q language.

The ability to represent any query as a function (or nested functions) gives us more flexibility when working with data. This is particularly handy for expressions which manipulate tables, the cornerstone of the query language. Let us take `select` as an example:

```
tabExample:([] a1: 1 2 3; a2: 4 5 6; a3: 7 8 9);
select a1 from tabExample where a2>=5
```

```
a1
--
2
3
```

This basic query makes perfect sense to us, and we can easily construct a number of similar queries. What if we want to have the selected columns or `where` constraints parameterised to be dynamic based on our desired input? The tools explored so far do not equip us with such flexibility, since a `select` statement can only reference explicit column names, not variables referring to those columns.

Thus,

```
select `a1 from tabExample
```

will attempt to select the symbol `` `a1`` from the table, as opposed to being a reference to selecting the `a1` column.

Functional `select` – and similarly functional `delete`, `upsert` and `update` – on the other hand, provide us with these options:

```
?[`tabExample;enlist (>=;`a2;5j);0b;(enlist `a1)!enlist `a1]
```

```
a1
--
2
3
```

and setting the column names as variables is now possible:

```
whereCol: `a2;
selectCol: `a1;
?[`tabExample;enlist (>=;whereCol;5j);0b;(enlist selectCol)!enlist
    ↪ selectCol]
```

```
a1
--
2
3
```

The query does not look intuitive; however, it gives us full flexibility as every element within `?[...]` can be formed dynamically. Understanding parse trees will be useful in becoming fluent with such expressions.

Should we use the query notation, like `select`, or its functional form? In terms of performance, it does not matter as q interpreter converts queries into a functional form. For code clarity when using basic queries, the SQL format of `select` is recommended. For more advanced – parameterised – queries, the functional form becomes inevitable.

Knowledge of parse trees is useful in appreciating the full elasticity of q and giving us access to its full repertoire. The following section introduces parse trees and then focuses on the functional evaluation of q-SQL queries.

10.1 DEFINITION

A parse tree is a list whose first element is a function, and the remaining entries are its arguments, expressed as tokens. This can be recursive so that the arguments can be functions themselves; therefore, the parse tree can be an elaborate construct spanning multiple levels and be challenging to represent graphically. Tokens are q's internal representation of constants and variables. There are two critical native operators which we need to know to be able to work with parse trees: `eval` and `parse`.

10.1.1 Evaluation

`eval` takes as an argument the parse tree itself and returns the value corresponding to the evaluated parse tree. The parse tree itself is not evaluated until explicitly done so by being passed as an argument to `eval`. Let us start with a basic example:

```
parseTree1: (:;`x;1j);
```

The parse tree is a mixed list:

```
type parseTree1
```

```
0h
```

The first element of the list is `:`, the assignment operator. The other elements of the list are arguments to the assignment operator. We can guess at this point that `parseTree1` represents q's internal representation of assigning `1j` to the variable `x`. We can verify it by using `eval`:

```
eval parseTree1
```

```
1
```

To verify there is a value assigned to the variable `x`, we can just run:

```
x
```

```
1
```

Evaluating `parseTree1` indeed assigned a value to variable `x`. The variable is called by reference, which makes the construction of the parse tree with assignment more flexible since the reference itself can be a variable which is dynamically assigned in our code. Let us consider the situation where we want to create the following list of variables: $x1 = 1, x2 = 2, x3 = 3, \ldots$ We may construct the k-th term as follows:

```
k:4;
name:`$"x",string k;
eval (:;name;k);
x4
```

```
4
```

We can embed this within a function which creates the variable:

```
parseTreeFunc1:{[k]
    eval (:;`$"x",string k;k);
 };
```

The function has a more cogent notation than the previous example. We can test it as

```
parseTreeFunc1[10];
x10
```

```
10
```

As proof of our understanding of essential parse trees, let us try to construct a parse tree analogous to the previous one for the statement:

```
1 + 2 * 3
```

```
7
```

The statement is the composition of two more elementary statements: since q parses from right to left, 2*3 is first evaluated and then the output becomes the second argument of the statement 1 + outputOfFirstStatement. We write this as a parse tree:

```
firstStatement:(*;2;3);
```

```
secondStatement:(+;1;firstStatement);
```

We now evaluate

```
eval secondStatement;
```

```
7
```

At this point, it is worth introducing the value function. This function is heavily overloaded as its functionality depends on the type of the argument which is passed in. Namely:

- *symbol* – it returns its value;
- *enumerated* – it returns the symbol list;
- *dictionary* – it returns values;
- *function* it returns a list of function meta such as bytecode, parameters, local variables, global variables, constants, and definition, as we saw in Chapter 5 and the .quantQ.debug.meta function;
- *primitive* – it returns its integer code;
  e.g.

```
value (+)
```

```
1
```

```
value (-)
```

```
2
```

```
value (%)
```

```
4
```

```
value value
```

```
19
```

- *string* – it evaluates the content of the string;

```
str:"cos acos -1"
```

we can evaluate it as

```
value str
```

```
-1
```

- *list of* *(func;arg1;arg2;...)* – it executes function `func` with arguments `arg1,arg2,...`.

We can see that the last case is similar in definition to a parse tree and both `value` and `eval` can evaluate the same expression. There are subtle differences, though, and the two functions do slightly different things: `eval` will always evaluate a correctly constructed parse tree. `value` will execute a list of functions and arguments and returns its result, as well as performing the other utilities described in the above list.

We can therefore have:

```
value "1+2"     / value the expression
```

```
3
```

```
eval "1+2"      / evaluate the constant string, just returns the constat
    ↪ string
```

```
"1+2"
```

```
eval (+;1;2)    / evaluation the parse-tree
```

```
3
```

```
value (:;`somevar;2)
```

```
2
```

```
somevar
```

```
'somevar    / variable doesnt exist
[0]  somevar
^
```

```
eval (:;`somevar;2)
```

```
2
```

```
somevar
```

```
2
```

10.1.2 Parse Tree Creation

We can get the parse tree of a statement using `parse`:

```
parse str
```

```
(cos;(acos;-1j))
```

```
eval parse str
```

```
-1f
```

This can be handy as a helper in creating *functional* `select` statements as we will illustrate later on.

10.1.3 Read-Only Evaluation

Read-only evaluation is performed with the function `reval` which has the same signature as `eval`. The verb `reval` simulates the effect of launching `q` with option `-b`, when accessing the instance remotely and running `eval`. By evaluating a parse tree using `reval`, the instance will block any incoming messages which attempt to amend global variables.

For instance, let us assume that we have a process with port number `5000`. We open a handle to the port:

```
z: hopen 5000
```

We then define a variable on the opened process:

```
z "a:1"
```

We have seen that this is equivalent to

```
z "eval(:;`aa;1)"
```

```
1
```

If we use `reval` instead, the command will fail:

```
z "reval(:;`aa;1)"
```

```
'noupdate: `. `aa
  [0]  z "reval(:;`aa;1)"
       ^
```

The same error is obtained when we use an IDE such as `qPad`, since it will connect to the given `q` instance. Running the same in qPad:

```
reval (:;`a;1)
```

```
ERROR: 'noupdate: `. `a
```

A commonly engineered implementation of the above concept is the usage of `reval` in connection with internal message handler `.z.pg`, which handles incoming client messages in a q process acting as a server. We can implement our version of this unary function – which is automatically called for synchronous client requests – and our implementation can always evaluate the incoming client messages using `reval`, ensuring that no client can modify server-side global variables.

10.2 FUNCTIONAL QUERIES

qSQL – i.e. the `select`, `update`, `delete` functions – enable us to easily aggregate table data and calculate overview statistics for stratified subsamples, with a query language. As mentioned, we want to generalise these functions to access dynamic arguments, such as column names, expressed as input variables. The *functional* version of these queries enables us with a programmatic approach to qSQL.

We build upon the example we showed at the start of this chapter. Assume the simple table

```
tab:([] a: til 10; b: desc til 10; c: 10#1);
tab
```

```
a b c
-----
0 9 1
1 8 1
2 7 1
3 6 1
4 5 1
5 4 1
6 3 1
7 2 1
8 1 1
9 0 1
```

Our task using qSQL query is to choose a variable, say `a`, from the table:

```
select a from tab
```

```
a
-
0
1
2
3
4
5
6
7
8
9
```

As illustrated, the problem with the query is that we cannot specify the variable to be chosen from the table as an argument using the `select` function. We, therefore, want a function of the form:

```
.quantQ.sql.select[tab;`a]
```

Similarly, `update`, `delete`, or `exec` fail in such instances. Let us discuss how we can resolve this using functional queries.

The way forward is to use `parse` function and parse trees corresponding to the qSQL queries. Let us get the parse tree for the select query we have used above:

```
parse "select a from tab"
```

```
?
`tab
()
0b
(,`a)!,`a
```

The output from the console is not very appealing. Most of the IDEs will present the result in a more appealing form:

```
(?;`tab;();0b;(enlist `a)!enlist `a)
```

The obtained parse tree can be evaluated back using `eval` function:

```
eval (?;`tab;();0b;(enlist `a)!enlist `a)
```

```
a
-
0
1
2
3
4
5
6
7
8
9
```

Function ? takes four arguments: First, the table we want to perform an operation on, followed by the where condition (in our example it is empty `()`, then the group variables as a dictionary with keys the new names and values the existing names (or false if no group-by), and finally a dictionary with selected columns (keys are new names and values are the existing column names). The table is passed by reference, i.e. `` `tab``, or value. Table columns are passed by reference.

We can use the parse tree version of the `select` to construct a function, which accepts as inputs the name of the table in the form of a string, and a list of columns to choose from the table:

```
.quantQ.sql.selectPT:{[t;vars]
    // t -- table name as a symbol or name
    // vars -- symbol vector of column names
    // functional select
    :eval (?;t;();0b;{x!x}vars);
 };
```

The second argument of the function is a list, and it is required from the user to ensure that. We encourage the readers to test their `q` skills and improve the function such that it can also expect an atom – e.g. `` `a `` – as an input.

Let us test the function as:

```
(select a,b from tab) ~ .quantQ.sql.selectPT[`tab;`a`b]
```

```
1b
```

The function returns the same output as the `qSQL` query.

Before we proceed further, we illustrate the parse tree version of a slightly more involved `qSQL` query:

```
select d:sum a by 2 xbar b from tab where b>3
```

```
b| d
-| -
4| 9
6| 5
8| 1
```

The function employs `by`, `xbar`, and `where`. The parse tree version of the query reads:

```
parse "select d:sum a by 2 xbar b from tab where b>3"
```

```
(?;`tab;enlist enlist (>;`b;3j);(enlist `b)!enlist (k){x*y div x:$[16h=abs[
    ↪ @x];"j"$x;x]};2j;`b);(enlist `d)!enlist (sum;`a))
```

We repeat the previous procedure and `eval` the query:

```
eval (?;`tab;enlist enlist (>;`b;3j);(enlist `b)!enlist ( k) {x*y div x:
    ↪ $[16h=abs[@x];"j"$x;x]};2j;`b);(enlist `d)!enlist (sum;`a))
```

The call will return error, which indicates unmatched number of `(` and `)`. We can verify it by inspecting the query. The reason for the error is due to `k)` meaning `k` expression within the code. The k expression comes from xbar within the original call. The parse function in this case returns the most "pure" version of the function:

```
parse "xbar"
```

```
k){x*y div x:$[16h=abs[@x];"j"$x;x]}
```

This confirms our claim why the k function is in the parse tree. We can overcome this problem by replacing the statement with k) by the xbar function. In the parse version of the qSQL call, we can keep some functions unparsed. In this case, we can keep the xbar explicitly and make the query running:

```
eval (?;`tab;enlist enlist (>;`b;3j);(enlist `b)!enlist ( xbar;2j;`b);(
    ↪ enlist `d)!enlist (sum;`a))
```

```
b| d
-| -
4| 9
6| 5
8| 1
```

The functional call works properly now.

The provided functionality gives us much flexibility; however, it is not very user-friendly. Luckily, the functional queries do not have to be run with the full eval machinery. The parsed version of the qSQL calls suggests that select can be replaced by the function ? with four arguments. In the following sections, we define this properly.

10.2.1 Functional Select

First, let us focus on the functional select. Our objective is as outlined in the previous paragraphs, we want to be able to run select flexibly with arguments being chosen as in the function. The functional analogue to select function is thus defined as:

```
?[table;where;group;columns]
```

where the four arguments are:

- table is referring to the table from which we want to select the data. The table is passed by reference or by value.
- where contains the filter criteria on which rows to choose from the table. Its form is a list of criteria in parse tree form. The table columns are passed by reference.
- group dictionary of the column names upon which the table is grouped by. The keys are the new column names while values are formed of the old names. The names are passed by reference.
- columns dictionary of columns to be chosen. The keys define the new names, e.g. a:, while values correspond to the statements on the right-hand side of the assign operator, e.g. :b+1. If an empty list is chosen, all columns are chosen.

When the functional query is called from within a function, it perceives `` `tab `` as a global variable. In such a case, we have to refer to the local variable within the function, and thus we pass the table name by value. We can illustrate it as follows: Let us call the functional select from within a dummy function, where we first pass the table by reference and then by value. Before we call the functional select, though, we define the local table with the same name as a global variable, `tab`.

The call where the table is passed by reference returns the globally defined table:

```
{[]
    tab: ([] aa:til 5);
    :?[`tab;();0b;()]
} ()
```

```
a b c
-----
0 9 1
1 8 1
2 7 1
3 6 1
4 5 1
5 4 1
6 3 1
7 2 1
8 1 1
9 0 1
```

On the other hand, when we pass the argument by value, we refer to the locally defined table:

```
{[]
    tab: ([] d:til 5);
    :?[tab;();0b;()]
} ()
```

```
d
-
0
1
2
3
4
```

We can confirm the difference by using the standard `select`:

```
{[]
    tab: ([] d:til 5);
    :select from tab
} ()
```

```
d
-
0
1
2
3
4
```

Let us illustrate several examples of how the functional select can be used as this is a powerful concept. If we want to turn the qSQL select query into its functional counterpart, we recommend to proceed as follows:

- Decompose the original query into the atomic parts. We can do that by building the query step by step.
- Apply parse function on the atomised elements. The parse tree of the simplified queries shows how the components of the full query are converted.
- There is no need to parse every function into the pure functional form. We can keep functions like xbar in its form instead of turning it into the k version. This makes the query more cogent and understandable.
- Since column names are passed by reference as symbols, we need to be able to make a distinction between referring to a column name or a symbol constant: we do this by using enlist on the symbol constants, as we will see in the example below.

The following examples illustrate functional queries. All the queries below return 1b. We encourage readers to run them on their own and see what the output is.

```
?[`tab;();0b;()] ~ select from tab
```

```
?[`tab;enlist (>;`a;`b);0b;()] ~ select from tab where a>b
```

```
?[`tab;((<;`b;8);(>;`a;`b));0b;()] ~ select from tab where a>b, b<8
```

```
?[`tab;((<;`b;(+;`a;`c));(>;`a;`b));0b;()] ~ select from tab where a>b, b<a
    ↪ +c
```

```
?[`tab;((within;`b;(1;6));(>;`a;`b));0b;()] ~ select from tab where a>b, b
    ↪ within (1;6)
```

```
?[`tab;();0b;(enlist `a)!(enlist `a)] ~ select a from tab
```

```
?[`tab;();0b;(enlist `newA)!(enlist `a)] ~ select newA:a from tab
```

```
?[`tab;();0b;(enlist `$"newA")!(enlist `a)] ~ select newA:a from tab
```

```
?[`tab;();0b;(`newA`b)!(`a;`b)] ~ select newA:a, b from tab
```

```
?[`tab;();0b;(enlist `newA)!(enlist (+;`a;`b))] ~ select newA:a+b from tab
```

```
?[`tab;();0b;(enlist `newA)!(enlist (cos;`a))] ~ select newA:cos a from tab
```

```
tab: update d:count[i]?`A`B`C from tab;
?[`tab;enlist (in;`d;enlist `A`B);0b;()] ~ select from tab where d in `A`B
```

This query cannot return one as it contains random number generator:

```
?[`tab;();0b;(enlist `newA)!(enlist (?;count[tab];1.0))] ~ select newA:
    ↪ count[tab]?1.0 from tab
```

However, two queries are functionally the same. Let us stress the difference when we run:

```
?[`tab;();0b;(enlist `newA)!(enlist (?;count[`tab];1.0))]
```

```
newA
---------
0.8056686
```

Further, let us focus on grouping within the table:

```
?[`tab;();0b;(enlist `a)!(enlist (sum;`a))] ~ select sum a from tab
```

```
?[`tab;();(enlist `b)!enlist `b;(enlist `a)!(enlist (sum;`a))] ~ select sum
    ↪  a by b from tab
```

```
?[`tab;();(enlist `b)!enlist (_:;(%;`b;3j));(enlist `a)!(enlist (sum;`a))]
    ↪ ~ select sum a by floor[b%3] from tab
```

```
?[`tab;();(enlist `newB)!enlist (_:;(%;`b;3j));(enlist `a)!(enlist (sum;`a)
    ↪ )] ~ select sum a by newB:floor[b%3] from tab
```

```
?[`tab;();(`newB`newD)!((_:;(%;`b;3j));(ceiling;(%;`b;3j)));(enlist `a)!(
    ↪ enlist (sum;`a))] ~ select sum a by newB:floor[b%3],newD:ceiling[b
    ↪ %3] from tab
```

This concludes our discourse into the functional select. Once we decompose a table into the atomic parts, construction of the functional counterpart is rather straightforward. In our experience, the biggest obstacle when constructing the functional query is not clear in the atomic elements of the query and how the perceived goal should be achieved.

In the next parts, we focus on the other qSQL calls.

10.2.2 Functional Exec

A similar function to qSQL select is the exec function. select will always return a table, but exec will return a dictionary, or a vector, if only 1 column is selected. The functional counterpart is the same as select:

```
?[table;where;group;columns]
```

where the four arguments are slightly different:

- table is referring to the table from which we want to select the data. The table is passed by reference or by value.
- where contains the filter criteria on which rows to choose from the table. Its form is a list of criteria in parse tree form. The table columns are passed by reference.
- group list of the column names upon which the table is grouped by, passed by reference.
- columns dictionary of column names to be chosen, or a single atom.

group has to be a list. When no group-by is needed, it takes value of empty list () as opposed to false 0b for the functional select. When we want to exec only one column from the table, columns is a symbol atom rather than a dictionary with a single element.

```
?[`tab;();();`a] ~ exec a from tab
```

Let us show how we cannot mix the select form, namely the group-by cannot be empty element when the selected column is not a dictionary.

```
?[`tab;();0b;`a]
```

```
`type error
```

Further, we cannot set the group-by input to be () when the selected columns are dictionary:

```
?[`tab;();();(enlist `a)!(enlist `a)]
```

```
a| 0 1 2 3 4 5 6 7 8 9
```

which does not have the form of

```
exec a from tab
```

```
0 1 2 3 4 5 6 7 8 9j
```

Let us continue with valid queries:

```
?[`tab;();();(`a`b)!(`a`b)] ~ exec a,b from tab
```

```
?[`tab;();0b;(`a`b)!(`a`b)] ~ select a,b from tab
```

```
?[`tab;();`b;(`a`b)!(`a`b)] ~ exec a,b by b from tab
```

```
?[`tab;();(floor;(%;`b;2.0));(`a`b)!(`a`b)] ~ exec a,b by floor[b%2] from
    ↪ tab
```

Testing the functionality of the `where` clause in the above examples is left as an exercise for the reader.

10.2.3 Functional Update

Another important `qSQL` functionality is the `update` function. The functional counterpart is given as:

```
![table;where;group;columns]
```

where the four arguments are:

- `table` is referring to the table from which we want to make an update. The table is passed by reference or value.
- `where` contains the filter criteria on which rows to choose from the table. Its form is a list of criteria in parse tree form. The table columns are passed by reference.
- `group` dictionary of the column names upon which the table is grouped by. The keys are the new column names while values are formed of the old names. The names are passed by reference.
- `columns` dictionary of columns to be updated. The keys define the new names, e.g. `a:`, while values correspond to the statements on the right-hand side of the assign operator, e.g. `:b+1`.

The input parameters are similar to the functional `select`. Let us provide a number of examples to illustrate how the functional update works:

```
![tab;();0b;()] ~ update from tab
```

This call actually gives error on both sides of ~ as this is not a valid `update`.

Further queries are valid:

```
![tab;();0b;(enlist `a)!(enlist `a)] ~ update a from tab  // update column
    ↪ a with itself
```

```
![tab;();0b;(enlist `newA)!(enlist `a)] ~ update newA:a from tab
```

```
![tab;();0b;(`newA`b)!(`a;`b)] ~ update newA:a, b from tab
```

```
![tab;();0b;(enlist `newA)!(enlist (+;`a;`b))] ~ update newA:a+b from tab
```

```
![tab;();0b;(enlist `a)!(enlist (sum;`a))] ~ update sum a from tab
```

```
![tab;();(enlist `b)!enlist (floor;(%;`b;3j));(enlist `a)!(enlist (sum;`a))
    ↪ ] ~ update sum a by floor[b%3] from tab
```

```
![tab;();(`newB`newD)!((floor;(%;`b;3j));(ceiling;(%;`b;3j)));(enlist `a)!(
    ↪ enlist (sum;`a))] ~ update sum a by newB:floor[b%3],newD:ceiling[b
    ↪ %3] from tab
```

```
![tab;((within;`b;(1;6));(>;`a;`b));0b;(enlist `a)!(enlist (sum;`a))] ~
    ↪ update a:sum a from tab where a>b, b within (1;6)
```

The examples cover the majority of cases we can encounter in real problems. It is essential to practise more examples, as in our experience, functional queries belong to the least user-friendly part of q, yet are extremely useful.

10.2.4 Functional Delete

The functional version of delete is:

```
![table;where;0b;columns]
```

where the four arguments are slightly different now:

- table is referring to the table from which we want to update. The table is passed by value.
- where contains the filter criteria on which rows to choose from the table. Its form is a list of criteria in parse tree form. The table columns are passed by reference.
- group is false 0b.
- columns list of columns to be chosen.

The function symbol ! is same as in functional update. In order to achieve the delete functionality, either where or columns has to be empty. Let us illustrate the functionality straight ahead:

```
![tab;enlist (>;`a;4);0b;`symbol$()] ~ delete from tab where a>4
```

```
![tab;();0b;`a`c] ~ delete a,c from tab
```

This concludes the functional form of qSQL operations. Throughout the text, we use such operations. We tend to stick to qSQL syntax as it is more accessible. We encourage readers to replace such operations by their functional counterpart when a generalisation is required.

CHAPTER 11

A Few Use Cases

We conclude the Data Operations part of the book by illustrating some common time series operations in kdb+/q and a demo of a real-time CEP engine.

11.1 ROLLING VWAP

The first example originates in high-frequency finance. Any update in the market will result in an update (*tick*) in our data. It is of fundamental importance for any market participant to understand the current state of the market. For this purpose, various statistics and indicators are needed to monitor market activity. Let us assume that we wish to calculate a moving VWAP (Volume Weighted Average Price) over a rolling window. We will cover two use cases.

11.1.1 N Tick VWAP

Here, we can make use of the msum function we saw in Chapter 3 to calculate the moving VWAP for, say, 2 consecutive ticks. Using our standard trades table trd from our hdb mydb:

```
trades: select from trd where date=2016.04.07;
trades
```

```
date       code  time         price  volume mktflag comments
-----------------------------------------------------------------------
2016.04.07 CLM16 10:20:00.329 38.3   4      E       "NYMEX/CME Group trade"
2016.04.07 CLM16 13:00:00.128 38.04  3      E       "NYMEX/CME Group trade"
2016.04.07 GCM16 12:00:00.055 1239.7 6      E       ""
2016.04.07 GCM16 12:37:02.106 1240.5 1      E       ""
2016.04.07 GCM16 14:35:01.241 1241.2 1      E       ""
2016.04.07 NEW   06:07:56.054 1      1      E       ""
2016.04.07 NEW   06:31:02.386 1      1      E       ""
2016.04.07 VXK16 13:22:05.617 18.85  5      E       ""
```

and the definition of a N-tick VWAP at tick i

$$VWAP_i = \frac{\sum_{j=i-N}^{i} volume \times price}{\sum_{j=i-N}^{i} volume}. \tag{11.1}$$

The 2-tick vwap for each symbol is

```
update vwap2tick: ( 2 msum  price * volume ) % 2 msum volume by code from
    ↪ trades
```

trades

```
date       code  time         price  volume mktflag comments                 vwap2tick
------------------------------------------------------------------------------------------
2016.04.07 CLM16 10:20:00.329 38.3   4      E       "NYMEX/CME Group trade" 38.3
2016.04.07 CLM16 13:00:00.128 38.04  3      E       "NYMEX/CME Group trade" 38.18857
2016.04.07 GCM16 12:00:00.055 1239.7 6      E       ""                      1239.7
2016.04.07 GCM16 12:37:02.106 1240.5 1      E       ""                      1239.814
2016.04.07 GCM16 14:35:01.241 1241.2 1      E       ""                      1240.85
2016.04.07 NEW   06:07:56.054 1      1      E       ""                      1
2016.04.07 NEW   06:31:02.386 1      1      E       ""                      1
2016.04.07 VXK16 13:22:05.617 18.85  5      E       ""                      18.85
```

11.1.2 Time Window VWAP

For a moving time-window VWAP, we need to aggregate over a sliding time window of, say, 1 hour. To do this, we use the window join function, and specifically, its `wj1` variation – this is a similar use-case to the TWAP example we saw in Chapter 7.

We use `wj1` instead of `wj` because we want the values within the 1-hour window prior to each record, but without including the as-of value, 1-hour prior to that record's time:

```
vwap: wj1 [ -01:00 0t +\: exec time from trades;
          `code`time; select code, time, price, volume from trades;
          ( select code, time, val: price * volume ,vol: volume from trades
              ↪ ;
          ( sum; `val); ( sum; `vol) ) ];
```

We examine the result of the window join:

```
vwap
```

```
code  time         price  volume val     vol
--------------------------------------------
CLM16 10:20:00.329 38.3   4      153.2   4
CLM16 13:00:00.128 38.04  3      114.12  3
GCM16 12:00:00.055 1239.7 6      7438.2  6
GCM16 12:37:02.106 1240.5 1      8678.7  7
GCM16 14:35:01.241 1241.2 1      1241.2  1
NEW   06:07:56.054 1      1      1       1
NEW   06:31:02.386 1      1      2       2
VXK16 13:22:05.617 18.85  5      94.25   5
```

VWAP can now be calculated as the ratio of the `val` and `vol` columns:

```
update vwap1h: val % vol from vwap
```

```
code  time         price  volume val    vol vwap1h
--------------------------------------------------
CLM16 10:20:00.329 38.3   4      153.2  4   38.3
CLM16 13:00:00.128 38.04  3      114.12 3   38.04
GCM16 12:00:00.055 1239.7 6      7438.2 6   1239.7
GCM16 12:37:02.106 1240.5 1      8678.7 7   1239.814
GCM16 14:35:01.241 1241.2 1      1241.2 1   1241.2
NEW   06:07:56.054 1      1      1      1   1
NEW   06:31:02.386 1      1      2      2   1
VXK16 13:22:05.617 18.85  5      94.25  5   18.85
```

11.2 WEIGHTED MID FOR N LEVELS OF AN ORDER BOOK

Let us recall that in a market, the interest in buying an asset or a realised trade of a certain amount of the underlying asset is expressed as a *quote* or a *trade* respectively. Our previous example saw how to calculate an N-tick moving VWAP on a series of trades. In contrast, the quote data usually represents the state of a limit order book, or LOB: the limit order book stores the market interest in buying or selling and this is expressed as a list of prices and corresponding amounts the market participants are willing to buy (bid) or sell at (ask).

When analysing the LOB, a standard extension to the top-of-book mid, i.e. the point which is equidistant between the best bid (higher price the participants are willing to buy at) and best ask (lowest price the participants are willing to sell at) of a LOB, is the weighted mid, or WMID. This mid can take into account the size which is placed on each side of the book and is, therefore, a weighted average. In our use case below, we generalise this concept to include two levels of depth, i.e. the best and second-best prices, respectively. In other words, we calculate the volume-weighted mid where we take into account the top 2 best levels of the LOB.

We define the weighted mid at each point in time `i`, as:

$$WMID_i = \frac{\sum_{j=1}^{N} bidSize_{i,j} \times bid_{i,j} + \sum_{j=1}^{N} askSize_{i,j} \times ask_{i,j}}{\sum_{j=1}^{N} bidSize_{i,j} + \sum_{j=1}^{N} askSize_{i,j}}, \tag{11.2}$$

where `N` are the levels of depth, in our case `N=2`. Let's create a quotes table with 2 levels of depth:

```
n: 10;
quote: ([] sym: n?`A`B; time: asc n?0t; bid1: n?10f; bidSize1: n?100 );
update bid2: 0 | bid1 - .1 * n ? 10, bidSize2: n?100, ask1: bid1 + .2 * n ?
    ↪ 10, askSize1: n?100
from `quote;
update ask2: ask1 + .1 * n ? 10, askSize2: n?100 from `quote;
quote
```

```
sym time         bid1     bidSize1 bid2     bidSize2 ask1     askSize1 ask2     askSize2
-----------------------------------------------------------------------------------------
B   02:36:22.237 2.329662 13       1.629662 91       2.329662 3        2.529662 71
B   02:55:16.871 2.50046  77       2.20046  83       3.50046  99       3.90046  12
A   05:01:01.940 0.737272 64       0.637272 76       0.937272 56       1.037272 2
A   05:10:14.172 3.186642 9        2.786642 88       3.586642 12       3.886642 47
A   08:19:58.169 1.872634 37       1.872634 4        2.272634 62       2.772634 4
A   09:12:36.839 8.416288 79       7.816288 56       8.416288 18       9.116288 85
B   10:59:00.065 7.250709 97       6.850709 32       7.850709 37       7.950709 21
A   18:09:32.544 4.81804  63       4.21804  30       6.41804  17       6.91804  47
B   20:40:09.995 9.351307 74       8.651307 97       9.551307 79       10.05131 25
B   20:57:52.099 7.093398 30       6.493398 31       8.293398 75       8.493398 18
```

We can now simply use the wavg function to implement the above WMID formula:

```
select sym,time, wmid: ( bidSize1; bidSize2; askSize1; askSize2 ) wavg (
    ↪ bid1; bid2; ask1; ask2)
from quote
```

```
sym time         wmid
--------------------------
B   02:36:22.237 2.051572
B   02:55:16.871 2.835884
A   05:01:01.940 0.7584841
A   05:10:14.172 3.202668
A   08:19:58.169 2.138055
A   09:12:36.839 8.525112
B   10:59:00.065 7.379586
A   18:09:32.544 5.505301
B   20:40:09.995 9.225489
B   20:57:52.099 7.720671
```

We note the beautiful feature of wavg, which allows us to work *in-depth* using a vectorised approach across multiple (in this case 2) dimensions!

Note that – in this case – our approach is much faster than using an iterative approach, i.e. each-both, on each record. To demonstrate this, we time the two approaches after first expanding our table to a more "realistic" number of 10 million records:

```
q:10000000#quote;    // ``take'' 10m records from quote table (this will
    ↪ repeatedly expand the table)
```

```
count q
```

```
10000000
```

We time our first approach:

```
\t res1: select sym,time, wmid: ( bidSize1; bidSize2; askSize1; askSize2 )
    ↪ wavg (bid1; bid2; ask1; ask2)
        from q
```

```
838
```

We now time an approach applying wavg on each domain of weights and prices (i.e. each table record). Note how we also need to transpose the lists of weights and prices to ensure that the operation can actually run record by record:

```
\t res2: select sym,time, wmid: flip[( bidSize1; bidSize2; askSize1;
    ↪ askSize2 )]
  wavg 'flip (bid1; bid2; ask1; ask2) from q
```

```
5436
```

```
res1~res2
```

```
1b
```

The results match. However, our recommended approach took around 800 milliseconds on a table with 10 million records and was more than 6 times faster than applying the function record by record. The ability of wavg to work in-depth across a 2-dimensional list is very welcome and reminds us that we should always use the simplest and natively supported approaches when available, instead of building our own.

11.3 CONSECUTIVE RUNS OF A RULE

Assume we have a time series – typically a series of observed metrics such as a price – and we want to calculate the time series points which obey a given rule for a number of consecutive occurrences in a row.

For example, in the following list of randomnly generated prices:

```
prices: 10?5;
```

```
4 4 1 4 4 0 2 2 0 4
```

We want to know if the time series is outside 50 percent of its five-point moving standard deviation, for two ticks in a row.

We first calculate the indices which are outside half of the moving standard deviation:

```
indices: { not x within (a-d;(a:5 mavg x)+d:.5*5 mdev x) } prices;
```

```
0011010011b
```

How would we now calculate the sequential occurrence of this rule? In other words, how do we find the indices where this rule holds for N times in a row?

The solution to this appears to require some recursion and thus brings adverbs into our mind. We recall a very useful optimisation of scan which we saw in Chapter 3 when presenting the exponential moving average, which was the fact that

```
{x y\z}
```

is an optimised shortcut to

```
{{z+y*x}\[x;y;z]}
```

We can therefore implement a trivial case of this on the indices vector itself, where x is our starting point (0 runs), y is the output of the last (recursive) call and z is the (recursive) element of the indices vector, *indices*$[i]$:

```
.quant.stats.runs:{0 x\x}"f"$;
```

which gives us the desired count of "truths" (1b's) for the time series:

```
.quant.stats.runs indices
```

```
0 0 1 2 0 1 0 0 1 2f
```

It is now simple to find the locations where that rule holds:

```
where 2=.quant.stats.runs indices
```

```
3 9
```

11.4 REAL-TIME SIGNALS AND ALERTS

In the previous section, we saw how one would perform standard tasks such as moving calculations and scanning data for consecutive runs of a given rule. This is useful for analysis of past data and to initially conclude which type of functions – or signals – we are interested in analysing and calibrating their parameters. Once we have done that, we would like to explore both signal creation in a real-time fashion, as well as a simulated scenario where we stream the data – just like it would be streamed in real-life – and then we run the calculations as the events happen. This enables us to create a real-time signal based on the result of our calculation. As mentioned, this signal could be either triggered in real-time or, for backtesting purposes, in a simulated run where our software is run just like it would be in a real-time scenario.

To perform such moving window calculations in real-time and create an actionable outcome – a signal or alert – we need a way to efficiently run such rules on the incoming updates, as soon as they arrive.

One way to perform this is to have an in-memory cache which effectively is a table upon which new incoming updates are joined and trigger our favourite computation in one go.

A way to store the in-memory cache is by having the time series of trade prices, their times and volumes, stored in a *nested* structure, keyed by sym.

Using our standard `trd` trade data, and pretending that this is now the result of all of today's *past* updates, stored in a cache, we can represent our cache as:

```
trades: select time,volume,price by sym from trd
```

```
sym  | time                                          volume price
-----| --------------------------------------------------------------
CLM16| 10:20:00.329 12:00:00.227 11:00:00.105 4 3 2  38.3   40.61 41.43
E    | 12:37:02.106 06:07:56.069 06:07:56.085 1 1 1  1240.5 1     1
GCM16| 13:00:00.128 15:20:02.000 16:00:00.044 3 3 1  38.04  40.78 1257.9
NEW  | 14:35:01.241 06:31:02.386 06:31:02.386 1 1 1  1241.2 1     1
VXK16| 12:00:00.055 10:13:01.048 16:28:34.311 6 3 1  1239.7 1240  1258.7
```

Assume we now want to run our *N*-tick VWAP calculation in real-time. Further, suppose that we have registered a *callback function*, which is a q function that gets called by our upstream data feed every time there is a new update from the market. The input of this function is a table with the newly arrived trades:

```
newdata: ([]sym:`VXK16`CLM16`GCM16;time:16:30:00 16:30:01 16:30:02t;volume
    ↪ :5 4 3h;price:1260 42.5 1270);
```

```
sym   time         volume price
-------------------------------
VXK16 16:30:00.000 5      1260
CLM16 16:30:01.000 4      42.5
GCM16 16:30:02.000 3      1270
```

We shall call this function `.quantQ.upd.trades`, where upd stands for update. Placing our function under this namespace enables us to create other such functions in the future for different types of updates.

```
.quantQ.upd.trades:{[new]
   // new -- the incoming data sent by the upstream feedhandler or
       ↪ tickerplant, in table type format
   // aggregate the new data by time,volume and price
   // then insert each list to each column for each key (record) of the
       ↪ global trades cache
   trades:: trades,'select time,volume,price by sym from new;
   // run a 3-tick moving vwap using each-both on every record
   :select sym, (-3#'volume) wavg'(-3#'price) from trades;
};
```

We run our function and observe the result:

```
.quantQ.upd.trades newdata
```

```
sym   price
--------------
CLM16 41.63222
E     414.1667
GCM16 741.4629
NEW   414.4
VXK16 1253.189
```

Checking our global cache, we see that the desired side effect of having appended the new trades is also there:

```
sym  | time                                                                volume   price
-----| ---------------------------------------------------------------------------------
CLM16| 10:20:00.329 12:00:00.227 11:00:00.105 16:30:01.000 4 3 2 4h 38.3 40.61 41.43 42.5
E    | 12:37:02.106 06:07:56.069 06:07:56.085              1 1 1h   1240.5 1 1
GCM16| 13:00:00.128 15:20:02.000 16:00:00.044 16:30:02.000 3 3 1 3h 38.04 40.78 1257.9 1270
NEW  | 14:35:01.241 06:31:02.386 06:31:02.386              1 1 1h   1241.2 1 1
VXK16| 12:00:00.055 10:13:01.048 16:28:34.311 16:30:00.000 6 3 1 5h 1239.7 1240 1258.7 1260
```

Notice the use of the global assignment `::` inside our function, since we wanted to update the global table `trades`. Besides, we may want to *clean up* our global cache to not contain past updates which are not relevant for our computation anymore. This is important since this cache can rapidly grow in size and cause significant memory usage throughout the day.

This can be achieved by updating the trades table to only keeping the last N ticks for each of the nested vectors in our cache:

```
.quantQ.upd.trades:{[new]
   // new -- the incoming data sent by the upstream feedhandler or
       ↪ tickerplant, in table type format
   // aggregate the new data by time,volume and price
   // then insert each list to each column for each key (record) of the
       ↪ global trades cache
   trades:: trades,''select time,volume,price by sym from new;
   // run a 3-tick moving vwap
   ret: select sym, (-3#'volume) wavg'(-3#'price) from trades;
   trades:: update -3#'time,-3#'volume,-3#'price from trades;
   :ret;
};
```

The advantage of storing incoming data in a single nested cache is that we can then run a series of rules, each looking at a variable window of recent data. Our cache can retain the history of observations only up to the maximum window size required by our rules.

PART Three

Data Science

CHAPTER 12

Basic Overview of Statistics

This chapter presents several tools which are useful when we need to go through the data at hand and get an initial understanding of the data content. The tools can be used individually or as an entire suite. It is an excellent habit to analyse the data before constructing a machine learning model. The tools presented in this chapter are a combination of statistics, tests and visualisation hints.

12.1 HISTOGRAM

A histogram is a representation of the data distribution, a visualisation tool for the data points in our sample. Theoretically, it represents an estimate of the probability distribution function for a continuous variable. It is, in fact, an empirical distribution function. In this chapter, we treat histograms as a visual tool which allows us to see and investigate the structure of our data.

A histogram function can have two inputs, the data and the bins (or buckets); it returns the number of data points per bin. The bins represent a scheme which will split the range interval of the data into a list of non-overlapping sub-intervals. Although the bins are not necessarily equal, in this section we will only consider equidistant intervals.

It is convenient to normalise the histogram so it can represent a probability distribution function, where every plot captures relative frequency. In such a case, the histogram is a kernel density estimator. Using some form of polynomials or splines, the kernel can be further enhanced to obtain smoothed histograms. In our example, we will use qPad, with the option "Bars", to obtain a visual representation of the histograms.

In our implementation, we use the `binr` verb, namely `x binr y`. The verb performs a binary search of `y` in list `x` and returns the index of the minimum element of `x`, which is `>=y`. The map between the data and the bins is thus mathematically expressed as $n : x \in (x_{n-1}, x_n]$. The function is implemented as follows:

```
.quantQ.stats.getHistogram:{[data;rule]
   // data -- array of data
   // rule -- function which takes data and returns bins
   // calculate bins
   bins: rule data;
```

```
    // return histogram table
    :update 0^histogram from
        ([bins:asc til count[bins]] x:bins) uj
        (select histogram: count bins by bins from ([] bins:bins binr data));
};
```

`getHistogram` wraps the `binr` verb. It accepts a vector of numbers and a function which creates the bins. There are a number of options on how to create the bins, and we list a few below. We implement each option as a function which takes one or more arguments. The last argument is the data while all but last arguments are optional parameters whose meaning depends on the binning scheme. When we call `getHistogram`, we specify all arguments except for the last and thus pass in the projected binning scheme.

A few implementations of bucketing schemes are:

Grid

We specify the grid for binning explicitly. In such a case, the optional parameter is the grid for binning itself. The data will not be taking any role:

```
.quantQ.stats.histGrid:{[bins;data]
    // bins -- explicit bins to use
    // data -- array of data (not used)
    // return bins
    :bins;
};
```

Width

We specify the width of the binning explicitly. The bins are then derived from the range of the data. The argument of the function is the width h:

```
.quantQ.stats.histWidth:{[h;data]
    // h -- width of bin
    // data -- array of data
    // return bins
    :min[data]+h*til 1+ceiling[(max[data]-min[data])%h];
};
```

Bins

We specify the number of equidistant bins n we want to plot. Since the function `binr` is considering semi-closed intervals, closed on the right, the number of bins created will be in fact $n + 1$, with elements being equal to *min* of the data falling into first bin:

```
.quantQ.stats.histBin:{[n;data]
    // n -- number of bins
    // data -- array of data
    // return bins
    :min[data]+((max[data]-min[data])%n)*til 1+n;
};
```

Square root

The number of bins is derived from the size of the sample using the square-root rule:

$$n = \lceil \sqrt{N} \rceil, \tag{12.1}$$

where $\lceil x \rceil$ denotes the smallest integer larger than x, and is implemented as:

```
.quantQ.stats.histSquareRoot:{[data]
   // data -- array of data
   // number of bins
   n:ceiling sqrt count data;
   // return bins
   :min[data]+((max[data]-min[data])%n)*til 1+n;
};
```

Sturge's formula

The number of bins is derived from the binomial distribution and provides reasonable histograms for large sizes and approximately normally distributed. The formula for number of bins reads:

$$n = 1 + \lceil \log_2 N \rceil, \tag{12.2}$$

implemented as:

```
.quantQ.stats.histSturge:{[data]
   // data -- array of data
   // number of bins
   n:1+ceiling xlog[2;count data];
   // return bins
   :min[data]+((max[data]-min[data])%n)*til 1+n;
};
```

Rice's rule

Similar outcome to Sturge's formula can be achieved by Rice's formula, where number of bins is given as:

$$n = \lceil N^{1/3} \rceil. \tag{12.3}$$

Function then reads:

```
.quantQ.stats.histRice:{[data]
   // data -- array of data
   // number of bins
   n:ceiling 2*xexp[count data;1.0%3.0];
   // return bins
   :min[data]+((max[data]-min[data])%n)*til 1+n;
};
```

Scott's rule

The final formula we implement is Scott's rule for normally distributed data, where the width of bins depends on the estimated sample variance $\hat{\sigma}^2$:

$$h = \frac{3.5\hat{\sigma}}{N^{1/3}}, \tag{12.4}$$

where we further derive the number of bins from its width and range of the data in the same way as for `histWidth` function:

```
.quantQ.stats.histScott:{[data]
   // data -- array of data
   // width of bins
   h:ceiling (3.5*dev data)%xexp[count data;1.0%3.0];
   // return bins
   :min[data]+h*til 1+ceiling[(max[data]-min[data])%h];
};
```

Let us illustrate the histogram on the example. First, we define data set:

```
data:(1000?3.0),(200?1.0),(2.0+300?1.0);
```

Figure 12.1 depicts `data` when transformed to the table using:

```
select i:i, data from ([] data)
```

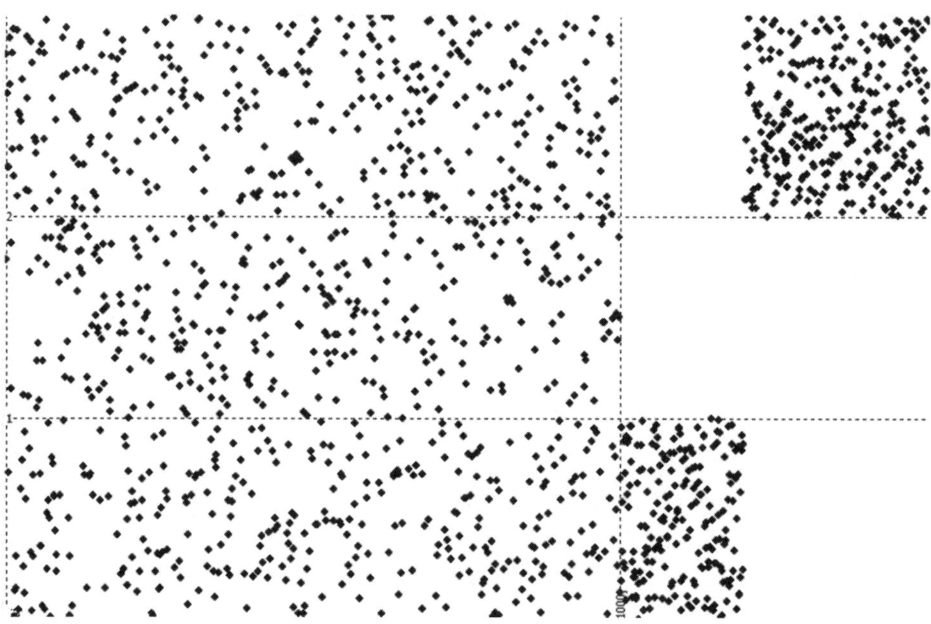

FIGURE 12.1 Visualisation of simulated `data`

We calculate the histograms for every bin scheme separately and store them into the separate tables:

```
histWidth: .quantQ.stats.getHistogram[data;.quantQ.stats.histWidth[0.2]];
histBin: .quantQ.stats.getHistogram[data;.quantQ.stats.histBin[20]];
histGrid:.quantQ.stats.getHistogram[data;.quantQ.stats.histGrid[0.1*til
    ↪ 40]];
histSquareRoot:.quantQ.stats.getHistogram[data;.quantQ.stats.histSquareRoot
    ↪ ];
histSturge:.quantQ.stats.getHistogram[data;.quantQ.stats.histSturge];
histRice:.quantQ.stats.getHistogram[data;.quantQ.stats.histRice];
histScott:.quantQ.stats.getHistogram[data;.quantQ.stats.histScott];
```

Figure 12.2 depicts four histograms using four different schemes for creating bins: Figure 12.2a captures `histWidth`, Figure 12.2b captures `histSquareRoot`, Figure 12.2c captures `histRice`, and Figure 12.2d captures `histScott`. The last method does not seem particularly useful. This is understandable as the underlying assumption behind Scott's rule is the normal distribution of the data. The `data` does not resemble the normal distribution by any mean as it is a union of three uniformly distributed sets. It is thus important to choose the method for bins carefully.

Finally, let us remind the reader that we have chosen the option "Bars" for plots. The default width of bars is rather tiny and thus barely visible. For that purpose, we

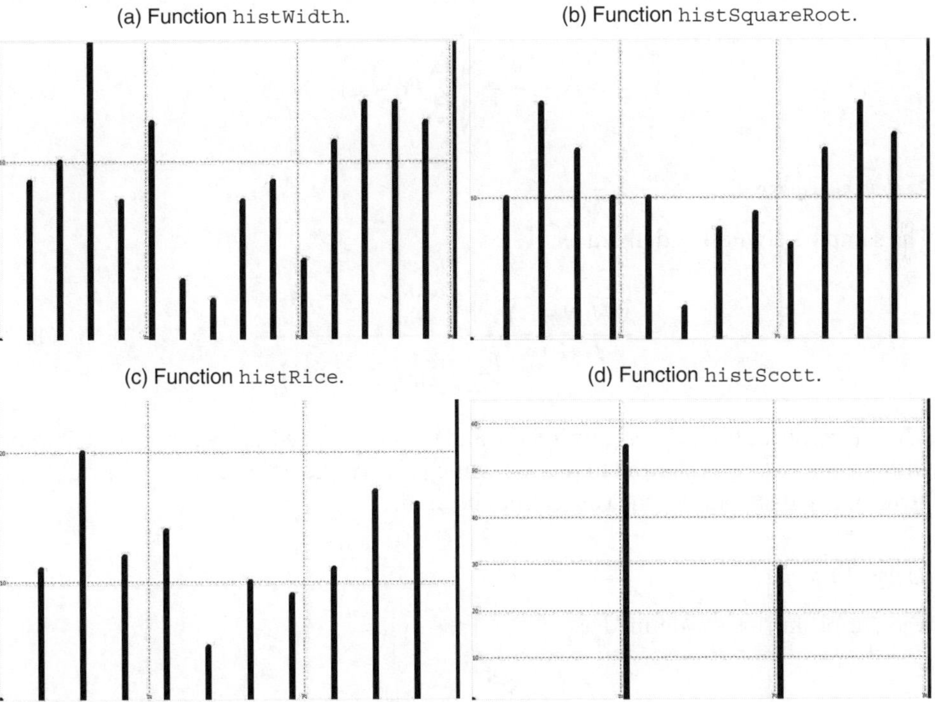

FIGURE 12.2 Examples of histograms using four functions

have changed the field "Line width:" to value 10. It is advised to explore this option when creating plots. Fine tuning of the graphics option may significantly improve the visibility of the chart and thus amplify the message conveyed.

12.2 FIRST MOMENTS

Let us define a useful utility function, which for a given numerical array returns a table with overview statistics. First, we define statistics used in the function itself and then implement it as one compact suite. Data are denoted as $(x_1, x_2, \ldots, x_K)$, where subset of $N \leq K$ observations are non-missing, $x_1, x_2, \ldots, x_N$.

Sample mean

The sample mean is defined as:

$$\mu = \frac{1}{N}\sum_{i=1}^{N} x_i. \tag{12.5}$$

Sample standard deviation

The sample standard deviation is defined as:

$$\sigma = \frac{1}{N-1}\sqrt{\sum_{i=1}^{N}(x_i - \mu)^2}. \tag{12.6}$$

Sample skewness

The sample skewness is defined as:

$$S = \frac{\sqrt{N(N-1)}}{N-1} \frac{\frac{1}{N}\sum_{i=1}^{N}(x_i - \mu)^3}{\left(\frac{1}{N-1}\sum_{i=1}^{N}(x_i - \mu)^2\right)^{3/2}} \tag{12.7}$$

where for distributions that are unimodal and not heavy tailed suggests that distribution with negative skew is skewed to the left while positive skew is skewed to the right. For heavy-tailed distribution, the rule cannot be used.

Sample kurtosis

The sample kurtosis is defined as:

$$K = \frac{\frac{1}{N}\sum_{i=1}^{N}(x_i - \mu)^4}{\left(\frac{1}{N-1}\sum_{i=1}^{N}(x_i - \mu)^2\right)^2} - 3 \tag{12.8}$$

and can be used to assess the heavy tails of the data. If the value is positive, the data are said to be leptokurtic, i.e. heavy-tailed relative to Gaussian distributions, while if value is negative, the data are said to be platykurtic, i.e. thin-tailed relative to Gaussian distribution.

Min

The minimum of the sample is derived from non-empty values.

Max

The maximum of the sample is derived from non-empty values.

Number of observations

The number of observations corresponds to K.

Missing observations

The number of missing observations is $K - N$.

The suite of tools is implemented in function overviewStats:

```
.quantQ.stats.overviewStats:{[data]
   // data -- array of numerical values
   // number of observations
   K: count data;
   // filter out missing data
   data: data where not null data;
   // number of non-missing data
   KminusN:K-count data;
   // sample average
   mu: avg data;
   // sample standard deviation
   sigma: dev data;
   // sample skewness
   tmp: (data-mu);
   N: count data;
   S: (xexp[N*N-1;0.5]%N-2)*((1.0%"f"$N)*sum tmp*tmp*tmp)%xexp[((1.0%"f"$N)
       ↪ *sum tmp*tmp);1.5];
   // sample kurtosis
   Kurt: (((1.0%"f"$N)*sum tmp*tmp*tmp*tmp)%xexp[((1.0%"f"$N)*sum tmp*tmp)
       ↪ ;2])-3.0;
   // sample min
   mn: min data;
   // sample max
   mx: max data;
   :([] statistics: ("Sample mean";"Sample standard deviation";"Sample
       ↪ skewness";"Sample kurtosis";
       "Sample min"; "Sample max";"Number of observations";"Number of
           ↪ missing observations");
       values: (mu; sigma; S;K; mn; mx; Kurt; KminusN));
};
```

We run the example query using the `data` we have defined for histograms:

```
.quantQ.stats.overviewStats[data]
```

which gives the following table:

```
statistics                         values
-------------------------------------------
"Sample mean"                      1.580707
"Sample standard deviation"        0.9362539
"Sample skewness"                  -0.1309539
"Sample kurtosis"                  -1.41629
"Sample min"                       0.0006490825
"Sample max"                       2.997296
"Number of observations"           1500
"Number of missing observations"   0
```

Data are slightly skewed to the left relative to its mean. Further, data are platykurtic, which naturally follows from the fact that the data come from the uniform distribution with no tails.

12.3 HYPOTHESIS TESTING

In this section, we focus on several useful routines, which are likely needed at the initial stage of data exploration. In such a stage, we need to review data quantitatively. Tests like comparing means of two samples, sign test or correlation between observations should be performed. We aim to provide tools which go beyond the usual comparison of two numbers. We aspire to encourage readers to formulate such comparison as tests and provide tools to evaluate such tests.

12.3.1 Normal *p*-values

For many statistics, we obtain a value which is asymptotically distributed as $N(0, 1)$. The question is how to form a statistical test to assess the statistical validity of the underlying test. Many tests result in statistics, which are in turn tested either against being different from zero or having a particular sign.

In this section, we focus on such test statistics. Generically, such statistics are under the null hypothesis distribution and standard normal variable. To assess whether we can reject the null hypothesis, we have to decide how likely it is for a given realised value to come from the standard normal distribution. To achieve this objective, we convert the normally distributed statistics into the p-value of a two-sided test numerically using the lookup table. This will allow us to statistically decide whether the statistics can likely come – with given confidence – from the standard normal distribution, i.e. implying that the null hypothesis cannot be rejected.

In order to calculate the p-value, we need to be able to calculate:

$$p = \Phi(x), \tag{12.9}$$

with Φ being the cumulative distribution function of $N(0, 1)$ distribution. More importantly, we need to calculate the inverse cumulative distribution function, or,

$$x = \Phi^{-1}(p). \tag{12.10}$$

We use a table of values to map the function of p and x as expressed in the previous display. The approach is suitable for assessing the significance of a statistical test as we are often interested in several values only corresponding to normal confidence levels. Typical values of choice found in the literature are 0.1%, 1%, 5% and 10%.

We define a table:

```
.quantQ.stats.normTable:((0.0005;3.290527);(0.005;2.575829);(0.01;2.326348)
   ↪ ;
...
;(0.495;0.01253347);(0.5;0))
```

where we have not listed the full map in the code snippet. Value `(0.0005;3.29052673149190)` denotes that probability to observe $P(z \geq 3.29052673149190) = 1 - 0.0005$, or, equivalently, $P(z \leq -3.29052673149190) = 0.0005$. For a two-sided test, we use $P(|z| \geq 3.29052673149190) = 0.001$. Keep in mind that we have defined the table within the name space of the book as it is a key and static object for the analysis.

We can thus use the table `normTable` to approximate $\Phi^{-1}(p)$. In particular, the algorithm to approximate the cumulative distribution function can proceed for a given non-negative x as follows. Go through the list of `normTable` element by element. Every element is a pair of numbers. Find the maximum second element such that it is smaller than x. Report corresponding first element. The cumulative distribution function is then 1− the value returned by the provided algorithm. For negative values, we can proceed the same way by using $|x|$ and not performing 1− operation at the end.

When applied for finding the confidence level of the given statistics, this approach is conservative, as it gives lower bound on the significance level. This is a good practice when we approximate distributions for assessing the test. In addition, if `normTable` will contain values for 0.1%, 1%, 5% and 10%, only, this will perform the usual econometric evaluation of the test.

Let us implement three functions, which perform the appropriate p-value calculation for two-sided test, one-sided test for a null hypothesis $z \leq 0$ ("left"), and one-sided test for null hypothesis $z \geq 0$ ("right"):

```
.quantQ.stats.pValueTwoSided:{[x]
    // x -- value of test statistics following N(0,1)
    // return corresponding p-value
    :2*(reverse first flip .quantQ.stats.normTable) neg[1]+
        (reverse last flip .quantQ.stats.normTable) binr x;
};
```

We test the two-sided test on values:

```
.quantQ.stats.pValueTwoSided[2.58]
```

```
0.01
```

```
.quantQ.stats.pValueTwoSided[10.0]
```

```
0.001
```

```
.quantQ.stats.pValueTwoSided[0.0]
```

```
1f
```

The pathological cases of smallest possible input 0 as well as large value are providing a valid outcome.

Further, the one-sided tests are given as:

```
.quantQ.stats.pValueLeftSided:{[x]
   // x -- value of test statistics following N(0,1)
   // return corresponding p-value for one-sided left hand side test
   :$[x>=0;1-(reverse first flip .quantQ.stats.normTable) neg[1]+
       (reverse last flip .quantQ.stats.normTable) binr x;(reverse first
           ↪ flip .quantQ.stats.normTable)
       neg[1]+(reverse last flip .quantQ.stats.normTable) binr abs x];
};
```

giving results:

```
.quantQ.stats.pValueLeftSided[-2.58]
```

```
0.005
```

```
.quantQ.stats.pValueLeftSided[2.58]
```

```
0.995
```

and, finally, the third version of the test:

```
.quantQ.stats.pValueRightSided:{[x]
   // x -- value of test statistics following N(0,1)
   // return corresponding p-value for one-sided right hand side test
   :$[x>=0;(reverse first flip .quantQ.stats.normTable) neg[1]+(reverse
       ↪ last flip .quantQ.stats.normTable)
       binr x;1-(reverse first flip .quantQ.stats.normTable) neg[1]+(
           ↪ reverse last flip .quantQ.stats.normTable)
       binr abs x];
};
```

gives on the provided examples:

```
.quantQ.stats.pValueRightSided[-2.58]
```

```
0.995
```

```
.quantQ.stats.pValueRightSided[2.58]
```

```
0.005
```

We can thus obtain the p-value for a given value of statistics with $N(0,1)$ asymptotic distribution.

12.3.2 Correlation

The basic tool we have at our disposal to assess the dependence between two variables X and Y is a correlation, or Pearson correlation, denoted as ρ_{XY}. Correlation is defined as the covariance of two random variables normalised by their respective variances:

$$\rho_{XY} = \frac{cov(X,Y)}{\sigma_X \sigma_Y}, \tag{12.11}$$

where cov stands for covariance, and σ_X and σ_Y stands for a square root of the variance of X and Y, respectively. Correlation is a definite quantity if the variance for both random variables exists.

Correlation is bounded to range $[-1, 1]$, where values close to 1 suggest perfect correlation, values close to -1 imply that variables are anti-correlated, while uncorrelated variables have correlation close to zero. The obvious null hypothesis to test is:

- H_0: Two random variables are uncorrelated.
- H_a: Two random variables are correlated.

Let us stress that we have formulated the alternative hypothesis in rather plain English. The proper formulation should be that we reject the null hypothesis.

In order to assess this hypothesis in statistical terms, we assume that we have two samples $x_1, x_2, \ldots, x_N$ and $y_1, y_2, \ldots, y_N$, two draws of random variables X and Y, respectively, and we have calculated the sample correlation ρ. We assume that true correlation is ρ_0. We centre the correlation around the true value and normalise it by the estimate of its standard error:

$$t_\rho = \frac{\rho - \rho_0}{\sigma_\rho} = \frac{\rho - \rho_0}{\sqrt{\frac{1-\rho^2}{N-2}}}. \tag{12.12}$$

This forms a statistic for which we need to know the asymptotic distribution. Its general form is rather complex. Luckily, the statistic t_ρ can be simplified for $\rho_0 = 0$:

$$t_\rho = \rho\sqrt{\frac{N-2}{1-\rho^2}}. \tag{12.13}$$

The centred and normalised correlation coefficient t_ρ follows distribution $\sim t_{N-2}$. We can thus use the statistics to form the following hypotheses:

- H_0: Two random variables have zero/non-negative/non-positive correlation.
- H_a: Two random variables have non-zero/positive/negative correlation.

The test is assessed by calculating t_ρ and comparing $|t_\rho| > t_{critical,N-2}$, $t_\rho > t_{critical,N-2}$, and $t_\rho < t_{critical,N-2}$, respectively. When the corresponding inequality is satisfied, we can reject the null hypothesis, where $t_{critical,N-2}$ is a corresponding critical value.

12.3.2.1 Implementation

The correlation is already implemented within q under the verb `cor`. Let us illustrate its use:

```
x:100?1.0;
y:(0.2*x)+0.8*100?1.0;
cor[x;y]
```

```
0.3384788
```

The result shows a value different from 0, suggesting positive correlation. In order to test it, we have to calculate the statistic t_ρ. We do that in function `tStatsCorr`, which has two arguments: calculated correlation and size of the sample (the true correlation under the null hypothesis is by definition $\rho_0 = 0$):

```
.quantQ.stats.tStatsCorr:{[rho;N]
   // rho -- estimated correlation
   // N -- size of sample
   :rho*sqrt[(N-2)%1-rho*rho];
 };
```

Let us test the hypothesis (two-sided) that the correlation observed above is different from 0. First, we calculate the statistic t_ρ:

```
.quantQ.stats.tStatsCorr[cor[x;y];count x]
```

```
3.560958
```

The value is large. We assess its significance level against the normal asymptotic behaviour using a two-sided test:

```
.quantQ.stats.pValueTwoSided abs .quantQ.stats.tStatsCorr[cor[x;y];count x]
```

```
0.001
```

The result clearly shows that we can reject the null hypothesis of correlation being zero. The derived p-value is 0.001, which is in fact the lowest number in our lookup table and thus stands for any p-value smaller than or equal to 0.001.

12.3.3 *t*-test: One Sample

Let us consider an independently drawn sample $x_1, \ldots, x_N$ representing N draws of a random variable X, which has a population mean μ and a standard deviation σ.

Our motivation is to form a hypothesis about the population mean inferred from the observed sample. The statistical procedure to achieve this objective is to use *t*-test.

In general, *t*-test is a statistical hypothesis test where the test statistics under the null hypothesis follow *t*-distribution. *t*-distribution is parameterised by one parameter n, denoted as degrees of freedom. For $n \nearrow$, the distribution converges to a normal distribution, while for n small, the distribution is fat-tailed.

Example of such a test statistic is the following variable:

$$t = \frac{\overline{x} - \mu}{\frac{\sigma}{\sqrt{N}}}, \tag{12.14}$$

where $\overline{x}$ is the sample average. The statistic under the null hypothesis is distributed as $\sim t_n$; these can be used in the following statistical test about the population average:

- H_0: The population mean is μ (given the sample size N and population standard deviation σ).
- H_a: The population mean is different from μ.

The test is inconvenient as it requires knowledge of a population standard deviation. This is, in practice, is hardly known and such an assumption in data analysis cannot be made. Fortunately, the *t*-statistic can be modified such that we can replace knowledge of population standard deviation by its estimator:

$$t' = \frac{\overline{X} - \mu}{s}, \tag{12.15}$$

where s is the standard deviation of the mean defined as:

$$s = \frac{1}{\sqrt{N}} \sqrt{\frac{1}{N-1} \sum_{i}^{N} (x_i - \overline{x})}. \tag{12.16}$$

Note that there is a factor $1/\sqrt{N}$ in front of the square root.

The adjusted statistic t' follows $\sim t_{N-1}$. The estimator of the standard deviation of the mean cost us one degree of freedom. The word "cost" is used as it worsens the asymptotic behaviour and makes the statistics further from the normal distribution.

We can form the following hypotheses to test using the t' statistic:

- H_0: The population mean is equal/smaller or equal/larger or equal to μ, given the sample size N.
- H_a: The population mean is different/larger/smaller relative to μ.

The three tests, i.e. a two-sided test and two one-sided tests, can be assessed as follows: we reject the null if $|t'| > t_{critical,N-1}$, $t' < -t_{critical,N-1}$, and $t' > t_{critical,N-1}$, respectively. The critical value $t_{critical,N-1}$ depends on the significance level. In the subsequent part, we will assume the asymptotic limit holds and use the normal distribution to derive the critical values.

12.3.3.1 Implementation

The calculation of the t' statistic is rather straightforward:

```
.quantQ.stats.tTestOneSample:{[x1;mean]
   // x1 -- array to be tested
   // mean -- mean
   // return t-statistics
   :(avg[x1]-mean)%(dev[x1]% sqrt count x1);
};
```

The input is the sample and the value of the mean we want to assess under the null hypothesis. The function returns the statistics. The assessment of the test is done using the function which maps the statistics to the corresponding p-value for a given test set-up. In this example, we use the two-sided test for μ being equal to 0.45. The value of the statistic can be calculated as:

```
.quantQ.stats.tTestOneSample[xTest:100?1.0;0.45]
```

```
1.929509
```

while the map to the corresponding p-value is:

```
.quantQ.stats.pValueTwoSided abs .quantQ.stats.tTestOneSample[xTest;0.45]
```

```
0.06
```

The p-value of the test is 6%, which suggests that we may reject the null hypothesis of mean being equal to 0.45 at 6% confidence level. Even though the true mean is 0.5, and the value tested 0.45 is smaller by 10%, the size of the sample prevents us from rejecting the null and inclines towards the difference confidently.

12.3.4 *t*-test: Two Samples

In the previous test, we tested one sample against a static mean value. In practice, we may want to test two samples that have the same mean. Let us consider an independently drawn sample $x_1, \ldots, x_N$ representing N draws of a random variable X, which has a population mean μ_1 and a standard deviation σ_1, and independently drawn sample $y_1, \ldots, y_M$ representing M draws of a random variable Y, which has a population mean μ_2 and a standard deviation σ_2.

The hypothesis to be tested is of the form:

- H_0: The population means are equal, $\mu_1 = \mu_2$.
- H_a: The population means are different.

The test is done by constructing a suitable test statistic. The form of the statistic depends on the assumptions imposed on N and M, and σ_1 and σ_2, respectively. The stronger the assumptions, the closer to asymptotic behaviour but more prone to model error. In this text, we focus on the least restricted version of the two-sample t-statistic, also known as Welch's test. In such a case, there is no assumption imposed on the relationship between N and M, and σ_1 and σ_2. The Welch t_W statistic is defined as:

$$t_W = \frac{\overline{x} - \overline{y}}{s_W}, \tag{12.17}$$

where s_W is defined as:

$$s_W = \sqrt{\frac{\frac{1}{N-1}\sum_i^N (x_i - \overline{x})}{N} + \frac{\frac{1}{M-1}\sum_i^M (y_i - \overline{y})}{M}}. \tag{12.18}$$

The Welch's t_W statistic follows under the null hypothesis $\sim t_{W_{df}}$, where the number of degrees of freedom is:

$$W_{df} = \frac{\left(\frac{\hat{\sigma}_1^2}{N} + \frac{\hat{\sigma}_2^2}{M}\right)^2}{\frac{(\hat{\sigma}_1^2)^2}{N-1} + \frac{(\hat{\sigma}_2^2)^2}{M-1}}. \tag{12.19}$$

We can again form following hypotheses to test using the t_W statistic:

- H_0: The population mean μ_1 is equal/smaller or equal/larger or equal to population mean μ_2.
- H_a: The population mean μ_1 is different/larger/smaller to population mean μ_2.

The three tests, i.e. the two-sided test and two one-sided tests, can be assessed as in the previous case. We reject the null if $|t_W| > t_{critical,W_{df}}$, $t_W < -t_{critical,W_{df}}$, and $t_W > t_{critical,W_{df}}$, respectively. The critical value $t_{critical,W_{df}}$ depends on the significance level. In the test, we will assume the asymptotic behaviour and consider the critical values based on a normal distribution.

12.3.4.1 Implementation

The calculation of the t_W statistic is given as:

```
.quantQ.stats.tTestTwoSample:{[x1;x2]
   // x1,x2 -- two arrays to be tested, unequal length
   // return Welch's statistics
   :(avg[x1]-avg[x2])%sqrt ((s*s:dev[x1])%count[x1])+(z*z:dev[x2])%count[x2
       ↪ ];
};
```

We test the function using two samples with the same mean but different size and variance:

```
.quantQ.stats.tTestTwoSample[xTest1:100?1.0;xTest2:neg[0.5]+1000?2.0]
```

```
-0.5628797
```

The value is then transformed into the corresponding p-value using the normal distribution:

```
.quantQ.stats.pValueTwoSided abs .quantQ.stats.tTestTwoSample[xTest1;xTest2
    ↪ ]
```

```
0.58
```

The result suggests that we cannot reject the null hypothesis and we thus conclude that two samples have the same mean as implied by the alternative hypothesis.

12.3.5 Sign Test

The sign test is a non-parametric test to assess the statistical difference between pairs of observations drawn from two related populations. For example, consider a set of investors who invest every month and report their PnL. The investors can subscribe to the advisory service. If the general market conditions remain the same, the effect of the advisory service can be estimated by comparing the performance – the PnL – before and after the advisory service was obtained for a sample of investors. If the effect of the advisory service is not material, then PnL before the advisory service and PnL after it comes for every investor from the same distribution. Since every investor can have a different distribution of PnL – different mean, sigma, or kurtosis, for example – we cannot compare PnL across investors. Instead, we should assess the statistical properties of the difference of the PnL before/after across the sample. In particular, if the effect of the advisory effect is irrelevant, the distribution of differences should be symmetric around zero. On the other hand, if the difference is positive/negative, the advisory effect is correspondingly negative/positive.

Let us formulate the sign test explicitly: consider two related populations, X and Y, and two related samples of pair draws, (x_i, y_i), with $i = 1, \ldots, N$. Each population is continuous, and the two populations are ordinal, i.e. we can order any pair (x_i, y_i). We further denote the order as inequality between x_i and y_i. For the sake of simplicity, we assume that $x_i = y_i$ is not possible (with probability 0), and discuss ties later in subsequent tests. Further, every two draws of pairs are independent of each other.

The ordinal variables may not be necessarily numeric. Consider for example a string of characters, which is not numeric, but we can easily sort a set of string alphabetically. We can always characterise the outcome of inequality numerically, in any case. We define the difference between x_i and y_i as $\delta_i = x_i - y_i$ for numerical variables while for non-numerical variables the difference can be defined as:

$$\delta_i = \begin{cases} +1, & x_i > y_i, \\ -1, & \text{otherwise.} \end{cases} \tag{12.20}$$

Then, the basic formulation of the sign test states:

- H_0: The difference between x_i and y_i, $\delta_i = x_i - y_i$, has the same probability to be positive as negative.
- H_0: The difference between x_i and y_i is skewed towards positive or negative values.

Alternatively, we can formulate one-sided tests:

- H_0: The difference between x_i and y_i, $\delta_i = x_i - y_i$, is more likely to be positive/negative.
- H_0: The difference between x_i and y_i is either equally distributed for positive and negative values, or skewed towards negative/positive values.

Since the test is concerned with the sign, we can encode the difference as:

$$z_i = \theta(\delta_i), \tag{12.21}$$

where θ is a Heaviside step function. For the purpose of the test, the draws with the same value, $\delta_i = 0$, are discarded.

Under the null hypothesis, the sample of sign variables z_i is drawn from the binomial distribution with $p = 0.5$. The (relevant) properties of the binomial distribution $binomial(N; p)$ can be summarised as follows:

- Mean of the sum: $\mu = N\,p$.
- Variance of the sum: $\sigma^2 = N\,p\,(1-p)$.

The binomial distribution can be approximated by the normal distribution $N(\mu, \sigma^2)$ for reasonably large N. In general, a population larger than 30 observations can be approximated by the normal distribution. This fact can be used to perform tests of the null hypothesis for symmetrically distributed differences δ_i.

When the sample is small the normal distribution cannot be used and we have to calculate the properties of the probability distribution function explicitly. Namely, the probability density function of the binomial distribution is defined as:

$$pdf(n, N; p) = \binom{N}{n} p^n (1-p)^{N-n}, \tag{12.22}$$

with the binomial number $\binom{N}{n}$ defined as

$$\binom{N}{n} = \frac{N!}{n!(N-n)!}. \tag{12.23}$$

We can use the knowledge of the binomial probability distribution function to calculate the probability to observe n cases of $z_i = 1$ in the sample of N observations under the null hypothesis of $p = 0.5$. Besides, we can use the binomial probability to calculate the p-values for one-sided and two-sided tests, respectively. For example, for a one-sided test of observing $z_i = 1$ less frequently than $z_i = 0$ given we have observed n instances with $z_i = 1$ out of N cases, we calculate:

$$\sum_{i=0}^{n} pdf(i, N; p = 0.5). \tag{12.24}$$

The cumulative probability gives the likelihood to observe more extreme outcomes when the null of equal probabilities for both types $z_i = 1$ and $z_i = 0$ holds. We can proceed analogously for the inverted one-sided test and/or two-sided test.

Example

Let us continue with the example of advisory service and investors. Consider the case where there are 10 investors who subscribed to the advisory service and 9 of them have shown improved PnL after the subscription to advisory service. The result shows in plain terms improvement, but is this improvement statistically significant? Let us formulate the test as two-sided. In such a case, we need to calculate probability for events as extreme as the outcome we have recorded or even more extreme. Thus, we need to calculate $pdf(n, 10, 0.5)$ for $n = 0, 1, 9, 10$:

$$\begin{aligned} P &= pdf(0,10,0.5) + pdf(1,10,0.5) + pdf(9,10,0.5) + pdf(10,10,0.5) \\ &= 0.00098 + 0.0097 + 0.0097 + 0.00098 \\ &= 0.02136. \end{aligned} \tag{12.25}$$

The value is below 2.2%, which suggests a high probability that positive outcome of investors is not a statistical coincidence. We are in fact interested in a one-sided test where null is that investors' performance is not improved, tested against the null of being improved (in plain English, the alternative is that we reject the null). The probability for the extreme outcome is 0.01063.

12.3.5.1 Implementation of the Test

In q language, the sign test can be implemented as follows. First, we define the calculator of the basic characteristics of the binomial distribution:

```
.quantQ.stats.characteristicsBinomial:{[n;N;p]
   // N -- population size
   // n -- number of "1"
   // p -- probability of "1" in every draw
   // first four moments: mean
   mean: N*p;
   // first four moments: variance
   variance: N*p*1-p;
   // sigma -- convenient
   sigma:sqrt variance;
   // first four moments: skewness
   skewness:(1-2.0*p)%sqrt[N*p*1-p];
   // first four moments: kurtosis
   kurtosis:(1-6.0*p*1-p)%N*p*1-p;
   // the output object
    :(`mean`variance`sigma`skewness`kurtosis)!(mean;variance;sigma;skewness
        ↪ ;kurtosis);
};
```

The function is rather for the completeness to have the binomial distribution fully covered. Further, we will need the probability distribution function of the binomial distribution:

```
.quantQ.stats.pdfBinomial:{[n;N;p]
   // N -- population size
   // n -- number of "1"
   // p -- probability of "1" in every draw
   :.quantQ.stats.coeffBinomial[N;n]*xexp[p;n]*xexp[1-p;N-n];
};
```

The binomial coefficient $\binom{a}{b}$ can be calculated as:

```
.quantQ.stats.coeffBinomial:{[a;b]
   // a, b -- integers
   // a choose b calculation
   :.quantQ.stats.factorial[a]%(.quantQ.stats.factorial[b]*.quantQ.stats.
       ↪ factorial[a-b]);
};
```

It works as expected:

```
.quantQ.stats.coeffBinomial[6;3]
```

```
20j
```

Further, we need the factorial function:

```
.quantQ.stats.factorial:{[n]
   // n  -- the integer input
   // for the purpose of calculation, the numbers are recast into float
   :prd "f"$1 + til n;
};
```

The factorial function takes as an input the integer valued number while the product is calculated in the float type. Otherwise, the factorial would not work since `21j`. The functionality of the factorial function can be illustrated:

```
.quantQ.stats.factorial[25]
```

```
1.551121e+025
```

Let us illustrate the functionality of the provided functions: we calculate the characteristics of the binomial distribution for a sample values:

```
.quantQ.stats.characteristicsBinomial[45;100;0.5]
```

```
mean    | 50
variance| 25
sigma   | 5
skewness| 0
kurtosis| -0.02
```

The reader can independently verify the calculated values. Before we perform the sign test, let us plot the binomial distribution:

```
tabBinom:([] t: til 100);
update Binom:.quantQ.stats.pdfBinomial[;100;0.5] each t from tabBinom
```

```
t  Binom
----------------
0  7.888609e-031
1  7.888609e-029
2  3.904861e-027
3  1.275588e-025
4  3.093301e-024
5  5.939138e-023
6  9.403635e-022
7  1.262774e-020
8  1.467975e-019
9  1.500596e-018
10 1.365543e-017
11 1.117262e-016
12 8.286361e-016
13 5.609229e-015
14 3.485735e-014
15 1.998488e-013
16 1.061697e-012
17 5.246031e-012
18 2.419003e-011
19 1.043991e-010
..
```

Figure 12.3 depicts the probability distribution function for the binomial distribution with $N = 100$. The shape of the distribution resembles the normal distribution centred around the value of $\mu = 50$.

We can formulate the calculation of the *p*-value for a given realisation as a sum of calls of *pdfBinomial* function over extreme events. The function thus has to primarily calculate an array of extreme events given `n` and `N`. Given two input parameters – number of the positive instances and size of the sample – function calculates the corresponding *p*-value for left-sided, right-sided and two-sided tests, respectively:

```
.quantQ.stats.pValSignTest:{[n;N]
   // n -- number of positive instances
   // N -- size of sample
   // calculate sets of extreme cases
   leftSample: z where n>=z:til N+1;
   rightSample: z where n<=z:til N+1;
   twoSample:asc distinct $[n<=N%2;(z where n>=z:til N+1),(z where (N-n)<=z
       ↪ :til N+1);
       (z where (N-n)>=z:til N+1),(z where n<=z:til N+1)];
   // return p-values
   :(`pValueLeft`pValueRight`pValueTwoSided)!(sum .quantQ.stats.pdfBinomial
       ↪ [;N;0.5]
       each leftSample;sum .quantQ.stats.pdfBinomial[;N;0.5] each
           ↪ rightSample;sum
       .quantQ.stats.pdfBinomial[;N;0.5] each twoSample);
};
```

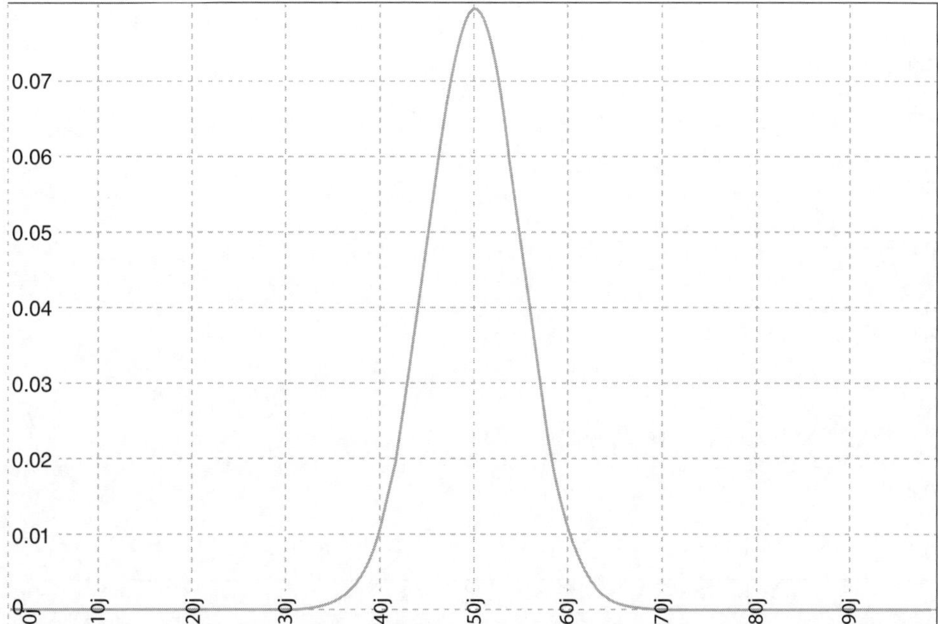

FIGURE 12.3 Probability distribution function of the binomial distribution with $N = 100$ and $p = 0.5$

Let us illustrate the functionality on the example of investors subscribing to an advisory service:

```
.quantQ.stats.pValSignTest[9;10]
```

```
pValueLeft     | 0.9990234
pValueRight    | 0.01074219
pValueTwoSided| 0.02148438
```

The outcome agrees with a general intuition and the numbers we have explicitly calculated above. The slight discrepancy is due to the rounding error we have performed in the calculation. The provided function thus can be used to perform the sign test and evaluate it.

12.3.5.2 Median Test

The sign test can be used as the test for the median against a certain threshold value. Namely, for a sample of data x_i, $i = 1, \dots, N$, we define a constant sample, $y_i = \eta$, $i = 1, \dots, N$. Then, a sign test applied on pairs of sample points (x_i, y_i) tests the following hypothesis:

- H_0: The median of the population from which x_i is drawn is η.
- H_0: The median is different from η.

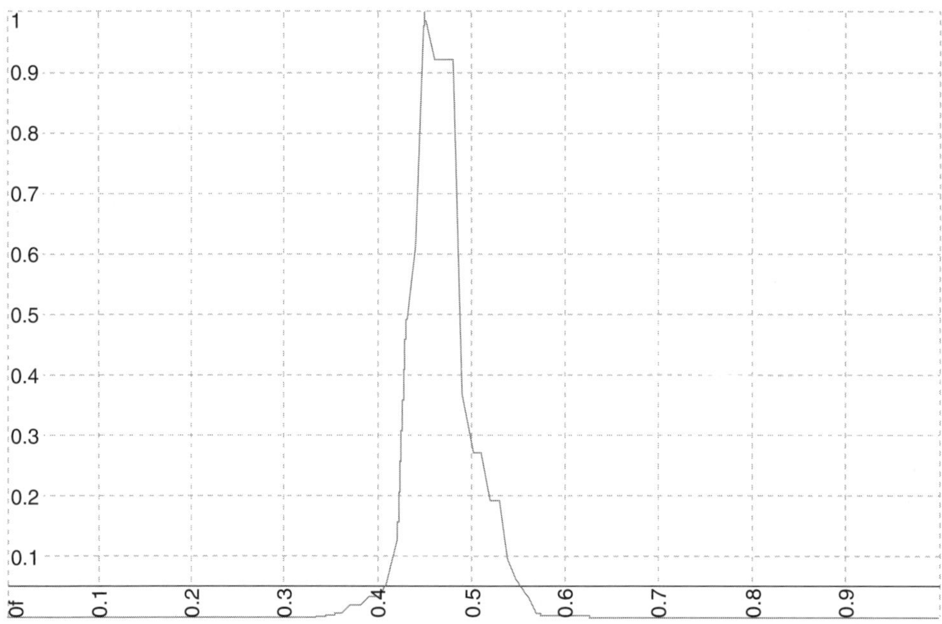

FIGURE 12.4 Median test: p-value as a function of tested value

First, the median is the value, which separates the higher half of the sample from the lower one. Thus, if we calculate the difference between the median and all the values in the sample, we get an equal number of positive and negative numbers. This is the nature of the sign test, and that is why we can quickly turn the sign test into the median test. The median test is considered by default to be a two-sided test. Further, it is clear that the median value as defined above is not unique for finite samples.

Further, we analyse the statistical power of the test given our sample size. We calculate the p-value of the median test for a range of tested median values `0.01 * til 101`. Figure 12.4 depicts the p-values against the tested median values. Also, the plot contains a constant horizontal line at 0.05, which stands for statistical significance. All the cases when p-values are above the line say that we cannot reject the null that the median of the array is given a tested value. This is true for values within $[0.41, 0.55]$ range, which shows the accuracy of our test – given we know the true median being 0.5. The data for the figure has been prepared as:

```
([] meds:0.01 * til 101; pVal: .quantQ.stats.testMedian[array;] each 0.01 *
    ↪  til 101; meds: 101#0.05)
```

12.3.6 Wilcoxon Signed-Rank Test

Wilcoxon signed-rank test is a paired difference test which is used to test the null hypothesis that for two related samples, their population mean ranks differ. It is an alternative for paired t-tests which cannot be assumed to be normally distributed. The test is used for paired samples, i.e. samples which are related, or repeated draws. The observations in pairs come from the same distribution, we can order the pair, and each pair is randomly and independently drawn. The Wilcoxon test states the following null and alternative hypotheses:

- H_0: The difference within the pair follows a symmetric distribution centred around zero.
- H_a: The difference within the pair does not follow a symmetric distribution centred around zero.

Consider the sample with related pairs (x_i, y_i), with $i = 1, \ldots, N$. Define the difference within i-th pair as $\delta_i = x_i - y_i$ and the sign of the difference $s_i = \text{signum}\delta_i$. Further, before we construct Wilcoxon statistics, we filter out all cases with $x_i = y_i$. Let us denote the subsample without ties as (x_i, y_i), with $i = 1, \ldots, N'$ and $N \geq N'$.

Then, we calculate the Wilcoxon statistics as:

$$W = \sum_{i}^{N'} (s_i \cdot r_i), \tag{12.26}$$

where r_i is the rank of the i-th pair, where differences have been sorted based on the absolute value of their difference, δ_i, with ties getting the average rank of the respective group.

The Wilcoxon statistic, W, has under the null hypothesis the underlying distribution with mean 0 and variance:

$$\sigma_W^2 = \sqrt{\frac{N'(N'+1)(2 \cdot N'+1)}{6}}. \tag{12.27}$$

For small samples, the reader has to consult with Wilcoxon (1950) to find critical values. We reject the null hypothesis (of a two-sided test) if $|W| > W_{critical}$, with $W_{critical}$ being critical value at a given confidence level.

For N' large, the distribution of the W statistics follows a normal distribution. If we normalise W by its standard deviation σ_W, we get $W/\sigma_W \sim N(0, 1)$. In such a case, we can use critical values from a standard normal distribution.

The Wilcoxon test is implemented in function `wilcoxonTest`. It accepts two arrays `x1` and `x2`, respectively, corresponding to x and y. The function calculates several outcomes arranged in the dictionary: Wilcoxon statistic W, size of sample, standard deviation σ_W, and normalized Wilcoxon statistic W/σ_W:

```
.quantQ.stats.wilcoxonTest:{[x1;x2]
  // x1,x2 -- arrays of sample 1 and sample 2, respectively, of the same
     ↪ length
  // the test is interpreted as a table
  intTab:([] x1;x2);
  // abs diff and the sign of the difference
  intTab: update absDif: abs[x1-x2], sign: signum[x1-x2] from intTab;
```

```
    // remove ties
    intTab: select from intTab where sign <>0;
    // sort
    intTab: `absDif xasc intTab;
    // add order of sorted table
    intTab: update rnk:i from intTab;
    // assign average rank to ties
    intTab: update avgRnk: avg rnk by absDif from intTab;
    // stat element of the stats
    w: exec sum avgRnk*sign from intTab;
    // elements of the test, number of observations
    n: count intTab;
    // elements of the test: variance of the test
    sigma: sqrt (1.0%6.0)*n*(n+1)*(1+2*n);
    // return dictionary with results
    :(`w`n`sigma`wNormalised)!(w;n;sigma;w%sigma);
};
```

Let us illustrate the functionality on two unrelated vectors:

```
wilcoxonTest:.quantQ.stats.wilcoxonTest[100?1.0;100?1.0];
wilcoxonTest
```

```
(`w`n`sigma`wNormalised)!(-902f;100j;581.6786;-1.550685)
```

The test itself does not produce the p-value; it is our responsibility to assess the validity of the test. For that purpose, we can utilise `pValueTwoSided` function to obtain the p-value estimate:

```
.quantQ.stats.pValueTwoSided abs wilcoxonTest`wNormalised
```

```
0.13
```

The test shows that we cannot reject the null at any significance level below 0.13, suggesting that we cannot reject the null hypothesis meaning, put plainly, that they have the same mean.

12.3.7 Rank Correlation and Somers' *D*

Previously mentioned measures aimed to work with numerical variables, i.e. cardinal numbers where we can sort and measure the difference between them. We have tacitly assumed to work with float types. In this section, we focus on ordinal variables and define some useful metrics to assess some hypothesis about them. Since for ordinal variables the notion of mean does not make much sense – though, we can still work with median – we focus our attention on the sorting of variables and ranking them.

Let us assume we have two ordinal variables X and Y; for each of them we observe sample of size N, i.e. $x_1, x_2, \ldots, x_N$ $y_1, y_2, \ldots, y_N$. Further, a pair (x_i, y_i) corresponds to the i-th draw of a pair (X, Y).

Somers' D is a measure of ordinal association between two random variables, see Somers (1962). It takes values $\in [-1, 1]$, where -1 corresponds to the case when all observed pairs of the variables disagree while 1 states for perfect agreement. The definition of the Somers' D is based on the notion of concordance. We say that two pairs (x_i, y_i) and (x_j, y_j) are concordant if the ranks of both elements agree, i.e., $x_i > x_j$ and $y_i > y_j$, or, $x_i < x_j$ and $y_i < y_j$. If the ranks disagree, i.e. $x_i < x_j$ and $y_i > y_j$, or, $x_i > x_j$ and $y_i < y_j$, we say that two pairs are discordant. If there is equality, $x_i = x_j$ and/or $y_i = y_j$, we say that pairs are neither concordant nor discordant.

Let us arrange two samples into pairs $(x_1, y_1), (x_2, y_2), \ldots, (x_N, y_N)$. Further, consider all possible pairs of pairs, i.e. if we denote pair $(x_i, y_i), (x_j, y_j)$ as (i, j), then all pairs of pairs are $(1, 2)$, $(1, 3)$, $\ldots$, $(2, 3)$, $\ldots$, $(N-1, N)$. There are $N(N-1)/2$ such combinations. Denote the number of concordant pairs out of all pairs as N_C and the number of discordant pairs as N_D.

First, let us define Kendall's τ rank correlation:

$$\tau(X, Y) = \frac{N_C - N_D}{\frac{N(N-1)}{2}}. \tag{12.28}$$

Kendall's τ is $\in [-1, 1]$.

Meaning of $\tau(X, X)$ is a measure of pairs within X with unequal numbers. We can then define Somers' $D(Y; X)$ as:

$$D(Y;X) = \frac{\tau(X, Y)}{\tau(X, X)}, \tag{12.29}$$

where the definition says that $D(Y; X)$ is the difference in the number of concordant and discordant pairs normalised by the number of unequal pairs in X. The role of normalisation is for the case of mass points in the distribution of X. For a continuously distributed variable which does not have "δ" function in its distribution, Somers' D and Kendall's τ rank coincide. The difference between the two is mainly for discrete observations.

Kendall's τ rank correlation is symmetric while Somers' D is asymmetric due to the normalisation factor. This is apparent for the case when one of the variables has mass points while the other one is continuously distributed. The distributions with mass points are a particular focus when Somers' D is being used.

There is a further simplified formula for the case where Y is discrete and X is binary. In such a case, Somers' D can be expressed as:

$$D(Y;X) = \frac{N_C - N_D}{N_C + N_D + N_T}, \tag{12.30}$$

where N_T is the number of neither concordant nor discordant pairs with $y_i = y_j$ while $x_i \neq x_j$.

Somers' D is being used for regression where the dependent variable is binary or discrete while the independent variable can be of any type. Alternatively, Somers' D can be used to evaluate the performance of classification models, i.e. to assign the degree of association between model and true values.

Finally, let us complement the definitions of the rank correlations by Kruskal's γ. It is another coefficient measuring the similarity of ordering of the data for a pair of ordinal variables; see Goodman and Kruskal (1954). The γ coefficient is defined as:

$$\gamma = \frac{N_C - N_D}{N_C + N_D}, \tag{12.31}$$

where N_C and N_D stand for a number of concordant and discordant pairs, respectively. Kruskal's γ ranges $\in [-1, 1]$. When there is no association between the two random variables, the γ is close to 0.

Somers' D, Kendall's τ, and Kurskal's γ are presented as descriptive statistics. In order to use them in the form of a test, we have two options. The first option is to calculate the small sample distribution of given statistics. Methods like bootstrap can be used. In such a case, we simulate a number of samples under the null hypothesis and evaluate the statistics for every simulation. Then, we collect the distribution of the statistics and create critical values based on the simulated distributions.

Alternatively, we may seek the analytic distributions of the test statistics. Its form may not be straightforward, and sometimes the analytic manipulations may be needed. Let us illustrate it for Kruskall's γ. We can define new statistics:

$$t_\gamma = \gamma \sqrt{\frac{N_C + N_D}{N(1 - \gamma^2)}}, \tag{12.32}$$

where all variables have been defined so far, with N being a number of observations. The statistics follows $\sim t_{N-1}$. For large N, the normal distribution can be used. We can then form the hypothesis:

- H_0: There is no ordinal association between two random variables.
- H_a: There is an ordinal association between two random variables.

The one-sided/two-sided test can be run by comparing t_γ against critical values $T_{critical;N-1}$.

12.3.7.1 Implementation

First, let us define the function, which determines whether a pair of pairs is concordant, discordant or neither of these:

```
.quantQ.stats.concordanceRoutine:{[row1;row2]
   // rowJ -- pair of observations (xJ;yJ) with J=1,2
   // explicitly extract x's and y's
   x1: first row1;
   y1: last row1;
   x2: first row2;
   y2: last row2;
```

```
    // concordance
    concordance: ((x1>x2) and (y1>y2)) or ((x1<x2) and (y1<y2));
    // discordance
    discordance: ((x1>x2) and (y1<y2)) or ((x1<x2) and (y1>y2));
    // output is triplet
    :(concordance;discordance;not concordance or discordance);
};
```

The outcome of the concordanceRoutine function is a triplet of binary numbers, where only one of the members of the triplet can be true, or 1b, denoting whether the pair of pairs is concordant/discordant/neither of these.

The example of the function is:

```
r1:(3.1;3.4);
r2:(3.3;5.7);
.quantQ.stats.concordanceRoutine[r1;r2]
```

giving:

```
100b
```

This denotes that the pair of pairs is concordant.

Further, we create a function for the calculation of Kendall's τ rank correlation. The function takes two arguments, sample for variable X and sample for variable Y:

```
.quantQ.stats.kendallTauRank:{[xS;yS]
    // xS, yS -- arrays of values to compare the rank
    // aggregate concordance statistics
    stats: sum raze {.quantQ.stats.concordanceRoutine/:[y;(1+x?y)_x]}[t]
       ↪ each t: flip(xS;yS);
    // return Kendall's Tau Rank
    :(stats[0]-stats[1])%0.5*count[xS]*count[xS]-1;
};
```

Calculate the τ coefficient for two randomly distributed vectors:

```
x: 100?1.0;
y: 100?1.0;
.quantQ.stats.kendallTauRank[x;y]
```

```
0.03676768
```

The value is close to zero, confirming the nature of the vectors x and y.

For the sake of completeness, we calculate the τ coefficient for perfectly aligned vectors:

```
x: 100?1.0;
y: x;
.quantQ.stats.kendallTauRank[x;y]
```

```
1f
```

Further, we utilise τ and define Somers' D in function somersD:

```
.quantQ.stats.somersD:{[yS;xS]
   // xS, yS -- arrays of values to calculate D
   // calculate Somers' D using Kendall's Tau Rank
   :.quantQ.stats.kendallTauRank[xS;yS]%.quantQ.stats.kendallTauRank[xS;xS];
};
```

We first test the implementation for two random vectors:

```
x: 100?1.0;
y: 100?1.0;
.quantQ.stats.somersD[y;x]
```

```
-0.02424242
```

The result verifies the independence of two vectors, though not in the form of a statistic but rather indicatively.

For two continuously distributed random variables without mass points, Somers' D is symmetric:

```
.quantQ.stats.somersD[x;y]
```

```
-0.02424242
```

The asymmetry appears when discretely observed points are assessed, with a possible overlap in sample values. Let us define a discrete sample now:

```
x: 100?2;
y: 100?3;
```

and calculate Somers' D relative to both X and Y:

```
.quantQ.stats.somersD[y;x]
```

```
0.1553156
```

and

```
.quantQ.stats.somersD[x;y]
```

```
0.1163116
```

There is an asymmetry in the outcome. On the other hand, Kendall's τ is symmetric:

```
.quantQ.stats.kendallTauRank[x;y]
```

```
0.1511111
```

and

```
.quantQ.stats.kendallTauRank[y;x]
```

```
0.1511111
```

Further, we proceed with Somers' D for X being binary variable:

```
.quantQ.stats.somersDBinaryX:{[yS;xS]
   // xS, yS -- arrays of values to calculate D, xS being binary
   // return modified Somers' D
   :0.5*1.0+.quantQ.stats.somersD[yS;xS];
};
```

which gives for a random sample:

```
x:100?2;
y:100?1.0;
.quantQ.stats.somersDBinaryX[y;x]
```

```
0.4611362
```

This suggests a seeming alignment in variables. Without critical values, though, there is no statistical power to support our claim.

Further, we implement the Somers' D for a case when X is binary, and Y is an integer. The modified definition has a different notion of a tie, which is calculated for the second argument array only. Before we proceed with the definition, we adjust the concordance routine:

```
.quantQ.stats.concordanceRoutineBinaryXIntegerY:{[row1;row2]
   // rowJ -- pair of observations (xJ;yJ) with J=1,2
   // XJ -- being binary
   // YJ -- being integers
   // explicitly x's and y's
   x1: first row1;
   y1: last row1;
   x2: first row2;
   y2: last row2;
   // concordance
   concordance: ((x1>x2) and (y1>y2)) or ((x1<x2) and (y1<y2));
   // discordance
   discordance: ((x1>x2) and (y1<y2)) or ((x1<x2) and (y1>y2));
   // tie
   tie: (x1<>x2) and (y1=y2);
   // output is triplet
   :(concordance;discordance;tie);
};
```

and then define the adjusted Somers' D:

```
.quantQ.stats.somersDBinaryXIntegerY:{[yS;xS]
   // xS, yS -- arrays of values to calculate D
   // xS -- being binary
   // yS being integer
   stats: sum raze {.quantQ.stats.concordanceRoutineBinaryXIntegerY/:[y;(1+
       ↪ x?y)_x]}[t]
       each t:flip (xS;yS);
   // Somers' D
   :("f"$stats[0]-stats[1])%("f"$stats[0]+stats[1]+stats[2]);
};
```

Let us run it for an example of randomly distributed arrays, one with binary outcome and the other one with integer values numbers:

```
x:100?2;
y:100?4;
.quantQ.stats.somersDBinaryXIntegerY[y;x]
```

```
0.1552377
```

The value is rather small, but without a statistical test, such an assertion is again descriptive.

Finally, we implement Kruskall's γ. First, function `kruskallGamma` takes two arguments: two samples of two random variables which are being examined:

```
.quantQ.stats.kruskallGamma:{[xS;yS]
   // xS, yS -- arrays of values to compare the rank
   // aggregate concordance statistics
   stats: sum raze {.quantQ.stats.concordanceRoutine/:[y;(1+x?y)_x]}[t]
       ↪ each t: flip(xS;yS);
   // return gamma Rank coefficient
   :(stats[0]-stats[1])%stats[0]+stats[1];
};
```

Let us test the function against a pair of random variables:

```
x:100?1.0;
y:100?1.0;
.quantQ.stats.kruskallGamma[x;y]
```

```
-0.004848485
```

The value is small and thus suggests no alignment between two variables. In order to test such a statement, we also implement t_γ:

```
.quantQ.stats.tKruskall:{[xS;yS]
   // xS, yS -- arrays of values to compare the rank
   // calculate Kruskall's gamma
   gamma: .quantQ.stats.kruskallGamma[xS;yS];
   // count number of combinations
   stats: sum raze {.quantQ.stats.concordanceRoutine/:[y;(1+x?y)_x]}[t]
       ↪ each t: flip(xS;yS);
   // return t_gamma
   :gamma*sqrt (stats[0]+stats[1])%(count[xS]*count[xS]*1-gamma*gamma);
};
```

The transformed γ then reads:

```
.quantQ.stats.tKruskall[x;y]
```

```
-0.003411252
```

In order to perform a proper two-sided test against normally distributed critical values, we run:

```
.quantQ.stats.pValueTwoSided abs .quantQ.stats.tKruskall[x;y]
```

```
1f
```

The outcome suggests we cannot reject the null hypothesis at any level. This confirms the true nature of the data, which are without any reciprocal link.

12.3.8 Multiple Hypothesis Testing

We finally mention an important problem which is crucial to be aware of when working with data. Let us imagine following setup: we have dependent variable Y and 1000 features, $X^{(1)}, X^{(2)}, \ldots, X^{(1000)}$. Further, let us assume that there is no true correlation between the dependent variable and any of the features. We calculate correlation between the dependent variable and each feature, one by one, and assess the statistical hypothesis that the correlation is equal to 0.0 using t_ρ. What will be the result? Let us illustrate it right now numerically using 100 observations for every variable:

First, we generate the dependent variable:

```
y:100?1.0;
```

and then generate 1000 features and assess it with the `tStatsCorr` function, where we calculate t_ρ based on correlation between `y` and new feature, and save it to an array:

```
draws: {[x] .quantQ.stats.tStatsCorr[cor[y;100?1.0];count 100?1.0]} each
    ↪ til 1000;
```

Figure 12.5 depicts the histogram of `draws` binned by `histBin` scheme with 40 bins. The values are distributed within a range spanning from −2.87 to 3.26. The histograms show a distribution similar in shape to the normal distribution. Importantly, it illustrates our assertion made previously that the statistic is a random variable drawn from a given distribution. This means that even under the null hypothesis, we find statistics with an extreme value given we made enough draws. Thus, if we perform hypothesis testing multiple times, we may end up with a false conclusion.

The histogram has been produced as:

```
.quantQ.stats.getHistogram[;.quantQ.stats.histBin[40]] draws
```

Let us further look on the outcome of the simulation exercise in more detail. The values of the t_ρ span interval $[-2.87, 3.26]$, which suggests that we may reject the null hypothesis for some values. The p-values for the left tail of the distribution are:

```
10#.quantQ.stats.pValueLeftSided each asc draws
```

```
0.005 0.005 0.005 0.005 0.005 0.005 0.005 0.005 0.005 0.01
```

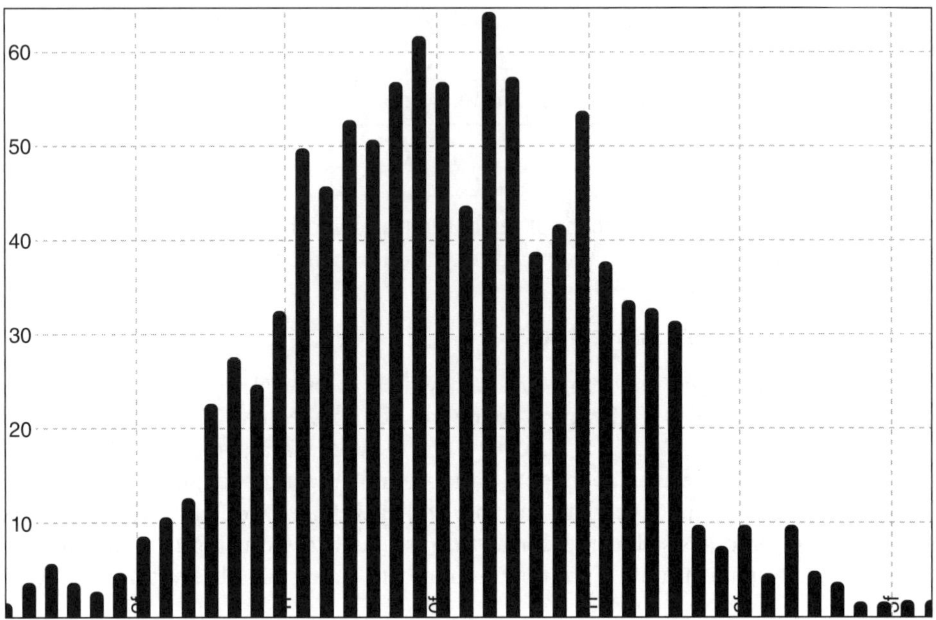

FIGURE 12.5 Histogram of t_ρ for 1000 realisations under the null hypothesis

and for the right tail of the distribution, where we properly adjust the *p*-value to correspond to percentile:

```
{1-x} each -10 # .quantQ.stats.pValueRightSided each asc draws
```

```
0.99 0.99 0.99 0.99 0.99 0.995 0.995 0.995 0.995 0.995
```

Given the value of 0.005 is the smallest value in the map between distribution value and *p*-values, we do realise very extreme values in the distribution. Every such observation on its own would correspond to an extreme value very unlikely to happen under the null hypothesis. How many such extreme values out of 1000 random realisations have exceeded the 0.05 confidence level to reject the null hypothesis? We can answer the question numerically as:

```
sum 0.05>=.quantQ.stats.pValueTwoSided abs draws
```

```
52
```

Thus, 52 out of 1000 observations are rejected. This corresponds to statistical properties of the t_ρ under null being distributed according to the given distribution. This numerical exercise does not contradict the asymptotic behaviour, i.e. normal distribution, which may be seen as verification (not proof though) of the presented statements.

The previous example illustrates the fundamental issue with multiple testing. The problem occurs when we simultaneously test the number of hypotheses, or family of hypotheses. By the nature of statistical testing, we may infer an erroneous conclusion. The significance level used for testing individual hypotheses does not correspond to the significance level at the family level. If we want to impose the confidence level on the family level, we have to adjust the confidence level for every individual hypothesis.

The important concept to define is the family-wise error rate, or *FWER*, which stands for the probability to make at least one error, or Type-I error, in the family of tests. Let us assume that the family contains m individual tests. Further, each test is independent of the other tests. Let us assume that the probability of Type-I error for the individual test is $\alpha_{individual}$. Then, the probability of observing at least one test to show Type-I error, α_{family}, is:

$$\alpha_{family} = 1 - (1 - \alpha_{individual})^m. \tag{12.33}$$

Let us illustrate it numerically for $\alpha_{family} = 0.05$ and m ranging from 1 to 100. Figure 12.6 depicts the dependence of the family-wise error rate, α_{family}, along the individual error rate, $\alpha_{individual}$, which is constant. As the size of the family progresses, the family-wise error rate is increasing and reaching towards 1.0. For a family of size 100, the probability of at least one test to fail is 0.9940795, which is a value very close to 1.0. Data for the figure has been generated as:

```
aIndividual:0.05;
([] familySize: 1+til 100; alphaIndividual: 100#aIndividual; alphaFamily:
    ↪ 1-(xexp[(1-aIndividual);] each  1+til 100))
```

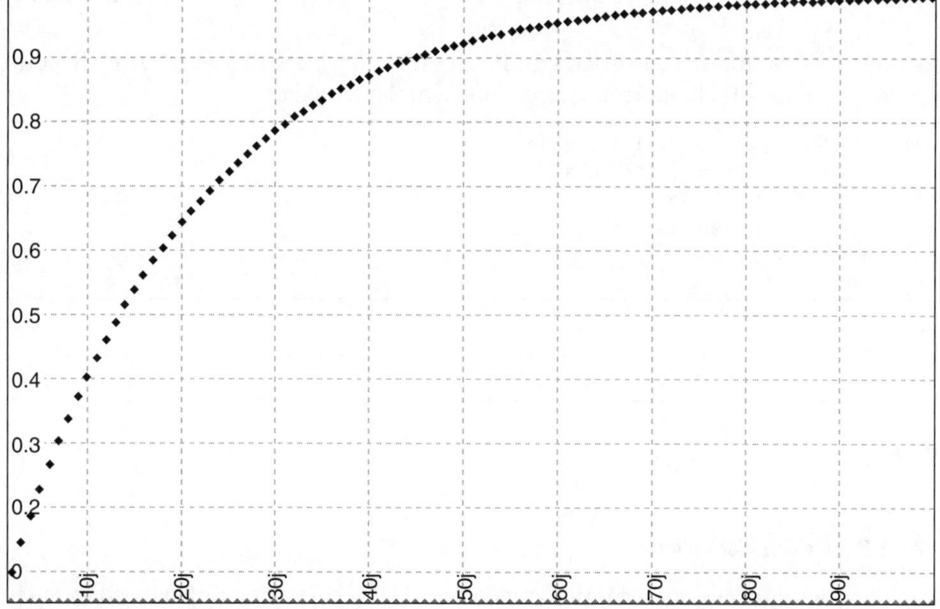

FIGURE 12.6 Individual error rate, $\alpha_{individual}$ (constant dotted line), and family-wise error rate, α_{family} (increasing dotted line), as a function of the size of the family

In the case of individual tests to be perfectly correlated, we would observe:

$$\alpha_{family} = \alpha_{individual}. \tag{12.34}$$

irrespective of the size of the family m. If we cannot assume that tests are independent but not perfectly correlated, one often employs Boole's inequality (the union bound) – for any finite set of tests, the probability that at least one of the tests fails is no greater than the sum of the probabilities of the individual error rates:

$$\alpha_{family} \leq m\alpha_{individual}. \tag{12.35}$$

In order to resolve the discrepancy between individual error rates and family-wise error rate, we present three possible solutions on how to resolve it. In every case below, we assume a family of m tests, and null hypothesis being true for each of them. This is a weaker formulation of the problem. For every test, we measure statistics and obtain set of p-values, p_i, with $i = 1, \dots, m$.

12.3.8.1 Bonferroni Correction

The classical solution to family-wise error rate is a Bonferroni correction, introduced in Dunn (1958). The Bonferroni correction is defined as follows: given we want to set the significance level for the family of tests as α_{family}, we reject the individual test when p_i satisfies:

$$p_i \leq \alpha_{Bonferroni} = \frac{\alpha_{family}}{m}, \tag{12.36}$$

for every i. We denote the corrected significance level at which we reject the null hypothesis as $\alpha_{Bonferroni}$. The Bonferroni correction is implemented as:

```
.quantQ.stats.pBonferroni:{[alpha;m]
   // alpha -- family-wise alpha
   // m -- size of family
   // return Bonferroni alpha
   :alpha%m;
};
```

giving

```
.quantQ.stats.pBonferroni[0.05;100]
```

```
0.0005
```

12.3.8.2 Šidák's Correction

Popular alternative to Bonferroni correction is Šidák's correction, introduced in Šidák (1967). The correction is exact when all tests are statistically independent. When individual tests are positively correlated, the outcome is conservative, while for negatively correlated tests, the outcome of the correction is less stringent and may not perform well. Given that we want to set the significance level for the family of tests as α_{family}, we reject the individual test when p_i satisfies:

$$p_i \leq \alpha_{\check{S}id\acute{a}k} = 1 - (1 - \alpha_{family})^{\frac{1}{m}}, \tag{12.37}$$

for every i. It is implemented as:

```
.quantQ.stats.pSidak:{[alpha;m]
   // alpha -- family-wise alpha
   // m -- size of family
   // return Sidak alpha
   :1-xexp[(1-alpha);1.0%m];
};
```

giving

```
.quantQ.stats.pSidak[0.05;100]
```

```
0.0005128014
```

12.3.8.3 Holm's Method

The Holm's method was introduced in Holm (1979) and provides an algorithm which assures that the family-wise error rate is α_{family}. The method works as follows:

- Sort in ascending order the p-values of all individual hypotheses: $p_{i_1} \leq p_{i_2} \leq \cdots \leq p_{i_m}$. The set of indices i_k orders the hypotheses accordingly, i.e. hypothesis H_{i_1} is the one with lowest p-value.
- For every index i_k, we define the critical value

$$\alpha_{i_k} = \frac{\alpha_{family}}{m + 1 - k}. \tag{12.38}$$

- Find the smallest index, such that

$$p_{i_k} > \alpha_{i_k}. \tag{12.39}$$

- Reject the hypotheses $H_{i_1}, \ldots, H_{i_{k-1}}$. In addition, H_{i_0} stands for no hypothesis to be rejected.

In order to implement the Holm's method, we need to provide an array of m p-values and the family-wise confidence level α_{family}. The implementation reads:

```
.quantQ.stats.pHolm:{[pArray;alpha]
   // alpha -- family-wise alpha
   // pArray -- m-dimensional array of p-values
   // return indices of hypothesis which are rejected
```

```
    :exec index from select from (update alphaHolm: alpha%(count[pArray]+1-i
        ↪ )
        from `pIndividual xasc ([] index: 1+til count[pArray]; pIndividual:
            ↪ pArray))
        where pIndividual<=alphaHolm;
};
```

Let us test the prescribed algorithm on two examples. The first example is composed of 100 random draws, where each draw is made from $U[0, 0.1]$ corresponding to an individual p-value. The second example is the same case but draws are made from $U[0, 0.05]$. The family-wise confidence level is chosen to be $\alpha_{family} = 0.05$. The first example gives:

```
.quantQ.stats.pHolm[100?0.1;0.05]
```

```
`long$()
```

There is no hypothesis which would be rejected such that family-wise confidence level is 0.05.

The second example gives:

```
.quantQ.stats.pHolm[100?0.01;0.05]
```

```
29j, 10j, 49j, 21j, 3j, 64j, 78j
```

There are seven hypotheses rejected altogether, such that the family-wise confidence level is at 0.05. If the underlying problem would be to find the factors, which are correlated with the dependent variable – see the problem at the beginning of this section – we would identify seven factors, which are correlated with the dependent variable at 0.05 confidence level.

12.3.8.4 Example

Finally, let us illustrate the multiple testing bias on the following example, which constitutes a moderately large number of features and still shows that multiple testing has to be performed properly. We have 10 features and 1 dependent variable. We want to make pairwise testing to find out whether there is a potentially dependent link between the feature(s) and the variable we want to model. We collect 1000 data points in our sample and choose confidence level $\alpha = 0.05$. Further, the true data generating process does not have any link between features and the dependent variable. Thus, all detected dependencies are due to Type-I error.

For the set of 10 features, we calculate t_ρ and get the corresponding p-values for a two-sided test against the null hypothesis $\rho = 0$. The question to answer is whether there is a dependence between one or more features and the dependent variable. We perform 1000 realisations of the test.

In the first stage, we collect 1000 arrays of size 10 containing the p-values of the individual tests:

```
pValues:{[x]
dataY:1000?1.0;
dataX:10 1000#10000?1.0;
.quantQ.stats.pValueTwoSided abs .quantQ.stats.tStatsCorr[;count dataY]
    ↪ each cor[dataY;] each dataX} each til 1000;
```

For every realisation of the test, we check whether there is at least one case with p-value below or equal to the confidence level chosen, 0.05. We record the number of realisations when at least one of the features shows statistical dependence:

```
sum {0.05>=min x} each pValues
```

```
413
```

In 41.3% of cases, we detect features which are significantly connected to the dependent variable. Thus, it is likely we may receive false results significantly many more times than the significance level would suggest. Ten features are far from what is usually perceived as a large number, and still, it may lead to a false conclusion quite frequently!

Let us repeat the test while making the Bonferroni correction:

```
sum {.quantQ.stats.pBonferroni[0.05;10]>=min x} each pValues
```

```
15
```

which leads to 15 cases, or, 0.15% cases in relative terms when a significant feature has been identified.

Šidák's correction is performed analogously:

```
sum {.quantQ.stats.pSidak[0.05;10]>=min x} each pValues
```

```
15
```

and leads to the same number of cases when a significant feature has been observed.

Finally, Holm's method has a different functional form to apply, but is still very straightforward:

```
sum {0<count .quantQ.stats.pHolm[x;0.05]} each pValues
```

```
15
```

The number of cases where a significant feature has been detected is the same.

The same results across the three methods is a consequence of our map between t-stats and the corresponding p-value. Our implementation through the lookup table is not granular enough to distinguish the nuances which are experienced in the current case. Nevertheless, all three methods significantly suppress the Type-I error and lead to the correct conclusion more often. We encourage readers to employ a more fine resolution of the map between t-statistic and p-values and thus confirm the difference between the methods. Finally, we encourage readers to explore other ways of applying the problem and observing different outcomes in the three methods.

CHAPTER 13

Linear Regression

In this chapter, we introduce the notion of linear regressions and implement it within q. The linear regression model should be a starting point for nearly any problem where we want to establish a relationship between factors on one side and a dependent variable on the other side. The linear regression is in nature close to understanding the correlation between variables. Why do we start with linear models which model the linear response of the system? The straightforward answer in the spirit of the famous physicist and Nobel prize winner Richard Feynman is "because we can solve them".

Linear regression corresponds to the modelling of a function based on the first-order Taylor expansion in the vicinity of a point x_0:

$$f(x) = f(x_0) + \sum_{i=1}^{n} \frac{\partial}{\partial x_i} f(x_0)(x_i - x_{0,i}) + \textit{residual}, \tag{13.1}$$

which can be ultimately recast into a linear model

$$f(x) \approx A_0 + A_1 x_1 + +A_2 x_2 + \cdots + A_n x_n, \tag{13.2}$$

where

$$A_0 = f(x_0) + \sum_{i=1}^{n} \frac{\partial}{\partial x_i} f(x_0)(-x_{0,i})$$

$$A_i = \frac{\partial}{\partial x_i} f(x_0).$$

In physics, making a linear approximation is a suitable tool to start to explore a new physical problem or to explain an observed phenomenon. Since we have mentioned Richard Feynman, see Veltman et al. (1994) for instance, famous Feynman diagrams for describing the interaction of the subatomic particles are a pictorial representation of an expansion of the interacting Hamiltonians in a small parameter (known as a perturbation expansion). The linear term in the expansion often provides enough insight to make reasonable physical assertions.

The linear models are easy to work with, easy to interpret and give us the first insight into our data. It is one of the most useful techniques in finance, economics and social sciences. Let us borrow a quote from Montgomery et al. (2012):

> Regression analysis is one of the most widely used techniques for analysing multi-factor data. Its broad appeal and usefulness result from the conceptually logical process of using an equation to express the relationship between a variable of interest (the response) and a set of related predictor variables. Regression analysis is also interesting theoretically because of elegant underlying mathematics and a well-developed statistical theory. Successful use of regression requires an appreciation of both the theory and the practical problems that typically arise when the technique is employed with real-world data.

The term "regression" was introduced in an 1886 paper on genetics, evolution, and natural selection, *Regression towards Mediocrity in Hereditary Stature*, Galton (1886). Galton used the word in the sense of "regression towards the mean" or, put more bluntly, "regression towards mediocrity". Galton was a pioneer in statistics. He computed correlations to make sense of empirical data and made extensive use of what would later become known as regression lines (Bulmer, 2003).

In this chapter, we provide the theory underlying the linear regression models and discuss its limitations. In the next chapter, we extend the material presented in this chapter and introduce the regularisation techniques. Regularisation can be considered as an extension, which helps us to generalise models such that they perform better on the unknown samples. This is an essential element to be introduced, and we encourage readers to not stop at this chapter but get straight ahead to the next one. Together, these chapters give the full and concise toolbox.

13.1 LINEAR REGRESSION

Let us start with the definition of the linear regression model. We use the matrix form to present the model. Let us denote $n \in \mathbb{N}*$ the number of data points, $p \in \mathbb{N}*$ the number of features, and $i \in [1, \ldots, n]$ number of observations. The true underlying data generating process reads

$$y_i = \beta_1 x_{i1} + \ldots + \beta_p x_{ip} + \epsilon_i, \tag{13.3}$$

where the variables in the equation are:

- $\boldsymbol{x}_i$ are referred to as the inputs, or also regressors, independent variables, or explanatory variables.
- y_i are referred to as the outputs, or also regressands, or dependent variables.
- ϵ_i are referred to as disturbance, or also noise, or error terms.

We can represent the model analogously in the matrix form:

$$\boldsymbol{y} = \boldsymbol{X}\boldsymbol{\beta} + \boldsymbol{\epsilon}, \tag{13.4}$$

where

$$\boldsymbol{y} = \begin{pmatrix} y_1 \\ y_2 \\ \vdots \\ y_n \end{pmatrix}, \quad \boldsymbol{X} = \begin{pmatrix} \boldsymbol{x}_1^\intercal \\ \boldsymbol{x}_2^\intercal \\ \vdots \\ \boldsymbol{x}_n^\intercal \end{pmatrix} = \begin{pmatrix} x_{11} & x_{12} & \cdots & x_{1p} \\ x_{21} & x_{22} & \cdots & x_{2p} \\ \vdots & \vdots & \ddots & \vdots \\ x_{n1} & x_{n2} & \cdots & x_{np} \end{pmatrix}, \quad \boldsymbol{\beta} = \begin{pmatrix} \beta_1 \\ \beta_2 \\ \vdots \\ \beta_p \end{pmatrix}, \quad \boldsymbol{\epsilon} = \begin{pmatrix} \epsilon_1 \\ \epsilon_2 \\ \vdots \\ \epsilon_n \end{pmatrix}. \tag{13.5}$$

The value of p determines the notation: for $p = 1$, the model is referred to as a simple linear regression model, while for $p > 1$, the model is referred to as a multivariate linear regression model. Variables $\boldsymbol{y}$ and $\boldsymbol{X}$ are given, i.e. provided in the data set. They are arranged in vector and matrix, respectively. On the other hand, vector $\boldsymbol{\epsilon}$ is composed of random variables.

Let us focus on the error terms and the different nature of disturbance and residuals. Let us notice that in eq. (13.4), the term $\boldsymbol{\epsilon}$ is a random vector variable modelling the difference between the regressand $\boldsymbol{y}$ and the deterministic function $\boldsymbol{X}\boldsymbol{\beta}$ involving the regressors $\boldsymbol{X}$. Since $\boldsymbol{y}$ depends on $\boldsymbol{\epsilon}$, it is itself a random variable. However, when we are given $\boldsymbol{y}$ as well as $\boldsymbol{X}$ as data, we can then compute the deterministic quantity

$$\hat{\boldsymbol{\epsilon}} = \boldsymbol{y} - \boldsymbol{X}\boldsymbol{\beta}, \tag{13.6}$$

which we call the residual. Confusingly enough, we use the same notation for $\boldsymbol{y}$ when it is a random variable as for its fixed sample when it is given. To recap, the disturbance is random while the residual is deterministic. Eq, (13.6) is all very well, but we don't actually know $\boldsymbol{\beta}$ in it. Given the data, $\boldsymbol{y}$ and $\boldsymbol{X}$, we need to fit the linear regression model and find a "good enough" estimate for $\boldsymbol{\beta}$, say $\hat{\boldsymbol{\beta}}$.

Eq, (13.6) is actually wrong; it should be

$$\hat{\boldsymbol{\epsilon}} = \boldsymbol{y} - \boldsymbol{X}\hat{\boldsymbol{\beta}}. \tag{13.7}$$

It remains to define the notion of "good enough". We do that by minimising a suitable function of residuals, which has a meaning of information loss between features and dependent variables. This brings us to the ordinary least squares method.

13.2 ORDINARY LEAST SQUARES

In order to formulate the ordinary least squares, we have to make several assumptions:

- for all $i \in [1, \dots, n]$, ϵ_i have a mean of zero, $\mathbb{E}[\epsilon_i] = 0$;
- for all $i \in [1, \dots, n]$, ϵ_i have the same finite variance, $\mathsf{Var}[\epsilon_i] = \sigma^2 < \infty$, in other words, the random variables ϵ_i are homoscedastic;

- for all $i, j \in [1, \ldots, n]$, $i \neq j$, the ϵ_i are uncorrelated, $\mathrm{Cov}[\epsilon_i, \epsilon_j] = 0$;
- the regressors are non-random and observable;
- the regressors are not perfectly linearly correlated with each other.

The ordinary least squares, or OLS, is constructed as follows: we aim to find such a $\boldsymbol{\beta}$ in

$$\boldsymbol{y} = \boldsymbol{X}\boldsymbol{\beta} + \boldsymbol{\epsilon}, \tag{13.8}$$

which will minimise a certain loss function of the residual $\hat{\boldsymbol{\epsilon}} := \boldsymbol{y} - \hat{\boldsymbol{y}}$. We use the squared error, which we'll now call the residual sum of squares (RSS)

$$\mathrm{RSS} = \hat{\boldsymbol{\epsilon}}^\intercal \hat{\boldsymbol{\epsilon}} = (\boldsymbol{y} - \boldsymbol{X}\hat{\boldsymbol{\beta}})^\intercal (\boldsymbol{y} - \boldsymbol{X}\hat{\boldsymbol{\beta}}). \tag{13.9}$$

We will refer to the estimate as $\hat{\boldsymbol{\beta}}$ that will give us the estimate of $\boldsymbol{y}$,

$$\hat{\boldsymbol{y}} := \boldsymbol{X}\hat{\boldsymbol{\beta}}. \tag{13.10}$$

The OLS estimator is given as:

$$\hat{\boldsymbol{\beta}} = (\boldsymbol{X}^\intercal \boldsymbol{X})^{-1} \boldsymbol{X}^\intercal \boldsymbol{y}. \tag{13.11}$$

We can prove this by first rewriting the RSS:

$$\mathrm{RSS} = \hat{\boldsymbol{\epsilon}}^\intercal \hat{\boldsymbol{\epsilon}} = (\boldsymbol{y} - \boldsymbol{X}\boldsymbol{\beta})^\intercal (\boldsymbol{y} - \boldsymbol{X}\boldsymbol{\beta}) = \boldsymbol{y}^\intercal \boldsymbol{y} - 2\boldsymbol{y}^\intercal \boldsymbol{X}\boldsymbol{\beta} + \boldsymbol{\beta}^\intercal \boldsymbol{X}^\intercal \boldsymbol{X}\boldsymbol{\beta}. \tag{13.12}$$

Using the denominator notation for vector-by-vector and scalar-by-vector derivatives,

$$\nabla_{\boldsymbol{\beta}} \mathrm{RSS} = \frac{\partial \mathrm{RSS}}{\partial \boldsymbol{\beta}} = -2\boldsymbol{X}^\intercal \boldsymbol{y} + 2\boldsymbol{X}^\intercal \boldsymbol{X}\boldsymbol{\beta}. \tag{13.13}$$

When $\nabla_{\boldsymbol{\beta}} \mathrm{RSS} = 0$, we get $\boldsymbol{X}^\intercal \boldsymbol{X}\boldsymbol{\beta} = \boldsymbol{X}^\intercal \boldsymbol{y}$ (this is the so-called normal equation), hence we obtain the solution $\boldsymbol{\beta} = (\boldsymbol{X}^\intercal \boldsymbol{X})^{-1} \boldsymbol{X}^\intercal \boldsymbol{y}$. To check that this critical point is a minimum, we examine the Hessian matrix

$$\frac{\partial}{\partial \boldsymbol{\beta}} \left(\frac{\partial \mathrm{RSS}}{\partial \boldsymbol{\beta}} \right) = 2\boldsymbol{X}^\intercal \boldsymbol{X}. \tag{13.14}$$

If $\boldsymbol{X}$ is full rank (i.e. has rank $p + 1$ if we allow the intercept and p if we don't; this implies that $\boldsymbol{X}$ is skinny or square), then $\boldsymbol{X}^\intercal \boldsymbol{X}$ is positive definite and the critical point is indeed a minimum.

The important feature of the OLS estimator is that it is unbiased, i.e. conditional expectation of the estimator is the true value:

$$\mathbb{E}[\hat{\boldsymbol{\beta}} \mid \boldsymbol{X}] = \mathbb{E}[(\boldsymbol{X}^\intercal \boldsymbol{X})^{-1} \boldsymbol{X}^\intercal \boldsymbol{y} \mid \boldsymbol{X}] \tag{13.15}$$

$$= (\boldsymbol{X}^\intercal \boldsymbol{X})^{-1} \boldsymbol{X}^\intercal \mathbb{E}[\boldsymbol{y} \mid \boldsymbol{X}] \tag{13.16}$$

$$= (\boldsymbol{X}^\intercal \boldsymbol{X})^{-1} \boldsymbol{X}^\intercal \boldsymbol{X}\boldsymbol{\beta} = \boldsymbol{\beta}. \tag{13.17}$$

The estimator of $\boldsymbol{\beta}$ is for a given sample random variable. The variance of the estimator can be derived as:

$$\begin{aligned}\mathsf{Var}[\hat{\boldsymbol{\beta}}] &:= \mathbb{E}[(\hat{\boldsymbol{\beta}} - \mathbb{E}[\hat{\boldsymbol{\beta}}])\,(\hat{\boldsymbol{\beta}} - \mathbb{E}[\hat{\boldsymbol{\beta}}])^{\intercal}] \\ &= \mathbb{E}[((\boldsymbol{X}^{\intercal}\boldsymbol{X})^{-1}\boldsymbol{X}^{\intercal}\boldsymbol{\epsilon})\,((\boldsymbol{X}^{\intercal}\boldsymbol{X})^{-1}\boldsymbol{X}^{\intercal}\boldsymbol{\epsilon})^{\intercal}] \\ &= \mathbb{E}[((\boldsymbol{X}^{\intercal}\boldsymbol{X})^{-1}\boldsymbol{X}^{\intercal}\boldsymbol{\epsilon})\,(\boldsymbol{\epsilon}^{\intercal}(\boldsymbol{X}^{\intercal})^{\intercal}((\boldsymbol{X}^{\intercal}\boldsymbol{X})^{-1})^{\intercal})] \\ &= \mathbb{E}[((\boldsymbol{X}^{\intercal}\boldsymbol{X})^{-1}\boldsymbol{X}^{\intercal}\boldsymbol{\epsilon})\,(\boldsymbol{\epsilon}^{\intercal}\boldsymbol{X}((\boldsymbol{X}^{\intercal}\boldsymbol{X})^{\intercal})^{-1})] \\ &= \mathbb{E}[((\boldsymbol{X}^{\intercal}\boldsymbol{X})^{-1}\boldsymbol{X}^{\intercal}\boldsymbol{\epsilon})\,(\boldsymbol{\epsilon}^{\intercal}\boldsymbol{X}(\boldsymbol{X}^{\intercal}\boldsymbol{X})^{-1})] \\ &= \mathbb{E}[((\boldsymbol{X}^{\intercal}\boldsymbol{X})^{-1}\boldsymbol{X}^{\intercal})\,(\boldsymbol{\epsilon}\boldsymbol{\epsilon}^{\intercal})(\boldsymbol{X}(\boldsymbol{X}^{\intercal}\boldsymbol{X})^{-1})].\end{aligned}$$

where we need assumptions imposed on the linear model to proceed with calculation, namely that $\mathbb{E}[\boldsymbol{\epsilon}] = \boldsymbol{0}_n$ and $\mathsf{Var}[\boldsymbol{\epsilon}] = \sigma^2\boldsymbol{I}_n$, for some constant $\sigma < \infty$, which is the case when the following three assumptions from the classical linear regression model (CLRM) hold:

- for all $i \in [1, \dots, n]$, ϵ_i have a mean of zero, $\mathbb{E}[\epsilon_i] = 0$;
- for all $i \in [1, \dots, n]$, ϵ_i have the same finite variance, $\mathsf{Var}[\epsilon_i] = \sigma^2 < \infty$, in other words, the random variables ϵ_i are homoscedastic;
- for all $i, j \in [1, \dots, n]$, $i \neq j$, the ϵ_i are uncorrelated, $\mathrm{Cov}[\epsilon_i, \epsilon_j] = 0$.

Then $\mathbb{E}[\boldsymbol{\epsilon}\boldsymbol{\epsilon}^{\intercal}] = \sigma^2\boldsymbol{I}_n$ and

$$\begin{aligned}\mathsf{Var}[\hat{\boldsymbol{\beta}}] &= \mathbb{E}[((\boldsymbol{X}^{\intercal}\boldsymbol{X})^{-1}\boldsymbol{X}^{\intercal})(\boldsymbol{\epsilon}\boldsymbol{\epsilon}^{\intercal})(\boldsymbol{X}(\boldsymbol{X}^{\intercal}\boldsymbol{X})^{-1})] \\ &= \mathbb{E}[((\boldsymbol{X}^{\intercal}\boldsymbol{X})^{-1}\boldsymbol{X}^{\intercal})(\sigma^2\boldsymbol{I}_n)(\boldsymbol{X}(\boldsymbol{X}^{\intercal}\boldsymbol{X})^{-1})] \\ &= \sigma^2\mathbb{E}[((\boldsymbol{X}^{\intercal}\boldsymbol{X})^{-1}\boldsymbol{X}^{\intercal})(\boldsymbol{X}(\boldsymbol{X}^{\intercal}\boldsymbol{X})^{-1})] \\ &= \sigma^2\mathbb{E}[(\boldsymbol{X}^{\intercal}\boldsymbol{X})^{-1}(\boldsymbol{X}^{\intercal}\boldsymbol{X})(\boldsymbol{X}^{\intercal}\boldsymbol{X})^{-1}] \\ &= \sigma^2\mathbb{E}[\boldsymbol{I}_p(\boldsymbol{X}^{\intercal}\boldsymbol{X})^{-1}] = \sigma^2\mathbb{E}[(\boldsymbol{X}^{\intercal}\boldsymbol{X})^{-1}].\end{aligned}$$

If we were also to assume that the regressors, $\boldsymbol{X}$, are non-random and observable (another assumption from CLRM), we could get rid of the expectation operator and write $\mathsf{Var}[\hat{\boldsymbol{\beta}}] = \sigma^2(\boldsymbol{X}^{\intercal}\boldsymbol{X})^{-1}$.

When we are writing $(\boldsymbol{X}^{\intercal}\boldsymbol{X})^{-1}$ anywhere, we are also making another assumption from CLRM: that the regressors are not perfectly linearly correlated with each other; thus $\boldsymbol{X}$ is full rank, and therefore the inverse of the Gram matrix does exist.

13.3 THE GEOMETRIC REPRESENTATION OF LINEAR REGRESSION

In order to work with linear regressions and make the most of it, it is fundamental to understand the geometric representation of the OLS. For that purpose, we will work with a simple example: we are given the linear model:

$$\boldsymbol{y} = \boldsymbol{X}\boldsymbol{\beta} + \boldsymbol{\epsilon}, \tag{13.18}$$

where

$$\boldsymbol{X} = \begin{pmatrix} 1 \\ 3 \\ 4 \end{pmatrix}, \boldsymbol{y} = \begin{pmatrix} 2 \\ 1 \\ 2 \end{pmatrix}, \boldsymbol{\epsilon} = \begin{pmatrix} \epsilon_1 \\ \epsilon_2 \\ \epsilon_3 \end{pmatrix}. \tag{13.19}$$

Our aim is to find an estimate $\boldsymbol{\beta}$. Here $p = 1$ (we have a single feature) and $n = 3$ (we have three data points). Our data set consists of three data points, three (x_i, y_i) pairs: $(1, 2), (3, 1), (4, 2)$. Because $p = 1$, all our x_i are univariate: 1, 3, and 4.

In the OLS procedure, we are fitting the regression line such that we are minimising the sum of squares of residuals. Figure 13.1 depicts the objective function of the OLS procedure: we minimise the distance of every point from the regression line. The distance is depicted as a dashed line in the figure.

It is worth stressing that we define the distance of a point to the fitted line using the projection on y axis. This is not the shortest distance we can come up with. Figure 13.2 depicts on the other hand the distance between the fitted line and the observed data defined as orthogonal projection, i.e. the shortest physical distance of a point to the fitted line. This objective function is used in other machine learning methods like Vector Support Machines or Principal Component Analysis (PCA).

The OLS solution to the presented problem reads:

$$\begin{aligned} \hat{\boldsymbol{\beta}} &= (\boldsymbol{X}^\top \boldsymbol{X})^{-1} \boldsymbol{X}^\top \boldsymbol{y} \\ &= (1^2 + 3^2 + 4^2)^{-1}(1 \cdot 2 + 3 \cdot 1 + 4 \cdot 2) = \frac{1}{2} \end{aligned}$$

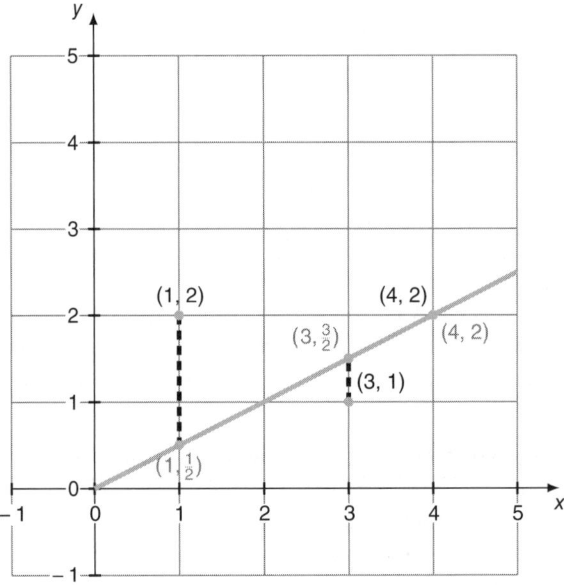

FIGURE 13.1 The objective of the OLS procedure

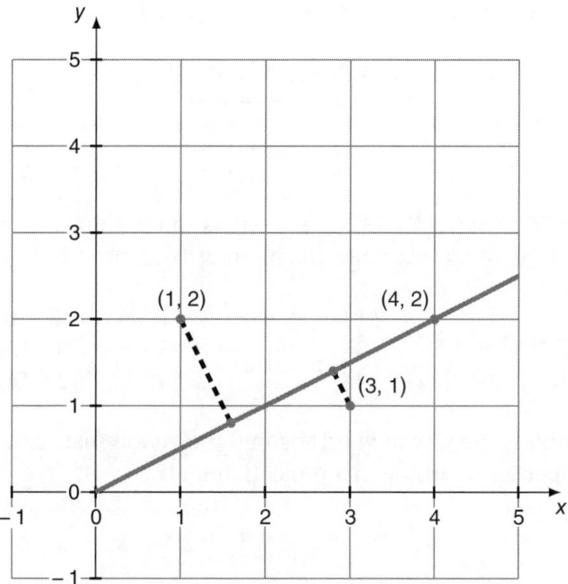

FIGURE 13.2 The orthogonal distance for linear fit

giving the projected values of $\boldsymbol{y}$

$$\hat{\boldsymbol{y}} = \boldsymbol{X}\hat{\boldsymbol{\beta}} = \begin{pmatrix} 1 \\ 3 \\ 4 \end{pmatrix} \cdot \frac{1}{2} = \begin{pmatrix} 1/2 \\ 3/2 \\ 2 \end{pmatrix}. \tag{13.20}$$

13.3.1 Moore–Penrose Pseudoinverse

Let's have a look at our $\hat{\boldsymbol{\beta}}$ in more detail:

$$\hat{\boldsymbol{\beta}} = \underbrace{(\boldsymbol{X}^\intercal \boldsymbol{X})^{-1}\boldsymbol{X}^\intercal}_{\boldsymbol{X}^+} \boldsymbol{y},$$

where $\boldsymbol{X}^+$ is called the Moore–Penrose pseudoinverse matrix of $\boldsymbol{X}$. In our example, we get

$$\boldsymbol{X}^+ = (\boldsymbol{X}^\intercal \boldsymbol{X})^{-1}\boldsymbol{X}^\intercal = (1^2 + 3^2 + 4^2)^{-1} \begin{pmatrix} 1 & 3 & 4 \end{pmatrix} = \begin{pmatrix} \frac{1}{26} & \frac{3}{26} & \frac{4}{26} \end{pmatrix}. \tag{13.21}$$

One of its properties is $(\boldsymbol{X}\boldsymbol{X}^+)\boldsymbol{X} = \boldsymbol{X}$; in other words, $\boldsymbol{X}\boldsymbol{X}^+$ maps all column vectors of $\boldsymbol{X}$ to themselves while $\boldsymbol{X}\boldsymbol{X}^+$ need not be the identity matrix. Namely,

$$(\boldsymbol{X}\boldsymbol{X}^+)\boldsymbol{X} = \left[\begin{pmatrix} 1 \\ 3 \\ 4 \end{pmatrix} \begin{pmatrix} \frac{1}{26} & \frac{3}{26} & \frac{4}{26} \end{pmatrix}\right] \begin{pmatrix} 1 \\ 3 \\ 4 \end{pmatrix} = \begin{pmatrix} 1/26 & 3/26 & 4/26 \\ 3/26 & 9/26 & 12/26 \\ 4/26 & 12/26 & 16/26 \end{pmatrix} \begin{pmatrix} 1 \\ 3 \\ 4 \end{pmatrix} = \begin{pmatrix} 1 \\ 3 \\ 4 \end{pmatrix}. \tag{13.22}$$

Then, we can explore the properties of the projected y:

$$\hat{\boldsymbol{y}} = \boldsymbol{X}\hat{\boldsymbol{\beta}} = \underbrace{\boldsymbol{X}\underbrace{(\boldsymbol{X}^\top\boldsymbol{X})^{-1}\boldsymbol{X}^\top}_{\boldsymbol{X}^+}}_{\boldsymbol{H}}\boldsymbol{y}, \tag{13.23}$$

where the matrix $\boldsymbol{H} := \boldsymbol{X}(\boldsymbol{X}^\top\boldsymbol{X})^{-1}\boldsymbol{X}^\top$ is known as the hat matrix – because it takes $\boldsymbol{y}$ and puts a hat on it, $\hat{\boldsymbol{y}}$. In our example, the hat matrix reads:

$$\boldsymbol{H} = \boldsymbol{X}(\boldsymbol{X}^\top\boldsymbol{X})^{-1}\boldsymbol{X}^\top = \boldsymbol{X}\boldsymbol{X}^+ = \begin{pmatrix}1\\3\\4\end{pmatrix}\begin{pmatrix}\frac{1}{26} & \frac{3}{26} & \frac{4}{26}\end{pmatrix} = \begin{pmatrix}1/26 & 3/26 & 4/26\\ 3/26 & 9/26 & 12/26\\ 4/26 & 12/26 & 16/26\end{pmatrix}. \tag{13.24}$$

Matrix $\boldsymbol{H}$ is one of the so-called orthogonal projection matrices. Let us check that it has the two properties of orthogonal projection matrices:

Symmetric

The matrix is symmetric as can be seen from:

$$\boldsymbol{H}^\top = (\boldsymbol{X}(\boldsymbol{X}^\top\boldsymbol{X})^{-1}\boldsymbol{X}^\top)^\top \tag{13.25}$$

$$= (\boldsymbol{X}^\top)^\top[(\boldsymbol{X}^\top\boldsymbol{X})^{-1}]^\top\boldsymbol{X}^\top \tag{13.26}$$

$$= \boldsymbol{X}[(\boldsymbol{X}^\top\boldsymbol{X})^\top]^{-1}\boldsymbol{X}^\top \tag{13.27}$$

$$= \boldsymbol{X}(\boldsymbol{X}^\top\boldsymbol{X})^{-1}\boldsymbol{X}^\top = \boldsymbol{H}. \tag{13.28}$$

Idempotent

The matrix is idempotent:

$$\boldsymbol{H}^2 = (\boldsymbol{X}(\boldsymbol{X}^\top\boldsymbol{X})^{-1}\boldsymbol{X}^\top)(\boldsymbol{X}(\boldsymbol{X}^\top\boldsymbol{X})^{-1}\boldsymbol{X}^\top) \tag{13.29}$$

$$= \boldsymbol{X}[(\boldsymbol{X}^\top\boldsymbol{X})^{-1}(\boldsymbol{X}^\top\boldsymbol{X})](\boldsymbol{X}^\top\boldsymbol{X})^{-1}\boldsymbol{X}^\top \tag{13.30}$$

$$= \boldsymbol{X}(\boldsymbol{X}^\top\boldsymbol{X})^{-1}\boldsymbol{X}^\top = \boldsymbol{H}. \tag{13.31}$$

It may seem to be confusing that $\boldsymbol{H}$ is orthogonal projection, though we actually decided to minimise the lengths defined in Figure 13.1, i.e. $\boldsymbol{y} - \hat{\boldsymbol{y}} = \boldsymbol{y} - \boldsymbol{X}\hat{\boldsymbol{\beta}}$, rather than the one in Figure 13.2.

The conflicting interpretation of the orthogonal projection is not real. The point of view hides orthogonal projection we took to visualise the data. In Figure 13.1, we use the plot which represents the so-called variable space view, $\mathbb{R}^p$, view of the linear regression: here each data point is indeed represented by a point, and the dimensions represent the features. Here we can see the regression line.

In order to see the orthogonal projection, we have to use the so-called subject space view, which is $\mathbb{R}^n$. It is of different dimension relative to the objective space.

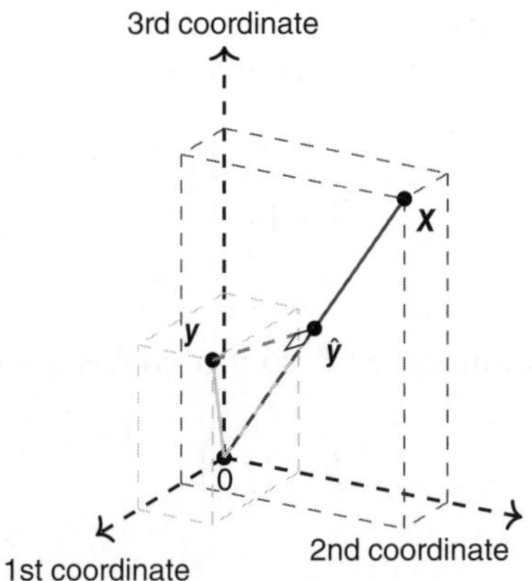

FIGURE 13.3 Visualisation of the linear regression in the subject space

Figure 13.3 depicts the regression problem we face in the variable space. Here y and $\hat{y}$ appear as vectors represented by lines and the dimensions represent the data points. The orthogonal projection was hidden on the variable space view but became revealed on the subject space view. This in itself is a useful lesson in data science.

In Figure 13.3, we find our OLS solution by orthogonally projecting $\boldsymbol{y}$ (the light gray line) onto the column space of $\boldsymbol{X}$ (the dark gray line or hyperplane) – see the dashed gray line on the right plot.

In summary:

- The hat matrix, $\boldsymbol{H}$ is an orthogonal projection matrix that projects $\boldsymbol{y}$ onto the column space of $\boldsymbol{X}$ – the space spanned by the column vectors of $\boldsymbol{X}$.
- The result, $\hat{\boldsymbol{y}}$, is a linear combination of the columns of $\boldsymbol{X}$.
- The weights in this linear combination are given by the elements of $\hat{\boldsymbol{\beta}}$.
- In our example, $p = 1$, so $\boldsymbol{X}$ has a single column. Thus the result, $\hat{\boldsymbol{y}}$, is a scalar multiple of that column, the scalar being our $\hat{\beta} = \frac{1}{2}$:

$$\hat{\boldsymbol{y}} = \boldsymbol{H}\boldsymbol{y} = \begin{pmatrix} 1/26 & 3/26 & 4/26 \\ 3/26 & 9/26 & 12/26 \\ 4/26 & 12/26 & 16/26 \end{pmatrix} \begin{pmatrix} 2 \\ 1 \\ 2 \end{pmatrix} = \begin{pmatrix} 1/2 \\ 3/2 \\ 2 \end{pmatrix} = \underbrace{\frac{1}{2}}_{\hat{\beta}} \underbrace{\begin{pmatrix} 1 \\ 3 \\ 4 \end{pmatrix}}_{\text{the single column of } \boldsymbol{X}}.$$

13.3.2 Adding Intercept

The solution we have defined so far is not the one we would likely use for practical considerations. If our goal is the line which fits the three data points the best, having $(x_1, \hat{y}_1) = (1, 1/2)$, $(x_2, \hat{y}_2) = (3, 3/2)$, $(x_3, \hat{y}_3) = (4, 2)$ is not the solution. The reason is that the chosen line goes through the origin. This is significant, and unless we want to impose it explicitly, we should release the intercept to take any value.

Including intercept within our framework is easy. We just prepend a column of ones to $\boldsymbol{X}$, so it becomes the $n \times (p+1)$-dimensional matrix:

$$\boldsymbol{X} = \begin{pmatrix} 1 & 1 \\ 1 & 3 \\ 1 & 4 \end{pmatrix}, \tag{13.32}$$

and prepend β_0 to the column vector $\hat{\boldsymbol{\beta}}$, so it becomes the $p+1$-dimensional column vector

$$\hat{\boldsymbol{\beta}} = \begin{pmatrix} \hat{\beta}_0 \\ \hat{\beta}_1 \end{pmatrix}. \tag{13.33}$$

We then proceed as before. In particular, for $n \in \mathbb{N}^*, p \in \mathbb{N}^*, i \in [1, \ldots, n]$,

$$y_i = \beta_0 + \beta_1 x_{i1} + \ldots + \beta_p x_{ip} + \epsilon_i, \tag{13.34}$$

or, in matrix form,

$$\boldsymbol{y} = \boldsymbol{X}\boldsymbol{\beta} + \boldsymbol{\epsilon},$$

where

$$\boldsymbol{y} = \begin{pmatrix} y_1 \\ y_2 \\ \vdots \\ y_n \end{pmatrix}, \quad \boldsymbol{X} = \begin{pmatrix} 1 & \boldsymbol{x}_1^\intercal \\ 1 & \boldsymbol{x}_2^\intercal \\ \vdots & \vdots \\ 1 & \boldsymbol{x}_n^\intercal \end{pmatrix} = \begin{pmatrix} 1 & x_{11} & x_{12} & \cdots & x_{1p} \\ 1 & x_{21} & x_{22} & \cdots & x_{2p} \\ \vdots & \vdots & \vdots & \ddots & \vdots \\ 1 & x_{n1} & x_{n2} & \cdots & x_{np} \end{pmatrix}, \quad \boldsymbol{\beta} = \begin{pmatrix} \beta_0 \\ \beta_1 \\ \vdots \\ \beta_p \end{pmatrix}, \quad \boldsymbol{\epsilon} = \begin{pmatrix} \epsilon_1 \\ \epsilon_2 \\ \vdots \\ \epsilon_n \end{pmatrix}.$$

We can calculate the Moore-Penrose pseudoinverse matrix of $\boldsymbol{X}$ as

$$\boldsymbol{X}^+ = (\boldsymbol{X}^\intercal\boldsymbol{X})^{-1}\boldsymbol{X}^\intercal = \left[\begin{pmatrix} 1 & 1 & 1 \\ 1 & 3 & 4 \end{pmatrix}\begin{pmatrix} 1 & 1 \\ 1 & 3 \\ 1 & 4 \end{pmatrix}\right]^{-1}\begin{pmatrix} 1 & 1 & 1 \\ 1 & 3 & 4 \end{pmatrix} \tag{13.35}$$

$$= \begin{pmatrix} 3 & 8 \\ 8 & 26 \end{pmatrix}^{-1}\begin{pmatrix} 1 & 1 & 1 \\ 1 & 3 & 4 \end{pmatrix} \tag{13.36}$$

$$= \frac{1}{14}\begin{pmatrix} 26 & -8 \\ -8 & 3 \end{pmatrix}\begin{pmatrix} 1 & 1 & 1 \\ 1 & 3 & 4 \end{pmatrix} \tag{13.37}$$

$$= \frac{1}{14}\begin{pmatrix} 18 & 2 & -6 \\ -5 & 1 & 4 \end{pmatrix}. \tag{13.38}$$

Hence

$$\hat{\boldsymbol{\beta}} = \boldsymbol{X}^+\boldsymbol{y} = \frac{1}{14}\begin{pmatrix} 18 & 2 & -6 \\ -5 & 1 & 4 \end{pmatrix}\begin{pmatrix} 2 \\ 1 \\ 2 \end{pmatrix} = \begin{pmatrix} 13/7 \\ -1/14 \end{pmatrix} = \begin{pmatrix} \beta_0 \\ \beta_1 \end{pmatrix}, \tag{13.39}$$

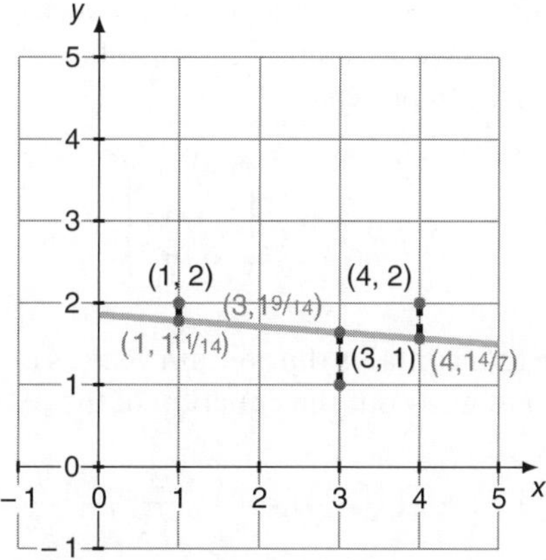

FIGURE 13.4 The OLS solution with intercept included

and

$$\hat{\boldsymbol{y}} = \boldsymbol{X}\hat{\boldsymbol{\beta}} = \begin{pmatrix} 1 & 1 \\ 1 & 3 \\ 1 & 4 \end{pmatrix} \begin{pmatrix} 13/7 \\ -1/14 \end{pmatrix} = \begin{pmatrix} 25/14 \\ 23/14 \\ 11/7 \end{pmatrix} = \hat{\beta}_0 \begin{pmatrix} 1 \\ 1 \\ 1 \end{pmatrix} + \hat{\beta}_1 \begin{pmatrix} 1 \\ 3 \\ 4 \end{pmatrix}. \tag{13.40}$$

We can visualise the solution in the variable space. Figure 13.4 depicts the regression line which is a solution to the OLS problem. The slope changed compared to the case when we enforced the fit going through the intercept. Visually, the distances of the observed points from the fitted line are significantly shorter compared to the restricted case. We thus obtain a better fit.

When we add the intercept, the hat matrix now projects onto a plane, not onto a line. Namely, the hat matrix becomes:

$$\boldsymbol{H} = \boldsymbol{X}(\boldsymbol{X}^\intercal \boldsymbol{X})^{-1}\boldsymbol{X}^\intercal \tag{13.41}$$

$$= \boldsymbol{X}\boldsymbol{X}^+ \tag{13.42}$$

$$= \begin{pmatrix} 1 & 1 \\ 1 & 3 \\ 1 & 4 \end{pmatrix} \left[\frac{1}{14} \begin{pmatrix} 18 & 2 & -6 \\ -5 & 1 & 4 \end{pmatrix} \right] \tag{13.43}$$

$$= \frac{1}{14} \begin{pmatrix} 13 & 3 & -2 \\ 3 & 5 & 6 \\ -2 & 6 & 10 \end{pmatrix}. \tag{13.44}$$

As before, it projects $\boldsymbol{y}$ onto the column space of $\boldsymbol{X}$, the resulting projection being $\hat{\boldsymbol{y}}$. However, now $\boldsymbol{X}$ has two (linearly independent) columns, not one, so the projection is onto a plane, not onto a line. If we increase p and add more columns to $\boldsymbol{X}$, if these columns are linearly independent, we will further increase the dimension of the column space of $\boldsymbol{X}$ onto which we project.

Recall that the equation of a plane orthogonal to a vector $\boldsymbol{a}$ and containing a point $\boldsymbol{x}_0$ is given by $\boldsymbol{a}^\intercal(\boldsymbol{x} - \boldsymbol{x}_0) = 0$. (We are simply stating a fact: $\boldsymbol{a}$ and $\boldsymbol{x} - \boldsymbol{x}_0$ (the latter lies on the plane) are orthogonal.) In our case,

$$\hat{\varepsilon} = \boldsymbol{y} - \hat{\boldsymbol{y}} = \begin{pmatrix} 3/14 \\ -9/14 \\ 3/7 \end{pmatrix}, \tag{13.45}$$

is orthogonal to the plane that contains the column vectors of $\boldsymbol{X}$: $(1\ 1\ 1)^\intercal$ and $(1\ 3\ 4)^\intercal$. We can use either of them to work out the equation of the plane:

$$\frac{3}{14}(x_1 - 1) - \frac{9}{14}(x_2 - 3) + \frac{3}{7}(x_3 - 4) = 0 \Rightarrow \frac{3}{14}x_1 - \frac{9}{14}x_2 + \frac{3}{7}x_3 = 0. \tag{13.46}$$

The resulting OLS solution is a linear combination of the columns of $\boldsymbol{X}$, the weights being given by the elements of $\hat{\boldsymbol{\beta}}$:

$$\hat{\boldsymbol{y}} = \boldsymbol{X}\hat{\boldsymbol{\beta}} = \begin{pmatrix} 25/14 \\ 23/14 \\ 11/7 \end{pmatrix} = \hat{\beta}_0 \begin{pmatrix} 1 \\ 1 \\ 1 \end{pmatrix} + \hat{\beta}_1 \begin{pmatrix} 1 \\ 3 \\ 4 \end{pmatrix}, \tag{13.47}$$

where $\hat{\beta}_0$ is, by construction, the y-intercept of the regression line and $\hat{\beta}_1$ is its gradient.

13.4 IMPLEMENTATION OF THE OLS

In this section, we implement the linear regression model in q. Following the underlying implementation, we discuss several advanced topics related to linear regression. Our final objective is to unite the code elements into an estimation suite which presents an alternative to linear regression toolboxes in other programming languages.

Before we start building the implementation in q, let us create a sample data set. Let us use the `multiNormal` function to generate the random sample and define independent variables:

```
simData: .quantQ.simul.multiNormal[4;1000;(1.0;neg[1.0];2.0;0.0);((1.0 0.0
    ↪ 0.0 0.0);(0.0 1.0 0.0 0.0);(0.0 0.0 1.0 0.0);(0.0 0.0 0.0 1.0))];
// create artificial dataset
x1:simData[`var1];
x2:simData[`var2];
x3:simData[`var3];
err:0.1*simData[`var4];
```

We choose a simple well-rounded linear model as the example used for the illustration of the OLS technique:

```
y:1.0+(1.0*x1)+(neg[1.0]*x2)+(2.0*x3)+err;
```

```
cor[x1;x2]
```

```
-0.03305148
```

```
cor[x1;x3]
```

```
0.03556649
```

```
cor[x2;x3]
```

```
0.03963119
```

```
cor[x1;y]
```

```
0.4386312
```

```
cor[x2;y]
```

```
-0.3844332
```

```
cor[x3;y]
```

```
0.8172105
```

The correlation reflects the model as we set it up. Let us remind the reader that the correlation coefficient does not correspond to the parameters of the linear model as the variance of the features is not normalised. Further, for convenience, we arrange the data into the table – a more natural data structure.

```
tabData:([] y:y; x1:x1;x2:x2;x3:x3);
```

Let us make an important note at this point about constants. In econometric literature, the constant plays a special role as it is frequently treated separately. For instance, a number of parameters in the linear model may be referred to a number of parameters corresponding to non-constant features. We thus remind the reader to check the convention when comparing different books. In the following text, we will consider constant as a regular feature, which is constant and equal to 1 for every observation. Thus, we add a constant term into our data table:

```
tabData: update const:1.0 from tabData;
tabData
```

```
y         x1         x2         x3       const
----------------------------------------------
11.82698 2.454263   -3.583155  2.456235  1
8.505473 3.91833    -0.7588861 1.390334  1
5.311374 0.5955665  0.1658444  2.04283   1
4.649372 -1.856926  -2.036408  1.723693  1
```

```
9.295402 -0.6730472 -1.952683  3.506369  1
6.65504  0.3517425  -2.000512  1.566093  1
7.12083  0.01475878 -1.554944  2.233064  1
8.331946 2.104604   -1.420382  1.810523  1
8.308305 1.870071   -1.473924  1.935104  1
13.51147 2.348974   -2.671633  3.728308  1
..
```

The OLS estimation is based on solving the system of linear equations with Moore–Penrose pseudoinverse of matrix $\boldsymbol{X}$. We take this opportunity to remind the reader that we can formulate the solution to the OLS as:

$$\hat{\boldsymbol{\beta}}^T = \boldsymbol{y}^T \boldsymbol{X}^{+T} = \boldsymbol{Y}^T \boldsymbol{X}(\boldsymbol{X}^T \boldsymbol{X})^{-1}. \tag{13.48}$$

We choose this formulation for convenience; this affects the two building blocks we have to define to calculate the solutions to the problem: first, we need to define $\boldsymbol{Y}^T \boldsymbol{X}$:

```
ytx: enlist tabData[`y] mmu flip[tabData[`const`x1`x2`x3]];
```

and then also $\boldsymbol{X}^T \boldsymbol{X}$

```
xtx: x mmu flip[x:tabData[`const`x1`x2`x3]];
```

We then solve the equation for the β's using the `lsq` verb corresponding to:

$$\boldsymbol{Y}^T \boldsymbol{X} = \hat{\boldsymbol{\beta}}^T (\boldsymbol{X}^T \boldsymbol{X}), \tag{13.49}$$

given as:

```
solution: ytx lsq xtx;
solution
```

```
enlist 1.010413 0.9998791 -0.9974519 1.996775
```

The solution is an enlisted list of estimated parameters corresponding to features `` `const`x1`x2`x3 ``, in a given order. The provided code allows us to find a solution for more than one set of dependent variables `y`, i.e. the column `` `y `` in the `tabData` table can be itself composed of lists instead of float atoms. The usual problems where we need OLS do not give us more than one dependent variable, and thus we restrict ourselves to situations where we will have just one. In such a case, we need to get the solution from the list:

```
beta:first solution;
beta
```

```
1.010413 0.9998791 -0.9974519 1.996775
```

We have thus obtained the solution in the form:

$$y = 1.010413 + 0.9998791 * x_1 - 0.9974519 * x_2 + 1.996775 * x_3. \tag{13.50}$$

The estimated coefficients truthfully reflect the true coefficients. The comparison is visual. In order to establish a statistical link, we need to estimate the properties of the estimator. In particular, we calculate the variance-covariance matrix of the estimate. The diagonal terms of the matrix are the errors of the estimated values, or rather its squares. The variance-covariance matrix reads:

```
varcov:(inv flip[xtx])*sum (1.0%(count[tabData[`y]]-count[beta]))*t*t:
    ↪ tabData[`y]-sum[beta*x: tabData[`const`x1`x2`x3]];
varcov
```

```
6.827689e-005   -9.232866e-006 1.015537e-005   -1.941069e-005
-9.232866e-006 1.028248e-005   3.473323e-007   -3.667938e-007
1.015537e-005   3.473323e-007   9.851538e-006   -3.972302e-007
-1.941069e-005 -3.667938e-007 -3.972302e-007 9.596056e-006
```

It is then straightforward to extract the sample errors of the estimated parameters:

```
errors:{sqrt x[y;y]}[varcov;] each til count varcov;
```

Let us make clear that the size of the sample does not normalise the errors. This will be done when we calculate the statistical properties of the estimates, namely, the t-statistic. Before we do that, let us summarise the results we have obtained so far in the form of a table:

```
([] variable: `x1`x2`x3`const;beta: beta; errors:{sqrt x[y;y]}[varcov;]
    ↪ each til count varcov)
```

```
variable beta       errors
------------------------------
x1       1.010413   0.008262983
x2       0.9998791  0.00320663
x3       -0.9974519 0.003138716
const    1.996775   0.00309775
```

This concludes the estimation of the parameters of the OLS problem for a linear equation. In the following sections, we define several additional features, which complement the statistical information about the estimates and the estimated model.

13.5 SIGNIFICANCE OF PARAMETERS

In the previous section we calculated the OLS estimates of the parameters of a linear model. In this section, we assess the significance of the estimated parameters. First, we calculate the t-statistic:

```
tStats:beta%errors%sqrt count y;
```

The t-statistic is distributed according to the t-distribution with degrees of freedom equal to a number of observations, N. We can evaluate the null hypothesis that a given coefficient comes from the distribution with zero mean. In order to evaluate the hypothesis, we need to be able to calculate the t-distribution with general degrees of freedom. We overcome this task by sticking to approximation $N \to \infty$, where the t-distribution converges to a normal distribution.

Further, we may not need the probability at which we may reject the null hypothesis itself, but rather to check whether we can reject the null at several benchmark values. In particular, we stick to 90%, 95%, 99% and 99.9%, respectively. We will use the "$*$" notation, where $*$ stands for a situation where we can reject the null at 90% confidence level, but not at a higher confidence level. Analogously, the case of $**$ corresponds to 95% confidence level, $***$ corresponds to 99%, and $****$ corresponds to 99.9%, respectively. Thus, having with every estimated parameter its corresponding number of "*" gives the easy-to-read statistical assessment of the estimated model.

We create a function which assigns the corresponding number of "*" for every given t-statistic under the asymptotic approximation:

```
.quantQ.ols.signLevels:{[ts]
   // ts -- list of t-statistics
   convertPDict:((0j;1j;2j;3j;4j)!("-";"* (90% c.l.)";"** (95% c.l.)";"***
       ↪ (99% c.l.)";
   "**** (99.9% c.l.)"));
   :convertPDict each binr[(1.282;1.645;2.326;3.091);] abs ts;
};
```

The confidence level of the estimated parameters thus reads:

```
signLevels: .quantQ.ols.signLevels[tStats];
signLevels
```

```
("**** (99.9% c.l.)";"**** (99.9% c.l.)";"**** (99.9% c.l.)";"**** (99.9% c
    ↪ .l.)")
```

The result shows that all four parameters are statistically significant, or, we can reject the null hypothesis at a very high confidence level. Given that all the assumptions hold, all the estimated parameters contained within the model are true values. Since we know it is the case by knowing the true model, this result is not surprising. Still, we cannot assess the overall quality of the model used. This will be done in the following sections.

13.6 HOW GOOD IS THE FIT: R^2

The question we have to answer is how good is the overall fit. The significance of individual parameters does not help. Imagine the model has four features, all significant. We include three of them into our model, where each of them will have coefficients significantly different from zero. This itself does not answer the question whether we have included all the features, or, in general, how much we do not know about the model. We can assert that we have acquired some knowledge about our model.

In order to answer the question about overall quality of the fit, we perform what is known as variance partitioning. Let $\bar{y} = \sum_{i=1}^{n} y_i$ be the sample mean, and let us define:

- Total Sum of Squares (TSS), sometimes also referred to as Sum of Squares, Total (SST, SSTO) and SYY: $\sum_{i=1}^{n} (y_i - \bar{y})^2$;
- Estimated Sum of Squares (ESS), sometimes also referred to as Sum of Squares, Model (SSM), Estimated Sum of Squares (ESS), and Sum of Squares, Regression (SSR, SSreg): $\sum_{i=1}^{n} (\hat{y}_i - \bar{y})^2$;
- Residual Sum of Squares (RSS), sometimes also referred to as Sum of Squares, Error (SSE): $\sum_{i=1}^{n} (y_i - \hat{y}_i)^2$.

Notice that the abbreviations used in the literature can be quite confusing: Does "E" stand for "estimated" or for "error"; does "R" stand for "regression" or for "residual"? To avoid confusion, we shall stick with Total Sum of Squares (TSS), Estimated Sum of Squares (ESS), and Residual Sum of Squares (RSS).

If we define $\bar{\boldsymbol{y}} \in \mathbb{R}^n$ as a vector all of whose elements are the sample mean $\bar{y}$, we can write these down in vector notation:

$$\text{TSS} = \sum_{i=1}^{n} (y_i - \bar{y})^2 = (\boldsymbol{y} - \bar{\boldsymbol{y}})^\intercal (\boldsymbol{y} - \bar{\boldsymbol{y}}), \tag{13.51}$$

$$\text{ESS} = \sum_{i=1}^{n} (\hat{y}_i - \bar{y})^2 = (\hat{\boldsymbol{y}} - \bar{\boldsymbol{y}})^\intercal (\hat{\boldsymbol{y}} - \bar{\boldsymbol{y}}), \tag{13.52}$$

$$\text{RSS} = \sum_{i=1}^{n} (y_i - \hat{y}_i)^2 = (\boldsymbol{y} - \hat{\boldsymbol{y}})^\intercal (\boldsymbol{y} - \hat{\boldsymbol{y}}). \tag{13.53}$$

Further, we notice that:

$$\text{TSS} = ||\boldsymbol{y} - \bar{\boldsymbol{y}}||^2 = ||\boldsymbol{y}||^2 - 2\boldsymbol{y}^\intercal \bar{\boldsymbol{y}} + ||\bar{\boldsymbol{y}}||^2, \tag{13.54}$$

$$\text{ESS} = ||\hat{\boldsymbol{y}} - \bar{\boldsymbol{y}}||^2 = ||\hat{\boldsymbol{y}}||^2 - 2\hat{\boldsymbol{y}}^\intercal \bar{\boldsymbol{y}} + ||\bar{\boldsymbol{y}}||^2, \tag{13.55}$$

$$\text{RSS} = ||\boldsymbol{y} - \hat{\boldsymbol{y}}||^2 = ||\epsilon||^2. \tag{13.56}$$

If the model includes the intercept, the first column of $\boldsymbol{X}$ is a column of ones and, since $\boldsymbol{X}^\intercal \hat{\epsilon} = \boldsymbol{0}$, the sum of the residuals is zero. This is equivalent to $\boldsymbol{y}^\intercal \bar{\boldsymbol{y}} = \hat{\boldsymbol{y}}^\intercal \bar{\boldsymbol{y}}$. By Pythagoras's theorem,

$$||\boldsymbol{y}||^2 = ||\hat{\boldsymbol{y}}||^2 + ||\hat{\epsilon}||^2, \tag{13.57}$$

hence

$$\text{TSS} = \text{ESS} + \text{RSS}, \tag{13.58}$$

which is a fundamental result known as variance partitioning. Irrespective of whether our model includes the intercept, if we centre $\boldsymbol{y}$ by subtracting the sample mean

$\bar{y} = \sum_{i=1}^{n} y_i$ from each element, we notice that TSS = ESS + RSS simply amounts to the above application of Pythagoras's theorem.

Recall that, in a right triangle,

$$\cos(\theta) = \frac{|\text{adjacent}|}{|\text{hypotenuse}|},$$

thus

$$(\cos\theta)^2 = \frac{||\hat{\boldsymbol{y}}||^2}{||\boldsymbol{y}||^2} = \frac{\text{ESS}}{\text{TSS}} = \frac{\text{TSS} - \text{RSS}}{\text{TSS}} = 1 - \frac{\text{RSS}}{\text{TSS}} =: R^2,$$

which is the quantity also known as the coefficient of determination. It indicates how much better the function predicts the dependent variable than the default predictor in the absence of any inputs – the mean value of the output. It is also sometimes described as the proportion of variance explained. This measure reflects how closely the model captures the data generating process.

Regression can be seen as an orthogonal projection of $\boldsymbol{y}$ onto the column space of $\boldsymbol{X}$. An orthogonal projection minimises the length of the vector that represents the difference between $\boldsymbol{y}$ and the fitted values, $\hat{\boldsymbol{y}}$, i.e. minimises $\boldsymbol{\epsilon}$. The fitted values are a vector in the column space of $\boldsymbol{X}$. If we add a column to $\boldsymbol{X}$, the column space of $\boldsymbol{X}$ either stays the same or gets more significant. Therefore, the orthogonal projection onto this new space cannot possibly be more extended since the original column space is a subspace of the new space.

The R^2 coefficient takes values between 0 and 1, where 0 means that the linear model does not explain the data, while coefficient close to 1 suggests that explanatory power of the model is reliable. Interestingly, for the univariate models, the R^2 coefficient is equal to the square of the Pearson correlation coefficient. The R^2 is also referred to as a goodness-of-fit coefficient. The estimation procedure thus aims to provide such a model, which gives the highest possible R^2. Using the R^2 as an objective of the researcher to maximise has its pitfalls. In particular, by adding one more variable into the model specification, the RSS term is decreasing – or, being precise, non-increasing. Thus, by adding more and more terms, the RSS is minimised. Ultimately, by adding n independent variables, we may achieve a holy grail of regression $RSS = 0$, i.e. seemingly explain all the uncertainty in the data.

This is, however, spurious goodness because by adding more and more independent features, the number of degrees of freedom is decreasing. Further, the primary objective of the data analysis is to introduce a model as parsimonious as possible, which explains as much as possible. Thus, there is a trade-off between a number of independent variables and the explanatory power of the model. The R^2 measure, as introduced above, ignores the number of independent variables and solely focuses on explanatory power.

The implementation in q is straightforward:

```
.quantQ.ols.rSquared:{[y;yHat]
   // y -- the underlying data
   // yHat -- the model
   // Total Sum of Squares
   TSS:sum t*t:y-avg[y];
```

```
    // Sum Square of Residuals
    RSS: sum t*t:y-yHat;
    // R squared
    :(TSS-RSS)%TSS;
};
```

and we can add this function into our OLS estimation suite.

```
.quantQ.ols.rSquared[y;sum beta*x]
```

```
0.9983963
```

The value is very high, close to the maximum value of 1.0. This measure thus suggests that the model we have used for estimation of the data generating process is very close to the true model and the estimated model explains 99.8% of variance.

13.6.1 Adjusted R-squared

There is a modification to the goodness-of-fit as introduced above which penalises the measure for the number of independent variables. The adjusted R^2 is based on the same principles as R^2, i.e. the ratio of unexplained variance to the total variance, except that the measure of variance is adjusted for the total number of degrees of freedom. In particular, let us denote the adjusted R^2 as $\overline{R}^2$ and define it as:

$$\begin{aligned} R^2 &= 1 - \frac{\overline{RSS}}{\overline{TSS}} \\ &= 1 - \frac{RSS/df_p}{TSS/df_0} \\ &= 1 - \frac{RSS}{TSS}\frac{n-1}{n-p-1}, \end{aligned}$$

where $\overline{RSS}$ denotes the adjusted residual sum of squares, $\overline{TSS}$ is the adjusted total sum of squares, df_p is the total number of degrees of freedom for a model with n data points, p independent variables and constant, $df_p = n - p - 1$, and df_0 is the total number of degrees of freedoms for a model equal to constant.

The adjusted R^2 is no longer equivalent to the square of the correlation coefficient for the univariate model, neither it is a non-increasing function with the number of independent variables added to the model. The adjusted measure contains the trade-off between the explanatory power of the model and its parsimoniousness; thus the adjusted R^2 is increasing with additional variables if the unexplained variance is decreasing faster than $\sim (n - p - 1)$.

It is worth noting that adjusted R^2 is no longer bounded within $[0, 1]$. The adjusted R^2 can be an objective of the researcher when modelling the data as the trade-off is fully reflected. However, we do not recommend to use the adjusted R^2 as the criteria to be maximised without further considerations. The main problem is that incremental improvement to the adjusted R^2 can still produce insignificant improvement of the model. The subsequent section considers a more appropriate tool to decide whether adding variables has a significant impact on the variance improvement.

We provide a function which implements the adjusted R^2 defined in the previous display as:

```
.quantQ.ols.rSquaredAdj:{[y;yHat;p]
   // y -- the underlying data
   // yHat -- the model
   // p -- the number of explanatory variables excluding constant
   // adjusted Total Sum of Squares
   adjTSS:(1.0%(count[y]-1))*sum t*t:y-avg[y];
   // adjusted Sum Square of Residuals
   adjRSS: (1.0%(count[y]-1-p))*sum t*t:y-yHat;
   // adjusted R squared
   :(adjTSS-adjRSS)%adjTSS;
};
```

The example under consideration shows very high adjusted R^2:

```
.quantQ.ols.rSquaredAdj[y;sum beta*x;count[beta]]
```

```
0.9983931
```

The adjusted value is close to the unadjusted value and very high. The estimated model explains most of the variance; the unexplained variance is white noise without any pattern.

13.7 RELATIONSHIP WITH MAXIMUM LIKELIHOOD ESTIMATION AND AIC WITH SMALL SAMPLE CORRECTION

Let us link the OLS procedure to the maximum likelihood estimation. This is interesting theoretically as well as useful from a practical perspective. It allows us to define additional criteria to assess the quality of the fit. Suppose that $\epsilon_1, \ldots, \epsilon_n \overset{\text{i.i.d.}}{\sim} \mathcal{N}(0, \sigma^2)$. Then, taking $\boldsymbol{x}_1, \ldots, \boldsymbol{x}_n$ as data, the observations have density functions $\varphi(y_i; \boldsymbol{x}_i^\top \boldsymbol{\beta}, \sigma^2)$, and the likelihood function of $\boldsymbol{\beta}$ and σ^2, based on the sample, is

$$\mathcal{L} = \prod_{i=1}^{n} \varphi(y_i; \boldsymbol{x}_i^\top \boldsymbol{\beta}, \sigma^2) = (2\pi\sigma^2)^{-n/2} \exp\left\{ -\frac{1}{2\sigma^2} (\boldsymbol{y} - \boldsymbol{X}\boldsymbol{\beta})^\top (\boldsymbol{y} - \boldsymbol{X}\boldsymbol{\beta}) \right\}. \tag{13.59}$$

It is convenient to take the logarithms and thus we obtain the log-likelihood

$$\ln(\mathcal{L}) = -\frac{n}{2}\ln(2\pi) - \frac{n}{2}\ln(\sigma^2) - \frac{1}{2\sigma^2}(\boldsymbol{y} - \boldsymbol{X}\boldsymbol{\beta})^\top (\boldsymbol{y} - \boldsymbol{X}\boldsymbol{\beta}) \tag{13.60}$$

$$= -\frac{n}{2}\ln(2\pi) - \frac{n}{2}\ln(\sigma^2) - \frac{1}{2\sigma^2}\text{RSS}. \tag{13.61}$$

We can use the log-likelihood to find the estimated parameters. To find the critical points, we compute the first partial derivatives:

$$\frac{\partial \ln(\mathcal{L})}{\partial \boldsymbol{\beta}} = -\frac{1}{2\sigma^2}\frac{\partial \text{RSS}}{\partial \boldsymbol{\beta}} = \frac{1}{\sigma^2}(\boldsymbol{X}^\top \boldsymbol{y} - \boldsymbol{X}^\top \boldsymbol{X}\boldsymbol{\beta}), \tag{13.62}$$

$$\frac{\partial \ln(\mathcal{L})}{\partial \sigma^2} = -\frac{n}{2\sigma^2} + \frac{1}{2\sigma^4}\text{RSS}. \tag{13.63}$$

In order to confirm that the solution is the global maximum of the log-likelihood and not just a saddle point, we have to add the Hessian matrix. This is not our objective at this point. We want to use knowledge of the log-likelihood to strengthen our knowledge about the quality of the fit.

The R^2 measure and its adjusted version serve to provide an absolute measure of how much variance was explained by the model. This measure, however, is not the only one we can use to evaluate models and decide which one to use. We introduce the Akaike Information Criteria, AIC, introduced by Akaike (1974).

Let us assume that we have a process at hand generated by a true model f_{true}. We choose a model f_1 and want to find out how good the model f_1 is to capture the dynamics of the data generated by model f_{true}. If we know both the true model and the chosen model, we can use the information theory and calculate information loss using the Kullback-Leibler divergence:

$$D_{KL}(f_{true} || f_1) = \int_{-\infty}^{\infty} f_{true}(x) \log \frac{f_{true}(x)}{f_1(x)} \, dx. \tag{13.64}$$

The knowledge of the true model is hardly known in reality. Thus calculating the information loss of a given model relative to the true model, i.e. having the absolute measure of quality for the chosen model, is not possible. Akaike showed that information loss as described above can be still utilised even when we do not know the true model. In particular, if we have two competing models f_1 and f_2 related to the same true and unknown model f_{true}, we can derive criteria that will help us to decide which of the two models f_1 and f_2 is causing less information loss. The measure does not allow us to say how good the models are; they can be both very poor or very close to the true model and the criteria only allow us to compare their difference.

For a given model f_1, Akaike defined the information criteria proportional to information loss implied by the model f_1 as:

$$AIC_1 = 2 \cdot p_1 - 2 \cdot \ln(\mathcal{L}_1), \tag{13.65}$$

where p_1 denotes the number of parameters in the model f_1, and $\ln(\mathcal{L}_1)$ is a log-likelihood of the model f_1.

For two competing models f_1 and f_2, we calculate the corresponding AICs, AIC_1 and AIC_2. The model with lower AIC is causing less information loss in the asymptotic limit of infinite sample size. This is the main result of Akaike.

The minimisation of the information criteria gives an intuitive explanation to two terms forming the AIC. The first term corresponds to a penalty which aims to discriminate in favour of complex models and prevent overfitting. The second term, on the other hand, corresponds to the quality of the fit. The AIC thus aims to balance the bias-variance trade-off and guide towards models which are truthful enough but not too complex.

The concept of comparing information criteria for two competing models does not constitute any form of hypothesis testing. The comparison brings a relative measure without any significance. The information criteria for two models can still be numerically interpreted. Let us assume we have two models f_1 and f_2 with similar information criteria AIC_1 and AIC_2. Without loss of generality, let us assume that $AIC_1 < AIC_2$. Then, the factor:

$$\exp \frac{AIC_1 - AIC_2}{2} \tag{13.66}$$

is proportional to probability that model f_2 minimises the information loss relative to model f_1.

For linear OLS-based models, the comparison based on the AIC results in similar comparison. The advantage of the AIC is that it can be used for non-nested models while measures derived from R^2 (see F-test below) can be used to compare nested models only.

Once we have obtained log-likelihood, we can then calculate the AIC for a given model. We can stick to $\ln(\mathcal{L}(beta)) = -\frac{n}{2}\log(\hat{\sigma}^2)$ as this is the term which will vary across models for a given sample. In the implementation below, however, we keep the full formula for log-likelihood:

```
logL:neg[log[2*acos -1]*count[y]%2.0]+neg[log[sqrt[SSR%count[y]]]*count[y
    ↪ ]]+neg[(1.0%(2.0%count[y]))];
logL
```

```
895.9121
```

It is convenient to create a function which calculates the log-likelihood, as it is one of the main concepts used in modern econometrics:

```
.quantQ.ols.logL:{[n;RSS]
   // n -- size of the sample
   // RSS -- Residual sum of squares
   :neg[log[2*acos-1]*n%2.0]+neg[log[sqrt[RSS%n]]*n]+neg[(1.0%(2.0%n))];
};
```

We can verify the function:

```
.quantQ.ols.logL[count[y];RSS]
```

```
895.9121
```

Having in hand the log-likelihood, we can formulate the AIC function:

```
.quantQ.ols.AIC:{[p;logL]
   // p -- number of parameters
   // logL -- log-likelihood
   :(2.0*p)-2.0*logL;
};
```

The AIC for the example listed in this section gives:

```
.quantQ.ols.AIC[count[beta];.quantQ.ols.logL[count[y];RSS]]
```

```
-1783.824
```

As we have mentioned in the paragraphs leading to this number, the AIC on its own does not give us any information. We cannot say whether −1783.824 is very small and thus information loss is small or if it is large and the model is unacceptable.

The calculation itself assumes the asymptotic holds, i.e. the size of the sample is infinite. This is not true as our sample contains 10^3 points. In such a case, the offset between the complexity of the model and its accuracy may adequately work. The small sample correction for AIC should thus be considered. In general, this task is very complicated and an analytic formula may not be possible to find for any model. Thus, methods like bootstrap are being used to have a numerical correction to AIC.

Fortunately, for the OLS model, or, for univariate model linear in parameters, where residuals are normally distributed, the analytic formula exists. In such a case, the AIC corrected for the small size of the sample, usually denoted as AICc, is defined as:

$$AICc = AIC + \frac{2p^2 + 2p}{n - p - 1}. \tag{13.67}$$

Several observations are at the place: $AICc \to AIC$ as $N \to \infty$, thus the small sample correction indeed works in the case of the finite sample. Further, the AICc is proportional to p^2 and thus can be considered as a second-order approximation to the relative information loss in the number of parameters.

The AICc implementation reads:

```
.quantQ.ols.AICC:{[n;sample;logL]
   // n -- number of parameters
   // sample -- sample size
   // logL -- log-likelihood
   :.quantQ.ols.AIC[n;logL]+("f"$2*(n*n)+n)%("f"$sample-1-n);
};
```

```
.quantQ.ols.AICC[count[beta];count[y];.quantQ.ols.logL[count[y];RSS]]
```

```
-1783.784
```

13.8 ESTIMATION SUITE

Finally, we put all the components together to create the entire regression suite of the ordinary least square regression including all the additional statistics. The output of the function is a dictionary with various variables. The dictionary corresponds to a chosen model. The advantage of this approach, in this case, is that we can later create statistics, which allows us to assess the accuracy of a model, or to compare two or more models, as the AIC suggests. The estimation suite consists of the measures and statistics introduced above, where some of them have been directly incorporated into the suite rather than re-use the functions introduced. We have also added treatment for missing values. In particular, whenever a missing value is observed among any feature, the row to which the missing value belongs is removed. This method is convenient when the data set has only a few missing entries. If the missing values are too frequent or present some pattern in the data, more sophisticated and tailored techniques will be needed.

```
.quantQ.ols.fit:{[y;x]
   // y -- array of dependent variables
   // x -- array of arrays of independent variables, constants has to be
       ↪ included
   whereMissing:raze (where y=0n; raze {where x=0n} each x);
   // remove the missing values
   y:y[(til count y) except whereMissing];
   x:{[whereMissing;x] x[(til count x) except whereMissing]}[whereMissing;]
       ↪ each x;
       // y^T X
       ytx: enlist y mmu flip[x];
       // X^T X
       xtx: x mmu flip[x];
       // solve the OLS equation
       solution: ytx lsq xtx;
       // beta
       beta:first solution;
       // var cov matrix
       varcov:(inv flip[xtx])*sum (1.0%(count[y]-count[beta]))*t*t:y-sum[
           ↪ beta*x];
       // errors for every estimation (sample standard deviation)
       errors:{sqrt x[y;y]}[varcov;] each til count varcov;
       // t-stat for every beta
       tStats:beta%errors;
       // TSS  or Total Sum of Squares
       TSS: sum t*t:y-avg[y];
       // RSS or Residual Sum of Squars
       RSS: sum t*t:y-sum beta*x;
       // R-squared
       Rsquared:1.0-RSS%TSS;
       // adjusted R-squared
       adjRsquared:1-(1-Rsquared)*(count[y]-1.0)%(count[y]-(count[beta]-1)
           ↪ -1.0);
       // significance level in normal approximation (econometric)
       convertPDict:((0j;1j;2j;3j;4j)!("-";"* (90% c.l.)";"** (95% c.l.)
           ↪ ";"*** (99% c.l.)";
           "**** (99.9% c.l.)"));
```

```
    signLevels: convertPDict each binr[(1.282;1.645;2.326;3.091);abs
        ↪ tStats];
    // log-likelihood
    logL:neg[log[2*acos -1]*count[y]%2.0]+neg[log[sqrt[RSS%count[y]]]*
        ↪ count[y]]+
        neg[(1.0%(2.0%count[y]))];
    // AIC from log-likelihood
    aic:(2.0*count[beta])-2.0*logL;
    // AIC with small sample correction - depends upon heavy assumptions
    aicc:aic+("f"$2*(k*k)+k)%("f"$count[y]-1-k:count[beta]);
  // output bucket
  bucket:(`beta`errors`varcov`nObservations`dfn`tStats`TSS`RSS`Rsquared`
      ↪ adjRsquared`signLevels`logL`aic`aicc!
        (beta;errors;varcov;count[y];count[beta];tStats;TSS;RSS;Rsquared;
            ↪ adjRsquared;signLevels;logL;aic;aicc));
  :bucket;
};
```

Let us run the suite for the example:

```
.quantQ.ols.fit[tabData[`y];tabData[`x1`x2`x3`const]]
```

with results in a comprised form that reads:

```
(`beta`errors`varcov`nObservations`dfn`tStats`TSS`RSS`Rsquared`adjRsquared`
    ↪ signLevels`logL`aic`aicc)!(0.9998791 -0.9974519 1.996775
    ↪ 1.010413;0.00320663 0.003138716 0.00309775 0.008262983;(1.028248e-05
    ↪  3.473323e-07 -3.667938e-07 -9.232866e-06;3.473323e-07 9.851538e-06
    ↪ -3.972302e-07 1.015537e-05;-3.667938e-07 -3.972302e-07 9.596056e-06
    ↪ -1.941069e-05;-9.232866e-06 1.015537e-05 -1.941069e-05 6.827689e-05)
    ↪ ;1000j;4j;9860.492 -10049.4 20383.69
    ↪ 3866.892;6084.551;9.757673;0.9983963;0.9983947;("**** (99.9% c.l.)
    ↪ ";"**** (99.9% c.l.)";"**** (99.9% c.l.)";"**** (99.9% c.l.)")
    ↪ ;895.9121;-1783.824;-1783.784)
```

The output is useful in terms of containing all the information in a comprised and easy-to-retrieve way, but still beyond readability by a human user. For that purpose, we summarise the full results in a more convenient and standardised form:

```
.quantQ.ols.olsTab:{[tab]
  // tab -- table with data
  // names
  yName:first cols tab;
  xNames:1_cols tab;
  // running regressions
  reg:.quantQ.ols.fit[tab[yName];tab[xNames]];
  // regression part of table
  tabReg:([] name:xNames; coeff:reg[`beta];error:reg[`errors];tStat:reg[`
      ↪ tStats];
    significance:reg[`signLevels]);
  // stats part of table
  tabStats:([] name:`STATISTICS`nObservations`nParameters`TSS`RSS`Rsquared
    `RsquaredAdjusted`logLikelihood`AIC`AICC; coeff:(0nf;"f"$count[y];"f
      ↪ "$reg[`dfn];
```

```
        "f"$reg[`TSS];"f"$reg[`RSS];reg[`Rsquared];reg[`adjRsquared];reg[`
            ↪ logL];reg[`aic];reg[`aicc]));
    // return the table with results
    :tabReg uj tabStats;
};
```

The comprehensive outcome of the estimation of the OLS model with supplementary measures and statistics can be finally obtained as:

```
.quantQ.ols.olsTab[select depVariable:y, variable1:x1, variable2:x2,
    ↪ variable3:x3, c:const from tabData]
```

```
name              coeff      error        tStat     significance
----------------------------------------------------------------------
variable1         0.9998791  0.00320663   9860.492  "**** (99.9% c.l.)"
variable2         -0.9974519 0.003138716  -10049.4  "**** (99.9% c.l.)"
variable3         1.996775   0.00309775   20383.69  "**** (99.9% c.l.)"
c                 1.010413   0.008262983  3866.892  "**** (99.9% c.l.)"
STATISTICS                                          ""
nObservations     1000                              ""
nParameters       4                                 ""
TSS               6084.551                          ""
RSS               9.757673                          ""
Rsquared          0.9983963                         ""
RsquaredAdjusted  0.9983947                         ""
logLikelihood     895.9121                          ""
AIC               -1783.824                         ""
AICC              -1783.784                         ""
```

We have achieved the estimation suite, which returns standard results for the estimation of the linear model using the OLS procedure. We can read from the output of all the relevant information. Further, the estimation suite can be easily extended for additional statistics and measures and readers can thus tailor the suite to their needs.

13.9 COMPARING TWO NESTED MODELS: TOWARDS A STOPPING RULE

The linear model and linear regression are very rarely run only once for a particular data set at hand. It is more common that the researcher has to estimate a series of various linear models and decide which model has the best explanatory power. A particular procedure may look as follows. We have a dependent variable and set of candidate features which may or may not explain the dependent variable. Among those features, we also count some higher power of the features themselves. The full model we can try is the full model with all the candidate features. Such a model will be likely too complex and overfit. We can thus try to remove some of the features or impose a constraint to set the parameters corresponding to those features to be zero, and run a restricted regression. Then, we can compare the outcomes and answer the question of whether the restricted model provides the same explanatory power as the full one. If it is so, we choose the restricted model as it is more parsimonious.

Using the R^2, or, better, the adjusted R^2 is one possible way to do so. Instead of comparing two numbers without any statistical insight, we can formulate a proper statistical test based on the same features as R^2, which allows us to choose between two models. The way to do so is to use the F-statistic.

The F-statistic is a statistic used to decide whether the nested model – indexed with index 1 – brings a statistically significant improvement in terms of the explained variance relative to the basic model – indexed with index 2. The statistics are defined in terms of the difference between the two variances as follows:

$$F = \frac{RSS_1 - RSS_2}{RSS_2} \frac{n - p_2}{p_2 - p_1}, \tag{13.68}$$

where RSS_1 is the residual sum of squares of the nested model, RSS_2 is the same quantity for the basis model from which the nested model was derived, and p_1, p_2 stands for the number of degrees of freedom including the constant for the nested and the basic models, respectively. Further, it holds $p_1 < p_2$.

The F-statistic follows the $\mathcal{F}$-distribution with $(p_2 - p_1, n - p_2)$ degrees of freedom, or,

$$F \sim \mathcal{F}_{(p_2 - p_1, n - p_2)}. \tag{13.69}$$

The test works as follows. We start with the basic model specification and estimate the properties of the model. Then, we propose an extension of the model by adding one or more independent variables into the regression specification and run the estimation procedure. Finally, we calculate the F-statistic and test the following hypothesis:

- H_0: The null hypothesis states that the nested model is not worse than the basic model in terms of the unexplained variance, or, $RSS_1 = RSS_2$.
- H_A: The alternative hypothesis states that the basic model is an improvement relative to the nested model and decreases the unexplained variance, $RSS_1 > RSS_2$.

The null hypothesis H_0 is rejected at significance level α when $F > F(p_2 - p_1, n - p_2; \alpha)$, where critical values are to be determined from statistical tables. When we reject the null hypothesis, the alternative hypothesis can be accepted as a result of the test.

The F-statistic for comparing two nested models estimated by our procedures is implemented as:

```
.quantQ.ols.fStatistics:{[model1;model2]
    // model1 -- the regression outcome of the nested model
    // model2 -- the regression outcome of the basis model
    // F-statistics
    :((count[model2[`nObservations]-model2[`dfn]])%(model2[`dfn]-model1[`dfn
        ↪ ]))*
        (model1[`RSS]-model2[`RSS])%model2[`RSS];
 };
```

Let us define the full model as the output of the `.quantQ.ols.fit` function as:

```
olsFull:.quantQ.ols.fit[tabData[`y];tabData[`x1`x2`x3`const]];
```

and the restricted model, which is a nested model derived from the `olsFull` by excluding the feature `` `x1`` from estimation:

```
olsConstrained:.quantQ.ols.fit[tabData[`y];tabData[`x2`x3`const]];
```

The F-statistic – and in fact the F-test itself – can be run:

```
.quantQ.ols.fStatistics[olsConstrained;olsFull]
```

```
97.61978
```

The value 97.61978 represents the value of the F-test to be compared against corresponding critical values. The statistics are under a null hypothesis a value drawn from $F_{1,996}$ distribution. If we set the confidence level at 99%, the corresponding critical value is 6.66039692. Since the statistics exceed the critical value, we can confidently reject the null hypothesis in favour of using the full model. This is in agreement with our knowledge of the model itself.

For the sake of completeness, let us show the adjusted R^2:

```
([] model: `Full`Constrained; adjRsquared: (olsFull[`adjRsquared];
    ↪ olsConstrained[`adjRsquared]))
```

```
model       adjRsquared
----------------------
Full        0.9983947
Constrained 0.8418454
```

The adjusted R^2 confirms the conclusion of the F-test.

13.9.1 Comparing Two General Models

Another alternative tool to choose between the competing models has already been mentioned: the Akaike Information Criteria. The AIC is derived on the premises of information theory, and it does not require that two compared models are nested. On the other hand, it does not constitute a proper statistical tool. Thus, AIC may prefer one model against the other, but the difference between the models can be insignificant.

Let us stick to the example from the F-statistic:

```
([] model: `Full`Constrained; AIC: (olsFull[`aic];olsConstrained[`aic]))
```

```
model       AIC
----------------------
Full        -1783.824
Constrained 2805.448
```

The full model, `olsFull`, shows lower values of the AIC and thus suggests lower information loss. Quantitatively, the difference between AICs is very large. Let us calculate the probability corresponding to the case when `olsConstrained` has less information loss compared to the full model `olsFull`:

```
exp(min[(olsFull[`aic];olsConstrained[`aic])]-max[(olsFull[`aic];
    ↪ olsConstrained[`aic])])%2.0
```

```
0f
```

The result suggests that the probability is equal to 0, which we have to interpret as very low rather than equal to zero.

13.10 IN-/OUT-OF-SAMPLE OPERATIONS

In many practical applications, we have to predict the dependent variables. The usual problem presents as follows. We have a data set, where we are provided with both independent and dependent variables. Let us further call this data set an "in-sample". This data set looks like the example we have used so far, and we can use all the functions developed to estimate the model. Beyond that, we are provided with another piece of data, where we know only the independent variables, i.e. features, but we do not know the dependent variable; let us call this data "out-of-sample." Our task is to predict the dependent variable for the out-of-sample data assuming that the data generating process is the same as for the in-sample data.

Let us create an additional out-of-sample data set. The data are driven by the same data generating process as we have used so far, but come entirely out of the sample and the random component is not related to the one drawn previously.

```
simDataOUT: .quantQ.simul.multiNormal[4;200;(1.0;neg[1.0];2.0;0.0);((1.0
    ↪ 0.0 0.0 0.0);(0.0 1.0 0.0 0.0);(0.0 0.0 1.0 0.0);(0.0 0.0 0.0 1.0))]
xOUT1:simDataOUT[`var1];
xOUT2:simDataOUT[`var2];
xOUT3:simDataOUT[`var3];
errOUT:0.1*simDataOUT[`var4];
```

We generate the dependent variable using the same parameters. We denote the out-of-sample data by appending `OUT` to the variable names:

```
yOUT:1.0+(1.0*xOUT1)+(neg[1.0]*xOUT2)+(2.0*xOUT3)+errOUT;
```

Conveniently, we arrange the data into a table and add a constant into the data set:

```
tabDataOUT:([] y:yOUT; x1:xOUT1;x2:xOUT2;x3:xOUT3);
tabDataOUT: update const:1.0 from tabDataOUT;
```

Even though we want to predict the dependent variable out-of-sample, i.e. using features we have not used for estimation of the model, we still model the true dependent variable. We will use the true values to compare how good the estimated model is at predicting the unknown values.

Let us re-run the OLS model and store the outcome:

```
regModel: .quantQ.ols.fit[tabData[`y];tabData[`x1`x2`x3`const]];
```

```
.quantQ.ols.predict:{[model;tabFeatures]
    // model -- outcome of the .quantQ.ols.fit function
    // tabFeatures -- table with features used to obtain model without y
    // create column in tabFeatures with Prediction
    :([] yPredicted:sum model[`beta]*tabFeatures[cols tabFeatures]),'
        ↪ tabFeatures;
};
```

Let us apply the estimated model on the out-of-sample data stored in tabDataOUT. We explore the values:

```
tabDataOUTwPred:.quantQ.ols.predict[regModel;select x1,x2,x3,const from
    ↪ tabDataOUT];
tabDataOUTwPred
```

```
yPredicted x1          x2          x3          const
-------------------------------------------------
10.08835   1.101371    -1.39889    3.296002    1
7.980847   0.8376526   0.8109236   3.476475    1
7.660068   0.2504282   -1.834959   2.288176    1
10.10229   2.823202    -1.104932   2.58762     1
6.164149   1.479903    -0.9100523  1.385373    1
4.129143   -0.7572189  -1.33482    1.274274    1
8.452925   -0.2415864  -2.172535   2.76299     1
2.246996   0.0663422   -0.07450187 0.5488536   1
5.815944   1.184231    -1.81366    0.9076661   1
1.562761   0.1379036   0.6896479   0.552066    1
..
```

Further, we need to compare the predicted variable with the true one (given we know the true data generating process). Let us add the true values into the table:

```
tabDataMODEL:(select y from tabDataOUT),'tabDataOUTwPred
tabDataMODEL
```

```
y         yPredicted x1          x2          x3          const
-----------------------------------------------------------
10.14239  10.08835   1.101371    -1.39889    3.296002    1
7.838523  7.980847   0.8376526   0.8109236   3.476475    1
7.506122  7.660068   0.2504282   -1.834959   2.288176    1
10.10861  10.10229   2.823202    -1.104932   2.58762     1
6.226893  6.164149   1.479903    -0.9100523  1.385373    1
4.024211  4.129143   -0.7572189  -1.33482    1.274274    1
8.471605  8.452925   -0.2415864  -2.172535   2.76299     1
2.191214  2.246996   0.0663422   -0.07450187 0.5488536   1
5.82039   5.815944   1.184231    -1.81366    0.9076661   1
1.400094  1.562761   0.1379036   0.6896479   0.552066    1
..
```

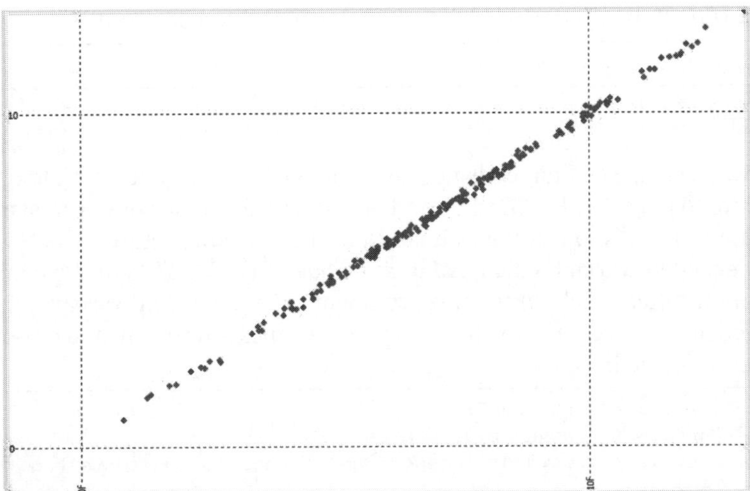

FIGURE 13.5 Comparison between true values and the predicted ones from table `tabDataMODEL`

Figure 13.5 depicts the scatter plot between the true values of the dependent variable `tabDataMODEL[`y]` and the predicted values `tabDataMODEL[`yPredicted]`. The points are scattered around the diagonal line suggesting accuracy in prediction. The Gaussian nature of the errors and the small size of the sample results in no outliers.

We further utilise the structure of the table `tabDataMODEL`. In particular, let us create a function which calculates the root mean-squared error, or *RMSE*, between the true and the predicted values. The *RMSE* is defined as:

$$RMSE = \sqrt{\frac{1}{N}\sum_{i=1}^{N}(y_i - yPredicted_i)^2}, \tag{13.70}$$

where y_i stands for i-th true value of the dependent variable, $yPredicted_i$ stands for i-th predicted value of the dependent variable, and there are altogether N observations.

The root-mean-squared error is a popular method to compare the predicted values to true ones. There is a number of alternatives in the literature, e.g. mean absolute error (MAE), which employs the sum of absolute values rather than the sum of squares and consequent square root. The reason for this stems from the sensitivity of the *RMSE* to outliers, which are amplified due to the squares present in the equation.

The *RMSE* is implemented as a function, which assumes that the first two columns in an input table are the relevant ones. In fact, due to the square and square root, the order of true and predicted variables does not matter. Further, the columns beyond the second one are not considered. The function reads:

```
.quantQ.ols.RMSE:{[tabModel]
   // tabModel -- table where first column is true dependent variable and
        ↪ second is the estimated one
   :sqrt t wavg t:tabModel[cols[tabModel][0]]-tabModel[cols[tabModel][1]];
};
```

The *RMSE* of the results in `tabDataMODEL` can be then obtained as:

```
.quantQ.ols.RMSE[tabDataMODEL]
```

```
0.09827836
```

The value we have obtained is not saying much when it stands isolated. We need some anchor to judge the *RMSE* value and how the model performs out-of-sample. The possible application is to run the estimation for two or more setups, which will differ by the independent variables included in the model. In order to do that, we implement an estimation suite, which takes three arguments: the dependent variable, the matrix of independent variables, and the flag which determines how the in- and out-of-sample splitting is performed:

```
.quantQ.ols.inOut:{[y;x;inOutFlag]
   // y -- array of dependent variables
   // x -- array of arrays of independent variables, constants has to be
       ↪ included
   // inOutFlag -- atom/array to form in/out sample, 1=out
   whereMissing:raze (where y=0n; raze {where x=0n} each x);
   // remove the missing values
   y:y[(til count y) except whereMissing];
   x:{[whereMissing;x] x[(til count x) except whereMissing]}[whereMissing;]
       ↪ each x;
   // inOutFlag is atom, in sample is randomly chosen inOutFlag fraction of
       ↪ sample
   if[(1=count[inOutFlag]);
       // split sample: OUT
       xOUT:flip ceiling[inOutFlag*count y] _ flip x;
       yOUT:ceiling[inOutFlag*count y] _ y;
       // split sample: IN
       x:flip ceiling[inOutFlag*count y]#flip x;
       y:ceiling[inOutFlag*count y]#y
   ];
   // inOutFlag is Boolean array with 1b being In/0b Out
   if[(1<count[inOutFlag]);
       inOutFlag:inOutFlag[(til count inOutFlag) except whereMissing];
       // split sample: OUT
       yOUT:y where inOutFlag;
       xOUT:flip flip[x] where inOutFlag;
       // split sample: IN
       y:y where not inOutFlag;
       x:flip flip[x] where not inOutFlag
   ];
   // IN sample regression
   regIN:.quantQ.ols.fit[y;x];
   // OUT sample prediction
   yPRED:sum regIN[`beta]*xOUT;
   RMSE:sqrt avg t*t:yOUT-yPRED;
   regOUT:(`RMSE`nObservationsOUT)!(RMSE;count[yOUT]);
   // output bucket
   bucket:regIN,regOUT;
   :bucket;
};
```

The in and out sample splitting can be done in two ways: if the `inOutFlag` variable is a scalar value, it should be between 0 and 1. Then, it represents the proportion of the data which are taken as in the sample or training sample. Data are taken from the beginning. This is motivated by the time series approach, where the out-of-sample data is conventionally taken as the most recent. Thus, the out-of-sample data is the remaining piece of the data.

On the other hand, we can specify explicitly which data to take as in-sample and which to take as out-of-sample. In that case, the `inOutFlag` variable is an array of boolean indicators, where true stands for being included in the training sample, and false to be in the out-of-sample. The array is used in conditional evaluation, and thus 0 serves as false while non-zero values are considered as true.

Let us show the example of the routine with 80% of the data to be training sample, and with remaining 20% being the verification sample:

```
regEx1a:.quantQ.ols.inOut[tabData[`y];tabData[`x1`x2`x3`const];0.8];
regEx1a
```

```
(`beta`errors`varcov`nObservations`dfn`tStats`TSS`RSS`Rsquared`adjRsquared`
    ↪ signLevels`logL`aic`aicc`RMSE`nObservationsOUT)!(1.00308 -0.9982089
    ↪ 1.99633 1.00899;0.003580111 0.00346714 0.003500768
    ↪ 0.009305881;(1.28172e-05 2.056495e-07 -4.601171e-07 -1.178749e
    ↪ -05;2.056495e-07 1.202106e-05 -1.744675e-07 1.227372e-05;-4.601171e
    ↪ -07 -1.744675e-07 1.225537e-05 -2.467186e-05;-1.178749e-05 1.227372e
    ↪ -05 -2.467186e-05 8.659943e-05);800j;4j;7924.723 -8143.2 16129.24
    ↪ 3066.72;4809.471;7.69077;0.9984009;0.9983989;("**** (99.9% c.l.)
    ↪ ";"**** (99.9% c.l.)";"**** (99.9% c.l.)";"**** (99.9% c.l.)")
    ↪ ;722.6855;-1437.371;-1437.321;0.1019856;200j)
```

Let us extract the *RMSE* value:

```
regEx1a[`RMSE]
```

```
0.1019856
```

Now, we remove the variable `x1` and re-run the regression:

```
regEx1b:.quantQ.ols.inOut[tabData[`y];tabData[`x2`x3`const];0.8];
regEx1b[`RMSE]
```

```
0.9911384
```

The value of *RMSE* is much worse compared to the case with `x1` being included. We can thus say that variable `x1` is essential to estimate the model. It brings the value out-of-sample.

It is worth further exploring the behaviour of the function, when there is no out-of-sample part of the data:

```
regEx1c:.quantQ.ols.inOut[tabData[`y];tabData[`x2`x3`const];1];
```

```
'length
   [1]  .quantQ.ols.inOut:
   // OUT sample prediction
   yPRED:sum regIN[`beta]*xOUT;
                           ^
   RMSE:sqrt t wavg t:yOUT-yPRED;
```

We encourage the reader to change our function, such that the function is resilient to such error and can work even in the case where the out-of-sample is empty. This will allow us to use the function for both the estimation as well as out-of-sample verification.

Let us also illustrate the estimation when the `inOutFlag` indicator is an array. We want to achieve the same result as when we use scalar value of `0.8`:

```
regEx2a:.quantQ.ols.inOut[tabData[`y];tabData[`x1`x2`x3`const];799>=neg[t]
    ↪ ? t:count tabData[`y]];
regEx2a
```

```
(`beta`errors`varcov`nObservations`dfn`tStats`TSS`RSS`Rsquared`adjRsquared`
    ↪ signLevels`logL`aic`aicc`RMSE`nObservationsOUT)!(0.997012 -0.9954925
    ↪  1.998253 1.013525;0.003549202 0.003535048 0.003385423
    ↪ 0.00904751;(1.259683e-05 1.868202e-07 -4.440448e-07 -1.189508e
    ↪ -05;1.868202e-07 1.249656e-05 -1.687987e-07 1.225569e-05;-4.440448e
    ↪ -07 -1.687987e-07 1.146109e-05 -2.271669e-05;-1.189508e-05 1.225569e
    ↪ -05 -2.271669e-05 8.185744e-05);800j;4j;7945.38 -7965.036 16694.85
    ↪ 3168.476;5026.822;7.723502;0.9984635;0.9984616;("**** (99.9% c.l.)
    ↪ ";"**** (99.9% c.l.)";"**** (99.9% c.l.)";"**** (99.9% c.l.)")
    ↪ ;720.9867;-1433.973;-1433.924;0.1012435;200j)
```

The two implementations of the `inOutFlag` flag variable may not necessarily exhaust all options we want to employ. It is straightforward, however, to extend the implementation and build in additional functionalities.

13.11 CROSS-VALIDATION

Finally, we extend the concept of in/out sample testing and introduce the cross-validation. The cross-validation is extended out-of-sample testing. The primary objective is to choose which model, among those provided, fits the model the best in terms of out-of-sample performance. The in/out sample splitting presented in the previous section relies on one particular type of splitting. The out-of-sample is fixed, and this may affect the outcome of the testing. If, for instance, the out-of-sample period is affected by some exogenous noise, the models tested can prove rather weak while they may be valid on the rest of the sample. It would thus make sense to try various in/out splitting schemes and derive the result from a sample of such outcomes.

Cross-validation aims to achieve exactly this. We implement one particular cross-validation scheme, which is the k-fold cross-validation. It is non-exhaustive cross-validation, as it involves k (chosen number) different schemes to split the sample into in- and out-of-sample parts. For every such split, the `olsInOut` function is being run and the *RMSE* recorded. Finally, an average over k such values is calculated and used as the *RMSE* for a tested model. Let us stress that for every splitting scheme, the estimated coefficients may be different. Our objective is to test the model, which plainly means the set of chosen features, and not the estimated values themselves.

The k-fold cross-validation works as follows:

- Set the parameter k.
- Split the sample into k equally sized parts. Parts are non-overlapping and cover the entire sample. Let us index them as Data_j, with $j = 1, \ldots, k$, such that $\text{Data} = \sum_j \text{Data}_j$.
- For $i = 1, \ldots, k$:
  - Define $\text{Data}_{in} = \sum_{j,j\neq i} \text{Data}_j$ and $\text{Data}_{out} = \text{Data}_i$.
  - Estimate the model on the Data_{in} and verify on the Data_{out}.
  - Get the corresponding $RMSE_i$.
- Calculate the average $RMSE_{CV} = \frac{1}{k}\sum_i RMSE_i$.

We judge the model based on the cross-validated value $RMSE_{CV}$.

We implement the k-fold cross-validation in the following function. It runs in the same manner as the `olsInOut` function. The third parameter is in this case an integer denoting the number of cross-validations k:

```
.quantQ.ols.cv:{[y;x;nCV]
   // y -- array of dependent variables
   // x -- array of arrays of independent variables, constants has to be
       ↪ included
   // nCV -- number of Cross-validation folds
   whereMissing:raze (where y=0n; raze {where x=0n} each x);
   // remove the missing values
   y:y[(til count y) except whereMissing];
   x:{[whereMissing;x] x[(til count x) except whereMissing]}[whereMissing;]
       ↪ each x;
   // create all the Flags for every fold
   foldFlag: (floor til[count y]%count[y]%nCV)=/:til nCV;
   // return list of coresponding RMSEs
   :(.quantQ.ols.inOut[y;x;] each foldFlag)[`RMSE];
};
```

The function returns an array of k *RMSE*s:

```
cvEx:.quantQ.ols.cv[tabData[`y];tabData[`x1`x2`x3`const];12];
cvEx
```

```
0.09982979 0.1008337 0.1017834 0.1017682 0.1020692 0.10122 0.09952369
    ↪ 0.1014075 0.1014641 0.1002764 0.102241 0.09999176
```

We can then calculate the average value and base our decision using the cross-validated *RMSE*:

```
avg cvEx
```

```
0.1010341
```

The value we obtained corresponds to the one we have obtained with the `olsInOut` with 80% of the sample being the in-sample. Since our sample is simulated as being homogeneous, this is the result we are expecting. The cross-validation reveals its power on more complex data with possible heteroscedastic nature.

13.12 CONCLUSION

We have implemented the ordinary least squares method in the form of an estimation suite. The suite contains a number of additional features, which helps us to assess the performance of a fit. This proves useful when we need to make an inference from the model. Besides, we have extended the routine for the in-sample/out-of-sample estimation and provided the k-fold cross-validation. This altogether allows us to use the suite for a number of tasks ranging from model estimation and statistical inference to robust model selection. Last but not least, it outlined a way to extend the existing framework for additional functionalities. We will illustrate the extension in a subsequent chapter, where we add regularisation into our linear models.

CHAPTER 14

Time Series Econometrics

`kdb+/q` is a very powerful language to store, manage and analyse large data sets. Time series are data sets containing a set of values of observation at discrete points in time. Time series are present in nearly all fields of applications that rely on a form of data that measures how things evolve. One of the main objectives of time series analysis is the forecast of future realisations of a random phenomenon. One typical example of time series analysis in finance is the forecast of the evolution of a financial asset based on its historical returns, sometimes with the help of exogenous variables such as macroeconomic factors or intrinsic values of the underlying instrument.

This chapter presents the main forecasting techniques in time series analysis and shows how they can be implemented in `q`. The chapter is divided into two parts. The first part introduces the autoregressive and moving average processes, stationarity and Granger causality tests and vector autoregressive models. The second part presents a possible implementation of the processes in `q`.

14.1 AUTOREGRESSIVE AND MOVING AVERAGE PROCESSES

14.1.1 Introduction

A time series is a sequential set of data constructed chronologically over consecutive times t=0,1,2,... denoted X_t. Time series can be discrete, where data are usually sampled at equally spaced time intervals, or continuous. Time series containing records of a single variable are called univariate. Multivariate time series refers to records of more than one variable. Time series are non-deterministic by nature and are generally affected by four main components: a trend, and cyclical, seasonal and random components. A trend measures the long-term variations in a time series. The cyclical variation of a time series describes the medium-term changes in the data set over time, such as business cycles. A cyclic pattern exists when data exhibit rises and falls that are not of a fixed period. Seasonal variations are always of the fixed and known period. They reflect the fluctuations within a year during the season. The random variations in a time series are caused by unpredictable behaviours of the data that do not follow a particular pattern.

The following sections present the class of univariate ARMA and multivariate VARMA models capable of handling trend, cyclical and seasonal behaviour of time series.

14.1.2 *AR*(*p*) Process

To efficiently forecast the future of a finite series of random variables we need to admit that these variables are somehow dependent from each other. If it is not the case, the series is purely random and not predictable. This section introduces autoregressive processes.

Formally, the autoregressive process of order p, denoted as $AR(p)$ is defined as:

$$X_t = c + \sum_{i=1}^{p} \phi_i X_{t-i} + \epsilon_t, \tag{14.1}$$

where $\phi_1, ..., \phi_p$ are the parameters of the model, c is a constant and $\{\epsilon_t\}$ the white noise, i.e. $\epsilon_t \sim W\mathbb{N}(0, \sigma_\epsilon^2)$, $E[X_t \epsilon_s] = 0,\ s < t$. Its expectation is $E[X_t] = c + \sum_{i=1}^{p} \phi_i E[X_{i-1}]$. If $|\phi_i| < 1, \forall i : i \in [1..p]$, the process 14.1 is wide-sense stationary and $E[X_t]$ is identical for all values of t. Denoting $E[X_t] = \mu$, $\mu = c + \mu \sum_{i=1}^{p} \phi_i$, i.e.

$$\mu = \frac{c}{1 - \sum_{i=1}^{p} \phi_i}. \tag{14.2}$$

The variance of (14.1) solves $Var[X_t] = \sum_{i=1}^{p} \phi_i^2 Var[X_{t-i}] + Var[\epsilon_t]$. If the process X_t is homoskedastic, i.e. $\forall t : Var[X_t] = \sigma^2$,

$$\sigma^2 = \frac{\sigma_\epsilon^2}{1 - \sum_{i=1}^{p} \phi_i^2}. \tag{14.3}$$

The autocovariance $E[X_t X_{t-n}]$ with $t > n$ solves:

$$\begin{aligned} E[X_t X_{t-n}] &= E[(c + \sum_{i=1}^{p} \phi_i X_{t-i} + \epsilon_t)(c + \sum_{i=1}^{p} \phi_i X_{t-i-n} + \epsilon_{t-n})] \\ &= c^2 + c\sum_{i=1}^{p} \phi_i E[X_{t-i}] + c\sum_{i=1}^{p} \phi_i E[X_{t-i-n}] + (\sum_{i=1}^{p} \phi_i E[X_{t-i}])(\sum_{i=1}^{p} \phi_i E[X_{t-i-n}]). \end{aligned} \tag{14.4}$$

If X_t is homoskedastic with mean μ:

$$E[X_t X_{t-n}] == (c + \mu \sum_{i=1}^{p} \phi_i)^2.$$

14.1.2.1 Simulation

The autoregressive model $X_t = 0.82X_{t-1} + \epsilon_t$ can be simulated as

```
0f {y+0.82*x}\eps
```

where eps is a list of random normal numbers. Given the following 5 normally distributed random numbers generated with genBoxMuller from simul namespace:

```
eps:-0.153913 2.22843 -0.320418 0.371417 0.573757;
0f {y+0.82*x}\eps
```

returns

```
-0.153913 2.102221 1.403403 1.522208 1.821967
```

which corresponds to -0.153913 (-0.153913*0.82)+2.22843 (2.102221*0.82) -0.320418 ...

An implementation of the simulation of an *AR*(*p*) model is given by the function simAR[phi;eps] presented in the second part of the chapter.

To illustrate the behaviour of an autoregressive process, we simulate 100 paths of the *AR*(2) process $X_t = 0.99X_{t-1} - 0.1X_{t-2}$:

```
.quantQ.ts.simAR[(0.99;-0.1);100?.quantQ.simul.genBoxMuller[]]
```

and depict this in Figure 14.1.

We see from the figure that the values at time t are strongly positively correlated with the previous value at time $t-1$ and slightly negatively correlated with the value at time $t-2$. As such, the process bounces positively and negatively depending on the value of the error term $\epsilon \sim \mathbb{N}(0, 1)$ given by 100?.quantQ.simul.genBoxMuller[].

Processes containing independent random variables are not predictable. Indeed, the *AR*(1) model with $\phi_1 = 0$ is the white noise $X_t = \epsilon_t$. To illustrate the phenomenon, let us simulate the *AR*(1) model $X_t = 0.001X_t + \epsilon_t$:

```
.quantQ.ts.simAR[{0.001};100?.quantQ.simul.genBoxMuller[]]
```

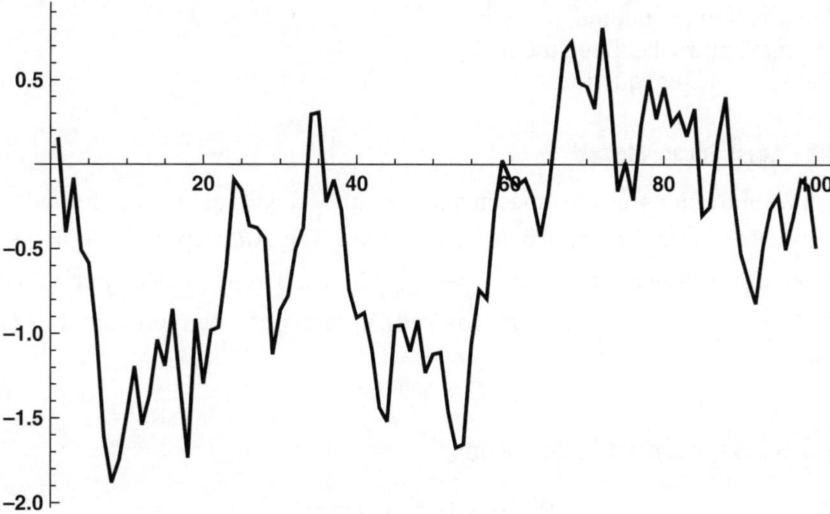

FIGURE 14.1 *AR*(2) simulated time series

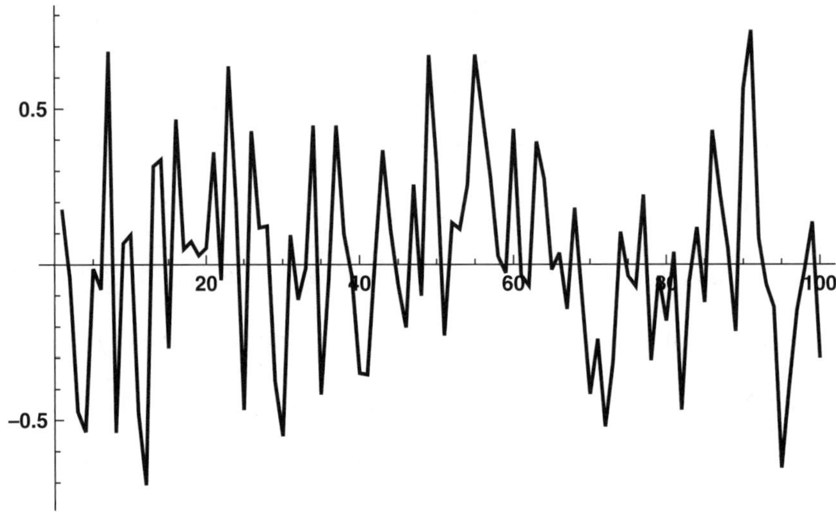

FIGURE 14.2 Simulated process $X_t = 0.001X_t + \epsilon_t$

Figure 14.2 captures the abovementioned $AR(1)$ process. We can clearly see that the process is nearly random. The low coefficient $\Phi_1 = 0.001$ does not add much information over the white noise ϵ_t.

14.1.2.2 Estimation of AR(p) Parameters

The parameters $\Phi_1, \Phi_2, ..., \Phi_p$ and σ^2 of the autoregressive process of order p presented in (14.1) can be estimated using:

- The least square method
- The maximum likelihood method
- The Yule-Walker equations

14.1.2.3 Least Square Method

Since the innovations ϵ_t are uncorrelated with X_{t-j}, $j = 1, ..., p$, the ordinary least square – OLS – can be applied to estimate Φ_i. The $AR(p)$ process $X_t = c + \sum_{i=1}^{p} \Phi_i X_{t-i} + \epsilon_t$ is equivalent to $\epsilon_t = X_t - c - \sum_{i=1}^{k} \Phi_i X_{t-i}$. The OLS estimator minimises $\sum_{t=k+1}^{n} \epsilon_t^2 = (X_t - c - \sum_{i=1}^{k} \Phi_i X_{t-i})^2$. The $AR(p)$ process can be represented in matrix form as:

$$\mathbf{X} = \mathbf{Y}\Phi + \epsilon, \tag{14.5}$$

where $\mathbf{Y}$ is a $n - p \times p + 1$ matrix defined as:

$$\mathbf{Y} = \begin{cases} y_{i,1} = 1 \ \forall i \in [1, n-p], \\ y_{i,j} = x_{i-j+1} \ \forall j \in [2, p+1]. \end{cases}$$

and $X = (x_p, x_{p+1}, ..., x_n)'$.

The OLS estimator of the parameters $\hat{\Phi} = (\hat{c}, \hat{\Phi}_1, \hat{\Phi}_2, ..., \hat{\Phi}_p)'$ solves:

$$\hat{\Phi} = (\mathbf{Y}'\mathbf{Y})^{-1}\mathbf{Y}'\mathbf{X}, \tag{14.6}$$

and the variance as:

$$\hat{\sigma}^2 = \frac{1}{n-p-1} \sum_{t=p+1}^{n} (\mathbf{X_t} - \hat{c} - \hat{\Phi}_1 \mathbf{X_{t-1}} - ... - \hat{\Phi}_p \mathbf{X_{t-p}})^2. \tag{14.7}$$

A q implementation of the OLS estimator of $AR(p)$ models is given by the function `.quantQ.ts.estARP[data;p]` explained in the second part of the chapter.

14.1.2.4 Example

To empirically verify the convergence of the implementation of the OLS estimator, we estimate 100,000 simulated values of an $AR(2)$ model:

$$X_t = 0.4X_{t-1} + 0.3X_{t-2} + \epsilon_t,$$

with $\epsilon_t \sim \mathbb{N}(0, 1)$.

```
simData:.quantQ.ts.simAR[(0.4;0.3);100000?.quantQ.simul.genBoxMuller[]];
.quantQ.ts.estARP[simData;2]
```

The estimated parameters $\hat{\Phi} = (\hat{c}, \hat{\Phi}_1, \hat{\Phi}_2)$

```
0.002898714 0.3967857 0.3017881
```

are close to $c = 0$, $\phi_1 = 0.4$ and $\phi_2 = 0.3$.

14.1.2.5 Maximum Likelihood Estimator

Assuming that the innovation $\epsilon_t \sim \mathbb{N}(0, \sigma^2)$ are independent, the likelihood function is:

$$l = \frac{1}{2\pi^{\frac{n}{2}}\sigma^n} e^{-\frac{1}{2\sigma^2}\sum_{t=p+1}^{n}(\mathbf{X_t} - \Phi_1\mathbf{X_{t-1}} - ... - \Phi_p\mathbf{X_{t-p}})^2}.$$

Maximising l means minimising $\sum_{t=p+1}^{n} (\mathbf{X_t} - \Phi_1\mathbf{X_{t-1}} - ... - \Phi_p\mathbf{X_{t-p}})^2$ and the method is equivalent to the least square estimator (14.6).

14.1.2.6 Yule-Walker Technique

Starting with the $AR(p)$ process $X_t = \Phi_1 X_{t-1} + ... + \Phi_p X_{t-p} + \epsilon_t$, we multiply both sides of the equation by X_{t-h}, $h > 0$ and take the expectation:

$$E[X_t X_{t-h}] = \Phi_1 E[X_{t-1}X_{t-h}] + \Phi_2 E[X_{t-2}X_{t-h-1}] + ... + \Phi_p E[X_{t-p}X_{t-h-p}] + E[\epsilon_t X_{t-h}]. \tag{14.8}$$

Let us denote the autocovariance of order h $E[X_t X_{t-h}]$ as $\gamma(h)$. The equation (14.8) can be rewritten as:

$$\gamma(h) = \Phi_1 \gamma(h-1) + ... + \Phi_p \gamma(h-p).$$

Dividing both sides by the variance $\gamma(0)$ and denoting the autocorrelation of order h by $\rho(h) = \frac{\gamma(h)}{\gamma(0)}$ we get:

$$\rho(h) = \Phi_1 \rho(h-1) + ... + \Phi_p \rho(h-p). \tag{14.9}$$

Since $\gamma(h) = \frac{E[X_t X_{t-h}]}{E[X_t^2]} = \gamma(-h) = \frac{E[X_t X_{t+h}]}{E[X_t^2]}$, $h = 1, ..., p$:

$$\begin{cases} \rho(1) &= \Phi_1 \rho(0) + ... + \Phi_p \rho(p-1) \\ ... &= ... \\ \rho(p) &= \Phi_1 \rho(p-1) + ... + \Phi_p \rho(0) \end{cases} \tag{14.10}$$

are called the Yule-Walker equations. If $\rho(h), h = 1, ..., p$ are known, $\mathbf{\Phi} = [\Phi_1, ..., \Phi_p]'$ are obtained by solving the system of p equations. Since $E[\epsilon_t X_t] = \sigma^2$, $\gamma(0) = \Phi_1 \gamma(1) + ... + \Phi_p \gamma(p) + \sigma^2$, hence:

$$\hat{\sigma}^2 = \gamma(0) - \Phi_1 \gamma(1) - ... - \Phi_p \gamma(p). \tag{14.11}$$

In general, $\rho(h)$ are unknown and need to be estimated from the sample. Denoting the sample autocorrelation $r(h) = \frac{\hat{\gamma}(h)}{\hat{\gamma}(0)}$ where $\hat{\gamma}(h) = \frac{1}{n} \sum_{t=1}^{n-h} (X_t - \overline{X})(X_{t+h} - \overline{X})$:

$$\begin{bmatrix} r(1) \\ r(2) \\ ... \\ r(p) \end{bmatrix} = \begin{bmatrix} r(0) & r(1) & ... & r(p-1) \\ r(1) & r(0) & ... & r(p-2) \\ ... & ... & ... & ... \\ r(p-1) & r(p-2) & ... & r(0) \end{bmatrix} \cdot \begin{bmatrix} \Phi_1 \\ \Phi_2 \\ ... \\ \Phi_p \end{bmatrix}. \tag{14.12}$$

The estimator of $\mathbf{\Phi} = [\Phi_1, ..., \Phi_p]'$ is $\hat{\Phi}_p = R_p^{-1} r_p$. As R is a Toeplitz matrix with non-null diagonal $r(0) = 1$, the Durbin-Levinson algorithm can be applied. Let us rewrite the $AR(p)$ process with a double suffix:

$$X_t = \Phi_{\mathbf{p},1} X_{t-1} + \Phi_{\mathbf{p},2} X_{t-2} + ... + \Phi_{\mathbf{p},p} X_{t-p} + \epsilon_t.$$

Starting recursively with $p = 1, 2, \ldots$ we have:

For $p = 1$, $\hat{\Phi}_{1,1} = r(1)$ with $\hat{\sigma}_1^2 = \hat{\gamma}(0)(1 - \hat{\Phi}_{1,1}^2)$.

For $p = 2$, $\hat{\Phi}_{2,2} = \frac{\hat{\gamma}(2) - \hat{\Phi}_{1,1} \hat{\gamma}(1)}{\hat{\sigma}_1^2}$ and $\hat{\Phi}_{2,1} = \hat{\Phi}_{1,1} - \hat{\Phi}_{2,2} \hat{\Phi}_{1,1}$ with $\hat{\sigma}_2^2 = \hat{\sigma}_1^2 (1 - \hat{\sigma}_{2,2}^2)$.

For any p, $\hat{\Phi}_{p,p} = \frac{\hat{\gamma}(p) - \sum_{j=1}^{p-1} \hat{\Phi}_{p-1,j} \hat{\gamma}(p-j)}{\hat{\sigma}_{p-1}^2}$ and

$$\begin{bmatrix} \hat{\Phi}_{p,1} \\ ... \\ \hat{\Phi}_{p,p-1} \end{bmatrix} = \begin{bmatrix} \hat{\Phi}_{p-1,1} \\ ... \\ \hat{\Phi}_{p-1,p-1} \end{bmatrix} - \hat{\Phi}_{p,p} \begin{bmatrix} \hat{\Phi}_{p-1,p-1} \\ ... \\ \hat{\Phi}_{p-1,1} \end{bmatrix},$$

with $\hat{\sigma}_p^2 = \hat{\sigma}_{p-1}^2 (1 - \hat{\Phi}_{p,p}^2)$.

A straightforward implementation of the Yule-Walker and Durbin-Levinson algorithms is given by the functions `.quantQ.ts.YuleWalker[p;data]` and `.quantQ.ts.DurbinLevinson[data;p]` described in the second part of the chapter. The least square method produces the same estimates of the *AR*(*p*) parameters as solving the Yule-Walker equations but is much slower than the iterative approach. The Durbin-Levinson algorithm is twice as fast as inverting the Toeplitz matrix $R_p^{-1} r_p$.

```
simData:.quantQ.ts.simAR[(0.4;0.3);100000?.quantQ.simul.genBoxMuller[]];
.quantQ.ts.estARP[simData;3]
.quantQ.ts.yuleWalker[simData;3]
.quantQ.ts.DurbinLevinson[simData;3]
```

returns:

```
0.002880853 0.3942897 0.2985167  0.008251775
0.3943002 0.2985118  0.008257555
0.3943002 0.2985118  0.008257555
```

However,

```
\t .quantQ.ts.estARP[data;3]
\t .quantQ.ts.yuleWalker[data;3]
\t .quantQ.ts.DurbinLevinson[data;3]
```

shows that it takes 913 milliseconds to estimate the parameters of 100,000 random numbers following the $ARMA(1,1)$ model $X_t = 0.4X_{t-1} + 0.3X_t + \epsilon_t$ by solving the OLS estimator while it takes 26 milliseconds by inverting the Toeplitz matrix and only 12 milliseconds by solving the Durbin-Levinson iterative algorithm:

```
913
26
12
```

14.1.3 *MA*(*q*) Process

Autoregressive processes are long memory models. They generally have an infinite non-zero autocorrelation decaying over time. Autoregressive processes cannot represent short memory series, where the current value of the series X_t is only correlated with a few past values X_{t-i}. This section presents moving average processes that are generally a function of a small number of past innovations.

A moving average process of order q, denoted as $MA(q)$, is defined as:

$$X_t = c + \epsilon_t + \alpha_1 \epsilon_{t-1} + \alpha_2 \epsilon_{t-2} + ... + \alpha_q \epsilon_{t-q}, \tag{14.13}$$

where $\alpha_1, \alpha_2, ..., \alpha_q$ are the parameters of the model, c a constant, and $\{\epsilon\}$ the white noise, i.e. $\epsilon_t \sim W\mathbb{N}(0, \sigma^2)$. The $MA(q)$ process is stationary by construction. Its expectation is $E[X_t] = c$ and variance is $Var[X_t] = \gamma(0) = \sigma^2(1 + \alpha_1^2 + \alpha_2^2 + ... + \alpha_q^2)$.

The autocorrelation $\gamma(s) = \begin{cases} \sigma^2(\alpha_s + \alpha_{s+1}\alpha_1 + \alpha_{s+2}\alpha_2 + ... + \alpha_q \alpha_{q-s}) & s \leq q \\ 0 & s > q \end{cases}$. Suppose that X_t is a zero-mean series with finite variance for each time t and $E[X_i X_j] = \gamma(i,j)$, where the matrix $[\gamma(i,j)]_{i,j=1}^n$ is non-singular for each $n = 1, 2, ...$

The one-step predictor of the $MA(q)$ process is given by:

$$\hat{X}_{n+1} = \begin{cases} 0 & n = 0 \\ \sum_{j=1}^{n} \hat{\alpha}_{nj}(X_{n+1-j} - \hat{X}_{n+1-j}) & n \geq 1 \end{cases}.$$

The one-step predictors $\hat{X}_1, \hat{X}_2, \ldots$ can be computed recursively once the coefficients $\hat{\alpha}_{ij}$ have been determined by the innovations algorithm (14.14).

14.1.3.1 Estimation of MA(q) Parameters

While the Durbin-Levinson algorithm gives the estimates of the coefficients in the representation:

$$\hat{X}_t = \sum_{j=1}^{p} \hat{\alpha}_{p,j} X_{t-j},$$

where $\hat{\alpha}_{p,j}, j = 1, \ldots, p$ are the parameters of the model, the innovations algorithm used to estimate the parameters of the $MA(q)$ process 14.13 considers the representation:

$$\hat{X}_t = \sum_{j=1}^{m} \hat{\theta}_{m,j}(X_{t-j} - \hat{X}_{t-j}).$$

As for the $AR(p)$ process, let us rewrite the $MA(q)$ process with a double suffix $X_t = \epsilon_t + \alpha_{q,1}\epsilon_{t-1} + \ldots + \alpha_{q,q}\epsilon_{t-q}$. Starting with $\hat{\sigma}_0^2 = \hat{\gamma}(0)$, the estimator of α recursively solves:

$$\hat{\alpha}_{q,q-k} = \frac{\hat{\gamma}(q-k) - \sum_{j=0}^{k-1} \hat{\alpha}_{q,q-j}\hat{\alpha}_{k,k-j}\hat{\sigma}_j^2}{\hat{\sigma}_k^2}, \tag{14.14}$$

for $q = 1, 2, 3, \ldots, k = 0, 1, \ldots, q-1$ and $\hat{\sigma}_q^2 = \hat{\gamma}(0) - \sum_{j=0}^{q-1} \hat{\alpha}_{q,q-j}^2 \hat{\sigma}_j^2$.

The innovations algorithm to estimate the parameters of the $MA(q)$ model is implemented with the function `.quantQ.ts.innovations[data;q]`.

14.1.3.2 Simulation

A moving average process of order 1 is simulated as:

$$X_1 = \epsilon_1 + \alpha_1\epsilon_0$$
$$X_2 = \epsilon_2 + \alpha_1\epsilon_1$$
$$\ldots$$
$$X_n = \epsilon_n + \alpha_1\epsilon_{n-1}.$$

Given a set of 5 random numbers $\epsilon_0, \ldots \epsilon_4$:

```
eps:-0.153913 2.22843 -0.320418 0.371417 0.573757;
```

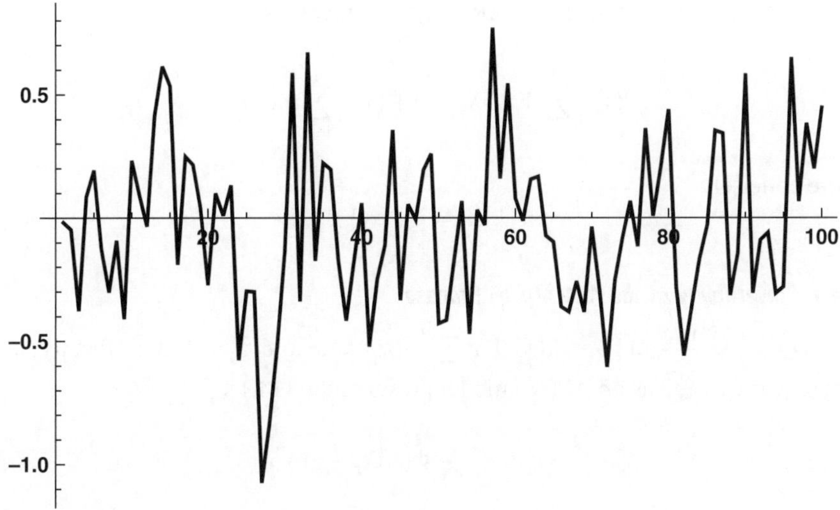

FIGURE 14.3 Simulated $MA(2)$ process $X_t = \epsilon_t + 0.5\epsilon_{t-1} + 0.3\epsilon_{t-2}$

An $MA(1)$ process is modelled as:

```
ma:{[alpha;eps] sum flip (1_eps,0),'(alpha*eps)}
```

For $\alpha = 0.9$, the function returns:

```
2.089908 1.685169 0.0830408 0.9080323 0.5163813
```

Generic $MA(q)$ models can be simulated with the recursive function `.quantQ.ts.simMA[q;alpha;eps]`.

14.1.3.3 Example

Figure 14.3 illustrates 100 simulated paths of an $MA(2)$ process:

$$X_t = \epsilon_t + 0.5\epsilon_{t-1} + 0.3\epsilon_{t-2},$$

generated with the function

```
.quantQ.ts.simMA[2;(0.5f;0.3f);100?.quantQ.simul.genBoxMuller[]]
```

14.1.4 *ARMA*(*p*, *q*) Process

The long memory $AR(p)$ model can be combined with the short memory $MA(q)$ process to produce a new family of tractable and flexible stationary processes called $ARMA(p, q)$. The autoregressive moving average process $ARMA(p, q)$ refers to the model with p autoregressive terms and q moving average terms:

$$X_t = c + \epsilon_t + \sum_{i=1}^{p} \Phi_i X_{t-i} + \sum_{i=1}^{q} \alpha_i \epsilon_{t-i}, \tag{14.15}$$

written with the lag operator L, the $ARMA(p, q)$ process is:

$$(1 - \sum_{i=1}^{p} \Phi_i L^i) X_t = c + (1 + \sum_{i=1}^{q} \alpha_i L^i)\epsilon_t,$$

or more concisely

$$\Phi(L)X_t = c + \alpha(L)\epsilon_t. \tag{14.16}$$

14.1.4.1 Invertibility of the ARMA(p, q) Process

Denoting $\pi(L) \equiv \frac{\Phi(L)}{\alpha(L)}$ and provided that $\sum_{j=0}^{\infty} |\pi_j| < \infty$ and $\pi_0 = 1$, the $ARMA(p, q)$ process can be presented as an $AR(\infty)$ model presented in (14.1):

$$\begin{aligned}\epsilon_t &= \frac{1}{\alpha(L)}(\Phi(L)X_t - c)\\ &= \pi(L)X_t - c\\ &= \sum_{j=0}^{\infty} \pi_j L^j X_t - c\\ &= \sum_{j=0}^{\infty} \pi_j X_{t-j} - c.\end{aligned}$$

14.1.4.2 Hannan-Rissanen Algorithm: Two-Step Regression Estimation

$ARMA(p, q)$ processes are a combination of autoregressive $AR(p)$ and moving average $MA(q)$ processes. The $p + q + 1$ parameters $\boldsymbol{\Phi} = (\Phi_1, ..., \Phi_p)'$, $\boldsymbol{\alpha} = (\alpha_1, ..., \alpha_q)'$ and σ^2 can be estimated with a two-step regression:

- Step 1: Regress x_t on its past values $x_{t-1}, ..., x_{t-m}$, $m > \max\{p, q\}$, and derive the OLS estimates of π_i, $i = 1, ..., m$ and the estimation of the residuals $\hat{\epsilon}_t = x_t - \sum_{i=1}^{m} \hat{\pi}_i x_{t-i}$.
- Step 2: Regress x_t on $x_{t-1}, ..., x_{t-p}$ and $\hat{\epsilon}_{t-1}, ..., \hat{\epsilon}_{t-q}$.

14.1.4.3 Yule-Walker Estimation

Following the same reasoning as for the $AR(p)$ process, the generalised Yule-Walker equations for the $ARMA(p, q)$ process are:

$$\begin{bmatrix} r(q+1) \\ r(q+2) \\ \cdots \\ r(q+p) \end{bmatrix} = \begin{bmatrix} r(q) & r(q-1) & \dots & r(q+2-p) & r(q+1-p) \\ r(q+1) & r(q) & \dots & r(q+3-p) & r(q+2-p) \\ \cdots & \cdots & \cdots & \cdots & \cdots \\ r(q+p-1) & r(q+p-2) & \dots & r(q+1) & r(q) \end{bmatrix} \cdot \begin{bmatrix} \Phi_1 \\ \Phi_2 \\ \cdots \\ \Phi_p \end{bmatrix}.$$

The Yule-Walker system of equations can be used to solve for Φ_i's given the autocorrelation function $r(i)$'s.

14.1.4.4 Maximum Likelihood Estimation

Let $\theta = (\Phi_1, ..., \Phi_p, \alpha_1, ..., \alpha_q, \sigma^2)'$ denote the parameters of the *ARMA*(p, q) process and let $\mathbf{x} = (x_1, ..., x_T)'$ be the observed sample of size T. The joint probability density function of the data given the parameter θ is $f(x_T, x_{T-1}, ...x_1|\theta)$. The likelihood function of the parameter θ given $\mathbf{x}$ is $L(\theta|\mathbf{x}) = f(x_T, x_{T-1}, ..., x_1|\theta)$. The maximum likelihood estimation is:

$$\hat{\theta}_{MLE} = \arg\max_{\theta\in\Theta} L(\theta|\mathbf{x}) = \arg\max_{\theta\in\Theta} \log L(\theta|\mathbf{x}).$$

Assuming that the error of the *ARMA*(p, q) process is Gaussian, $\epsilon_t \sim WN(0, \sigma^2)$, the likelihood is:

$$L(\theta|\mathbf{x}) = (2\pi)^{-T/2}|\Gamma(\theta)|^{-1/2}\exp(-\frac{1}{2}\mathbf{x}'\Gamma(\theta)^{-1}\mathbf{x}),$$

where the $T \times T$ variance-covariance matrix of x is $\Gamma(\theta) = E[\mathbf{x}\mathbf{x}']$. The log-likelihood to optimise is:

$$l(\theta|\mathbf{x}) = \log L(\theta|\mathbf{x}) = -\frac{1}{2}(T(\log(2\pi) + \log|\Gamma(\theta)| + \mathbf{x}'\Gamma(\theta)^{-1}\mathbf{x}). \quad (14.17)$$

14.1.4.5 Simulation

ARMA(p, q)processes are simulated with the q function `.quantQ.ts.simARMA[phi; alpha;eps]`. Figure 14.4 illustrates 100 simulated paths of a *ARMA*$(1, 1)$ process:

$$X_t = \epsilon_t - 0.4\epsilon_{t-1} + 0.99X_{t-1},$$

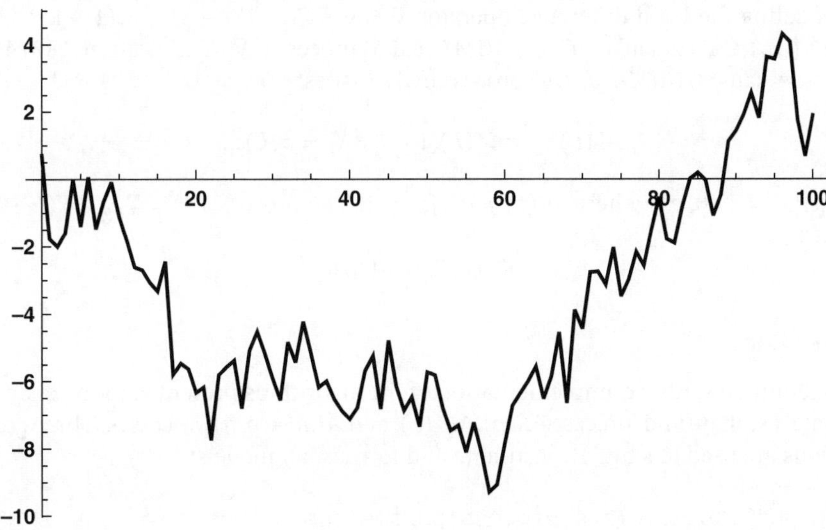

FIGURE 14.4 Simulated *ARMA*$(1, 1)$ process $X_t = \epsilon_t - 0.4\epsilon_{t-1} + 0.99X_{t-1}$

generated with the function

```
.quantQ.ts.simARMA[(enlist 0.99);(enlist -0.4);100?.quantQ.simul.
    ↪ genBoxMuller[]]
```

14.1.4.6 *Forecast*

The innovations algorithm (14.14) used to estimate and forecast the $MA(q)$ process can be adapted to forecast the $ARMA(p,q)$ model. The one-step predictor is given by:

$$\hat{X}_{n+1} = \begin{cases} \sum_{j=1}^{n} \hat{\alpha}_{nj}(X_{n+1-j} - \hat{X}_{n+1-j}) & 1 \leq n < m = \max\{p,q\} \\ \Phi_1 X_n + \ldots + \Phi_p X_{n+1-p} + \sum_{j=1}^{n} \hat{\alpha}_{nj}(X_{n+1-j} - \hat{X}_{n+1-j}) & n \geq m \end{cases}.$$

$\hat{\alpha}_{nj}$ is given in the innovations algorithm (14.14) with:

$$\hat{\gamma}(i,j) = \begin{cases} \sigma^{-2}\gamma(i-j) & 1 \leq i,j \leq m \\ \sigma^{-2}[\gamma(i-j) - \sum_{r=1}^{p} \Phi_r \gamma(r - |i-j|)] & \min\{i,j\} \leq m < \max\{i,j\} \leq 2m \\ \sum_{r=0}^{q} \hat{\alpha}_r \hat{\alpha}_{r+|i-j|} & \min\{i,j\} > m \\ 0 & \text{otherwise} \end{cases}.$$

14.1.5 *ARIMA*(p, d, q) Process

The autoregressive integrated moving average process is a generalisation of the $ARMA(p,q)$ process. It is defined with three parameters: as for the ARMA process, p is the order of the autoregressive component and q is the order of the moving average of the process. The parameter d indicates the order of the integration of the series. Let us define the lag-d difference operator ∇_d by $\nabla_d X_t = X_t - X_{t-d} = (1 - L^d)X_t$. The process $\{X_t, t \in \mathbb{Z}\}$ is said to be an ARIMA(p,d,q) process if $\nabla_d X_t$ is a causal $ARMA(p,q)$ process. A causal $ARIMA(p,d,q)$ process $\{X_t\}$ satisfies:

$$\Phi(L)X_t = \Phi^*(L)(1-L)^d X_t = \alpha(L)\epsilon_t,$$

with $\{\epsilon_t\} \sim W\mathbb{N}(0,\sigma^2)$ where $\Phi^*(z) \neq 0 \ \forall |z| \leq 1$. The process $Y_t := \nabla_d X_t = (I-L)^d X_t$ satisfies

$$\Phi^*(L)Y_t = \alpha(L)\epsilon_t. \tag{14.18}$$

14.1.6 Code

This section presents a q implementation of the algorithms presented in the chapter to simulate, estimate and forecast $AR(p)$, $MA(q)$, and $ARMA(p,q)$ processes. Three generic functions are used to simulate, estimate and forecast all models:

- `.quantQ.ts.simulate[process;params;eps]`
- `.quantQ.ts.estimate[data;process;lags]`
- `.quantQ.ts.forecast[data;period;process;lags]`.

14.1.6.1 Simulation

The generic function `.quantQ.ts.simulate` simulates autoregressive, moving average and ARMA processes covered in the chapter. The function takes three arguments. The first argument `process` takes the value `` `AR``, `` `MA`` and `` `ARMA``. The second parameter `params` contains the parameters of the model as a list of floating numbers. For ARMA models, `params` is of the form ((AR params; MA params)), where each sublist contains floating numbers.

```
.quantQ.ts.simulate:{[process;params;eps]
   // process -- type of process to simulate. Accepted values: `AR,`MA or `
       ↪ ARMA
   // params -- list of floating numbers containing the parameters of the
       ↪ process
   // eps -- list of random normal numbers
   $[process=`AR;
       $[9h=type params;
           :.quantQ.ts.simAR[params;eps];
           '"wrong type for params"        // note the single tick (') which
               ↪ is used to return an exception
];
       $[process=`MA;
           $[9h=type params;
               :.quantQ.ts.simMA[count params;params;eps];
               '"wrong type of params"
           ];
           $[process=`ARMA;
               $[(2=count params) & (9h = type params[0]) & (9h = type
                   ↪ params[1]);
                   :.quantQ.ts.simARMA[params[0];params[1];eps];
                   '"wrong type of params"
                   ];
                   '"process is `AR, `MA or `ARMA"
           ]
       ]
   ]
};
```

The simulation of $AR(p)$ model is performed by the function `.quant.ts.simAR`. The function simulates (14.1) given the list of parameters Φ_i, $i \in [1..p]$ and white noise ϵ.

```
.quantQ.ts.simAR:{[phi;eps]
   // phi -- list of parameters (phi1;...,phip)
   // eps -- list of random normal numbers
   p:count phi;
   x:(count eps)#0f;
   t:p;
   while[t<(count eps);
       // here all the error terms are used, can be replace with eps[t]
       x[t]:(x[(t-p)+til p] mmu phi)+eps[t-p];
       t:t+1];
   :x;
};
```

The simulation of moving average process (14.13) is computed recursively as follows:

```
.quantQ.ts.simMA:{[q;alpha;eps]
    // q -- order of the MA(q) process to simulate. q is an integer.
    // alpha -- list of parameters of the MA process (alpha1,...,alphaq)
    // eps -- list of random normal numbers
    :sum flip $[q>1;
        (,')[(q _eps,q#0);((q-1) _alpha[q-1]*eps,(q-1)#0)],'.quantQ.ts.simMA
            ↪ [q-1;alpha;eps];
        (,')[(q _eps,0);(q-1) _alpha[q-1]*eps]];
};
```

The $ARMA(p,q)$ process (14.15) is simulated given the white noise process ϵ and list of parameters for autoregressive coefficients Φ_i, $i \in [1..p]$ and moving average α_i, $i \in [1..q]$:

```
.quantQ.ts.simARMA:{[phi;alpha;eps]
    // phi -- list of parameters of the AR(p) process.
    // alpha -- list of parameters of the MA(q) process
    // eps -- list of random numbers
    p:count phi;
    q:count alpha;
    x:(count eps)#0f;
    t:p;
    while[t<(count eps);
        x[t]:(x[(t-p)+til p] mmu phi)+(eps[(t-q)+til q] mmu alpha);
        t:t+1];
    :x;
}
```

14.1.6.2 Estimation

The generic function `.quantQ.ts.estimate` estimates the coefficients of the autoregressive, moving average and ARMA processes. The function estimates the coefficients on the list of floating point numbers provided in the first argument. The second parameter `process` takes the value `` `AR``, `` `MA`` or `` `ARMA`` depending on the type of process to be estimated. The third parameter contains either an integer corresponding to the order of the autoregressive or moving average process or a list of two integers for the two lags of the $ARMA(p,q)$ process.

```
.quantQ.ts.estimate:{[data;process;lags]
    // data -- historical data (list of floating numbers) used to estimate
        ↪ the process.
    // process -- type of process to simulate. Accepted values: `AR,`MA or `
        ↪ ARMA
    // lags -- order of the process. integer for AR and MA process. List of
        ↪ two integers for ARMA
    $[process=`AR;
        $[-7h = type lags;
            :.quantQ.ts.DurbinLevinson[data;lags];
            $[7h = type lags;
```

```
            :.quantQ.ts.DurbinLevinson[data;first lags];
            :'"wrong type of the parameter lags"]
        ];
      $[process=`MA;
          $[-7h = type lags;
              :.quantQ.ts.innovations[data;lags];
              $[7h = type lags;
                  :quantQ.ts.innovations[data;first lags];
                  :'"wrong type of the parameter lags"]
          ];
          $[process=`ARMA;
              $[7h = type lags;
                  :.quantQ.ts.HannanRissanen[data;lags[0];lags[1]];
                  :'"The estimation of ARMA(p,q) processes requires a list
                      ↪ of two integers for the lag parameter"
              ];
              :'"unknown process type. Accepted values: `AR; `MA and `ARMA
                  ↪ "
          ]
      ]
   ]
};
```

The autoregressive process *AR*(*p*) is estimated with the Durbin-Levinson algorithm by default as the procedure is quicker than solving the Yule-Walker equation or inverting the matrix (14.6) to compute the OLS estimator. The Durbin-Levinson algorithm is implemented as follows:

```
.quantQ.ts.DurbinLevinson:{[data;p]
   // data -- historical data (list of floating numbers) used to estimate
      ↪ the AR(p) process.
   // p -- order of the AR(p) model.
   p:p+1;
   phi:(p;p)#0f;
   v:p#0f;
   phi[1;1]:.quantQ.ts.gamma[1;data]%.quantQ.ts.gamma[0;data];
   v[0]:.quantQ.ts.gamma[0;data];
   n:1;
   s:0f;
   while[n<p;
       j:1;
       while[j<n;
           s:s+phi[n-1;j]*.quantQ.ts.gamma[n-j;data];
           j:j+1];
       phi[n;n]:(.quantQ.ts.gamma[n;data]-s)%v[n-1];
       s:0f;
       v[n]:v[n-1]*(1f-(phi[n;n] xexp 2));
       j:1;
       while[j<n;
           phi[n;j]:phi[n-1;j]-phi[n;n]*phi[n-1;n-j];
           j:j+1];
       n:n+1];
   :1_phi[p-1;];
};
```

Given the function `.quantQ.ts.toeplitz` to build the Toeplitz matrix (14.12) of sample autocorrelation `.quantQ.ts.r`, first, we define the sample autocovariance function of order `h`:

```
.quantQ.ts.gamma:{[h;data]
   // h -- order of autocorrelation
   // data -- data
   :(neg[h]_data) cov (h _data);
};
```

then the sample autocorrelation function of order `h`:

```
.quantQ.ts.r:{[data;h]
   // h -- order of autocorrelation
   // data -- data
   :.quantQ.ts.gamma[h;data]%.quantQ.ts.gamma[0;data];
};
```

and, finally, the Toeplitz matrix:

```
.quantQ.ts.toeplitz:{[data;p]
   // data -- historical data (list of floating numbers)
   // p -- order of the AR(p) process
   t:abs (til p)-/:(til p);
   :(p;p)#{[x;data].quantQ.ts.r[data;x]}[;data] each raze t;
};
```

The Yule-Walker equations can be solved as follows:

```
.quantQ.ts.yuleWalker:{[data;p]
   // data -- historical data (list of floating numbers)
   // p -- order of the AR(p) model
   :inv[.quantQ.ts.toeplitz[data;p]] mmu (.quantQ.ts.r[data;] each 1+til p)
       ↪ ;
};
```

Finally, the OLS estimator (14.6) can be implemented as:

```
.quantQ.ts.estARP:{[data;p]
   // data -- historical data (list of floating numbers) used to estimate
       ↪ the AR(p) model
   // p -- order of the AR(p) process
   n:count data;
   dim:(n-p;p+1);
   x:dim#0f;
   i:0;j:1;
   while[i<(n-p);
       x[i;0]:1f;
       while[j<p+1;
           $[0<=i-j;
               x[i;j]:data[i-j];
           x[i;j]:0f];
        j:j+1];
```

```
    j:1;
    i:i+1];
    y:neg[p]_ data;
    :inv[(flip x) mmu x] mmu (flip x) mmu y;
};
```

An implementation of the innovations algorithm (14.14) to estimate the coefficients of the *MA*(*q*) process is provided as:

```
.quantQ.ts.innovations:{[data;q]
   // data -- historical data (list of floating numbers) used to estimate
       ↪ the MA(q) process
   // q -- order of the MA(q) process
   p:10*q; // until convergence
   v:(p+1)#0f;
   alpha:(p+1;p+1)#0f;
   v[0]:.quantQ.ts.gamma[0;data];
   n:1;
   k:0;
   while[n<=p;
       k:0;
       while[k<n;
           j:0; s:0f;
           while[j<k;
               s:s+(alpha[k;k-j]*alpha[n;n-j]*v[j]);
               j:j+1;
           ];
           alpha[n;n-k]:(.quantQ.ts.gamma[n-k;data] - s)%v[k];
           k:k+1;
           s:0f; j:0;
           while[j<n;
               s:s+(alpha[n;n-j] xexp 2)*v[j];
               j:j+1;
           ];
           v[n]:.quantQ.ts.gamma[0;data]-s;
       ];
       n:n+1;
   ];
   :alpha[p-1;1+ til q];
};
```

The innovations algorithm converges more slowly than the number of lags of the moving average process. Thus, we multiply the number of lags q by 10 to improve the estimator and select the q first element of the alpha matrix.

The parameters of the *ARMA*(p, q) are estimated by solving the Hannan-Rissanen algorithm with a two-step regression:

```
.quantQ.ts.HannanRissanen:{[data;p;q]
   // data -- historical data (list of floating numbers) used to estimate
       ↪ the ARMA(p,q) process
   // p -- order of the AR(p) process
   // q -- order of the MA(q) process
```

```
    // Step 1 - Estimate AR(max(p+q)+1)
    lags:1+(p|q);
    arEst:.quantQ.ts.DurbinLevinson[data;lags];
    res:.quantQ.ts.residualsAR[arEst;data];
    res:(lags#0f),res;
    // Step 2 - regress data[t] on (data[t-1],...,data[t-p],res[t-1],...,res
        ↪ [t-q])
    // for t = lag+q, ..., n by OLS
    t:(lags+q) _ til count data;
    x:(reverse each .quantQ.ts.matrix[t;p;data]),'(reverse each .quantQ.ts.
        ↪ matrix[t;q;res]);
    :(inv[(flip x) mmu x] mmu flip x) mmu data[t];
};
```

where the recursive helper function `.quantQ.ts.matrix` stacks the series d into a matrix and computes `(d[t-q];d[t-q-1];...;d[t-1])`:

```
.quantQ.ts.matrix:{[t;q;d]
    // t -- index
    // q -- order of the MA(q) process
    // d -- series
    :$[q>1; d[t-q],'.quantQ.ts.matrix[t;q-1;d];d[t-1]];
};
```

The implementation of the estimator for the *ARIMA*(p, d, q) process is left as an exercise for our readers. It can be estimated by modifying the Yule-Walker equation of the *ARMA*(p, q) process or by adapting the Hannan-Rissanen algorithm.

14.1.6.3 Forecast

The generic function `.quantQ.ts.forecast[data;period;process;lags]` forecasts `period`-step ahead the process of order `lags` based on the data set `data`. The parameter `data` is a list of floating numbers. The argument `period` is a positive integer. The variable `process` contains the values `` `AR`` for autoregressive process, `` `MA`` for moving average process or `` `ARMA`` for autoregressive moving average processes. The fourth parameter `lags` is positive integer or list of two positive integers for *ARMA*(p, q) models.

```
.quantQ.ts.forecast:{[data;period;process;lags]
    // data -- historical data (list of floating numbers) used to forecast
        ↪ the process
    // period -- forecast period-step ahead the process where period is a
        ↪ positive integer.
    // process -- type of process to simulate. Accepted values: `AR,`MA or `
        ↪ ARMA
    // lags -- order of the process. integer for AR and MA process. List of
        ↪ two integers for ARMA.
    $[process=`AR;
        $[(-7h=type period) & (period > 0);
            $[-7h = type lags;
                :.quantQ.ts.forecastAR[data;period;lags];
               $[7h = type lags;
```

```
                    :.quantQ.ts.forecastAR[data;period;first lags];
                    '"wrong type of the parameter lags for AR processes"]
            ];
            '"period needs to be a positive integer"
        ];
        $[process=`MA;
            $[(-7h=type period) & (period > 0);
                $[-7h = type lags;
                    :.quantQ.ts.forecastMA[data;period;lags];
                    $[7h = type lags;
                        :.quantQ.ts.forecastMA[data;period;first lags];
                        '"wrong type of the parameter lags for MA processes
                            ↪ "]
                ];
                '"period needs to be a positive integer"
            ];
            $[process=`ARMA;
                $[(-7h=type period) & (period > 0);
                    $[7h = type lags;
                        :.quantQ.ts.forecastARMA[data;period;lags[0];lags
                            ↪ [1]];
                        '"lags needs to be a list of two positive integers
                            ↪ for ARMA(p,q) process"
                    ];
                    '"period needs to be a positive integer"
                ];
                '"unknown process type. Accepted values `AR; `MA and `ARMA"
            ]
        ]
    ]
};
```

The autoregressive forecasting subroutine is implemented recursively as:

```
.quantQ.ts.forecastAR:{[data;period;lags]
   // data --  historical data (list of floating) used to forecast the AR(
        ↪ lags) model
   // period -- number of steps (positive integer) forecasted
   // lags -- positive integer containing the order of the autoregressive
        ↪ process
   forecast:((neg lags)#data) mmu .quantQ.ts.DurbinLevinson[data;lags];
   data:data,forecast;
   $[period=1;
        :forecast;
        :forecast,.quantQ.ts.forecastAR[data;period-1;lags]
   ]
};
```

To forecast a *MA*(q) process, we assume that the estimated model is the true model and fill in unknown values with predictions. Let's take an *MA*(2) process as an example:

$$X_t = c + \epsilon_t + \alpha_1 \epsilon_{t-1} + \alpha_2 \epsilon_{t-2}.$$

The one-step forecast is:

$$X_{n+1} = c + \epsilon_{n+1} + \alpha_1\epsilon_n + \alpha_2\epsilon_{n-1}$$
$$\hat{X}_{n+1} = c + 0 + \alpha_1\epsilon_n + \alpha_2\epsilon_{n-1},$$

with $\epsilon_{n+1} = X_{n+1} - \hat{X}_{n+1}$ and variance $Var(X_{n+1} - \hat{X}_{n+1}) = \sigma$. The two-step forecast solves:

$$X_{n+2} = c + \epsilon_{n+2} + \alpha_1\epsilon_{n+1} + \alpha_2\epsilon_n$$
$$\hat{X}_{n+2} = c + 0 + \alpha_1 \cdot 0 + \alpha_2\epsilon_n.$$

The forecasted error is $X_{n+2} - \hat{X}_{n+2} = \epsilon_{n+2} + \alpha_1\epsilon_{n+1}$. The variance of the error $Var(X_{n+2} - \hat{X}_{n+2}) = \sigma^2(1 - \alpha_1^2)$ as explained in 14.1.3. The third step forecasts:

$$X_{n+3} = c + \epsilon_{n+3} + \alpha_1\epsilon_{n+2} + \alpha_2\epsilon_{n+1}$$
$$\hat{X}_{n+3} = c.$$

The forecasted error is $X_{n+3} - \hat{X}_{n+3} = \epsilon_{n+3} + \alpha_1\epsilon_{n+2} + \alpha_2\epsilon_{n+1}$ and the variance of the error $Var(X_{n+3} - \hat{X}_{n+3}) = \sigma^2(1 - \alpha_1^2 - \alpha_2^2)$.

The code to forecast an $MA(q)$ model can, therefore, be implemented as follows:

```
.quantQ.ts.forecastMA:{[data;q]
    // data -- historical data (list of floating) used to forecast the AR(
        ↪ lags) model
    // q -- degree of MA
    est:(q+2)#0f;
    v:(q+1)#0f;
    alpha:(q+1;q+1)#0f;
    v[0]:.quantQ.ts.gamma[0;data];
    n:1;
    k:0;
    while[n<=q;
        k:0;
        while[k<n;
            j:0; s:0f;
            while[j<k;
                s:s+(alpha[k;k-j]*alpha[n;n-j]*v[j]);
                j:j+1;
            ];
        alpha[n;n-k]:(.quantQ.ts.gamma[n-k;data] - s)%v[k];
        k:k+1;
        s:0f; j:0;
            while[j<n;
                s:s+(alpha[n;n-j] xexp 2)*v[j];
                j:j+1;
            ];
            v[n]:.quantQ.ts.gamma[0;data]-s;
        ];
        n:n+1;
    ];
```

```
    // one-step predictor of MA(q)
    n:1;
    while[n <= q;
        j:1;s:0f;
        while[j <= n;
            s:s+(alpha[n;j]*(data[j]-est[j]));
            j:j+1];
        est[n+1]:s;
        n:n+1;
        s:0f
    ];
    :1_est;
};
```

Forecasting the ARMA process follows the same principle. Given the ARMA process

$$X_t = \Phi_1 X_{t-1} + ... + \Phi_p X_{t-p} + \epsilon_t + \alpha_1 \epsilon_{t-1} + ... + \alpha_q \epsilon_{t-q},$$

the one-step ahead forecast is $\hat{X}_{n+1} = \Phi_1 X_n + ... + \Phi_p X_{n-p+1} + (\hat{\epsilon}_{n+1} = 0) + \alpha_1 \hat{\epsilon}_n + ... + \alpha_q \epsilon_{n-q+1}$. The two-step ahead forecast is $\hat{X}_{n+2} = \Phi_1 \hat{X}_{n+1} + ... + \Phi_p X_{n-p+2} + (\hat{\epsilon}_{n+2} = 0) + \alpha_1(\hat{\epsilon}_{n+1} = 0) + ... + \alpha_q \epsilon_{n-q+2}$. The third-step ahead forecast is $\hat{X}_{n+3} = \Phi_1 \hat{X}_{n+2} + \Phi_2 \hat{X}_{n+1} + ... + \Phi_p X_{n-p+3} + (\hat{\epsilon}_{n+3} = 0) + \alpha_1(\hat{\epsilon}_{n+2} = 0) + \alpha_2(\hat{\epsilon}_{n+1} = 0) + ... + \alpha_q \epsilon_{n-q+3}$. The $q+1$ step ahead forecast is $\hat{X}_{n+q+1} = \Phi_1 \hat{X}_{n+q} + \Phi_2 \hat{X}_{n+q-1} + ... + \Phi_p X_{n-p+q+1} + (\hat{\epsilon}_{n+q+1} = 0) + \alpha_1(\hat{\epsilon}_{n+q} = 0) + \alpha_2(\hat{\epsilon}_{n+q-1} = 0) + ... + \alpha_q(\hat{\epsilon}_{n+1} = 0)$. We clearly see that the moving average terms disappear. The implementation of this function is left as an advanced exercise for our readers. If the function `.quantQ.ts.forecastARMA` will not be implemented, the function `.quantQ.ts.forecast` has to be simply amended to tackle the case of `ARMA`.

14.2 STATIONARITY AND GRANGER CAUSALITY

14.2.1 Stationarity

A stochastic process is said to be stationary if its statistical properties do not change with time. Formally, a time series X_t, $t \in \mathbb{Z}$ is weakly stationary or wide sense stationary if:

- It has a finite variance: $Var(X_t) < \infty \; \forall t \in \mathbb{Z}$.
- The mean is constant: $\mu_X(t) = \mu, \forall t \in \mathbb{Z}$.
- The autocovariance does not depend on time $Cov(X_t, X_{t+h}) = Cov(X_{t+r}, X_{t+r+h})$, $\forall r \in \mathbb{Z}$.

A process is said to be strictly stationary if any finite collection $(X_{n_1}, ..., X_{n_k})$ has the same distribution as $(X_{n_1+t}, ..., X_{n_k+t})$ for any $k \geq 1$ and $(n_1, ..., n_k, t) \in \mathbb{Z}$.

14.2.2 Test of Stationarity – Dickey-Fuller and Augmented Dickey-Fuller Tests

The Dickey-Fuller (DF) test tests the null hypothesis that a unit root is present in an autoregressive model. The test estimates three models:

- The first model is an $AR(1)$ process without constant: $y_t = \rho_1 y_{t-1} + \epsilon_t$.
- The second model is an $AR(1)$ process with constant: $y_t = \beta_2 + \rho_2 y_{t-1} + \epsilon_t$.
- The third model adds a trend to the $AR(1)$ with constant: $y_t = \mu_1 t + \beta_3 + \rho_3 y_{t-1} + \epsilon_t$.

The first model can be rewritten as $\Delta y_t = (\rho_1 - 1)y_{t-1} + \epsilon_t = \phi_1 y_{t-1} + \epsilon_t$, the second model $\Delta y_t = \mu_1 + \phi_2 y_{t-1} + \epsilon_t$ and the third $\Delta y_t = \mu_2 + \beta t + \phi_3 y_{t-1} + \epsilon_t$.

The DF test tests the stationarity of $AR(1)$ processes. The test can be augmented to detect unit root for $AR(p)$. It is called Augmented Dickey–Fuller (ADF) test. The ADF test estimates three models:

- The $AR(p)$ model without constant: $\Delta y_t = \phi y_{t-1} + \sum_{j=2}^{p} \beta_j \Delta y_{t-j+1} + \epsilon_t$.
- The $AR(p)$ model with constant: $\Delta y_t = \mu_1 + \phi y_{t-1} + \sum_{j=2}^{p} \beta_j \Delta y_{t-j+1} + \epsilon_t$.
- The $AR(p)$ model with constant and trend: $\Delta y_t = \mu_2 + \beta(t - p - \frac{T-p+1}{2}) + \phi y_{t-1} + \sum_{j=2}^{p} \beta_j \Delta y_{t-j+1} + \epsilon_t$.

The null hypothesis of the ADF test is the non-stationarity (unit root) of the variable y_t, i.e. $H_0 : \phi = 0$. The ADF test compares the Student-t associated with the parameter ϕ with the tabulated values of the statistics given by MacKinnon (1996). The null hypothesis of non-stationarity is rejected at 5% if $t_{obs} < ADF_{0.05}$. The optimal number of lags of $AR(p)$ can be determined with the AIC test described in Chapter 13 dedicated to linear regression and implemented with the function `.quantQ.ols.AIC:[p;logL]`.

To determine whether to retain the hypothesis of a unit root with or without a constant, the Student-t associated with the constant μ_1 is compared with the tabulated values of the statistics. For the third model, the ADF test checks whether the estimated values of the coefficients associated with the constant (μ_2) and trend (β) are significantly different from zero with $H_0 : \mu_2 = 0$ and $H_0 : \beta_0$.

The Δ of a time series `data` is simply `deltas data`. The three autoregressive models can be estimated with the function `.quantQ.ts.DurbinLevinson[data;q]`. Tabulated values of the statistics given by MacKinnon can be stored in a dictionary and compared with the t-stat t_{obs} as implemented in the function `.quantQ.ols.fit`.

14.2.3 Granger Causality

The models presented so far are, somehow, limited. They only use past realisations of a random variable to explain its current and future values. In addition to the use of past values of a random variable to forecast its future, a model can often be improved by adding historical values of external factors, also called exogenous variables. An autoregressive process of order p with exogenous variables, denoted as $ARX(p)$, is given by:

$$Y_t = a_0 + a_1 Y_{t-1} + ... + a_p Y_{t-p} + b_1 X_{t-1} + ... + b_p X_{t-p} + \epsilon_t. \tag{14.19}$$

By the same token, an $ARMAX(p, q)$ process is defined as:

$$Y_t = a_0 + \epsilon_t + \sum_{i=1}^{p} a_i Y_{t-i} + \sum_{i=1}^{p} b_i X_{t-i} + \sum_{i=1}^{q} c_i \epsilon_{t-i}. \tag{14.20}$$

The parameters of these two models with exogenous variables can be estimated with the same methods as their based models. To determine whether the lagged values of an exogenous variable explain the current and future values of a random variable, we introduce the Granger Causality test. The Granger Causality test is a statistical hypothesis test for determining whether an external time series $X(t)$ is useful in forecasting another, say $Y(t)$. A time series X is said to Granger-cause Y if it can be shown, by running a t-test or an F-test on lagged values of X, that those historical values of X provide statistically significant information about future values of Y. To find out whether X Granger-uses Y, we compare the $AR(p)$ model with the corresponding $ARX(p)$ model and perform a t-test for individual coefficients with the null hypothesis $H_0 : b_1 = ... = b_p = 0$ against the alternative hypothesis H_1 that at least one coefficient is non-zero.

We can also run an F-test:

$$F = \frac{(R^2_{fullModel} - R^2_{restrictedModel})/nbAdditionalVariables}{(1 - R^2_{fullModel})/(nbObs - nbParamsFullModel)},$$

and compare it with $F^*(nbAddedParams, nbObs - nbParamsFullModels)$. The null hypothesis of no Granger causality is rejected if $F > F^*$. Note that the Granger Causality test suffers from some limitations such as:

- Granger Causality is not necessarily true causality.
- The Granger Causality often fails if an exogenous variable X affects Y through another time series Z.
- When X(t) is autocorrelated, the impact of lagged values of X on Y(t) is simply a consequence of the impact of X(t) on Y(t).

A q implementation of the F-test presented in the previous chapter is `.quantQ.ols.fStatistics`.

14.3 VECTOR AUTOREGRESSION

This chapter generalises the univariate autoregressive and moving average process to capture the linear interdependencies among multiple time series. Simply speaking a vector autoregressive model $VAR(p)$ is a generalisation of an $AR(p)$ process where the random variable X_t is replaced with a vector of random variables $X_t = (X_{1t}, ..., X_{Kt})$.

14.3.1 *VAR*(*p*) Process

The vector autoregressive process (VAR) of order p is given by

$$Y_t = \nu + A_1 Y_{t-1} + \dots + A_p Y_{t-p} + u_t, \tag{14.21}$$

for $t = 0, 1, 2, \dots$ where $u_t = (u_{1t}, \dots, u_{Kt})'$ is a K-dimensional white noise or innovation process with $E[u_t] = 0$, $E[u_t u_t'] = \Sigma_u$ and $E[u_t u_s'] = 0$ for $s \neq t$.

14.3.1.1 Notation

Let us assume that $y_1, \dots, y_T$ is available for each of the K variables for the same sample period. We introduce the following notations:

- $Y := (y_1, \dots, y_T)'$ a $K \times T$ matrix
- $B := (\nu, A_1, \dots, A_p)$ a $K \times (Kp + 1)$ matrix
- $Z_t = \begin{bmatrix} 1 \\ y_t \\ \dots \\ y_{t-p+1} \end{bmatrix}$ a $(Kp + 1) \times 1$ matrix
- $Z := (Z_0, \dots, Z_{T-1})$ a $(K + 1) \times T$ matrix
- $U := (u_1, \dots, u_T)$ a $K \times T$ matrix
- $y := vec(Y)$ a $KT \times 1$ matrix
- $\beta := vec(B)$ a $(K^2 p + K) \times 1$ matrix
- $b := vec(B')$ a $(K^2 p + K) \times 1$ matrix
- $u := vec(U)$ a $KT \times 1$ matrix.

14.3.1.2 Estimator

An unbiased estimator of a *VAR*(*p*) process defined in (14.21) is

$$\hat{B} = YZ'(ZZ')^{-1}. \tag{14.22}$$

The estimator of the variance-covariance matrix of the residual is given by:

$$\hat{\Sigma}_U = \frac{1}{T - Kp - 1}(YY' - YZ'(ZZ')^{-1}ZY'). \tag{14.23}$$

To estimate whether the estimated coefficients $\hat{B}$ of the model are significant, we can compare the associated element of t-ratios matrix

$$\frac{\hat{B}}{\sqrt{diag(\hat{\Sigma}_u \otimes (ZZ')^{-1})}}, \tag{14.24}$$

with the critical values from a t-distribution with $KT - K^2 p - K$ degrees of freedom. The operator $\otimes$ is the Kronecker product and diag is the diagonal of the matrix

$\hat{\Sigma}_u \otimes (ZZ')^{-1}$. Assuming that y_t is Gaussian, an approximation of a $(1-\alpha)$ interval forecast h-step ahead for k-th component $y_{k,t}$ is $[\hat{y}_{k,t}(h) \pm z_{(\alpha/2)}\hat{\sigma}_k(h)]$. $\hat{\sigma}_k(h)$ is the square root of the k-th diagonal element of $\hat{\Sigma}_{\hat{y}}(h)$ and $z_{(\alpha/2)}$ is the $(\alpha/2)^{th}$ quantile of the normal distribution.

$$\hat{\Sigma}_{\hat{y}}(h) = \hat{\Sigma}_y(h) + \frac{1}{T}\hat{\Omega}(h)$$

$$\hat{\Omega}(h) = \sum_{i=0}^{h-1}\sum_{j=0}^{h-1} tr[(\hat{\mathbf{B}}')^{h-1-i}\hat{\Gamma}^{-1}\hat{\mathbf{B}}^{h-1-j}\hat{\Gamma}]\hat{\phi}_i\hat{\Sigma}_u\hat{\phi}_j',$$

with $\Gamma = E[Z_t Z_t']$, $\hat{\phi}_i = J_1 \hat{\mathbf{B}}^{\mathbf{i}} J_1'$, $J_1 = [0_{K\times1} : I_K : 0_{K\times1} : ... : 0_{K\times1}]$ a $K \times (Kp+1)$ matrix.

The order of a *VAR(p)* process is usually unknown and needs to be determined. Choosing an unnecessarily large value of p reduces the forecast precision the model. Y_t is called a *VAR(p)* process if $A_p \neq 0$ and $A_i = 0$ for $i > p$ so that the p is the smallest possible order. The likelihood ratio statistic determines the correct VAR order by testing the significance of coefficient A_M of an upper bound VAR order M. The null hypothesis $H_0^{M-m-1} : A_m = 0$ versus the alternative hypothesis $H_1^{M-m-1} : A_m \neq 0$ is tested for decreasing values of $m \in [M, M-1, ...1]$ conditionally on the previous values being true. If H_0^{M-m-1} is rejected, the order $\hat{p} = m$ is chosen as the optimal order of the VAR process. The likelihood ratio test statistic for testing the $M-m-1$-th null hypothesis solves:

$$\lambda_{LR}(M-m-1) = T[\log det(\tilde{\Sigma}_u(m-2)) - \log det(\tilde{\Sigma}_u(m-1))], \tag{14.25}$$

where T is the length of the time series and $\tilde{\Sigma}_u$ is the least square estimator

$$\tilde{\Sigma}_u = \frac{1}{T}(Y(I_T - Z')(ZZ')^{-1}Z)Y. \tag{14.26}$$

The likelihood ratio test λ_{LR} follows a χ^2 distribution with K degrees of freedom.

14.3.1.3 Example

To illustrate the *VAR(p)* model, let us model the quarterly and seasonally adjusted West German fixed investment, disposable income and consumption expenditures given in file `e1.csv` available on the book website. The data set comes from Helmut (2005) and is present on the author's website, http://www.jmulti.de/download/datasets/e1.dat.

```
// store the content of the file in a table
data:flip (`invest`income`consumption)!("III";";") 0:`:e1.csv;
// add the dates
data:`date xkey update date:`date$(`month$1960.01.01) + 3*til count data
    ↪ from data;
```

We only take the data from 1960 until 1978 and compute the log-return for the three time series. The data set is a 3×75 matrix:

```
// compute the log return of the data
ldata:`date xkey 1_(select date from data),'deltas log value data;
// only select data from 1960 until end of 1978
ldata:select from ldata where date within (1960.04.01;1978.12.01);
// only select the values of the data
d:value[ldata][(cols ldata) except keys ldata];
```

Figure 14.5 captures the evolution of the Investment (dashed line), disposable income (bold-dashed line), and consumption expenditure (dotted line) between years 1960 and 1978 for West Germany as given by the variable `data`. The log-return version of the data is presented in Figure 14.6.

We first want to determine the optimal order of the vector autoregressive process for the data set `ldata` containing the three time series: investment (S), disposable income

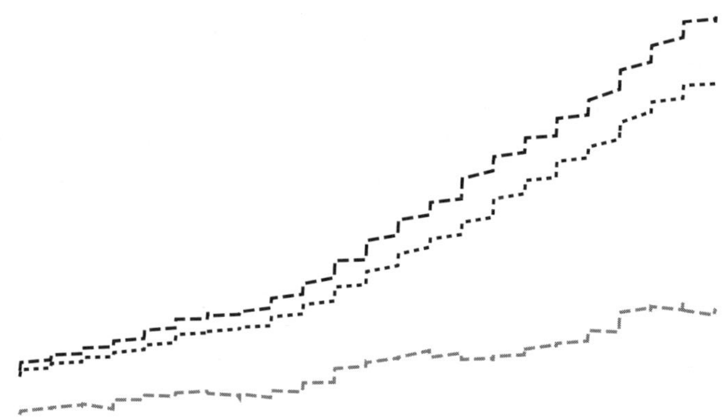

FIGURE 14.5 Investment (dashed line), disposable income (bold-dashed line), and consumption expenditure (dotted line) between years 1960 and 1978 for West Germany as given by the variable `data`

FIGURE 14.6 Log-return of the investment, the income, and the consumption between years 1960 and 1978 for West Germany as given by the variable `ldata`

(I) and consumption expenditure (C). The optimal number of lags is the number p such that the parameters $A_i \neq 0$, $i \in [1, ..., p]$:

$$\begin{pmatrix} S_{t+p} & I_{t+p} & C_{t+p} \\ S_{t+p+1} & I_{t+p+1} & C_{t+p+1} \\ \dots & \dots & \dots \\ S_T & I_T & C_T \end{pmatrix} = \hat{\nu} + \hat{A}_1 \begin{pmatrix} S_{t+p-1} & I_{t+p-1} & C_{t+p-1} \\ S_{t+p} & I_{t+p} & C_{t+p} \\ \dots & \dots & \dots \\ S_T & I_T & C_T \end{pmatrix} + \dots + \hat{A}_p \begin{pmatrix} S_t & I_t & C_t \\ S_{t+1} & I_{t+1} & C_{t+1} \\ \dots & \dots & \dots \\ S_T & I_T & C_T \end{pmatrix}.$$

Given an upper bound order M, the function `.quantQ.ts.varOrder[y;M]` computes the likelihood ratio test statistic LR given in (14.25) for $p = [1; M]$ and the associated p-value. The order p is significant at a 0.05 level if $lr(p) > q\chi_{95\%}(K^2)$. Based on the p-value, `.quantQ.ts.varOrder[d;4]` shows that the optimal number of lags is 2.

```
p| lr       pvalue
-| --------------------
0| 14.47595 0.1070603
1| 4.032504 -0.07941333
2| 29.10602 0.000621964
3| 22.597   0.007169783
```

We then forecast the three time series (S, I and C) with a $VAR(2)$ model and measure the precision of the estimation by computing an interval of confidence for the forecasted values. The function `.quantQ.ts.tRatios[y;p]` computes the matrix of t-ratios (14.24) for a matrix of incoming data y and lag p.

The result of `.quantQ.ts.tRatios[d;2]` is

```
-0.9707203 -2.547745   0.2675425 1.446943  -1.285368 0.2143873 1.4049
3.604272   1.37891     -1.102199 1.71015   1.577281  0.1411818 -0.06041993
3.666287   -0.09435428 2.013052  -1.941514 1.32533   3.243976  -0.1633121
```

The critical values of the t-distribution with $(3 \times 75) + (9 \times 2) - 3 = 240$ degrees of freedom is around 2. The first column corresponds to the t-ratios of the intercept ν, the 3 next columns equate the t-ratios of A_1. The last three columns are the t-ratios of A_2. The estimator of the $VAR(2)$ model with the log-return times series `ldata`

```
varp:.quantQ.ts.varpest[d;2]
```

returns

```
-0.01672199 -0.319631    0.1459888  0.961219   -0.1605511 0.114605
    ↪ 0.9343938
0.01576719  0.04393106   -0.1527319 0.2885016  0.05003084 0.01916576
    ↪ -0.01020487
0.01292586  -0.002422666 0.2248127  -0.2639675 0.03388041 0.3549124
    ↪ -0.02223012
```

It means that the intercept ν, first parameter A_1 and second parameter A_2 are estimated as:

$$\hat{\nu} = \begin{pmatrix} -0.01672199 \\ 0.01576719 \\ 0.01292586 \end{pmatrix}; A_1 = \begin{pmatrix} -0.319631 & 0.1459888 & 0.961219 \\ 0.04393106 & -0.1527319 & 0.2885016 \\ -0.002422666 & 0.2248127 & -0.2639675 \end{pmatrix}$$

and

$$A_2 = \begin{pmatrix} -0.1605511 & 0.114605 & 0.9343938 \\ 0.05003084 & 0.01916576 & -0.01020487 \\ 0.03388041 & 0.3549124 & -0.02223012 \end{pmatrix}$$

The function `.quantQ.ts.estimate[y;p]` returns the one-step prediction of the *VAR(p)* model. Hence, `.quantQ.ts.estimate[d;2]` forecasts the next values of d with a *VAR*(2) model:

```
-0.01081094 0.01991084 0.02162873
```

It computes $\hat{\nu} + \hat{A}_1 y_T + A_2 y_{T-1}$:

```
nu:varp[;0];
a1:varp[;(1;2;3)];
a2:varp[;(4;5;6)];
y2:d[;(count d[0])-2];
y1:d[;(count d[0])-1];
nu + (a1 mmu y2) + (a2 mmu y1)
```

The function `.quantQ.ts.confInterval[y;p]` computes the 95% confidence interval of the *VAR(p)* model, i.e. $[\hat{y}_{k,t}(h) \pm 1.96\hat{\sigma}_k(h)]$

```
.quantQ.ts.confInterval[d;2]
```

returns

```
-0.1054982   0.08387633
-0.004134704 0.04395638
0.002249761  0.04100769
```

It means that one-period ahead forecast of the log-return investment is within $[-0.1054982; 0.08387633]$, log-return of income within $[-0.004134704; 0.04395638]$ and log-return consumption within $[0.002249761; 0.04100769]$.

The second step forecast is based on the previous forecast $\hat{\nu} + \hat{A}_1 \hat{y}_T(1) + \hat{A}_2 y_t$:

```
nu + (a1 mmu y1) + (a2 mmu (nu + (a1 mmu y2) + (a2 mmu y1) ))
```

The recursive function `.quantQ.ts.estimateN[n;y;p]` computes the n-step forecast of an VAR(p) based on the data y. The second and third period forecast of the VAR(2) model:

```
.quantQ.ts.estimateN[2;d;2]
.quantQ.ts.estimateN[3;d;2]
```

returns:

```
0.01078091 0.02034868 0.01465388
0.0211157 0.01698059 0.01982574
```

14.3.1.4 Code

The unbiased estimator of the *VAR*(*p*) process given in (14.22) is implemented in the function `.quantQ.ts.varpest`. It uses the vectorisation matrices *Y* and *Z* introduced in the notation section. First, we implement a vectorisation of a matrix *a* denoted as *vec*(*a*) in the notation section:

```
.quantQ.ts.vec:{[a]
    // a -- matrix
    i:(count raze a);
    j:1;
    v:(flip a)[0;];
    while[j<i;
        v:v,/(flip a)[j;];
        j:j+1];
    :v;
};
```

Then, we compute `Zt = (1,y(t),...,y(t-p+1))'`:

```
.quantQ.ts.zt:{[y;t;p]
    // y -- historical data (list of floating numbers)
    // t -- time point (positive integer)
    // p -- lags (positive integer) corresponding to the order of the VAR(p)
        ↪ process
    :1f,.quantQ.ts.vec[y[;(t-1)-til p]];
};
```

and compute `Z = (zt(y;0;p),...,zt(y;T-p;p))`:

```
.quantQ.ts.Z:{[y;p]
    // y -- historical data (list of floating numbers)
    // p -- lags (positive integer) corresponding to the order of the VAR(p)
        ↪ process
    :flip {[y;i;p]
        .quantQ.ts.zt[y;i;p]}[y;;p] each p + til (count y[0])-p;
};
```

followed by the computation of `Y = (y(1),...y(T-p))'`:

```
.quantQ.ts.Y:{[y;p]
    // y -- historical data (list of floating numbers)
    // p -- lags (positive integer) corresponding to the order of the VAR(p)
        ↪ process
    :y[;p+til (count y[0;])-p];
};
```

We can now implement the estimator of the *VAR*(*p*) model:

```
.quantQ.ts.varpest:{[y;p]
    // y -- historical data (list of floating numbers) used to estimate the
        ↪ VAR(p) model.
    // p -- order of the VAR(p) model
    :.quantQ.ts.Y[y;p] mmu (flip .quantQ.ts.Z[y;p]) mmu
        inv[.quantQ.ts.Z[y;p] mmu flip .quantQ.ts.Z[y;p]];
};
```

The estimator of the variance-covariance matrix of residual (14.23) is implemented as follows:

```
.quantQ.ts.covarianceResidual:{[y;p]
   // y -- historical data (list of floating numbers)
   // p -- order of the VAR(p) process
   T:(count y[0])-p;
   K:count y;
   coef:1f%((T-K*p)-1f);
   :coef*(.quantQ.ts.Y[y;p] mmu flip .quantQ.ts.Y[y;p]) -
       (.quantQ.ts.Y[y;p] mmu flip .quantQ.ts.Z[y;p]) mmu
       inv[.quantQ.ts.Z[y;p] mmu flip .quantQ.ts.Z[y;p]] mmu
       (.quantQ.ts.Z[y;p] mmu flip .quantQ.ts.Y[y;p]);
};
```

The Likelihood Ratio test statistic used to determine the optimal order of the *VAR*(*p*) process is implemented in `.quantQ.ts.varOrder[y;m]` as a function of the least square or the maximum likelihood estimator of the error (14.26). The function returns a table of three columns. The first column *p* returns the order of the *VAR*(*p*) model, the second column computes $\lambda_{LR}(p)$ as given in (14.25) and the third the *p*-value of $\lambda_{LR}(p)$.

First, we implement the identity matrix of rank *k*:

```
.quantQ.ts.eye:{[k]
   // k -- rank of matrix
   :`float$(til k)=/:til k;
};
```

Then, we provide a definition of the least square estimator of the error:

```
.quantQ.ts.beta:{[y;p]
   // y -- historical data (list of floating numbers)
   // p -- order of the VAR(p) process
   :(1f%(count y[0])-p) * (.quantQ.ts.Y[y;p] mmu
   (.quantQ.ts.eye[(count y[0])-p] - ((flip .quantQ.ts.Z[y;p]) mmu
       inv[.quantQ.ts.Z[y;p] mmu flip .quantQ.ts.Z[y;p]] mmu
       .quantQ.ts.Z[y;p]))) mmu flip .quantQ.ts.Y[y;p];
};
```

The estimator of the optimal order of the VAR model then reads:

```
.quantQ.ts.varOrder:{[y;m]
   // y -- historical data (list of floating numbers
   // m -- maximum order of the VAR process
   T:count y[0];
   K:count y;
   i:m;
   k:v1:v2:();
   while[i>0;
       lr:T*(log .quantQ.mat.det[.quantQ.ts.beta[y;i-1]])-(log .quantQ.mat.
           ↪ det[.quantQ.ts.beta[y;i]]);
       k:k,(m-i);
       v1:v1,lr;
       v2:v2,.quantQ.ts.pValueChi2[lr;K*K];
       i:i-1];
   :([p:k]lr:v1;pvalue:v2);
};
```

The p-value of a χ^2 distribution with k degrees of freedom is approximated using the formula

$$\frac{e^{v-u}}{p\sqrt{2\pi}}\left(\frac{u}{v}\right)^{v}\left(1-\frac{v-1}{p^2+2u}\right)\left(\frac{12v^{3/2}}{12v+1}\right), \tag{14.27}$$

with $u = \frac{\chi^2}{2}$, $2v = k$ and $p = u - v + 1$ described in Gray et al. (1969) and implemented as:

```
.quantQ.ts.pValueChi2:{[chi;nu]
   // chi -- instance of distribution (floating)
   // nu -- degrees of freedom of the Chi2 distribution
   u:chi%2f;
   v:nu%2f;
   p:(u-v)+1f;
   pi:3.141592654f;
   term1:exp[v-u]%(p*sqrt[2*pi]);
   term2:(u % v) xexp v;
   term3:1f-((v-1f)%((p*p)+2f*u));
   term4:(12f*(v xexp 1.5f))%((12f*v)+1);
   :term1*term2*term3*term4;
};
```

The matrix of t-ratios (14.24) indicating the statistical significance of the coefficients of the *VAR*(p) model is implemented as a function of the t-statistic:

```
.quantQ.ts.tstat:{[y;p]
   // y -- historical data (list of floating numbers)
   // p -- order of the VAR(p) process
   :.quantQ.ts.kron[.quantQ.ts.covarianceResidual[y;p]; inv[.quantQ.ts.Z[y;
       ↪ p] mmu
       flip .quantQ.ts.Z[y;p]]];
};
```

```
.quantQ.ts.tRatios:{[y;p]
   // y -- historical data (list of floating numbers)
   // p -- order of the VAR(p) process
   varp:.quantQ.ts.varpest[y;p];
   diag:(count varp;count varp[0])#sqrt[.quantQ.ts.diag[.quantQ.ts.tstat[y;
       ↪ p]]];
   :varp%diag;
};
```

where the Kronecker product and the diagonal of a matrix are:

```
.quantQ.ts.kron:{[a;b]
   // a -- matrix of floating numbers
   // b -- matrix of floating numbers
   // calculating Kronecker product
   nbcols:(count b[0;])*(count a[0;]);
   nbrows:(count b[;0])*(count a[;0]);
   :(nbrows;nbcols) #(raze over) {[i;a;b](,/)(flip (flip a)[;i]*\:b)}[;a;b]
       ↪ each til count a;
};
```

and the diagonal matrix

```
.quantQ.ts.diag:{[m]
   // m -- array of numbers to put on diagonal
   :{[i;m] m[i;i]}[;m] each til count m;
 };
```

The 1-step and n-step forecasts estimate the coefficients $\hat{B}$ of the $VAR(p)$ model based on the data set y and predict its future values. First, the implementation of the 1-step forecast reads:

```
.quantQ.ts.estimate1:{[y;p]
   // y -- historical data (list of floating numbers)
   // p -- order of the VAR(p) process
   b:.quantQ.ts.varpest[y;p];
   v:b[;0];
   k:count b;
   :v+sum {[i;y;b;k]b[;(1+k*i)+til k] mmu y[;(count y[0])-(1+i)]}[;y;b;k]
       ↪ each til p;
 };
```

Further, we implement the n-step forecast of the $VAR(p)$ model:

```
.quantQ.ts.estimateN:{[n;y;p]
   // n -- positive integer indicating a n-step ahead forecast
   // y -- historical data (list of floating numbers)
   // p -- order of the VAR(p) process
   output:.quantQ.ts.estimate1[y;p];
   :$[n>1;
       .quantQ.ts.estimateN[n-1;y,'output;p];
       output];
 };
```

The accuracy of the 1-step forecast is determined with the MSE function:

```
.quantQ.ts.forecastMSE:{[y;p]
   // y -- historical data (list of floating numbers)
   // p -- order of the VAR(p) process
   T:(count y[0])-p;
   K:count y;
   coef:(T+(K*p)+1)%T;
   :coef*.quantQ.ts.covarianceResidual[y;p];
 };
```

The corresponding 95% confidence interval of the 1-step forecast is:

```
.quantQ.ts.confInterval:{[y;p]
   // y -- historical data (list of floating numbers)
   // p -- order of the VAR(p) process
   mse:1.96*sqrt[.quantQ.ts.diag[.quantQ.ts.forecastMSE[y;p]]];
   forecast:.quantQ.ts.estimate1[d;2];
   :flip ((forecast-mse);(forecast+mse));
 };
```

14.3.2 *VARX*(*p*, *q*) Process

The VAR model assumes that all stochastic variables of a system (A_i in our case) have essentially the same status in that they are all determined within the system. With a VAR model only past values determine its future values. In practice, the generation process may be affected by other observable variables which are determined outside the system of interest. Such variables are called exogenous or unmodelled variables. In contrast, the variables determined within the system are called endogenous. A vector autoregressive process with exogenous variables $VARX(p,q)$ has the following reduced form:

$$y_t = A_1 y_{t-1} + ... + A_p y_{t-p} + B_0 x_t + ... + B_q x_{t-q} + u_t, \tag{14.28}$$

where $A_i, i = 1..p$ and $B_j, j = 0..q, y_t = (y_{1t}, ..., y_{Kt})'$ is a K-dimensional vector of endogenous variables, $x_t = (x_{1t}, ..., x_{Mt})'$ is an M-dimensional vector of exogenous variables and u_t is white noise.

These types of models are also called transfer function models or distributed lag. In lag operator notation, the reduced form can be written as:

$$A(L)y_t = B(L)x_t + u_t,$$

where $A(L) := I_K - A_1 L - ... - A_p L^p$ and $B(L) := B_0 + B_1 L + ... + B_q L^q$.

The final form of the system is given by:

$$y_t = D(L)x_t + A(L)^{-1} u_t,$$

where $D(L) := A(L)^{-1}B(L)$. The coefficient matrices D_i of the transfer operator $D(L) = \sum_{i=0}^{\infty} D_i L^i$ contain the effects that changes in the exogenous variables have on the endogenous variables.

14.3.2.1 Estimator

The reduced form of a $VARX(p,q)$ model can be rewritten as:

$$y_t = AY_{t-1} + BX_{t-1} + B_0 x_t + u_t, \tag{14.29}$$

where $A := [A_1, ..., A_p], B := [B_1, ..., B_q]$.

$$Y_t := \begin{bmatrix} y_t \\ ... \\ y_{t-p+1} \end{bmatrix} \text{and } X_t := \begin{bmatrix} x_t \\ ... \\ x_t - q + 1 \end{bmatrix}.$$

For a sample of size T, the system can be written compactly as $Y = [A, B, B_0]Z + U$ where $Y := [y_1, ..., y_T]$, $Z := \begin{bmatrix} Y_0, ..., Y_{T-1} \\ X_0, ..., X_{T-1} \\ x_1, ..., x_T \end{bmatrix}$ and $U := [u_1, ..., u_T]$. Let $\beta := vec(A, B, B_0) = R\gamma$. The reduced form can be vectorised as $y = (Z' \otimes I_K)\beta + u = (Z' \otimes I_K)R\gamma + u$ with $y = vec(Y)$ and $u = vec(U)$.

The generalised least squares (GLS) estimator of γ is:

$$\hat{\gamma} = [R'(ZZ' \otimes \Sigma_U^{-1})R]^{-1}R'(Z \otimes \Sigma_U^{-1})y.$$

The variance-covariance matrix of the residual Σ_u is unknown and can be estimated by OLS. Given the residuals $\tilde{u} = vec(\tilde{U}) = y - (Z' \otimes I_K)R\hat{\gamma}$, the estimated generalised least squares (EGLS) estimator of γ becomes:

$$\tilde{\gamma} = [R'(ZZ' \otimes \widetilde{\Sigma_u^{-1}})R]^{-1}R'(Z \otimes \widetilde{\Sigma_u^{-1}})y,$$

with $\tilde{\Sigma}_u = \tilde{U}\tilde{U}'/T$.

14.3.2.2 Code

The implementation of the *VARX(p, q)* model closely follows the structure of the *VAR(p)* process. The function `.quantQ.ts.varXest` provides the unbiased estimate of the *VARX(p, q)* model. It uses an extension of the vectorisation matrices Y and Z of the *VAR(p)*. Below is defined a suite of functions:

```
.quantQ.ts.zt:{[y0;t;p;flag]
   // y0 -- vectorisation of y0
   // t -- time (positive integer)
   // p -- number of lags (positive integer)
   // flag -- boolean value deciding whether a leading 1 needs to be set.
   :$[flag;
       1f,.quantQ.ts.vec[y0[;(t-1)-til p]];
       .quantQ.ts.vec[y0[;(t-1)-til p]]];
};
```

```
.quantQ.ts.Z:{[y;p;flag]
   // y -- historical data of the endogenous variable (list of floating
       ↪ numbers)
   // p -- order of the VAR(p) process
   // flag -- boolean value deciding whether a leading 1 needs to be set
       ↪ for zt.
   :flip {[y;i;p;flag].quantQ.ts.zt[y;i;p;flag]}[y;;p;flag] each p + til (
       ↪ count y[0])-p;
};
```

```
.quantQ.ts.ZX:{[x;y;q;p]
   // x -- historical data of the exogenous variable (list of floating
       ↪ numbers)
   // y -- historical data of the endogenous variable (list of floating
       ↪ numbers)
   // q -- order of exogenous process
   // p -- order of the VAR(p) process
   :.quantQ.ts.Z[y;p;1b],.quantQ.ts.Z[x;q;0b],x[;q+til (count x[0])-q];
};
```

```
.quantQ.ts.Y:{[y;p]
   // y -- historical data of the endogenous variable (list of floating
        ↪ numbers)
   // p -- order of the VAR(p) process
   :y[;p+til (count y[;0])+1-p];
};
```

The estimator of the *VARX*(p, q) model is implemented as:

```
.quantQ.varXest:{[x;y;q;p]
   // x -- historical data of the exogenous variable (list of floating
        ↪ numbers)
   // y -- historical data of the endogenous variable (list of floating
        ↪ numbers)
   // q -- order of the exogenous process
   // p -- order of the VAR(p) process
   z0:.quantQ.ts.ZX[x;y;q;p];
   :y[;p+til (count y[0])-p] mmu flip z0 mmu inv (flip z0) mmu z0;
};
```

The estimator of the variance-covariance matrix of residual is adapted to include the q exogenous variables:

```
.quantQ.ts.covarianceResidual:{[x;y;q;p]
   // x -- historical data of the exogenous variable (list of floating
        ↪ numbers)
   // y -- historical data of the endogenous variable (list of floating
        ↪ numbers)
   // q -- order of exogenous process
   // p -- order of the VAR(p) process
   yp0:.quantQ.ts.Y[y;p];
   z0:.quantQ.ts.ZX[x;y;q;p];
   T:count y[0];
   K:count y;
   coef:1%(T-(K*p)-1f);
   :coef*(yp0 mmu flip yp0) - yp0 mmu (flip z0) mmu inv[z0 mmu flip z0] mmu
         ↪ z0 mmu flip yp0;
};
```

The corresponding 1-step and n-step forecasting functions of the *VARX*(p, q) model based on the data set y and exogenous time series x are given by following two functions: first, the 1-step forecast of a *VARX*(p, q) model:

```
.quantQ.ts.estimateX:{[x;y;q;p]
   // x -- historical data of the exogenous variable (list of floating
        ↪ numbers)
   // y -- historical data of the endogenous variable (list of floating
        ↪ numbers)
   // q -- order of exogenous process
   // p -- order of the VAR(p) process
   M:.quantQ.ts.varXest[x;y;q;p];
   v:M[;0];
   k:count y;
   m:count x;
```

```
    :v+sum[{[i]M[;(1+k*i)+til k] mmu y[;(count y[0])-(1+i)]} each til p]+
        sum[{[i]M[;1+(k*p)+(m*i)+til m] mmu x[;(count x[0])-(1+i)]} each til
            ↪ q]+
        M[;1+(k*p)+(m*q)+til m] mmu x[;0];
};
```

Second, the n-step forecast of a $VARX(p, q)$ model:

```
.quantQ.ts.estimateNX:{[n;x;y;q;p]
    // n -- positive integer indicating the number of steps of the foreast
    // x -- historical data of the exogenous variable (list of floating
        ↪ numbers)
    // y -- historical data of the endogenous variable (list of floating
        ↪ numbers)
    // q -- order of exogenous process
    // p -- order of the VAR(p) process
    output:.quantQ.ts.estimateX[x;y;q;p];
    :$[n>1;
    {
        newx:.quantQ.ts.estimateN[(n-1);q;x];
        .quantQ.ts.estimateNX[n-1;x,'newx;y,'output;q;p];
    };
    output];
};
```

CHAPTER 15

Fourier Transform

In this chapter, we introduce the implementation of the Fourier Transform, in particular, the discrete Fourier transform (DFT) and illustrate its usage for time series analysis. The DFT allows us to transform a time series from a time domain into a frequency domain and understand the periodicity, if any, of the contributing components. In order to be able to introduce the DFT, we first start with complex numbers. After introducing the DFT, we conclude with a bonus section on quaternions and fractals.

15.1 COMPLEX NUMBERS

Complex numbers are native to some languages, but this is not the case in q, which does not go beyond real numbers. What is a complex number? For a full answer, see for example Agarwal et al. (2011). In a nutshell, a complex number is a number which can be written as $a + bi$, where a and b are real numbers and $i^2 = -1$. It is the last property of i, which distinguishes complex numbers from reals as there is no real number i which would satisfy this condition.

Alternatively, we may define a complex number z as a linear polynomial in a single indeterminate variable x:

$$z = a + bx, \tag{15.1}$$

where additional constraint on x is imposed:

$$x^2 + 1 = 0. \tag{15.2}$$

We can thus treat complex numbers as polynomials. The algebraic operations for complex numbers can be derived from those defined for polynomials. It is convenient to denote the variable x as i and tacitly assume that $i^2 = -1$.

An example of a complex number is $1 + 2i$. The number 1 is called the real part of the complex number, and the number 2 is the imaginary part of the complex number. The word "imaginary" does not mean that complex numbers are not useful. On the contrary, they have proven to be important in physics and mathematics.

From a mathematical perspective, the system of complex numbers is an algebraic extension of real numbers by an imaginary number i. This gives rise to an analogy between complex numbers and polynomials with i and allows the system of complex numbers to form a field. Every field has well-defined operations of adding two elements and multiplying two elements. Complex numbers can also be divided by a non-zero complex number, i.e., the notion of an opposite number exists.

Complex numbers form the fundamental theorem of algebra: every non-constant polynomial equation with complex coefficients has a complex solution. There is no real number i which will solve $i^2 = -1$, yet this theorem also holds for a real number whose imaginary part is equal to zero. Another interpretation of complex numbers is geometric. Real numbers are defined in one dimension while complex numbers span the two-dimensional plane. The real part of the complex number is a projection of the complex number on the real axis (x-axis) while the imaginary part is a projection on the imaginary axis, which is perpendicular to the real one (y-axis). The geometric interpretation gives us an intuitive interpretation of how complex numbers extend real numbers. Algebraic operations on complex numbers then correspond to operations on two-dimensional vectors. Further, the two-dimensional interpretation of complex numbers results in a polar representation, where complex numbers are defined as vectors originating at $(0, 0)$ with a given radius and angle to the positive part of the real axis.

Let us provide some useful formulas which allow us to work with complex numbers. Since the formulas are rather straightforward, we will provide along with them the q implementation.

15.1.1 Properties of Complex Numbers

Complex numbers are represented in two parts: a real and an imaginary part. Our implementation, therefore, uses a dictionary to represent the two parts. The first key which we denote by `` `re `` corresponds to the real part while the second key `` `im `` represents the imaginary part. Let us define a few examples:

```
cx1:`re`im!1 0f;
cx2:`re`im!0 1f;
cx3:`re`im!neg[0.5]+2?1.0;
```

The first complex number `cx1` is equivalent to the real number 1.0, the second complex number `cx2` is the pure imaginary number i, and the last complex number is a randomly generated one:

```
cx3
```

```
re| -0.1072476
im| 0.01709112
```

In the following paragraphs, we define the set of utility functions for operations on complex numbers. The convention is such that all the functions are prepended with `.quantQ.complex`. The first algebraic operation to define is adding two complex numbers. Mathematically, the sum of two complex numbers is:

$$z_1 + z_2 = (a_1 + b_1 i) + (a_2 + b_2 i) = (a_1 + a_2) + (b_1 + b_2)i. \tag{15.3}$$

We can therefore simply do:

```
cx1 + cx2
```

```
re| 1
im| 1
```

The second algebraic operation to define is multiplying two complex numbers. It is defined as:

$$z_1 * z_2 = (a_1 + b_1 i) * (a_2 + b_2 i) = (a_1 * a_2 - b_1 * b_2) + (a_1 * b_2 + a_2 * b_1)i, \quad (15.4)$$

with straightforward implementation:

```
.quantQ.complex.mult:{`re`im!(1 -1 wsum x*y;x wsum reverse value y)};
```

Let us provide two examples for illustration:

```
.quantQ.complex.mult[cx1;cx2]
```

```
re| 0
im| 1
```

```
.quantQ.complex.mult[cx3;cx3]
```

```
re| 0.01120995
im| -0.003665964
```

Further, we have to define the division of two numbers. The formula for division is:

$$\frac{z_1}{z_2} = \frac{a_1 + b_1 i}{a_2 + b_2 i} = \frac{a_1 * a_2 + b_1 * b_2}{a_2^2 + b_2^2} + \frac{b_1 * a_2 - a_1 * b_2}{a_2^2 + b_2^2} i, \quad (15.5)$$

with corresponding function

```
.quantQ.complex.div:{[num;den]
   // num -- numerator
   // den -- denominator
   :`re`im!(wsum[num;den]%yy;(1 -1 wsum den*reverse value num)%yy:den wsum
       ↪ den);
};
```

We first verify complex division on two real numbers:

```
.quantQ.complex.div[`re`im!2 0f;`re`im!4 0f]
```

```
re| 0.5
im| 0
```

For complex numbers, we get:

```
.quantQ.complex.div[cx2;cx3]
```

```
re| 1.449117
im| -9.093283
```

Further, we define the complex conjugate of the complex number as:

$$z^* = (a + bi)^* = (a - bi). \tag{15.6}$$

In the geometric interpretation, the complex conjugate is a reflection around the real axis. Further, the following relationship $z^* = z$ is equivalent to stating that the complex number z is real. We can get the real and imaginary parts as:

$$a = \frac{z + z^*}{2}, a = \frac{z - z^*}{2i}. \tag{15.7}$$

The complex conjugate function is then provided as:

```
.quantQ.complex.conjugate:{@[x;`im;neg]}
```

giving:

```
.quantQ.complex.conjugate[cx3]
```

```
re| -0.1072476
im| -0.01709112
```

The geometric interpretation of the complex numbers would require a few functions, in particular, to convert a complex number into polar coordinates:

$$z = (a + bi) = re^{i\phi}, \tag{15.8}$$

where r is the modulus of the complex number and ϕ is the polar angle. When a complex number is interpreted as a vector on the two-dimensional plane originating at $(0, 0)$, then r is the length of the vector, and ϕ is the angle of the vector with the positive part of the real axis.

The modulus is given as:

$$r = |z| = z * z^* = a^2 + b^2. \tag{15.9}$$

In order to obtain the polar angle, we have to employ a trigonometric formula whose form depends on the complex number itself:

$$\phi = \begin{cases} \arctan\left(\frac{b}{a}\right) & \text{if } a > 0, \\ \arctan\left(\frac{b}{a}\right) + \pi & \text{if } a < 0 \text{ and } b \geq 0, \\ \arctan\left(\frac{b}{a}\right) - \pi & \text{if } a < 0 \text{ and } b < 0, \\ \frac{\pi}{2} & \text{if } a = 0 \text{ and } b > 0, \\ -\frac{\pi}{2} & \text{if } a = 0 \text{ and } b < 0, \\ \text{not defined} & \text{if } a = 0 \text{ and } b = 0, \end{cases} \tag{15.10}$$

where ϕ is defined within the interval $(-\pi, \pi]$.

The trigonometric form of the complex number is given as:

$$z = r(\cos\phi + i\sin\phi). \tag{15.11}$$

We implement the polar decomposition, which returns a dictionary of the radius and the angle:

```
.quantQ.complex.polar:{[cx]
   // cx -- complex number
   // radial part
   r: sqrt cx wsum cx;
   // angular part
   phi:$[0<cx`re;atan cx[`im]%cx[`re];
       0>cx`re;$[0<=cx`im;
           atan[cx[`im]%cx[`re]] + .quantQ.pi;
           atan[cx[`im]%cx[`re]] - .quantQ.pi];
       0=cx`re;$[0<cx`im;  .5 * .quantQ.pi;
           0>cx`im; -.5 * .quantQ.pi;
           0n];
       0n];
   :`radius`angle!(r;phi);
};
```

Let us calculate a couple of examples:

```
.quantQ.complex.polar[cx1]
```

```
radius| 1
angle | 0
```

```
.quantQ.complex.polar[cx2]
```

```
radius| 1
angle | 1.570796
```

```
.quantQ.complex.polar[`re`im!0 0f]
```

```
radius| 0
angle | 0n
```

For the sake of completeness, we provide a function which converts the polar coordinates to regular form using the trigonometric form:

```
.quantQ.complex.polar2Canonical:{[polar]
   // polar -- complex number in polar coordinates
   :`re`im!polar[`radius]*(cos;sin)@\:polar`angle;
};
```

and verify its functionality:

```
.quantQ.complex.polar2Canonical[`radius`angle!(2;0.25*3.14152)]
```

```
re| 1.414239
im| 1.414188
```

It is convenient to also define the Euler formula:

$$e^{i\phi} = \cos\phi + i\sin\phi, \tag{15.12}$$

as:

```
.quantQ.complex.realExp:{[phi]
   // phi -- angular component
   :`re`im!(cos;sin)@\:phi;
};
```

which gives

```
.quantQ.complex.realExp[0.25*3.14152]
```

```
re| 0.7071196
im| 0.7070939
```

The function is defined for real arguments only and thus we use the name RealExp. The Euler formula is useful when considered as an exponent of the complex number:

$$u = e^z = e^{a+bi} = e^a * e^{bi}, \tag{15.13}$$

which is then basis for transformations based on exponential functions. We thus implement the complex analogy to exp as:

```
.quantQ.complex.exp:{[cx]
   // cx -- complex number
   :exp[cx`re]*.quantQ.complex.realExp cx`im;
};
```

and illustrate it on:

```
.quantQ.complex.exp[cx1]
```

```
re| 2.718282
im| 0
```

and

```
.quantQ.complex.exp[cx3]
```

```
re| 0.898172
im| 0.01535226
```

Having in hand an implementation of complex exp, we need the complex equivalent of logarithm. Euler's formula allows us to obtain this in a straightforward manner:

$$\log(z) = \log(re^{i\phi}) = \log(r) + i\phi. \tag{15.14}$$

This solution is not unique, though. The ambiguity comes from periodicity of the cos and sin functions, or, alternatively, the rotation in the complex plane $e^{i\pi} = e^{3i\pi} = e^{5i\pi} = \ldots$. This results in a multivalued definition of the logarithm:

$$\log(z) = \log(r) + i(\phi + 2\pi k) \text{ with } k \in \mathbb{Z}. \tag{15.15}$$

The function for complex logarithm has two arguments: the first argument is the complex number z while the second argument is the branch cut k as defined in the previous display. The default value of choice for the branch cut is 0.

```
.quantQ.complex.log:{[cx;k]
   // cx -- complex number
   // k -- branching cut
   polar:.quantQ.complex.polar cx;
   :`re`im!(log polar`radius;polar[`angle] + 2 * .quantQ.pi * k);
};
```

```
.quantQ.complex.log[cx1;0]
```

```
re| 0
im| 0
```

```
.quantQ.complex.log[cx1;1]
```

```
re| 0
im| 6.283185
```

Finally, we check the identity $z = e^{\log z}$:

```
.quantQ.complex.exp[.quantQ.complex.log[cx1;1]]
```

```
re| 1
im| -2.449294e-16
```

The discrepancy comes from the rounding error.

The verification of the formula for a logarithm of a complex number is the following formula:

$$\log(i) = \frac{\pi}{2}i, \tag{15.16}$$

```
.quantQ.complex.log[cx2;0]
```

```
re| 0
im| 1.570796
```

which is confirmed. It is worth mentioning that when implementing algebraic concepts, it is useful to have some identities ready which allow us to test the code. In our opinion, the provided identity is suitable for implementation of algebraic formulas dealing with complex numbers.

Finally, we provide a non-mathematical utility function which turns a real number – float – into our definition of the complex number:

```
.quantQ.complex.real2Cx:{[real]
   // real -- real number
   :`re`im!(`float$real;$[0>type real;0f;count[real]#0f]);
 };
```

giving

```
.quantQ.complex.real2Cx[1]
```

```
re| 1
im| 0f
```

This function allows us to convert float vectors into "complex vectors", i.e. dictionaries with vector elements. This will prove useful in the next section, where the discrete Fourier transform will be introduced for analysing time series.

15.2 DISCRETE FOURIER TRANSFORM

We are now equipped with formalism to treat complex numbers in q. We can proceed with introducing the discrete Fourier transform (DFT). The DFT is a special example of Fourier analysis applied on sampled points of a continuous process. We start with introducing the DFT and then proceed with its discrete version. For references, we encourage the reader to go through Arfken (1985) or Flannery et al. (1988) for a more empirical approach.

The Fourier transform consists of a continuous function of time – denoted as signal – and decomposes it into its frequency components, see Bracewell and Bracewell (1986) or Grafakos (2008). The DFT thus transforms the function from the temporal coordinates into the frequency domain. The DFT of a function is a complex function, hence the motivation to introduce complex numbers first.

Introducing the DFT opens up the way for some useful tools across different fields. Among others, the differentiation of a function in the time domain is simply multiplication in the frequency domain. Thus, transforming the differentiation of a function into the frequency domain will result in multiplication instead of differentiation. This is a very useful property in signal processing. The DFT deserves more space than we can afford and we thus restrict our interpretation of the DFT as a filter, which allows us to decompose a function of time into the frequency components and find the leading frequencies forming the time series. We can then identify periodicity in a signal. In financial time series, this could correspond to the mean reversion frequency, for instance.

Let us proceed to define a DFT. Let f be an integrable real function $f : \boldsymbol{R} \rightarrow \mathbb{C}$, then its Fourier Transform $\hat{f}$ is defined as:

$$\hat{f}(\zeta) = \int_{-\infty}^{\infty} f(t)e^{-2\pi it\zeta}\,dt, \tag{15.17}$$

with ζ being any real number.

The variable ζ corresponds to frequency in suitable units. Let us further define the inverse DFT, which is transforming function from the frequency domain back into the time domain:

$$f(t) = \int_{-\infty}^{\infty} f(\zeta)e^{2\pi it\zeta}d\zeta. \tag{15.18}$$

The definition above assumes that we are equipped with the full knowledge of f across $(-\infty,\infty)$. In practical applications, we rather observe a finite sample $f_0, f_1, f_2, f_3, \dots, f_{N-1}$ of equidistant sample points of the process f. The sample points can be in general complex. The DFT can be therefore thought of as a sequence $F_0, F_1, F_2, F_3, \dots, F_{N-1}$ given as:

$$F_k = \sum_{n=0}^{N-1} f_n e^{-\frac{2\pi ikn}{N}}. \tag{15.19}$$

The component of the DFT can be interpreted as a correlation of the input sequence with the complex sinusoid of a frequency $\frac{k}{N}$. It filters out the frequency contribution to the given frequency amplitude. Further, every coefficient F_k is a complex number encoding the amplitude and phase of a complex periodic component $e^{-\frac{2\pi ikn}{N}}$ of the original series. The DFT is defined on the domain $k \in 0, 1, \dots, N-1$. The transform can be extended outside of the domain, considering the sequence to be N-periodic, i.e. repeating itself every N points.

Let us illustrate the DFT in an example. First, we implement a function which takes as an argument a complex series and returns one component of the DFT:

```
.quantQ.complex.dft1k:{[cxs;n;tiln;k]
   // cxs -- series of complex numbers
   // n -- length of the series
   // tiln -- index of the series
   // k -- coefficient of the DFT coefficient
   :sum .quantQ.complex.mult'[cxs;flip .quantQ.complex.realExp neg (2 * .
      ↪ quantQ.pi * k * tiln)%n];
 };
```

and then wrap it to get the full set of DFT coefficients:

```
.quantQ.complex.dft:{[cxs]
   // cxs -- series of complex numbers to be transformed
   :.quantQ.complex.dft1k[cxs;N;til N] peach til N:count cxs;
 };
```

Note the use of `peach` to provide multithreaded concurrent processing when starting `q` with n slave threads (`q -s n`).

Let us define a sequence of complex numbers:

```
cxSeries: flip `re`im!flip (0.2421429 0.3013791;0.1102202
   ↪ 0.9201851;0.6466032 0.3515431;0.8917427 0.3049351;0.05981635
   ↪ 0.2161336;0.7835583 0.1152005;0.244422 0.5292301;0.230607
   ↪ 0.82064;0.4140276 0.2774816;0.9143396 0.6609365);
```

and transform it:

```
.quantQ.complex.dft[cxSeries]
```

```
re         im
---------------------
4.53748    4.497665
-0.4294141 0.4400665
0.5612426  0.5570959
-0.5056962 1.795277
0.4007738  -0.9668292
-1.323456  -1.14613
0.8497442  -0.8799416
-0.9224544 -1.136011
-1.220734  -1.125092
0.4739435  0.9776904
```

The example proves that the outcome of the function is a complex series of the same length. Note that the beautiful attribute of q to treat a list of dictionaries as a table automatically formats the result as a table which we can now plot. For that purpose, we define the function which conveniently extracts those series, i.e. the outcome is a triplet of series of floats:

```
.quantQ.complex.dftTs:{[dfts]
   // dfts -- DFT series
   :update i from dfts,'.quantQ.complex.polar each dfts;
};
```

Let us apply it on the outcome of the DFT obtained above:

```
.quantQ.complex.dftTs[.quantQ.complex.dft[cxSeries]];
```

and plot it.

Figure 15.1 depicts the real part, the imaginary part and the modulus of the transformed series. The series is short, and thus it is difficult to interpret the results from the figure. In the following paragraphs, we will move towards a more realistic example with an intuitive interpretation.

Let us consider an example, where the input time series is characterised by both the time index and the signal itself. The signal is a real-valued time series. In order to interpret the results, let us define the time series as a periodic function composed of two sinusoids with different frequencies. The time series is defined in a table:

```
t: 0.0+(1.0%1000)*til 5001;
pi: acos[-1];
xt: cos[2*pi*2*t]+0.5*cos[2*pi*4*t];
tabXt:([] t;xt);
```

The signal xt is composed of 5001 points spanning the time interval $t_0 = 0$ to $t_{5001} = 10$. The function is periodic with a frequency of 2 and 4, respectively, where the component with frequency 2 has twice the amplitude compared to the other one. Figure 15.2 depicts the time series xt against the corresponding time t. The two frequency modes

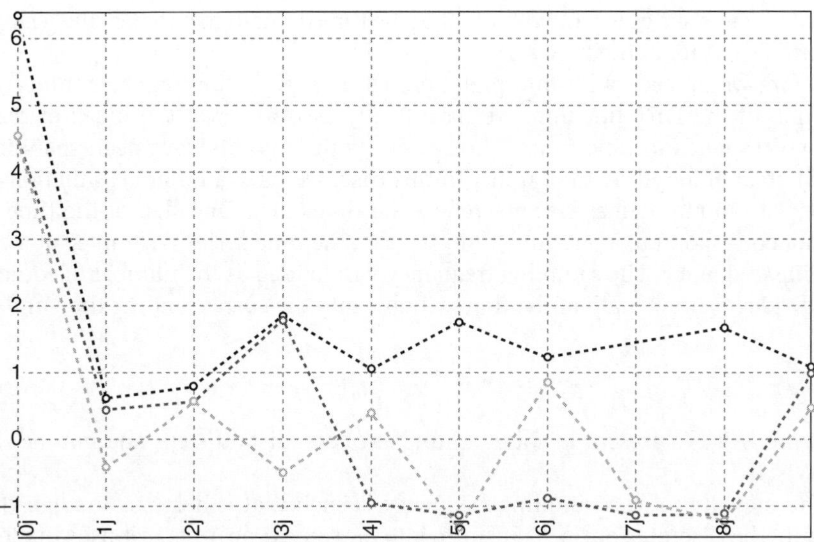

FIGURE 15.1 The real part (light gray), the imaginary part (dark gray) and the modulus (black) of the Discrete Fourier Transform of the complex series `cxSeries`

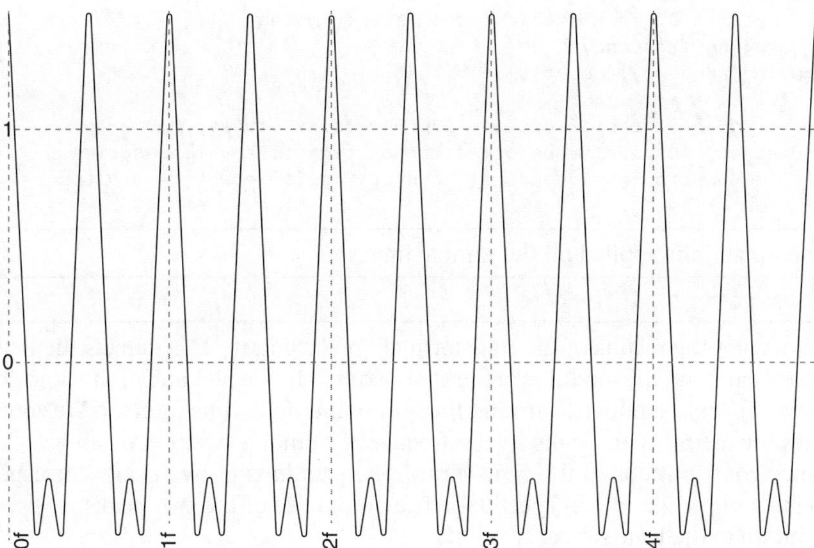

FIGURE 15.2 The time series `xt`

are visible. Time series is plotted for half of the time domain to enhance the visibility of the periodic nature of the time series.

Before we proceed with interpretation, let us explain the frequency units. In the definition of the DFT function, we have tacitly assumed that the index of the time series corresponds to time units. Thus, series with N points have been spanning the time interval of length N time units. In this case, we have a different situation as the number of sample points does not reflect the time span. One step of the time series does not correspond to a one-time unit. Instead, the time series is sampled at a certain sampling frequency. The sampling frequency ν is defined as the number of equidistant steps divided by the length of the time window into the corresponding time units:

$$\nu = \frac{N-1}{t_N - t_0}, \tag{15.20}$$

where the $N-1$ is present to count a number of equidistant steps and not the sample points itself.

The meaning of the sampling frequency is such that it helps us to align the frequency of the Discrete Fourier Transform into the same time units as is used in the input time series. This is implemented as a function, which takes as an argument table with time and real-valued signal and returns the real part, imaginary part, and the modulus of the Discrete Fourier Transform:

```
.quantQ.complex.dftTab:{[tab]
   // tab -- sorted time-series table with 2 columns (t and xt)
   t:tab`t;
   xt:update im:0f from `re xcol delete t from tab;
   // sampling frequency
   samplingFrequency:(count[t]-1)%(last[t]-first[t]);
   // dft
   dftts: .quantQ.complex.dftTs .quantQ.complex.dft xt;
   // discrete fourier transform decomposition of the time series
   :(([] f:samplingFrequency*(til count t)%neg[1]+count[t]),'dftts);
};
```

The function is applied on the sample time series:

```
.quantQ.complex.dftTab[tabXt]
```

Let us plot the results of the transform of `tabXt`. Figure 15.3 depicts the real part, imaginary part, and the modulus of the DFT of `dftTab`. We plot half of the time domain as the transform is symmetric around the mid-point of the time interval. We zoom into the relevant region with peaks in the frequency domain, where we can see the two frequency contributions to the time series. The positions of two peaks correspond to the coefficients of 2 and 4, respectively. The amplitude of the two peaks reflects their contribution to the time series.

Although we are now equipped with a toolset to analyse the frequency contributions of a time series, we should keep in mind that there are two phenomena which can spoil the interpretations of our results:

- Aliasing
- Leakage

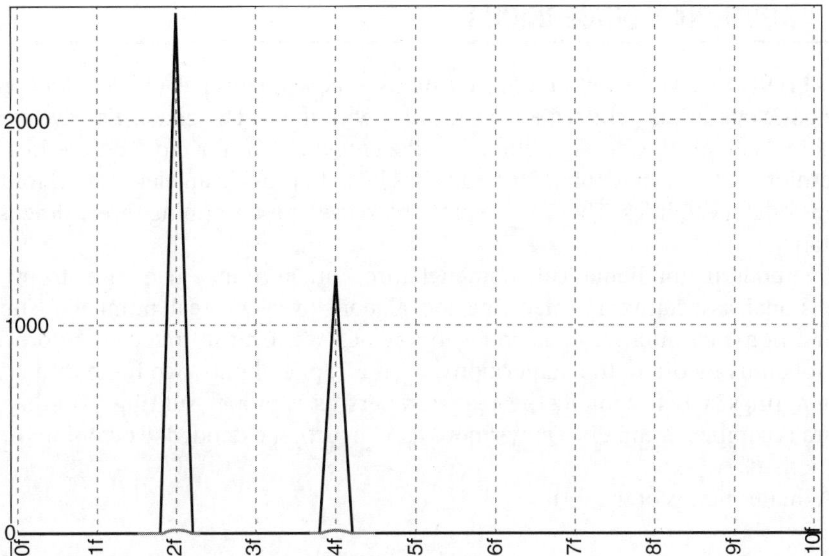

FIGURE 15.3 The decomposition of the DFT of dftTabZoom (real, imaginary and modulus of the DFT, respectively); the positions of two peaks correspond to the coefficients of 2 and 4, respectively

Aliasing

In a plot of modulus vs frequency, e.g. Figure 15.3, aliasing is a false translation of the power we observe in the filter coming from the signal outside the frequency range, essentially a distortion effect. Aliasing is caused by discrete sampling below the Nyquist frequency. The Nyquist frequency is half of the sampling rate of a discrete time series. Aliasing can be removed by either increasing the underlying sampling rate or pre-filtering the signal to eliminate high-frequency components using anti-aliasing filters, such as a low-pass filter.

Leakage

Spectral leakage is smearing of modulus across a frequency spectrum. It takes place when the signal is not periodic within the time domain. This is a very common error, and it cannot be simply eliminated.

We encourage the reader to employ the Discrete Fourier Transform on a time series of their interest and perform its frequency analysis. Using the provided functions, this analysis is straightforward, but we should always keep in mind aliasing and spectral leakage when interpreting results.

In the next section, we provide an extension to complex numbers and introduce quaternions. Its implementation in q is again straightforward and serves as a nice exercise of our q skills motivated by intriguing mathematical concepts.

15.3 ADDENDUM: QUATERNIONS

Let us briefly review the notion of quaternions – see Kuipers et al. (1999) – and provide some basic operations which allow us to work with them. The quaternions were introduced by William Rowan Hamilton; see Rosenfeld (1988) for more on the history of quaternions. The purpose of quaternions has been to provide an elegant tool for three-dimensional mechanics. They are, in particular, used for describing three-dimensional rotations.

In modern mathematical nomenclature, quaternions give rise to a four-dimensional associative normed division algebra over the real numbers. They are the first non-commutative division algebra which was ever introduced. As proven by the Frobenius theorem, the quaternions algebra is one of only two finite-dimensional division rings which contain the real numbers as a proper subring. Another such algebra is complex numbers. Quaternions can be further extended to octonions or even sedenions.

A quaternion is of the form:

$$a + b\mathbf{i} + c\mathbf{j} + d\mathbf{k}, \tag{15.21}$$

where a, b, c, and d are real numbers and $\mathbf{i}$, $\mathbf{j}$, and $\mathbf{k}$ are symbols denoting the three additional dimensions of quaternions.

According to legend, Hamilton wrote the following formula on the stone at the Brougham Bridge as the idea behind quaternions settled in his mind:

$$\mathbf{i}^2 = \mathbf{j}^2 = \mathbf{k}^2 = \mathbf{ijk} = -1. \tag{15.22}$$

The previous display reflects the properties of the quaternion symbols for extra dimensions. Furthermore, multiplication of the cross-symbol combinations is governed by a set of rules:

$$\mathbf{ij} = \mathbf{k}, \tag{15.23}$$

$$\mathbf{ji} = -\mathbf{k}, \tag{15.24}$$

$$\mathbf{jk} = \mathbf{i}, \tag{15.25}$$

$$\mathbf{kj} = -\mathbf{i}, \tag{15.26}$$

$$\mathbf{ki} = \mathbf{j}, \tag{15.27}$$

$$\mathbf{ik} = -\mathbf{j}. \tag{15.28}$$

The quaternion symbols are not commutative and thus the multiplication of two quaternion results in a non-trivial formula, the so-called Hamilton product, which is a direct consequence of the above rules. For two quaternions $q_1 = a_1 + b_1\mathbf{i} + c_1\mathbf{j} + d_1\mathbf{k}$ and $q_2 = a_2 + b_2\mathbf{i} + c_2\mathbf{j} + d_2\mathbf{k}$, it is given as:

$$q_1 q_2 = a_1a_2 - b_1b_2 - c_1c_2 - d_1d_2 \tag{15.29}$$
$$+ (a_1b_2 + b_1a_2 + c_1d_2 - d_1c_2)\mathbf{i} \tag{15.30}$$
$$+ (a_1c_2 - b_1d_2 + c_1a_2 + d_1b_2)\mathbf{j} \tag{15.31}$$
$$+ (a_1d_2 + b_1c_2 - c_1b_2 + d_1a_2)\mathbf{k}. \tag{15.32}$$

There is also the notion of the cross-product in the quaternion space. The cross-product is defined for purely "imaginary" quaternions, i.e. those with zero real part $a = 0$. In such a case, the cross-product is defined as:

$$(0 + a_1\mathbf{i} + b_1\mathbf{j} + c_1\mathbf{k}) \times (0 + a_1\mathbf{i} + b_1\mathbf{j} + c_1\mathbf{k}) = (c_1d_2 - d_1c_2)\mathbf{i}$$
$$+ (d_1b_2 - b_1d - 2)\mathbf{j} + (b_1c_2 - c_1b_2)\mathbf{k}. \tag{15.33}$$

Let us illustrate quaternions and introduce the basic algebraic operations on quaternions. We will use the notation `.quantQ.quat`, which will be prepended to the function names. Using a similar approach to complex numbers, we represent a quaternion as a dictionary, but with expanded keys: `` `r`i`j`k``.

Let us define three sample quaternions:

```
quat1:`r`i`j`k!1 0 0 0f;
quat2:`r`i`j`k!1 1 1 1f;
quat3:`r`i`j`k!neg[1]+2*4?1.0;
```

It will be useful to have better visualisation of the quaternion, namely, to see all three extra dimensions. For that purpose, we provide a simple utility function which converts any quaternion into a formatted string:

```
.quantQ.quat.visual:{raze (enlist[""],("+";"")(-1=signum 1_value x)),'
    ↪ string[value x],'enlist[""],string 1_key x};
```

and works as follows:

```
.quantQ.quat.visual[quat3]
```

```
"0.570066+0.06941923i+0.4223433j-0.176806k"
```

giving a string-formatted and easy to understand quaternion.

Addition flows naturally, and multiplication is algebraic operations which require an implementation. First, adding two quaternions can be done element-wise:

```
quat1 + quat2
```

```
r| 2
i| 1
j| 1
k| 1
```

Second, we implement the product of two quaternions. In particular, the product is defined using the Hamilton formula:

```
.quantQ.quat.mult:{[qt1;qt2]
   // qt1,qt2 -- pair of quaternions
   :`r`i`j`k!(
       {x[`r]-x[`i]-x[`j]-x[`k]}qt1*qt2;
       (qt1[`r]*qt2[`i])+(qt1[`i]*qt2[`r])+(qt1[`j]*qt2[`k])-qt1[`k]*qt[`j
           ↪ ];
       (qt1[`r]*qt2[`j])-(qt1[`i]*qt2[`k])+(qt1[`j]*qt2[`r])+qt1[`k]*qt2[`i
           ↪ ];
       {x[`r]+x[`i]-x[`j]+x[`k]}qt1*key[qt2]!reverse value qt2);
};
```

and testing it on a pair of sample quaternions:

```
.quantQ.complex.quatMulti[quat1;quat3]
```

```
r| 0.570066
i| 0.06941923
j| 0.4223433
k| -0.176806
```

The existence of the Hamilton product allows us to introduce the inverse product. The inverse product is defined with respect to the Hamilton product and for a quaternion $q = a + b\mathbf{i} + c\mathbf{j} + d\mathbf{k}$ is defined as:

$$q^{-1} = (a + b\mathbf{i} + c\mathbf{j} + d\mathbf{k})^{-1} = \frac{a - b\mathbf{i} - c\mathbf{j} - d\mathbf{k}}{a^2 + b^2 + c^2 + d^2}, \tag{15.34}$$

and is implemented as:

```
.quantQ.quat.inverse:{[qt]
   // qt -- quaternion
   :@[qt;`i`j`k;neg]%qt wsum qt;
};
```

The inverse of the third quaternion we have defined `quat3` is then calculated:

```
.quantQ.quat.inverse[quat3]
```

```
r| 1.056796
i| -0.1286903
j| -0.7829458
k| 0.3277655
```

We leave it to our readers to show the Hamilton product of a quaternion and its inverse.

Analogously to complex numbers, we may define the norm of the quaternion or its modulus. The norm corresponds to the geometric interpretation of the quaternion as a vector in a four-dimensional space:

```
.quantQ.complex.norm:{ sqrt x wsum x};
```

The norm of the quaternion quat2 is defined as L_2-norm:

$$|q| = |a + b\mathbf{i} + c\mathbf{j} + d\mathbf{k}| = \sqrt{a^2 + b^2 + c^2 + d^2}, \tag{15.35}$$

and implemented in the following function:

```
.quantQ.quat.norm[quat2]
```

```
2f
```

The conjugate of the quaternion is similar to what we have defined for complex numbers:

$$q^* = (a + b\mathbf{i} + c\mathbf{j} + d\mathbf{k})^* = a - b\mathbf{i} - c\mathbf{j} - d\mathbf{k}. \tag{15.36}$$

The conjugation can be expressed through addition and multiplication:

$$q^* = -\frac{1}{2}(q + \mathbf{i}q\mathbf{i} + \mathbf{j}q\mathbf{j} + \mathbf{k}q\mathbf{k}). \tag{15.37}$$

The conjugate can also be used to define the norm introduced previously:

$$|q| = \sqrt{qq^*}. \tag{15.38}$$

The implementation then follows as:

```
.quantQ.quat.conjugate:{@[x;`i`j`k;neg]};
```

and its functionality on the quaternion with all the coefficients equal to 1 reads:

```
.quantQ.quat.conjugate[quat2]
```

```
r| 1
i| -1
j| -1
k| -1
```

Quaternions also have a notion of polar decomposition. The polar decomposition means that we rewrite the quaternion q as pair of two numbers $(|q|, \overline{q})$, where $|q|$ is a norm of the quaternion and $\overline{q}$ is a unit quaternion given as:

$$\overline{q} = \frac{q}{|q|}. \tag{15.39}$$

The polar decomposition thus does not correspond to a radius and polar angles, yet is still useful when we interpret quaternions as vectors and are interested in linear dependence.

```
.quantQ.quat.polarDecomp:{[qt]
   // qt -- quaternion
   norm: .quantQ.quat.norm qt;
   // return a norm and unit quaternion
   :(norm; qt%norm);
};
```

The polar decomposition of a quaternion with unit coefficients:

```
.quantQ.quat.polarDecomp[quat2]
```

```
( 2f ; `r`i`j`k!0.5 0.5 0.5 0.5 )
```

In the geometric interpretation of quaternions, it is convenient to focus on the "imaginary" part of quaternions, i.e. coefficients b, c and d, while considering $a = 0$. The algebraic operations for such quaternions resemble the three-dimensional geometry. We can then define the dot product and the vector product.

The dot-product for a pair of imaginary quaternions $q_1 = b_1\mathbf{i} + c_1\mathbf{j} + d_1\mathbf{k}$ and $q_2 = b_2\mathbf{i} + c_2\mathbf{j} + d_2\mathbf{k}$ is defined as:

$$q_1 \cdot q_2 = b_1 b_2 + c_1 c_2 + d_1 d_2, \tag{15.40}$$

or

$$q_1 \cdot q_2 = \frac{1}{2}(q_1 q_2^* + q_2 q_1^*) = \frac{1}{2}(q_1^* q_2 + q_2^* q_1), \tag{15.41}$$

where the function in q reads as simply the weighted sum function and is trivial:

```
(`r`i`j`k!0 1.0 1.0 1.0) wsum (`r`i`j`k!0 1.0 -1.0 2.0)
```

```
2f
```

Secondly, we introduce the cross product, as it is known from three-dimensional geometry. The cross product of two imaginary quaternions is useful when we want to use them to express the rotations in a three-dimensional space. The generalisation beyond the purely imaginary cross product would need insight into the wedge products, which can be perceived as generalisation of cross product in any dimension. This is beyond the scope of this book, though, and we stick to dealing with purely imaginary quaternions. The cross product is defined as:

$$q_1 \times q_2 = (b_1\mathbf{i} + c_1\mathbf{j} + d_1\mathbf{k}) \times (b_2\mathbf{i} + c_2\mathbf{j} + d_2\mathbf{k}) \tag{15.42}$$

$$= (c_1 d_2 - d_1 c_2)\mathbf{i} + (d_1 b_2 - b_1 d_2)\mathbf{j} + (b_1 c_2 - c_1 b_2)\mathbf{k}. \tag{15.43}$$

The cross product of the imaginary part of a quaternion results in an imaginary part of a quaternion as well. A symbolic definition of the cross product using conjugate reads:

$$q_1 \times q_2 = \frac{1}{2}(pq - q^* p^*). \tag{15.44}$$

The function for the cross product `crossProduct` takes as an argument two full quaternions and ignores the real part of quaternions. In the output, the real part is set to zero by definition, and thus the real part does not affect the calculation:

```
.quantQ.quat.crossProduct:{[qt1;qt2]
    // qt1, qt2 -- quaternion
    // the real part is ignored and in the output set to zero
    :`r`i`j`k!(0.0;(qt1[`j]*qt2[`k])-(qt1[`k]*qt2[`j]);(qt1[`k]*qt2[`i])-(
        ↪ qt1[`i]*qt2[`k]);
        (qt1[`i]*qt2[`j])-(qt1[`j]*qt2[`i]));
};
```

We can then calculate the cross product of two quaternions which have the real part:

```
.quantQ.quat.crossProduct[quat2;quat3]
```

```
r| 0
i| -0.5991493
j| 0.2462253
k| 0.3529241
```

where the real part has not been considered in the calculation as expected.

In order to develop reasonable calculus with quaternions, it is convenient to have exponential and logarithmic functions, as many functions can be expressed through them. The exponential function of a quaternion is defined as:

$$\exp(q) = \exp(a + b\mathbf{i} + c\mathbf{j} + d\mathbf{k}) \tag{15.45}$$

$$= \sum_{n=0}^{\infty} \frac{q^n}{n!} \tag{15.46}$$

$$= \exp(a)\left(\cos|b\mathbf{i} + c\mathbf{j} + d\mathbf{k}| + \frac{b\mathbf{i} + c\mathbf{j} + d\mathbf{k}}{|b\mathbf{i} + c\mathbf{j} + d\mathbf{k}|}\sin|b\mathbf{i} + c\mathbf{j} + d\mathbf{k}|\right), \tag{15.47}$$

where the cos term in the last row is the real part of the resultant quaternion while the sin term corresponds to the purely imaginary part of the quaternion. Implementing:

```
.quantQ.quat.exp:{[qt]
    // qt -- quaternion
    realPart: qt`r;
    imPart: `r _qt;
    newRealPart: enlist[`r]!enlist cos sqrt imPart wsum imPart;
    newImPart: $[0=normImPart:sqrt sum imPart*imPart;imPart;(imPart%
        ↪ normImPart)*
        sin[sqrt sum imPart*imPart]];
    // return exp of quaternion
    :exp[realPart]*newRealPart,newImPart;
};
```

and applying it to the two sample quaternions we have defined in the beginning:

```
.quantQ.quat.exp[quat1]
```

```
r| 2.718282
i| 0
j| 0
k| 0
```

and

```
.quantQ.quat.exp[quat3]
```

```
r| 1.582131
i| 0.1184189
j| 0.7204552
k| -0.301605
```

The second function we need to define is the quaternion logarithm. The function reads:

$$\log(q) = \log|q| + \frac{b\mathbf{i} + c\mathbf{j} + d\mathbf{k}}{|b\mathbf{i} + c\mathbf{j} + d\mathbf{k}|} \arccos\frac{a}{|q|}, \tag{15.48}$$

and is provided in the next display:

```
.quantQ.quat.log:{[qt]
   // qt -- quaternion
   realPart: qt`r;
   imPart: `r _qt;
   // exp of quaternion
   newRealPart: enlist[`r]!enlist log .quantQ.quat.norm qt ;
   newImPart: $[0=normImPart:sqrt sum imPart*imPart;0.0*imPart;
       (imPart%normImPart)]*acos[realPart % .quantQ.quat.norm qt];
   :newRealPart,newImPart;
};
```

The logarithm of two sample quaternions:

```
.quantQ.quat.log[quat1]
```

```
r| 0
i| 0
j| 0
k| 0
```

and

```
.quantQ.quat.log[quat2]
```

```
r| 0.6931472
i| 0.6045998
j| 0.6045998
k| 0.6045998
```

We verify the functionality on log(i), the previously mentioned identity:

```
.quantQ.quat.log[`r`i`j`k!0.0 1.0 0.0 0.0 ]
```

giving $\frac{\pi}{2}i$:

```
r| 0
i| 1.570796
j| 0
k| 0
```

This concludes the section on quaternions. We encourage readers interested in the concept of quaternions to study this matter in more detail. An interesting exercise would be to implement the "octonions", the 8-dimensional extension of quaternions, constructed in a similar way we have proceeded from complex numbers to quaternions.

15.4 ADDENDUM: FRACTALS

We close this chapter with a brief reference to fractals and specifically the famous Mandelbrot set, due to its close relationship with complex numbers. Fractals have fascinated generations of scientists with their interesting properties and frequent occurrence in nature. They have a wide range of applications, with acoustics, networks, neuroscience, geometry, fMRI and price analysis being just a few examples of areas where fractal analysis is used to identify fractal patterns. Their potential applicability to long-memory processes in time series analysis and Fractal Brownian Motion also make them an interesting area for further exploration. For further reading, see Mandelbrot (1982).

A fractal is usually defined as a recursive set which exhibits self-similarity. It is usually nowhere differentiable and will exhibit a dimension which is not necessarily an integer, known as a fractal dimension. The interesting property of fractals – which relates to their dimension – comes from the observation that zooming into their shape results in the same pattern, making it hard to distinguish any differences. This can be infinitely recursive.

We will attempt to generate the Mandelbrot set, one of the most recognisable fractal geometries, named after Benoit Mandelbrot, who first coined the name "fractal" as a way of describing their roughness and fragmented nature.

The set is defined in the complex plane, so our new complex functions will come in handy. The quadratic set we shall iterate over is:

$$z_{new} = (z_{old}^2) + c, \tag{15.49}$$

where z is a complex number and c is a constant.

In our implementation, we will use the concept of a computer screen's pixel resolution to represent the complex plane. Our algorithm shall iterate over all pixels for each row and column in our screen and the values for which the set is bounded at 2 (its norm is less than 2) will be returned as true `1b`.

We start with the quadratic function iteration using the over adverb (/) and exit the iteration if the norm is less than 2.

```
.quantQ.complex.fractal:{[cx]
   // cx -- complex offset
   // iterate z_n+1= (z_n^2)+ c and exit if the norm converges or hits max
       ↪ number of iterations
   :{[c;list]
      newp: .quantQ.complex.mult[p;p:first list] + c;
      if[(50<i:last list) or 2<.quantQ.complex.norm newp;:list];
      :(newp;1+i)
   }[cx]/[(`re`im!0 0f;0)];
};
```

Note the addition of a cap of 50 on a maximum number of iterations for the case where the norm does not converge. We encourage the reader to generalise the function such that bound on the norm and the maximum size of the list enter the function as parameters, preferably through a dictionary.

We write two wrapper functions which will re-centre our screen and return an output of 1b or 0b, depending on whether the norm converged for that particular pair of pixels on our screen. Our value for z_0 is (0,0):

```
.quantQ.complex.mandelbrot_:{[p;r;i]
   // p -- starting point for iteration
   // r -- real part
   // i -- imaginary part
   :`row`col`res!(r;i;50<last .quantQ.complex.fractal[`re`im!(r;i)])
};
```

We can now iterate over the whole screen: h and w are the height and width of our computer screen:

```
.quantQ.complex.mandelbrot:{[h;w]
   // h -- screen height
   // w -- screen width
   // iterate over all rows and columns
   // set the constant c by scaling the row and column and centre to 0
   c:{[h;w;row;col] ((row - .5 * w ) * 4.0 % w; (col - .5 * h) * 4.0 % w)}[
       ↪ h;w]. flip t cross t:til w;
   // iterate over all rows and columns
   :.quantQ.complex.mandelbrot_\[0 0;c 0;c 1]
};
```

Let's try and run it, using a "resolution" of height and width of 600x600:

```
mandelbrot:.quantQ.complex.mandelbrot[600;600]
```

```
select from mandelbrot where res
```

```
row       col res
-----------------
-2        0   1
-1.993333 0   1
```

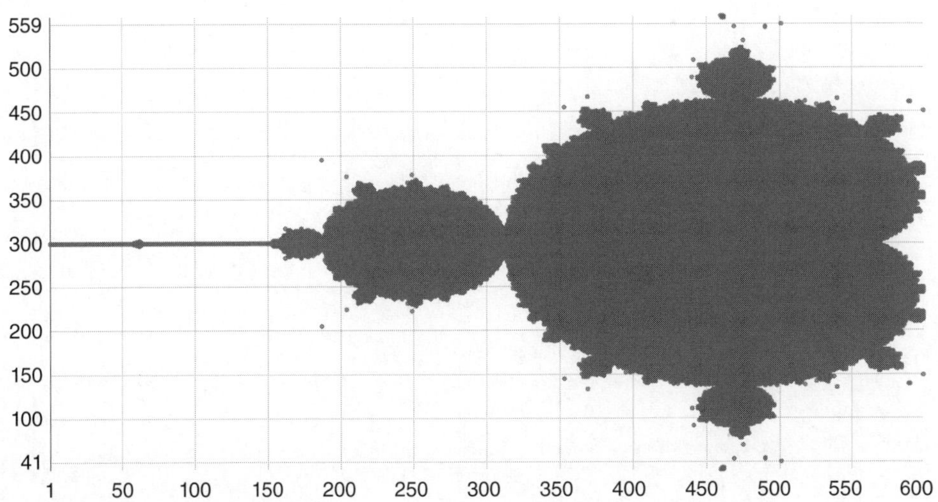

FIGURE 15.4 The points plot shows how the canvas points whose norm converged are highlighted in gray (`res = 1b`) while the rest are left blank

```
-1.986667 0   1
-1.98     0   1
-1.973333 0   1
-1.966667 0   1
-1.96     0   1
-1.953333 0   1
-1.946667 0   1
-1.94     0   1
-1.933333 0   1
-1.926667 0   1
-1.92     0   1
-1.913333 0   1
..
```

Figure 15.4 shows the result of plotting the above table for all the values where `res` is true – the resultant shape is indeed the famous fractal!

As an exercise, one can consider an alternative approach to the above recursion, which may be more memory efficient. Additionally, a more elaborate colour scheme can be introduced, where the number of iterations before convergence can represent a colour code, instead of the simpler binary approach demonstrated here.

We encourage the reader to continue exploring the beautiful world of fractals and their potential applications to their relative field. To borrow a quote from Mandelbrot (1982):

> Clouds are not spheres, mountains are not cones, coastlines are not circles, and bark is not smooth, nor does lightning travel in a straight line.

CHAPTER 16

Eigensystem and PCA

In this section, we provide an algorithm to solve the eigensystem, i.e. for any square matrix $\boldsymbol{A}$, we find the eigenvalues and the corresponding eigenvectors. We utilise the eigensystem for the principal component analysis (PCA) decomposition, which is a powerful tool to analyse data.

16.1 THEORY

Matrices and matrix equations are everyday objects we encounter in statistics and data science. Square matrices play a unique role, and it is thus convenient to get more familiar with their properties and be able to deal with them numerically. The covariance matrix is a particular example of the square matrix, which we meet whenever we get our hands on any data set. It is particularly useful to calculate the eigensystem of square matrices as they allow us to make inferences about their properties. When applied to the covariance matrix, we derive the basis for the PCA, which gives insight into the source of variation in the data set.

Let us start with a definition of eigenvalues and eigenvectors, or the eigensystem, for a square matrix. The notion of eigenvectors and eigensystems can be defined for a general linear transformation, but for our purpose, we consider the finite-dimensional linear transformations which can be expressed as square matrices. Let us consider a $p \times p$ matrix $\boldsymbol{A}$, which can contain in general complex numbers, and a p-dimensional column vector $\boldsymbol{x}$ which can be viewed as another $p \times 1$ matrix. The product of a matrix $\boldsymbol{A}$ and a vector $\boldsymbol{x}$ is:

$$\boldsymbol{A}\boldsymbol{x} = \boldsymbol{b}, \tag{16.1}$$

where $\boldsymbol{b}$ is a vector of the same dimension as $\boldsymbol{x}$. The matrix $\boldsymbol{A}$ represents linear transformation which transforms one vector into another one in the same vector space.

We say that vector $\boldsymbol{v}$ is an *eigenvector*, when

$$\boldsymbol{A}\boldsymbol{v} = \lambda_v \boldsymbol{v}, \tag{16.2}$$

and λ_v is a scalar number, which is known as *eigenvalue*. The eigenvector is a special vector, which is transformed by the matrix $\boldsymbol{A}$ in a special way: it is rather stretched. It represents a special direction of the matrix $\boldsymbol{A}$ in the vector space.

We can immediately say that if $\boldsymbol{v}$ is an eigenvector, then any multiple of such a vector is an eigenvector as well with the same eigenvalue, or

$$\boldsymbol{Av} = \lambda_v \boldsymbol{v} \;\Rightarrow\; \boldsymbol{A}a\boldsymbol{v} = \lambda_v a\boldsymbol{v}. \tag{16.3}$$

Further, eq. (16.2) can be rewritten as:

$$(\boldsymbol{A} - \lambda \boldsymbol{I}_p)\boldsymbol{v} = 0, \tag{16.4}$$

where $\boldsymbol{I}_p$ is an identity matrix. The eq. (16.4) has a non-trivial solution $\boldsymbol{v}$ if the matrix $(\boldsymbol{A} - \lambda \boldsymbol{I}_p)$ is singular. For non-singular matrices, only trivial solutions can satisfy the equality.

To be precise, the matrix is said to be singular when it is not invertible. In other words, some of its columns can be written as a linear combination of the remaining columns. This implies that such a matrix is not of the full rank. An equivalent definition is that its determinant is equal to zero (see the Appendix to this chapter for more about determinants and their implementation in q). We can thus say that for a square matrix $\boldsymbol{A}$ the vector $\boldsymbol{v}$ is an eigenvector corresponding to the eigenvalue λ if

$$|\boldsymbol{A} - \lambda \boldsymbol{I}_p| = 0, \tag{16.5}$$

where $|\boldsymbol{A}|$ stands for the determinant of the square matrix $\boldsymbol{A}$. This equation is known as a characteristic polynomial. This comes from the fact that the determinant in eq. (16.5) is a polynomial of order p in λ.

It is due to the fundamental theorem of algebra which says that we can rewrite eq. (16.5) as a product of:

$$|\boldsymbol{A} - \lambda \boldsymbol{I}_p| = (\lambda - \lambda_1)(\lambda - \lambda_2)\cdots(\lambda - \lambda_p), \tag{16.6}$$

where λ_i are roots of the polynomial. The roots can be all distinct or degenerate, and they can take complex values. When the root is degenerate, i.e. there is sequence of $(\lambda - \lambda_i)^{p_i}$, we say that the root has non-trivial algebraic multiplicity, p_i. The sum of all multiplicities is equal to the rank of the matrix.

It is further important to introduce the notion of null space. For a given eigenvalue λ_i, we define the subspace:

$$\boldsymbol{v}_i : (\boldsymbol{A} - \lambda_i \boldsymbol{I}_p)\boldsymbol{v}_i = 0. \tag{16.7}$$

This space of all such $\boldsymbol{v}_i$'s is further known as eigenspace of λ_i. The eigenspace is closed under addition and multiplication by scalar. Thus, if we have two vectors $\boldsymbol{v}_i^1$ and $\boldsymbol{v}_i^2$, both eigenvectors of λ_i, then their linear combination is also an eigenvector of λ_i.

The consequence of this observation is such that for a square complex matrix $\boldsymbol{A}$, the entire vector space (of dimension p) can be written as a cartesian product of all eigenspaces corresponding to all eigenvalues. Further, any p-dimensional vector can be written as a linear combination of eigenvectors of $\boldsymbol{A}$. In other words, linearly independent eigenvectors of $\boldsymbol{A}$ form the eigenbasis of a p-dimensional vector space.

Let us mention a number of useful properties of the eigensystem. Below, we assume that $\boldsymbol{A}$ is a p-dimensional square matrix.

Determinant

(discussed at the end of this chapter) of the matrix $\boldsymbol{A}$ can be written as:

$$\det \boldsymbol{A} = \prod_{i}^{p} \lambda_i, \tag{16.8}$$

where λ_i are eigenvalues of the matrix $\boldsymbol{A}$.

Trace

of the matrix $\boldsymbol{A}$ can be written as:

$$\operatorname{trace} \boldsymbol{A} = \sum_{i}^{p} \lambda_i, \tag{16.9}$$

where λ_i are eigenvalues of the matrix $\boldsymbol{A}$.

Hermitian

matrix $\boldsymbol{A}$, i.e. a matrix such that $\boldsymbol{A} = \boldsymbol{A}^*$, have all the eigenvalues real. If the matrix is positive-definite/ positive-semidefinite/ negative-definite/ negative-semidefinite, then every eigenvalue is positive/ non-negative/ negative/ non-positive.

Unitary

matrix $\boldsymbol{A}$ has all eigenvalues with modulo equal to 1.

Power

of the matrix $\boldsymbol{A}$, i.e. $\boldsymbol{A}^k$, has the eigenvalues $\lambda_1^k, \lambda_2^k, \ldots, \lambda_p^k$.

Invertibility

of the matrix $\boldsymbol{A}$ is equivalent to a situation where every eigenvalue λ_i is non-zero. Further, for an invertible matrix $\boldsymbol{A}$, the eigenvalues of $\boldsymbol{A}^{-1}$ are $\lambda_1^{-1}, \lambda_2^{-1}, \ldots, \lambda_p^{-1}$. The algebraic multiplicity of the inverse eigenvalues coincides with the direct counterparts.

In the next section, we proceed with numerical algorithms to find out the eigensystem. We focus on the QR algorithm to find out the eigenvalues and the inverse iteration algorithm to find out the corresponding eigenvectors.

16.2 ALGORITHMS

In order to find the eigensystem of the real matrix $\boldsymbol{A}$, we proceed in two steps. First, we run the QR algorithm to find the eigenvalues of the matrix $\boldsymbol{A}$. Once we obtain the eigenvalues, we find the corresponding eigenvectors using the inverse iteration algorithm. In the next two subsections, we introduce both algorithms.

16.2.1 QR Decomposition

Given a square real matrix $\boldsymbol{A}$, the QR decomposition is a factorisation of the matrix into a product of $\boldsymbol{QR}$, where $\boldsymbol{Q}$ is an orthogonal matrix and $\boldsymbol{R}$ is an upper triangular matrix. Symbolically, it reads:

$$\boldsymbol{A} = \boldsymbol{QR}. \tag{16.10}$$

The decomposition is useful for many applications, and in particular, it is a basis for the QR algorithm to find eigenvalues of the square matrix.

There is a number of procedures to find the QR decomposition. The favoured method is, for instance, Householder reflection, which is a transformation that takes a vector and reflects it about some plane or hyperplane. The hyperplane is chosen such that the sub-diagonal part of $\boldsymbol{A}$ disappears. Another popular method is the numerically unstable Gram-Schmidt orthogonalisation process, which can be turned into an expression for the matrix $\boldsymbol{R}$. Last but not least, there is a method based on Givens rotations, which will be utilised in this chapter.

Givens rotation

The notion of Givens rotation is a general concept which stands for a rotation in a plane spanned by two coordinate axes. In the case of three dimensions with axes denoted as x, y, and z, Givens rotation is for example rotation in $x-y$ plane, where all z coordinates of a rotated object are constant. In linear algebra, rotation can be represented by a square matrix. For Givens rotation, such a matrix has the form of:

$$\boldsymbol{G}(i,j;\theta) = \begin{pmatrix} 1 & \cdots & 0 & \dots & 0 & \cdots & 0 \\ \vdots & \ddots & 0 & & \vdots & & \vdots \\ 0 & \cdots & \cos(\theta) & \cdots & -\sin(\theta) & \cdots & 0 \\ \vdots & & 0 & \ddots & \vdots & & \vdots \\ 0 & \cdots & \sin(\theta) & \cdots & \cos(\theta) & \cdots & 0 \\ \vdots & & 0 & & \vdots & \ddots & \vdots \\ 0 & \cdots & 0 & \cdots & 0 & \cdots & 1 \end{pmatrix}, \tag{16.11}$$

where the matrix $\boldsymbol{G}$ has a unit on the diagonal for every row but i-th and j-th one, respectively. The two selected rows denote the plane in which the rotation takes place. The rotation in a two-dimensional space is given by

$$\boldsymbol{R}(\theta) = \begin{pmatrix} \cos(\theta) & -\sin(\theta) \\ \sin(\theta) & \cos(\theta) \end{pmatrix}. \tag{16.12}$$

The rotation matrix is thus present in i-th and j-th rows/columns.

The QR decomposition can be found as follows:

- Start with the matrix $\boldsymbol{A}$.
- Start with the first column.

- Start with the last row, indexed with p. Find Givens rotation $\boldsymbol{G}_{(p,1)} = \boldsymbol{G}(p, 1; \theta_{(p,1)})$, which zeros the $(p, 1)$ element of the matrix $\boldsymbol{A}$: $\{\boldsymbol{G}_{(p,1)}\boldsymbol{A}\}_{(p,1)} = 0$.
- Take the outcome of the previous step and find a Givens rotation $G_{(p-1,1)}$ (we use compact notation from now onwards), which zeros the $(p-1, 1)$ element of the matrix. Thus, $\{\boldsymbol{G}_{(p_1,1)}\boldsymbol{G}_{(p,1)}\boldsymbol{A}\}_{(p-1,1)} = 0$. By nature of the Givens rotation matrix, it will hold $\{\boldsymbol{G}_{(p_1,1)}\boldsymbol{G}_{(p,1)}\boldsymbol{A}\}_{(p,1)} = 0$ as well.
- Proceed upwards until the $(2, 1)$ element. At the end of this step, we have a matrix where the first column has all elements but the diagonal one is equal to zero.

- Proceed with the second column and construct Givens rotations such that elements $(p, 2), \ldots, (p-2, 2)$ are zero, starting with $(p, 2)$ element. Since this procedure does not involve any element with index 1, the property of the first column remains unchanged.
- Proceed with the same procedure right to $p-1$-st column.
- Recollect the results.

At the end of the algorithm, we have

$$\boldsymbol{R} = \boldsymbol{G}_{(1,p-1)} \cdots \boldsymbol{G}_{(p_1,1)}\boldsymbol{G}_{(p,1)}\boldsymbol{A}. \tag{16.13}$$

The matrix $\boldsymbol{R}$ is an upper diagonal matrix by construction. If we further denote

$$\boldsymbol{Q}^{\mathsf{T}} = \boldsymbol{G}_{(1,p-1)} \cdots \boldsymbol{G}_{(p_1,1)}\boldsymbol{G}_{(p,1)}, \tag{16.14}$$

we get

$$\boldsymbol{R} = \boldsymbol{Q}^{\mathsf{T}}\boldsymbol{A}, \tag{16.15}$$

which is the decomposition we were looking for once we will de-transpose the matrix $\boldsymbol{Q}^{\mathsf{T}}$, i.e. by transposing it one more time.

It remains to specify how to find the particular form of the Givens rotation matrix which will make the (i,j) element zero. Let us consider the input matrix $\boldsymbol{A}$, and our objective to find $\boldsymbol{G} = \boldsymbol{G}(i,j; \theta_{(i,j)})$ such that $\{\boldsymbol{G}\boldsymbol{A}\}_{(i,j)} = 0$. If we recall the form of the matrix $\boldsymbol{G}$ in equation (16.11), we write directly the equation for the (i,j) element to be zero:

$$\sin(\theta_{(i,j)})a_{(i,i)} + \cos(\theta_{(i,j)})a_{(i,j)} = 0, \tag{16.16}$$

which can be used to find $\theta_{(i,j)}$,

$$\theta_{(i,j)} = \arctan\left(-\frac{a_{(i,j)}}{a_{(i,i)}}\right). \tag{16.17}$$

This concludes the algorithm which allows us to obtain the QR decomposition for any real square matrix.

16.2.2 QR Algorithm for Eigenvalues

We can proceed with the QR algorithm, which allows us to calculate all eigenvalues for a given real square matrix $\boldsymbol{A}$. The QR algorithm works as follows:

- We initialise the algorithm as $\boldsymbol{A}_0 = \boldsymbol{A}$.
- The algorithm proceeds in iterative steps, with k denoting the iteration step, starting at $k = 0$:
  - Calculate the QR decomposition: $\boldsymbol{A}_k = \boldsymbol{Q}_k\boldsymbol{R}_k$.
  - Update the matrix: $\boldsymbol{A}_{k+1} = \boldsymbol{R}_k\boldsymbol{Q}_k$.
  - Increase k and iterate.
- The diagonal of the matrix $\boldsymbol{A}_{k+1}$ converges to the Schur form of $\boldsymbol{A}$ with eigenvalues being on the diagonal.

The algorithm is based on the similarity of the matrix $\boldsymbol{A}_k$ and $\boldsymbol{A}_{k+1}$ within the iteration steps. The similarity can be shown as:

$$\boldsymbol{A}_{k+1} = \boldsymbol{R}_k\boldsymbol{Q}_k \tag{16.18}$$

$$= (\boldsymbol{Q}_k^{-1}\boldsymbol{Q}_k)\boldsymbol{R}_k\boldsymbol{Q}_k \tag{16.19}$$

$$= \boldsymbol{Q}_k^{-1}\boldsymbol{A}_k\boldsymbol{Q}_k. \tag{16.20}$$

The matrices are similar; they represent the same operator expressed in two different bases. The algorithm thus transforms the matrix into a different basis. Further, the two matrices have the same eigenvalues.

If the matrix $\boldsymbol{A}$ has distinct real eigenvalues, the QR algorithm converges to the upper triangular matrix – the Schur form. The QR algorithm cannot produce complex values as it involves only addition and multiplication of real numbers. If the real matrix has complex eigenvalues, or conjugate pairs of eigenvalues, the QR algorithm does not converge to the upper triangular matrix. In such a case, the matrix will converge to a block-upper triangular form. Elements in the block will never converge – they correspond to the oscillation in the complex plane while those outside of the block carry the information about eigenvalues.

The convergence criteria of the algorithm cannot thus be formed merely by checking the upper diagonal form as the blocks may be present and are perfectly valid. Thus, it is more suitable to monitor the performance of the algorithm in a controlled way with regularly overseeing the outcome of the algorithm. Alternatively, we may use some upper bound on the errors and construct the indicator for the shape of the matrix. The algorithm as is formulated above is simple, but we have to pay the price by rather expensive calculations and oversight. There are specific techniques which speed up convergence in terms of numerical cost but they are beyond our scope.

The QR algorithm aims to find all the eigenvalues at the same time. It is possible to formulate a simplified version of the algorithm, when only the largest value is being sought. In such a case, instead of multiplying by the matrix, we multiply the matrix $\boldsymbol{A}$ by a vector. When the vector is normalised after every iteration step, the iteration converges towards the eigenvector corresponding to the largest eigenvalue. This simplified method is thus suitable for searching the properties of the largest eigenvalue only.

The QR algorithm has an obvious weakness in the underlying assumption imposed on the matrix $\boldsymbol{A}$. If the matrix does not have distinct real eigenvalues, the method fails. In such a case, a more advanced method is needed. The purpose of this section is to introduce the reader into the numerical calculations of eigensystems. In order to cover all the possibilities and provide efficient algorithms in such cases, we would have to devote the entire book to this goal.

16.2.3 Inverse Iteration

Let us assume that we are equipped with the knowledge of the complete set of distinct real eigenvalues. Our objective is to find corresponding eigenvectors. We will focus on the inverse (power) iteration algorithm. The algorithm is an iterative procedure which for a given approximation of the eigenvalue finds the corresponding eigenvector, or its approximation. Let us consider the square real $p \times p$ matrix $\boldsymbol{A}$ with true eigenvalues $\lambda_1, \ldots, \lambda_p$. Further, we denote the approximation of the eigenvalue by indexing the variable with bar, i.e. $\lambda^{‘}$ being a close approximation to λ.

The following procedure describes the inverse iteration algorithm:

- Start with the approximated eigenvalue $\lambda^{‘}$ to the matrix $\boldsymbol{A}$.
- Initialise the eigenvector $\boldsymbol{v}_0$.
- The algorithm proceeds in iterative steps, with k denoting the iteration step, starting at $k = 0$:
  - Calculate the updated vector: $\boldsymbol{v}_{k+1} = (\boldsymbol{A} - \lambda^{‘}\boldsymbol{I}_p)^{-1}v_k$.
  - Normalise vector $\boldsymbol{v}_{k+1}$ by its norm: $\boldsymbol{v}_{k+1} = \frac{\boldsymbol{v}_{k+1}}{\|\boldsymbol{v}_{k+1}\|}$.
- Vector $\boldsymbol{v}_{k+1}$ converges to $\boldsymbol{v}_\lambda$.

The numerical procedure requires us to calculate $\boldsymbol{v}_{k+1} = (\boldsymbol{A} - \lambda^{‘}\boldsymbol{I}_p)^{-1}v_k$. This can be done either by solving

$$(\boldsymbol{A} - \lambda^{‘}\boldsymbol{I}_p)\boldsymbol{v}_{k+1} = v_k, \tag{16.21}$$

or by calculating the inverse of $\boldsymbol{A} - \lambda^{‘}\boldsymbol{I}_p$. Both approaches are valid; they differ by the numerical implementations.

Further, the closer $\lambda^{‘}$ is to λ, the faster is the convergence. The algorithm can for very good approximations of eigenvalue converge in very few steps. If, on the other hand, the approximation is not good, the algorithm can converge to an eigenvector of another eigenvalue. The iteration also involves normalisation. We have chosen the L_1 norm, where other normalisations are possible as well. The normalisation assures that convergence proceeds in terms of the orientation of the iterated vector and prevents an explosion of the vector in its norm.

In the next section, we implement both methods.

16.3 IMPLEMENTATION OF EIGENSYSTEM CALCULATION

We implement the numerical procedure to calculate the eigensystem for a real matrix $\boldsymbol{A}$ of dimension p. First, we need to generate a unit matrix:

```
.quantQ.mat.diagMatrix:{[dim]
   // dim -- dimension of diagonal matrix
   :"f"$v=/:v:til dim
};
```

which works as expected:

```
unitMatrix:.quantQ.mat.diagMatrix[4];
unitMatrix
```

```
1 0 0 0
0 1 0 0
0 0 1 0
0 0 0 1
```

We have stored the unit matrix into a temporary variable for further numerical checks. For the sake of curiosity, let us provide an alternative implementation of the unit matrix:

```
.quantQ.mat.diagMatrix2:{[dimM]
   // dimM -- dimension of diagonal matrix
   :{[x;y] t:x#0.0; t[y]:1.0; t}[dimM;] each til dimM;
};
```

The definition is identical to the first one, as we can see from

```
unitMatrix~.quantQ.mat.diagMatrix2[4]
```

```
1b
```

We encourage readers to compare and time the two approaches above and come up with further definitions using other verbs and/or adverbs.

The QR algorithm as introduced above is built upon the Givens rotation. We implement a function, which takes four arguments: the dimension of the matrix, the two coordinates i and j, and the angle of rotation θ, and returns the matrix with Givens rotation:

```
.quantQ.mat.givensRotation:{[dimM;i;j;theta]
   // dimM -- dimension of the matrix
   // i -- dim1 (0 to dimM-1)
   // j -- dim2 (0 to dimM-1)
   // theta -- angle of rotation
   // unit matrix
   givens: .quantQ.mat.diagMatrix[dimM];
   // insert cos
   givens[i;i]:cos[theta];
   givens[j;j]:cos[theta];
```

```
    // insert sin
    givens[min[(i;j)];max[(i;j)]]:neg[sin[theta]];
    givens[max[(i;j)];min[(i;j)]]:sin[theta];
    // rotation matrix
    :givens;
};
```

Let us produce the Givens matrix in a 4-dimensional space with a rotation in the space spanned by 2nd and 4th axis by angle of $\pi/4$:

```
.quantQ.mat.givensRotation[4;1;3;0.25*acos[-1]]
```

```
1 0         0 0
0 0.7071068 0 -0.7071068
0 0         1 0
0 0.7071068 0 0.7071068
```

The form of the matrix is as expected. Let us rotate the unit matrix by such a matrix:

```
.quantQ.mat.givensRotation[4;1;3;0.25*acos[-1]] mmu unitMatrix
```

```
1 0         0 0
0 0.7071068 0 -0.7071068
0 0         1 0
0 0.7071068 0 0.7071068
```

The rotated unit matrix is equal to the rotation matrix itself. The example also reminds us of the mmu verb we use to multiply two matrices in q.

16.3.1 QR Decomposition

Let us proceed with the QR decomposition. Function QRdecomp implements the procedure. The input is the matrix we wish to decompose. The outcome of the function is three matrices: the original matrix, the rotated matrix, and the rotation matrix. The function itself contains iterative procedure, where we iterate over all coordinates which need to be set to zero. We have kept the iterated function within the main function and not separated it. The reason that it is important to run the function as coord is defined. We have stressed that in the description of the algorithm.

```
.quantQ.mat.QRdecomp:{[matt]
   // matt -- input matrix
   // calculate dimension of the matrix
   dimM: count[matt];
   // list of coordinates to iterate over
   coord: raze {[dimM;x]     {[x;y] (y;x)}[x]'[t where x<t:reverse til dimM
      ↪ ]}[dimM;] each til dimM;
   // inputmatrix
   inputMat:matt;
   // initialised rotation matrix
   rotMat:.quantQ.mat.diagMatrix[dimM];
   // counter for bucket
   counter:0;
```

```
    // bucket with four variables for iterative procedure
    bucket:((`inputMat`rotMat`coord`counter)!(inputMat;rotMat;coord;counter)
        ↪ );
    // iteration to find QR decomposition
    bucket:({[bucket]
        // coordinates at the given step
        i:first bucket[`coord][bucket[`counter]];
        j:last bucket[`coord][bucket[`counter]];
        // theta to rotate the matrix
        theta:atan[neg[bucket[`inputMat][i;j]]%bucket[`inputMat][min[(i;j)];
            ↪ min[(i;j)]]];
        // dimension of the problem
        dimM: count bucket[`inputMat];
        // rotation matrix at the given step
        rotTMP:.quantQ.mat.givensRotation[dimM;j;i;theta];
        // update inputMat
        bucket[`inputMat]:rotTMP mmu bucket[`inputMat];
        // update rotMat
        bucket[`rotMat]:rotTMP mmu bucket[`rotMat];  // tohle bylo prehozene
        // increase counter
        bucket[`counter]:bucket[`counter]+1;
        // return bucket
        :bucket
    }/)[count[coord];bucket];
    // output bucket: initial matrix, rotated matrix and rotation matrix
    :((`matrix`matrixRotated`rotationMatrix)!(matt;bucket[`inputMat];bucket
        ↪ [`rotMat]));
};
```

Let us apply the QR decomposition function on the product of two Givens rotation matrices. The first acts in 2nd and 4th coordinate space with angle $\pi/4$ while the second one acts in 2nd and 3rd coordinate space with the same angle $\pi/4$.

```
output: .quantQ.mat.QRdecomp[.quantQ.mat.givensRotation[4;1;3;0.25*acos
    ↪ [-1]] mmu .quantQ.mat.givensRotation[4;1;2;0.25*acos[-1]]];
```

We have saved the outcome into a temporary variable as it contains three matrices, which we will explore one by one. First, the input matrix reads:

```
output[`matrix]
```

```
1 0         0         0
0 0.5       -0.5      -0.7071068
0 0.7071068 0.7071068 0
0 0.5       -0.5      0.7071068
```

We encourage reader to verify that this matrix indeed corresponds to a stacked ration.

The second matrix contained in the outcome of the function is the rotated matrix. The matrix should be upper diagonal. Since we have created the matrix as two Givens rotations, the outcome matrix will be unit matrix (which is upper diagonal):

```
output[`matrixRotated]
```

```
1 0 0 0
0 1 0 0
0 0 1 0
0 0 0 1
```

Finally, the last matrix which is returned by the function is the rotation matrix:

```
output[`rotationMatrix]
```

```
1 0          0         0
0 0.5        0.7071068 0.5
0 -0.5       0.7071068 -0.5
0 -0.7071068 0         0.7071068
```

The rotation matrix corresponds to unwinding the two rotations: First, we rotate in the space spanned by the 2nd and 3rd coordinate by angle $-\pi/4$. Then, we rotate in the 2nd and 4th coordinate space by angle $-\pi/4$. We can verify it as:

```
(.quantQ.mat.givensRotation[4;1;2;neg 0.25*acos[-1]] mmu .quantQ.mat.
    ↪ givensRotation[4;1;3;neg 0.25*acos[-1]]) ~ output[`rotationMatrix]
```

```
1b
```

This verifies the functionality of the QR decomposition function.

We will use the QR decomposition to obtain the eigenvalues. The QR algorithm is an iterative procedure which iteratively employs the QR decomposition and updates the matrix. First, we implement the iteration. The input is the dictionary with a matrix, which is input in the function `QRdecomp`. In the beginning, the input matrix is being read. The QR decomposition is then found and the new iterated matrix is calculated as a product of the upper triangular matrix and the transposed orthogonal matrix. Besides, it contains counter to be able to control the iterations:

```
.quantQ.mat.iterQR:{[bucket]
   // bucket -- contains matrix and counter
   // QR decomposition
   bucketTMP:.quantQ.mat.QRdecomp[bucket[`matrix]];
   // define Q and R
   Q:flip bucketTMP[`rotationMatrix];
   R: bucketTMP[`matrixRotated];
   // QT:bucket[`rotationMatrix];
   // define new matrix, similar to original one
   bucket[`matrix]:R mmu Q;
   // increase counter
   bucket[`counter]:bucket[`counter]+1;
   // return bucket
   :bucket;
};
```

Let us define an example matrix we will use for the rest of this chapter for eigensystem calculation.

```
matExa: (1.0 -2.0 0.0 5.0;0.0 7.0 1.0 5.0; 0.0 4.0 4.0 0.0;0.0 0.0 0.0 2.0)
    ↪ ;
matExa
```

```
1 -2 0 5
0 7  1 5
0 4  4 0
0 0  0 2
```

Initialise the bucket in order to run the function:

```
bucket:(`matrix`counter!(matExa;0j));
```

and run the function explicitly in ten iterations:

```
bucket:(.quantQ.mat.iterQR/)[10;bucket];
bucket[`matrix]
```

which gives following output:

```
1 -1.414262     1.414165  5
0 8.000103      -2.999828 3.535655
0 0.0001718623 2.999897   -3.535412
0 0             0         2
```

The matrix is getting shape close to the upper diagonal matrix. There are elements below the main diagonal which are very small. We need to wrap the iteration into a function which will control for precision. Function algoQR is such a function, which accepts as an argument dictionary with matrix to be decomposed, counter, and two control variables: the maximum number of iterations and the numerical precision:

```
.quantQ.mat.algoQR:{[bucket]
   // bucket -- contains matrix, counter, max number of iterations and
       ↪ precision
   // QR decomposition
   bucketTMP:.quantQ.mat.QRdecomp[bucket[`matrix]];
   // define Q and R
   Q:flip bucketTMP[`rotationMatrix];
   R: bucketTMP[`matrixRotated];
   dimM: count bucket[`matrix];
   // define new matrix, similar to original one
   bucket[`matrix]:R mmu Q;
   // increase counter
   bucket[`counter]:bucket[`counter]+1;
   // decide if continue
   // criterion 1: counts
   $[bucket[`counter]>=bucket[`maxCounts];bucket[`continue]:0b;];
   // criterion 2: precision
   $[bucket[`thresholdZero]>max abs {[matt;coord] matt[first[coord];last[
       ↪ coord]]}[bucket[`matrix];]
       each raze {[dimM;x]    {[x;y] (y;x)}[x]'[t where x<t:reverse til
           ↪ dimM]
       }[dimM;] each til count[bucket[`matrix]];bucket[`continue]:0b;];
   :bucket;
};
```

Function iteratively transforms matrix by using the QR algorithm. There are two checks for the iterations to stop. The algorithm stops if the number of iterations exceeds the threshold or all the numbers below the diagonal are within a specialised numerical precision.

We initialise the input bucket:

```
bucket:((`matrix`counter`maxCounts`thresholdZero`continue)!(matExa;0j;10000
    ↪ j;1e-10;1b));
```

and run the function, where we are interested in the upper diagonal matrix:

```
bucket:(.quantQ.mat.algoQR/)[{x[`continue]};bucket];
bucket[`matrix]
```

The matrix which is produced by the algorithm reads:

```
1 -1.414214     1.414214 5
0 8             -3       3.535534
0 7.008607e-011 3        -3.535534
0 0             0        2
```

The elements below diagonal are smaller than the precision. The elements on the diagonal are the eigenvalues of the matrix `matExa`. We provide finally a routine which will extract the eigenvalues from the bucket and sort the eigenvalues in a descending order:

```
.quantQ.mat.extractEigenvalQR:{[bucket]
   // bucket -- outcome from algoQR
   // extract diagonal and sort
   :desc {x[y;y]}[bucket[`matrix];] each til count bucket[`matrix];
};
```

where eigenvalues are being produced as:

```
eigenvalues:.quantQ.mat.extractEigenvalQR[bucket]
eigenvalues
```

```
8 3 2 1f
```

16.3.2 Inverse Iteration

At this step, we are equipped with the eigenvalues calculated by the QR algorithm. We will now implement the inverse iteration algorithm, which will for every eigenvalue numerically recover the eigenvector.

First, we define an L_1 matrix norm, which we need within the algorithm:

```
.quantQ.mat.normL1:{[matt]
   // matt -- matrix
   // return L1 (column norm)
   :max sum abs matt;
};
```

and verify it on the matrix we use:

```
.quantQ.mat.normL1[matExa]
```

```
13f
```

We define the `inverseIteration` function, which takes four arguments: the matrix, the eigenvalues, the numerical tolerance, and the maximum number of iterations. Our implementation of the iterative algorithm uses the inverse matrix, `inv`. The problem using the matrix inversion occurs in the situation when we are provided with the exact eigenvalue. In such a case, the matrix $(\boldsymbol{A} - \lambda^{`}\boldsymbol{I}_p)$ is singular and cannot be inverted.

In order to overcome the singularity in the iterative algorithm, we have introduced perturbation into the eigenvalue. Thus, when we are provided with the exact eigenvalue, we distort it such that we have only an approximate solution. For such a solution, the iterative algorithm works and can proceed. We perform the check `0<sum{[x] (x=0nf) or (x=0wf) or (x=-0wf)} each raze inv[invMat]` at the beginning of each iteration. The perturbation is applied only during the initial call as it amends the eigenvalue directly. The function returns the eigenvector and we are thus not exposed to the perturbed value.

The normalisation within the iterations is using L_1 matrix norm. Besides, in order to prevent flipping of the eigenvector by a multiplicative factor -1, we enforce the first element of the eigenvector to be non-negative. The function starts with a random vector with components being independently drawn from the uniform distribution defined over $[-1; 1]$. At the end of the iterations, the eigenvector is normalised by L_2 norm to the unit modulus.

The function reads:

```
.quantQ.mat.inverseIteration:{[mattInit;eigenValue;toler;maxIter]
    // mattInit -- the matrix
    // eigenValue -- the eigenvalue
    // toler -- numerical tolerance
    // maxIter -- maximum number of iterations
    // dimension of the matrix
    dimM: count mattInit;
    // initial starting vector, random
    vecB:neg[1.0]+dimM?2.0;
    // set the first element of the random vector to be positive
    $[0<=first vecB; ; vecB:neg vecB];
    // prepare the bucket
    bucketI:((`matrix`eigenVal`vecB`tolerance`counter`maxIter`continue)!(
        ↪ mattInit;eigenValue;vecB;toler;0j;maxIter;1b));
    bucketI:({[bucketI]
        // the matrix for inverse iteration
        invMat:(bucketI[`matrix]-bucketI[`eigenVal]*.quantQ.mat.diagMatrix[
            ↪ count[bucketI[`matrix]]]);
        // the inverse iteration method works for non-singular matrices
        $[0<sum{[x] (x=0nf) or (x=0wf) or (x=-0wf)} each raze inv[invMat];
            // introduce random perturbation
            bucketI[`eigenVal]:bucketI[`eigenVal]+(1e-7)*(neg[1.0]+first
                ↪ 1?2.0);
```

```
        [
            vecBOld:bucketI[`vecB];
            vecB: (1.0% .quantQ.mat.normL1[t])*t:(inv[invMat] mmu vecBOld);
            // set the first element of the random vector to be positive
            $[0<=first vecB; ; vecB:neg vecB];
            // plug into bucket
            bucketI[`vecB]:vecB;
            // increase counter
            bucketI[`counter]:bucketI[`counter]+1;
            // switch off iteration
            $[((max[abs[vecBOld-vecB]])<bucketI[`tolerance]) or (bucketI[`
                ↪ counter]>bucketI[`maxIter]);bucketI[`continue]:0b; ];
            // in the last step, normalize to L2=1
            $[bucketI[`continue]=0b; bucketI[`vecB]:bucketI[`vecB]*(1.0%sqrt
                ↪ [sum bucketI[`vecB]*bucketI[`vecB]]); ]
        ]
        ];
        // output bucket
        : bucketI
        }/)[{x[`continue]};bucketI];
    // eigenvector
    :bucketI[`vecB];
};
```

We calculate the eigenvectors to eigenvalues we have found in the previous section:

```
eigenvectors: .quantQ.mat.inverseIteration[matExa;;1e-10;10000j] each
    ↪ eigenvalues
```

and revise the eigenvectors one by one:

```
eigenvectors[0]
```

```
0.1980295 -0.6931033 -0.6931033 -1.059117e-08
```

```
eigenvectors[1]
```

```
0.2357023 -0.2357023 0.942809 5.291795e-09
```

```
eigenvectors[2]
```

```
0.9074425 -0.1814885 0.362977 0.1088931
```

```
eigenvectors[3]
```

```
1 -5.400702e-09 2.054183e-08 -1.031521e-10
```

We can verify the eigenvectors by checking the property of eigenvectors, i.e. when the eigenvector is multiplied by the matrix itself and divided by the corresponding eigenvalue, the eigenvector is recovered.

```
(matExa mmu eigenvectors[0])%eigenvalues[0]
```

```
0.1980295 -0.6931033 -0.6931033 -2.647794e-09
```

```
(matExa mmu eigenvectors[1])%eigenvalues[1]
```

```
0.2357023 -0.2357023 0.942809 3.527864e-09
```

```
(matExa mmu eigenvectors[2])%eigenvalues[2]
```

```
0.9074425 -0.1814885 0.362977 0.1088931
```

```
(matExa mmu eigenvectors[3])%eigenvalues[3]
```

```
1 -1.777885e-08 6.05645e-08 -2.063043e-10
```

Indeed, the eigenvectors are recovered within the working numerical precision. That is why we have not used ~ to compare the eigenvectors with their numerically recovered values.

Finally, we wrap the functions into a numerical suite which accepts as an input the matrix and returns sorted the list of eigenvectors in descending order, and a corresponding list of eigenvectors. The values are wrapped in the dictionary:

```
.quantQ.mat.eigenSystem:{[matt]
   // matt -- input matrix
   // set the bucket, default controls
   bucket:((`matrix`counter`maxCounts`thresholdZero`continue)!(matt;0j
       ↪ ;10000j;1e-10;1b));
   // solve for eigenvalues
   bucket:(.quantQ.mat.algoQR/)[{x[`continue]};bucket];
   // extract eigenvalues
   eigenvalues:.quantQ.mat.extractEigenvalQR[bucket];
   // solve for eigenvectors
   eigenvectors: .quantQ.mat.inverseIteration[matt;;1e-10;10000j] each
       ↪ eigenvalues;
   // output bucket
   :((`eigenvalues`eigenvectors)!(eigenvalues;eigenvectors));
};
```

Finally, we obtain the full solution with the eigensystem of the matrix:

```
flip .quantQ.mat.eigenSystem[matExa]
```

```
eigenvalues eigenvectors
-------------------------------------------------------------
8           0.1980295 -0.6931033     -0.6931033    3.884289e-009
3           0.2357022 -0.2357023     0.9428091     -5.887847e-017
2           0.9074425 -0.1814885     0.362977      0.1088931
1           1         -1.252761e-009 2.246023e-010 8.945528e-010
```

We have flipped the dictionary to present the result in the form of a table. Every row corresponds to the different eigenvalue/eigenvector.

We encourage the readers to review the provided functions and suggest the generalisations. The obvious place to improve the provided algorithms is in the fact where we are perturbing the case when we have the correct eigenvalue. The more suitable solution would be to use the correct eigenvalues directly. Further, the algorithm does not work perfectly when there is a degenerate eigenvalue. This is a place for improvement as well.

16.4 THE DATA MATRIX AND THE PRINCIPAL COMPONENT ANALYSIS

The principal component analysis (PCA) is a popular statistical technique which transforms a set of data into a new orthogonal basis such that directions of the new basis are ordered in terms of variance contribution to the overall variance. This was introduced by Pearson (1901). In this section, we consider a p-dimensional vector of features, where each feature is observed n times. Let us denote the $n \times p$ dimensional matrix of data as $\boldsymbol{X}$. First, we discuss the data matrix and its properties and then use the findings to introduce the PCA.

16.4.1 The Data Matrix

In general, the data matrix $\boldsymbol{X}$ is rectangular – not necessarily square. Eigenvalues, as we have seen in previous paragraphs, are not defined for rectangular matrices. There is thus another, closely related notion: singular values. The right and left singular values for a rectangular matrix $\boldsymbol{X}$ are the square roots of the eigenvalues of $\boldsymbol{X}^\top\boldsymbol{X}$ and $\boldsymbol{X}\boldsymbol{X}^\top$, respectively. The eigenvectors corresponding to those eigenvalues are referred to as the right and left singular vectors, respectively. What exactly do these matrices, $\boldsymbol{X}^\top\boldsymbol{X}$ and $\boldsymbol{X}\boldsymbol{X}^\top$, mean in terms of statistics if $\boldsymbol{X}$ is a data matrix?

Mathematically, we could model our observations as a p-dimensional vector random variable $\boldsymbol{x}$. While it is customary to use uppercase letters for random variables, we shall use a lowercase letter for now, to distinguish the random variable $\boldsymbol{x}$ from the data matrix $\boldsymbol{X}$. It is also customary to deal with column vectors, rather than with row vectors, so we shall assume that $\boldsymbol{x}$ is a column vector, i.e. $\boldsymbol{x} \in \mathbb{R}^{p\times 1}$. Let us denote that this is inconsistent with the way the data is presented in the data matrix: the samples – which we model as realisations of the random variable $\boldsymbol{x}$ – occur as the rows of $\boldsymbol{X}$, not as columns.

Let us define the covariance matrix. Namely, let $\boldsymbol{x}$ be a p-dimensional random vector, $\boldsymbol{x} \in \mathbb{R}^{p\times 1}$. Its covariance matrix is given by

$$\boldsymbol{\Sigma} := \mathsf{Cov}[\boldsymbol{x}] := \mathsf{Var}[\boldsymbol{x}] = \mathbb{E}[(\boldsymbol{x} - \mathbb{E}[\boldsymbol{x}])(\boldsymbol{x} - \mathbb{E}[\boldsymbol{x}])^\top] \in \mathbb{R}^{p\times p}. \tag{16.22}$$

The covariance matrix is a generalisation of the variance for higher (than one) dimensional random variables: we may still write $\mathsf{Var}[\boldsymbol{x}]$ instead of $\mathsf{Cov}[\boldsymbol{x}]$. It has nothing to do with a specific data sample (equivalently, with a specific data matrix); it has everything to do with the random variable $\boldsymbol{x}$ used to model the data. This random variable is a mathematical abstraction/idealisation, unlike a specific data sample.

The covariance matrix is not a random quantity, but we can only write down a specific covariance matrix if we assume that we "know" the distribution of the random variable $\boldsymbol{x}$; quite often we only pretend that we know it. Here we assumed that $\boldsymbol{x}$ is a column vector, i.e. $\boldsymbol{x} \in \mathbb{R}^{p\times 1}$.

First, let us answer the question, what is the significance of the (i,j)-th entry of the covariance matrix $\boldsymbol{\Sigma}$? If we write the p-dimensional random vector $\boldsymbol{x}$ as

$$\boldsymbol{x} = \begin{pmatrix} x^{(1)} \\ x^{(2)} \\ x^{(3)} \\ \vdots \\ x^{(p)} \end{pmatrix}, \tag{16.23}$$

then the (i,j)-th entry of $\boldsymbol{\Sigma}$ is the covariance between the scalar random variables $x^{(i)}$ and $x^{(j)}$:

$$\boldsymbol{\Sigma}^{(i,j)} = \mathsf{Cov}[x^{(i)}, x^{(j)}] := \mathbb{E}[(x^{(i)} - \mathbb{E}[x^{(i)}])(x^{(j)} - \mathbb{E}[x^{(j)}])], \tag{16.24}$$

where we notice that, in this notation for covariance of two random variables, Cov has two arguments, whereas, in the notation $\mathsf{Cov}[\boldsymbol{x}]$ for the covariance matrix, Cov has a single argument.

The key properties of covariance matrices are: first, it is symmetric, and second, it is positive semidefinite. To show that $\boldsymbol{\Sigma}$ is symmetric:

$$\boldsymbol{\Sigma}^{\intercal} = \{\mathbb{E}[(\boldsymbol{x} - \mathbb{E}[\boldsymbol{x}])(\boldsymbol{x} - \mathbb{E}[\boldsymbol{x}])^{\intercal}]\}^{\intercal} \tag{16.25}$$

$$= \mathbb{E}[\{(\boldsymbol{x} - \mathbb{E}[\boldsymbol{x}])^{\intercal}\}^{\intercal}(\boldsymbol{x} - \mathbb{E}[\boldsymbol{x}])^{\intercal}] \tag{16.26}$$

$$= \mathbb{E}[(\boldsymbol{x} - \mathbb{E}[\boldsymbol{x}])(\boldsymbol{x} - \mathbb{E}[\boldsymbol{x}])^{\intercal}] = \boldsymbol{\Sigma}, \tag{16.27}$$

and to show that $\boldsymbol{\Sigma}$ is positive semidefinite, let $\boldsymbol{u} \in \mathbb{R}^p$ be a nonzero vector. Then

$$\boldsymbol{u}^{\intercal}\boldsymbol{\Sigma}\boldsymbol{u} = \boldsymbol{u}^{\intercal}\{\mathbb{E}[(\boldsymbol{x} - \mathbb{E}[\boldsymbol{x}])(\boldsymbol{x} - \mathbb{E}[\boldsymbol{x}])^{\intercal}]\}\boldsymbol{u} \tag{16.28}$$

$$= \mathbb{E}[\{(\boldsymbol{x} - \mathbb{E}[\boldsymbol{x}])^{\intercal}\boldsymbol{u}\}^{\intercal}\{(\boldsymbol{x} - \mathbb{E}[\boldsymbol{x}])^{\intercal}\boldsymbol{u}\}] \tag{16.29}$$

$$= \mathbb{E}\left[\left\{\underbrace{(\boldsymbol{x} - \mathbb{E}[\boldsymbol{x}])^{\intercal}\boldsymbol{u}}_{\text{scalar}}\right\}^2\right] \geq 0. \tag{16.30}$$

When we work with data, we often say we calculate covariance matrix and talk about values of the covariance matrix coming from the given sample. In this case, we talk about the sample covariance matrix, which is given by

$$\boldsymbol{Q} = \frac{1}{n-1}\sum_{i=1}^{n}(\boldsymbol{x}_i - \overline{\boldsymbol{x}})(\boldsymbol{x}_i - \overline{\boldsymbol{x}})^{\intercal} \in \mathbb{R}^{p\times p}, \tag{16.31}$$

where $\boldsymbol{x}_i$ is the i-th row of the data matrix $\boldsymbol{X}$ written as a column vector and $\overline{\boldsymbol{x}}$ is the sample mean, also written as a column vector. We are still modelling $\boldsymbol{x}_i$ as a random variable, but now we have a data sample; for a concrete data sample (for a concrete data matrix $\boldsymbol{X}$), we could obtain a specific matrix $\boldsymbol{Q}$ and use it as an estimator of the covariance matrix $\mathsf{Cov}[\boldsymbol{x}]$ of the hypothetical random variable $\boldsymbol{x}$.

Thus the sample covariance matrix is a generalisation of the sample covariance, whereas the covariance matrix is a generalisation of the variance of a random variable. However, people often use the term "covariance matrix" for both these things, so beware of the confusion!

The sample covariance matrix is symmetric and positive semidefinite. We will leave it to the reader to construct proof of this assertion. Please keep in mind that we have to use sums over all realisations in the sample data $\boldsymbol{X}$. Another important feature of the sample covariance matrix is to be an unbiased estimator of the true covariance matrix $\mathsf{Cov}[\boldsymbol{x}]$, $\boldsymbol{x}$. This assertion follows from:

$$\mathbb{E}[\boldsymbol{Q}] = \frac{1}{n-1}\mathbb{E}\left[\sum_{i=1}^{n}(\boldsymbol{x}_i - \overline{\boldsymbol{x}})(\boldsymbol{x}_i - \overline{\boldsymbol{x}})^{\mathsf{T}}\right] \tag{16.32}$$

$$= \frac{1}{n-1}\mathbb{E}\left[\sum_{i=1}^{n}\boldsymbol{x}_i\boldsymbol{x}_i^{\mathsf{T}} - n\overline{\boldsymbol{x}}\overline{\boldsymbol{x}}^{\mathsf{T}} - n\overline{\boldsymbol{x}}\overline{\boldsymbol{x}}^{\mathsf{T}} + n\overline{\boldsymbol{x}}\overline{\boldsymbol{x}}^{\mathsf{T}}\right] \tag{16.33}$$

$$= \frac{1}{n-1}\sum_{i=1}^{n}\mathbb{E}[\boldsymbol{x}_i\boldsymbol{x}_i^{\mathsf{T}}] - n\mathbb{E}[\overline{\boldsymbol{x}}\overline{\boldsymbol{x}}^{\mathsf{T}}] \tag{16.34}$$

$$= \frac{1}{n-1}\sum_{i=1}^{n}(\boldsymbol{\Sigma} + \boldsymbol{\mu}\boldsymbol{\mu}^{\mathsf{T}}) - n\left(\frac{1}{n}\boldsymbol{\Sigma} + \boldsymbol{\mu}\boldsymbol{\mu}^{\mathsf{T}}\right) \tag{16.35}$$

$$= \frac{1}{n-1}\{n\boldsymbol{\Sigma} + n\boldsymbol{\mu}\boldsymbol{\mu}^{\mathsf{T}} - \boldsymbol{\Sigma} - n\boldsymbol{\mu}\boldsymbol{\mu}^{\mathsf{T}}\} = \boldsymbol{\Sigma}, \tag{16.36}$$

so $\boldsymbol{Q}$ is an unbiased estimator of $\boldsymbol{\Sigma}$.

Further, closely related to the covariance matrix is the correlation matrix. The correlation matrix, the matrix of Pearson product-moment correlation coefficients between each element in the random vector $\boldsymbol{x}$, can be written as:

$$\mathsf{Cor}[\boldsymbol{x}] = (\boldsymbol{\Sigma}^{(\text{diag})})^{-\frac{1}{2}}\,\boldsymbol{\Sigma}\,(\boldsymbol{\Sigma}^{(\text{diag})})^{-\frac{1}{2}}, \tag{16.37}$$

where $\boldsymbol{\Sigma}^{(\text{diag})}$ is the matrix of the diagonal elements of $\boldsymbol{\Sigma}$, i.e. a diagonal matrix of the variances of x_i for each i-th element of $\boldsymbol{x}$. The sample correlation matrix is obtained accordingly from the sample covariance matrix. By construction, the correlation matrix and the sample correlation matrix are also symmetric and positive semidefinite. Further, all diagonal entries in these matrices are equal to 1. If the variances of all elements of $\boldsymbol{x}$ were equal to 1, then the covariance matrix would be equal to the variance matrix. The correlation matrix is thus a rescaling of the covariance matrix forcing all element variances to be equal.

It is worth establishing a connection between the sample covariance matrix and Gram matrix, $(\boldsymbol{X}')^{\mathsf{T}}\boldsymbol{X}'$. In particular, when the data is centred ($\boldsymbol{X} = \boldsymbol{X}'$), the unbiased sample covariance matrix is given by a scalar multiple of the Gram matrix, namely $\frac{1}{n-1}\boldsymbol{X}^\top\boldsymbol{X}$.

16.4.2 PCA: The First Principal Component

Let us introduce the principal components of the data set provided. We focus on the calculation of the first principal component (PCA), which we will then extend to higher components. For the sake of clarity, let us once again stress that we have p features. We shall model our data as a p-dimensional random variable $\boldsymbol{x} \in \mathbb{R}^{p\times 1}$.

The objective behind the PCA is to look for a vector of weights $\boldsymbol{w}_{(1)} \in \mathbb{R}^{p\times 1}$ such that the variance of the scalar random variable $\boldsymbol{x}^\top\boldsymbol{w}_{(1)}$ is maximised. Thus our objective is to find

$$\max_{\boldsymbol{w}_{(1)}} \mathsf{Var}[\boldsymbol{x}^\top\boldsymbol{w}_{(1)}]. \tag{16.38}$$

We assume that we are given a data matrix with n observations, $\boldsymbol{X} \in \mathbb{R}^{n\times p}$. Let us centre this data to obtain the centred data matrix $\boldsymbol{X}'$. We have already argued that the sample covariance matrix:

$$\boldsymbol{Q} = \frac{1}{n-1}(\boldsymbol{X}')^\top\boldsymbol{X}' \tag{16.39}$$

is an unbiased estimator of the covariance matrix $\mathsf{Var}[\boldsymbol{x}]$. Moreover, by the properties of variances,

$$\mathsf{Var}[\boldsymbol{x}^\top\boldsymbol{w}_{(1)}] = \boldsymbol{w}_{(1)}^\top\mathsf{Var}[\boldsymbol{x}]\boldsymbol{w}_{(1)} = \boldsymbol{w}_{(1)}^\top\,\boldsymbol{\Sigma}\,\boldsymbol{w}_{(1)}. \tag{16.40}$$

In practice, however, we don't have access to $\boldsymbol{\Sigma}$. At best, we can approximate it by some matrix $\boldsymbol{C}$, say by the unbiased estimator – the sample covariance matrix:

$$\boldsymbol{C} = \boldsymbol{Q} := \frac{1}{n-1}(\boldsymbol{X}')^\top\boldsymbol{X}'. \tag{16.41}$$

Thus our maximisation problem becomes:

$$\max_{\boldsymbol{w}_{(1)}} \boldsymbol{w}_{(1)}^\top\boldsymbol{C}\boldsymbol{w}_{(1)}. \tag{16.42}$$

This is not enough; let us add another requirement (in optimisation parlance, another constraint): we want our weights, $\boldsymbol{w}_{(1)}$, to be a unit vector:

$$\boldsymbol{w}_{(1)}^\top\boldsymbol{w}_{(1)} = 1. \tag{16.43}$$

Equivalently, we can add a penalty to our (again, in optimisation parlance) objective function for any deviation from zero of $\boldsymbol{w}_{(1)}^\top\boldsymbol{w}_{(1)} - 1$. The optimisation problem then becomes

$$\max_{\boldsymbol{w}_{(1)}} \boldsymbol{w}_{(1)}^\top\boldsymbol{C}\boldsymbol{w}_{(1)} - \lambda_{(1)}(\boldsymbol{w}_{(1)}^\top\boldsymbol{w}_{(1)} - 1), \tag{16.44}$$

where the constant $\lambda_{(1)}$ is a Lagrange multiplier. (This method of including a constraint within the objective function is called the Lagrange multipliers technique.)

Let us now solve this optimisation problem. If $\boldsymbol{w}_{(1)}$ maximises our objective function, then

$$\frac{\partial}{\partial \boldsymbol{w}_{(1)}}(\boldsymbol{w}_{(1)}^{\mathsf{T}}\boldsymbol{C}\boldsymbol{w}_{(1)} - \lambda_{(1)}(\boldsymbol{w}_{(1)}^{\mathsf{T}}\boldsymbol{w}_{(1)} - 1)) = 0, \tag{16.45}$$

and, computing the partial derivative on the left-hand side, we get

$$\boldsymbol{C}\boldsymbol{w}_{(1)} - \lambda_{(1)}\boldsymbol{w}_{(1)} = \boldsymbol{0}. \tag{16.46}$$

Rearranging this equation,

$$\boldsymbol{C}\boldsymbol{w}_{(1)} = \lambda_{(1)}\boldsymbol{w}_{(1)}, \tag{16.47}$$

we see that $\boldsymbol{w}_{(1)}$ is an eigenvector of $\boldsymbol{C}$ and $\lambda_{(1)}$ the corresponding eigenvalue. And so

$$\mathsf{Var}[\boldsymbol{x}^{\mathsf{T}}\boldsymbol{w}_{(1)}] \approx \boldsymbol{w}_{(1)}^{\mathsf{T}}\boldsymbol{C}\boldsymbol{w}_{(1)} = \boldsymbol{w}_{(1)}^{\mathsf{T}}\lambda_{(1)}\boldsymbol{w}_{(1)} = \lambda_{(1)}\boldsymbol{w}_{(1)}^{\mathsf{T}}\boldsymbol{w}_{(1)} = \lambda_{(1)}. \tag{16.48}$$

From this, since we must maximise $\mathsf{Var}[\boldsymbol{x}^{\mathsf{T}}\boldsymbol{w}_{(1)}]$, we see that $\lambda_{(1)}$ is not just any eigenvalue of $\boldsymbol{C}$, but the largest eigenvalue (and $\boldsymbol{w}_{(1)}$ the corresponding eigenvector). We have thus established that $\lambda_{(1)}$ is the *largest eigenvalue* of $\boldsymbol{C}$ and $\boldsymbol{w}_{(1)}$ the corresponding eigenvector.

Note that, if $\boldsymbol{A}$ is a matrix and α a non-zero scalar, then

$$\boldsymbol{A}\boldsymbol{v} = \lambda\boldsymbol{v} \iff (\alpha\boldsymbol{A})\boldsymbol{v} = (\alpha\lambda)\boldsymbol{v}, \tag{16.49}$$

so the eigenvectors of $\alpha\boldsymbol{A}$ are precisely the eigenvectors of $\boldsymbol{A}$ but the corresponding eigenvalues of $\alpha\boldsymbol{A}$ are α times the corresponding eigenvalues of $\boldsymbol{A}$. Thus, if we take $\boldsymbol{C} = \boldsymbol{Q} = \frac{1}{n-1}(\boldsymbol{X}')^{\mathsf{T}}\boldsymbol{X}'$, $\lambda_{(1)}$ is $\lambda_{(1)} = \frac{1}{n-1}\lambda_1$, where λ_1 is the largest eigenvalue of $(\boldsymbol{X}')^{\mathsf{T}}\boldsymbol{X}'$.

Equivalently, $\lambda_{(1)}$ is $\frac{1}{n-1}$ times the square of the largest right singular value of $\boldsymbol{X}'$ and $\boldsymbol{w}_{(1)}$ the corresponding right singular vector of $\boldsymbol{X}'$. Recall that, since $\boldsymbol{C}$ is symmetric positive (semi)definite, $\lambda_{(1)}$ is positive (non-negative). Recall also that, since $\boldsymbol{C}$ is symmetric positive (semi)definite, all its eigenvectors are mutually orthogonal.

16.4.3 Second Principal Component

We shall now look for a vector of weights $\boldsymbol{w}_{(2)} \in \mathbb{R}^{p\times 1}$ such that $\boldsymbol{w}_{(2)}$ is orthogonal to $\boldsymbol{w}_{(2)}$ and the variance of the scalar random variable $\boldsymbol{x}^{\mathsf{T}}\boldsymbol{w}_{(2)}$ is maximised. We want this vector to be a unit vector, $\boldsymbol{w}_{(2)}^{\mathsf{T}}\boldsymbol{w}_{(2)} = 1$. Since it is orthogonal to $\boldsymbol{w}_{(1)}$, $\boldsymbol{w}_{(1)}^{\mathsf{T}}\boldsymbol{w}_{(2)} = 0$. We can add this as a constraint to our optimisation problem. We add both constraints to our objective problem using the Lagrange multipliers technique, thus obtaining the objective function:

$$\max_{\boldsymbol{w}_{(2)}} \boldsymbol{w}_{(2)}^{\mathsf{T}}\boldsymbol{C}\boldsymbol{w}_{(2)} - \lambda_{(2)}(\boldsymbol{w}_{(2)}^{\mathsf{T}}\boldsymbol{w}_{(2)} - 1) - \nu_{(1)}\boldsymbol{w}_{(1)}^{\mathsf{T}}\boldsymbol{w}_{(2)}, \tag{16.50}$$

where $\lambda_{(2)}$ is the Lagrange multiplier corresponding to the unit vector constraint and $\nu_{(1)}$ the Lagrange multiplier corresponding to the orthogonality constraint.

If $\boldsymbol{w}_{(2)}$ maximises our objective function, then

$$\frac{\partial}{\partial \boldsymbol{w}_{(2)}}\left(\boldsymbol{w}_{(2)}^{\mathsf{T}}\boldsymbol{C}\boldsymbol{w}_{(2)} - \lambda_{(2)}(\boldsymbol{w}_{(2)}^{\mathsf{T}}\boldsymbol{w}_{(2)} - 1) - \nu_{(1)}\boldsymbol{w}_{(1)}^{\mathsf{T}}\boldsymbol{w}_{(2)}\right) = 0. \tag{16.51}$$

Computing the partial derivative on the left-hand side, we get

$$\boldsymbol{C}\boldsymbol{w}_{(2)} - \lambda_{(2)}\boldsymbol{w}_{(2)} - \nu_{(1)}\boldsymbol{w}_{(1)} = \boldsymbol{0}. \tag{16.52}$$

Let us multiply both sides of this equation by $\boldsymbol{w}_{(1)}^{\mathsf{T}}$ on the left:

$$\boldsymbol{w}_{(1)}^{\mathsf{T}}\boldsymbol{C}\boldsymbol{w}_{(2)} - \lambda_{(2)}\boldsymbol{w}_{(1)}^{\mathsf{T}}\boldsymbol{w}_{(2)} - \nu_{(1)}\boldsymbol{w}_{(1)}^{\mathsf{T}}\boldsymbol{w}_{(1)} = 0. \tag{16.53}$$

Here,

$$\boldsymbol{w}_{(1)}^{\mathsf{T}}\boldsymbol{C}\boldsymbol{w}_{(2)} = \boldsymbol{w}_{(2)}^{\mathsf{T}}\boldsymbol{C}\boldsymbol{w}_{(1)} = \tag{16.54}$$

$$\boldsymbol{w}_{(2)}^{\mathsf{T}}(\boldsymbol{C}\boldsymbol{w}_{(1)}) = \boldsymbol{w}_{(2)}^{\mathsf{T}}(\lambda_{(1)}\boldsymbol{w}_{(1)}) = \lambda_{(1)}(\boldsymbol{w}_{(2)}^{\mathsf{T}}\boldsymbol{w}_{(1)}) = \lambda_{(1)} \cdot 0 = 0. \tag{16.55}$$

Moreover, since $\boldsymbol{w}_{(1)}$ and $\boldsymbol{w}_{(2)}$ are orthogonal and $\boldsymbol{w}_{(2)}$ is a unit vector, we get

$$\boldsymbol{w}_{(1)}^{\mathsf{T}}\boldsymbol{w}_{(2)} = 0, \quad \boldsymbol{w}_{(2)}^{\mathsf{T}}\boldsymbol{w}_{(2)} = 1, \tag{16.56}$$

and the equation becomes $\nu_{(1)} = 0$. Hence

$$\boldsymbol{C}\boldsymbol{w}_{(2)} - \lambda_{(2)}\boldsymbol{w}_{(2)} = \boldsymbol{0}. \tag{16.57}$$

Rearranging this equation,

$$\boldsymbol{C}\boldsymbol{w}_{(2)} = \lambda_{(2)}\boldsymbol{w}_{(2)}, \tag{16.58}$$

we see that $\boldsymbol{w}_{(2)}$ is an eigenvector of $\boldsymbol{C}$ and $\lambda_{(2)}$ the corresponding eigenvalue. And so

$$\mathsf{Var}[\boldsymbol{x}^{\mathsf{T}}\boldsymbol{w}_{(2)}] \approx \boldsymbol{w}_{(2)}^{\mathsf{T}}\boldsymbol{C}\boldsymbol{w}_{(2)} = \boldsymbol{w}_{(2)}^{\mathsf{T}}\lambda_{(2)}\boldsymbol{w}_{(2)} = \lambda_{(2)}\boldsymbol{w}_{(2)}^{\mathsf{T}}\boldsymbol{w}_{(2)} = \lambda_{(2)}. \tag{16.59}$$

From this, since we must maximise $\mathsf{Var}[\boldsymbol{x}^{\mathsf{T}}\boldsymbol{w}_{(2)}]$, we see that $\lambda_{(2)}$ is not just any eigenvalue of $\boldsymbol{C}$, but the next largest eigenvalue (after excluding the eigenvalue $\lambda_{(1)}$) (and $\boldsymbol{w}_{(2)}$ the corresponding eigenvector). The eigenvalue $\lambda_{(1)}$ is excluded from consideration by the orthogonality constraints on the eigenvectors. Although it may (or may not) happen that $\lambda_{(2)} = \lambda_{(1)}$.

We can generalise this process and obtain:

- The eigenvalue, $\lambda_{(1)}$, and the corresponding eigenvector $\boldsymbol{w}_{(1)}$, of $\boldsymbol{C}$, such that $\mathsf{Var}[\boldsymbol{x}^\mathsf{T}\boldsymbol{w}_{(1)}] \approx \boldsymbol{w}_{(1)}^\mathsf{T}\boldsymbol{C}\boldsymbol{w}_{(1)} = \lambda_{(1)}$;
- The eigenvalue, $\lambda_{(2)} \leq \lambda_{(1)}$, and the corresponding eigenvector $\boldsymbol{w}_{(2)}$, of $\boldsymbol{C}$, such that $\mathsf{Var}[\boldsymbol{x}^\mathsf{T}\boldsymbol{w}_{(2)}] \approx \boldsymbol{w}_{(2)}^\mathsf{T}\boldsymbol{C}\boldsymbol{w}_{(2)} = \lambda_{(2)}$;
- The eigenvalue, $\lambda_{(3)} \leq \lambda_{(2)}$, and the corresponding eigenvector $\boldsymbol{w}_{(3)}$, of $\boldsymbol{C}$, such that $\mathsf{Var}[\boldsymbol{x}^\mathsf{T}\boldsymbol{w}_{(3)}] \approx \boldsymbol{w}_{(3)}^\mathsf{T}\boldsymbol{C}\boldsymbol{w}_{(3)} = \lambda_{(3)}$;
- $\vdots$
- The eigenvalue, $\lambda_{(p)} \leq \lambda_{(p-1)}$, and the corresponding eigenvector $\boldsymbol{w}_{(p)}$, of $\boldsymbol{C}$, such that $\mathsf{Var}[\boldsymbol{x}^\mathsf{T}\boldsymbol{w}_{(p)}] \approx \boldsymbol{w}_{(p)}^\mathsf{T}\boldsymbol{C}\boldsymbol{w}_{(p)} = \lambda_{(p)}$.

16.4.4 Terminology and Explained Variance

It is worth summarising the common terminology used when the PCA is applied. Let $\boldsymbol{W}$ be the matrix with weights – $\boldsymbol{C}$'s eigenvectors – as its columns,

$$\boldsymbol{W} = \begin{pmatrix} | & | & & | \\ \boldsymbol{w}_{(1)} & \boldsymbol{w}_{(2)} & \cdots & \boldsymbol{w}_{(p)} \\ | & | & & | \end{pmatrix} \in \mathbb{R}^{p\times p}. \tag{16.60}$$

The transformation of the p-dimensional random vector $\boldsymbol{x}$, centred (corrected for its mean $\boldsymbol{\mu}$),

$$\boldsymbol{y} = \boldsymbol{W}^\mathsf{T}(\boldsymbol{x} - \boldsymbol{\mu}) \in \mathbb{R}^{p\times 1}, \tag{16.61}$$

the p-dimensional random vector $\boldsymbol{y}$, is called the vector of $\boldsymbol{x}$'s principal components or principal component (PC) scores. The i-th element of $\boldsymbol{y}$ is then the i-th principal component or the i-th PC score of $\boldsymbol{x}$.

For the centred data matrix $\boldsymbol{X}' \in \mathbb{R}^{n\times p}$, the principal components or principal component (PC) scores are given by the matrix

$$\boldsymbol{Z} := \boldsymbol{X}'\boldsymbol{W} \in \mathbb{R}^{n\times p}, \tag{16.62}$$

so that the (i,j)-th entry of $\boldsymbol{Z}$,

$$Z_{i,j} = \boldsymbol{x}'_{i,:}\boldsymbol{w}_{(j)}, \tag{16.63}$$

with $1 \leq i \leq n, 1 \leq j \leq p$, where $\boldsymbol{x}'_{i,:}$ is the i-th row of $\boldsymbol{X}'$, is the j-th principal component (j-th PC score) of the i-th observation (the i-th row of $\boldsymbol{X}'$). The j-th column of $\boldsymbol{Z}$, $1 \leq j \leq p$, $\boldsymbol{z}_{(j)}$, is sometimes referred to as the j-th principal component of the data. Thus the j-th weight vector, $\boldsymbol{w}_{(j)} \in \mathbb{R}^{p\times 1}$, maps the data to the j-th principal component (PC score).

Since $\boldsymbol{W}$ is an orthogonal matrix, its inverse is given by its transpose, $\boldsymbol{W}^{-1} = \boldsymbol{W}^{\intercal}$, and so the inverse transform is obtained from

$$\boldsymbol{X}' = \boldsymbol{Z}\boldsymbol{W}^{\intercal} = \boldsymbol{X}'\boldsymbol{W}\boldsymbol{W}^{\intercal} = \boldsymbol{X}'. \tag{16.64}$$

Sometimes the weights – the columns of $\boldsymbol{W}$, $\boldsymbol{w}_{(1)}, \boldsymbol{w}_{(2)}, \ldots, \boldsymbol{w}_{(p)}$ – are referred to as loadings. However, it is possible to find also the following as loadings – the columns of $\boldsymbol{W}$ scaled up by the square roots of the corresponding eigenvalues:

$$\boldsymbol{L} = \begin{pmatrix} | & | & & | \\ \sqrt{\lambda_{(1)}}\boldsymbol{w}_{(1)} & \sqrt{\lambda_{(2)}}\boldsymbol{w}_{(2)} & \cdots & \sqrt{\lambda_{(p)}}\boldsymbol{w}_{(p)} \\ | & | & & | \end{pmatrix} \in \mathbb{R}^{p \times p}. \tag{16.65}$$

Because of this ambiguity, we shall avoid this term altogether. Note that there is quite a lot of ambiguity and confusion in the terminology associated with the PCA, especially across different fields.

It is worth noting that the principal components are uncorrelated: Since, for $1 \leq j \neq k \leq p$,

$$\begin{aligned}
\mathsf{Cov}[\boldsymbol{z}_{(j)}, \boldsymbol{z}_{(k)}] &\propto (\boldsymbol{X}'\boldsymbol{w}_{(j)})^{\intercal}(\boldsymbol{X}'\boldsymbol{w}_{(k)}) && (16.66)\\
&= \boldsymbol{w}_{(j)}^{\intercal}(\boldsymbol{X}')^{\intercal}\boldsymbol{X}\boldsymbol{w}_{(k)} && (16.67)\\
&= \boldsymbol{w}_{(j)}^{\intercal}\lambda_{(k)}\boldsymbol{w}_{(k)} && (16.68)\\
&= \lambda_{(k)}\boldsymbol{w}_{(j)}^{\intercal}\boldsymbol{w}_{(k)} && (16.69)\\
&= \lambda_{(k)}\boldsymbol{w}_{(j)}^{\intercal}\boldsymbol{w}_{(k)} && (16.70)\\
&= \lambda_{(k)} \cdot 0 && (16.71)
\end{aligned}$$

by orthogonality, the distinct principal components are uncorrelated.

It also common to connect the PCA with explanation of variance. The question arises: In what sense do the principal components "explain the variance"? It is a fact from linear algebra that, since $\boldsymbol{C}$ is symmetric positive, it is diagonalisable as

$$\boldsymbol{C} = \boldsymbol{W}\boldsymbol{\Lambda}\boldsymbol{W}^{\intercal} = \sum_{i=1}^{p} \lambda_{(i)}\boldsymbol{w}_{(i)}\boldsymbol{w}_{(i)}^{\intercal}, \tag{16.72}$$

where $\boldsymbol{W}$ is a matrix with $\boldsymbol{C}$'s eigenvectors as its columns:

$$\boldsymbol{W} = \begin{pmatrix} | & | & & | \\ \boldsymbol{w}_{(1)} & \boldsymbol{w}_{(2)} & \cdots & \boldsymbol{w}_{(p)} \\ | & | & & | \end{pmatrix}, \tag{16.73}$$

and $\boldsymbol{\Lambda}$ a diagonal matrix with $\boldsymbol{C}$'s eigenvalues as its diagonal entries:

$$\boldsymbol{\Lambda} = \begin{pmatrix} \lambda_{(1)} & & & \\ & \lambda_{(2)} & & \\ & & \ddots & \\ & & & \lambda_{(p)} \end{pmatrix}. \tag{16.74}$$

Since, for any matrices $\boldsymbol{A}$ and $\boldsymbol{B}$, such that both products $\boldsymbol{AB}$ and $\boldsymbol{BA}$ exist, $\operatorname{tr}\boldsymbol{AB} = \operatorname{tr}\boldsymbol{BA}$,

$$\operatorname{tr}\boldsymbol{C} = \operatorname{tr}\boldsymbol{W}\boldsymbol{\Lambda}\boldsymbol{W}^{\intercal} = \operatorname{tr}\boldsymbol{\Lambda}\boldsymbol{W}^{\intercal}\boldsymbol{W} = \operatorname{tr}\boldsymbol{\Lambda}. \tag{16.75}$$

Thus the first d, $1 \leq d \leq p$, principal components account for the proportion

$$\frac{\lambda_{(1)} + \lambda_{(2)} + \ldots + \lambda_{(d)}}{\lambda_{(1)} + \lambda_{(2)} + \ldots + \lambda_{(p)}} = \frac{\sum_{i=1}^{d} \lambda_{(i)}}{\sum_{i=1}^{p} \lambda_{(i)}} \tag{16.76}$$

of the total variation.

16.4.5 Dimensionality Reduction

Finding the patterns in the data which can help us to explain the dependent variable suffers the bias-variance trade-off. This can be explained as follows. The squared bias typically decreases with increasing model complexity, and variance increases with increasing model complexity, and total error is the sum of the squared bias and variance components, so there is usually an optimal model complexity at which the total error is minimised.

Restricting complexity can be achieved by considering only a subset of available features. In particular, we may truncate our vector at $1 \leq d < p$ columns by removing the columns $d + 1, d + 2, \ldots, p$:

$$\boldsymbol{W}_d = \begin{pmatrix} | & | & & | \\ \boldsymbol{w}_{(1)} & \boldsymbol{w}_{(2)} & \cdots & \boldsymbol{w}_{(d)} \\ | & | & & | \end{pmatrix} \in \mathbb{R}^{p \times p}. \tag{16.77}$$

Thus we keep only the first d principal components:

$$\boldsymbol{Z}_d := \boldsymbol{X}'\boldsymbol{W}_d \in \mathbb{R}^{n \times d}. \tag{16.78}$$

Since

$$\mathsf{Var}[\boldsymbol{Z}] = \mathsf{Var}[\boldsymbol{X}'\boldsymbol{W}] = \boldsymbol{W}^{\intercal}\mathsf{Var}[\boldsymbol{X}']\boldsymbol{W} \approx \boldsymbol{W}^{\intercal}\boldsymbol{C}\boldsymbol{W} = \boldsymbol{\Lambda}, \tag{16.79}$$

and, similarly,

$$\mathsf{Var}[\boldsymbol{Z}_d] = \boldsymbol{\Lambda}_d, \tag{16.80}$$

the truncated principal components decrease variance

$$\text{tr}\boldsymbol{\Lambda}_d < \boldsymbol{\Lambda},$$

at the expense of introducing bias.

16.4.6 PCA Regression (PCR)

The natural extension of the dimensionality reduction using the PCA is the PCA regression, or PCR. Recall that, in linear regression, we work with the model

$$\boldsymbol{y} = \overset{*}{\boldsymbol{X}}\boldsymbol{\beta} + \boldsymbol{\epsilon}, \tag{16.81}$$

where $\boldsymbol{y} \in \mathbb{R}^n$ is the output vector; $\overset{*}{\boldsymbol{X}} \in \mathbb{R}^{n \times p^*}$ is the data matrix $\boldsymbol{X}$ – our input, possibly augmented with a vector of ones on the left to allow intercept (in which case $p^* = p + 1$) or not (in which case $p^* = p$); $\boldsymbol{\beta} \in \mathbb{R}^{p^*}$ is the vector of parameters of the model, and it is our task to estimate this vector; and $\boldsymbol{\epsilon} \in \mathbb{R}^n$ is the vector random variable representing some noise or disturbance.

Instead of regressing $\boldsymbol{y}$ on $\boldsymbol{X}$, we could regress $\boldsymbol{y}$ on $\boldsymbol{Z}_d$:

$$\boldsymbol{y} = \overset{*}{\boldsymbol{Z}}_d\boldsymbol{\gamma}_d + \boldsymbol{\eta}, \tag{16.82}$$

where $\overset{*}{\boldsymbol{Z}}_d \in \mathbb{R}^{n \times d^*}$ is the matrix of principal component scores $\boldsymbol{Z}$, possibly augmented with a vector of ones on the left to allow intercept (in which case $d^* = d + 1$) or not (in which case $d^* = d$); $\boldsymbol{\gamma} \in \mathbb{R}^{d^*}$ is the vector of parameters of the model, and it is our task to estimate this vector; and $\boldsymbol{\eta} \in \mathbb{R}^n$ is the vector random variable representing some noise or disturbance.

The properties of the estimator $\hat{\boldsymbol{\gamma}}_d$ can be derived as follows: from linear regression theory, we know that the ordinary least squares (OLS) estimator of $\boldsymbol{\gamma}_d$ is

$$\hat{\boldsymbol{\gamma}}_d = (\overset{*}{\boldsymbol{Z}}{}_d^{\mathsf{T}}\overset{*}{\boldsymbol{Z}}_d)^{-1}\overset{*}{\boldsymbol{Z}}{}_d^{\mathsf{T}}\boldsymbol{y}. \tag{16.83}$$

We know that this estimator is unbiased,

$$\mathbb{E}[\hat{\boldsymbol{\gamma}}_d \,|\, \boldsymbol{Z}_d] = \mathbb{E}[\hat{\boldsymbol{\gamma}}_d | \boldsymbol{X}] = \boldsymbol{\gamma}_d, \tag{16.84}$$

and that its variance is given by

$$\text{Var}[\hat{\boldsymbol{\gamma}}_d] = \sigma_\eta^2(\overset{*}{\boldsymbol{Z}}{}_d^{\mathsf{T}}\overset{*}{\boldsymbol{Z}}_d)^{-1}. \tag{16.85}$$

This concludes the theory behind the PCA. Since this is a popular method, we have devoted more space to several related topics. In the following section, we utilise our implementation of the eigensystem and provide utility for calculation of the PCA.

16.5 IMPLEMENTATION OF PCA

Let us implement the basics of PCA. We use the calculation of eigensystem provided at the initial part of this chapter. Let us start with simulating the sample data we use:

```
data:.quantQ.simul.multiNormal[3;1000;3?2.0;(2.0 -1.0 0.0;-1.0 3.0 -1.0;0.0
    ↪ -1.0 4.0)][`var1`var2`var3];
```

Let us provide a function, which calculates the covariance matrix efficiently:

```
.quantQ.mat.covarianceMatrixFast:{[data]
   // data -- array of data
   :(data+flip(not n=\:n)*data:(n#'0.0),'(data$/:'(n:til count data)_\:data
       ↪ )%count first data)
       -a*\:a:avg each data;
};
```

The PCA is in fact applying the eigensystem decomposition on the sample covariance matrix:

```
pcaTab:flip .quantQ.mat.eigenSystem[.quantQ.mat.covarianceMatrixFast[data]]
pcaTab
```

```
eigenvalues eigenvectors
--------------------------------------------
4.735611    0.2559419 -0.6260256 0.7366042
3.250099    0.5447843 -0.4957256 -0.6763625
1.238536    0.7879696 0.5785655  0.2106323
```

We have stated that the eigenvectors corresponding to the individual principal components are orthogonal – in fact, they are orthonormal due to unit norm. We can verify this as:

```
wsum[first[t];] each t:pcaTab[`eigenvectors]
```

```
1 -0.04844146 -0.005369745
```

The second and third components are not zero. This is due to our small sample and our numerical precision. Let us centre the data set:

```
dataNorm: data - avg each data
```

We can verify the data are centred as:

```
avg each dataNorm
```

```
-1.65068e-15 1.49214e-16 -3.409273e-15
```

We can now apply the principal components to calculate the variance captured by each of the components: the first component captures

```
var pcaTab[`eigenvectors][0] wsum dataNorm
```

```
4.732024
```

variance. Analogously for second and third components, we get:

```
var pcaTab[`eigenvectors][1] wsum dataNorm
```

```
3.250099
```

and

```
var pcaTab[`eigenvectors][2] wsum dataNorm
```

```
1.238536
```

respectively.

Let us confirm the properties of the principal components. In particular, the correlation of the first principal component with itself is obviously one:

```
cor[sum[pcaTab[`eigenvectors][0]*dataNorm];sum[pcaTab[`eigenvectors][0]*
    ↪ dataNorm]]
```

```
1f
```

where the correlation between the first and second component is close to zero:

```
cor[sum[pcaTab[`eigenvectors][0]*dataNorm];sum[pcaTab[`eigenvectors][1]*
    ↪ dataNorm]]
```

```
-0.04014597
```

despite the fact that data itself is correlated:

```
cor[dataNorm[0];dataNorm[1]]
```

```
-0.4577103
```

We can finally construct the routine which provides the PCA decomposition and on top of that the relative variance each component captures. The following function takes as an argument the matrix with data and returns the PCA decomposition:

```
.quantQ.mat.pca:{[data]
   // data -- array of input data
   // calculate eigensytem
   pTab:flip .quantQ.mat.eigenSystem[.quantQ.mat.covarianceMatrixFast[data
       ↪ ]];
```

```
    // normalised data
    dataNorm: data - avg each data;
    // add variance for each eigenvector (eigenvalues)
    pTab: update variance: {var y wsum x}[dataNorm;] each eigenvectors from
        ↪ pTab;
    // caluclate cumulative variance
    pTab: update relVariance: variance%sum variance from pTab;
    // output format
    pTab:select variance, weights:eigenvectors, relVariance from pTab;
    // transformed data
    dataTransformed: wsum[;data] each pTab[`weights];
    // return overview data and transformed data
    :(`tab`dataTransformed)!(pTab;dataTransformed);
};
```

Let us apply the function on our sample data.

```
pca:.quantQ.mat.pca[data];
```

First, we examine the `` `tab ``, which contains the PCA decomposition and basic information about each component:

```
pca[`tab]
```

```
variance weights                          relVariance
------------------------------------------------------
4.732024 0.2559419 -0.6260256 0.7366042  0.5131981
3.250099 0.5447843 -0.4957256 -0.6763625 0.3524801
1.238536 0.7879696 0.5785655  0.2106323  0.1343219
```

We see that first component is capturing slightly more than 50% of total variance while the first two components are together describing approximately 86% of variance.

Further, the PCA function returns as well the `` `dataTransformed `` element, which is the table with transformed data, component by component. We can see that by examining the correlation between the first two columns of the transformed data set:

```
pca[`dataTransformed][0] cor pca[`dataTransformed][1]
```

```
-0.04014598
```

while original data carry correlation:

```
data[0] cor data[1]
```

```
-0.4577103
```

This concludes the PCA in `q`. We leave it to readers as an interesting exercise to develop the routine to perform the PCR. All the necessary components are within this book; they just need to be appropriately piped together. Such a routine will nicely complement the provided algorithms.

16.6 APPENDIX: DETERMINANT

In this section, we provide an algorithm to calculate the determinant of the matrix. We need a determinant in the central part of this chapter to calculate eigensystems. The determinant of a matrix also proves a necessary piece of theory/toolset for data analytics.

16.6.1 Theory

Let us consider a square real matrix $\boldsymbol{A}$:

$$\boldsymbol{A} = \begin{pmatrix} A_{11} & A_{12} & \cdots & A_{1n} \\ A_{21} & A_{22} & \cdots & A_{2n} \\ \vdots & \vdots & \ddots & \vdots \\ A_{n1} & A_{n2} & \cdots & A_{nn} \end{pmatrix}. \tag{16.86}$$

For every square real-valued matrix (we do omit the complex matrices in this section, though the determinant can be extended to complex matrix domain), we can define the determinant as a real-valued function, with inputs being the elements of the matrix. The determinant is a polynomial of the order 2 in entries of the matrix $\boldsymbol{A}$. The determinant is usually denoted as $\det(\boldsymbol{A})$, or, $|\boldsymbol{A}|$. The determinant is met across the various topics in the linear algebra. In this chapter, we have encountered the determinant when we have been constructing the algorithm to calculate the eigensystem of a real matrix. It can be further used to determine the linear independence of a system of n vectors, or calculating Jacobians.

The determinant also has a geometric interpretation. Let us consider a unit n-dimensional cube and n-dimensional square matrix $\boldsymbol{A}$. The columns of the matrix can be considered as edges which define the parallelotope, with one corner being at the origin. The parallelotope is a deformed cube, which is deformed by the matrix transformation $\boldsymbol{A}$. In 2-dimensions, the parallelotope is a parallelogram, which is nothing but deformed square. Then, the determinant is the volume of such a parallelotope.

Before we dive into the definition of the determinant, we first present the useful properties of the determinant:

- $\det(\boldsymbol{I}) = 1$ for any unit matrix $\boldsymbol{I}$.
- $\det(\boldsymbol{A}^\intercal) = \det(\boldsymbol{A})$.
- $\det(\boldsymbol{A}^{-1}) = \frac{1}{\det(\boldsymbol{A})} = \det(\boldsymbol{A})^{-1}$.
- $\det(\boldsymbol{AB}) = \det(\boldsymbol{A})\det(\boldsymbol{B})$ where matrices $\boldsymbol{A}$ and $\boldsymbol{B}$ are square matrices of the same dimension.
- $\det(c\boldsymbol{A}) = c^n\det(\boldsymbol{A})$ with c being a constant.
- $\det(\boldsymbol{A} + \boldsymbol{B}) \geq \det(\boldsymbol{A}) + \det(\boldsymbol{B})$ for matrices $\boldsymbol{A}$ and $\boldsymbol{B}$ being of the same size and both positive semidefinite.
- $\mathrm{tr}(A) = \log(\det(\exp(A)))$ with tr being the trace of a square matrix.
- $\det(A) = \prod_{i=1}^{n} \lambda_i$ where λ_i are eigenvalues of the matrix $\boldsymbol{A}$.

The listed properties are useful when we manipulate with determinants.

16.6.2 Techniques to Calculate a Determinant

In the following, we consider matrix $\boldsymbol{A}$ to be a square matrix of the dimension n. Let us define a procedure to calculate the determinant recursively.

Trivial case

Let us start with trivial case of $n = 1$. In such a case, we can consider a scalar number to be a matrix of the dimension 1×1. The determinant in this case is obvious:

$$\begin{vmatrix} a_{11} \end{vmatrix} = a_{11}, \tag{16.87}$$

i.e. the constant itself.

We have stated in the introductory part that a determinant is a polynomial of order n in the matrix elements. This is satisfied in this case.

Leibniz formula

Let us proceed with $n = 2$. In this case, the determinant is defined as:

$$\begin{vmatrix} A_{11} & A_{12} \\ A_{21} & A_{22} \end{vmatrix} = a_{11}a_{22} - a12a_{21}, \tag{16.88}$$

which is polynomial of order 2 in the matrix elements.

Sarrus rule

In the case of $n = 3$, the determinant is given as:

$$\begin{vmatrix} a_{11} & a_{12} & a_{13} \\ a_{21} & a_{22} & a_{23} \\ a_{31} & a_{32} & a_{33} \end{vmatrix} = a_{11}a_{22}a_{33} + a_{12}a_{23}a_{31} + a_{13}a_{21}a_{32} - a_{13}a_{22}a_{31} - a_{12}a_{21}a_{33} - a_{11}a_{23}a_{32}. \tag{16.89}$$

The formula is polynomial of order 3 in matrix elements and it becomes quite cumbersome. Luckily, there is simple tool to get this formula, called Sarrus rule. We start with a matrix $\boldsymbol{A}$ and append the first and the second column to the right-hand side of the matrix:

$$\begin{vmatrix} a_{11} & a_{12} & a_{13} \\ a_{21} & a_{22} & a_{23} \\ a_{31} & a_{32} & a_{33} \end{vmatrix} \rightarrow \begin{vmatrix} a_{11} & a_{12} & a_{13} & a_{11} & a_{12} \\ a_{21} & a_{22} & a_{23} & a_{21} & a_{22} \\ a_{31} & a_{32} & a_{33} & a_{31} & a_{32} \end{vmatrix}, \tag{16.90}$$

and then we form three products of elements placed on the diagonals: $a_{11}a_{22}a_{33}$, $a_{12}a_{23}a_{31}$, and $a_{13}a_{21}a_{32}$, respectively. Then, we form three analogous products lying on the anti-diagonal $a_{13}a_{22}a_{31}$, $a_{12}a_{21}a_{33}$, and $a_{11}a_{23}a_{32}$, respectively. Finally, the determinant is calculated as a sum of the six products, where those originating from the diagonal are added with + sign while those from the anti-diagonal come with – sign.

Laplace formula

For the general case of n (which includes any $n \geq 1$), we can use recursive Laplace formula to calculate the determinant. First, we define a minor of a matrix. For a square $n \times n$ matrix $\boldsymbol{A}$, the minor $\boldsymbol{M}_{i,j}$ is the determinant of $(n-1) \times (n-1)$ matrix, which is obtained from the matrix $\boldsymbol{A}$ by removing all $A_{i\bullet}$ and $A_{\bullet j}$ elements, i.e. by removing i-th row and j-th column.

Second, we define the cofactor, which is defined as $(-1)^{i+j}\boldsymbol{M}_{i,j}$. Then, the determinant of a matrix $\boldsymbol{A}$ is defined as expansion along the i-th row:

$$\det(\boldsymbol{A}) = \sum_{j=1}^{n} A_{ij}(-1)^{i+j}\boldsymbol{M}_{i,j}. \tag{16.91}$$

Alternatively, we may define expansion along the j-th column as

$$\det(\boldsymbol{A}) = \sum_{i=1}^{n} A_{ij}(-1)^{i+j}\boldsymbol{M}_{i,j}. \tag{16.92}$$

The determinant of the $n \times n$ matrix is thus expressed as a sum of cofactors, where each cofactor is in fact determinant of the $(n-1) \times (n-1)$ matrix. This is a basis of a recursive formula we can use to calculate any determinant.

16.6.3 Implementation of the Determinant

Let us implement the calculation of the determinant for a square matrix $\boldsymbol{A}$. In the implementation below, we use the recursive relationship provided in equation (16.91). We expand the matrix always along the first row. This is easy to implement but not the most efficient approach, as expansion along the row/column with the most significant proportion of zeros can save computational time.

Let us proceed with the function which takes as an input a square matrix, and two indices for row/column, and returns a matrix which is used to calculate the minor:

```
.quantQ.mat.minorMatrix:{[mat;i;j]
   // mat -- square matrix
   // i -- row index
   // j -- column index
   :mat[(t where not i=t:til count[mat]);(s where not j=s:til count[mat])];
};
```

Let us test it:

```
.quantQ.mat.minorMatrix[((1 2 3);(4 5 6);(7 8 9));0;0]
```

```
5 6
8 9
```

Then, we proceed directly with the function, which calculates the determinant. In order to illustrate the methods for calculating the determinant discussed in the previous section, we use different methods based on the dimensionality of the problem. In particular, for $n = 3$, we use the Sarrus rule explicitly, even though it is not necessary, as the Laplace expansion would be sufficient. For the Laplace expansion, we use recursion. In particular, we use `.z.s`, which refers to the function itself when called from within the function. We could use the name of the function itself instead of the "dotzetdotes" construct. The function reads:

```
.quantQ.mat.det:{[mat]
   // mat - square matrix
   // dimension of matrix
   dimM: count mat;
   // split based on the dimension of the problem
   // default output value
   det:0.0;
   // dim=1
   $[dimM=1;det:mat; ];
   // dim=2
   $[dimM=2;det:(mat[0;0]*mat[1;1])-(mat[0;1]*mat[1;0]); ];
   // dim=3, Sarrus rule
   $[dimM=3;
       [
       // extend matrix
       mat:raze (mat ; mat);
       // positive diagonal
       posDiagonal:sum {[mat;dimM;offset]  prd {[mat;offset;i] mat[i+offset
           ↪ ;i]}[mat;offset;] each til dimM}[mat;dimM;]  each til dimM;
       // negative diagonal
       negDiagonal:sum {[mat;dimM;offset]  prd {[mat;offset;i] mat[(count[
           ↪ flip mat]-i)+offset;i]}[mat;offset;] each til dimM}[mat;dimM
           ↪ ;]  each til dimM;
       // determinant
       det:posDiagonal-negDiagonal
       ];
   ];
   // dim>3, Laplace expansion, always use first row
   $[dimM>3;
       [
       rowPivot:0;
       signFact: {[rowPivot;x]xexp[neg[1.0];(rowPivot+1+x+1)] }[rowPivot;]
           ↪ each til dimM;
       det:sum mat[rowPivot]*signFact*(.z.s each .quantQ.mat.minorMatrix[
           ↪ mat;rowPivot;] each til dimM);
       ];
   ];
   // output determinant
   :det;
};
```

Let us test the calculation of the determinant for $n = 3$:

```
.quantQ.mat.det ((2 2 2);(-1 1 0);(1 2 3))
```

```
6
```

and for $n = 5$:

```
.quantQ.mat.det[((1.0;0.0;2.0;0.0;0.0);(0.0;1.0;0.0;0.0;0.0)
    ↪ ;(2.0;0.0;1.0;0.0;0.0);(0.0;0.0;0.0;1.0;0.0);(0.0;0.0;0.0;0.0;1.0))]
```

```
-3
```

In addition, we can test the linear independence of the rows of the table as:

```
.quantQ.mat.det[5 5 # til 25]
```

```
0
```

which shows that the rows of such a matrix are linearly dependent. We leave it for readers to show the exact dependence of the rows and how we can express any row as a linear combination of other rows.

CHAPTER 17

Outlier Detection

Outlier detection, or anomaly detection, is a data science technique aiming to identify observations which do not fit into the data set and are way too different from the "normal" data. In general, there are two reasons why such nonconformity in the data may exist. First, the anomalous data points can be produced by some technical error, where, for example, the data recording technique failed, or the survey has not been correctly scanned, among others. A particular example can be limit order book data, where bid price is recorded as −999. Such a datum corresponds to a failed print rather than to a situation where the interest in the particular asset is negative. Such a transaction would not be technically possible in properly working venues.

Second, the more critical reason corresponds to actual anomalous behaviour in the data. This may correspond, for example, to cases of bank frauds in the context of bank activity records. When a fraudster commits the unlawful act, she often tries to make the transaction to look usual. This, however, is not possible as the knowledge of usual transactions is not publicly available. The outliers may thus appear in the data analysis as records with the unusual size of the transaction, timing of trades, or their frequency do not fit into the common patterns.

The outlier detection is by its nature a data science technique, where the objective "being outlier" is rather vaguely defined. It is thus without surprise that outlier detection technique mimics the machine learning techniques. The non-supervised outlier detection techniques work with unlabelled data. The majority of data is assumed to be valid, and the property of being an outlier is understood relative to the majority. Such a method can be illustrated by a PCA technique for dimensionality reduction. The reduced set of principal components replaces the data. Then, every observation is recovered back from the reduced set, and the error of the reduction is recorded. The outliers are then observations with significant errors.

The supervised outlier detection techniques assume that we have a labelled training set, where data are labelled as "normal" or "outlier". One can then formulate a model, either theoretical or econometric, for "being outlier" and estimate the parameters. The typical choice can be a logistic regression model, which is well suited for modelling binary dependent variables. The usual problem for such techniques rests in the need for correct classification and presence of outliers, which are often very rare. The techniques thus have to be able to deal with unbalanced data sets, where one of the classes is present sparsely. The alternative methods model probability, or likelihood, for an observation to be outlier instead of the discrete decision rule of "normal/outlier". One can also formulate outlier detection techniques based on Bayesian principles.

The examples of the outlier detection techniques are:

- Cluster analysis–based outlier detection, Campello et al. (2015).
- Support vector machines–based models, Schölkopf et al. (2001).
- Correlation-based outlier detection techniques, Kriegel et al. (2012).
- Feature bagging–based techniques, Lazarevic and Kumar (2005).
- Bayesian networks, Hawkins et al. (2002).
- Density-based techniques (k-nearest-neighbour based), Knorr et al. (2000), and local outlier factor, which is explained in detail below.

17.1 LOCAL OUTLIER FACTOR

In this section, we delve into the details of the local outlier factor – see Breunig et al. (2000) – and implement the method directly along with its explanation. The local outlier factor technique estimates the local density of the data and determines the property of "being outlier" from the anomalous values of the data point density. The local density is derived based on the k-nearest neighbours principles (see subsequent chapters for more details). The density of a point within a data set is derived from the distance between the point and its local neighbourhood relative to the density of the neighbourhood itself. The values, which are far from their neighbours relative to the distance among the neighbours, are deemed to be considered outliers. On the other hand, one can define the inverted notion of "inliers" as observations, where the distance between the point and its local neighbourhood relative to the density of the neighbourhood itself is unusually small. The method calls the distance mentioned above as the reachability distance.

Let us assume a data set of N features, $x_1, x_2, \ldots, x_N$ spanning the N-dimensional space. First, we need to define a notion of distance between two N-dimensional points. The distance has to be data-sensible definition of the length between two observations, and it has to satisfy the usual properties imposed on distance metric. The suitable candidates are any of the L_p norms:

$$d(X, Y) = \left(\sum_{i=1}^{N} |X_i - Y_i|^p \right)^{1/p}, \tag{17.1}$$

where X and Y are two N-dimensional points in the feature space.

Let us stress at this point that we cannot just take features as they are but rather to normalise them across the board. The distance based on any L_p tacitly assumes that all dimensions have the same scale. The features in this method thus have to be normalised such that the distance in the different directions (features) are comparable. The normalisation to be done is rather a matter of art; there is no clear recipe and method chosen should reflect the data. The two possible candidate methods are:

- For each feature, demean the observations and divide them by the sample standard deviation.
- For each feature, demean the observations and divide the observations by the sample range.

The essential element of the two methods above is division by scale – either standard deviation or range. The demeaning part is applied to be able to apply the scale. If any of the methods is applied, every new data point has to be normalised in the same way. The common mistake appears especially for splitting the sample into in-sample, where the model is calibrated, and out-of-sample, where the model is tested. Still, many researchers take the entire sample, calculate the sample mean and sample scale – range or variance – and normalise the entire sample. Then, they split the normalised sample into two pieces. This approach is wrong, as the in-sample uses information coming from the out-of-sample and thus the calibration of the model in the in-sample is not independent of the out-sample.

We introduce the local outlier factor technique along with the example implementation. For the sake of clarity, we restrict ourselves to $N = 2$, where we can depict the data. First, we define the model data set in which we apply our method. The data set is composed of two features `` `x0`x1 ``, defined on the square $[0, 1]^2$. The data are formed of two dense clusters overlaying the noisy background.

The first cluster is defined within the lower left corner of the support set:

```
// cluster 1
cluster1:([] x0:0.5*1000?1.0;x1:0.5*1000?1.0 );
```

The second cluster is defined in the upper-right corner of the support set:

```
// cluster 2
cluster2:([] x0:0.5+0.5*100?1.0;x1:0.5+0.5*100?1.0 );
```

and the noise is evenly spread over the support space:

```
// noise
noise:([] x0:100?1.0;x1:100?1.0 );
```

Finally, we merge the data into a unique table:

```
// dataSet
dataSet:cluster1,cluster2,noise;
```

Figure 17.1 depicts the `dataSet`. The objective of the outlier detection technique is to recognise points within each cluster as not outliers and those being on the boundaries as well as those outside the clusters as outliers.

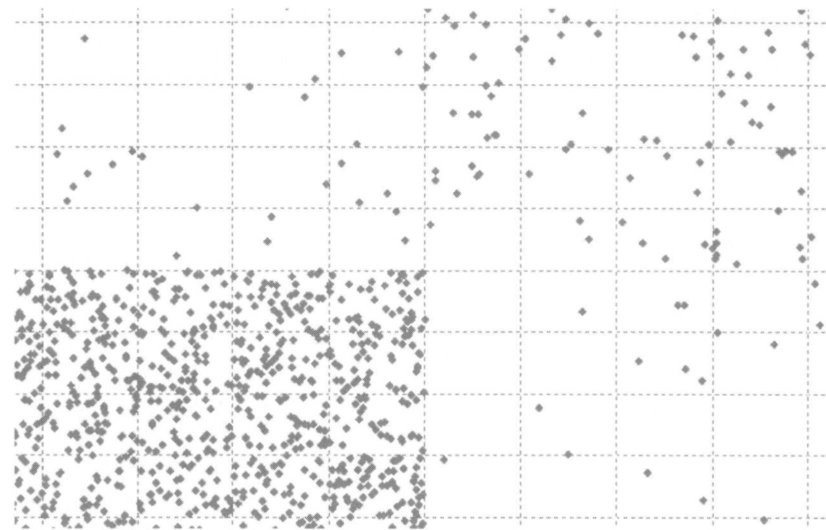

FIGURE 17.1 Scatter plot of the dataSet, which is composed of two data clusters and the background noise

In order to define the local outlier factor, we have to fix the definition of the distance between two points in the feature space. We employ the one based on the L_p-norm, and in particular we set $p = 2$, i.e.

$$d(X, Y) = \left(\sum_{i=1}^{N} |X_i - Y_i|^2 \right)^{1/2}, \tag{17.2}$$

for any two points X and Y.

For our purpose, we implement the L_2-norm as a function of two arguments, where the first one is a reference point and the other is a vector of points. The function calculates the distance between the reference point and each point of an array:

```
.quantQ.lof.L2distance:{[point;dataVector]
   // point -- reference point
   // dataVector -- vector of data
   :sqrt t wsum t:flip[dataVector]-point;
};
```

We can verify the implementation against the test point by updating the table dataSet by extra column distanceToPoint, which contains the distance between the test point and the feature array `` `x0`x1``:

```
testPoint:(0.5;0.5);
// calculate distance to each point
dataSet: update distanceToPoint: .quantQ.lof.L2distance[testPoint;(x0,'x1)]
    ↪ from dataSet;
dataSet
```

```
x0         x1         distanceToPoint
-------------------------------------
0.03849788 0.2307442  0.534306
0.1649356  0.0318651  0.5756895
0.402105   0.4755074  0.1009124
0.3134949  0.3519337  0.2381339
0.2059655  0.2207454  0.4055113
0.4279761  0.2826131  0.2290077
0.2718751  0.3608687  0.2672049
0.1318884  0.3937577  0.3831365
0.1884478  0.3601324  0.341508
0.2362291  0.3795504  0.289971
...
```

The `distanceToPoint` thus contains the distance to the reference point. We can sort the table and identify the nearest neighbours, or inspect the histogram of the distances.

The local outlier factor is based on the k-nearest neighbours. We choose k conveniently as:

```
k:12;
```

where the neighbourhood will be defined as 12 nearest points in the sense of L_2-norm. The value is arbitrary, and we encourage the reader to vary the parameter in the exercise.

Being equipped with the distance, we define the k-distance of the point X to be the distance of X from k-th nearest neighbour. It may happen that within the k-distance of the point X, there is more than k elements; let us denote the number of such points as $n_k(X)$. This happens when data points lie on the circle of radius k-distance with X being in origin.

We implement the k-distance of the point X and the number of points within the k-distance within one function:

```
.quantQ.lof.getKNNProperties:{[k;data;point]
   // k -- the parameter of the kNN
   // data -- the data set with one column x, each observation is a list of
       ↪ features
   // point -- reference point
   // calculate distance to point and sort it
   data: `distanceToPoint xasc update distanceToPoint: .quantQ.lof.
       ↪ L2distance[point;x] from data;
   // distance to k-th
   distanceToK: data[`distanceToPoint][min[(k-1;count[data])]];
   // number of elements within the distance
   numberToK: count select from data where distanceToPoint<=distanceToK;
   // return values
   :(`distanceToK`numberToK)!(distanceToK;numberToK);
};
```

The function has three arguments: first, the size of the neighbourhood `k`, data-set `data`, and the reference point denoted as `point`. The reference point does not have to be part of the data set and is considered as a separate point. We illustrate the use of the function `getKNNProperties` as follows:

```
.quantQ.lof.getKNNProperties[k;select x:(x0,'x1) from dataSet;testPoint]
```

```
distanceToK| 0.002619135
numberToK  | 12
```

Further, we define the reachability distance of the point X from the point Y as:

$$\text{reachability}_k(X, Y) = \max(d(X, Y), k\text{-distance}(Y)), \tag{17.3}$$

where the meaning is such that the reachability between the two points is a maximum of their true distance and the k-distance of the point Y. The meaning of this definition is such that the k-distance is the minimum distance around the point Y, or the recognition scale of the neighbourhood of the point Y. Any point within the k-distance is considered to be the same.

We implement the `reachability` distance as a function of three arguments: the point `X`, the index of the point `Y` within the data-set `data`, and the size of the neighbourhood `k`:

```
.quantQ.lof.reachabilityDistance:{[X;indexY;data;k]
   // X -- point to find distance, can be out of data
   // indexY -- index of the point Y, it has to come from data
   // data -- the data set with one column x, each observation is a row of
       ↪ features
   // k -- the parameter of the kNN
   // extract point Y
   Y: first exec x from data where i=indexY;
   // component 1: distance between X and Y
   distanceXY: first .quantQ.lof.L2distance[X;enlist Y];
   // component 2: k-th distance of Y within dataset
   kDistanceY: .quantQ.lof.getKNNProperties[k;data;Y][`distanceToK];
   // return the reachability distance
   :max[(distanceXY;kDistanceY)];
   };
```

In the table `data`, we assume that the features are in the common column `x`, each observation being an array of the features for a given observation.

We can illustrate the function by using a test point and the first row of the `dataSet`:

```
.quantQ.lof.reachabilityDistance[testPoint;0;select x:(x0,'x1) from dataSet
    ↪ ;k]
```

```
0.534306
```

We use the reachability distance to define the local reachability density of the observation X as:

$$\rho(X) = \frac{1}{\left(\frac{\sum_{Y\in n_k(X)} \text{reachability}_k(X,Y)}{n_k(X)}\right)}, \tag{17.4}$$

where the density ρ is the inverse of the average reachability distance of the observation X from its neighbours. The definition can show singularity for the identical points. The density ρ is implemented as:

```
.quantQ.lof.localReachabilityDensity:{[X;data;k]
   // X -- point to find distance, can be out of data
   // data -- the data set with one column x, each observation is a row of
       ↪ features
   // k -- the parameter of the kNN
   // update distance to point to data
   data: update distanceToPoint: .quantQ.lof.L2distance[X;x] from data;
   // find k-neighbourhood of X
   neighbourhood: .quantQ.lof.getKNNProperties[k;data;X];
   // indices of k-neighbours -- contains neighbourhood[`numberToK]
       ↪ elements
   indicesB: exec i from data where distanceToPoint<=neighbourhood[`
       ↪ distanceToK];
   // return density
   :1.0%(sum .quantQ.lof.reachabilityDistance[X; ;data;k] each indicesB)%
       ↪ neighbourhood[`numberToK];
};
```

Let us illustrate the calculation of the density ρ for the reference point used above:

```
.quantQ.lof.localReachabilityDensity[testPoint;select x:(x0,'x1) from
    ↪ dataSet;k]
```

```
21.77545
```

Finally, we define the local outlier factor, or LOF, as the average local reachability distance of the neighbourhood of point X normalized by the local reachability distance of the point X itself:

$$LOF_k(X) = \frac{\frac{\sum_{Y \in_k(X)} \rho(Y)}{n_k(X)}}{\rho(X)}. \tag{17.5}$$

The value of LOF_k around 1 implies that the observation is comparable to its neighbours. This means that the point is not an outlier. On the other hand, values above 1 indicate an outlier with the observation having a lower density relative to its neighbourhood. Further, we can interpret the values smaller than one as "inliers" – points which have higher density compared to their neighbourhood.

We implement the LOF_k function as follows:

```
.quantQ.lof.LOF:{[X;data;k]
   // X -- point to find distance, can be out of data
   // data -- the data set with one column x, each observation is a row of
       ↪ features
   // k -- the parameter of the kNN
   // update distance to point to data
   data: update distanceToPoint: .quantQ.lof.L2distance[X;x] from data;
   // find k-neighbourhood of X
   neighbourhood: .quantQ.lof.getKNNProperties[k;data;X];
```

```
    // indices of k-neighbours -- contains neighbourhood[`numberToK] elements
    indicesY: exec i from data where distanceToPoint<=neighbourhood[`
        ↪ distanceToK];
    // return LOF
    :sum[.quantQ.lof.localReachabilityDensity[ ;data;k] each (exec x from
        ↪ data)[indicesY]]
        %neighbourhood[`numberToK]*.quantQ.lof.localReachabilityDensity[X;
            ↪ data;k];
};
```

Let us calculate the LOF to the reference point `(0.5;0.5)`:

```
.quantQ.lof.LOF[testPoint;select x:(x0,'x1) from dataSet;k]
```

```
1.175787
```

The point lies in the middle of the square, in the corner of two clusters. This point is thus hard to be identified as an outlier, in particular when $k = 12$ neighbours are considered. Let us increase the size of the neighbourhood to $k = 100$:

```
.quantQ.lof.LOF[testPoint;select x:(x0,'x1) from dataSet;100]
```

```
1.250251
```

The values increase as intuition suggests as the neighbourhood "sees" the vast region around itself and references itself to a broader set.

Let us further calculate the local outlier factor for list of points:

```
listPoints:((0.15;0.15);(0.85;0.85);(0.15;0.85);(0.85;0.15));
```

The first two points from the list lie in one of the clusters `cluster1` and `cluster2`, respectively. The remaining two points lie outside of the clusters and are produced by the noise background only. The list of the corresponding LOFs reads:

```
.quantQ.lof.LOF[;select x:(x0,'x1) from dataSet;k] each listPoints
```

```
1.061019 0.9856536 1.149604 1.40695
```

The results clearly support our intuition, where the LOF of the first two points is lower than the LOF of those coming from the noise background. The result is more prominent with larger neighbourhood:

```
.quantQ.lof.LOF[;select x:(x0,'x1) from dataSet;100] each ((0.15;0.15)
    ↪ ;(0.85;0.85);(0.15;0.85);(0.85;0.15))
```

```
0.985998 1.021251 2.763716 3.052752
```

With larger neighbourhood, the difference between the points is prominent and straightforward criteria can be defined. Further, the `cluster1` is denser than the other cluster, `cluster2`, and as such, the *LOF* reaches a value below 1, suggesting the dense region.

Finally, we illustrate how to calculate the LOF for every point of the data set `data`:

```
.quantQ.lof.LOFdata:{[data;k]
    // data -- the data set with one column x, each observation is a row of
        ↪ features
    // k -- the parameter of the kNN
```

```
    // LOF for every row of data
    LOFarray:{[dataSet;k;j] .quantQ.lof.LOF[(exec x from dataSet)[j];select
        ↪ from dataSet where i<>j;k]}
        [data;k;] each til count[data];
    // update table and publish
    :update LOF:LOFarray from data;
};
```

The table dataSet updated by the LOF for each of its points is then obtained as:

```
.quantQ.lof.LOFdata[select x:(x0,'x1) from dataSet;k]
```

```
x                      LOF
------------------------------
0.03849788 0.2307442  0.9865357
0.1649356  0.0318651  1.113023
0.402105   0.4755074  1.061303
0.3134949  0.3519337  1.007823
0.2059655  0.2207454  1.035789
0.4279761  0.2826131  1.024151
0.2718751  0.3608687  1.093017
0.1318884  0.3937577  1.007277
0.1884478  0.3601324  1.099363
0.2362291  0.3795504  1.028475
...
```

In order to illustrate the power of the LOF technique, we calculate the LOF for every observation of the table with $k = 100$, and select the observation with values above 2. We have chosen 2 as an ad hoc parameter without fine-tuning:

```
select x0: first each x, x1: last each x from .quantQ.lof.LOFdata[dataSet;
    ↪ 100] where LOF>2
```

Figure 17.2 depicts the subset of dataSet with points with $LOF > 2$. The points chosen are those outside of the dense clusters. Those points do not have a dense neighbourhood and are by definition outliers.

Figure 17.3 depicts the subset of dataSet with points with LOF>1.5. In this case, we have slightly relaxed the selection criteria. This is reflected on the number of points classified as outliers, in this case 45, compared to 17 with the former choice of the threshold. The points identified as outliers lie in the same region; more points are identified, though, for a more strict threshold.

The number of examples presented here suggests that choosing the hyper-parameters of the local outlier factors, namely the size of the neighbourhood and the threshold, is a matter of art. They require fine-tuning, possibly on the in-sample, where we are aware of the true outliers. Further, the selected outliers are aimed to be investigated by some detailed, and likely costly, methods or procedures. Good intuition is needed if one wants to use the provided method in some production applications, where the algorithm will entirely rely on the outcome of the technique.

The selected method has been illustrated for a few numbers of hyper-parameters as space provided by the book does not allow for more. We encourage the reader to go through more hyper-parameter settings. The features to look for are the number of the identified outliers as a function of the threshold and the size of the neighbourhood.

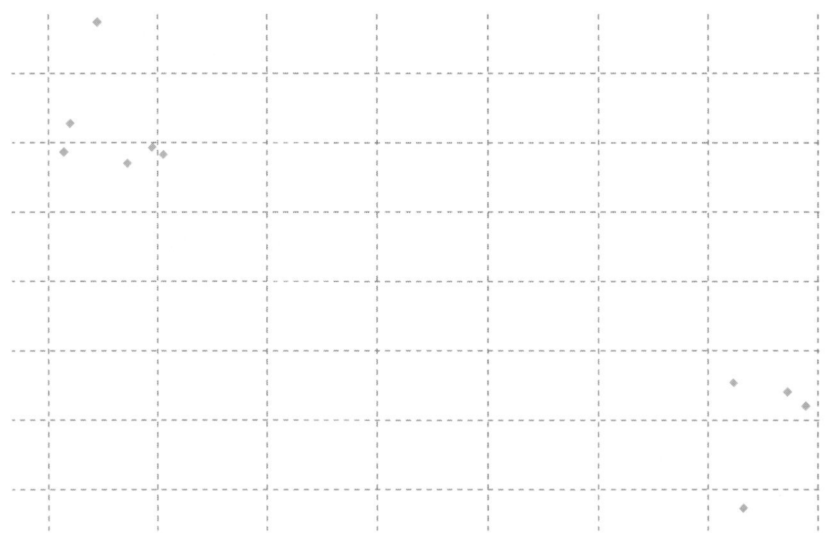

FIGURE 17.2 Scatter plot of the subset of `dataSet` with values of local outlier factor above 2

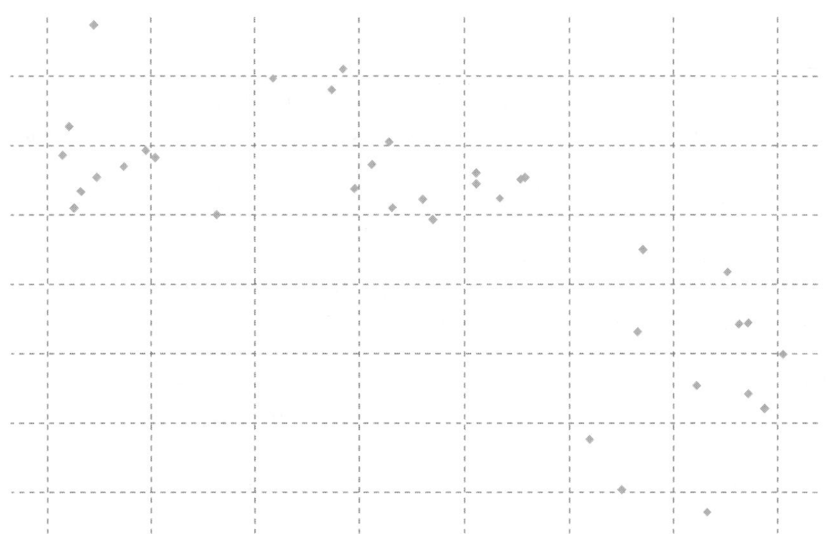

FIGURE 17.3 Scatter plot of the subset of `dataSet` with values of local outlier factor above 1.5

The above-provided technique will fail if the distance between points is 0. This can occur, for example, if we work with integer-typed features. How would the provided techniques be changed to catch the "zero distance" exceptions and provide more data-resilient technique? We keep this problem open and encourage readers to solve it.

CHAPTER 18

Simulating Asset Prices

In this chapter, we provide a framework to simulate multivariate stochastic volatility process with jumps. We build the framework step by step, and wherever we need to introduce some new functions, we build them on the fly. This chapter is motivated by Novotny and Urga (2017). The paper provides a test for co-jumps in asset prices. One section of the paper is a simulation exercise to assess the size and power of the tests. In order to do that, we need to simulate a realistic price generating process. The choice was made for a stochastic volatility process with price jumps in both the price and volatility. This chapter illustrates that q can be naturally used for academic research as well.

18.1 STOCHASTIC VOLATILITY PROCESS WITH PRICE JUMPS

We start with a simulation of the Stochastic Volatility Model with an intraday volatility pattern and price jumps both in the volatility process and the price process, as proposed by Andersen et al. (2012). The price generating process is defined by the following equations:

$$d\log P_t^{(i)} = u_t\sigma_t^{(i)}dW_t^{(i)} + U_{P,t}^{(i)}dJ_{P,t}^{(i)}, \tag{18.1}$$

$$d\sigma_t^{(i)2} = \kappa^{(i)}(\theta^{(i)} - \sigma_t^{(i)2})dt + \omega^{(i)}\sigma_t^{(i)}dB_t^{(i)} + U_{\sigma,t}^{(i)}dJ_{\sigma,t}^{(i)}, \tag{18.2}$$

$$E[dW_t^{(i)}dB_t^{(i)}] = \rho^{(i)}dt, \tag{18.3}$$

$$E[dW_t^{(i)}dB_t^{(j)}] = 0, i \neq j, \tag{18.4}$$

$$E[dW_t^{(i)}dW_t^{(j)}] = \rho_W^{(i,j)}dt, \tag{18.5}$$

where $i = 1, \ldots, N$, and

$$u_t = c_1 + c_{open}\exp(-a_{open}(t - t_{open})) + c_{close}(-a_{close}(t_{close} - t)), \tag{18.6}$$

where t denotes the time in the trading day, t_{open} is the opening time, and t_{close} is the closing time.

The model contains a large number of parameters which have to be set according to the underlying process which is supposed to be simulated. In order to get the specific numbers, we employ the calibration used by Novotny and Urga (2017) with $N = 3$ based on Eraker (2004) and Lee (2011). In particular, the intra-day pattern is set as $c_1 = 0.8892$, $c_{open} = 0.75$, $c_{close} = 0.25$, $a_{open} = 10$, and $a_{close} = 10$. We consider the same volatility pattern for each asset. The following parameters for each asset are the same: $\kappa^{(i)} = \kappa = 10 \cdot 0.0162$, $\theta^{(i)} = \theta = 0.573$, $\omega^{(i)} = \omega = 0.58$, and $\rho^{(i)} = \rho_{vol} = -0.46$. This ensures that the portfolio has N assets of the same type. The correlation coefficients, $\rho_W^{(i,j)}$, are the same for every pair, $\rho_W^{(i,j)} = 0.2$. The parameters are normalised to $T = 1\ day$.

The magnitude of the jump $U_{P,t}^{(i)}$ is set relative to the prevailing level of stochastic volatility as $U_{P,t}^{(i)} = \nu\sigma_{t-}^{(i)}$, where $\sigma_{t-}^{(i)}$ is the prevailing volatility immediately before the jump occurs, and ν is the parameter common to all assets, for which we consider $\nu_1 = 4$, $\nu_{2i} = 8$, and $\nu_{3i} = 12$, respectively. The magnitude of the volatility jumps $U_{\sigma,t}^{(i)}$ follows for every i an exponential distribution with mean $\mu_\sigma = 0.0167$. For every asset, we assume that $U_{\sigma,t}^{(i)}$ is drawn independently of each other. Further, for each asset i, the arrival process $dJ_{P,t}^{(i)}$ and $dJ_{\sigma,t}^{(i)}$ is assumed to be driven by the same stochastic intensity function $d\Lambda_t^{(i)}$. In our setup, the price jump arrivals are drawn simultaneously.

In the provided specification, we consider positive price jumps only in both the price process and the volatility process. This means that the price is increasing due to the price jumps. In the case of volatility, the volatility spikes up when the price jump arrives and then converges back to the long-term value due to the mean-reverting property of the price process.

The data generating process is being simulated at a 5-minute frequency; the first tick is at `tIni:09:00:00` and the last one at `tFin:16:30:00`, with 90 time increments at each day. We further consider that the last tick of a day and the first tick of the following day are two identical ticks.

This excludes the accumulation of the economic events overnight which materialises as jumps on the opening. We encourage the reader to extend the provided model by adding an overnight tick and explicit price jumps in the price process at the opening tick. Such a change allows us to treat two consecutive days more realistically.

The provided parameters are captured in the following dictionary:

```
stochVolPars:`Tday`tIni`tFin`c1`cOpen`cClose`aOpen`aClose`kappaInp`thetaInp
    ↪ `omegaInp`rhoInp`sigma0InitInp`rho12`rho13`rho23`nu1`nu2`nu3`expDist
!(90;09:00:00;16:30:00;0.8892;0.75;0.25;10.0;10.0;0.0162;0.573;0.58;(neg
    ↪ 0.46);sqrt[0.573];0.2;0.2;0.2;4.0;8.0;12.0;1.25);
```

Any change of parameters of the data generating process itself is done through the provided parameters dictionary. The parameters further contain some basic setup parameters, like the initial and final time of the trading hours.

18.2 TOWARDS THE NUMERICAL EXAMPLE

We need to define several functions before we start generating the prices. We start with the intra-day volatility pattern function, which imposes a deterministic shape on the volatility during a trading day:

```
.quantQ.simul.stochVolIntraPatt:{[time;isFlag;params]
   // time -- time tick
   // isFlag -- boolean flag
   // params -- dictionary with parameters
   // define intraday time
   tIntra:("f"$"j"$time-params[`tIni])%(1000*"f"$"j"$params[`tFin]-params[`
       ↪ tIni]);
   // return intraday volatility pattern (point at given time)
   :$[isFlag=1b;params[`c1]+(params[`cOpen]*exp[neg params[`aOpen]*tIntra])
       +(params[`cClose]*exp[neg params[`aClose]*(1.0 - tIntra)]);1];
};
```

A little bit more challenging is a function which would generate a multivariate normal process, Y, with a specific variance-covariance matrix Σ and zero mean (in practical cases, we usually need a process with zero mean, even though we define a general routine which can deal with non-zero mean). Such a process can be obtained as a projection prescribed by:

$$Y = L \cdot X, \tag{18.7}$$

where X is a multivariate uncorrelated normal process, and lower triangular matrix L is obtained as a Cholesky decomposition of Σ. The Cholesky decomposition – see Flannery et al. (1988) for reference – is for a Hermitian positive-definite matrix B given as:

$$B = LL*, \tag{18.8}$$

where L is a lower triangular matrix with real and positive diagonal. For positive semidefinite matrix B, some diagonal entries are zero. Alternative Cholesky decomposition is given as:

$$B = LDL*, \tag{18.9}$$

where L is lower triangular with unit diagonal and D is a diagonal matrix. In the following sections, we stick to the former definition.

18.2.1 Numerical Preliminaries

We implement the Cholesky decomposition using the Cholesky-Banachiewicz algorithm, which starts in the upper left corner and calculates the matrix L row by row, where in each row, the algorithm proceeds from left to right. The last element to be calculated for a given row is the diagonal element. The algorithm can be expressed as:

$$L_{j,j} = \sqrt{\Sigma_{j,j} - \sum_{k=1}^{j-1} L_{j,k}^2}, \tag{18.10}$$

$$L_{i,j} = \frac{1}{L_{j,j}} \left(\Sigma_{i,j} - \sum_{k=1}^{j-1} L_{i,k} L_{j,k} \right). \tag{18.11}$$

The algorithm is implemented in the following function, which takes a single argument, the matrix A; this is a real positive definite square matrix. The user is responsible for providing such a matrix, or encouraged to extend the functionality for the relevant checks.

The function produces the lower-diagonal matrix L:

```
.quantQ.simul.choleskyChB:{[A]
   // A -- matrix to be decomposed
   L:0f*A;
   i:j:0;
   do[floor (N*1+N:count A)%2;
       L[i;j]: $[b:i=j; sqrt A[i;j] - {x mmu x} j#L[j] ;
           reciprocal[L[j;j]] * A[i;j] - (i#L i)mmu i#L j];
       i:i+b;
       j:(j+nb)*nb:not b;
   ];
   :L;
};
```

The Cholesky decomposition implementation operates using a do loop, which – although not in the pure spirit of q – operates efficiently. Our code repo offers alternative approaches to a Cholesky decomposition using q's iterators.

We can verify the decomposition simply as:

```
mat:((4;12;-16);(12;37;-43);(-16;-43;98));
.quantQ.simul.choleskyChB[mat]
```

```
(2 0 0f;6 1 0f;-8 5 3f)
```

giving together with the transposed counterpart the original matrix

```
mat=.quantQ.simul.choleskyChB[mat] mmu (flip .quantQ.simul.choleskyChB[mat
    ↪ ])
```

```
(111b;111b;111b)
```

showing us that we can recover the original matrix element by element.

Having in hand a function for the Cholesky decomposition, we can generate a random variate following the N-dimensional multivariate normal distribution function with mean μ and variance-covariance matrix Σ. We are primarily interested in having data in the form of a table, and thus the function produces a table with nRows rows.

```
.quantQ.simul.multiNormal:{[N;nRows;mu;Sigma]
   // N -- number of variables
   // nRows -- number of observations
   // mu -- array of means
   // Sigma -- variance-covariance matrix
   // generate N times nRows array
   multinormalVariate:{[nRows;x].quantQ.simul.getNormalVariate[nRows]}[
       ↪ nRows;] each til N;
   // multiply the multinormal variate by the Cholesky lower diagonal
       ↪ matrix
   multinormalVariateCorr:(.quantQ.simul.choleskyChB[Sigma]) mmu
       ↪ multinormalVariate;
   // add a mean of each process
   multinormalVariateCorr:multinormalVariateCorr+mu;
   // create a table, variables are named var1, var2,...
   :flip ({`$"var",string x} each 1+til N)!multinormalVariateCorr;
};
```

The function generates N independent 1-dimensional normally distributed random variates, each following $N(0,1)$. Those are then transformed into the correlated process using the lower-diagonal matrix from the Cholesky decomposition. The array with *nRows* rows of $N(0,1)$ variate is defined as:

```
.quantQ.simul.getNormalVariate:{[nRows]
   // nRows -- dimension of the array
   // the Box-Muller procedure; we have to call it (nRows%2) round-up times
   nCall:ceiling nRows%2;
   // nCall calls of .quantQ.simul.genBoxMuller and then taking the first
       ↪ nRows outcomes
   :(raze {.quantQ.simul.genBoxMuller[]} each til nCall)[til nRows];
};
```

The Box-Muller transformation is used to generate the normal random variable, $N(0,1)$, from the uniform random variable defined on $[-1,1]$. The transformation takes as an input two independent uniform variables $x_i \sim U[-1,1]$, with $i=1,2$, which are constrained as $0 < x_1^2 + x_2^2 < 1$, and outputs two independent normally distributed random variables $z_i \sim N(0,1)$, with $i=1,2$:

$$z_1 = x_1 \cdot \sqrt{\frac{-2 * \ln(x_1^2 + x_2^2)}{(x_1^2 + x_2^2)}},$$

$$z_2 = x_2 \cdot \sqrt{\frac{-2 * \ln(x_1^2 + x_2^2)}{(x_1^2 + x_2^2)}}.$$

The function which employs the Box-Muller polar transform is given as:

```
.quantQ.simul.genBoxMuller:{[x]
   // x -- two-dimensional array to transform
   // generate 2-dimensional array with radius within (0,1) using
       ↪ convergence
```

```
    x1x2:{[x] (2?2f)-1.0}/[{((((x[0]*x[0])+(x[1]*x[1])))>=1) or (((x[0]*x[0])
        ↪ +(x[1]*x[1]))=0.0)};(0.0;0.0)];
    // use it as an input into .quantQ.simul.BoxMuller
    :.quantQ.simul.BoxMuller[x1x2];
};
```

with the transformation being implemented as:

```
.quantQ.simul.BoxMuller:{[x1x2]
    // x1x2 -- 2-dimensional array of uniform numbers
    // the radius of point in 2D space
    rad:(x1x2[0]*x1x2[0])+x1x2[1]*x1x2[1];
    // the output is a 2-dimensional array
    z1z2:(0 0f);
    // the first normal variable
    z1z2[0]:x1x2[0]*sqrt[(neg 2*log[rad])%rad];
    // the second normal variable
    z1z2[1]:x1x2[1]*sqrt[(neg 2*log[rad])%rad];
    :z1z2;
};
```

and can be tested as:

```
.quantQ.simul.genBoxMuller[]
```

```
0.1511711 -0.8011183
```

In the function generateBoxMuller, we have used the iterator function over, /, to find the first pair of independent uniform random variables with radius within interval (0, 1). We encourage readers to implement an alternative approach using self-reference as an interesting exercise.

At this point, we can generate the multidimensional normal variate with a general variance-covariance matrix and drift using .quantQ.simul.multiNormal. The variance-covariance matrix for the problem we aim to simulate is given from the parameters dictionary stochVolPars as:

```
varcov:((1.0; stochVolPars[`rhoInp];stochVolPars[`rho12]; 0.0;stochVolPars
    ↪ [`rho13]; 0.0);
        (stochVolPars[`rhoInp]; 1.0; 0.0; 0.0;0.0;0.0);
        (stochVolPars[`rho12]; 0.0; 1.0;stochVolPars[`rhoInp];stochVolPars[`
            ↪ rho23]; 0.0);
        (0.0; 0.0;stochVolPars[`rhoInp]; 1.0; 0.0;0.0);
        (stochVolPars[`rho13];0.0;stochVolPars[`rho23]; 0.0; 1.0;
            ↪ stochVolPars[`rhoInp]);
        (0.0; 0.0; 0.0; 0.0;stochVolPars[`rhoInp]; 1.0));
```

where the parameters are ordered such that we simulate: $dW_t^{(1)}, dB_t^{(1)}, \ldots, dW_t^{(3)}, dB_t^{(3)}$.

18.2.2 Implementing Stochastic Volatility Process with Jumps

In our simulation, we will work with a realistic time index. The time index is thus a timestamp, where we start counting our time on 2000.01.01 and for the sake of simplicity, we assume trading 7 days a week. The simulation will be done in a table such that we end up with our data having a format we are used to in our empirical analysis. We aim to simulate 100 days of data:

```
nDays:100;
```

Let us first define the table with time index:

```
tableSimul:([]time:{(first x)+(last x)} each
          (2000.01.01+til nDays) cross
          stochVolPars[`tIni] +
           "t"$1000 * (("j"$stochVolPars[`tFin]-stochVolPars[`tIni])%
                    (stochVolPars[`Tday]))
                   * til 1+stochVolPars[`Tday]);
```

where we have used cross to combine the list of dates with all times within a day. The table contains 9100 rows; each day contains stochVolPars[`Tday]+1 ticks.

In the next step, we simulate the $dW_t^{(1)}, dB_t^{(1)}, \dots, dW_t^{(3)}, dB_t^{(3)}$ variables:

```
tableSimul:`time`dW1`dB1`dW2`dB2`dW3`dB3 xcol tableSimul,'.quantQ.simul.
    ↪ multiNormal[count varcov;count tableSimul;(count varcov)#0.0;varcov
    ↪ ];
```

The stochastic volatility jumps process requires simulation of another random process, which is the arrival of price jumps; in particular, we need to define $dJ_{P,t}^{(i)}, dJ_{\sigma,t}^{(i)}$, for $i = 1, 2, 3$. We restrict ourselves to the situation where we observe exactly one price jump per day per process, and, further, the price jumps in the price process and in the volatility process at the same time for each asset.

```
// asset 1
tableSimul: update dJs1: raze {[x] tmp:((1+stochVolPars[`Tday])#0);
tmp[first 1?(1+stochVolPars[`Tday])]:1;
:tmp} each til nDays from tableSimul;
tableSimul: update dJp1:"f"$dJs1 from tableSimul;
// asset 2
tableSimul: update dJs2: raze {[x] tmp:((1+stochVolPars[`Tday])#0);
tmp[first 1?(1+stochVolPars[`Tday])]:1;
:tmp} each til nDays from tableSimul;
tableSimul: update dJp2:"f"$dJs2 from tableSimul;
// asset 3
tableSimul: update dJs3: raze {[x] tmp:((1+stochVolPars[`Tday])#0);
tmp[first 1?(1+stochVolPars[`Tday])]:1;
:tmp} each til nDays from tableSimul;
tableSimul: update dJp3:"f"$dJs3 from tableSimul;
```

This code snippet implements the price jumps with a positive sign. We encourage readers to adjust the code such that the sign of price jumps may alternate. This brings many challenges: Should we alternate the sign for volatility price jumps as well? What adjustments may this bring? Are we supposed to make additional checks for the price process itself? How would we prevent the price from becoming negative?

Let us continue with our objective. Further, $dJ^{(i)}_{\sigma,t}$ are multiplied by ν_i, and $dJ^{(i)}_{P,t}$ are each time when they take value equal to 1 multiplied by a random realisation of the exponential distribution $Exp[1.25]$. The first task is simply achieved by

```
tableSimul: update dJs1:dJs1*stochVolPars[`nu1] from tableSimul;
tableSimul: update dJs2:dJs2*stochVolPars[`nu2] from tableSimul;
tableSimul: update dJs3:dJs3*stochVolPars[`nu3] from tableSimul;
```

To achieve the second task, we need to generate the exponential random variate:

```
.quantQ.simul.expRandomVariate:{[lambda]
   // lambda -- parameter of exponential distribution
   :neg[log[first 1?1f]]%lambda;
};
```

which takes the $U[0,1]$ random variable and transforms it into distributed according to an exponential distribution, $Exp[\lambda]$:

$$Exp[\lambda] = \lambda e^{-\lambda x} \text{ for } x \geq 0. \tag{18.12}$$

```
tableSimul: update dJp1:{.quantQ.simul.expRandomVariate[stochVolPars[`
    ↪ expDist]]} each til nDays
            from tableSimul where dJp1=1;
tableSimul: update dJp2:{.quantQ.simul.expRandomVariate[stochVolPars[`
    ↪ expDist]]} each til nDays
            from tableSimul where dJp2=1;
tableSimul: update dJp3:{.quantQ.simul.expRandomVariate[stochVolPars[`
    ↪ expDist]]} each til nDays
            from tableSimul where dJp3=1;
```

The table `tableSimul` contains 13 variables, one time index and 12 random variables driving the randomness of the process under scrutiny. The remaining part of the simulation process is deterministic conditional on the simulated random variables. Out of the six processes we have to calculate – three price processes and three volatilities – the price process time series are easy to vectorise while the volatility time series cannot be directly vectorised as it contains feedback in terms of autorecursion. The feedback is implemented using the iteration parameter:

```
tableSimul: update volSq1:
   {[x;y;z]
   // the squared volatility cannot be negative and we thus reflect the
       ↪ volatility path at zero
   max[((
   // the current value of volatility
   x
   // plus the update from the mean-reverting trend
   +(100*stochVolPars[`kappaInp]*(stochVolPars[`thetaInp]-x)*(1.0%
       ↪ stochVolPars[`Tday]))
   // plus the update from gaussian noise
   +(stochVolPars[`omegaInp]*sqrt[x]*sqrt[1%stochVolPars[`Tday]]*y)
   // plus the update from jumps
   +z
   );0.0)]}\[stochVolPars[`sigma0InitInp];]'[dB1;dJp1] from tableSimul;
```

We have used `stochVolPars[`sigma0InitInp]` as a starting value. We perform analogous updates for other assets. We start with the second asset:

```
tableSimul: update volSq2:{[x;y;z] max[((x+(100*stochVolPars[`kappaInp] *
                    (stochVolPars[`thetaInp]-x)*(1.0%stochVolPars[`
                        ↪ Tday]))+
                    (stochVolPars[`omegaInp]*sqrt[x]*sqrt[1%
                        ↪ stochVolPars[`Tday]]*y)+z);0.0)]}\
                    [stochVolPars[`sigma0InitInp];]'[dB2;dJp2] from
                        ↪ tableSimul;
```

and for the last asset:

```
tableSimul: update volSq3:{[x;y;z] max[((x+(100*stochVolPars[`kappaInp] *
                    (stochVolPars[`thetaInp]-x)*(1.0%stochVolPars[`
                        ↪ Tday]))+
                    (stochVolPars[`omegaInp]*sqrt[x]*sqrt[1%
                        ↪ stochVolPars[`Tday]]*y)+z);0.0)]}\
                    [stochVolPars[`sigma0InitInp];]'[dB3;dJp3] from
                        ↪ tableSimul;
```

Then, we recover the log-price process as:

```
// price process of the asset 1
tableSimul: update logP1: 0^0.01 *
                    (dW1*sqrt[volSq1] *
                     .quantQ.simul.stochVolIntraPatt[`time$time;1b;
                         ↪ stochVolPars])
                     + (prev[sqrt[volSq1]] * (1.0%stochVolPars[`Tday])
                         ↪  * stochVolPars[`nu1]*dJs1)
            from tableSimul;
// price process of the asset 2
tableSimul: update logP2: 0^0.01 *
                    (dW2*sqrt[volSq2] *
                     .quantQ.simul.stochVolIntraPatt[`time$time;1b;
                         ↪ stochVolPars])
                     + (prev[sqrt[volSq2]] * (1.0%stochVolPars[`Tday])
                         ↪  * stochVolPars[`nu2]*dJs2)
            from tableSimul;
// price process of the asset 3
tableSimul: update logP3: 0^0.01 *
                    (dW3*sqrt[volSq3] *
                     .quantQ.simul.stochVolIntraPatt[`time$time;1b;
                         ↪ stochVolPars])
                     + (prev[sqrt[volSq3]] * (1.0%stochVolPars[`Tday])
                         ↪ *stochVolPars[`nu3]*dJs3)
            from tableSimul;
```

The price process is driven by a vectorised equation without the need for iteration. The parameters are such that the log-prices are expressed as a percentage. We multiply the equation by a factor of `0.01*`, which assures that price changes are normalised to one.

As we have pointed out in the beginning, the price jumps in the price process are scaled to the prevailing value of volatility calculated as the previous value of the volatility. This value is not available on the first tick, and we thus have to replace the first missing entry, which is done using the zero-fill function `0^`. Since the volatility is such

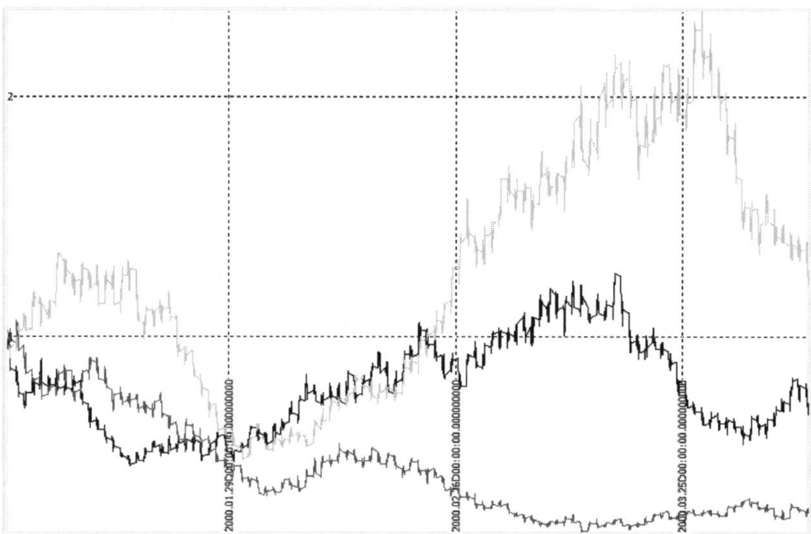

FIGURE 18.1 Depicted are price paths for three assets from table `tableSimul`

that the value σ corresponds to a value normalised to one trading day, we have to provide an extra scaling factor of $1/\sqrt{\Delta t}$. Besides, the jumps are always positive. This means that the price process is always increasing and the price is increasing.

If we normalise the price to start at value \$1, we may recover the price path as:

```
// price path asset 1
tableSimul: update price1: exp sums logP1 from tableSimul;
// price path asset 2
tableSimul: update price2: exp sums logP2 from tableSimul;
// price path asset 3
tableSimul: update price3: exp sums logP3 from tableSimul;
```

Figure 18.1 contains an illustration of the price paths for three assets. The x-axis is in calendar time, and thus the price path is discontinuous. Even though the price jumps are always positive, we see price paths which decline. This is because price jumps are scaled to the current volatility and thus jumps represent a rather minor correction. The shift towards positive values would thus be visible in a large sample of paths. We may also change the magnitude of price jumps to make them more dominant. We encourage readers to explore the price evolution by varying the different parameters.

18.3 CONCLUSION

The chapter introduced some routines which allow us to simulate a stochastic volatility process with jumps. This is useful in a number of financial applications as well as in testing research ideas. In particular, in the current chapter, we have focused on the simulation of the process itself. It is then a natural step to develop a suite of functions, which would create a proper Monte Carlo framework. If, on the other hand, an enhancement of the data generating process is needed, we can build it on the existing functions as well. q is thus very well suited as a data analytics language for research and data generation.

PART Four

Machine Learning

CHAPTER 19

Basic Principles of Machine Learning

In the following chapters, we will focus our attention on topics which commonly fall under the machine learning literature. Although q is not a typical candidate for implementing machine learning methods, we aim to show that many techniques can be easily implemented in q, which gives us the advantage of using smart algorithms sitting next to the data, quickly writing, modifying and adapting our logic while at the same time we crunch and review large data sets.

In this chapter, we prepare the ground by introducing two concepts. First, we discuss the various data types we meet in our empirical work and how to (pre-)process them. We then walk through the general programming technique we use to implement the algorithms. This will lay the foundation for subsequent algorithms and adjust our mindset for further exploratory journeys in q.

19.1 NON-NUMERIC FEATURES AND NORMALISATION

Let us first discuss two technical tricks which are useful to cover before we dive into the machine learning methods themselves: dealing with non-numeric features, and the normalisation of features. For both, we provide q functions.

19.1.1 Non-Numeric Features

When working with large and rich data sets, we often encounter features which do not have a numerical representation. In the context of finance, such a feature can be the venue where a financial transaction took place: some assets are traded at the same time on several exchanges, which – due to regulatory or exchange/venue related rules or other constraints – may lead to a different price discovery process. Other examples are the day of the week, which itself is a non-numeric characteristic, or the output of a questionnaire submitted by analysts. Machine learning methods have to be able to deal with such features, and thus we briefly outline how to incorporate non-numeric features into the learning algorithms.

In general, we may encounter two types of non-numeric variables: ordinal variables and categorical variables. The former stands for variables which are ordered and thus a quantitative measure of the difference between values can be assigned. Such an example is investment grade, which tends to have an alphabetical representation – e.g. $AAA+$, AAA, AA, ... The difference between two assets of grade $AAA+$ and AAA is smaller than the difference between two assets of grade $AAA+$ and AA.

The latter, on the other hand, do not have any such property and we cannot establish any intuitive distance between different values. Days of the week fall under this category, as we may easily say that market activity on Monday is different to Wednesday's, but we cannot say that market activity on Tuesday lies just between them.

19.1.1.1 Ordinal Features

A common approach to turn the ordinal variables into numerical ones is to use integer representation for them, i.e., to provide a map between features and integers. As an example of such a procedure, let us assume variable `grade`, which captures the quality of an asset. The variable takes values from a set $A, \ldots, E$, where the best quality is represented by A and the worst one by E. Let us generate a random list of 15 features:

```
feature: 15?`A`B`C`D`E;
```

where `feature` may contain the following set:

```
`C`A`B`B`C`B`A`A`B`C`D`E`E`C`E
```

We have used symbols for convenience, as the values may be repetitive. A step further would be to restrict ourselves to the `enum` type and we encourage the reader to extend the example with such a type. In order to turn the feature into an integer list, we need a dictionary which maps the values onto integers. In our case, we may achieve this programmatically as we know that alphabetic ordering is the right one:

```
.quantQ.preml.alpha2Int:{[list]
   // list -- the input list of all non-numeric features, underlying list
       ↪ is alphabetically ordered ordinal variable
   listIndep: asc distinct list;
   // dictionary mapping the underlying list on the integers
   :listIndep!til count listIndep;
};
```

This gives:

```
.quantQ.preml.alpha2Int[feature]
```

```
(`s#`A`B`C`D`E)!0j, 1j, 2j, 3j, 4j
```

where the dictionary also contains the sorting attribute as a side effect of calling the `asc` function on the unique types from `` `A `` to `` `E ``.

We can then map the underlying arrays by

```
.quantQ.preml.alpha2Int[feature] feature
```

giving

```
2j, 0j, 1j, 1j, 2j, 1j, 0j, 0j, 1j, 2j, 3j, 4j, 4j, 2j, 4j
```

The mapped array is then numeric, and we can thus now treat it as an ordinary numerical vector. We may use the numerical distance measures between different observations to assess how much the assets' grades differ. Thus, the difference between `` `A `` and `` `C `` is the same as the difference between `` `B `` and `` `D ``. We introduce the distance measure functions in the subsequent paragraphs.

It is our responsibility to ensure that the underlying ordinal variables are sorted in the proper order. There may not be a general way to do this programmatically, i.e. alphabetical ordering is not always feasible. Accurate ordering is required for a correct representation of the data, even if in some cases this is cumbersome to do.

19.1.1.2 Categorical Features

In the case of categorical variables, we may use the same approach as above to turn the values into integers; however, this does not have much meaning as we cannot assess any intuitive distance between different values. The plausible way to assign the difference between different observations is to check whether the observations agree. If they agree, we assign the distance to 0 and 1 otherwise. One implementation of the categorical distance can be:

```
.quantQ.preml.distanceCategorical:{[point;list]
   // point --- a reference symbol
   // list -- array of symbols
   :point=list;
};
```

This is applied as

```
.quantQ.preml.distanceCategorical[`A;feature]
```

```
010000110000000b
```

The function works in the case of multidimensional arrays as well:

```
.quantQ.preml.distanceCategorical[`A`B;(feature;feature)]
```

```
(010000110000000b;001101001000000b)
```

19.1.2 Normalisation

Features used in machine learning are very often of different scale. When calculating the difference between observations, we need to normalise different features to make them comparable and easy to use within a single algorithm. There are a number of different normalisation techniques; we illustrate two of the most popular ones: the normal score–based method, and the range-based normalisation.

In the implementation below, we always provide two types of functions. One performs normalisation in the sample, i.e. the entire sample is used to provide normalisation parameters. Thus, if the underlying data are a time series, both past and future values are used. This approach is convenient for all calibration and learning purposes. However, this is not convenient for out-of-sample testing or online learning unless we want to change the normalisation with every new observation. For that purpose, we provide functions which have static parameters specified externally.

19.1.2.1 Normal Score

The most common type of normalisation is based on the normal score, or z-score. The purpose of the normalisation is to demean the variables and scale the variables to have unit variance. The z-score is defined as

$$z = \frac{X - \mu}{\sigma} \tag{19.1}$$

where μ is the mean of the variable X, and σ is the standard deviation of the variable X. If both variables are known, we can provide them explicitly. The most common situation is the case when both are unknown and have to be estimated from the sample. Thus, equation (19.1) takes the form of

$$z = \frac{X - \hat{\mu}}{\hat{\sigma}} \tag{19.2}$$

with $\hat{x}$ being the sample, or the estimated, versions of variable x.

The q version of the in-sample z-score normalization is given as:

```
.quantQ.preml.zScoreNorm:{[sample]
   // sample -- array of values to normalize
   :(sample - avg[sample])%sdev[sample];
};
```

Let us test the function:

```
testArray:1.0+100?2.0;
(avg[testArray];sdev[testArray])
```

```
1.938569 0.5695563
```

The normalized array is then obtained as

```
testArrayNorm:.quantQ.preml.zScoreNorm[testArray];
(avg[testArrayNorm];sdev[testArrayNorm])
```

```
1.559863e-016 1
```

The static version of the normalisation is implemented as

```
.quantQ.preml.zScoreNormExt:{[sample;params]
   // sample -- array of values to normalize
   // params -- dictionary with `mean and `std
   : (sample - params[`mean])%params[`std];
};
```

where we have provided the parameters through a dictionary. For example:

```
testArrayNorm2:.quantQ.preml.zScoreNormExt[testArray;`mean`std!(2.0;1%sqrt
    ↪ [3])];
(avg[testArrayNorm2];sdev[testArrayNorm2])
```

```
-0.1064008 0.9865005
```

19.1.2.2 Range Scaling

The second normalisation technique is the normalisation of the variable to fall into a provided range of $[a, b]$. The formula is given as

$$\tilde{X} = a + \frac{(X - \min X)(b - a)}{(\max X - \min X)}, \tag{19.3}$$

where we assume the existence of finite $\min X$ and $\max X$ values. The implementation reads

```
.quantQ.preml.rangeScaleNorm:{[sample;range]
   // sample -- array of values to normalize
   // range -- two-dimensional array of a and b
   :range[0] + ((sample-min[sample])*(range[1]-range[0]))%(max[sample]-min[
        ↪ sample]);
};
```

and it can be applied as:

```
testArrayNorm3:.quantQ.preml.rangeScaleNorm[testArray;(-1.0;3.0)];
(min[testArrayNorm3]; max[testArrayNorm3];avg[testArrayNorm3];sdev[
    ↪ testArrayNorm3])
```

```
-1 3 0.8718423 1.142799
```

The static version of the range-based normalisation is provided as

```
.quantQ.preml.rangeScaleNormExt:{[sample;range;params]
   // sample -- array of values to normalize
   // range -- two-dimensional array of a and b
   // params -- dictionary with `min and `max
  :range[0] + ((sample-params[`min])*(range[1]-range[0]))%(params[`max]-
       ↪ params[`min]);
};
```

with illustration:

```
testArrayNorm4:.quantQ.preml.rangeScaleNormExt[testArray;(-1.0;3.0);`min`
    ↪ max!(1.0 3.0)];
(min[testArrayNorm4]; max[testArrayNorm4];avg[testArrayNorm4];sdev[
    ↪ testArrayNorm4])
```

```
-0.9886659 2.998433 0.877139 1.139113
```

19.2 ITERATION: CONSTRUCTING MACHINE LEARNING ALGORITHMS

In this section, we review the functionality of the iteration function and discuss its importance during construction of machine learning algorithms.

19.2.1 Iteration

As seen in Chapter 3, the backslash operator \ and the forward slash operator /, when applied on monadic functions, act as a loop by iteratively calling the function, where the argument is the past evaluation of the function. The difference between the two is such that the backslash prints out all the intermediate steps and the final value, while the forward slash prints out the final value only.

Conceptually, we illustrate this as:

```
({f[]}\)[terminal;initValue]
```

where `f[]` is a monadic function whose argument (input) datatype matches its output, i.e. a map of a `` `float `` on `` `float ``, the variable `initValue` is a starting value for the iteration and `terminal` is a terminal condition. q allows us to use two types of terminal conditions:

- Number of iterations
- A logical condition

To use the first, `terminal` should be of type long:

```
type terminal
```

```
-7h
```

On the other hand, if we want to use a while-type constraint, i.e. to continue the iteration while a particular condition is met, `terminal` is a function which accepts as an argument the output of the function `f` and returns a boolean.

Let us illustrate the concept of iteration using the following simple function

```
f:{[x] 2*x}
```

which accepts a number of any type and multiplies it by 2:

```
f[3]
```

```
6
```

In order to iteratively employ the function five times with a starting value of 1.0, we run

```
f/[5;1.0]
```

and obtain

```
32f
```

To monitor the intermediate outputs, we replace the forward slash with a backslash:

```
f\[5;1.0]
```

giving

```
1 2 4 8 16 32f
```

The code returns the initial value along with the following 5 iterations.

Alternatively, we may want to continue execution while an output of the function is below a certain threshold, say 100. This can be achieved as

```
f\[{x<100};1.0]
```

resulting in

```
2 4 8 16 32 64 128
```

The result shows the initial value and all iterations up until the condition is false. The iteration stops at the first value where the condition gets broken. The forward slash suppresses the intermediate outputs. The condition is thus a function, which takes a single input, evaluates it, and produces a boolean output.

Using the while-type condition carries a risk of providing the wrong specification, where, if the condition is always true, the loop will never stop.

Let's take a look at two similar examples, where integer overflow results in a different behaviour. For instance, the following specification with implicit integer type will terminate:

```
f/[{x>-1};2]
```

with the output

```
0N
```

while the specification using a float initial value will hang our process:

```
f/[{x>-1};2.0]
```

In many situations, we may want to combine both types of conditions. For that purpose, we can use the following approach: the argument of the function to be iterated is a dictionary, which contains an entry for the function value, and an entry for the counter. Whenever the function is called, the function value is evaluated, and the counter is updated. The f function may read as follows:

```
f:{[argument]
   // argument -- dictionary with arguments
   // perform the function operation itself
   valueTmp:2*argument[`value];
   // update the counter
   counterTmp:argument[`counter]+:1;
   // update the argument
   :`value`counter!(valueTmp;counterTmp);
};
```

Calling the function with `value:2.0` and `counter:0`

```
f[`value`counter!(2.0;0)]
```

results in

```
`value`counter!(4f;1j)
```

which updates the `value` as intended and updates the `counter` while the output keeps the same format as the input.

We can then add the while-type evaluation of the iteration with a circuit-breaker for too many iterations. We achieve that by defining a constraint in the following way:

```
constraint:{[constr;cnt;argument] (argument[`value]<constr) and (argument[`
    ↪ counter]<cnt)};
```

and then setting the iteration with initial value of 2.0, the terminal constraint for the `value` set at 10.0, while keeping the maximum number of iterations

```
(f/)[constraint[10.0;10;];`value`counter!(2.0;0)]
```

with the output

```
`value`counter!(16f;3)
```

summarising both the output value and the number of iterations done.

If we mistakenly specify the constraint such that the constraint will hold true all the time, the limitation on the number iterations kicks in:

```
(f/)[{[argument] (argument[`value]>0.0f) and (argument[`counter]<20)};`
    ↪ value`counter!(2.0;0)]
```

with the output

```
`value`counter!(2097152f;20)
```

preventing the iteration from running indefinitely.

Lastly, observe that using the backslash operator with a dictionary as the argument of the iterated function results in the table where each row of the table corresponds to the step in the iteration:

```
(f\)[constraint[10.0;10;];`value`counter!(2.0;0)]
```

leading to

```
value counter
-------------
2     0
4     1
8     2
16    3
```

The above result is due to a table being equivalent to a list of dictionaries, as seen in Chapter 2.

19.2.2 Constructing Machine Learning Algorithms

In the following chapters, we introduce and implement a number of machine learning methods. Nearly every machine learning algorithm can be written as a sequence of iterative steps. Algorithms can be quickly implemented with the use of the iteration operators introduced above.

The data type which we will use to iterate is usually a dictionary. Such a dictionary may contain all the necessary data needed for the iteration. This includes the data set itself, the parameters of the model, as well as temporary variables, which help us to propagate the system from one iteration step to the next. Due to q's efficient memory management (which is managing memory through reference counting), large data sets and not copied when passed in as function parameters and thus including the data into the input dictionary is "memory safe".

It is also useful to include some parameters which help monitor the convergence of the algorithm. There are two types of such parameters. First, the algorithm should converge in terms of some objective function. This can be a loss function or some form of prediction error. The variable itself depends on the algorithm, but most of the machine learning algorithms do have such a well-defined error.

Further, the second type of variables used for monitoring convergence is the counter for number of steps. Even though we can run an iteration in "run the function N times" mode, it is preferable to monitor the number of steps explicitly. The reason is that a well-constructed algorithm should contain both types of control variables to control the run time of the algorithm. There should be an objective to be met, i.e. the prediction error on the dedicated data set has to be below the provided threshold. Besides, there are cases when the algorithm does not converge. This can occur for a number of reasons, for instance, wrongly set initial parameters or maybe a bug in the algorithm itself. In such a case, the error will never get below the threshold, and the iteration would run indefinitely.

The best approach is to combine the convergence rate in terms of error and, at the same time, control for the maximum number of iterations. The program will therefore be protected against an infinite loop. Keeping an exact track of the number of iterations also allows us to adjust the algorithm during the iterations. A textbook example of such modifications is the changing learning rate during calibration of neural networks. We will illustrate this example later on in our neural network routines. In a nutshell, we aim to achieve more significant steps during the initial stage of the algorithm's lifetime while later on we would instead prefer refining the parameters found.

But let us now start with machine learning.

CHAPTER 20

Linear Regression with Regularisation

In Chapter 13, we have introduced the linear regression model and the ordinary least squares (OLS) method. In this section, we build on this framework and introduce two popular regularisation methods: the ridge regression, and the lasso regression. The regularisation aims to improve the out-of-sample performance of the models.

We encourage readers to familiarise themselves with Chapter 13, as this one extends the framework and codebase introduced previously. Let us recall the main results of the linear regression chapter. We consider a model between dependent and independent variables, where for $n \in \mathbb{N}^*$, $p \in \mathbb{N}^*$, $i \in [1, \ldots, n]$, the data generating process is given as:

$$y_i = \beta_0 + \beta_1 x_{i1} + \ldots + \beta_p x_{ip} + \epsilon_i, \tag{20.1}$$

or, in a matrix form,

$$\boldsymbol{y} = \boldsymbol{X}\boldsymbol{\beta} + \boldsymbol{\epsilon}, \tag{20.2}$$

where

$$\boldsymbol{y} = \begin{pmatrix} y_1 \\ y_2 \\ \vdots \\ y_n \end{pmatrix}, \quad \boldsymbol{X} = \begin{pmatrix} 1 & \boldsymbol{x}_1^\intercal \\ 1 & \boldsymbol{x}_2^\intercal \\ \vdots & \vdots \\ 1 & \boldsymbol{x}_n^\intercal \end{pmatrix} = \begin{pmatrix} 1 & x_{11} & x_{12} & \cdots & x_{1p} \\ 1 & x_{21} & x_{22} & \cdots & x_{2p} \\ \vdots & \vdots & \vdots & \ddots & \vdots \\ 1 & x_{n1} & x_{n2} & \cdots & x_{np} \end{pmatrix}, \quad \boldsymbol{\beta} = \begin{pmatrix} \beta_0 \\ \beta_1 \\ \vdots \\ \beta_p \end{pmatrix}, \quad \boldsymbol{\epsilon} = \begin{pmatrix} \epsilon_1 \\ \epsilon_2 \\ \vdots \\ \epsilon_n \end{pmatrix}. \tag{20.3}$$

The estimator of the vector of parameters $\boldsymbol{\beta}$ is given as minimisation of the residual sum of squares and reads:

$$\hat{\boldsymbol{\beta}} = (\boldsymbol{X}^\intercal \boldsymbol{X})^{-1} \boldsymbol{X}^\intercal \boldsymbol{y}, \tag{20.4}$$

with the corresponding variance

$$\mathsf{Var}[\hat{\boldsymbol{\beta}}] = \sigma^2 (\boldsymbol{X}^\intercal \boldsymbol{X})^{-1}. \tag{20.5}$$

20.1 BIAS-VARIANCE TRADE-OFF

Consider the general case where we want to predict Y using X. Assume there is a relationship: $Y = f(X) + \epsilon$, where $\epsilon \sim N(0, \sigma_\epsilon^2)$. We may estimate our model $f(X)$ as $\hat{f}(X)$ and want to understand how well $\hat{f}(\cdot)$ fits some future random observation (x_0, y_0). If $\hat{f}(X)$ is a good model, then $\hat{f}(x_0)$ should be close to y_0 – this is the notion of prediction error. The prediction error is estimated as

$$PE(x_0) = E[(Y - \hat{f}(x_0))^2]. \tag{20.6}$$

When we deal with supervised machine learning, it is important to understand prediction errors, which can be decomposed into two main components:

- Error due to "Bias": The error due to bias is taken as the difference between the expected (or average) prediction of our model and the correct value which we are trying to predict. Bias measures how far off, in general, these models' predictions are from the correct value. High bias can cause an algorithm to miss the relevant relations between features and target outputs. This is connected to the so-called "underfitting" of the model.
- Error due to "Variance": This error is the counterpart of the error due to bias and stems from sensitivity to small fluctuations in the training set. The high variance of the model means that the algorithm models complexity in the training data which is due to random noise, rather than a genuine link between dependent and independent variables. This is also known as model "overfitting".

Let us derive the bias–variance trade-off explicitly:

$$PE(x_0) = E[(Y - \hat{f}(x_0))^2] \tag{20.7}$$

$$= E[Y^2 + \hat{f}(x_0)^2 - 2Y\hat{f}(x_0)] \tag{20.8}$$

$$= E[Y^2] + E[\hat{f}(x_0)^2] - E[2Y\hat{f}(x_0)] \tag{20.9}$$

$$= \mathrm{Var}[Y] + (E[Y])^2 + \mathrm{Var}[\hat{f}(x_0)] + (E[\hat{f}(x_0)])^2 - 2f(x_0)E[\hat{f}(x_0)] \tag{20.10}$$

$$= \mathrm{Var}[Y] + \mathrm{Var}[\hat{f}(x_0)] + (f(x_o) - E[\hat{f}(x_0)])^2 \tag{20.11}$$

$$= \sigma_\epsilon^2 + Variance + Bias^2. \tag{20.12}$$

Let us stress that σ_ϵ^2 is the irreducible error, the noise term that cannot fundamentally be reduced by any model. Given the true model and infinite data to calibrate it, we should be able to reduce both the bias and variance terms to 0. However, in a world with imperfect models and finite data, there is a trade-off between minimizing the bias and minimizing the variance:

- As a model becomes more complex (more terms included), local structure/curvature can be picked up;
- However, coefficient estimates suffer from high variance as more terms are included in the model.

This is the fundamental reason underlying the bias–variance trade-off. In Chapter 13, we introduced cross-validation. This technique is the method of choice for controlling the bias–variance trade-off. However, it was introduced in a way where we do not have much control of the trade-off itself. We have introduced it for the sake of understanding it. We could make binary decisions either to include a given feature or not. This can control the trade-off, but we can do better than making binary decisions. Regularisation is an approach introduced to balance the bias–variance trade-off in a much smoother and more controlled way. The smoothness, in this case, means that if the model is driven by two (not entirely) correlated variables, we want to reduce their mutual contribution to the regression model rather than exclude one of them.

20.2 REGULARISATION

The regularisation is a method for solving problems of overfitting or problems with significant variance. The method involves introducing an additional penalty in the form of shrinkage of the coefficient estimates. The shrinkage is controlled by an additional parameter, which allows for smooth (not necessarily in the mathematical sense) control of the trade-off.

Generally, an L_p regularization is used: $L_p = (\sum |\beta_i|^p)^{\frac{1}{p}}$. For any regularisation, it is important to have the data normalised as we do not want to punish the coefficient just because the corresponding regressors are large in magnitude.

The solution to the OLS is found by minimising the residual sum of squares:

$$\hat{\boldsymbol{\beta}} = \arg\min_{\boldsymbol{\beta}'} \text{RSS} = \arg\min_{\boldsymbol{\beta}'} (\boldsymbol{y} - \boldsymbol{X}\boldsymbol{\beta}')^{\mathsf{T}}(\boldsymbol{y} - \boldsymbol{X}\boldsymbol{\beta}'). \tag{20.13}$$

The optimisation problem in eq. (20.13) is unconstrained optimisation. With regularisation, we introduce the constraint on the solution:

$$\hat{\boldsymbol{\beta}} = \arg\min_{\boldsymbol{\beta}'} (\boldsymbol{y} - \boldsymbol{X}\boldsymbol{\beta}')^{\mathsf{T}}(\boldsymbol{y} - \boldsymbol{X}\boldsymbol{\beta}') \tag{20.14}$$

$$\text{s.t. } L_p(\boldsymbol{\beta}) \leq t, \tag{20.15}$$

where parameter t controls shrinkage and p drives how we constrain the vector of parameters. Equivalently, we can rewrite eq. (20.14) into the more familiar form:

$$\hat{\boldsymbol{\beta}} = \arg\min_{\boldsymbol{\beta}'} (\boldsymbol{y} - \boldsymbol{X}\boldsymbol{\beta}')^{\mathsf{T}}(\boldsymbol{y} - \boldsymbol{X}\boldsymbol{\beta}') + \lambda L_p(\boldsymbol{\beta}), \tag{20.16}$$

where the last term $\lambda L_p(\boldsymbol{\beta})$ introduces the penalty. The more weight we put on the estimated parameters, the more prone we are to increase variance out of the sample. Parameter λ is a free parameter, which has to be chosen carefully to make the most out of the penalty. If $\lambda = 0$, we recover the original OLS solution, while for $\lambda \to \infty$, the parameters are infinitely penalised and the model prefers trivial solution.

Let us make an important remark at this point. The penalty in a regularisation optimisation problem expressed in eq. (20.16) cannot be applied to the intercept.

For that purpose, it is convenient to demean the dependent variable first by calculating and subtracting the mean from every variable in the data set. Once the variables are demeaned, the constrained estimation is performed and the mean added back to the equation when we predict the dependent variable.

The regularisation as introduced so far is also known as shrinkage method. The objective is to shrink the estimated parameters and thus control the overfitting of the model. In the next sections, we present two of the most popular methods: the ridge regression, and the lasso regression, respectively.

20.3 RIDGE REGRESSION

Ridge regression is a formulation of the OLS solution where an additional penalty on the estimated parameters is imposed and has the form of an L_2 norm. A parameter estimated in this way is also known as a ridge estimator.

The ridge estimator is a solution to the problem:

$$\hat{\boldsymbol{\beta}}_{\lambda}^{Ridge} = \arg\min_{\boldsymbol{\beta}'} (\boldsymbol{y} - \boldsymbol{X}\boldsymbol{\beta}')^{\mathsf{T}}(\boldsymbol{y} - \boldsymbol{X}\boldsymbol{\beta}') + \lambda\boldsymbol{\beta}^{\mathsf{T}}\boldsymbol{\beta}, \tag{20.17}$$

where term $\lambda\boldsymbol{\beta}^{\mathsf{T}}\boldsymbol{\beta}$ corresponds to $L_2(\boldsymbol{\beta})$ distance. We keep the explicit dependence of the estimator on the parameter λ present in the expression in the form of an index. This reminds us that we have added a parameter which has to be properly considered.

The solution to the optimisation (20.17) can be written as:

$$\hat{\beta}_{\lambda}^{Ridge} = (\boldsymbol{X}^{\mathsf{T}}\boldsymbol{X} + \lambda\boldsymbol{I}_{\boldsymbol{p}})^{-1}\boldsymbol{X}^{\mathsf{T}}\boldsymbol{y} \tag{20.18}$$

where $\boldsymbol{I}_p$ is a unit matrix of dimension p.

The ridge estimator has a very convenient form. We can quickly solve it by matrix manipulations using the same sort of techniques we have used to find the OLS solution. This brings literally no extra effort as we do not have to perform any optimisation search when estimating the ridge estimator.

The matrix representation of the ridge estimator also reveals its original motivation. Imagine the situation where the features used in the data are linearly dependent or perfectly collinear, using the terminology of a regression framework. In such a case, we can express one or more features as a linear combination of other features. Such features are redundant; they do not bring any additional information into the model. Another consequence of that is that the matrix $\boldsymbol{X}^{\mathsf{T}}\boldsymbol{X}$ is not full rank and thus the inverse does not exist. Adding the term $\lambda\boldsymbol{I}_p$ returns the full rank to the matrix and allows for a calculation of the Moore–Penrose pseudoinverse matrix. The parameters can then be solved. The ridge regularisation can be thus perceived as a solution to the perfect collinearity in the data. Presence of collinearity in the data amplifies the importance of bias–variance trade-off, and thus it is tightly linked to our initial objective.

Finally, it is worth pointing out that ridge regression (not the estimator!) can be viewed as an application of the dropout technique, popular in neural networks. Without going into too much detail, imagine we set a probability to drop an observation with a certain probability p. Then, after some manipulations, we end up with the formulation of the regression, which is exactly like the one in eq. (20.17). We let the readers show the link between the probability to drop an observation p and the regularisation parameter λ. We may then understand the usefulness of the dropout regularisation technique for neural networks calibration, through the lenses of our linear regression knowledge built in this chapter.

Next, let us explore the properties of the ridge estimator. First, we can show that the estimator is biased:

$$\begin{aligned}
\hat{\beta}_\lambda^{Ridge} &= (\boldsymbol{X}^\intercal\boldsymbol{X} + \lambda\boldsymbol{I_p})^{-1}\boldsymbol{X}^\intercal\boldsymbol{y} && (20.19)\\
&= (\boldsymbol{A} + \lambda\boldsymbol{I_p})^{-1}\boldsymbol{A}(\boldsymbol{A}^{-1}\boldsymbol{X}^\intercal\boldsymbol{y}) && (20.20)\\
&= [\boldsymbol{A}(\boldsymbol{I_p} + \lambda\boldsymbol{A}^{-1})]^{-1}\boldsymbol{A}[(\boldsymbol{X}^\intercal\boldsymbol{X})^{-1}\boldsymbol{X}^\intercal\boldsymbol{y}] && (20.21)\\
&= (\boldsymbol{I_p} + \lambda\boldsymbol{A}^{-1})^{-1}\boldsymbol{A}^{-1}\boldsymbol{A}\hat{\beta}^{OLS} && (20.22)\\
&= (\boldsymbol{I_p} + \lambda\boldsymbol{A}^{-1})^{-1}\hat{\beta}^{OLS}E[\hat{\beta}_\lambda^{Ridge}] && (20.23)\\
&= (\boldsymbol{I_p} + \lambda\boldsymbol{A}^{-1})^{-1}\beta, && (20.24)
\end{aligned}$$

where $\boldsymbol{A} = \boldsymbol{X}^\intercal\boldsymbol{X}$ and unless $\lambda = 0$, there is a bias in the estimate.

The variance of the $\hat{\beta}_\lambda^{Ridge}$ estimator can be also expressed using matrix manipulations:

$$\begin{aligned}
\mathsf{Var}[\hat{\beta}_\lambda^{Ridge}] &= \mathsf{Var}[(\boldsymbol{I_p} + \boldsymbol{\lambda A^{-1}})^{-1}\hat{\beta}^{OLS}] && (20.25)\\
&= (\boldsymbol{I_p} + \boldsymbol{\lambda A^{-1}})^{-1}\mathsf{Var}[\hat{\beta}^{OLS}](\boldsymbol{I_p} + \boldsymbol{\lambda A^{-1}})^{-1^\intercal} && (20.26)\\
&= \sigma^2(\boldsymbol{I_p} + \boldsymbol{\lambda A^{-1}})^{-1}(\boldsymbol{X}^\intercal\boldsymbol{X})^{-1}(\boldsymbol{I_p} + \boldsymbol{\lambda A^{-1}})^{-1^\intercal} && (20.27)\\
&= \sigma^2[\boldsymbol{X}^\intercal\boldsymbol{X} + \lambda\boldsymbol{I_p}]^{-1}\boldsymbol{X}^\intercal\boldsymbol{X}([\boldsymbol{X}^\intercal\boldsymbol{X} + \lambda\boldsymbol{I_p}]^{-1})^T. && (20.28)
\end{aligned}$$

Let us recall the bias–variance formula for the MSE of estimators:

$$\begin{aligned}
MSE = E[(\hat{\Theta} - \Theta)^2] &= E[((\hat{\Theta} - E[\hat{\Theta}]) - (\Theta - E[\hat{\Theta}]))^2] && (20.29)\\
&= E[\hat{\Theta} - E[\hat{\Theta}]]^2 + E[(\Theta - E[\hat{\Theta}])^2] - 2E[(\hat{\Theta} - E[\hat{\Theta}])(\Theta - E[\hat{\Theta}])] && (20.30)\\
&= Var[\hat{\Theta}] + [Bias(\hat{\Theta})]^2. && (20.31)
\end{aligned}$$

It appears that there exists λ^* such that $MSE[\hat{\beta}_{\lambda^*}^{Ridge}] < MSE[\hat{\beta}^{OLS}]$. This is (one of) the reasons the ridge regression is useful.

It remains to answer the obvious question, how to identify the value of such λ^*. The performance of the model for a given λ has to be assessed in the out-of-sample context. An intuitive tool to use is the cross-validation technique we have discussed in the previous section. It is convenient to perform the cross-validation estimation across a grid of λ values and optimise for λ based on the estimated landscape in terms of chosen measure like *RMSE*. We will show the details in the implementation section.

In conclusion, the ridge regression is a friendly and easy to implement method to deal with bias–variance trade-off. The method imposes a penalty in terms of shrinking the regression coefficients. The ridge regression shrinks the entire vector of parameters at the same time, trying to balance the proper mixture of re-weighted parameters. The ridge regression is not functional when our objective is to select a subset of regressors.

20.4 IMPLEMENTATION OF THE RIDGE REGRESSION

We implement the ridge regression suite of functions within the namespace `.quantQ.reg`. Let us first start with the data set we will employ. We will build upon the data set created in Chapter 13, but we will add another feature, `` `x4 ``, which is identical to feature `` `x3 ``. The data set thus contains perfectly collinear data, where features are linearly dependent. Let us denote the new data table `tabData2` and define it as follows:

```
tabData2:([] y:y; x1:x1;x2:x2;x3:x3;x4:x3);
```

We have to add a constant term as well:

```
tabData2: update const:1.0 from tabData2;
tabData2
```

```
y         x1          x2          x3        x4        const
-----------------------------------------------------------
11.82698 2.454263   -3.583155  2.456235  2.456235  1
8.505473 3.91833    -0.7588861 1.390334  1.390334  1
5.311374 0.5955665  0.1658444  2.04283   2.04283   1
4.649372 -1.856926  -2.036408  1.723693  1.723693  1
9.295402 -0.6730472 -1.952683  3.506369  3.506369  1
6.65504  0.3517425  -2.000512  1.566093  1.566093  1
7.12083  0.01475878 -1.554944  2.233064  2.233064  1
8.331946 2.104604   -1.420382  1.810523  1.810523  1
8.308305 1.870071   -1.473924  1.935104  1.935104  1
13.51147 2.348974   -2.671633  3.728308  3.728308  1
..
```

The consequence of linear dependence among features is that the rank of the `xtx` matrix is less than the number of features and this matrix cannot be inverted. The OLS fails in such a case, and the algorithm for the OLS calculation cannot be used. Let us illustrate it as follows:

```
ytx: enlist tabData2[`y] mmu flip[tabData2[`const`x1`x2`x3`x4]];
xtx: x mmu flip[x:tabData2[`const`x1`x2`x3`x4]];
```

and we can solve the OLS by:

```
solution: ytx lsq xtx;
beta:first solution;
beta
```

```
0n 0n 0n 0n 0nf
```

The solution is a list of missing values. This indicates that the method has not been able to find any solution and the entire procedure fails. The reason the method fails is the rank of the matrix `xtx`. We can introduce a perturbation along the matrix diagonal such that the rank of the matrix will be full, i.e. equal to many features:

$$\boldsymbol{X}^{\mathsf{T}}\boldsymbol{X} \rightarrow \boldsymbol{X}^{\mathsf{T}}\boldsymbol{X} + \alpha \boldsymbol{I}_p, \tag{20.32}$$

where α is a perturbation parameter and the matrix $\boldsymbol{I}_p$ is a unit matrix. The regularised term is of full rank, and the OLS procedure can be used as usual. Let us explore the regularisation in the code. We will need a function which calculates the diagonal matrix. This was introduced in Chapter 16:

```
.quantQ.mat.diagMatrix[count xtx]
```

```
1 0 0 0 0
0 1 0 0 0
0 0 1 0 0
0 0 0 1 0
0 0 0 0 1
```

We can now solve the OLS with a regularised term and perturbation parameter 0.1 as:

```
solution2: ytx lsq (xtx+0.1*.quantQ.mat.diagMatrix[count xtx]);
solution2
```

```
enlist 1.010104 0.9998766 -0.9974558 0.9984387 0.9984387
```

Let us explore explicitly the value of the parameters for the 3rd and 4th component, respectively. The true value in the data generating process is 2. We have introduced `` `x3 `` and `` `x4 `` to be identical and thus we expect that the sum of the two coefficients adds up to a value close to 2. This is indeed the case:

```
beta: first solution2;
beta[3]+beta[4]
1.996877
```

the value is close to 2. The regularisation thus leads to a meaningful solution.

We have illustrated the ridge regression at a semi-manual level. Let us automate the process and define the function which performs the regularised ridge regression – an analogue to the OLS function. The function has an additional parameter which is a regularisation parameter (recall that we kept that parameter explicitly in the ridge estimator):

```
.quantQ.reg.ridge:{[y;x;reg]
   // y -- array of dependent variables
   // x -- array of arrays of independent variables, constants has to be
       ↪ included
   // reg -- regularization parameter for Ridge regression
   whereMissing:raze (where y=0n; raze {where x=0n} each x);
   // remove the missing values
   y:y[(til count y) except whereMissing];
```

```
    x:{[whereMissing;x] x[(til count x) except whereMissing]}[whereMissing;]
        ↪ each x;
    // y^T X
    ytx: enlist y mmu flip[x];
    // X^T X
    xtx: x mmu flip[x];
    // regularization
    xtx: (xtx+reg*.quantQ.mat.diagMatrix[count xtx]);
    // solve the regularised OLS equation
    solution: ytx lsq xtx;
    // beta
    beta:first solution;
    // output bucket
    bucket:(`beta`nObservations`dfn`regParameter!(beta;count[y];count[beta];
        ↪ reg));
    :bucket;
};
```

The function returns a dictionary with four keys: the estimated parameters, number of observations, number of degrees of freedom, and regularisation parameter. We can verify the functionality of the function at this point. First, we run the function using the data set employed for the OLS algorithm and with a regularisation parameter set to 0.0. In such a case, the function returns the usual OLS output:

```
regRidge1: .quantQ.reg.ridge[tabData2[`y];tabData2[`const`x1`x2`x3];0.0];
regRidge1
```

```
(`beta`nObservations`dfn`regParameter)!(1.010413 0.9998791 -0.9974519
    ↪ 1.996775;1000j;4j;0f)
```

Let us check the regularised solution with the OLS one explicitly:

```
.quantQ.ols.fit[tabData[`y];tabData[`const`x1`x2`x3]][`beta] ~ .quantQ.reg.
    ↪ ridge[tabData2[`y];tabData2[`const`x1`x2`x3];0.0][`beta]
```

```
1b
```

The ridge regression function is thus equal to the OLS regression, at least in the provided example, when regularisation is set to 0.0.

In the next step, we introduce a collinear variable and run regression with regularisation set to 0.0, corresponding to no regularisation:

```
regRidge2: .quantQ.reg.ridge[tabData2[`y];tabData2[`const`x1`x2`x3`x4
    ↪ ];0.0];
regRidge2
```

```
(`beta`nObservations`dfn`regParameter)!(0n 0n 0n 0n 0nf;1000j;5j;0f)
```

The outcome is as expected; non-regularised regression is not able to provide a meaningful estimate, and we thus see missing values. It is worth remembering that missing parameters may imply collinearity in the data set.

Let us add some non-zero regularisation. We choose a value of 0.1 as an initial value to explore the outcome:

```
regRidge3: .quantQ.reg.ridge[tabData2[`y];tabData2[`const`x1`x2`x3`x4
    ↪ ];0.1];
regRidge3
```

```
(`beta`nObservations`dfn`regParameter)!(1.010104 0.9998766 -0.9974558
    ↪ 0.9984387 0.9984387;1000j;5j;0.1)
```

The estimated numbers are close to the correct data generating process. The regularisation thus makes sense and should enter our toolkit of useful routines. We should not stop at this point, though, and try to understand what value to choose for our regularisation parameter . Our value of 0.1 seems to provide a meaningful result; however, in a general case we do not know the correct data generating process, and we need some statistical assessment.

Let us start with the notion of in-/out-of-sample and implement a function analogous to `.quantQ.ols.inOut`. We split the sample into two parts: the in-sample part is used to fit the model. The out-of-sample part is used to evaluate the model using the data which has not been used to calibrate the model.

It is also important to stress that regularisation is used only during training. Once the parameters (regularised) are found, they are used on the out-of-sample data while λ is ignored. When the model is applied to predict values and compare them with the correct values, regularisation does not play any role. In fact, at this point, the estimated parameters are treated the same as if they came from the plain OLS model. The regularisation parameter does not enter any measure we use to assess the performance of the model.

We implement the in/out procedure in the following function. The additional parameter is `inOutFlag`, which works in the same way as for `olsInOut`. It decides how we split the sample into two subsamples; it adds the *RMSE* statistics into the output bucket to be able to judge the quality of a fit:

```
.quantQ.reg.ridgeInOut:{[y;x;reg;inOutFlag]
   // y -- array of dependent variables
   // x -- array of arrays of independent variables, constants has to be
       ↪ included
   // reg -- regularization parameter for Ridge regression
   // inOutFlag -- atom/array to form in/out sample, 1=out
   whereMissing:raze (where y=0n; raze {where x=0n} each x);
   // remove the missing values
   y:y[(til count y) except whereMissing];
   x:{[whereMissing;x] x[(til count x) except whereMissing]}[whereMissing;]
       ↪  each x;
   // inOutFlag is atom, in sample is randomly chosen inOutFlag fraction of
       ↪  sample
   if[(1=count[inOutFlag]);
       // split sample: OUT
       xOUT:flip ceiling[inOutFlag*count y] _ flip x;
       yOUT:ceiling[inOutFlag*count y] _ y;
```

```
        // split sample: IN
        x:flip ceiling[inOutFlag*count y]#flip x;
        y:ceiling[inOutFlag*count y]#y
    ];
    // inOutFlag is Boolean array with 1b being In/0b Out
    if[(1<count[inOutFlag]);
        inOutFlag:inOutFlag[(til count inOutFlag) except whereMissing];
        // split sample: OUT
        yOUT:y where inOutFlag;
        xOUT:flip flip[x] where inOutFlag;
        // split sample: IN
        y:y where not inOutFlag;
        x:flip flip[x] where not inOutFlag
    ];
    // IN sample Ridge regression
    regIN:.quantQ.reg.ridge[y;x;reg];
    // OUT sample prediction
    yPRED:sum regIN[`beta]*xOUT;
    RMSE:sqrt avg t*t:yOUT-yPRED;
    regOUT:(`RMSE`nObservationsOUT)!(RMSE;count[yOUT]);
    // output bucket
    bucket:regIN,regOUT;
    :bucket;
};
```

and apply it on our test data set. We use a scalar value for `inOutFlag` to take the initial 80% of the data set as a training set and the remaining part as a test data set:

```
ridgeEx1:.quantQ.reg.ridgeInOut[tabData2[`y];tabData2[`const`x1`x2`x3`x4
    ↪ ];0.1;0.8];
ridgeEx1
```

```
(`beta`nObservations`dfn`regParameter`RMSE`nObservationsOUT)!(1.00859
    ↪ 1.003077 -0.9982131 0.998231 0.9982325;800j;5j;0.1;0.1019728;200j
```

and focus on *RMSE*:

```
ridgeEx1[`RMSE]
```

```
0.1019728
```

The value we have obtained is very close to the one obtained with a fully specified OLS model. We can use this procedure to test several values for the regularisation parameter. We keep this as an exercise for the reader and proceed directly with cross-validation, which gives us the tool we ultimately want to achieve and use on our data.

We take the `ridgeInOut` function and wrap it within a routine which is preparing *k*-fold splits of the data. The routine further collects the values of *RMSE* from every run and returns them back to the user for further analysis:

```
.quantQ.reg.ridgeCV:{[y;x;reg;nCV]
    // y -- array of dependent variables
    // x -- array of arrays of independent variables, constants has to be
        ↪ included
```

```
    // reg -- regularization parameter for Ridge regression
    // nCV -- number of Cross-validation folds
    whereMissing:raze (where y=0n; raze {where x=0n} each x);
    // remove the missing values
    y:y[(til count y) except whereMissing];
    x:{[whereMissing;x] x[(til count x) except whereMissing]}[whereMissing;]
        ↪ each x;
    // create all the Flags for every fold
    foldFlag: (floor til[count y]%count[y]%nCV)=/:til nCV;
    // return list of coresponding RMSEs
    :(.quantQ.reg.ridgeInOut[y;x;reg;] each foldFlag)[`RMSE];
};
```

In our example, we can run a 12-fold cross-validation as:

```
cvRidgeEx:.quantQ.reg.ridgeCV[tabData[`y];tabData[`x1`x2`x3`const];0.1;12];
cvRidgeEx
```

```
0.09968289 0.1007171 0.1018614 0.101703 0.1019981 0.1013131 0.09956029
    ↪ 0.1013994 0.1013774 0.1004144 0.1023408 0.09987965
```

The outcome is an array of 12 values of *RMSE*s. The average value is:

```
avg cvRidgeEx
```

```
0.1010206
```

Again, the value is close to the ones obtained previously. This can be considered as a verification test of our implementation.

20.4.1 Optimisation of the Regularisation Parameter

The cross-validation technique is used as a procedure to find out the meta-parameters in estimations. The regularisation parameter is such a parameter. In order to find the optimal value of the regularisation parameter, we want to solve the following equation:

$$\arg\min_{\alpha} RMSE(nF;\alpha), \tag{20.33}$$

where $RMSE(nF;\alpha)$ stands for the cross-validated *RMSE* across the entire sample using nF folds with regularisation parameter equal to α. In this exercise, we fix nF even though this parameter can be optimised in the same way as we do for α. The cross-validated *RMSE* is defined as the average *RMSE* across folds for a given α.

The optimisation expressed in the previous display can be tested on our existing example. In particular, we choose the full model with features `tabData2[`x1`x2`x3 `const]`. The corresponding $\boldsymbol{X}^{\top}\boldsymbol{X}$ matrix is regular and thus does not need regularisation; however, since the model is finite, we may still see some improvement when regularisation is being applied. We choose this problem as opposed to the one with additional collinear variable `` `x4 `` because we know the correct solution. It is also the problem where we would likely use the OLS without any hesitation.

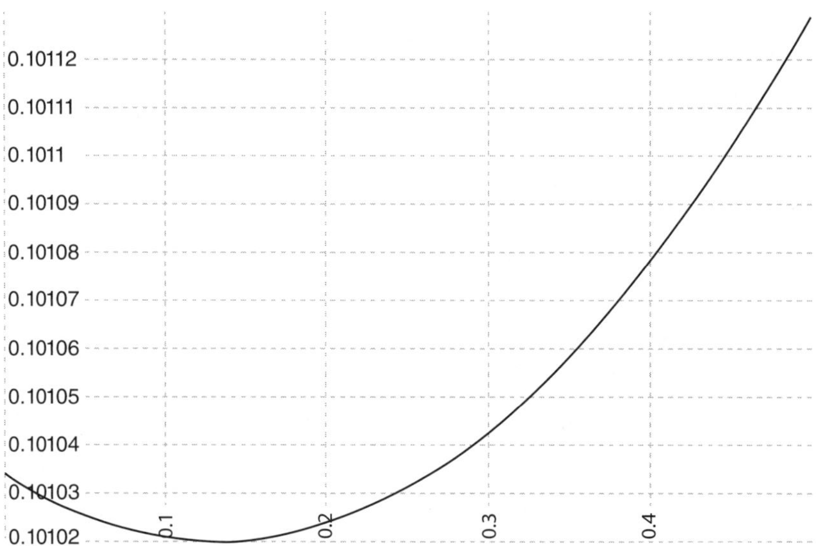

FIGURE 20.1 *RMSE* as a function of the regularisation parameter in a cross-validation with 12 folds

Let us explore the optimisation graphically. We run the `.quantQ.reg.ridgeCV` function across a range of regularisation parameters and plot the average of the *RMSE* for every regularisation parameter as a function of the regularisation parameter. We create a simple table:

```
ridgeOptimum: ([] (0.001*til 500); avg each .quantQ.reg.ridgeCV[tabData[`y
    ↪ ];tabData[`x1`x2`x3`const];;12] each (0.001*til 500));
ridgeOptimum
```

Figure 20.1 depicts the average *RMSE* in a cross-validation run with 12 folds as a function of the regularisation parameter. The function has a global minimum over the range of plotted values, and the minimum is different from zero. This means that even though we know the true model, we may obtain better results in terms of minimising *RMSE* when we will use some form of regularisation.

The value of the regularisation parameter which minimises the cross-validated RMSE can be found by exploring the outcome stored in table `ridgeOptimum`. Using the precision in the previous queries, we see that the global minimum is rather shallow and several values of regularisation parameter solve the problem:

```
`x1 xasc ridgeOptimum
```

```
param     rmse
---------------
0.132 0.1010198
0.131 0.1010198
0.133 0.1010198
0.13  0.1010198
```

```
0.134 0.1010198
0.129 0.1010198
0.135 0.1010198
0.128 0.1010198
0.136 0.1010198
0.127 0.1010198
0.137 0.1010198
0.126 0.1010198
0.138 0.1010198
0.125 0.1010198
0.139 0.1010198
0.124 0.1010198
0.14  0.1010198
0.123 0.1010199
0.141 0.1010199
0.122 0.1010199
..
```

Values from 0.124 to 0.14 are within our precision the possible solutions as suitable candidates, which improves the out-of-sample quality of the fit. We could narrow the search and iterate the procedure around the candidate values. The procedure shows that we can get a better outcome in terms of overall model performance when we use regularisation.

We encourage the reader to repeat the exercise we have run when `x4 is included. The regularisation, in this case, is needed, where value $\lambda = 0$ will not produce a model which could be used outside of the sample. In particular, the question which is to be answered is whether the optimal $\lambda$ when `x4 is included will be the same as in the case of `x4 being missing and thus having the regular data set.

Note that our function does not have explicit demeaning within the estimation routines. The data enter the functions with the assumption of having a zero mean. The function thus needs to be extended to handle demeaning properly. We leave this as an exercise for the reader as the change is straightforward and rewarding.

20.5 LASSO REGRESSION

The second regularisation technique we introduce is the lasso regression. First of all, why do we introduce a new technique given the ridge regression is straightforward to implement and apply? The main reason is that ridge regression tends to penalise all the coefficients across the board, but in many instances, it may be suitable to select a subset of features, i.e. remove some of the features instead of suppressing them significantly but still keeping them within the model. More importantly, feature selection can frequently be our starting point when working with advanced machine learning methods. The lasso regression assists us in feature selection as it has a different way to impose a penalty.

The lasso regression is a formulation of the OLS solution with imposed penalty having a form of an L_1 norm. The lasso estimator is a solution to the problem:

$$\hat{\boldsymbol{\beta}}_{\lambda}^{Lasso} = \arg\min_{\boldsymbol{\beta}'} (\boldsymbol{y} - \boldsymbol{X}\boldsymbol{\beta}')^{\intercal}(\boldsymbol{y} - \boldsymbol{X}\boldsymbol{\beta}') + \lambda \sum_{j=1}^{p} |\boldsymbol{\beta}_j|, \tag{20.34}$$

where term $\lambda \sum_{j=1}^{p} |\boldsymbol{\beta}_j|$ corresponds to the $L_1(\boldsymbol{\beta})$ distance. Analogously to ridge regression, we keep an explicit dependence on λ.

When $\lambda = 0$, we recover the OLS solution, while for large values λ, the parameters are suppressed significantly, ultimately leading to a trivial solution. We still tacitly impose demeaning on the dependent and independent variables. This will be stressed in the implementation part again.

We are tempted to ask for the analytic solution to the lasso regression. It is, however, challenging to obtain such a solution, so we are left with solving the problem numerically. The lasso optimisation, as in eq. (20.34), is *NP*-hard and thus is on the frontier of solvable numerical problems. If we want to implement this, we need a reliable optimisation technique. Luckily for us, there is another, lesser known regularisation technique, least angle regression, or LAR, which is close to the lasso regression (there is an interesting theoretical relationship), which does not need optimisation to provide a solution and mimics the lasso solution. Further, thanks to its construction it helps us to make feature selection.

The least angle regression was introduced by Efron et al. (2004). The method emerges from forward stepwise regression. Forward stepwise regression starts with no feature selected and tests addition of a variable into the active set of features. The one with the most significant contribution to the fit is then added. The process continues until a stopping rule. The procedure also allows us at every step to test removing a feature from an active set.

The LAR, on the other hand, is defined as follows: it starts with an empty active set of features. First, it identifies the variable which is the most correlated with the dependent variable. A small portion of the variable is added to the model and residuals are generated. The procedure is repeated. When another variable reaches comparable correlation to the first variable, the second variable joins the active set. The two variables are then added in a tied manner and contribute to the model by small portions. This continues until all the variables are in the model. In the end, the model reaches the OLS fit.

The notion of a small portion in the description above is best understood as an infinitesimal step, which would imply that the variable contribution to the model is continuously increasing. This is not feasible in a statistical procedure, and thus a small step is taken. The procedure works even if $p > n - 1$ because zero residuals will be reached during the iteration and the entire algorithm stops.

Let us demonstrate the mechanics of the least angle regression using pseudocode:

- Demean and normalise data with independent variables.
- Set residuals $\boldsymbol{\epsilon} = \boldsymbol{y} - \text{avg}(\boldsymbol{y})$ and the parameters $\beta_1, \ldots, \beta_p = 0$.
- Find $\boldsymbol{x}_j$ which is the most correlated to $\boldsymbol{\epsilon}$.
- Change β_j from 0 towards the OLS solution of $\boldsymbol{\epsilon} = \beta_j' \boldsymbol{x}_j + \varepsilon$. The value chosen, β_j^*, is such that there is a new variable $\boldsymbol{x}_k$, which has the same correlation with $\boldsymbol{\epsilon} - \beta_j^* \boldsymbol{x}_j$ as $\boldsymbol{x}_j$ itself.

- Change β_j and β_k jointly. The OLS coefficients give the direction $\epsilon = \beta_j' \boldsymbol{x}_j + \beta_k' \boldsymbol{x}_k + \varepsilon$ with residuals being updated by the previous steps. The value is updated until there is another variable $\boldsymbol{x}_m$, which has the same correlation with updated residuals as the two variables.
- This process continues until all variables have been included ($p > n - 1$, then the process stops when $n - 1$ variables have been included).

The procedure outlined above can be stopped at any iteration step. At the initial stage, the situation corresponds to $\lambda \to \infty$. The more we progress in the iteration and keep adding $\boldsymbol{\beta}$'s, the outcome corresponds to lower and lower λ. In the end, we end up with a full OLS solution which corresponds to $\lambda = 0$. If we keep track of estimated coefficients $\boldsymbol{\beta}$ during the iteration process, and for every such vector of $\boldsymbol{\beta}$ we perform a cross-validation test, we can reach the optimally regularised estimator. The process is similar to choosing λ for lasso procedure itself.

The least angle regression will be giving the same results as the lasso procedure until the first coefficient goes through zero. At this point, solutions start to deviate from each other and least angle regression will be a different regularisation scheme. There is a possible correction to the presented algorithm which makes the solution mimic lasso regression precisely:

- Once any coefficient β_k crosses zero, it is excluded from the active set. At this point, the linear regression for the remaining set is recalculated without β_k.

Once this rule is added, the lasso procedure is recovered. Excluding β_k does not mean it may not return to the active set later. Given our stopping rule is to include all the variables (if $p \leq n - 1$), it will return into the active set. In the following section, we implement the least angle regression procedure.

We encourage the reader to extend the provided algorithm and implement the lasso correction. It will be a rewarding project, at the end of which the reader will strengthen their knowledge of regularisation and the lasso implementation, an inherently *NP*-hard problem.

20.6 IMPLEMENTATION OF THE LASSO REGRESSION

In this section, we implement the other regularisation scheme, which is the least angle regression. The least angle regression is a numerically feasible proxy for the lasso regression, as we have argued. We continue using the `.quantQ.reg` namespace.

We prepare a test data set. We use the `.quantQ.simul.multiNormal` function to generate randomly distributed features and error term. We prepare a different data set to illustrate another way of using the previously developed functions to verify the implemented functionalities.

First, we simulate the 4-dimensional random array, where each of the array has 1000 observations:

```
simData: .quantQ.simul.multiNormal[4;1000;4#0.0;((1.0 0.0 0.0 0.0);(0.0 1.0
    ↪  0.0 0.0);(0.0 0.0 1.0 0.0);(0.0 0.0 0.0 1.0))];
```

and combine the data into a linearly dependent data set. We ultimately obtain three features and one error term:

```
x1:simData[`var1];
x2:(0.3*simData[`var1])+(0.7*simData[`var2]);
x3:(0.5*simData[`var1])+(0.4*simData[`var2])+(0.1*simData[`var3]);
err:simData[`var4];
```

All three features have by construction zero mean. Features x2 and x3 are created as a linear combination of more than one underlying random array, thus introducing the explicit correlation between features. The dependent variable y is defined as:

```
y:2.0+(1.0*x1)+(neg 1.2*x2)+(0.2*x3)+err;
```

Let us further analyse the correlation between the variables used in the definition of y:

```
cor[x1;x2]
```

```
0.393036
```

```
cor[x1;x3]
```

```
0.7705068
```

```
cor[x2;x3]
```

```
0.8716451
```

```
cor[x1;y]
```

```
0.5256652
```

```
cor[x2;y]
```

```
-0.2787934
```

```
cor[x3;y]
```

```
0.08457488
```

We arrange the dependent and independent variables into a table, which is the format we will face in real situations:

```
tabData:([] y:y; x1:x1;x2:x2;x3:x3);
```

We add a constant feature into the table such that we can more easily incorporate the constant term into regressions.

```
tabData: update const:1.0 from tabData;
```

We run a simple OLS on the data created:

```
solutionOLS: .quantQ.ols.fit[tabData[`y];(tabData[`x1];tabData[`x2];tabData
    ↪ [`x3];tabData[`const])];
solutionOLS[`beta]
```

```
0.902613 -1.470181 0.5879043 2.033987
```

The values are in principle close to the real parameters; however, the error term of the estimated parameters is large due to the magnitude of the error term. Let us measure the L_2 distance between the true solution and the estimate:

```
sqrt sum {x*x} each (1; -1.2;0.2;2)-solutionOLS[`beta]
```

```
0.4838462
```

We proceed now with the implementation of the least angle regression algorithm. The algorithm is implemented as a function which performs one iteration step. The argument of the function is a dictionary with all the model parameters and variables, referred to as `bucket`. One step is an update of the vector of $\boldsymbol{\beta}$ by an amount which is normalised in every step using an L_1 measure. The amount by which the parameters are updated is in `bucket[`step]`.

The algorithm distinguishes three regimes:

- `step 1, find the first variable`: This corresponds to the initial stage of the algorithm. Only one variable is in the active set.
- `step 2++, there is space for improvement`: This corresponds to the stage of the algorithm when the new variable can enter the active set. The algorithm tries to include new variables into the active set.
- `step 2++, there is no space for improvement`: This is the last stage of the algorithm when there are no variables to be included, and the algorithm thus tries to finish the run by adding as much of the features loading as possible.

The dictionary `bucket` contains several variables monitoring the state of the iteration; they are needed during the iterations only. The function utilises the `ols` function in order to find the common direction in which to increase the parameters. The decision to include the variable or continue in the present direction is done using the built-in `cor` function. The algorithm is aimed to work with finite sets, and thus the notion correlation is a random variable with a certain error. We use $n^{-1/2}$ criteria to decide whether the correlation is significant or not. Once correlation is within $[-n^{-1/2}, n^{-1/2}]$, the two variables are considered uncorrelated.

Demeaning of variables is not part of the one step of the iteration. This has to be done before engaging with the iteration. We will discuss it later on within a wrapper which creates the estimation suite for the entire LAR algorithm. At the end of every iteration, the vector of residuals `r` is updated accordingly. The vector of residuals thus contains a cumulative unexplained part of variance at the end of each step. The algorithm is supposed to stop once we cannot find any more correlation of the remaining residuals to the data (within our precision).

```
.quantQ.reg.oneStepLAR:{[bucket]
   // bucket -- all the variables
   beta:bucket[`beta];
   betaUsed:bucket[`betaUsed];
   betaDir:bucket[`betaDir];
   y:bucket[`y];
   xS:bucket[`xS];
   r:bucket[`r];
   path:bucket[`path];
   continue:bucket[`continue];
   step:bucket[`step];
   // set the significance limit
   corThr:1.0%sqrt "f"$count y;
   // step 1, find first variable
   $[1=count path;[
       // find variable with largest correlation
       betaUsed:z=max z:abs cor[r;] each xS;
       // set the direction
       betaDir:"f"$betaUsed;
       // update r
       r-:sum step*betaDir*xS;
       // update beta
       beta+:step*betaDir;
       // update path
       path,:([] step:1+last path[`step];beta: enlist beta)
   ];];
   // step 2++, there is space for improvement
   $[(1<count path) and (0=prd betaUsed);
       [
       // correlation with existing direction
       corDir: abs cor[r;sum betaDir*xS];
       // best correlation with the candidate directions
       corNew: max z:not[betaUsed]* abs cor[r;] each (),xS;
       corNewWhere: z=max z;
       // decide whether to continue
       $[corThr>max[(corDir;corNew)];
           // stop the algorithm
           continue:0;
           // continue algorithm, decide the direction
           [
           $[corDir>corNew;
           // old direction
               [
```

```
            // update r
            r-:sum step*betaDir*xS;
            // update beta
            beta+:step*betaDir;
            // update path
            path,:([] step:1+last path[`step];beta: enlist beta)
            ];
        // new direction
            [
            // new set of variables
            betaUsed:betaUsed or corNewWhere;
            // new direction
            newDir:.quantQ.ols.fit[y;xS where betaUsed][`beta];
            // normalize by L1 to make steps comparable
            newDir:newDir%(sum abs newDir);
            // new beta direction
            betaDir:(count[betaUsed]#0.0);
            betaDir[where 1=betaUsed]:newDir;
            // update r
            r-:sum step*betaDir*xS;
            // update beta
            beta+:step*betaDir;
            // update path
            path,:([] step:1+last path[`step];beta: enlist beta)
            ]
        ]
        ]
    ];
];
];
// step 2++, there is no space for improvement
$[(1<count path) and (1=prd betaUsed);
    [
    // correlation with existing direction
    corDir: abs cor[r;sum betaDir*xS];
    $[corThr>corDir;
        // stop the algorithm
        continue:0;
        // continue algorithm
        [
        // update r
        r-:sum step*betaDir*xS;
        // update beta
        beta+:step*betaDir;
        // update path
        path,:([] step:1+last path[`step];beta: enlist beta)
        ]
    ]
    ];
];
// update bucket
bucket[`beta]:beta;
bucket[`betaUsed]:betaUsed;
bucket[`betaDir]:betaDir;
bucket[`r]:r;
```

```
    bucket[`path]:path;
    bucket[`continue]:continue;
    // return bucket
    :bucket;
};
```

Let us run the LAR algorithm altogether. We need to first initialise the `bucket` with all the variables:

```
// set the step
step:0.0001;
// dependent variable
y:tabData first cols tabData;
// independent variables without constant
xS:  (),tabData -1_1_cols tabData;
// create empty vector with beta
beta: ((count flip tabData)-2)#0.0;
// vector with beta in a given iteration
betaDir: ((count flip tabData)-2)#0.0;
// used independent variables;
betaUsed:((count flip tabData)-2)#0b;
// demeaning y, return meanY
y:y-meanY:avg y;
// define residual variable
r:y;
// table with entire path
path:([] step:0;beta:enlist beta);
```

and combine all the individual variables into the dictionary:

```
bucket: ((`beta`betaUsed`betaDir`y`xS`r`path`continue`step)!(beta;betaUsed;
    ↪ betaDir;y;xS;r;path;1;step));
```

Having among the variables the flag `continue`, we can use iteration to run the algorithm until all the possible dependence in the data is exploited:

```
bucketExample:(.quantQ.reg.oneStepLAR/)[{x[`continue]};bucket];
```

The results of the LAR algorithm can be now reviewed. First, the mean of the dependent variable is in the `meanY` variable:

```
meanY
```

```
1.949716
```

Second, the estimated βs read:

```
bucketExample[`beta]
```

```
1.115732 -0.9479582 0.06770964
```

The parameters are visually of the same magnitude as those obtained by the standard OLS. We can confirm it by calculating the L_2-distance to the true solution:

```
sqrt sum {x*x} each (1; -1.2;0.2;2)-raze (bucketExample[`beta];meanY)
```

```
0.3113651
```

The result is improved compared to the one corresponding to the OLS case. For convenience, we create a table with the estimated path which will be indexed by the `arcLength`. This stands for the cumulative sum of `bucket[`step]` performed during the iteration so far. First, we extract the betas from the `path` table:

```
pathLAR: update beta1:beta[;0],beta2:beta[;1],beta3:beta[;2] from
    ↪ bucketExample[`path];
```

then add the `arcLength`:

```
pathLAR: update arcLength: sums abs[deltas[beta1]]+abs[deltas[beta2]]+abs[
    ↪ deltas[beta3]] from pathLAR;
```

When we select a subset from the table, we get the full estimation path:

```
select arcLength, beta1, beta2, beta3 from pathLAR
```

Figure 20.2 depicts the entire path we have obtained using the LAR algorithm as captured by table `pathLAR`. The colour convention used is as follows: light gray colour

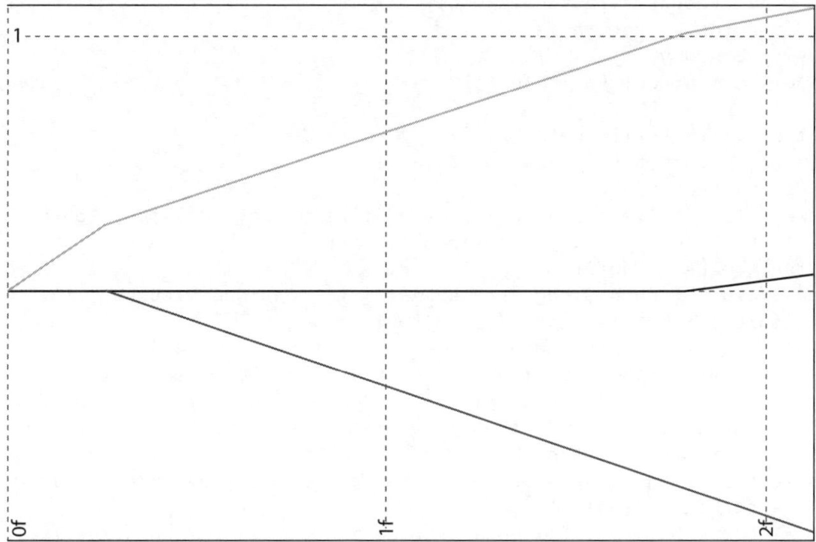

FIGURE 20.2 The plot of the entire path of the LAR algorithm for `tabData`. Light gray colour corresponds to `beta1`, dark gray colour corresponds to `beta2`, and black colour corresponds to `beta3`

corresponds to beta1 coefficient, dark gray colour corresponds to beta2 coefficient, and black colour corresponds to beta3 coefficient.

At this point, we would like to encourage the reader to run the oneStepLAR function step by step with large step and see how the estimation path emerges. A possible weakness of the oneStepLAR function is that there is no limit on the number of steps the function can take. The function can in the extreme case run indefinitely. It is wise to amend the function such that there is a safety feature to prevent this case.

We wrap the algorithm into a function. The function will have two arguments: the table with data, where the first column is the dependent variable, and the remaining columns capture the features in the linear relationship to be estimated. The second argument is the size of the step. Due to the normalisation, it determines the arcLength the algorithm moves in every iteration:

```
.quantQ.reg.LAR:{[tab;step]
   // tab -- table with data with (y,'xS)
   // step -- the step of the LAR algorithm
   // dependent variable - first column of tab
   y:tab first cols tab;
   // independent variables - remaining columns
   xS:  (),tab 1_cols tab;
   // create empty vector with beta
   beta: ((count flip tab)-1)#0.0;
   // vector with beta in a given iteration
   betaDir: ((count flip tab)-1)#0.0;
   // used independent variables;
   betaUsed:((count flip tab)-1)#0b;
   // demeaning y, return meanY
   y:y-meanY:avg y;
   // define residual variable
   r:y;
   // table with entire path
   path:([] step:0;beta:enlist beta);
   // define bucket
   bucket: ((`beta`betaUsed`betaDir`y`xS`r`path`continue`step)!(beta;
        ↪ betaUsed;betaDir;y;xS;r;path;1;step));
   // run the LAR algorithm
   bucketResult:(.quantQ.reg.oneStepLAR/)[{x[`continue]};bucket];
   // result is the re-arranged path table
   pathTab: bucketResult[`path];
   // create ArcLength, add meanY, and individual betas and return table:
        ↪ the L1 arc-length of piecewise-linear LAR coefficient profile
        ↪ amounts to summing the L1 norms of the changes in coefficients
        ↪ from step to step
   :(select arcLength: sums sum each abs deltas beta, beta0:meanY from
        ↪ pathTab),'(eval
        (?;pathTab;();0b;({`$"beta",string x} each 1+til count[xS])!{(`beta
            ↪ ;::;x)} each til count[xS]));
};
```

The function is tested on the same data set tabData. We explicitly keep the constant feature among the variables even though the function performs demeaning before engaging in the iterative process:

```
pathLAR2:.quantQ.reg.LAR[tabData;0.0001];
```

Viewing the last 10 rows of the table pathLAR2:

```
-10#pathLAR2
```

```
arcLength beta0       beta1       beta2         beta3        beta4
-------------------------------------------------------------------
2.1305    1.949716    1.115456    -0.9475115    0.06753275    0
2.1306    1.949716    1.115486    -0.9475611    0.0675524     0
2.1307    1.949716    1.115517    -0.9476107    0.06757206    0
2.1308    1.949716    1.115548    -0.9476604    0.06759171    0
2.1309    1.949716    1.115579    -0.9477100    0.06761137    0
2.1310    1.949716    1.115609    -0.9477597    0.06763102    0
2.1311    1.949716    1.115640    -0.9478093    0.06765068    0
2.1312    1.949716    1.115671    -0.9478589    0.06767033    0
2.1313    1.949716    1.115701    -0.9479086    0.06768999    0
2.1314    1.949716    1.115732    -0.9479582    0.06770964    0
```

We have obtained the same result. There is a 0 coefficient on the constant term, which means that the function operating on the demeaned time series does not assign any value to the constant feature. It can thus ignore irrelevant features. This shows that even though the constant feature is not in fact demeaned, the algorithm performs well.

Following the previous sections, we further develop a function which tests the validity of regularisation on the out-of-sample data. The function performs the same regularisation path as in the LAR function using the in-sample data while the validity of the given regularisation is assessed using the *RMSE* measure on the out-of-sample part of the data. The outcome of the function is a table with a regularisation path, where each point of the path got assigned the *RMSE* value.

```
.quantQ.reg.LARInOut:{[tab;step;inOutFlag]
   // tab -- table with data with (y,'xS)
   // step -- the step of the LAR algorithm
   // inOutFlag -- atom/array to form in/out sample, 1=out
   // dependent variable - first column of tab
   y:tab first cols tab;
   // independent variables - remaining columns
   xS:  (),tab 1_cols tab;
   whereMissing:raze (where y=0n; raze {where x=0n} each xS);
   // remove the missing values
   y:y[(til count y) except whereMissing];
   xS:{[whereMissing;xS] xS[(til count xS) except whereMissing]}[
       ↪ whereMissing;] each xS;
   // inOutFlag is atom, in sample is randomly chosen inOutFlag fraction of
       ↪  sample
   if[(1=count[inOutFlag]);
       // split sample: OUT
       xSOUT:flip ceiling[inOutFlag*count y] _ flip xS;
       yOUT:ceiling[inOutFlag*count y] _ y;
       // split sample: IN
       xS:flip ceiling[inOutFlag*count y]#flip xS;
       y:ceiling[inOutFlag*count y]#y
   ];
   // inOutFlag is Boolean array with 1b being In/0b Out
   if[(1<count[inOutFlag]);
       inOutFlag:inOutFlag[(til count inOutFlag) except whereMissing];
```

```
        // split sample: OUT
        yOUT:y where inOutFlag;
        xSOUT:flip flip[xS] where inOutFlag;
        // split sample: IN
        y:y where not inOutFlag;
        xS:flip flip[xS] where not inOutFlag
    ];
    // run LAR algorithm on in-sample
    inLAR: .quantQ.reg.LAR[([] y),'flip ({`$"x",string[x]} each til count[xS
        ↪ ])!xS;step];
    // evaluate out -sample for every row of inLAR and calculate RMSE
   :update RMSE:{[yOUT;xSOUT;betas] :sqrt avg t*t:yOUT- betas[0] +sum (1
        ↪ _betas)*xSOUT;}
        [yOUT;xSOUT;] each flip 1_value flip inLAR from inLAR;
};
```

The function has two modes of operation depending on the format of the `inOutFlag` variable. We calculate an example using the first 80% of the sample as the in-sample, and the results are verified on the 20% of the sample outside the training part.

```
exLARInOut:.quantQ.reg.LARInOut[tabData;0.0001;0.8];
```

We plot the outcome of `LARInOut`:

```
select arcLength, RMSE from exLARInOut
```

Figure 20.3 depicts the regularisation path. The y-axis corresponds to the *RMSE* on the out-of-sample part of the data while the x-axis is equal to the `arcLength`. The model is estimated for every value of the `arcLength` on the in-sample data.

The model shows the optimal *RMSE* value, i.e. the lowest value, at the end of the path. This means that the optimal regularisation is no regularisation. The optimal model is instead the one corresponding to the OLS.

Further, we provide a routine which employs cross-validation to explore the validity of the regularisation path. For every fold, the sample is split into in-sample and out-of-sample. For such a split, the `LARInOut` function is used. In the end, the *RMSE* is averaged across the validation folds:

```
// LARS regression with CV
.quantQ.reg.LARCV:{[tab;step;nCV]
    // tab -- table with data with (y,'xS)
    // step -- the step of the LAR algorithm
    // nCV -- number of Cross-validation folds
    // dependent variable - first column of tab
    y:tab first cols tab;
    // independent variables - remaining columns
    xS: (),tab 1_cols tab;
    whereMissing:raze (where y=0n; raze {where x=0n} each xS);
    // remove the missing values
    y:y[(til count y) except whereMissing];
    xS:{[whereMissing;xS] xS[(til count xS) except whereMissing]}[
        ↪ whereMissing;] each xS;
    // create all the Flags for every fold
    foldFlag: (floor til[count y]%count[y]%nCV)=/:til nCV;
```

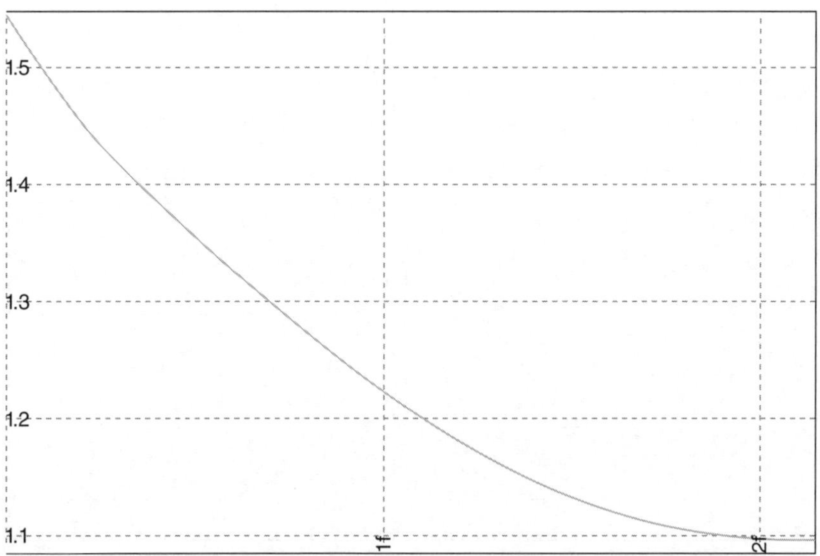

FIGURE 20.3 *RMSE* as function of the arcLength within the LAR algorithm tested out of sample

```
    // run evalaution for every fold
    outCV: (,/){[f;nflag] show first nflag; eval (!;f[last nflag];();0b;(
        ↪ enlist `fold)!enlist first nflag) }[.quantQ.reg.LARInOut[([] y),'
        ↪ flip ({`$"x",string[x]} each til count[xS])!xS;step;];] each flip
        ↪  ((til count foldFlag);foldFlag);
    // create frame (avoid rounding due to arcLength being float) using step
        ↪  and nfolds
    frame: flip (`arcLength`fold)!flip (exec arcLength*step from select
        ↪ distinct "j"$arcLength%step from outCV) cross (til count foldFlag
        ↪ );
    // aj outCV with frame for every fold separately
    fullCV: (,/){[frame;outCV;n] aj[`arcLength;`arcLength xasc select from
        ↪ frame where fold=n;select arcLength, RMSE from outCV where fold=n
        ↪ ]  }[frame;outCV;] peach (til count foldFlag);
    // return RMSE as a function of arcLength averaged across folds
    :select avg RMSE by arcLength from fullCV;
};
```

There are some points to be made. First, for every validation fold, the regularisation path can be of different length. In order to be able to aggregate across different paths, we extend the regularisation path beyond the last estimated point using the last value. This approximation corresponds to the fact that the larger the arcLength value, the less regularisation and the last point of the regularisation path is equal to the plain OLS model. The OLS plays the role of the asymptotic model. In q, this can be achieved by fills. Besides, the values of the arcLength are float numbers. This may cause numerical discrepancies between the values coming from different folds. Thus, we round the arcLength at the step precision explicitly before we use select ... by arcLength ... functionality. Finally, the average value of the *RMSE* by arcLength across the folds is calculated and populated for the regularisation path.

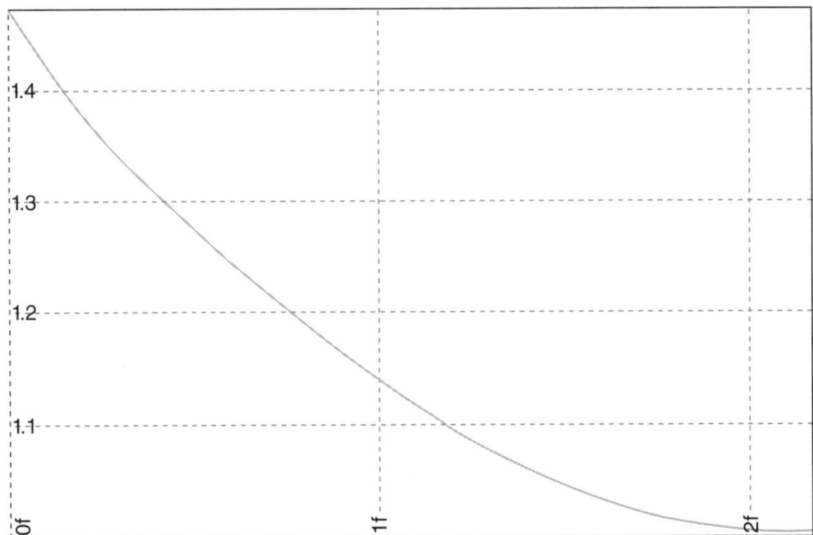

FIGURE 20.4 *RMSE* as function of the `arcLength` within the LAR algorithm using the cross-validation with 12 folds

Let us calculate the example with 12 folds in the cross-validation:

```
exLARCV1: .quantQ.reg.LARCV[tabData;0.0001;12];
```

Figure 20.4 depicts the full regularisation path. The path captures the average *RMSE* as a function of the `arcLength`, calculated across 12 folds of the cross-validation scheme. Figure 20.5 zooms in on the end of the regularisation path. There is a visible minimum. The cross-validation scheme thus shows that optimal linear regression is the one with regularisation, though quite small. The result corresponds to the conclusion we have made with the ridge regression, where optimal linear regression was the one with small regularisation.

The value of the optimal `arcLength` can be recovered as:

```
`RMSE xasc exLARCV1
```

```
arcLength| RMSE
---------| --------
2.1224   | 1.003023
2.1223   | 1.003023
2.1222   | 1.003023
2.1221   | 1.003023
2.122    | 1.003023
2.1219   | 1.003023
2.1218   | 1.003023
2.1217   | 1.003023
2.1216   | 1.003023
2.1215   | 1.003023
..
```

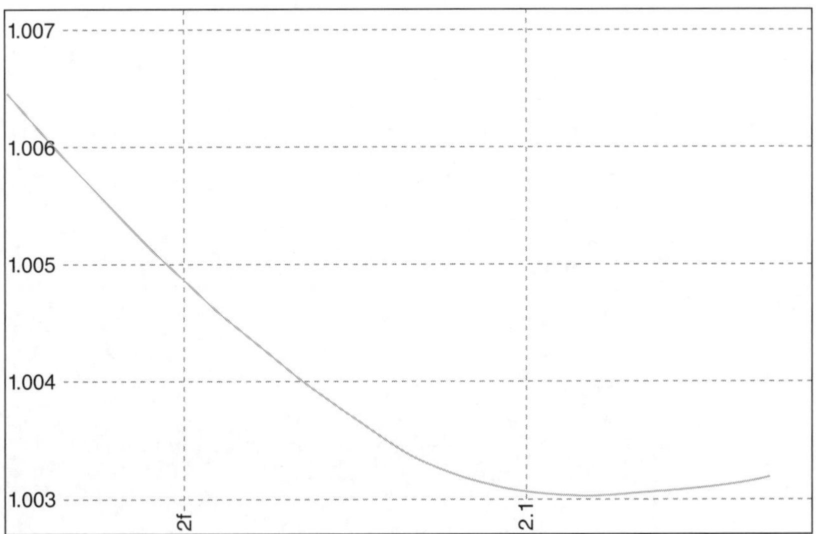

FIGURE 20.5 *RMSE* as function of the `arcLength` within the LAR algorithm using the cross-validation with 12 folds with a focus around the minimum

The precision we use suggests many values be used. Thus, for a given chosen value of `arcLength`, we take the estimated parameters as the estimator of the model. We can choose different criteria to stop the iteration. Imagine we are provided with p variables, and we want to make a feature selection such that we want to use the subset of features of size p'. We run the algorithm but as a stopping rule, we adjust `bucket[`continue]` to work with `sum not 0=bucket[`beta]`. We can alternatively run the full algorithm as it stands and then find a first row in the output table, which has p' non-zero $\boldsymbol{\beta}$ coefficients. Those components will consist of the chosen subset.

Similar to ridge regression, we have not included the demeaning and normalisation of the features within the functions. This part is left as an extension. In particular, the regularisation has to be included in the provided function, including in-/out-of-sample and cross-validated ones. The implementation should not, at any step, mix any information from out-the-sample into the in-sample. A common mistake is to calculate the average of variables across the entire data, demean the data and *then* split them into a training sample and validation sample. Such an approach has information leakage from the validation part into the training one through the global mean.

The provided algorithm opens many possible applications which have to be tailored to the problem at hand. We encourage the reader to implement an extension of the algorithm to mimic the lasso regularisation path as is described in the introduction. We can then explore the deviation of the two algorithms and link their predictive accuracy. Even without doing the last step, the least angle regression implemented in this chapter provides a tool which regularises the model and can perform robust feature selection.

CHAPTER 21

Nearest Neighbours

Nearest neighbours algorithms are popular with data exploration and pattern recognition. In this chapter, we cover the foundation of the nearest neighbours techniques and present three particular algorithms. These methods are by definition model free. We only need to impose mild – or no – assumptions on the data. The outcome is fully derived from the data set itself. The inevitable consequence of this is the black-box nature of the model. We can barely introduce a narrative for the link between independent and dependent variables without looking into the raw data itself.

The nearest neighbour–based algorithms are quite successful in classification problems. They can be used for regression, but the power of the algorithm is not as good as it is with classification. In particular, high-dimensional problems are challenging for nearest neighbour–based regressions. A regression is thus better to be run with other methods discussed in this book, such as linear regression (with regularisation), trees/forests, or neural networks.

In this section, we present three specific algorithms based on the principles of nearest neighbours and implement them in `q`:

- *k*-nearest neighbours classifier
- Prototype clustering
- Feature selection based on the local nearest neighbourhood

21.1 *k*-NEAREST NEIGHBOURS CLASSIFIER

The first method of the machine learning approach we present is the k-nearest neighbours, or *kNN*, one of the most simple and basic machine learning algorithms. The *kNN* is a non-parametric method for classification and/or regression of the data. For the object which we want to classify or for which we want to regress the characteristic value, we use voting based on the set of objects from the nearest neighbourhood.

The *kNN* is very simple in terms of no model being inferred from the data, and all computation is postponed. Whenever the inference has to be drawn, the entire training set is used, and the neighbourhood is identified. Therefore, the method itself is very intensive in terms of computational resources needed to deal with the full training data set when the method is employed during the inference stage. When the problem at hand requires dealing with extensive data, both in cross-sectional dimension and number of samples, the method becomes infeasible for languages which are not able to deal with a large volume of data quickly. This is where q will show it is powerful in dealing with large in-memory data sets.

Assume we are equipped with a training data set, which contains N independent variables, x_i, all of numeric type, and one dependent variable, f, also of numeric type. We defer discussion of non-numeric types until the end of this section. A typical data set will take the following form:

```
tableFunction:([] x1:"f"$();x2:"f"$();x3:"f"$();...;f:"f"$());
```

kNN prescribes the following procedure: consider an out-of-sample observation `point`, which is an array of features `x1; x2;...;xN`. From the training sample `tableFunction`, we identify the subset of k entries closest to the out-of-sample point. The subset then determines our expectation of the value f corresponding to the `point`. The expectations have to be derived from the values in the neighbourhood: this can be based on a majority vote, or we can use probability derived from the proportions within the neighbourhood.

In order to find the subset of observations close to `point`, we use a distance measure, given in general as L_X, i.e.

$$d(x,y) \equiv \left(\sum_{i=1}^{N} |x_i - y_i|^X \right)^{\frac{1}{X}}. \tag{21.1}$$

We consider the general form of a distance metric as we introduce the voting system and the value of X will play the role of a metaparameter of the model. $X = 2$ recovers the standard Euclidean distance, for $X = 1$ the distance metric is derived from absolute values, while for $X \nearrow$, the maximum of the distances of individual feature differences is chosen.

We implement the L_X-distance as a function which takes a `point` and training sample and returns a vector of distances of the `point` from each entry in the training sample:

```
.quantQ.knn.distanceLX:{[point;trainingSampleX;LX]
   // point -- N-dimensional array
   // trainingSampleX -- matrix of training sample points
   // LX -- parameter of the distance measure
   :xexp[;1%LX] sum xexp[;LX] abs point-trainingSampleX;
};
```

We illustrate the distance measure for three values $X = 1$, $X = 2$, and $X = 10$. We use point `(0.2;0.3;0.0)` and a randomly generated table with three rows.

```
update dist1: .quantQ.knn.distanceLX[(0.2;0.3;0.0);(x1;x2;x3);1],
      dist2: .quantQ.knn.distanceLX[(0.2;0.3;0.0);(x1;x2;x3);2],
      dist10: .quantQ.knn.distanceLX[(0.2;0.3;0.0);(x1;x2;x3);10] from
      tableFunction:([] x1:3?1.0;x2:3?1.0;x3:3?1.0;f:3?1.0)
```

```
x1        x2        x3        f         dist1    dist2     dist10
--------------------------------------------------------------------
0.3811122 0.7867853 0.5295997 0.2223885 1.197497 0.7417798 0.5489021
0.313977  0.6996214 0.6139158 0.7827882 1.127514 0.7413371 0.6147492
0.1812966 0.5284474 0.8214644 0.5669183 1.068615 0.8528433 0.8214646
```

Ordering of points based on their distance to the `point` depends on the value of parameter X. The third row is classified as the closest observation by choice of $X = 1$ while the other measures classify the same point as the most distant. The choice of the parameter X thus may affect results, and its role has to be investigated.

We can proceed with construction of the k-nearest neighbour classifier. The implementation is done in two steps:

- Identify the k neighbourhood of the test point.
- Classify the point.

In the first step, we consider the given point and calculate the distance to every point in the training sample. Then, we select k points from the training sample which are closest to the given point. We have to store only the value of a dependent variable for every chosen point and the distance to the point. The following function captures such a procedure:

```
.quantQ.knn.kNNneighbours:{[point;tableFunction;LX;k]
   // point -- N-dimensional array
   // tableFunction -- table with training data, first N are features, N+1-
       ↪ st is dependent
   // LX -- parameter of the distance measure
   // k -- number of nearest neighbours to be selected
   // returns dictionary with dependent variable (`f) and distance (`dist)
   :flip select[k] from `dist xasc
    ([] f: tableFunction[last cols tableFunction];
     dist: .quantQ.knn.distanceLX[point;tableFunction[cols[tableFunction]
         ↪ except `f];LX]);
};
```

The function takes four arguments: the point for which the neighbourhood is being sought, the training sample with data in the form of a table, the parameter of the distance measure, and the size of the neighbourhood to be returned. The output is a dictionary of classes and corresponding distances.

Let us examine an example. First, define a point to be classified,

```
point:(0.2;0.3;0);
```

then, the training data. We use a randomly generated table without any pattern,

```
n:10000;
tableFunction:([] x1:n?1.0;x2:n?1.0;x3:n?1.0;f:n?4);
```

and then find the corresponding neighbourhood of size `10` and with Euclidean distance metrics:

```
.quantQ.knn.kNNneighbours[point;tableFunction;2;10]
```

```
(`f`dist)!(3j, 2j, 1j, 3j, 3j, 3j, 0j, 3j, 1j, 2j;0.1984643 0.2137866
    ↪ 0.2309698 0.2360172 0.2433415 0.2647322 0.2927005 0.3046259
    ↪ 0.3178132 0.3303349)
```

The neighbourhood is sorted by distance.

In the second step, we proceed with classification based on the selected neighbourhood. The conventional approach is the majority vote: the point is classified based on the most common class within the selected neighbourhood. If there is a tie between two or more classes, one is chosen randomly.

Function `kNNclassifyMajorityVote` takes as an argument the outcome of function `kNNneighbours` and returns class based on the majority vote. The function is implemented as follows:

```
.quantQ.knn.kNNclassifyMajorityVote:{[kNN]
   // kNN -- output of kNNneighbours function
   // sort classes by number of votes obtained
   votesTab: 0!`cntF xdesc select cntF:count f by f from flip kNN;
   // return class which was favoured by votes (select randomly if more
       ↪ than one)
   :first 1?exec f from votesTab where cntF=max votesTab[`cntF];
};
```

Continuing with the setup introduced above:

```
.quantQ.knn.kNNclassifyMajorityVote .quantQ.knn.kNNneighbours[point;
    ↪ tableFunction;2;10]
```

which returns class:

```
3j
```

The majority vote is not the only option we can use to classify the unknown observation. The distance-weighted rule looks not at just the number of points in the neighbourhood of the given class, but also their distance to the point itself. The distance-weighted classification works as follows: consider n points in the selected neighbourhood, where each point is described by two values (c_i, d_i), with $i = 1, \ldots, n$ and d_i being the distance of i-th point, and c_i its class. First, we normalise the distances to sum up to 1:

$$d'_i = \frac{d_i}{\sum_i d_i}, \tag{21.2}$$

with d'_i being normalised distances.

The distance-weighted scheme chooses the class based on the following formula:

$$\tilde{c} = \arg\min_{c'} \sum_{i,c_i=c'} (1 - d'_i). \tag{21.3}$$

The weight in the scheme is $(1 - d_i')$. The higher the weight, the closer the given point is. We consider such quantity as "proximity". The class is chosen based on the overall amount of proximity within the chosen neighbourhood. The alternative explanation for $(1 - d_i')$ is a probability to classify i-th neighbourhood point as c_i and $1 - (1 - d_i')$ otherwise.

The distance-weighted decision rule is implemented in function `kNNclassifyDistanceWeighted`, which works in the same manner as `kNNclassifyMajorityVote`.

```
.quantQ.knn.kNNclassifyDistanceWeighted:{[kNN]
   // kNN -- output of kNNneighbours function
   // normalize distances to sum up to one
   normDist:exec sum dist from flip kNN;
   // sort classes by total weight of votes
   votesTab: 0!`cntF xdesc select cntF:sum weight by f from update weight
      ↪ :1-dist%normDist from flip kNN;
   // return class which was favoured by weighted votes (select randomly if
      ↪ more than one)
   :first 1?exec f from votesTab where cntF=max votesTab[`cntF];
 };
```

Let us continue in the example above and classify `point` based on the distance-weighted scheme:

```
.quantQ.knn.kNNclassifyDistanceWeighted .quantQ.knn.kNNneighbours[point;
    ↪ tableFunction;2;10]
```

gives the same class as the method above.

```
3j
```

The two rules can be wrapped within one function. For example, we can create a dictionary, and the classification function is in fact a dictionary with a chosen argument. We encourage the reader to construct such a dictionary as an exercise.

21.2 PROTOTYPE CLUSTERING

The previous method is compelling as it does not assume any parametric form and can be tuned well to fit many examples. Both regression and classification have the same functional form. The distinct disadvantage is a requirement to have the large data set in memory as a "model" (training sample used on the fly), and whenever the classification/regression is performed, we have to work with the full sample. Depending on how much RAM we have availble on our processing server, this may become problematic.

In this section, we focus on the prototype method, which is a classification method where we identify regions in the parametric space which exhibit the same support of the dependent variable. The centre then characterises such a region. Every region may have several centres, which are learned in the training sample. In the prediction/out-of-sample step, the predicted value of the dependent variable is determined by the value of the nearest centre.

Let us proceed more specifically, where we are equipped with a training data set as in the previous method, which contains N independent variables, x_i, all of the numeric type. Let us further assume that these variables are each normalised using the z-score. Further, the data set contains one dependent variable, f, which is of integer value. The support of f is finite, and we further assume that cardinality of each value of the variable f is rather large. This is not a mathematical constraint but rather a practical constraint, where the reader should appropriately treat all the pathological cases with having isolated values. Let us assume the dependent variable f takes L different values which we need to classify.

The following algorithm defines the prototype method based on the nearest neighbours:

- Split the sample by the value of the dependent variable f into L subsamples. Further, proceed for each subsample independently:
  - For a given subsample, choose R observations randomly. Those observations are centres or the prototypes for a given subsample.
  - For each centre, find k nearest neighbours from the subsample.
  - Replace the centre by the new centre, which is the average of the k neighbours and the centre itself.
  - Iterate this procedure until convergence.
- Replace the training sample by $L \times R$ centres. Each centre carries information about the value of f.
- Predict the class of the out-of-sample observation by the class of the nearest neighbour.

This procedure is known in the literature as k-means clustering.

Let us implement the prototype method using the following case: each observation is formed by (x_1, x_2, f), where $x_i \in [0, 1]$, for $i = 1, 2$, and the dependent variable is defined as

$$f = I_{\{x_1^2+x_2^2<=1\}}, \tag{21.4}$$

where I is the indicator function taking value one when the argument is true and zero otherwise. We thus have a dependent variable which classifies whether the point – in feature space – lies within a circle with centre in origin and radius equal to one. In q, such data can be generated as follows:

```
tableKNN:([] x1:10000?1.0;x2:10000?1.0);
tableKNN: update f:1>(x1*x1)+(x2*x2) from tableKNN;
```

We have generated 10,000 points. We can illustrate the data using the following "trick":

```
(select x1,x2_0:x2 from tableKNN where f=0 ) uj (select x1,x2_1:x2 from
    ↪ tableKNN where f=1 )
```

which can be depicted with the scatter plot option. Figure 21.1 depicts the result, where all points within the unit circle are dark gray and the remaining ones are plotted in light gray.

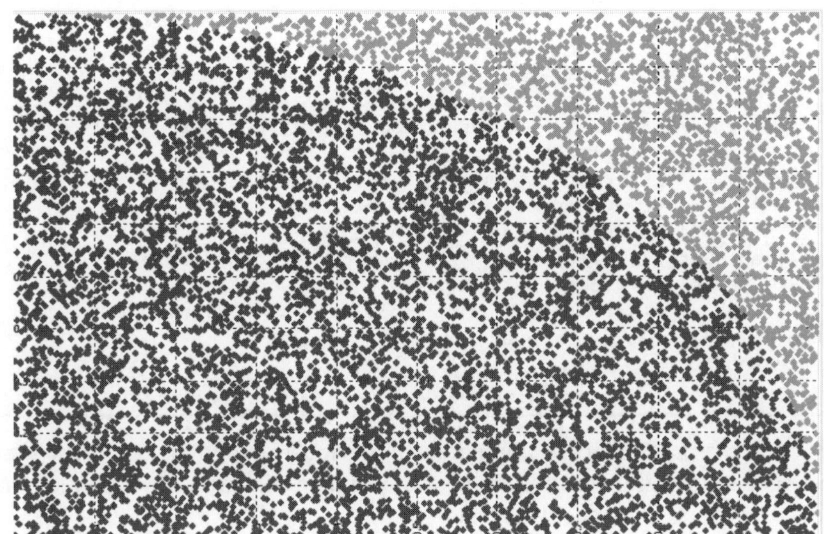

FIGURE 21.1 Scatter plot of true clusters as defined in `tableKNN`

It is convenient to work with the following data arrangement,

```
tableKNN: select x:flip (x1;x2),f from tableKNN;
```

where we have only two variables: the first one is an array of the factors, the second one being the classifier, in our case the binary variable f. The implementation assumes such a form of data where array x is of any dimension. The q function reads:

LISTING 21.1

```
.quantQ.knn.prototypeKNN:{[table;k;R;iterations]
    // table -- the training data with array of features x and the
        ↪ classifier (dependent variable) f
    // k -- the size of the neighbourhood
    // R -- the number of centres per each class
    // iterations -- the number of iterations
    // all distinct values
    valuesF: exec distinct f from table;
    // "parallel loop" over all distinct values of dependent variable
    tableGlobalOut:raze {[table;k;R;iterations;fRealization]
        // create a sub-sample
        tableSub: select centre:x from table where f=fRealization;
        // output table, contains initial draws of centres
        tableOut: update centreID:1+i from (neg R)?(select centre:x,f from
            ↪ table where f=fRealization);
        // loop over each centre
        centresNew:{[tableSub;k;iterations;centre]
            // for each centre, iterate search using neighbours
            {[tableSub;k;centreX]
```

```
                tableX:update distVect:.quantQ.knn.distanceLX[centreX;;2]
                    ↪ flip centre from tableSub;
                // sort table
                tableX:`distVect xasc tableX;
                // choose the neighbourhood, include centre itself
                tableX: tableX[til k+1];
                // calculate the mean of the neighbourhood
                :exec avg centre from tableX;
            }[tableSub;k]/[iterations;centre]
        }[tableSub;k;iterations;] each exec centre from tableOut;
        // update the tableOut by setting the new centres
        update centre:centresNew from tableOut
    }[table;k;R;iterations;] peach valuesF;
    :tableGlobalOut;
};
```

The function uses L_2 distance as implemented previously in distanceLX. The function is also prepared for parallelisation in the topmost loop where peach is applied over all distinct values of the dependent variable.

We can run an example for $R = 6$ centres; each centre is found using $k = 12$ nearest neighbours, and each search is iterated 1000 times:

```
resultKNN:.quantQ.knn.prototypeKNN[tableKNN;12;6;1000];
resultKNN
```

```
centre                     f  centreID
----------------------------------
0.3251196 0.3038678        1  1
0.7374341 0.650928         1  2
0.1197821 0.6141843        1  3
0.6798257 0.6033659        1  4
0.2202886 0.0632962        1  5
0.3205736 0.7321857        1  6
0.8268309 0.8217146        0  1
0.9843239 0.6751862        0  2
0.912804 0.7239548         0  3
0.5214162 0.9187594        0  4
0.9451731 0.8858281        0  5
0.9756126 0.7372355        0  6
```

The graphical output can be obtained by scatter plot option using the table transformed by the following:

```
(select x1:centre[;0], x2_k0:centre[;1] from resultKNN where f=0)
uj
(select x1:centre[;0], x2_k1:centre[;1] from resultKNN where f=1)
uj
([] x1:0.01*til 100; x2_boundary:sqrt[1-(0.01*til 100) xexp 2])
```

We have explicitly generated points on the boundary, so we see where the centres were identified. The graphical output from qPad can be seen in Figure 21.2, which contains the trained centres using the function prototypeKNN. The black points correspond to the case of $f = 0$ and gray ones to $f = 1$.

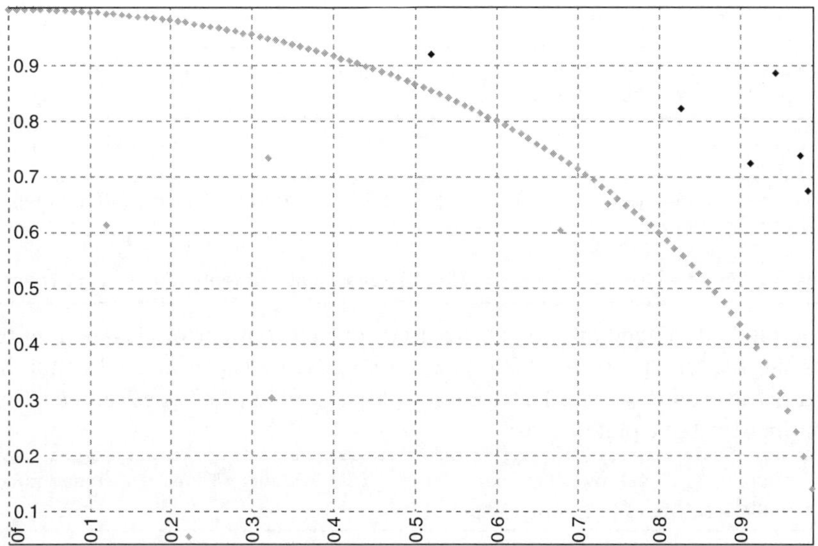

FIGURE 21.2 Black and gray plots are the prototypes for each class as identified by `.quantQ.knn.prototypeKNN` function

The trained points are not sufficient to serve as trustworthy and accurate prototypes to the two regions selected. This can be solved by increasing the number of prototypes. Let us illustrate how the prototypes perform for the out-of-sample test. Let us create a function which assigns a class to a point based on the proximity to the trained centres.

```
.quantQ.knn.getPrototypeKNN:{[tablesCentre;point]
   // tablesCentre -- the table with trained centres, contains variables
       ↪ centre and f
   // point -- the array to classify
   // table with proximity of a point to the centres
   tablesCentreX:`distVect xasc update distVect:.quantQ.knn.distanceLX[
       ↪ point;;2]
       flip centre from tablesCentre;
   // class of nearest centre
   :first exec f from tablesCentreX;
};
```

Moreover, we can test it as

```
.quantQ.knn.getPrototypeKNN[resultKNN;.2 .3]
```

```
1b
```

To see how the trained prototype centres classify region, we perform a following sweep through the entire space $[0, 1] \times [0, 1]$:

```
tableSweep:([] points:((0.01*til 100) cross (0.01*til 100)));
```

assign class for every point,

```
tableSweep: update fTrained: .quantQ.knn.getPrototypeKNN[resultKNN; ] each
    ↪ points from tableSweep;
```

and depict the table:

```
tableSweepPlot:(select x1:points[;0], x2_k0:points[;1] from tableSweep
    ↪ where fTrained=0)
uj
(select x1:points[;0], x2_k1:points[;1] from tableSweep where fTrained=1);
```

The method is general and can be used for any number of classes. Figure 21.3 depicts the scatter plot of the table `tableSweepPlot`. The recovered shape indeed resembles the original shape. The accuracy of the trained prototypes can be seen from the contingency table obtained as:

```
select count fTrained by fTrained,fTrue from update fTrue: {1.0>sum x*x}
    ↪ each points  from tableSweep
```

```
fTrained fTrue|     fTrained
--------------|--------------
0        0    |     1817
0        1    |     389
1        0    |     234
1        1    |     7560
```

We see that accuracy in assigning the correct class is 93.7%, which is not bad given we have replaced the structure in the entire region by 10 points–centres. A further step

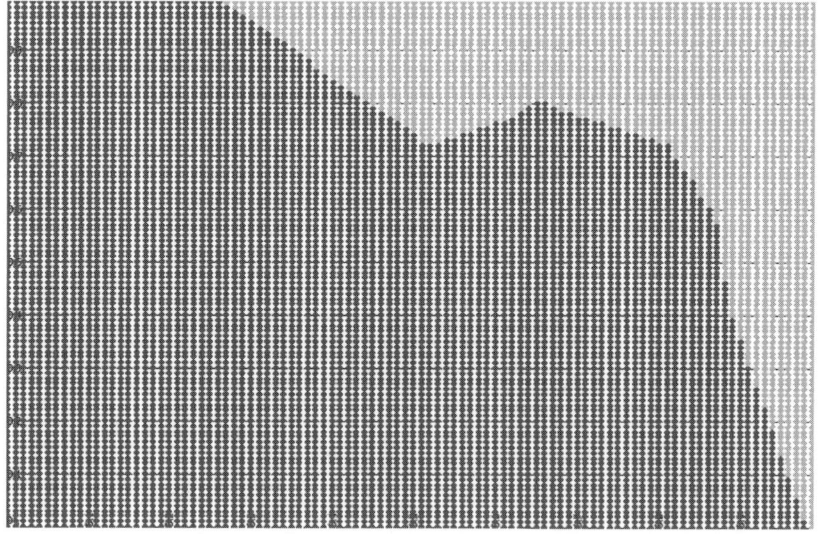

FIGURE 21.3 The two clusters identified by the classification algorithm as defined in `tableKNN`

could be to explore the tools in more depth by finding out what the optimal size of R is in terms of the power of the out-of-sample test and various regions/number of classes.

21.3 FEATURE SELECTION: LOCAL NEAREST NEIGHBOURS APPROACH

The concept of nearest neighbours as introduced above is a rather brute force approach which aims to exploit similarity between past observations for the prediction of future states. This can be used out-of-sample or even in real time. In this section, we employ the nearest neighbours for feature selection as was introduced by Navot et al. (2006). The aim of the presented method is not a prediction, but dimensionality reduction in the space of the independent variables.

The method comes from the field of biostatistics; it was invented for analysing cortical neural activity, namely, to search through the high-dimensional space of neural features and explain the particular neural activity. The proposed algorithm extends the leave-one-out algorithm with mean-squared-error, where the optimal feature set is found using the forward selection algorithm, investigating the importance of features one by one. The proposed algorithm assigns weights to features and also a score. This makes the problem differentiable, so the gradient can be calculated analytically and gradient descent type of algorithms can be used to find the optimal weights. The features can therefore be sorted based on the assigned weights.

The method can be also viewed as an extension of the *kNN* regression, which assigns the value of a dependent variable for a point x, being n-dimensional vector of independent variables, based on the average value of the neighbourhood N as:

$$\hat{y} = \frac{1}{\text{card } N} \sum_{x' \in N} y(x'), \tag{21.5}$$

the average of the value of the dependent variables in the neighbourhood of $y(x)$. The neighbourhood is defined in the same way as in the previous sections. Analogously to the distance-weighted function `kNNclassifyDistanceWeighted`, we can define the weighted average for regression based on the proximity, L_2 distance, as:

$$\hat{y} = \frac{1}{\sum_{x' \in N} e^{-\frac{1}{\beta}\|x-x'\|^2}} \sum_{x' \in N} y(x') e^{-\frac{1}{\beta}\|x-x'\|^2}. \tag{21.6}$$

The factor in front of the sum normalises the estimate – average – based on the weights derived from $\|x - x'\|$. The weights themselves do not have to be normalised.

The purpose of the algorithm is to assess the importance of individual independent variables. We thus introduce the weighted norm:

$$\|x - x'\|_w^2 = \sum (x_i - x_i')^2 \, w_i^2, \tag{21.7}$$

where w_i is an n-dimensional vector of weights, which puts different emphasis on different independent variables. We do not need to impose any normalisation on weights.

Having in hand the weighted norm, we define the weighted regression equation:

$$\hat{y}_w = \frac{1}{\sum_{x' \in N} e^{-\frac{1}{\beta}||x-x'||^2_w}} \sum_{x' \in N} y(x') e^{-\frac{1}{\beta}||x-x'||^2_w}. \tag{21.8}$$

Finally, we define a score function which assesses the performance of each vector of weights, w. The score is defined as the negative mean-squared error:

$$e(w) = -\frac{1}{2} \sum_x (y(x) - \hat{y}_w(x))^2, \tag{21.9}$$

where we have used a factor of $1/2$ for convenience. The method itself incorporates leave-one-out cross-validation approach as the estimated value of y for a given x does not use x itself.

Further, it is important to stress that the function is continuous in w. This is an essential feature as it allows us to obtain an analytic expression for the first derivative of the score concerning weights. Gradient-descent type of methods can be employed in order to find out weights, which optimise score. This is detailed below.

The algorithm for feature selection can be specified as follows:

- Initialize $w = (1, 1, \dots, 1)$, set $K = 1$.
- Perform an update of weights:
  - Pick datum x from the training set.
  - Calculate the gradient of the loss function (L_2 norm) as a function of weights

$$\nabla e(w) = -\sum_x \left(f(x) - \hat{f}_w(x)\right) \nabla_w \hat{f}_w(x), \tag{21.10}$$

$$\nabla_w \hat{f}_w(x) = \frac{-\frac{4}{\beta}\sum_{x'',x'} f(x'') a(x', x'') u(x', x'')}{\sum_{x'',x'} a(x', x'')}, \tag{21.11}$$

with

$$a(x', x'') = \exp(-(||x - x'||^2_w + ||x - x''||^2_w)/\beta), \tag{21.12}$$

and vector u with components

$$u_i = w_i[(x - x')^2 + (x - x'')^2]. \tag{21.13}$$

  - Update $w = w + \eta_K \nabla e(w) = w(1 + \eta_K \nabla_w \hat{f}_w(x))$.
- Update the counter $K = K + 1$ and repeat the update of weights until convergence is achieved.

21.3.1 Implementation

In the following part we implement the procedure in q. We build the implementation in several steps for the sake of illustration. We encourage the reader to simplify the code into one robust and optimised function.

Let us consider our data set to be of the following format:

```
tableFunction:([] coord1:"f"$();coord2:"f"$();coord3:"f"$();...; val:"f"$()
    ↪ );
```

where we consider n independent variables `coordi` and one dependent variable `val`. We further assume that dependent variables are normalized using one of the normalization techniques. The feature selection based on nearest neighbours is built as follows.

First, we define the weighted L_2-norm, $||x - x'||_w^2$, as:

```
.quantQ.knn.weightedL2norm:{[x;y;weight]
   // x, y -- n-dimensional arrrays (two points in feature space)
   // weight -- n-dimensional array of weights
   :t wsum t:weight*x-y;
};
```

where `x`, `y`, `weight` are three vectors of the same length, n, and the function returns $||x - y||_w^2$.

We implement a local estimator of the value function in the neighbourhood coordinates of a given point, $\hat{y}_w$, where the neighbourhood is weighted by its proximity to the point using the weighted L_2-norm as calculated by `weightedL2norm`:

```
.quantQ.knn.kNNMeanFunction:{[coordX;coordY;valueY;weights;beta]
   // coordX -- n-dimensional array (point to make regression)
   // coordY -- kNN x n array, k observations of n-dimensional arrays
   // valueY -- kNN-dimensional array of dependent variables
   // weights -- n-dimensional array of weights
   // beta -- parameter of the algorithm
   // returns MSE-based score
   :(1%(sum exp neg (1%beta)*.quantQ.knn.weightedL2norm[coordX;;weights]
       ↪ each coordY))*sum
       valueY*exp neg (1%beta) *.quantQ.knn.weightedL2norm[coordX;;weights
           ↪ ] each coordY;
};
```

In order to implement the algorithm, we have to implement several building blocks. In particular, we define five separate functions which form the basis of the algorithm. First, we implement the error function, $e(w)$, a negative of the mean-squared error of the weighted estimator and unweighted one. The function has the same arguments as the previous function `kNNMeanFunction`:

```
.quantQ.knn.errorLocal:{[coordX;coordY;valueY;weights;beta]
   // coordX -- n-dimensional array (point to make regression)
   // coordY -- kNN x n array, k observations of n-dimensional arrays
   // valueY -- kNN-dimensional array of dependent variables
   // weights -- n-dimensional array of weights
   // beta -- parameter of the algorithm
   // returns error at local point
   :neg 0.5*t*t:(.quantQ.knn.kNNMeanFunction[coordX;coordY;valueY;weights;
       ↪ beta]-
       .quantQ.knn.kNNMeanFunction[coordX;coordY;valueY;(count weight)#1;
           ↪ beta]);
};
```

Let us further define an a function and u function, respectively:

```
.quantQ.knn.aFunc:{[coordX;coordXb;coordXbb;beta;weights]
   // coordX, coordXb, and coordXbb -- n-dimensional arrays (three points)
   // weights -- n-dimensional array of weights
   // beta -- parameter of the algorithm
   // returns aFunc
   :exp neg ((.quantQ.knn.weightedL2norm[coordX;coordXb;weights]+
       .quantQ.knn.weightedL2norm[coordX;coordXbb;weights])%beta);
};
```

```
.quantQ.knn.uFunc:{[coordX;coordXb;coordXbb;weights]
   // coordX, coordXb, and coordXbb -- n-dimensional arrays (three points)
   // weight -- n-dimensional array of weights
   // returns uFunc
   :weights*(t*t:(coordX-coordXb))+(u*u:(coordX-coordXbb));
};
```

We can proceed with the definition of the gradient of the function, $\nabla_w \hat{f}_w(x)$:

```
.quantQ.knn.gradFunc:{[coordX;coordY;valueY;weights;beta]
   // coordX -- n-dimensional array
   // coordY -- kNN x n array, k observations of n-dimensional arrays
   // valueY -- kNN-dimensional array of dependent variables
   // weights -- n-dimensional array of weights
   // beta -- parameter of the algorithm
   // returns gradient of a function
   :(1%sum {[coordX;coordY;beta;weights;x]
            .quantQ.knn.aFunc[coordX;coordY[x[0]];coordY[x[1]];beta;weights
                ↪ ]
          }[coordX;coordY;beta;weights;] each
          (t cross t:til count coordY))*neg (4%beta)*
        sum {[valueY;coordX;coordY;beta;weights;x]
              valueY[x[1]]*
              .quantQ.knn.aFunc[coordX;coordY[x[0]];coordY[x[1]];beta;
                  ↪ weights]*
              .quantQ.knn.uFunc[coordX;coordY[x[0]];coordY[x[1]];weights]
              }[valueY;coordX;coordY;beta;weights;] each
              (t cross t:til count coordY);
};
```

Finally, we construct the gradient of the error, $\nabla e(w)$, along which we will search for the features explaining most of the dependent variables:

```
.quantQ.knn.gradError:{[coordFull;valueFull;weights;beta;fractionS;kNN]
   // coordFull -- k x n array, k observations of n-dimensional arrays
   // valueFull -- k-dimensional array of dependent variables
   // fractionS -- relative size of the data used in assessing the score
   // kNN -- number of nearest neighbours used for regression around each
       ↪ point
   // weight -- n-dimensional array of weights
   // beta -- parameter of the algorithm
   dim: count coordFull;
   setS: asc(neg ceiling[fractionS*dim])?dim;
```

```
    // returns gradient of error at given weights
    :neg sum{[coordFull;valueFull;weights;beta;i;kNN]
        coordX:coordFull[i];
        valueX:valueFull[i];
        dim: count coordFull;
        vecDist: .quantQ.knn.weightedL2norm[coordFull[i];;weights] each
            ↪ coordFull;
        neighbourhood: where vecDist<=(first (kNN-1)_(asc vecDist));
        x1:coordFull[neighbourhood];
        y1:valueFull[neighbourhood];
        :.quantQ.knn.gradFunc[coordX;x1;y1;weights;beta]*(valueX-
            .quantQ.knn.kNNMeanFunction[coordX;x1;y1;weights;beta]);
    }[coordFull;valueFull;weights;beta;;kNN] each setS;
};
```

We combine all the above-defined functions into the iterative algorithm to select the features following the gradient descent approach from data set `coordFull` and `valueFull`. The iterative algorithm initiates the weights to 1. The function defines an internal function `kNNUpdateWeights`, which represents one run of the algorithm, i.e. one update of weights. The updating is based on the gradient of the error, where the updates are being weighted by the decaying learning ratio, driven by `learningRatio` and `decay`. The algorithm relies on nearest neighbours and the size of the neighbourhood used for the *kNN* regressions is given by `kNN`, which enters as another parameter. Further, the parameter β, or inverse temperature, is provided as `beta`. In every iteration, we need to calculate the properties of score measure and the derivatives. We do not use the full sample for these calculations, but a fraction of the entire data set, `fractionS`. Finally, we specify as the last input the number of iterations, `nIterations`, the algorithm will take. The parameters are wrapped within a dictionary for convenience.

```
.quantQ.knn.kNNFeatureSelection:{[bucket]
    // bucket -- dictionary with variables of the model
    // bucket[`coordFull] -- k x n array, k observations of n-dimensional
        ↪ arrays
    // bucket[`valueFull] -- k-dimensional array of dependent variables
    // bucket[`learningRatio] -- learning ratio
    // bucket[`decay] -- parameter for decaying learning ratio
    // bucket[`kNN] -- number of nearest neighbours used for regression
        ↪ around each point
    // bucket[`beta] -- parameter of the algorithm
    // bucket[`fractionS] -- relative size of the data used in each
        ↪ iteration of the algorithm
    // bucket[`nIterations] -- number of iterations
    nFeatures: count flip bucket[`coordFull];
    // initiate weights with 1's
    weightInit:nFeatures#1.0;
    // one-iteration function, defined internally
    kNNUpdateWeights:{[coordFull;valueFull;learningRatio;decay;kNN;beta;
        ↪ fractionS;bucket]
        :`weight`cnt!(bucket[`weight]+learningRatio*(decay xexp bucket[`cnt
            ↪ ])*
            .quantQ.knn.gradError[coordFull;valueFull;bucket[`weight];beta;
                ↪ fractionS;kNN];bucket[`cnt]+1);
    };
```

```
    // loop to iterate the algorithm nIterations times, return outcome
    :(kNNUpdateWeights[bucket[`coordFull];bucket[`valueFull];bucket[`
        ↪ learningRatio];
        bucket[`decay];bucket[`kNN];bucket[`beta];bucket[`fractionS];]\)[
            ↪ bucket[`nIterations];
        `weight`cnt!(weightInit;0)];
};
```

Time to illustrate its usage with an example. We define a data set with three independent variables and one dependent variable:

```
coord1:100?1.0;
coord2:100?1.0;
coord3:100?1.0;
val: (0.2*coord1)+(0.5*coord2)+(100?0.3);
```

The dependent variable `val` does not depend on variable `coord3` while the strongest link is with `coord2`. Let us then pack the variables within a table:

```
tableFunction:([] coord1;coord2;coord3; val);
```

The `kNNFeatureSelection` function requires as an input dictionary with number of parameters. Defining the following values:

```
coordFull: flip value exec coord1, coord2, coord3 from tableFunction;
valueFull: exec val from tableFunction;
kNN:5;
learningRatio:0.01;
decay:1;
beta:0.05;
fractionS:0.5;
nIterations:100;
```

and wrapping them into the dictionary:

```
bucket:(`coordFull`valueFull`kNN`learningRatio`decay`beta`fractionS`
    ↪ nIterations)!
      (coordFull;valueFull;kNN;learningRatio;decay;beta;fractionS;
          ↪ nIterations);
```

The values chosen, among others, do not provide any decay of the learning ratio. The number of iterations is fixed to 100 while the *kNN* neighbourhood size is to be small, 5. In every iteration, half of the sample is used.

The iteration is run as:

```
kNNtab:.quantQ.knn.kNNFeatureSelection[bucket]
```

saving the result into the table `kNNtab`.

We can explore the outcome:

```
last kNNtab
```

```
(`weight`cnt)!(1.122086 1.209277 1.036502;100j)
```

The weights for three features are `coord1:1.122086`, `coord2:1.209277`, and `coord3:1.036502`. The second feature gets the highest weight, suggesting the largest importance, while least importance is on the third feature. This conforms with the underlying data structure.

Let us depict the evolution of weights:

```
select cnt, w1:weight[;0], w2:weight[;1], w3:weight[;2] from  kNNtab
```

Figure 21.4 depicts the evolution of three weights corresponding to the three features as a function of the number of iterations taken. The three lines are `coord1` (light gray line), `coord2` (black line), and `coord3` (dark gray line). The figure shows that the difference between three weights is growing in absolute value. The values are not by any means saturated and the system is still evolving. Since the weights are not forced to be normalised, the value of interest is rather the relative difference between the weights.

The exercise can be further extended for more complex problems. It is also interesting to investigate the evolution of weights. They are random as we are using only a fraction (random one) of the data set in each iteration. It is also worth considering renormalisation of the weights in every iteration step, for instance, to fix $\|w\| = 1$. The absolute values of weights could be then used to assess the importance of features across different problems.

To motivate readers to extend the presented exercise, Figure 21.5 depicts the evolution of three weights corresponding to the three features as a function of the number of iterations taken for 10,000 steps. The three lines are `coord1` (light gray line), `coord2` (black line), and `coord3` (dark gray line). Compared to Figure 21.4, current figure has weights normalised as $\|w\| = 1$, where normalisation was done ex post. The dynamics

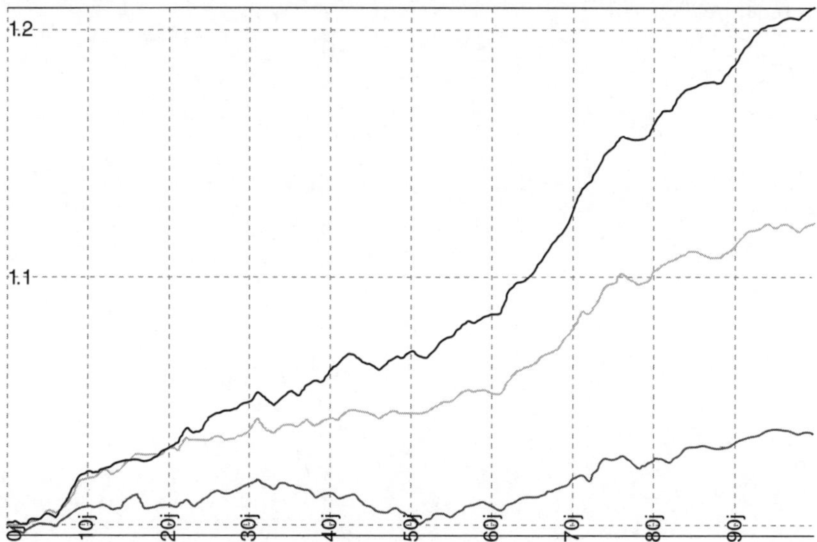

FIGURE 21.4 Evolution of weights for three features `coord1` (light gray), `coord2` (black), and `coord3` (dark gray), as a function of number of iterations

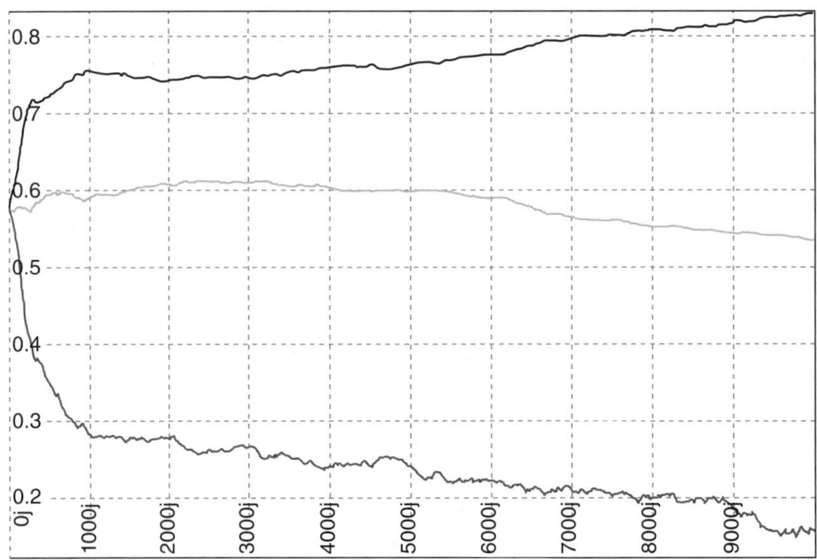

FIGURE 21.5 Evolution of normalised weights for three features `coord1` (light gray), `coord2` (black), and `coord3` (dark gray), as a function of number of iterations, for 10,000 runs

of weights get more stable after approximately 1000 runs. The weight for the third feature tends to 0 as expected while the other two features have weights different from zero, both sorted by value according to their importance. The figure suggests an extension towards an algorithm where we iterate for as long as we eliminate features with weights reaching 0.

CHAPTER 22

Neural Networks

The focus of this chapter is nothing less than neural networks. The term covers a number of related methods and techniques and represents one of the most rapidly growing domains in the machine learning literature. In this chapter, we aim to convince the reader that q can be used to work with neural networks as well. We implement a neural network–based classifier and regressor within a few lines of code and successfully apply it in practice.

We do not claim that q on its own is the language of choice for neural networks and their applications to complex problems. Deep networks, convoluted neural networks, or long short-term memory (LSTM) could be programmed in q, but their implementation would require a significant time investment. This is beyond the scope of our book, and we keep this for future work.

The terminology of neural networks comes from their original purpose: to model the functions of the human brain. The model was microscopic, i.e. modelling each neuron explicitly and parameterising how the signal spreads across the network of neurons. The most straightforward implementation was using step functions with certain thresholds as models for neurons' responses. The terminology from its original purpose persisted into current days; further, it gives the neural network models a certain metaphysical flavour.

22.1 THEORETICAL INTRODUCTION

Let us start with an introduction to neural networks. Our objective is to acquire an understanding of neural networks with a single hidden layer. It is called hidden, because it is neither the input nor the output layer, but appears inside the neural network. This is a slightly simplified setup while there are a plethora of more elaborate setups of neural networks in the literature. We encourage interested readers to fulfil their curiosity in specialised publications; see, for instance, Aggarwal (2018).

Despite the simplicity of our choice, neural networks with a single hidden layer capture all nonlinear relationships between the dependent variable and features. Thus we shall restrict our attention to neural networks with a single hidden layer.

We are provided with an M-dimensional array of features $X_1, \dots, X_M$, and our aim is to predict L dependent variables $Y_1, \dots, Y_L$. The general dimension of the dependent variable allows us to formulate regression and L-class classification within one framework. For regression we usually set $L = 1$ while for L-class classification each l, with $l = 1, \dots, L$, corresponds to one of the classes.

The application of a neural network is a two-stage procedure:

- *The first stage:* Map between the input features and the hidden layer.
- *The second stage:* Map between the hidden layer and the dependent variable.

The neural network is frequently depicted using the following scheme:

$$\begin{bmatrix} X_0 \\ X_1 \\ \vdots \\ X_M \end{bmatrix} \overset{\text{Stage 1:}\eta}{\rightarrow} \begin{bmatrix} Z_0 \\ Z_1 \\ \vdots \\ Z_N \end{bmatrix} \overset{\text{Stage 2:}\tau}{\rightarrow} \begin{bmatrix} Y_1 \\ \vdots \\ Y_L \end{bmatrix}. \tag{22.1}$$

We have added X_0 and Z_0, respectively. Those variables are frequently referred to as the bias and represent a constant shift in the model. The vector Z corresponds to the hidden layer. This layer is not visible outside of the model and corresponds to the latent variables of the model. This layer is essential to capture nonlinearities. For more complex neural network topologies, the hidden layers encapsulate memory and perception of general features.

The first stage

First, the map between the observed data, $X_0, X_1, \dots, X_M$, and the hidden layer, $Z_1, \dots, Z_N$, is provided. The map is modelled as:

$$Z_n = \eta\left(\alpha_0^{(n)} X_0 + \alpha_1^{(n)} X_1 + \cdots + \alpha_M^{(n)} X_M\right), \tag{22.2}$$

where $n = 1, \dots, N$, and $\alpha_m^{(n)}$ are parameters of the map. The activation function η can be thought of as neuron. There are a number of popular choices:

- Sigmoid function: $\eta(x) = \frac{1}{1+\exp(-x)}$.
- Hyperbolic tangent function: $\eta(x) = \frac{\exp(x)-\exp(-x)}{\exp(x)+\exp(-x)}$.
- RELU, or rectified linear unit function: $\eta(x) = \max(0, x)$.

Thus, in general, every node of the hidden layer, Z_n, is a function of all input nodes and the bias node. The hidden layer nodes serve as input for the second stage with the output layer.

The second stage

Second, the map between the hidden layer, $Z_0, Z_1, \dots, Z_N$, and the dependent variable(s), $Y_1, \dots, Y_L$, is defined. The form of the function τ depends on the problem at hand and the particular neurons can have the following form (the function in the output layer is usually also called an activation function):

- Regression with $L = 1$: Linear activation function:

$$\tau(\beta_0 Z_0 + \beta_1 Z_1 + \cdots + \beta_N Z_N) = \beta_0 Z_0 + \beta_1 Z_1 + \cdots + \beta_N Z_N. \tag{22.3}$$

- Classification with L classes: Softmax function assigning probability to every class:

$$\tau_l = \frac{\beta_0^{(l)} Z_0 + \beta_1^{(l)} Z_1 + \cdots + \beta_N^{(l)} Z_N}{\sum_{l'=1}^{L} \beta_0^{(l')} Z_0 + \beta_1^{(l')} Z_1 + \cdots + \beta_N^{(l')} Z_N}. \tag{22.4}$$

The provided functions are for illustration. In general, the activation function of the output layer depends on the cost function. We require that the first derivative of the cost function with respect to the hidden layer be easy to compute. For instance, for $L = 1$, we set the cost function to be the square of the difference between the predicted output value and the true value:

$$Loss(Y, Z) = \frac{1}{2}(y - \tau(Z))^2, \tag{22.5}$$

then the first derivative reads:

$$\frac{\partial Loss(Y, Z)}{\partial Z} = \tau(Z) - y, \tag{22.6}$$

which is a straightforward expression to operate with. Analogously, the same argument can be applied to classification and the cross-entropy cost function.

Keep in mind that the activation function may affect the performance of the algorithm and thus its form is a hyper- or meta-parameter of the model. It is worth trying several forms based on the problem at hand.

There are many ways to interpret a neural network. For regression, we can think of the neural network as a standard linear regression, where independent variables entering the regression is a "neuron" expansion of the original input variables. This method is similar to methods where input variables are expanded in a particular basis, and the expansion is used in the linear model. It can thus be thought of as some form of generalisation of the linear regression, where nonlinearity is brought in through the basis – neuron – expansion. For classification problems, we may interpret the neural network as an "advisory committee" where individual "advisors" – nodes in the hidden layer – are weighted according to an activation function.

The hidden nodes thus play an important role, either as a basis for the expansions or as "advisors". They are referred to as hidden as they are not directly observable. They can, however, play a significant role and in specific problems they may be needed to be known explicitly. In particular, if $N < M$, the map from the input data to the hidden layer is a compression, since we reduce the dimensionality of the data. This itself can be utilised in dimensionality reduction problems (in fact, the autoencoder neural network with one hidden layer containing n neurons would be similar to extracting first n

components within principal component analysis (PCA), which is frequently used for dimensionality reduction).

22.1.1 Calibration

The neural network itself is rather intuitive, and two-stage regression/classification interpretation makes it transparent. What is less clear, however, is the procedure for the calibration of the weights, as the parameters of this model are frequently called. There are all together

$$N_{params} = L \cdot (N+1) + N \cdot (M+1) \tag{22.7}$$

parameters. The dimensionality of the problem is large.

Let us first propose an exact solution. We index the observations by index t, with $t = 1, \ldots, T$ observations in total.

Regression

Let us assume we want to regress the L-dimensional dependent variable Y_l. The loss function used is the sum of squared residuals:

$$\begin{aligned} Loss_{reg}(Y,X;\Theta) &= \sum_{t=1}^{T} R_t(Y,X;\Theta) \\ &= \sum_{t=1}^{T} R(y_t^{(1)},\ldots,y_t^{(L)},x_t^{(1)},\ldots,x_t^{(M)};\Theta) \\ &= \sum_{t=1}^{T}\sum_{l=1}^{L} (y_t^{(l)} - \tau_l(\beta_0^{(l)} Z_0(X;\alpha) + \beta_1^{(l)} Z_1(X;\alpha) + \cdots + \beta_N^{(l)} Z_N(X;\alpha)))^2, \end{aligned} \tag{22.8}$$

where each $Z_n(X;\alpha)$ is a further function of the input data X and parameters α, expressed symbolically for brevity, and Θ comprises all the parameters in the model. The linear activation function usually works well for regression problems. The loss function $Loss_{reg}(Y,X;\Theta)$ is minimised with respect to all the parameters Θ.

Classification

When we want to classify the L-dimensional dependent variable Y_l into L classes, a convenient loss function is the cross-entropy function:

$$Loss_{class}(Y,X;\Theta) = -\sum_{t=1}^{T}\sum_{l=1}^{L} y_t^{(l)} \log \tau_l\left(\beta_0^{(l)} Z_0(X;\alpha) + \beta_1^{(l)} Z_1(X;\alpha) + \cdots + \beta_N^{(l)} Z_N(X;\alpha)\right), \tag{22.9}$$

where the same description as for the regression holds. The choice of the activation function will affect the resulting model. Using the softmax function defined in eq. (22.4) and the majority vote, i.e. choosing the class according to:

$$\hat{L} = \arg\max_{l} \tau_l, \tag{22.10}$$

is a convenient choice. In addition, it affects the interpretability of the model. The model can be understood as a logistic regression in Z_l. This corresponds to a class of models which are extensively studied in the literature and are frequently used in practice.

22.1.1.1 Backpropagation

The exact solution for the parameter set Θ may not always be accessible or optimal. The solution can be overfitted as the neural network contains a large number of parameters and the expression for the parameters themselves may be cumbersome. A better approach is based on Rumelhart et al. (1986), a technique for backpropagation of errors for training neural networks. It is based on the optimisation method of gradient descent. It works as follows:

- Set the parameters of the model randomly.
- Propagate forward the input data and calculate the error of prediction at the output layer.
- Propagate backwards the errors through the network.
- Update the parameters of the model throughout the network based on the gradient of the error at each part of the network.

This mechanism, where the propagation goes forward and then backward, gives rise to an alternative name of the procedure, the *forward-backward* propagation. The procedure requires the knowledge of the gradient at each node. This is technically feasible for neural networks as chain rule can be used for calculating derivatives at each node. The procedure allows us to progress layer-by-layer and the information relevant for a given layer/node can be stored.

Let us derive the equations needed for the backpropagation algorithm, namely the gradients at each node. For that purpose, we will employ the square loss function for the regression problem with L dependent variables. Further, we need to express the equations describing the neural network for each observation. Thus, we denote every feature and dependent variable observed as $X_m = (x_{m1}, x_{m2}, \ldots, x_{mT})'$ and $Y_l = (y_{l1}, y_{l2}, \ldots, y_{lT})'$, respectively, where the observations are indexed by t. Analogously, the state of the hidden node of the neural network when t-th observation is read by the network follows:

$$z_{nt} = \eta\left(\alpha_0^{(n)} x_{0t} + \alpha_1^{(n)} x_{1t} + \cdots + \alpha_M^{(n)} x_{Mt}\right). \tag{22.11}$$

The gradient to be calculated is derived from eq. (22.8). We need to calculate derivatives with respect to the parameters α and β, respectively. We will use the chain rule for derivatives and thus will derive derivatives starting at the output node and proceeding towards the input node. Every node is chained to the previous one: the first derivative with respect to the parameter $\beta_n^{(l)}$ driving the error of the activation function reads

$$\frac{\partial R_t}{\partial \beta_n^{(l)}} = -2\left(y_t^{(l)} - \tau_l\left(\beta_0^{(l)} z_{0t}(X;\alpha) + \beta_1^{(l)} z_{1t}(X;\alpha) + \cdots + \beta_N^{(l)} z_{Nt}(X;\alpha)\right)\right) \times \tag{22.12}$$

$$\tau_l'\left(\beta_0^{(l)} z_{0t}(X;\alpha) + \beta_1^{(l)} z_{1t}(X;\alpha) + \cdots + \beta_N^{(l)} z_{Nt}(X;\alpha)\right) z_{nt}. \tag{22.13}$$

Then, using the chain rule, we can write down the first derivative with respect to $\alpha_m^{(n)}$:

$$\frac{\partial R_t}{\partial \alpha_m^{(n)}} = -2\sum_{l=1}^{L}\left(y_t^{(l)} - \tau_l\left(\beta_0^{(l)} z_{0t}(X;\alpha) + \beta_1^{(l)} z_{1t}(X;\alpha) + \cdots + \beta_N^{(l)} z_{Nt}(X;\alpha)\right)\right) \times \tag{22.14}$$

$$\tau_l'\left(\beta_0^{(l)} z_{0t}(X;\alpha) + \beta_1^{(l)} z_{1t}(X;\alpha) + \cdots + \beta_N^{(l)} z_{Nt}(X;\alpha)\right) \times \tag{22.15}$$

$$\beta_n^{(l)} \eta'\left(\alpha_0^{(n)} x_{0t} + \alpha_1^{(n)} X_{1t} + \cdots + \alpha_M^{(n)} X_{Mt}\right) x_{mt}. \tag{22.16}$$

Both derivatives allow us to quantify how much each node contributes to the error obtained by evaluating t-th observation. It drives the correction of the parameter(s) to be made in response to the observed error:

$$\frac{\partial R_t}{\partial \beta_n^{(l)}} = \Delta_{lt}^{(z)} z_{nt}, \tag{22.17}$$

$$\frac{\partial R_t}{\partial \alpha_m^{(n)}} = \Delta_{nt}^{(x)} x_{mt}. \tag{22.18}$$

We have written two derivatives as a product of the error for the current model evaluated against the t-th data point, $\Delta^{(z)}$ and $\Delta^{(x)}$, respectively, and the value of the node. We can define the iterative procedure to update the parameters according to the gradient of the error:

$$\beta_n^{(l)} \to \beta_n^{(l)} - \lambda \sum_{t=1}^{T} \frac{\partial R_t}{\partial \beta_n^{(l)}} \tag{22.19}$$

$$\alpha_m^{(n)} \to \alpha_m^{(n)} - \lambda \sum_{t=1}^{T} \frac{\partial R_t}{\partial \alpha_m^{(n)}}, \tag{22.20}$$

where we keep the ordering of the equations from the output layer towards the input layer. The parameter λ is the learning rate. It reflects how much we want to update the parameter as a function of the error. We consider the parameter constant at this stage, but we cease this assumption below. The set of equations for classification is derived analogously. We will see the functional form when we discuss the implementation below.

The updating procedure then works as advertised. In the forward stage, we use the current model and propagate observations forwards through the network until we produce output values. Thus, we obtain τ_l's from which we can calculate errors. Then, we calculate $\Delta^{(z)}$ and $\Delta^{(x)}$, respectively, and the corresponding values at nodes (input layer is given and does not have to be calculated while the hidden nodes have to be). Finally, we update the parameters according to eqs. (22.20) and (22.19). The entire procedure is simple to implement, as we will demonstrate in the following section.

Further, eqs. (22.20) and (22.19) contain a sum over the sample used in the training phase. We have used the full sample in those equations, but we can implement different setups. For instance, we can use one observation at a time, and the procedure can be performed in an *online* manner, where the current observation updates the network and is forgotten. This allows us to use large data sets which do not fit into memory. Another technique for dealing with large data sets is to use batches. A batch is a subset of the training sample. The learning by batches works so that we perform a single update of the parameters using a batch of data. The iteration then progresses to the next step, when another batch is chosen and the parameters are further updated. It is convenient to refer as an epoch to the set of iterations which went through the entire training data set.

22.1.2 The Learning Rate Parameter

The critical parameter in the backpropagation algorithm is the learning rate λ. If the parameter is too big, the update is massive and may respond too harshly to the errors. This would be unpleasant especially when we are close to the solution: we would be forced to step over the optimum. On the other hand, a small value will cause the convergence to be too slow and thus numerically inefficient.

These problems could be overcome by letting λ depend on the progress through iterations. Let us denote the index of the iteration by ν. Then, we denote λ_ν the learning rate parameter as a function of the iteration stage. It was shown in Robbins and Monro (1985) that for $\lambda_\nu \to 0$ as $\nu \to \infty$, such that $\sum_\nu \lambda_\nu = \infty$ and $\sum_\nu \lambda_\nu^2 < \infty$, the gradient search will converge.

We can also consider more advanced procedures. The learning rate parameter can depend on the error and be progressively chosen as needed. Besides, it can contain elements of stochastic annealing, where even when converging to a specific value, the learning rate parameter can be suddenly increased, thus trying to probe the neighbourhood and prevent being stuck in the local solution. Even more advanced techniques, suitable for deep networks, would involve periodically decreasing λ_ν and then resetting it into the initial value while at every instance when λ_ν reaches its minimum the solution is taken and stored. The set of all such solutions then constitutes the set of weak learners, which can be combined as trees in the forest.

22.1.3 Initialisation

The iteration starts with a specific choice of parameters (weights). The natural choice is to set all of them to 0.0. We encourage the reader to explore what form the updating equations take. The derivatives will be zero, and the iteration will get stuck at zero values. It is therefore necessary to choose nonzero values. Initialising the starting parameters at random values, rather small, allows the algorithm to pick up and navigate through the parametric space.

Let us mention one more item related to initialisation. The input parameters should be normalised such that they are demeaned and the variance is normalised to 1.0. This assures that parameters in the network are operating at the same scale and the same initial random initialisation can be used for every parameter.

22.1.4 Overfitting

Neural networks are prone to overfit the model. They potentially contain a large number of parameters and fully connected networks tend to adapt to the data too much. A popular choice is weight decay, where the loss function $Loss(Y,X;\Theta)$ contains additional penalty proportional to the magnitude of the parameters of the model:

$$Loss(Y,X;\Theta) \rightarrow Loss(Y,X;\Theta) + \rho \left(\sum_{ln} (\beta_n^{(l)})^2 + \sum_{nm} (\alpha_m^{(n)})^2 \right), \tag{22.21}$$

with ρ driving the regularisation.

Another popular method is dropout, see Srivastava et al. (2014). The dropout is de facto equivalent to ridge regression and works as follows. At every iteration step, we select which nodes will be updated according to a predetermined probability p (this is a parameter of the regularisation analogous to ρ in the preceding paragraph). The nodes which have not been selected are physically removed from the network with all the connections and are not updated during the given iteration step. After the iteration, the updated nodes are merged with the nodes which have been excluded.

Further, excluding the node from training means that we lose some information and tend to emphasise the effect of the nodes which have been preserved. This means that we have to weigh the output of all nodes at the end by probability p. This will create a fully connected network with all the nodes included in the training situation.

Additional to regularisation, with $p = 0.5$, we cut the number of parameters to half, which may significantly speed up the calibration. Dropout technique is both a regularisation method as well as a speed-up improvement and is gaining popularity in the machine learning community, especially for complex networks.

22.1.5 Dimension of the Hidden Layer(s)

We consider the neural network with one hidden layer. In general, nothing prevents us from creating a topology of the neural network with more hidden layers. It is in fact topology with a large number of hidden layers which brought fame to neural networks. Deep networks – how the neural networks with a large number of hidden layers are known – can learn very complex patterns and, mainly, generalise the concepts. It is still not fully understood what makes the deep networks so successful in generalisation.

Let us put aside deep networks and discuss the dimension of the hidden layer(s). Going beyond one hidden layer allows us to create a network able to model highly complex and nonlinear features. This brings the need for optimisation of a large number of weights. For this, not only a huge data set is needed, but also proper training techniques and regularisations have to be well thought out.

For the case of one hidden layer, the question is what should be the dimension of the hidden layer, N. Since the dimension of the input (features) is M, we compare the dimension of the hidden layer relative to the size of the input. In the case of $N < M$, there is information suppression in the hidden layer as we aim to represent M-dimensional input through the N-dimensional variables. Thus, it is recommended to have $N > M$ such that we can model nonlinear dependencies in the features.

There is, in fact, a reason to use $N < M$. Imagine the case when $Y = X$ and thus $L = M$. Such a setup aims to model the input variables and use the features to explain themselves. If we set $N < M$, the role of the hidden layer is to compress the input such that we can recover the input as much as possible. This is nothing but dimensionality reduction, given we can use the hidden layer to represent the input data. It can be shown that this is equivalent to the PCA. We can thus obtain PCA without the need to perform advanced matrix manipulations. The extreme case of $N = 1$ means that we want to compress the input into a single scalar factor.

22.2 IMPLEMENTATION OF NEURAL NETWORKS

In this section, we turn the theory of the previous paragraphs into functional code. We implement a function which can perform either classification or regression. It is further convenient to split the classification of the binary variable and general classification for $M > 2$.

First, we define some useful routines and functions, which will then be wrapped into the function comprehending the neural network training. We aim to add a few extra features into learner functions in order to achieve various functionalities. All will be wrapped in a user-friendly interface with several options to choose from using a simple set of switches.

22.2.1 Multivariate Encoder

It is convenient to map the M-class classification problem, where the dependent variable can take M discrete values into an M-dimensional variable where every individual component is a binary variable. Such a transformation is not the most economical one; we waste at least one dimension. Models are conveniently simple ones, and the extra dimension of the dependent variable does not cause in most of the situations problems during learning.

To implement the multivariate classifier, we will need to encode the M-class discrete variable into M binary variables. The function `encoderMulti` takes as an argument list (M discrete cases of the dependent variable) and returns a dictionary, which can be itself used as a function to create a list of binary variables:

```
.quantQ.nn.encoderMulti:{[arg]
   // arg -- list of classes to be encoded
   :arg!`float$arg=/:arg;
};
```

The construction `arg=/:arg` works as follows: the list `arg` is compared with each element of the list `arg` and creates boolean lists marking the match of the compared elements. Namely,

```
1 2 3=/:(1 2 3)
```

```
(100b;010b;001b)
```

We can test the function using the simple case where the argument of the function is a list of elements which are to be classified:

```
.quantQ.nn.encoderMulti[`t1`t2`t3]
```

and creates a dictionary which has for each element of the list entering the function an entry:

```
t1 | 1 0 0
t2 | 0 1 0
t3 | 0 0 1
```

We use the encoder function to convert the column containing the categorical variable into an array of indicator time series:

```
t:([] index: 1 2 3 4 5;val: 100 200 100 300 100);
update class: (.quantQ.nn.encoderMulti distinct exec val from t) val from t
```

```
index val class
---------------
1     100 1 0 0
2     200 0 1 0
3     100 1 0 0
4     300 0 0 1
5     100 1 0 0
```

The map is for a variable `val`, which has three distinct values. As the outcome of the encoding procedure, we have created a new variable `class`, which has for every atom a three-dimensional array of binary variables. The array has always one of the elements equal to `1b` while the rest are zero, denoting which class is present.

22.2.2 Neurons

The critical component of any neural network is neurons. These are functions which transform a signal coming from different nodes into a response. We consider both hidden layer neurons and the activation function (the neurons mapping the hidden layer into the output variable) as neurons. In addition to the response of the neuron itself, we also need first derivatives to calculate the gradient of the errors for backward propagation.

Binary classification

First, we specify the functional form of function η for classification problem. We consider the so-called sigmoid function

$$\eta_{binary}(x) = \frac{1}{1+e^{-x}}. \tag{22.22}$$

In addition to the multi-encoder, we define the objective functions which will be used for either of the three modes. Further, for each objective function, we have to define the error function which allows us to train the neural network based on the error feedback.

For bivariate classifier, the objective function used is based on the typical sigmoid function. The function reads:

```
.quantQ.nn.sigmoid:{[arg]
   // arg -- argument of the function
   :1%1+exp neg arg;
 };
```

and the corresponding error function used for training of the network is the cross-entropy function $Loss_{class}$ provided in eq. (22.9):

```
.quantQ.nn.sigmoidErr:{[argX;argY]
   // argX -- array of true values
   // argY -- array of predicted values
   :neg sum sum flip (argX*log argY) + ((1.0-argX)*log[1.0 - argY]);
 };
```

M-class classification

In the case of multivariate classification, we use the softmax function defined in eq. (22.4) for response of neurons:

```
.quantQ.nn.softmax:{[arg]
   // arg -- input argument (array with entry for every class)
   :exp[arg]%sum flip exp[arg];
 };
```

Corresponding error function, the cross-entropy, is functionally similar to the bivariate classification case:

```
.quantQ.nn.softmaxErr:{[argX;argY]
   // argX -- true value
   // argY -- predicted values
   :neg sum sum flip argX*log[argY];
 };
```

Regression

Finally, we utilise the neural network for regression. The output of the neuron is thus a simple pass by the input argument:

```
.quantQ.nn.linearNN:{[arg]
   // arg -- input argument
   :arg;
 };
```

with the corresponding squared error function:

```
.quantQ.nn.linearNNErr:{[argX;argY]
   // argX -- true value
   // argY -- predicted values
   :sum sum z*z:(argX-argY);
 };
```

Finally, we wrap the functions and the error function terms into two dictionaries. We will call corresponding functions based on the purpose the neural network is used for, i.e. as a `` `classifier``, `` `multiClassifier``, or `` `nonlinearReg``:

```
.quantQ.nn.funcNN: `classifier`multiClassifier`nonlinearReg!
                  (.quantQ.nn.sigmoid;.quantQ.nn.softmax;.quantQ.nn.
                     ↪ linearNN);
.quantQ.nn.funcErrNN: `classifier`multiClassifier`nonlinearReg!
                     (.quantQ.nn.sigmoidErr;.quantQ.nn.softmaxErr;.quantQ.
                        ↪ nn.linearNNErr);
```

The purpose of dictionaries is to put the functional forms under the surface and make the functions more convenient for users.

22.2.3 Training the Neural Network

We can proceed with implementing the training procedure for the neural network itself. At the beginning of the iteration procedure, we need to initialise the parameters of the neural network. Function `weightNNInit` takes two arguments: the size of the input nodes, `argIn`, and the size of the layer itself, `argOut`. The output is the array for a given layer, where every parameter is initialised as a random number drawn from $U[0,1]$:

```
.quantQ.nn.weightNNInit:{[argIn;argOut]
   // argIn -- number of input arguments
   // argOut -- number of output arguments
   :flip flip[weights]-avg weights:{[x;y]x?1.0}[argOut;]each til argIn;
 };
```

We proceed with defining one iteration of the gradient descent update. The function `forwardBackwardNNwError` performs one iteration. It takes the following arguments: the input and output arrays, `inputValue` and `outputValue`, respectively, `learningRatio` being the constant learning rate parameter, `func` standing for the type of the problem to solve in order to choose a correct function for the neuron and the gradient of the error for learning (choose from three options `classifier, `multiClassifier, and `nonlinearReg, respectively), and dictionary of parameters, params, which are updated during iteration. The dictionary contains the output of the model, `out, parameters of the hidden layer and of the activation function, `parsHid2out and `parsIn2Hid, respectively, error from *Loss* function, `Error, and a counter of iteration `Counter.

```
.quantQ.nn.forwardBackwardNNwError:{[inputValue;outputValue;learningRate;
    ↪ func;params]
   // inputValue -- array of input values
   // outputValue -- array of output values
   // learningRate -- learning rate for update
   // func -- purpose of the NN: `classifier`multiClassifier`nonlinearReg
   // params -- bucket of parameters to be updated
   // Forward stage
   // mapping Input -> Hidden using current parameters
   hiddenLayer:1.0,/:.quantQ.nn.sigmoid[inputValue mmu params[`parsIn2Hid
       ↪ ]];
   // mapping Hidden -> Output using current parameters
   outputLayer:.quantQ.nn.funcNN[func][hiddenLayer mmu params[`parsHid2Out
       ↪ ]];
   // Backward stage
   // error Hidden -> Output
   deltaLayerH2O:(outputValue-outputLayer);
   // error Input -> Hidden
   deltaLayerI2H:1_/:$[deltaLayerH2O;flip params[`parsHid2Out]]*hiddenLayer
       ↪ *1-hiddenLayer;
   // updating the model
   :`out`parsHid2Out`parsIn2Hid`Error`Counter!(outputLayer;params[`
       ↪ parsHid2Out]+learningRate*
       flip[hiddenLayer] mmu deltaLayerH2O;params[`parsIn2Hid]+learningRate
           ↪ *flip[inputValue] mmu
       deltaLayerI2H;.quantQ.nn.funcErrNN[func][outputValue;outputLayer];
           ↪ params[`Counter]+1);
};
```

The hidden layer uses by the default sigmoid activation function. This can be easily changed if needed by modifying the definition of hiddenLayer and deltaLayerI2H accordingly. The function performs three steps. First, the forward step is done by propagating the input value through the network by stacking the layers atop each other. Then, the error is recorded and propagated back, keeping track of the gradient in each node. Finally, the parameters in dictionary params are updated and iteration is concluded.

We further wrap the one iteration step into the complete function modelNN. Similarly to one iteration step, the function has a number of input arguments to be specified: the input and output arrays, input and output, respectively; the number of neurons of the hidden layer, nNeurons; the control for the terminal condition and corresponding parameter of the terminal condition, typeTerminal and argTerminal, respectively; a binary variable to track the progress during convergence, monitorConvergence; and, finally, specification of the problem, func (choose from three options `classifier, `multiClassifier, and `nonlinearReg, respectively).

There are two terminal conditions supported: `count, standing for a case where provided number of iterations is performed, and `relativeError, being the required minimum error to be achieved during the convergence process. The function is implemented as follows:

```
.quantQ.nn.modelNN:{[input;output;nNeurons;typeTerminal;argTerminal;
    ↪ learningRate;monitorConvergence;func]
   // input -- array of input values
   // output -- array of output values
   // nNeurons -- number of neurons in hiddne layer
   // typeTerminal -- type of terminal condition:`count`relativeError
   // argTerminal -- parameter for terminal condition
   // learningRate -- learning rate for update
   // monitorConvergence -- binary variable to monitor convergence
   // func -- purpose of the NN: `classifier`multiClassifier`nonlinearReg
   // adding bias/intercept to the input data
   input:1.0,'input;
   // counting dimension of the input including intercept
   nInput: count flip input;
   // counting dimension of the output
   nOutput: count first output;
   // initialization of layer: Input -> Hidden
   layerI2H:.quantQ.nn.weightNNInit[nInput;nNeurons];
   // initialization of layer: Hidden (with bias neuron) -> Output
   layerH2O:.quantQ.nn.weightNNInit[1+nNeurons;nOutput];
   // decide between two specified terminal conditions
   $[typeTerminal=`count;terminus:argTerminal;];
       $[typeTerminal=`relativeError;terminus:{[argTerminal;param] param[`
           ↪ Error]>argTerminal}[argTerminal;];
   ];
   // training the network and return output (depends on monitoring the
       ↪ convergence):
   $[monitorConvergence=1;
       :(.quantQ.nn.forwardBackwardNNwError[input;output;learningRate;func
           ↪ ]\)[terminus;`out`parsHid2Out`parsIn2Hid`Error`Counter!(0,();
           ↪ layerH2O;layerI2H;1f;0)];
       :(.quantQ.nn.forwardBackwardNNwError[input;output;learningRate;func
           ↪ ]/)[terminus;`out`parsHid2Out`parsIn2Hid`Error`Counter!(0,();
           ↪ layerH2O;layerI2H;1f;0)]
   ];
};
```

The function proceeds as follows: First, the initial parameters are instantiated using weightNNInit. Then, the terminal condition is decided and the appropriate rule for the iteration procedure is defined. This step can be potentially outsourced into another function. Then, depending on the choice whether we want to see every iteration step or not, based on the value of variable monitorConvergence, the iteration is performed. When we aim for monitoring convergence, we do record the dictionary params in every step. From this record, we can understand the evolution of errors as well as variance in the parameters. This is a useful option when we want to gain intuition about the problem itself.

22.3 EXAMPLES

Finally, we illustrate the neural network on three cases, each exploiting one possible option defined for neural networks: `` `classifier ``, `` `multiClassifier ``, and `` `nonlinearReg ``, i.e., options for the neuron functions and the error terms.

22.3.1 Binary Classification

We test the binary classification model on the following setup. We consider four features. Each feature can take two values only; we can treat them as *true* and *false*. The dependent variable is defined as *XOR* operator with four input arguments:

$$y = XOR(x_1, x_2, x_3, x_4) = \begin{cases} 1, & \text{if } x_1 + x_2 + x_3 + x_4 = 1 \\ 0, & \text{otherwise,} \end{cases} \tag{22.23}$$

where x_i are variables taking values $\{0, 1\}$. In the case of having two arguments only, the operation would be the logical operator *XOR*.

We first define four input features x_i. Instead of using the range of variables for every feature as $\{0, 1\}$, we define the variables to be taking values $\{-1, 1\}$. Value of -1 corresponds to logical *false* while 1 is *true*. The advantage of the redefined range is the zero mean of the input features, which is suitable for neural networks. We define them as:

```
xA1:500?-1 1;
xA2:500?-1 1;
xA3:500?-1 1;
xA4:500?-1 1;
```

and define the dependent variable as being *true* when sum of the four features is -2, which corresponds to *XOR* function:

```
yA:?[neg[2]=xA1+xA2+xA3+xA4;1;0];
```

The probability of observing *true* value of `yA` is $p = 0.25$, as can be verified by simple algebra. We can verify this assertion by:

```
sum yA
```

```
125
```

Having the data set comprising four input features `xA1`, `xA2`, `xA3`, and `xA4`, and dependent variable `yA`, we can train the neural network. We use 6 neurons in the hidden layer (excluding bias), which exceeds the dimension of the features. As a terminal rule, we use `` `count `` and 1000 iterations. The learning rate is 0.01, and we do monitor the output of every iteration step. Further, the problem is binary classification, which has to be specified as a last argument for the function. The following call invokes the learning of the neural network:

```
modelA:.quantQ.nn.modelNN[flip "f"$(xA1;xA2;xA3;xA4);yA;6;`count
    ↪ ;1000;0.01;1;`classifier];
```

The outcome is stored into object `modelA`, which is nothing but a table:

```
meta modelA
```

```
c          | t f a
-----------| -----
out        | J
parsHid2Out|
parsIn2Hid |
Error      | f
Counter    | j
```

The table has a single row for every iteration step. The first row is the initialisation of the routine. The columns correspond to the `pars` dictionary defined above. Let us focus on the `Error` and analyse how it evolves during the iteration of the algorithm. This can be done as:

```
select Counter, Error from modelA where i>0
```

where we have excluded the first row of the table.

Figure 22.1 depicts the error during the learning process of the neural network. The error is depicted against the iteration index. The reason to exclude the first row is because `Error` is set to 0.0, which does not have any meaning. The error drops during the initial stages of the learning, approximately the first 20 steps. Then, the steepness of the error descent slows down while the model keeps improving. From approximately 200 steps, the improvement of the model slows down significantly; the model reaches

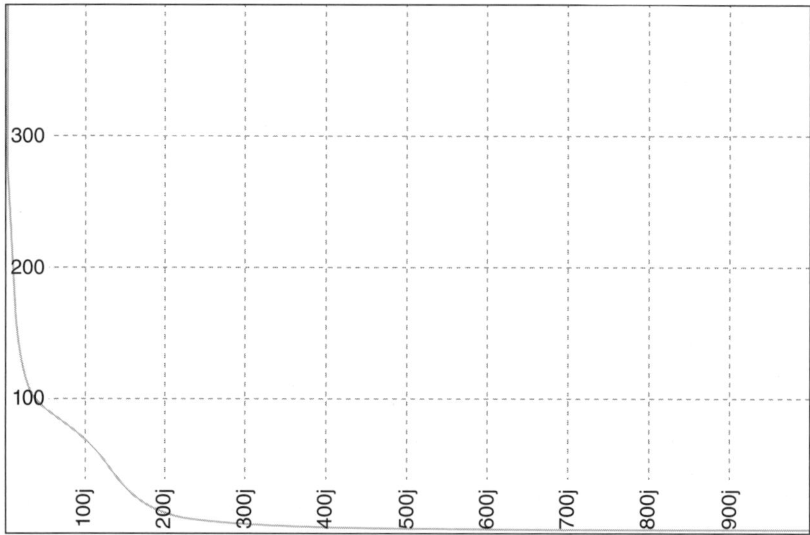

FIGURE 22.1 Learning path (errors) for classification problem of four binary variables with *XOR* operation

a plateau with no further progress. The optimal learning should avoid overtraining. Training should stop before reaching the plateau.

Once we have trained the model, we need to verify the validity of the model on the test data set. Our data set is rather trivial in the sense that the space of possible values is limited. The features can take 16 different configurations and thus the size of our sample is largely overshot. We encourage the reader to repeat the exercise once small noise is introduced to the features.

Our focus is rather the implementation itself, though. We extract the model parameters and weights at the end of the training (what we would observe under the option of not monitoring performance). The weights are recovered as:

```
pHid2OutA: exec last parsHid2Out from modelA;
pIn2HidA: exec last parsIn2Hid from modelA;
```

Defining a table with all 16 configurations of our feature space:

```
tmpA:flip t cross t cross t cross t:(-1.0 1.0);
tabA:update y:?[neg[2]=x1+x2+x3+x4;1;0] from ([] x1: tmpA[0]; x2: tmpA[1];
    ↪ x3: tmpA[2]; x4: tmpA[3]);
```

we can list the full table:

```
tabA
```

```
x1 x2 x3 x4 y
-------------
-1 -1 -1 -1 0
-1 -1 -1 1  1
-1 -1 1  -1 1
-1 -1 1  1  0
-1 1  -1 -1 1
-1 1  -1 1  0
-1 1  1  -1 0
-1 1  1  1  0
1  -1 -1 -1 1
1  -1 -1 1  0
1  -1 1  -1 0
1  -1 1  1  0
1  1  -1 -1 0
1  1  -1 1  0
1  1  1  -1 0
1  1  1  1  0
```

We add to the table tabA an extra column which is the prediction of the dependent variable; we call it yPredict. The prediction is simply stacking the neural network layer by layer and evaluating it on the input data:

```
tabA: update yPredict: .quantQ.nn.funcNN[`classifier][(1.0,/:.quantQ.nn.
    ↪ sigmoid[(1.0,'flip[tmpA]) mmu pIn2HidA]) mmu pHid2OutA] from tabA;
```

The updated table and validity of the prediction can be in this case eye-checked:

```
tabA
```

```
x1 x2 x3 x4 y yPredict
---------------------------
-1 -1 -1 -1 0 0.01066704
-1 -1 -1 1  1 0.9987026
-1 -1 1  -1 1 0.9980297
-1 -1 1  1  0 0.0003424803
-1 1  -1 -1 1 0.9936351
-1 1  -1 1  0 0.000139613
-1 1  1  -1 0 0.0001762468
-1 1  1  1  0 0.0004901187
1  -1 -1 -1 1 0.9980993
1  -1 -1 1  0 0.0003461194
1  -1 1  -1 0 0.0002189907
1  -1 1  1  0 1.850549e-005
1  1  -1 -1 0 0.0002024397
1  1  -1 1  0 0.0004997925
1  1  1  -1 0 7.439039e-005
1  1  1  1  0 0.0007311004
```

The predicted value is a real-valued number from $[0,1]$. We could further round the number to integers 0 and 1, respectively, to get the corresponding number format. Table `tabA` shows perfect agreement between `y` and `yPredict` as we can consider the small values to correspond to true 0 while values very close to 1 can be treated as true 1.

22.3.2 *M*-class Classification

The second example involves testing the M-classification, where the dependent variable can take M distinct values. We test our implementation on Fisher's Iris data set iri. Let us recall the meaning of the variables in the data set:

- *Feature 1:* sepal length in cm,
- *Feature 2:* sepal width in cm,
- *Feature 3:* petal length in cm,
- *Feature 4:* petal width in cm,
- *Dependent variable:* class: Iris Setosa, Iris Versicolour, and Iris Virginica, respectively.

The data set has 150 rows. We assume we have the data on the local drive (in root directory). First, we load the data:

```
irisData:("FFFFS"; enlist ",") 0:`$"C:\\irisData.csv"
```

and verify the structure of the table with all the names of variables:

```
meta irisData
```

```
c          | t f a
-----------| -----
sepalLength| f
sepalWidth | f
```

```
petalLength| f
petalWidth | f
class      | s
```

Further, we split the data set into a training sample with 100 observations, and test sample with 50 observations. Since the data set itself can be sorted based on the class, we do the random split of the data:

```
randomDraw100:neg[100]?count irisData;
irisDataIN: select from irisData where i in randomDraw100;
irisDataOUT: select from irisData where not i in randomDraw100;
```

We verify that all three classes are represented in the training sample:

```
distinctClass:distinct irisDataIN`class;
distinctClass
```

```
`Iris-setosa`Iris-versicolor`Iris-virginica
```

We train the model using 8 neurons in the hidden layer with learning rate parameter 0.01 and run the algorithm for 1000 steps. We monitor the convergence of the algorithm:

```
modelB:.quantQ.nn.modelNN[flip (irisDataIN`sepalLength;irisDataIN`
    sepalWidth;irisDataIN`petalLength;irisDataIN`petalWidth);.quantQ.nn.
    encoderMulti[distinctClass] irisDataIN`class;8;`count;1000;0.01;1;`
    multiClassifier];
```

Figure 22.2 depicts the error during the learning process of the neural network for the iris data set. The learning pattern shows complex episodes during the iterations.

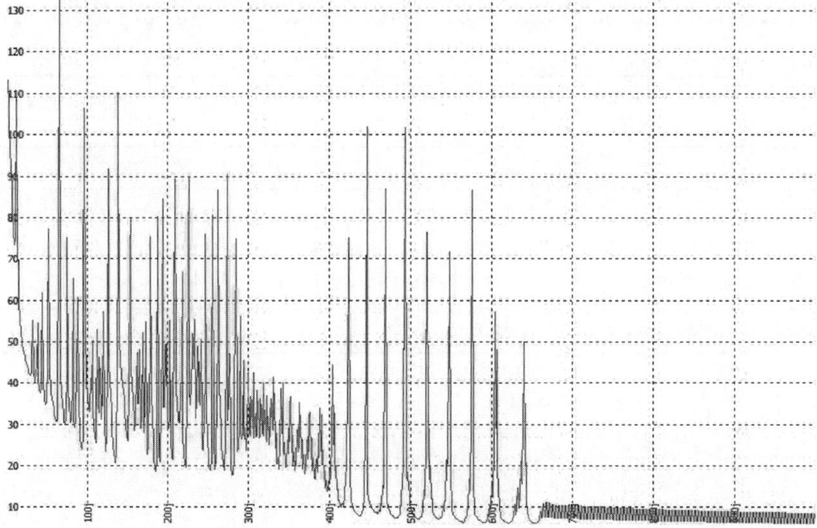

FIGURE 22.2 Learning path (errors) for M-class classification of the Iris data set

The improvement is somewhat volatile and shows a brief burst when the error gets worse though the overall improvement is apparent. During the final stages of the learning process, the error oscillates around two values, both representing improvement. This suggests that the algorithm cannot rest in the optimum but slightly oscillates around it. This could be prevented by having the learning rate decreasing during the last stages of the iteration process.

The data have been extracted as:

```
select Counter, Error from modelB where i>0
```

Further, we extract the model parameters at the end of the training process:

```
pHid2OutB: exec last parsHid2Out from modelB;
pIn2HidB: exec last parsIn2Hid from modelB;
```

We arrange the out-of-sample data into a new table `tabB`, and add an encoded dependent variable:

```
tabB:update classEnc: .quantQ.nn.encoderMulti[distinctClass] class from
    ↪ irisDataOUT;
```

Then, we predict the class of the iris using the trained model. The prediction is done by stacking the network together:

```
tabB: update classEncPredict: .quantQ.nn.funcNN[`multiClassifier][(1.0,/:.
    ↪ quantQ.nn.sigmoid[(1.0,'flip[(irisDataOUT`sepalLength;irisDataOUT`
    ↪ sepalWidth;irisDataOUT`petalLength;irisDataOUT`petalWidth)]
) mmu pIn2HidB]) mmu pHid2OutB] from tabB;
```

The predicted variable `classEncPredict` is an encoded array of three values, where each value represents probability that given observation is of a given class. The class with highest probability wins. We can check the accuracy of our prediction model as:

```
exec sum {(where y=max y)=(where x=max x)}'[classEncPredict;classEnc] from
    ↪ tabB
```

```
enlist 47
```

The model predicts correctly 47 out of 50 cases, i.e. 94% accuracy. Let us further inspect the table itself; we view 10 random rows for illustration:

```
10?select classEncPredict, classEnc from tabB
```

```
classEncPredict                         classEnc
------------------------------------------------
0.00434627    0.9956356   1.813319e-005 0 1 0
0.9973335     0.002666495 1.273018e-009 1 0 0
0.006007452   0.9939817   1.080583e-005 0 1 0
0.006007452   0.9939817   1.080583e-005 0 1 0
3.073432e-005 0.6700523   0.3299169     0 0 1
0.009888061   0.9901043   7.592463e-006 0 1 0
```

```
8.104051e-008 0.01313227  0.9868677     0 0 1
3.073432e-005 0.6700523   0.3299169     0 0 1
0.9973873     0.002612676 1.243462e-009 1 0 0
0.9973153     0.002684707 1.284016e-009 1 0 0
```

It is worth noting that 5th and 8th row represent a case where the model does not work. In the cases where the model works, the probability for a correct class is usually close to 1, while in the confused case, the probabilities are instead distributed across classes. This fact can be further utilised in interpreting and adding some measure of uncertainty for every prediction.

22.3.3 Regression

The third case to explore is the regression, where the dependent variable is a real-valued array. We have mentioned in the introductory part that by suitable choice of the neural network parameters, we can turn the neural network into a dimensionality reduction tool. We explore this situation in our example as it provides a handy and practical tool.

In particular, we stick to the case of four real-valued features. Each feature is constructed as a linear combination of a common factor and an idiosyncratic noise:

$$x_i = \alpha_i \cdot \phi + \sqrt{1 - \alpha_i^2} \cdot e_i \text{ with } i = 1, \ldots, 4, \tag{22.24}$$

where α_i is a parameter within $[0, 1]$, e_i is an idiosyncratic noise, and ϕ is a factor shared across different features. The factor and the idiosyncratic noise have the same variance and thus all the features have the same variance as well.

We employ the uniform distribution to define factors and idiosyncratic noise variables:

```
factor:neg[1]+2*500?1.0;
tmpC1:neg[1]+2*500?1.0;
tmpC2:neg[1]+2*500?1.0;
tmpC3:neg[1]+2*500?1.0;
tmpC4:neg[1]+2*500?1.0;
```

The features themselves are defined as linear combinations defined in eq. (22.24) with corresponding coefficients:

```
c1:0.2;
c2:0.4;
c3:0.6;
c4:0.0;
xC1:(c1*factor)+sqrt[1-c1*c1]*tmpC1;
xC2:(c2*factor)+sqrt[1-c2*c2]*tmpC2;
xC3:(c3*factor)+sqrt[1-c3*c3]*tmpC3;
xC4:(c4*factor)+sqrt[1-c4*c4]*tmpC4;
```

The last feature is not correlated to the common factor. Let us confirm that the correlation between factor and the features reflects the corresponding factors:

```
cor[xC1;factor]
```

```
0.1872497
```

```
cor[xC2;factor]
```

```
0.3850902
```

```
cor[xC3;factor]
```

```
0.5670842
```

```
cor[xC4;factor]
```

```
-0.01085183
```

We can proceed to train the neural network. We start with a similar parametric set-up as in the binary classification case. In particular, we choose 1 neuron in the hidden layer:

```
modelC1:.quantQ.nn.modelNN[flip "f"$(xC1;xC2;xC3;xC4);flip "f"$(xC1;xC2;xC3
    ↪ ;xC4);1;`count;100;0.01;1;`nonlinearReg];
```

The focus is on the evaluation of the error during the iteration. The provided model does not converge, as the reader could realise when the number of iteration steps would be set too large. This brings a useful insight: we should start with a smaller case using a few iteration steps and investigate the evolution of the training. Then, set the full-scale learning.

Figure 22.3 depicts the learning path as a function of the iteration index. Contrary to previous cases, we plot log of the error in order to visualise the divergence of errors. The model does not converge, and thus we have to change the parameters of learning. The suspected parameter to be changed is the learning rate which may be too coarse, thus dragging us from the optimal values.

The data for the figure has been extracted as:

```
select Counter, log Error from modelC1 where i>0
```

Let us repeat the training of the model with smaller learning rate parameter, in this case 0.01. We show the run of the model for 3000 steps:

```
modelC2:.quantQ.nn.modelNN[flip "f"$(xC1;xC2;xC3;xC4);flip "f"$(xC1;xC2;xC3
    ↪ ;xC4);1;`count;3000;0.001;1;`nonlinearReg];
```

Figure 22.4 depicts the learning path (error without the log transformation) as it progresses during the iterations. The procedure converges in this case; the model is learning. The improvement of the error is approximately 50%, relatively mediocre improvement compared to all the previous cases when the improvements have been in the orders of magnitude. This confirms the failure to converge for large learning

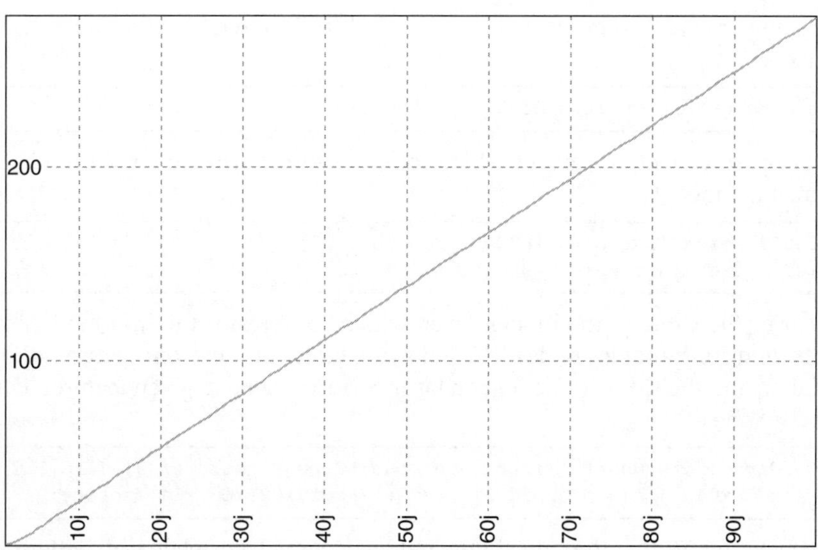

FIGURE 22.3 Learning path (*log* errors) for dimensionality reduction and large learning rate

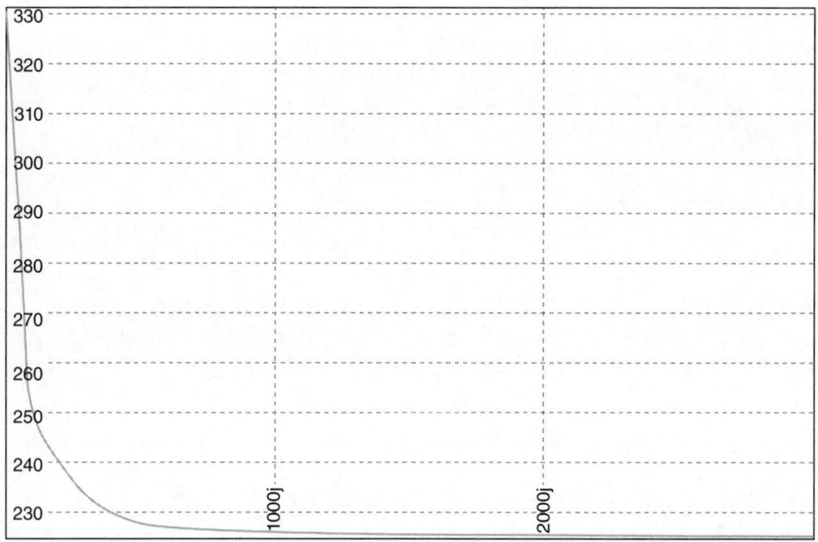

FIGURE 22.4 Learning path (errors) for dimensionality reduction and moderate learning rate

rate parameter as the improvement is rather subtle. The data for the figure has been extracted as:

```
select Counter, Error from modelC2 where i>0
```

Having the converging model, which compress the information in the hidden layer, we extract the model:

```
pHid2OutC2: exec last parsHid2Out from modelC2;
pIn2HidC2: exec last parsIn2Hid from modelC2;
```

and recover the value in the hidden layer, which compresses the information of four features (and constant bias node). The following table contains four features, the common factor, and the value in the hidden layer corresponding to given features, denoted as `factorModel`:

```
tabC: update factorModel: first each .quantQ.nn.sigmoid[(1.0,'flip[(xC1;xC2
    ↪ ;xC3;xC4)]) mmu pIn2HidC2] from ([] xC1;xC2;xC3;xC4;factor);
```

We hypothesise that the value in the hidden layer will correlate well with the `factor`. Figure 22.5 depicts the scatter plot of `factor` vs. `factorModel`. There is a clear positive correlation between the two variables, though dependency is rather noisy.

We can check the correlations between the factor, the hidden value and the features:

```
cor[tabC`factor;tabC`factorModel]
```

```
0.6119059
```

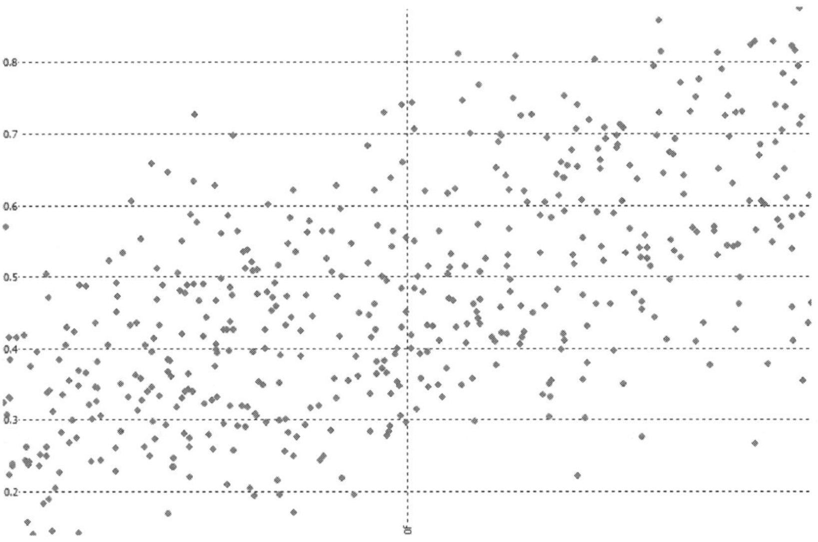

FIGURE 22.5 Scatter diagram of `factor` vs `factorModel`

the correlation between the factor variables and the factorModel values is rather large, exceeding 60%. This is a reasonable value given we have not a priori used any correlation or covariance criteria to train the hidden layer.

On the other hand, the correlation between individual features and the factorModel values is more complex:

```
cor[tabC`xC1;tabC`factorModel]
```

```
0.407073
```

```
cor[tabC`xC2;tabC`factorModel]
```

```
0.7539911
```

```
cor[tabC`xC3;tabC`factorModel]
```

```
0.7009646
```

```
cor[tabC`xC4;tabC`factorModel]
```

```
-0.1458108
```

In particular, the feature xC2 is more correlated to factorModel than the feature xC3 is. The underlying data, however, would suggest otherwise. This means that the value in the hidden layer does not manifest in our numerical exercise as a correlation preserving proxy for factor. This was not an objective during the training.

In summary, the extracted featureModel value correlates to the common factor, factor, well. It allows us to reduce the dimension of the data set, in our case from 4 to 1. For the sake of completeness, let us explore the case where we want to model the four features on itself. We can do it by setting number of neurons in the hidden layer to be greater than 4, namely, we choose 8:

```
modelC3:.quantQ.nn.modelNN[flip "f"$(xC1;xC2;xC3;xC4);flip "f"$(xC1;xC2;xC3
    ↪ ;xC4);8;`count;1000;0.001;1;`nonlinearReg];
```

Figure 22.6 depicts the learning path as a function of the iteration index. The procedure converges well; the improvement is back to orders of magnitude as we would normally expect. The number of iterations is set to be large again. The underlying data have been obtained from table modelC3 as:

```
select Counter, Error from modelC3 where i>0
```

We extract the model:

```
pHid2OutC3: exec last parsHid2Out from modelC3;
pIn2HidC3: exec last parsIn2Hid from modelC3;
```

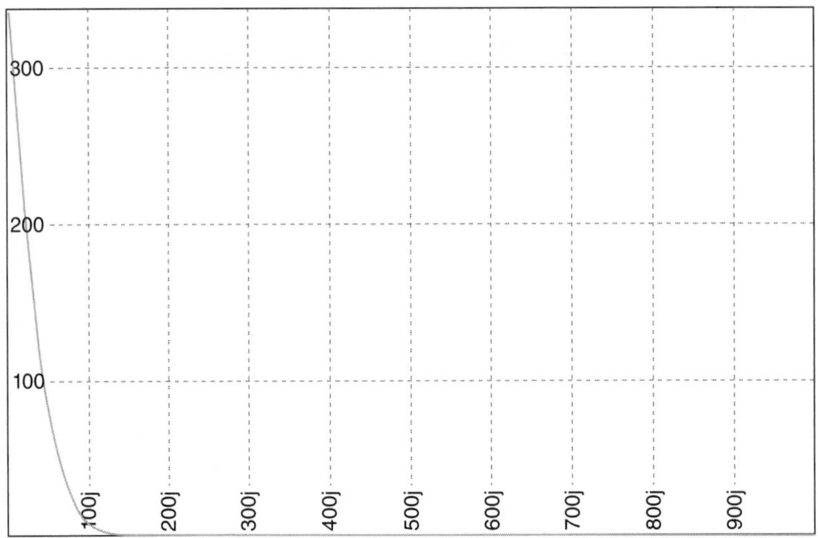

FIGURE 22.6 Learning path (errors) for modelling the input on itself with 8 hidden neurons

and recover the four features using the trained model:

```
tabC3: update factorC1:factorModel[;0], factorC2:factorModel[;1], factorC3:
    ↪ factorModel[;2], factorC4:factorModel[;3] from update factorModel: .
    ↪ quantQ.nn.funcNN[`nonlinearReg][(1.0,/:.quantQ.nn.sigmoid[(1.0,'flip
    ↪ [(xC1;xC2;xC3;xC4)]) mmu pIn2HidC3]) mmu pHid2OutC3] from ([] xC1;
    ↪ xC2;xC3;xC4;factor);
```

Finally, we confirm that the trained neural network models the input well. We calculate the correlation between the component of the input and the corresponding modelled value:

```
cor[tabC3`xC1;tabC3`factorC1]
```

```
0.9985345
```

```
cor[tabC3`xC2;tabC3`factorC2]
```

```
0.9992018
```

```
cor[tabC3`xC3;tabC3`factorC3]
```

```
0.9987443
```

```
cor[tabC3`xC4;tabC3`factorC4]
```

```
0.9989041
```

In all four cases, the correlation is very close to 1.0. We can thus confidently say the model recovers the input values. We keep in mind that the exercise is performed in the sample. The purpose of the exercise was to validate the implementation rather than show the power of the neural networks.

22.4 POSSIBLE SUGGESTIONS

Our implementation of the neural networks narrows to the vanilla case of single hidden layer topology. There is a plethora of possible extensions:

- Accessing the trained model and applying it on the out-of-sample data is done manually. It would be more convenient to have a suitable function, where stacking the neural network together would be hidden from the user.
- The learning rate is implemented as constant. The function for training network contains an iterations counter. It would be worth extending the function such that the learning rate is a function of the iteration step. A suitable candidate is a function where the learning rate will be inversely proportional to the iteration steps.
- It is worth exploring the dimensionality reduction when more than 1 neuron is used in the hidden layer. The measure of overall correlation captured by more than one value would be higher. The proper exercise can be through measuring R^2 in linear regression using value(s) from hidden layers. We further encourage readers to verify the dimensionality reduction results with the PCA analysis introduced in Chapter 16.

CHAPTER 23

AdaBoost with Stumps

In this section, we introduce a particular machine learning technique called AdaBoost and apply it on stumps. We aim to provide a working example of the AdaBoost technique with a simple weak learner – a binary decision stump. There are numerous extensions of this technique as well as interesting theory to be covered, which are not within our scope. This chapter serves as a gentle introduction for the next section, which focuses on decision trees and related techniques.

23.1 BOOSTING

Boosting, in general, is one of the most powerful techniques for machine learning. In practice, we have the frequently available number of "weak" classifiers, each of them being able to explain a small fraction of the dependent variable. Forming a suitable committee of such weak classifiers which can appropriately combine their power will provide a considerable advantage.

In principle, the Boosting algorithm works as follows. Let us assume we have a set of weak classifiers denoted as G_l, with $l = 1, \ldots, L$ and the data set. Boosting uses the following logic:

- Start with the original data set.
- Apply the first weak classifier G_1 using the original data set, adjust the data set by the outcome of the weak classifier.
- Apply the second weak classifier G_2 using the adjusted data set from the previous step, adjust the data set by the outcome of the second weak classifier.
- Continue with third, fourth, fifth, etc.
- Apply the L-th weak classifier G_L using the adjusted data set from the previous step, adjust the data set by the outcome of the last weak classifier.
- Combine the weak classifiers with appropriate scheme reflecting how each classifier performed.

The AdaBoost, or Adaptive Boosting was introduced by Freund and Schapire (1997). The boosting was originally introduced for classification problems, but it was successfully extended to regression problems as well. In our example, we stick to the classification problem where we aim to explain and predict a binary dependent variable. The weak classifier we implement in this section is a decision stump.

23.2 DECISION STUMPS

A decision stump is a one-level decision tree. The rule is formed by a root node and two child nodes. Each node corresponds to a class predicted by the rule based on the one-dimensional feature split according to a chosen threshold. For the sake of simplicity, let us consider a case where we have a binary variable y taking values -1 and 1 and single real-valued feature x. The decision stump g:

$$\hat{y} = g(x; \xi) = \begin{cases} -1, \text{if } x \leq \xi \\ 1, \text{if } x > \xi \end{cases}, \tag{23.1}$$

where ξ is a threshold of the decision stump.

Let us implement the stump function as follows:

```
.quantQ.ada.stump:{[variable;threshold]
   // variable -- array of variables
   // threshold -- threshold for > operation
   :neg[1]+2*eval (>;variable;threshold);
};
```

where we have defined the stump as a function of two variables, the array of features and the threshold. The inequality in the stump is fixed. For that reason, we define later on every feature its negative counterpart. This gives us flexibility in terms of inverted proportionality between feature values and the class.

Let us create a small sample, contained in the following table:

```
tabSmall: ([] x:10?1.0);
```

and add the stump using the threshold of 0.5

```
update stump: .quantQ.ada.stump[;0.5] x from tabSmall
```

```
x          stump
----------------
0.7788857    1
0.8886694    1
0.1858148   -1
0.5734651    1
0.1926813   -1
0.2416352   -1
0.6666029    1
0.5038234    1
0.9015700    1
0.2610908   -1
```

The stump is thus classifying the observations according to the value of the selected feature. The stump then constitutes our weak classifier. Further, the function allows us to operate on the features stored in the table.

23.3 ADABOOST

We now introduce the discrete version of the AdaBoost algorithm. Let us consider a case where we have a binary variable y taking values -1 and 1 and a set of features $x_0, x_1, \ldots, x_N$. The range of variable y is chosen for convenience, and any binary variable can be easily recast into this form. Concerning variables representing features, we require them to be of any ordinal type, i.e. such that we can order them and apply the inequality operation. Thus, aside from obvious candidates of floats, integers, and various date and time types – which are either floats or integers under the surface – we also allow for strings and characters.

The ultimate aim of the model we want to develop is to find the relationship between x_i and y such that we can write:

$$y = G(x_1, x_2, \ldots, x_N), \tag{23.2}$$

where function G models the relationship between features and the dependent variable.

Let us assume that we are equipped with weak classifiers $g_l(x_i; \xi_l)$, where l indexes the weak classifier, ξ_l is the corresponding parameter set (in the case of stumps the threshold), and x_i is the feature chosen for the given classifier.

Let us define the loss function for a general single-valued classifier g at sample point $(x_i)_j$:

$$E(g(x_{i,j}), y_j) = \exp(-y_j g(x_{i,j})), \tag{23.3}$$

where the loss function distinguishes the sign and not the numerical value itself, and j indexes observation points with $j = 1, \ldots, M$. We do not need to restrict ourselves to any numerical values for the model. In the case of regression, the corresponding loss function would be the square of the differences, the one used with a least squares method or neural networks. Using the exponential function implies that the error of the additive model is the product of error at each stage. Thus, AdaBoost aims to minimise the exponential loss function by iterative updates of the model. It brings a computational advantage for additive modelling as the model is consecutively re-weighted as estimation progresses. It is also noted that AdaBoost with an exponential loss function is equivalent to forward stagewise additive modelling.

AdaBoost is defined as follows:

- Initialise every observation weight $w_j = 1/M$, with $j = 1, \ldots, M$.
- Initialise the model $G_0 \equiv 0$.
- For $l = 1, \ldots, L_{AdB}$:
  - Fit classifier $g_l(x_i; \xi_l)$ to the data that minimises sum of errors for misclassified observations:

$$err_l = \sum_j^M w_j 1(g_l(x_{i,j}; \xi_l) \neq y_j). \tag{23.4}$$

- Compute parameter $\alpha_l = \frac{1}{2}\log\left(\frac{1-err_l}{err_l}\right)$.
- Update the ensemble of models as: $G_l = G_{l-1} + \alpha_l\, g_l(x_i;\xi_l)$.
- Update the observation weights $w_j \leftarrow w_j \exp(-\alpha_l y_j g_l(x_i;\xi_l))$ for every observation j.
- Normalise weights as $w_j \leftarrow \frac{w_j}{\sum_j^M w_j}$ for every observation j.

- The model G_l is the AdaBoost model for the data set.

Finally, the model determines the class based on the sign of G_l, i.e.

$$\hat{y} = signum\ G_l(x), \tag{23.5}$$

where the case of zero means indecisive outcome. We decide the value in such a case randomly; however, the probability to obtain such a case is theoretically zero (numerically, it is still possible).

Let us note that L_{AdB} is a meta-parameter of the algorithm. A suitable way to determine it is through the cross-validation technique.

23.4 IMPLEMENTATION OF ADABOOST

We start by specifying the format of the data set. The hypothetical meta of the data table reads:

```
c      | t f a
-------| -----
y      | j
weights| f
x0     | f
...
xN     | f
```

The first column corresponds to the dependent variable y taking values $\{-1, 1\}$. The second column is a vector of weights w_j. The third and further columns correspond to the independent variables or features. Due to the nature of the stump, we need to add for every column its negative counterpart. Such a construction allows us to capture both direct proportionality as well as inverse proportionality. Adding the negative features is done through the function addNegFeatureTable:

```
.quantQ.ada.addNegFeatureTable:{[tab]
   // tab -- input table, 3rd column onwards are features
   colsx: 2_cols tab;
   coly: first 1#cols tab;
   //add negative features
   :tab,'flip raze{[tab;yy;name] flip
    eval (?;tab;();0b;(enlist`$string[name],"n")!enlist (-:;name))
    }[tab;coly;] each colsx;
};
```

Let us create a sample data set with two independent variables. The data set contains 110 observations, where 100 observations are pure random noise while

10 observations reveal a strong link between features and the dependent variable. In addition, the data set contains the column of weights, each having the same value 1/110. The data set is stored in the table `tab`:

```
tab:([] y:neg[1]+2*(10#1),100?2; weights:1.0%110;x0:(10#0.98),100?1.0;x1
    ↪ :(10#0.98),100?1.0);
```

Let us add the negative counterparts for two features:

```
tab: .quantQ.ada.addNegFeatureTable[tab];
```

and print out a subset of the data. This time, we choose 10 random entries from the table:

```
10? tab
```

```
y  weights     x0          x1        x0n          x1n
------------------------------------------------------------
-1 0.009090909 0.3195925   0.8284666 -0.3195925   -0.8284666
1  0.009090909 0.2830818   0.4046644 -0.2830818   -0.4046644
1  0.009090909 0.98        0.98      -0.98        -0.98
1  0.009090909 0.6331422   0.5682244 -0.6331422   -0.5682244
1  0.009090909 0.5322796   0.896032  -0.5322796   -0.896032
-1 0.009090909 0.1225951   0.2057899 -0.1225951   -0.2057899
-1 0.009090909 0.5794445   0.2037281 -0.5794445   -0.2037281
1  0.009090909 0.002197345 0.8420655 -0.002197345 -0.8420655
1  0.009090909 0.5691882   0.8579086 -0.5691882   -0.8579086
1  0.009090909 0.06563834  0.5046616 -0.06563834  -0.5046616
```

The `weights` column in the table will be updated during the AdaBoost algorithm. Besides the table `tab`, we need to store the individual weak classifiers – the feature used and the corresponding threshold – as well as corresponding α's. We keep this information in the following table:

```
ada: ([] i:"j"$(); alpha: "f"$();stump:());
```

During the run of the algorithm, new selected weak classifiers will be added one by one into the table. The complete model will be then recovered from the table.

Further, we follow the procedure used throughout this book and create a dictionary which will contain both tables. The AdaBoost algorithm will then process the dictionary and update it.

```
bucket:(`tab`ada)!(tab;ada);
```

Before we implement the algorithm itself, we define the loss function, which is optimised when the weak classifier is being fit. The loss function is in plain terms equal to the sum of weights for observations, which are not correctly predicted. The function is implemented as follows:

```
.quantQ.ada.weightedError:{[tab;prediction]
   // tab -- table with data and current weights
   // prediction -- array of predictions
   :sum tab[`weights] where tab[`y]<>prediction;
};
```

We have all the components we need to implement one iteration of the AdaBoost algorithm outlined above. The function runOneAdaBoost takes as an input the dictionary bucket and identifies the new weak classifier using stumps and appends it into the existing model. Along the way, we update the weights.

```
.quantQ.ada.runOneAdaBoost:{[bucket]
   // bucket -- dictionary with tab and ada tables
   tab:bucket[`tab];
   ada:bucket[`ada];
   // get names of features and of the dependent variable
   colsx: 2_cols tab;
   coly: first 1#cols tab;
   //randomly choose feature to split
   feature: first 1?colsx;
   // iterate through possible stumps and find the best one, if more than
       ↪ exists, choose randomly one
   optimalStump: first 1?(flip (t;z)) where (min[t])=t:.quantQ.ada.
       ↪ weightedError[tab;] each
       .quantQ.ada.stump[tab[feature];] each z: distinct asc tab[feature];
   // error of the optimal stump
   err: optimalStump[0];
   //split point
   splitPoint:optimalStump[1];
   // alpha of the adaBoost
   alpha: 0.5*log[(1-err)%err];
   // correction to weights
   corr2w: exp neg alpha*tab[coly]*.quantQ.ada.stump[tab[feature];
       ↪ splitPoint];
   // update data table
   tab:update weights: (weights*corr2w)%sum[weights*corr2w] from tab;
   // update ada table
   ada: ada,([] i:(1+count ada);alpha: alpha;stump: enlist(feature;
       ↪ splitPoint;err));
   // return bucket
   :((`tab`ada)!(tab;ada));
};
```

It is worth making several comments. First, feature: first 1?colsx implements how the feature for a given stump is chosen, namely, we choose a feature randomly. This simplifies the code we are using. It keeps randomness in the model. The apparent disadvantage is that our implementation of the AdaBoost does not allow us to use it as a feature selection technique, though the validity of the technique is still preserved. Second, given the feature chosen, the optimal stump is chosen by iterating through all the possible splitting points – which are nothing but the unique values of the feature itself – and chooses the one with least loss. Finally, all the variables are updated.

Let us use the data set we have created so far and run AdaBoost with $L_{AdB} = 10$, i.e., to add 10 weak stump classifiers and create their boosted committee. The procedure can be run as:

```
outBucket:(.quantQ.ada.runOneAdaBoost/)[10;bucket]
```

Let us first explore the information about the weak classifiers stored in the `` `ada `` variable:

```
outBucket[`ada]
```

```
i  alpha      stump
---------------------------------------
1  0.240919   `x1  0.938132     0.3818182
2  0.2088676  `x1n -0.9949916  0.3970588
3  0.0711613  `x0n -0.2983847  0.4644793
4  0.1551251  `x1  0.7430824    0.4230537
5  0.0786616  `x1  0.01909514   0.4607501
6  0.1273026  `x1n -0.5907093  0.4366903
7  0.09619632 `x1n -0.04598392 0.4520497
8  0.1007024  `x1n -0.9949916  0.4498183
9  0.1666662  `x1  0.938132     0.41743
10 0.2373138  `x0  0.4720859    0.3835215
```

We can reconstruct the stumps from the provided table. The first split is based on feature `` `x1 ``, split at the threshold $\xi_1 = 0.938132$. The given split gives loss function, or error, of the size 0.3818182. This number itself can be interpreted as an overall error as the weights have been initialised being equal and normalised to 1. In the subsequent iterations, it cannot be interpreted in the same way as weights are not equal. Due to the overall normalisation, the value of error should be decreasing over time for improving the algorithm. If we accept this premise, the outcome of the algorithm suggests that the algorithm is not improving much beyond the first stump. This is highly likely given how we have constructed the data set, where one of two features split around threshold close to 0.98 is sufficient choice. We encourage the reader to run the function with a large L_{AdB} and graphically explore the evolution of errors.

The step which we miss is a function which would give us the prediction based on the entire AdaBoost committee we have collected by the algorithm. This is done in the following function, which takes as the input `bucket` and returns a table with four columns: `` `res `` containing the numerical value provided by the model, `` `y `` containing true value of the dependent variable, `` `prediction `` containing the predicted dependent variable based on sign of the numerical value, and `` `isPredicted `` column, which shows whether the observation has been correctly predicted, value 1, or not, value −1.

```
.quantQ.ada.adaBoostPrediction:{[bucket]
   // bucket -- dictionary with tab and ada tables
   tab:bucket[`tab];
   ada:bucket[`ada];
   // calculate the sum of the individual predictions
   res: sum {[tab;config] config[0]*.quantQ.ada.stump[tab[config[1]];config
       ↪ [2]]}[tab;] each
       (ada[`alpha],'ada[`stump]);
   // add prediction to tab table
   :update isPredicted: prediction*y from update prediction: signum res
       ↪ from ([] res:res; y:tab[`y]);
};
```

Let us predict the dependent variable using the example:

```
tabAdaPrediction:.quantQ.ada.adaBoostPrediction[outBucket];
tabAdaPrediction
```

```
res        y  prediction isPredicted
------------------------------------
0.8935955  1  1          1
0.8935955  1  1          1
0.8935955  1  1          1
0.8935955  1  1          1
0.8935955  1  1          1
0.8935955  1  1          1
0.8935955  1  1          1
0.8935955  1  1          1
0.8935955  1  1          1
0.8935955  1  1          1
-0.2318251 -1 -1         1
-0.25388   1  -1         -1
-0.3095249 -1 -1         1
-0.2594549 1  -1         -1
0.2151728  1  1          1
0.02278013 1  1          1
-0.25388   1  -1         -1
-0.3095249 -1 -1         1
-0.2318251 1  -1         -1
0.07842508 -1 1          -1
..
```

The first ten observations are perfectly predicted. Those observations are ones with a straight link between dependent and independent variables. The rest does not show any apparent pattern. Let us create the following table:

```
select i:i, sums isPredicted from .quantQ.ada.adaBoostPrediction[outBucket]
```

which contains index `i`, and the cumulative sum of the `` `isPredicted `` column.

Figure 23.1 depicts the cumulative sum of `` `isPredicted `` variable as a function of the index. Besides the straight improvement at the beginning of the sample, there are a few episodes where the algorithm picked up the dependent variable successfully. Due to the randomness in the data set, this can be a symptom of overfitting. The results thus have to be interpreted carefully. At the end of the sample, the cumulative sum reaches a value of 38. The maximum possible value is 110 and value equal to 0 corresponds to no predictive power. In this case, the model is visually interpreted as predictive.

In order to understand the results, we finally implement the function which returns the series of useful statistics based on the contingency table. In particular, the function provides a dictionary with the following items:

- `` `truePositive `` – number of correctly identified cases of $y = 1$.
- `` `trueNegative `` – number of correctly identified cases of $y = -1$.
- `` `falsePositive `` – number of incorrectly identified cases of $y = 1$.
- `` `falseNegative `` – number of incorrectly identified cases of $y = -1$.

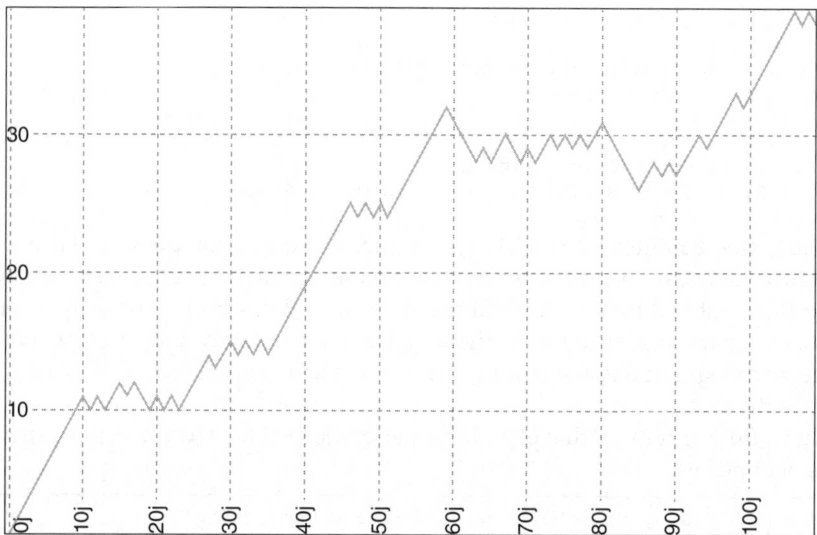

FIGURE 23.1 The cumulative sum of `` `isPredicted`` variable for AdaBoost across the sample

- `` `accuracy`` – the proportion of true cases among the total number of cases tested.
- `` `recall`` – proportion of true positives to number of true cases with $y = 1$.
- `` `precision`` – proportion of true positives to number of cases predicted as $\hat{y} = 1$.
- `` `specificity`` – proportion of true negatives to number of true cases with $y = -1$.
- `` `F1score`` – harmonic average of precision and recall.

The function is implemented as follows:

```
.quantQ.ada.adaPredictionStats:{[tabAdaPrediction]
   // tabAdaPrediction -- output of .quantQ.ada.adaBoostPrediction function
   truePositive:sum (tabAdaPrediction[`y]=tabAdaPrediction[`prediction])
       ↪ and (tabAdaPrediction[`y]=1);
   trueNegative:sum (tabAdaPrediction[`y]=tabAdaPrediction[`prediction])
       ↪ and (tabAdaPrediction[`y]=-1);
   falsePositive:sum (tabAdaPrediction[`y]=1) and (tabAdaPrediction[`
       ↪ prediction]=-1);
   falseNegative:sum (tabAdaPrediction[`y]=-1) and (tabAdaPrediction[`
       ↪ prediction]=1);
   accuracy:("f"$truePositive+trueNegative)%"f"$count tabAdaPrediction;
   recall:("f"$truePositive)%"f"$(truePositive+falseNegative);
   precision: ("f"$truePositive)%"f"$(truePositive+falsePositive);
   specificity: ("f"$trueNegative)%"f"$falsePositive+trueNegative;
   F1score:2.0%((1.0%recall)+(1.0%precision));
   // output is dictionary with all measures
   :`truePositive`trueNegative`falsePositive`falseNegative`accuracy`recall`
       ↪ precision`specificity
       `F1score!(truePositive;trueNegative;falsePositive;falseNegative;
          ↪ accuracy;recall;
       precision;specificity;F1score);
};
```

and gives for the case under examination:

```
.quantQ.ada.adaPredictionStats[tabAdaPrediction]
```

```
(`truePositive`trueNegative`falsePositive`falseNegative`accuracy`recall`
    ↪ precision`specificity`F1score)
    ↪ !(37;37;18;18;0.6727273;0.6727273;0.6727273;0.6727273;0.6727273)
```

The predicted outcome is fairly symmetric. The algorithm does not favour either of the two classes. It aims to provide a balanced estimate which has been achieved in our synthetic table. Further, the analysis of the model has been done fully in-sample. We encourage the reader to repeat the exercise independently and assess whether the symmetry encountered in the output is just coincidence or native to the data set (Hint: former is the case).

Let us further remark that clear information needed to view the contingency table can be obtained as:

```
select count res by y, prediction from tabAdaPrediction
```

```
y  prediction| res
-------------| ---
-1 -1        | 37
-1 1         | 18
1  -1        | 18
1  1         | 37
```

If we investigate the part of the table which is purely random, we obtain:

```
select count res by y, prediction from tabAdaPrediction where i>9
```

```
y  prediction| res
-------------| ---
-1 -1        | 37
-1 1         | 18
1  -1        | 18
1  1         | 27
```

suggesting that the portion of true positives corresponds to the observations with a strong link between dependent and independent variables.

23.5 RECOMMENDATION FOR READERS

We suggest several extensions for readers:

- *Random feature* – The implementation of the AdaBoost algorithm selects features randomly. It would be more optimal to select the best feature, using the same criteria as is used for threshold selection.

- *Meta-parameter selection* – The number of weak classifiers, L_{AdB}, is chosen by the user. This may not necessarily provide the optimal number, as overfitting may be encountered. The cross-validation is a possible technique which can be used to find an optimal value for L_{AdB}. AdaBoost can be wrapped into the cross-validation utility function, which will split the sample into parts and verify the accuracy out-of-sample.
- *Subsampling* – The data set can be split into batches, and each weak classifier can be trained on the different batch. This will strengthen the power of the technique.
- *Regression* – The provided method is for binary classification only. The AdaBoost technique can be well-defined for regressions as well. Current functions can be thus extended for regressions.

The recommended extensions would strengthen the power of the provided algorithm and encourage readers to master their skills writing the machine learning techniques in q.

CHAPTER 24

Trees

In Chapter 23, we have introduced the notion of decision stumps and their use within the AdaBoost algorithm. A decision stump is the simplest example of a decision tree. In this chapter, we will cover decision trees in more detail; see Morgan and Sonquist (1963) for illustration of first works in this direction, or Brieman et al. (1984) and Loh (2011). We present methods for both classification and regression. We start with a theoretical introduction and proceed with an implementation in q. The functions we will use to represent trees are based on the concept of treetables, first introduced by Stevan Apter; see Apter (2010).

24.1 INTRODUCTION TO TREES

Let us consider a feature space spanned over the features $x_1, \ldots, x_N$. Tree-based methods partition the space into rectangle-shaped domains and then assign a simple model to each domain. The simple model is usually constant and fits over observations belonging to the given domain. This corresponds to CART, or the Classification And Regression Tree approach.

Figure 24.1 illustrates partitioning for a case of $N = 2$, where $x_i \in [-1, 1]$ for $i = 1, 2$. We have produced this partitioning by using the following script:

```
// grid
xGrid: -1 + 0.001*til 2001;
xyGrid: xGrid cross xGrid;
// table
tabTree2D:flip `x`y!flip xyGrid;
// fill domains
tabTree2D: update y1:y from tabTree2D where x>0.5, y>-0.2;
tabTree2D: update y2:y from tabTree2D where x>0.5, y<=-0.2;
tabTree2D: update y3:y from tabTree2D where x<=0.5, x>-0.1,y>0;
tabTree2D: update y4:y from tabTree2D where x<=0.5, x>-0.1,y<=0;
tabTree2D: update y5:y from tabTree2D where x<=-0.1, x>-0.8;
tabTree2D: update y6:y from tabTree2D where x<=-0.8,y>-0.7;
tabTree2D: update y7:y from tabTree2D where x<=-0.8,y<=-0.7;
```

where the shade of grey in the figure is increasing with the index of y.

The way we constructed `tabTree2D` table reflects the underlying decision:

- Case: $x > 0.5$
  - **Case**: $y > -0.2$
  - **Case**: $y \leq -0.2$
- Case: $x \leq 0.5$
  - Case: $x > -0.1$
    * **Case**: $y > 0$
    * **Case**: $y \leq 0$
  - Case: $x \leq -0.1$
    * **Case**: $y > -0.8$
    * Case: $y \leq -0.8$
      - **Case**: $y > -0.7$
      - **Case**: $y \leq -0.7$

where in bold font, we have denoted the "leaf" nodes, i.e. those which have been depicted in Figure 24.1.

Let us further assume that we are in fact solving a regression problem, where we have two features x_1, x_2, both defined in $[-1, 1]^2$, and one dependent variable y, i.e. the model for the data looks like:

$$y = f(x_1, x_2). \tag{24.1}$$

We can use the tree structure built in the previous paragraph to model y as a function of x_1, x_2. The regression model is such that we approximate the true function in every domain by a constant c_i:

$$\hat{y} = \hat{f}(x_1, x_2) = \sum_{i=1}^{7} c_i \; 1((x_1, x_2) \in \text{domain}_i), \tag{24.2}$$

where 1() is the indicator function used to model the tree domains.

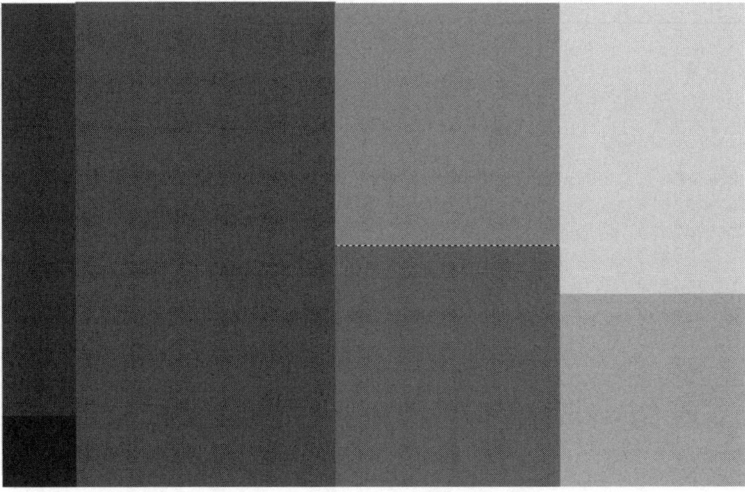

FIGURE 24.1 Example of the tree-based partitioning for a two-dimensional case

The regression is expressed in such a way that we start with the full data set. We then apply the decision rules expressed in the itemised list above. Every decision rule is binary and assigns a value to every observation of a corresponding branch. The progress is made step-by-step towards more indented rules. The decision process ends with the leaf nodes.

Creating domains using decision trees is a synthetic restriction, which affects the shape of the domains. The ease of interpreting results compensates the perceived disadvantage. If features are descriptive characteristics of a subject, the decision tree reflects the way a human analyst would classify the subject based on features. This is true in medicine, for instance, where diagnosis for a disease is based on the presence of various symptoms and measurements.

In the following subsections, we outline in detail how to build a tree which can be used to fit regression and classification problems.

24.2 REGRESSION TREES

Let us consider the following problem. We have N features $x_1, \ldots, x_N$, and a dependent variable y, each observation indexed by j, with $j = 1, \ldots, \mathcal{T}$. The dependent variable can take any value; here we will assume it is real-valued. In order to fit the regression model, we have to determine the loss function, i.e. how well or bad the model denoted by f approximated the true data generating process. We consider the loss function in the form of sum of squares:

$$Loss = \sum_{j=1}^{\mathcal{T}} (y_j - f(x_{1j}, \ldots, x_{N,j}))^2. \tag{24.3}$$

The decision tree model thus has to achieve the minimum loss. Let us assume we are already provided with a given decision tree, e.g. the scheme to split the domain into leaf nodes:

$$f(x_{1j}, \ldots, x_{Nj}) = \sum_{i=1}^{N_d} c_i 1((x_{1j}, \ldots, x_{Nj}) \in \text{domain}_i), \tag{24.4}$$

where constants c_i remain to be determined.

In fact, if we fix the tree itself, the constants are easy to find; they are simply given as:

$$c_i = \text{mean } y_j 1((x_{1j}, \ldots, x_{Nj}) \in \text{domain}_i), \tag{24.5}$$

i.e. the mean over all observations within the corresponding domain.

This does not allow us yet to form a decision. In particular, it remains to answer how branches are formed, how many of them, and how deep the tree should be. Before we discuss these, let us point out that we tacitly consider binary recursive trees, which are created as follows:

- First, we split the space into two halves; the way to split the space – variable and threshold – is decided based on the chosen loss function.
- Second, we model the response by the mean in each domain.
- Each region is further split (or not) using the procedure above.
- This process is recursively applied until a stopping rule is reached.

The optimisation of the outcome – the entire decision tree and the corresponding means – is not computationally feasible to be achieved in one go. The problem is highly non-linear and data-dependent, which will be exploited in the next chapter when we bag trees. It is thus more convenient to proceed with a greedy algorithm, which does not aim to provide a global minimum. It instead reaches a satisfactory level for the loss function in a numerically possible manner.

The greedy algorithm for a decision tree is constructed as follows:

- Start with root node – the entire data set.
- Set the feature i, with $i \in \{1, \dots, N\}$, and the threshold ξ_i to define the binary choice:

$$\text{domain}_1(i, \xi_i) = \{x | x_i \leq \xi_i\}, \tag{24.6}$$

$$\text{domain}_2(i, \xi_i) = \{x | x_i > \xi_i\}. \tag{24.7}$$

  – The feature index i and corresponding ξ_i is found as a solution to:

$$\min_{i,\xi_i} \left[\min_{c_1} \sum_{x_j \in \text{domain}_1(i,\xi_i)} (y_j - c_1)^2 + \min_{c_2} \sum_{x_j \in \text{domain}_2(i,\xi_i)} (y_j - c_2)^2 \right]. \tag{24.8}$$

  – The inner minimisation is indeed trivial:

$$c_l = \text{mean}\ (x_i) \text{ with } x_j \in \text{domain}_l(i, \xi_i) \text{ for } l = 1, 2. \tag{24.9}$$

  – For a given i, the split ξ_i is found by minimising the sum of squares across possible splits.
- The procedure is iteratively repeated on both domains.
- The algorithm proceeds until the stopping rule is reached.

Let us point out that the procedure itself can produce trees which will have one observation per leaf node. This will provide a seemingly optimal regression tree as every average value will be formed by one value only. This is not feasible since the number of parameters needed to achieve such a tree will exploit all degrees of freedom of the data set. This constitutes an overfit, which will be seen when tested out-of-sample.

The stopping rule is thus needed, and it represents a hyperparameter of the model. The first choice is some threshold on the improvement of the loss function itself. This is in line with the greedy approach; when a given step does not provide short-term profit, the algorithm stops. The disadvantage of the approach is that a split which does not improve the overall loss function much may well open up significant improvements in subsequent splits.

The preferred algorithm is following a slightly different philosophy. First, the decision tree is grown maximally, with the stopping rule being a minimum size of leaf nodes. The fully grown decision tree is then subsequently pruned. The motivation is to build a maximum tree and then merge any branches which do not bring significant improvements. The way to perform this operation is called “cost-complexity” pruning.

24.2.1 Cost-Complexity Pruning

In order to introduce the cost-complexity measure, which governs the pruning mechanism, we have to first introduce the relevant terminology for describing trees. The provided terminology is necessary to understand this measure and will give the reader a deeper understanding of the decision tree universe in general. Let us stress that trees have proven to be useful in the construction of a wide range of different algorithms.

Full tree

Let us denote the fully grown tree as T_0.

Subtree

The subtree of a tree T is formed by nodes and edges, which are a subset of those in the tree T.

Cardinality of tree

The cardinality of a tree $|T|$ stands for the number of leaf nodes in the tree T.

Descendant

A node t' is a descendant of a node t in the tree T, if there exists a connected path down the tree from t to t'.

Ancestor

A node t is an ancestor of a node t' in the tree T, if t' is a descendant of t.

Branch

A branch T_t of the tree T is a subtree with a node t being a root node and all descendants of t from T.

Pruning

Process of pruning a branch T_t of the tree T consists of deleting all descendants of t from T.

Pruned tree

A tree T' is a pruned subtree from the tree T, if some branches of the tree T have been pruned off. We denote it as $T' \subset T$.

We are now fully equipped to define the cost-complexity measure. The measure governs the second part of the algorithm outlined above:

Cost-complexity measure

The cost-complexity measure is defined as:

$$R_\alpha(T) = \sum_{l=1}^{|T|} \left[\sum_{x_j \in \text{domain}_l(i,\xi_i)} Loss_l(T) \right] + \alpha|T| \tag{24.10}$$

$$= \sum_{l=1}^{|T|} \left[\sum_{x_j \in \text{domain}_l(i,\xi_i)} \left(y_j - \frac{1}{\sum_{x_j \in \text{domain}_l(i,\xi_i)}} \sum_{x_j \in \text{domain}_l(i,\xi_i)} y_j \right) \right] + \alpha|T|. \tag{24.11}$$

The cost-complexity pruning algorithm thus starts with a fully grown tree and aims to find for every α the pruned tree T_α, i.e., $T_\alpha \subset T$ such that $R_\alpha(T)$ is minimised. The role of the parameter α is apparent: the parameter governs the trade-off between the tree size and how well it performs in fitting the data. When $\alpha \to 0$, the fully grown tree is preferred. On the other hand, as α grows the size is penalised more, up to the point when the tree with root node only is chosen.

The cost-complexity pruning algorithm works as follows:

- Grow a fully grown tree T_0.
- Choose a range of values for α.
  - For every α, find a unique smallest subtree $T_\alpha \subset T_0$, which minimises $R_\alpha(T_\alpha)$.
  - The subtree is found by pruning: the nodes are successively collapsed in a sequence, where we collapse a node, which produces the smallest per-node increase of the loss function – sum of squares. The sequence of collapsing the tree continues until the tree with root node only is obtained. This procedure contains a sequence of subtrees and the optimal tree is contained in this sequence.
- Given the sequence of trees T_α, each of them optimising the cost-complexity measure, the optimal α is found by cross-validation.

In the following section, we discuss the formulation of the decision trees for the classification problems.

24.3 CLASSIFICATION TREE

Let us focus on the classification problem. This means that the dependent variable y is assumed to take integer values $k = 1, \ldots, K$. This can correspond to the dependent variable being an array of K words or symbols, for instance. Without loss of generality, we will operate with an integer-valued dependent variable. In order to employ the decision tree on classification problems, we have to decide which loss function to use.

First, we define the proportion of class k observations in node m:

$$\hat{p}_{mk} = \frac{1}{\sum_{x_j \in \text{domain}_m(i,\xi_i)}} \sum_{x_i \in \text{domain}_m(i,\xi_i)} 1(y_j = k). \tag{24.12}$$

The decision rule based on majority vote classifies the node to be such a class, which maximises:

$$k(m) = \arg\max_k \hat{p}_{mk}. \tag{24.13}$$

We can now define the loss function, $Loss(T)$, which can be used within the cost-complexity pruning algorithm to find an optimal tree structure. Unlike regression, where the sum of squares of residuals keeps its monopolistic position, the classification problem offers several comparable measures, each with different advantages and disadvantages.

Misclassification error:

$$Loss_l(T) = 1 - \hat{p}_{mk}. \tag{24.14}$$

Gini index:

$$Loss_l(T) = \sum_{k \neq k'} \hat{p}_{mk}\hat{p}_{mk'} = \sum_{k=1}^{K} \hat{p}_{mk}(1 - \hat{p}_{mk}). \tag{24.15}$$

Cross-entropy:

$$Loss_l(T) = -\sum_{k=1}^{K} \hat{p}_{mk} \log(\hat{p}_{mk}). \tag{24.16}$$

In the case of two classes, $K = 2$, with p denoting the proportion in the second class, the three functions collapse into the intuitive functions:

$$\text{Misclassification error: } Loss_l(T) = 1 - \max(p, 1 - p), \tag{24.17}$$

$$\text{Gini index: } Loss_l(T) = 2p(1 - p), \tag{24.18}$$

$$\text{Cross-entropy: } Loss_l(T) = -p\log(p) - (1 - p)\log(1 - p). \tag{24.19}$$

We believe the reader may be curious about the shape of the functions. We encourage the reader to plot the above functions in q – implementation should be trivial.

Let us illustrate the difference using the following example. Consider a case with $K = 2$, where there are 400 observations in each class (denoted as (400,400)). Further, suppose that Split 1 creates nodes (300,100) and (100,300) while Split 2 creates nodes (200,400) and (200, 0). The following statements hold:

- Cross-entropy and the Gini index are more sensitive to changes in the node probabilities than the misclassification error.
- Both splits produce a misclassification rate of 0.25; however, Split 2 produces a pure node. This can be in many cases the preferable choice.
- The Gini index and cross-entropy are lower for Split 2.

As a rule of thumb, it is recommended that for growing the tree, the Gini index or cross-entropy are used. For the cost-complexity pruning algorithm, any measure can be used. Many researchers prefer the misclassification rate, though.

It is worth it to denote that the Gini index can be obtained as a consequence of changing the majority vote into probabilistic interpretation. Namely, if we interpret the outcome of a node in terms of probability to classify node m as class k, i.e., $\hat{p}_{mk}$, then the training error rate of this rule in the node is $\sum_{k\neq k'}\hat{p}_{mk}\hat{p}_{mk'}$. If observation is coded as 1 for class k and 0 otherwise, the variance within the node is $\hat{p}_{mk}(1-\hat{p}_{mk})$. We can sum the variance of all nodes and obtain the Gini index.

24.4 MISCELLANEOUS

Let us summarise several observations which are useful when considering using the decision trees on real examples. In this section we have covered CART, or Classification And Regression Tree, algorithm. There are other alternative successful methods to construct trees, for example, C4.5; see Quinlan (2014).

Beyond binary trees

It is not practical to use trees which split into more than two branches at each node. The tree will cause considerable fragmentation and not enough structure can be built due to the insufficient amount of data.

Categorical predictors

The dependent variable can be composed of categorical variables. If the dependent variable is formed of Q possible unordered values, then there are $2^{Q-1}-1$ possible partitions. If Q is large, this becomes numerically infeasible.

The loss matrix

In practical problems, the different outcomes can have a different impact. For example, in medicine, we want to minimise Type 2 error, i.e. failing to detect disease is more costly as opposed to producing false alarms. On the other hand, in the judicial system, Type 1 error is not acceptable as releasing a guilty person may be preferable to sentencing an innocent one.

In order to take this into account, we may define a $K\times K$ loss matrix L, with $L_{kk'}$ being the loss for classifying a true class k as class k'. The diagonal of K contains zeros. Consequently, the Gini index is modified as:

$$Loss_l(T) = \sum_{k\neq k'} L_{kk'}\hat{p}_{mk}\hat{p}_{mk'}. \tag{24.20}$$

The loss matrix K can be interpreted in Bayesian language as prior probabilities imposed on the classes.

Additive structure

Decision trees can successfully describe non-linear patterns in the data. However, the trees have a blind spot, which is nothing but models with additive structure. Let us illustrate it on a simple example where the dependent variable is a function of two factors x_1 and x_2 where the underlying data generating process reads:

$$y_i = c_1 \, 1(x_{1i} < \xi_1) + c_2 \, 1(x_{2i} < \xi_2) + \epsilon_i, \tag{24.21}$$

where ϵ_i is a zero-mean noise. It is not difficult to see that the decision tree needed such a model. In the case of more complex additive models, the decision trees needed may need a large amount of data to work. A more suitable method is using Multivariate Adaptive Splines; see Friedman (1991). This method provides smoother models as opposed to decision trees, which are by nature rough.

Data dependence

Decision trees are data dependent, where small variation in a data set can easily result in a completely different decision tree structure. This instability is a disadvantage when we want to interpret the tree as a set of rules. On the other hand, the data dependence which allows us to construct forests of trees will lead to a significant improvement in fitting various models. The next chapter will be devoted to forests and how they adress this issue.

However, before we do that, let us illustrate a way to build trees using q.

24.5 IMPLEMENTATION OF TREES

We now look at a sample use case, using the famous Iris data set, and build our q code around that. First, we load our data:

```
iris:("FFFFS";enlist csv)0:`:irisData.csv;
```

```
iris
```

```
sepalLength sepalWidth petalLength petalWidth class
-----------------------------------------------------
5.1         3.5        1.4         0.2        Iris-setosa
4.9         3          1.4         0.2        Iris-setosa
4.7         3.2        1.3         0.2        Iris-setosa
4.6         3.1        1.5         0.2        Iris-setosa
5           3.6        1.4         0.2        Iris-setosa
5.4         3.9        1.7         0.4        Iris-setosa
4.6         3.4        1.4         0.3        Iris-setosa
5           3.4        1.5         0.2        Iris-setosa
4.4         2.9        1.4         0.2        Iris-setosa
4.9         3.1        1.5         0.1        Iris-setosa
5.4         3.7        1.5         0.2        Iris-setosa
```

```
4.8         3.4         1.6         0.2         Iris-setosa
4.8         3           1.4         0.1         Iris-setosa
4.3         3           1.1         0.1         Iris-setosa
..
```

We start our q sample implementation by creating a function which can classify a vector of real values into distinct integer values. This will enable us to fit a classification where our sampled predicted variable y takes values $k = 0, \ldots, K - 1$ using 0 as the first class, in line with q's natural indexing.

```
.quantQ.trees.classify:{[breakpoints;y] asc[breakpoints] binr y};
```

For our loss function, we chose to implement a function which calculates entropy according to the formula we gave earlier:

```
.quantQ.trees.entropy:{[y;classes]
   // y -- vector of sampled predicted variable
   // classes -- domain we wish to classify y, the distinct classes
   p:{sum[x=y]%count x}[y]each classes;
   :neg p wsum 2 xlog p;
};
```

Information gain for a given classification in each split is given by:

```
.quantQ.trees.infogain:{[yp;ysplit;classes]
   // yp -- the parent node classification set of attributes
   // ysplit -- the child nodes classifications set of attributes after the
       ↪ split
   // classes -- the set of classes
   uncond: .quantQ.trees.entropy[yp;classes];
   cond:  (wsum). flip ({count[y]%count x}[yp];.quantQ.trees.entropy[;
       ↪ classes])@\:/:ysplit;
   :uncond - cond;
};
```

Let us validate these definitions with a few intuitive examples. The entropy of a sample from classes 0 1 2 only containing 1's is 0:

```
0=.quantQ.trees.entropy[1 1 1 1;0 1 2]
```

```
1b
```

Increasing the randomness increases the entropy:

```
.quantQ.trees.entropy[0 1 1 1;0 1 2]
```

```
0.8112781
```

```
.quantQ.trees.entropy[0 1 2;0 1 2]
```

```
1.584963
```

Similarly, we observe an increase of information gain as we lower the entropy which we create when splitting a parent node into children:

```
.quantQ.trees.infogain[1 1 1 2;(enlist 1;1 1 2);0 1 2]
```

```
0.1225562
```

```
.quantQ.trees.infogain[1 1 1 2;(1 1;1 2);0 1 2]
```

```
0.3112781
```

```
.quantQ.trees.infogain[1 1 1 2;(1 1 1;enlist 2);0 1 2]
```

```
0.8112781
```

We also define a couple of utility functions which will apply our splitting rule of choice:

```
.quantQ.trees.applyRule:{[cbm;bmi;xi;rule;j]
   // cbm -- count of the bitmap: number of sampled points for predicted
       ↪ and predictor variable
   // bmi -- bitmap indicating indices of the sampled variables at this
       ↪ node
   // xi -- the ith predicted variable
   // rule -- rule to split on
   // j -- split xi at point j based on rule
   :(`bitmap`appliedrule!( @[zb; bmi;:;] not b; not);
       `bitmap`appliedrule!( @[zb:cbm#0b; bmi;:;] b:eval (rule;xi;j); (::))
           ↪ );
};
```

```
.quantQ.trees.runRule:{[rule;i;j;x] rule[x i;j]}
```

Note in the above definition of `applyRule` we also carry a bitmap of indices of the initial sample data and return a dictionary – choosing to do so allows us to visualise the tree structure and contents at each node, enabling us to observe and study the tree at every step.

We can now move on to the higher level functions of choosing the split and finally growing the tree:

```
.quantQ.trees.chooseSplitXi:{[yy;y;cbm;bmi;rule;classes;xi]
   // yy -- predicted variable, all sample points
   // y -- predicted variable at node
   // cbm -- count of the bitmap: number of sampled points for predicted
       ↪ and predictor variable
   // bmi -- bitmap indicating indices of the sampled variables at this
       ↪ node
   // rule -- the logical rule to apply
   // classes -- the k classification classes for y
   // xi -- the ith predicted variable
```

```
    j:asc distinct xi;
    info:{[yy;y;cbm;bmi;xi;rule;classes;j]
        split: .quantQ.trees.applyRule[cbm;bmi;xi;rule;j];
        (.quantQ.trees.infogain[y;{x where y}[yy] each split[`bitmap];
            ↪ classes];split)
        }[yy;y;cbm;bmi;xi;rule;classes] each j;
    :(j;info)@\:first idesc flip[info]0;
};
```

Choose optimal split for a node and find the split which maximises information gain by iterating over all splits

```
// Choose optimal split for a node
.quantQ.trees.chooseSplit:{[xy;treeinput]
    // treeinput -- dictionary with splitting information
    // xy -- dictionary of
    //          predictor (`x) set
    //          predicted (`y) vector
    //          distinct vector of k classification classes (`classes)
    //          number of predictor vectors to sample (`m)
    bm: treeinput`bitmap;
    x: xy[`x][;bmi: where bm];
    y: xy[`y][bmi];
    classes: xy`classes;
    m: xy`m;
    // the logical rule to apply
    rule: treeinput`rule;rulepath: treeinput`rulepath;
    cx:count x;
    info: .quantQ.trees.chooseSplitXi[xy`y;y;count bm;bmi;rule;classes]peach
        ↪ x@sampled:asc neg[m]?cx;
    is:info[;1;0];
    summary: (`infogains`xi`j`infogain!enlist[sampled!is],i,(-1_r)),/:last r
        ↪ :raze info i:first idesc is;
    cnt: count summary;
    rulepathfunc:{[rp;ar;r;i;j] rp,enlist (ar;(`.quantQ.trees.runRule;r;i;j)
        ↪ )};
    :update rule:rule,
        rulepath:rulepathfunc[rulepath]'[appliedrule;rule;xi;j] from summary
            ↪ ;
};
```

and

```
.quantQ.trees.growTree:{[xy;treeinput]
    // treeinput -- dictionary with splitting information
    // xy -- dictionary of
    //        predictor (`x) set
    //        predicted (`y) vector
    //        distinct vector of k classification classes (`classes)
    //        number of predictor vectors to sample (`m)
    //        maximum tree depth (`maxdepth)
    :{[xy;r]
        if[(1>=count distinct xy[`y]where r`bitmap)
            or xy[`maxdepth]<=count r`rulepath;
            :r];
```

```
        enlist[r],$[98h<>type rr:.quantQ.trees.growTree[xy;r];raze @[rr;
            ↪ where 99h=type each rr;enlist];rr]
    }[xy]each  r:.quantQ.trees.chooseSplit[xy;treeinput];
};
```

We can now learn a tree: for each of the records in the initial split, we iterate until we reach pure nodes (leaves) or until the maximum specified level (`` `maxdepth `` key) is reached. When we reach a leaf, we return a flattened result and then recurse over the next split record until there are none left. The flattened tree should contain all the paths and a tree-like structure with all indices `i` and parents `p`. The provided function takes as an input a dictionary with the index of the predictor `x`, its indices `i` and `j`, the information gain, and four parameters which are carried through:

```
.quantQ.trees.learnTree:{[params]
    // params -- dictionary with parameters for learning the tree
    // m -- number of features to randomly select defaults to all features
    // maxdepth -- maximum depth of tree if pure nodes not reached defaults
        ↪ to 100
    params[`m]: $[`m in key params;params`m;count params`x];
    params[`maxdepth]: $[`maxdepth in key params;params`maxdepth;100];
    r0: `infogains`xi`j`infogain`bitmap`x`y`appliedrule`rule`rulepath`
        ↪ classes`m`maxdepth#
        params,
        `infogains`xi`j`infogain`bitmap`appliedrule`rulepath!(()!();0N;0N;0n
            ↪ ;count[params`y]#1b;::;());
    tree: enlist[r0],
    $[ 98<>type r:.quantQ.trees.growTree[; r0:dc _r0] (dc:`x`y`classes`m`
        ↪ maxdepth)#r0;
        raze @[r;where 99h=type each r;enlist];
        r];
    tree: update p:{x?-1_'x} rulepath  from tree;
    :`i`p`path xcols update path:{(x scan)each til count x}p,i:i from tree;
};
```

We will now create a dictionary of the parameters we need to fit, or *learn* the tree:

```
dataset:()!();
dataset[`x]:value flip delete class from iris;
dataset[`y]:{distinct[x]?x} iris[`class];
params: dataset,`rule`classes!(>;asc distinct dataset`y);
```

View our features:

```
flip params`x
```

```
5.1 3.5 1.4 0.2
4.9 3   1.4 0.2
4.7 3.2 1.3 0.2
4.6 3.1 1.5 0.2
5   3.6 1.4 0.2
5.4 3.9 1.7 0.4
4.6 3.4 1.4 0.3
5   3.4 1.5 0.2
4.4 2.9 1.4 0.2
```

```
4.9 3.1 1.5 0.1
5.4 3.7 1.5 0.2
4.8 3.4 1.6 0.2
4.8 3   1.4 0.1
4.3 3   1.1 0.1
5.8 4   1.2 0.2
5.7 4.4 1.5 0.4
..
```

and the classification of our predicted variable:

```
distinct params`y
```

```
0 1 2
```

and visualising as a table:

```
flip @[`x`y#params;`x;flip]
```

```
x               y
-----------------
5.1 3.5 1.4 0.2 0
4.9 3   1.4 0.2 0
4.7 3.2 1.3 0.2 0
4.6 3.1 1.5 0.2 0
5   3.6 1.4 0.2 0
5.4 3.9 1.7 0.4 0
4.6 3.4 1.4 0.3 0
5   3.4 1.5 0.2 0
4.4 2.9 1.4 0.2 0
4.9 3.1 1.5 0.1 0
5.4 3.7 1.5 0.2 0
4.8 3.4 1.6 0.2 0
4.8 3   1.4 0.1 0
4.3 3   1.1 0.1 0
..
```

We grow (learn) a tree and observe its meta. We can see that columns returned for this treetable include the params as well as intermediate steps which are useful for exploration of each node:

```
tree:.quantQ.trees.learnTree params
```

```
meta tree
```

```
c          | t f a
-----------| -----
i          | j
p          | j
path       | J
```

```
infogains   |
xi          | j
j           |
infogain    | f
bitmap      | B
appliedrule|
rule        |
rulepath    |
```

We can inspect our fields of choice, e.g. the full rule path along with the associated applied rules:

```
select i,p,path,xi,j,rulepath from tree
```

```
x  p  path          xi j   rulepath
   ↪                                                                 ..
-------------------------------------------------------------------------..
0  0  ,0               0N  ()
   ↪
   ↪ ..
1  0  1 0           2  1.9 ,(~:;(`.quantQ.trees.runRule;>;2;1.9))
   ↪                                          ..
2  0  2 0           2  1.9 ,(::;(`.quantQ.trees.runRule;>;2;1.9))
   ↪                                          ..
3  2  3 2 0         3  1.7 ((::;(`.quantQ.trees.runRule;>;2;1.9));(~:;(`.
   ↪ quantQ.trees.runRule;>;3;..
4  3  4 3 2 0       2  4.9 ((::;(`.quantQ.trees.runRule;>;2;1.9));(~:;(`.
   ↪ quantQ.trees.runRule;>;3;..
5  4  5 4 3 2 0     3  1.6 ((::;(`.quantQ.trees.runRule;>;2;1.9));(~:;(`.
   ↪ quantQ.trees.runRule;>;3;..
6  4  6 4 3 2 0     3  1.6 ((::;(`.quantQ.trees.runRule;>;2;1.9));(~:;(`.
   ↪ quantQ.trees.runRule;>;3;..
7  3  7 3 2 0       2  4.9 ((::;(`.quantQ.trees.runRule;>;2;1.9));(~:;(`.
   ↪ quantQ.trees.runRule;>;3;..
8  7  8 7 3 2 0     3  1.5 ((::;(`.quantQ.trees.runRule;>;2;1.9));(~:;(`.
   ↪ quantQ.trees.runRule;>;3;..
9  7  9 7 3 2 0     3  1.5 ((::;(`.quantQ.trees.runRule;>;2;1.9));(~:;(`.
   ↪ quantQ.trees.runRule;>;3;..
10 9  10 9 7 3 2 0 0  6.7 ((::;(`.quantQ.trees.runRule;>;2;1.9));(~:;(`.
   ↪ quantQ.trees.runRule;>;3;..
11 9  11 9 7 3 2 0 0  6.7 ((::;(`.quantQ.trees.runRule;>;2;1.9));(~:;(`.
   ↪ quantQ.trees.runRule;>;3;..
12 2  12 2 0        3  1.7 ((::;(`.quantQ.trees.runRule;>;2;1.9));(::;(`.
   ↪ quantQ.trees.runRule;>;3;..
13 12 13 12 2 0     2  4.8 ((::;(`.quantQ.trees.runRule;>;2;1.9));(::;(`.
   ↪ quantQ.trees.runRule;>;3;..
14 13 14 13 12 2 0 0  5.9 ((::;(`.quantQ.trees.runRule;>;2;1.9));(::;(`.
   ↪ quantQ.trees.runRule;>;3;..
15 13 15 13 12 2 0 0  5.9 ((::;(`.quantQ.trees.runRule;>;2;1.9));(::;(`.
   ↪ quantQ.trees.runRule;>;3;..
16 12 16 12 2 0     2  4.8 ((::;(`.quantQ.trees.runRule;>;2;1.9));(::;(`.
   ↪ quantQ.trees.runRule;>;3;..
```

We can return a subtree T' which contains only the leaves:

```
.quantQ.trees.leaves:{[tree]
   // tree -- decision tree
   :select from tree where i in til[count p]except p
 };
```

where p here is the parent node of that node and we therefore select all the nodes which are not parents:

```
.quantQ.trees.leaves tree
```

```
i  p  path          infogains
   ↪ xi j   infogain   bitma..
-----------------------------------------------------------------------..
1  0  1 0            `s#0 1 2 3!0.5572327 0.2679114 0.9182958 0.9182958     2
   ↪    1.9 0.9182958  11111..
5  4  5 4 3 2 0      `s#0 1 2 3!0.1044276 0.03781815 0.02834482 0.1460943   3
   ↪    1.6 0.1460943  00000..
6  4  6 4 3 2 0      `s#0 1 2 3!0.1044276 0.03781815 0.02834482 0.1460943   3
   ↪    1.6 0.1460943  00000..
8  7  8 7 3 2 0      `s#0 1 2 3!0.1091703 0.2516292 0.2516292 0.4591479     3
   ↪    1.5 0.4591479  00000..
10 9  10 9 7 3 2 0 `s#0 1 2 3!0.9182958 0.2516292 0.9182958 0.2516292      0
   ↪    6.7 0.9182958  00000..
11 9  11 9 7 3 2 0 `s#0 1 2 3!0.9182958 0.2516292 0.9182958 0.2516292      0
   ↪    6.7 0.9182958  00000..
14 13 14 13 12 2 0 `s#0 1 2 3!0.9182958 0.9182958 0 0                      0
   ↪    5.9 0.9182958  00000..
15 13 15 13 12 2 0 `s#0 1 2 3!0.9182958 0.9182958 0 0                      0
   ↪    5.9 0.9182958  00000..
16 12 16 12 2 0      `s#0 1 2 3!0.06105981 0.03811322 0.09120811 0.04314475 2
   ↪    4.8 0.09120811 00000..
```

Let us predict a value. We start by looking at the average values for each feature, grouping by the predicted variable, and then predict:

```
select avg sepalLength,avg sepalWidth,avg petalLength,avg petalWidth by
   ↪ class from iris
```

```
class          | sepalLength sepalWidth petalLength petalWidth
---------------| ------------------------------------------
Iris-setosa    | 5.006       3.418      1.464       0.244
Iris-versicolor| 5.936       2.77       4.26        1.326
Iris-virginica | 6.588       2.974      5.552       2.026
```

Let X_i denote a tuple of the features at a data point i denoting the node identifier. Now to predict a value, we apply the rules of the tree to X_i using the previously constructed `rulepath field and return the tree record containing the classification. Predict Y (classify) given a tree and an input X_i:

```
.quantQ.trees.predictOnTree:{[tree;x]
   // tree -- a previously grown tree
   // x -- a tuple of the features at a data point i, ie X[i]
   :({[x;tree]
       if[1=count tree;:tree];
       @[tree;`rulepath;1_'] where {value y[0],value[y 1]x}[x]each tree[`
           ↪ rulepath][;0]
       }[x]over)[.quantQ.trees.leaves tree];
};
```

We can now take an *x* tuple and predict the value of *y*

```
select i:i,path,y:{distinct x where y}[params`y]each bitmap from .quantQ.
    ↪ trees.predictOnTree[tree] 5.936 2.77 4.26 1.326
```

```
i path      y
-------------
0 5 4 3 2 0 1
```

The predicted class is 1, which is versicolor. This is in line with what we expected since the sample we chose was the average value for that class.

We can also write a quick test to check whether all features are predicted correctly:

```
all {[x;y;i]
       predicted: .quantQ.trees.predictOnTree[tree] flip[x] i ;
       y[i]=first distinct y where first predicted`bitmap
   }[dataset`x;dataset`y]each til count iris
```

```
1b
```

We have thus built an initial toolset to allow us to grow a tree and use the resultant tree to predict values. We have previously also performed classification with the use of neural networks. We are now equipped with two machine learning techniques for classification with the same sample data set. We encourage readers to perform a numerical comparison between the two methods to assess their strengths and weaknesses.

CHAPTER 25

Forests

In Chapter 24, we introduced the concept of decision trees. They represent a useful method for capturing and modelling non-linear data generating processes. They also provide results which can be easily read and interpreted by human analysts. The notion of decision trees can be extended further into a more powerful concept – the ensemble of trees – random forests; see Breiman (2001). They give rise to a method of estimation which is very powerful, due to its numerical ease in obtaining the fit and its explanatory power. Random forests attempt to address one of the main challenges of decision trees, which is overfitting, using the statistical concept of bootstrapping. In this section, building upon the previous chapter on trees, we introduce the theoretical foundations behind random forests and demonstrate an implementation.

25.1 BOOTSTRAP

Let us start with the concept of bootstrapping as it is introduced in statistics; see Efron (1992). This will equip us with the intuition on how it can be used to improve the performance of decision trees. The concept of bootstrapping stands for testing which involves random sampling with replacement. It is particularly useful when we need to estimate the sampling distribution for a particular measure or statistic. Consequently, we can obtain the significance level for sample statistics and test the various hypotheses on the given sample. The bootstrap is a general procedure and an alternative to asymptotic methods which use a parametric model for the underlying statistics. In some cases, it produces better results than a traditional normal approximation of the statistic's properties while in others we may obtain dubious results.

In order to understand the bootstrap, let us assume a random variable X generated by some distribution function G and statistic θ. We consider N realisations of the random variable X – the observations – which we denote as $x_1, \ldots, x_N$ and calculate the sample statistic $\hat{\theta}$. In order to make plausible inference about the statistic, we need to understand the statistical properties of $\hat{\theta}$ calculated from a sample of size N. The particular variable of interest here is the variability of the sample statistic.

The sample statistic is a function of the sample, i.e., $\hat{\theta} = \theta(x_1, \ldots, x_N)$, and thus the sample statistic is a random variable with a certain sampling distribution function, denoted as τ. Such a function depends on the size of the sample and the underlying distribution function G, i.e., $\tau = \tau(N, G)$. There are two possible cases which can make the inference of the sampling distribution function complex:

- G is known, but $\hat{\theta}(x_1, \dots, x_N)$ is too complicated to derive the sampling distribution $\tau(N, G)$.
- G is unknown.

In both cases, τ cannot be analytically derived. Let us stress that the asymptotic theory aims to derive the function analytically and assess its properties. The function converges to the normal distribution with variance proportional to $N^{-\alpha}$ in many cases. This is not the case in the subsequent paragraphs.

G is known, $\hat{\theta}$ complex

Since the analytic derivations are not possible, we can derive properties of $\hat{\theta}$ numerically. In particular, we generate B samples $x_1^b, \dots, x_N^b$, with $b = 1, \dots, B$ by sampling *with replacement*. For every sample, we calculate corresponding $\hat{\theta}_b$.

Having in hand $\hat{\theta}_b$, we can approximate $\hat{\tau}$ using the empirical distribution function of the observed sample. Obtaining the variability of $\hat{\theta}$ is then straightforward; we can read it from the sample. We may therefore test a hypothesis about the value of $\hat{\theta}$. It is worth pointing out that it is our numerical limitations which affect the accuracy of the approximation: the higher B is, the more accurate the approximation is.

G is unknown

We now restrict our knowledge even more and assume that we do not know G. There are two possible causes of our ignorance of G. First, we may know the functional form of G up to the parameter(s) ν. If we know that parameter, we can proceed in the way outlined in the previous paragraph. In many cases, however, we can obtain an estimate of the parameter, $\hat{\nu}$. In such a case, we can employ the *parametric bootstrap* and assume that data are coming from $G(\cdot|\hat{\nu})$. We then proceed as above.

Let us consider a more interesting case, where we do not possess any knowledge of G. The only knowledge about G is encoded in the sample $x_1, \dots, x_N$. The way to assess the statistical properties of $\hat{\theta}$ is to employ a *nonparametric bootstrap*. First, we form the empirical distribution function G_N from the observed sample. Such a function assigns equal probability $1/N$ to every value x_i, with $i = 1, \dots, N$. We consider G_N as approximation of G. Then, we proceed as above: we sample B samples of size N from G_N. For every sample, we calculate θ_b^*. Then, we can assess $\hat{\theta}$ from the empirical distribution function derived from sequence θ_b^*. For instance, the standard deviation of $\hat{\theta}$ is given as:

$$\sigma_{\hat{\theta}} = \sqrt{\frac{1}{B}\sum_{b=1}^{B}\left(\theta_b^* - \frac{1}{B}\sum_{b=1}^{B}\theta_b^*\right)^2}. \tag{25.1}$$

Generating a bootstrap sample from G_N means sampling from $x_1, \dots, x_N$ with replacement.

Tossing coins

Let us illustrate the bootstrap with a simple example. We toss a coin and denote 1 for heads and 0 for tails. We are interested in the properties of the estimator of the average value when we toss a coin N-times. Tossing the coin N-times is equivalent to recording the series $x_1, x_2, \ldots, x_N$, with $x_i = 0, 1$. The statistic of interest is:

$$\mu_N = \frac{1}{N}\sum_{i=1}^{N} x_i \ . \tag{25.2}$$

In order to assess the statistical properties of μ_N, we draw B samples with replacement from $x_1, \ldots, x_N$. Such a bootstrapped sample may read: $\tilde{X}_b = x_3, x_4, x_1, x_N, x_1, \ldots$. We repeat the procedure $B - 1$ times and collect $\mu_{N,1}, \ldots, \mu_{N,B}$. The empirical distribution function of $\mu_{N,b}$, with $b = 1, \ldots, B$ can be used to approximate $\hat{\theta}_{\mu}$.

We can illustrate this example numerically for $N = 10$ and $p_{tail} = 0.6$. We are interested in the standard deviation of the estimator for the mean. The following code gives the answer:

```
B:100;
dev {avg ((N:10)?1.0)<0.6} each til B
```

```
0.1527711
```

where we can change N or B accordingly.

An important assumption which underlyies the bootstrap is that the samples with replacement obtained from the observed sample have to be independent. It is appealing to use the bootstrap in regression problems. However, there are cases where the plain bootstrap outlined above does not work, due to this lack of independence or the presence of heteroscedasticity. For that purpose, alternative bootstrapping schemes have been derived; among others, we may list:

- Wild bootstrap
- Bayesian bootstrap
- White-noise bootstrap

The bootstrap is challenging when the underlying regression problem is performed on time series data, which are not stationary. A popular method is Block bootstrap where entire consecutive blocks are drawn from the sample rather than individual observations. Another method derived in Bergamelli et al. (2015) proposes a method called Maximum Non-Extensive Entropy Block Bootstrap. The basis of the bootstrap is to use entropy of the empirical distribution function, which allows us to preserve the rank correlation between the sample and the bootstrapped sample locally. Further, the method can be extended for fat-tailed non-stationary distributions by using non-extensive entropy.

The bootstrap technique can essentially be used to improve the accuracy of the estimator, which will be addressed in the next section.

25.2 BAGGING

Bagging, or bootstrap aggregation, is a procedure to improve the accuracy of a regression or classification algorithm introduced in Breiman (1996). We will illustrate the notion of bagging on decision trees, but the method is general and can be used for any estimation technique. The estimators for which bagging, in particular, shows the most significant improvement are estimators with large variance and low bias. Decision trees fall into this category due to the provision of a very good fit on the training data when grown fully. This fit, however, may result in high variance across samples, which is why training sets and out-of-sample validation are critical for decision trees, as well as pruning, as mentioned in Chapter 24. Bagging helps us address these challenges.

Bagging differs in nature from boosting, introduced in Chapter 23, as it does not require any sequential estimation and the primary motivation is not to improve the properties of weak estimators, but rather improve the variance of unstable estimators. The bagging method averages the noisy unbiased estimators. Boosting is in many cases more powerful; however, the appealing feature of bagging rests in its simplicity.

The bagging of estimators works as follows:

- Create B samples with replacement from the original sample of data.
- For every sample, estimate the model of interest, i.e. either regression or classification.
- Average the result across the bootstrap samples.

The procedure thus assumes that by creating bootstrapped samples and then estimating the model, we obtain a sample of individual models, where each comes from the same underlying distribution, i.e. having the same bias and (potentially large) variance. This stresses the difference to boosting, where the estimators are estimated in sequence and every estimator aims to efficiently remove bias left after the previous estimators have been taken into account.

The improvement in the variance of the bagged estimators is due to the same underlying reason that makes hedging so popular among asset managers and why we rely upon portfolio theory. Let us consider B draws of a random variable, each with variance σ^2. There is also a correlation between observations ρ, and let us consider the case of non-negative correlation only. The variance of the average is given:

$$\sigma_B^2 = \rho\sigma^2 + \frac{1-\rho}{B}\sigma^2 \,. \tag{25.3}$$

For given B, the variance is decreased when $\rho \to 0$. On the other hand, for $\rho = 1$ the variance remains unchanged. If we want to achieve given variance reduction, then random variables with higher pairwise correlation require large sample B.

In the case of bagging, this means that effective variance reduction occurs for uncorrelated estimators. If the underlying estimator is, for example, linear regression, the bootstrapped estimates are highly correlated, and thus variance improvement is minor. On the other hand, in the case of decision trees, the trees are noisy and non-linear in data. When we change the sample slightly, we end up growing a tree with a very different structure. Often, even a tiny fraction of data changed can lead to a very different tree topology.

The technique of random forests employs trees which optimise equation 25.3. In particular, the trees grown on every bootstrapped sample are grown such that correlation between any other sample is reduced, given the variance is not affected much. A radical version of the random forest is to grow the individual trees randomly without any optimisation and then bag such trees. This, however, increases the variance of individual trees too much and thus the entire technique does not result in significant improvement. The recommended procedure is:

- Given the sample data consisting of N observations of M-dimensional vector of features $x_{1n}, \ldots, x_{Mn}$ and dependent variable y_n, with $n = 1, \ldots, N$, we draw the bootstrapped sample – random sample with replacement – of size N from the sample, denoted for simplicity as $(X, Y)^*$.
- Using the bootstrapped sample $(X, Y)^*$, grow a tree using the following procedure:
  - For every leaf node of a tree, select m out of M features and select the best split of the node by optimising a chosen *Loss* function.
  - Split the node into two nodes, which will constitute new leaf nodes.
  - Repeat procedure until the tree with a minimum leaf node size n_{min} is grown.
  - Denote the tree as T_b^*.
- Get all the bootstrapped trees T_b^*, with $b = 1, \ldots, B$ and predict the outcome based on average value – for regression problems; or majority vote – for classification problems.

Trees are grown such that the correlation between two different trees is minimised. Considering in every split only a subset of variables amplifies the data dependence of the tree topology while it does not introduce a significant increase of individual variances. The suitable choice of m is $\sqrt{M}$ for classifications and $M/3$ for regressions.

25.2.1 Out-of-Bag

Throughout the book we have already seen the use of N-fold cross-validation as a means to determine out-of-sample performance of a given method. Alternatively, we have used it as a way to determine the best possible value for meta-parameters. The cost we had to pay for running the cross-validation is the general need to re-estimate the model N-times, each time for different folds.

The out-of-bag method provides a suitable alternative in the case of random forests. In order to calculate the error of an in-sample observation, we construct the random forest and predict the value only from those trees where the observation has not appeared among bootstrapped samples. Thus, if we keep for every tree an indicator of the observations used in the corresponding bootstrap, we can estimate the random forest only once, and we are already equipped with cross-validation error estimates – up to vector manipulations of aggregating the proper trees.

An alternative approach to constructing the out-of-bag estimate is to calculate the errors on the fly. Namely, after we grow the tree from the bootstrapped sample, the part of the sample not used in the bootstrap is then used to test the out-of-sample error.

The error is noted. In the end, the errors are aggregated. This approach does not require storing additional data to indicate which tree has used a given observation.

We can use the out-of-bag approach to assess the importance of every variable within the data set. In particular, when we grow a given tree, we store which observations have been "in-the-bag". We calculate the error of the prediction. We then choose a feature x_n and reshuffle the observations in the out-of-bag part of the sample. We denote the error for the case with reshuffled n-th feature. Comparing two errors shows how important the n-th feature is in predicting the dependent variable.

25.3 IMPLEMENTATION

We start our implementation by first creating the bootstrapping function which will sample our data for each tree's growth:

```
.quantQ.rf.sampleTree:{[s;n]
   // s -- sample dictionary with predictor and predicted variables
   // n -- sample size
   z:`x`y!(s[`x][;i];s[`y]i:n?n);
   :z,`oobi`ibi!((til n) except distinct i; i);
};
```

This function returns a dictionary of the sampled x and y for size N, but also the out-of-bag indices of the features which were not selected and the in-the-bag indices of the features that *were* selected.

To create a given "bootstrap" tree, we now draw a bootstrap sample of size N from the training data using the function above and calculate the out-of-bag error. For all features which were not sampled for that tree (out-of-bag), we predict their values and measure the prediction error:

```
.quantQ.rf.bootstrapTree:{[params;m;n;B]
   // params -- same as the ones required by .quantQ.trees.learnTree
   // m -- select m of the features in each split
   // n -- sample size
   // B -- size of bootstrap: create B bootstrap sample trees
   z: .quantQ.rf.sampleTree[`x`y#params;n];
   tree_b:   .quantQ.trees.learnTree @[params;`x`y;:;z`x`y],enlist[`m]!
       ↪ enlist m;
   tree_oob: raze .quantQ.trees.predictOnTree[tree_b]each flip params[`x;;z
       ↪ `oobi];
   tree_oob: update pred_error: abs obs_y-{first x where y}[z`y]each bitmap
       ↪ from
       update obs_y:params[`y]z`oobi from tree_oob;
   :`tree`oob`ibi!
       (`B xcols update B from tree_b;
       `B xcols update B from tree_oob;
       enlist[B]!enlist z`ibi);
};
```

The function returns a dictionary where the first key `` `tree `` is our tree for bootstrap sample *b*. It also returns a key `` `oob `` containing the out-of-bag predictions and their prediction error, and a third entry denoted by `` `ibi ``, which contains the in-the-bag indices for each sample. It "tags" the tree with the value of the correponding *b* under column `B`.

The procedure is then repeated until all B trees have been created:

```
.quantQ.rf.randomForest:{[params]
   // params dictionary,
   ensemble: .quantQ.rf.bootstrapTree[params;params`m;params`n] peach til
       ↪ params`B;
   :raze each flip ensemble;
};
```

Using the Iris data set, we can now create a random forest of 10 trees by running the following code, which samples 3 features out of 4, `m = 3`:

```
//  sampling size = count of data sample
//  start with sampling 3/4 features in every breakpoint search
//  n == count iris
forest: .quantQ.rf.randomForest params,`m`n`B!(3;150;10)
```

Examining the result, we see that it is a dictionary with 3 keys, the trees ensemble, the out-of-bag predictions and the "in-the-bag" indices, i.e., the indices selected for each bootstrap sample:

```
type forest
```

```
99h
```

```
key forest
```

```
`tree`oob`ibi
```

The ensemble of trees – a table of treetables – and the out-of-bag predictions are both themselves, tables:

```
type each forest
```

```
tree| 98
oob | 98
ibi | 99
```

The `` `ibi `` key is a dictionary (`type=99`) of indices used for each tree `B`.

Let us store the ensemble of trees:

```
rf: forest`tree
rf
```

```
B i  p  path                  infogains                                   xi j
    ↪ infogain  bi..
-----------------------------------------------------------------------------..
0 0  0  ,0                    ()!()                                          0N
    ↪            11..
0 1  0  1 0                   `s#0 2 3!0.5263125 0.9043815 0.9043815   1  1.9
    ↪ 0.9043815 11..
0 2  0  2 0                   `s#0 2 3!0.5263125 0.9043815 0.9043815   1  1.9
    ↪ 0.9043815 00..
0 3  2  3 2 0                 `s#0 1 2!0.2264283 0.1015524 0.6978655   2  4.7
    ↪ 0.6978655 00..
0 4  2  4 2 0                 `s#0 1 2!0.2264283 0.1015524 0.6978655   2  4.7
    ↪ 0.6978655 00..
0 5  4  5 4 2 0               `s#0 1 3!0.05228595 0.04691776 0.2107031 2  1.8
    ↪ 0.2107031 00..
0 6  5  6 5 4 2 0             `s#1 2 3!0.1669034 0.1864743 0.1166423   1  5f
    ↪ 0.1864743 00..
0 7  6  7 6 5 4 2 0           `s#0 1 2!0.4307766 0.3033074 0.03482766  0  6.1
    ↪ 0.4307766 00..
0 8  7  8 7 6 5 4 2 0         `s#0 1 3!0.5435644 0.5435644 0.1379254   0  5.9
    ↪ 0.5435644 00..
0 9  7  9 7 6 5 4 2 0         `s#0 1 3!0.5435644 0.5435644 0.1379254   0  5.9
    ↪ 0.5435644 00..
0 10 6  10 6 5 4 2 0          `s#0 1 2!0.4307766 0.3033074 0.03482766  0  6.1
    ↪ 0.4307766 00..
0 11 10 11 10 6 5 4 2 0       `s#0 1 2!0.1981174 0.1981174 0.07600985  0  6.3
    ↪ 0.1981174 00..
0 12 11 12 11 10 6 5 4 2 0 `s#1 2 3!0.9182958 0 0.9182958             0  2.5
    ↪ 0.9182958 00..
0 13 11 13 11 10 6 5 4 2 0 `s#1 2 3!0.9182958 0 0.9182958             0  2.5
    ↪ 0.9182958 00..
..
```

We can then access the nodes of all trees:

```
show each {[rf;b] .quantQ.trees.leaves select from rf where B=b}[rf]each
    ↪ exec distinct B from rf
```

```
B i  p  path          infogains                                  xi j
    ↪ infogain  bitmap  ..
-----------------------------------------------------------------------------..
0 1  0  1 0           `s#1 2 3!0.2805016 0.9248187 0.9248187   1  1.7
    ↪ 0.9248187 01101000..
0 5  4  5 4 3 2 0     `s#0 1 3!0.1044276 0.04537619 0.1460943  2  1.6
    ↪ 0.1460943 10010110..
0 6  4  6 4 3 2 0     `s#0 1 3!0.1044276 0.04537619 0.1460943  2  1.6
    ↪ 0.1460943 00000000..
0 8  7  8 7 3 2 0     `s#0 2 3!0.07600985 0.291692 0.4695652   2  1.5
    ↪ 0.4695652 00000000..
0 10 9  10 9 7 3 2 0 `s#1 2 3!0.2516292 0.9182958 0.2516292   1  5.1
    ↪ 0.9182958 00000000..
0 11 9  11 9 7 3 2 0 `s#1 2 3!0.2516292 0.9182958 0.2516292   1  5.1
    ↪ 0.9182958 00000000..
```

```
0 14 13 14 13 12 2 0 `s#0 1 2!1 1 0f                           0  5.9 1
   ↪         00000000..
0 15 13 15 13 12 2 0 `s#0 1 2!1 1 0f                           0  5.9 1
   ↪         00000000..
0 16 12 16 12 2 0    `s#1 2 3!0.04089637 0.1110365 0.05355186 1  4.8
   ↪ 0.1110365 00000001..
B i  p  path          infogains                                 xi j
   ↪ infogain  bitmap..
-------------------------------------------------------------------------..
1 1  0  1 0           `s#0 2 3!0.6040432 0.8729883 0.8729883    1  1.7
   ↪ 0.8729883  000100..
1 5  4  5 4 3 2 0     `s#0 1 2!0.06381 0.1607048 0.3867211      2  4.4
   ↪ 0.3867211  000000..
1 7  6  7 6 4 3 2 0   `s#0 1 3!0.9709506 0.1709506 0.1709506    0  6.1
   ↪ 0.9709506  000000..
1 8  6  8 6 4 3 2 0   `s#0 1 3!0.9709506 0.1709506 0.1709506    0  6.1
   ↪ 0.9709506  000000..
1 9  3  9 3 2 0       `s#1 2 3!0.09817123 0.08305719 0.04552503 0  2.6
   ↪ 0.09817123 000010..
1 12 11 12 11 10 2 0 `s#0 1 2!0.2364528 0.7219281 0.7219281    1  3
   ↪ 0.7219281  000000..
1 13 11 13 11 10 2 0 `s#0 1 2!0.2364528 0.7219281 0.7219281    1  3
   ↪ 0.7219281  000000..
1 14 10 14 10 2 0    `s#0 1 3!0.0956002 0.07148017 0.06089513  0  5.9
   ↪ 0.0956002  111001..
B i  p  path                 infogains                               xi j
   ↪ infogain  bi..
-------------------------------------------------------------------------..
2 1  0  1 0                  `s#0 1 3!0.6051125 0.2930229 0.9709506  2  0.6
   ↪ 0.9709506 10..
..
```

25.3.1 Prediction

We use the built random forest to predict the classification of a new data point. The data point will traverse every tree in the random forest and the final classification will be based on a *majority vote*.

```
.quantQ.rf.predictOnRF:{[y;ensemble;data]
   // y -- predicted variable vector
   // ensemble -- a random forest: a dictionary of
   //              `tree: list of treetables, a table itself
   //              `oob:  the table of out-of-bag predictions
   //              `ibi:  in-the-bag indices for each sample B
   // data -- a tuple of the features at a data point i, ie X[i]
   // returns a classification of data X based on majority rule
   rf:{[data;tree;ibi;b]
       prediction: .quantQ.trees.predictOnTree[select from tree where B=b]
           ↪ data;
       update ibi: enlist ibi b from prediction
      }[data;tree;ensemble`ibi] each exec distinct B from tree:ensemble`
          ↪ tree;
```

```
    prediction: {first where x=max x}count each
        group exec {first x[y] where z}[y]'[ibi; bitmap] from raze rf;
    :`prediction`mean_error`dev_error!
        enlist[prediction],value exec avg pred_error,dev pred_error from
            ↪ ensemble`oob;
};
```

Recall that the out-of-bag samples are stored as a separate key and used to validate the prediction ability of the learnt tree by running the prediction on them.

Now let us see how well our small random forest of bootstrap size 10 performs:

```
\ts forest: .quantQ.rf.randomForest params,`m`n`B!(3;150;10)
```

```
169 110320
```

Using our familiar Iris data set, we will attempt to predict the classification by inputting the same average values per species we also used in the previous chapter, when predicting on trees:

```
select avgSepalL: avg sepalLength, devSepalL: dev sepalLength, avgSepalW:
    ↪ avg sepalWidth, devSepalW: dev sepalWidth, avgPetalL: avg
    ↪ petalLength, devPetalL: dev petalLength, avgPetalW: avg petalWidth,
    ↪ devPetalW: dev petalWidth by class from iris
```

```
class          | avgSepalL devSepalL avgSepalW devSepalW avgPetalL
    ↪ devPetalL avgPetalW devPetalW
---------------|
    ↪ ------------------------------------------------------------------
Iris-setosa    | 5.006     0.348947  3.418     0.3771949 1.464
    ↪ 0.1717673 0.244     0.106132
Iris-versicolor| 5.936     0.5109834 2.77      0.3106445 4.26
    ↪ 0.4651881 1.326     0.1957652
Iris-virginica | 6.588     0.6294887 2.974     0.3192554 5.552
    ↪ 0.5463479 2.026     0.2718897
```

```
.quantQ.rf.predictOnRF[params`y; forest;5.006 3.418 1.464 0.244]
```

```
prediction| 1
mean_error| 0.5155709
dev_error | 0.5738835
```

The prediction is incorrect, since the output is 1 (versicolor), whereas our input was the average observed value for the 0 group (setosa).

```
.quantQ.rf.predictOnRF[params`y; forest;5.936 2.77 4.26 1.326]
```

```
prediction| 2
mean_error| 0.5155709
dev_error | 0.5738835
```

Alas, the prediction is again incorrect, since the output is 2 (virginica), whereas our input was the average observed value for the 1 group (versicolor).

Finally,

```
.quantQ.rf.predictOnRF[params`y; forest;6.588 2.974 5.552 2.026]
```

```
prediction| 2
mean_error| 0.5155709
dev_error | 0.5738835
```

gives us the correct prediction of group 2.

Looking at the mean error and standard deviation of the out-of-bag errors, we observe that their values are too high for a reliable result. This is in line with our above experiment, which yielded only 1 correct prediction out of 3.

Let us try and use all features in the sample, yet keep computation cost inline – even reducing it – by selecting a smaller data sample:

```
\ts forest: .quantQ.rf.randomForest params,`m`n`B!(4;125;10)
140 56560
```

Above we have reduced the sample size from 150 to 125, but kept all 4 features in our selection criteria for each tree's node splits. By reducing the sample size the performance of our code has actually slightly improved, even though we are now sampling all 4 features. Has our prediction accuracy improved, too?

Let us see:

```
.quantQ.rf.predictOnRF[params`y; forest;5.006 3.418 1.464 0.244]
```

```
prediction| 0
mean_error| 0.04646018
dev_error | 0.2104795
```

```
.quantQ.rf.predictOnRF[params`y; forest;5.936 2.77 4.26 1.326]
```

```
prediction| 1
mean_error| 0.04646018
dev_error | 0.2104795
```

```
.quantQ.rf.predictOnRF[params`y; forest;6.588 2.974 5.552 2.026]
```

```
prediction| 2
mean_error| 0.04646018
dev_error | 0.2104795
```

We observe that both the mean and deviation of our errors have been considerably reduced. More importantly, our predictions now are 100% correct.

25.3.2 Feature Selection

During the construction of each tree in the forest, a field of interest is the `` `infogains `` column. For each node split in a tree, we keep track of the information gain for all features. At the end, after the tree – and indeed, whole forest – construction is completed, we can use the total information gain of each feature to make inferences on the importance of each feature in our algorithm.

We can assess the importance of each feature by summing their total information gains:

```
desc sum each exec (,'/)infogains from forest`tree
```

```
2| 47.28814
3| 47.00419
0| 42.77091
1| 33.62626
```

with the forest's average prediction error shown earlier above. We know that using all features we were able to acurately predict the 3 chosen tuples into their respective classes.

What if we repeat this experiment, but by using only features 3 and 4 (indexed 2 and 3 respectively), which appear to have the most information gain during tree construction? We adjust our input parameters and reconstruct the random forest:

```
params34: @[params;`x;2_]
count each params34
```

```
x      | 2
y      | 150
rule   | 1
classes| 3
```

```
\ts forest34: .quantQ.rf.randomForest params34,`m`n`B!(2;125;10)
```

```
99 56560
```

The prediction error is reduced in this case:

```
select avg pred_error from forest34`oob
```

```
pred_error
----------
0.02850877
```

And prediction is able to correctly place the 3 test tuples into their classes:

```
.quantQ.rf.predictOnRF[params34`y; forest34; 1.464 0.244]
```

```
prediction| 0
mean_error| 0.02850877
dev_error | 0.1664212
```

```
.quantQ.rf.predictOnRF[params34`y; forest34; 4.26 1.326]
```

```
prediction| 1
mean_error| 0.02850877
dev_error | 0.1664212
```

```
.quantQ.rf.predictOnRF[params34`y; forest34;5.552 2.026]
```

```
prediction| 2
mean_error| 0.02850877
dev_error | 0.1664212
```

If instead we choose features 1 and 2, which have lower total information gain, the results are not so good:

```
params12:@[params;`x;-2_]
count each params12
```

```
x       | 2
y       | 150
rule    | 1
classes| 3
```

```
\ts forest12: .quantQ.rf.randomForest params12,`m`n`B!(2;150;10)
```

```
5307 1207024
```

```
select avg pred_error from forest12`oob
```

```
pred_error
----------
0.3180147
```

The prediction error has increased; the predicted value is now not always correct:

```
.quantQ.rf.predictOnRF[params12`y; forest12;5.006 3.418]
```

```
prediction| 0
mean_error| 0.3180147
dev_error | 0.4925613
```

```
.quantQ.rf.predictOnRF[params12`y; forest12;5.936 2.77]
```

```
prediction| 1
mean_error| 0.3180147
dev_error | 0.4925613
```

```
.quantQ.rf.predictOnRF[params12`y; forest12;6.588 2.974]
```

```
prediction| 1
mean_error| 0.3180147
dev_error | 0.4925613
```

In conclusion, our random forest implementation has equiped us both with a way to deal with the high variance of individual trees, and also a built-in mechanism to validate our prediciton through measuring the prediction error of out-of-bag samples. In addition, keeping track of information gains across the whole feature vector enables us to focus on the features that may be more powerful predictors and potentially get rid of others which may play a lesser role. In practice, this tool is useful for us to narrow down the feature space when modelling a prediction based on multiple features.

CHAPTER 26

Unsupervised Machine Learning: The Apriori Algorithm

Chapters on Linear Regression, Decision Trees, Random Forests, AdaBoost, Neural Networks and k-Nearest Neighbours belong to the supervised machine learning algorithms family. In such cases, we are equipped with two types of variables in the data set: the M-dimensional vector of features, $x_1, \ldots, x_M$, and, the K-dimensional vector of dependent variables (usually $K = 1$). Given the data set of N observations of both features and corresponding dependent variables, we calibrate the chosen model using both types of data. The relationship between the features and the dependent variable is then learnt.

Our objective for this chapter is to assume that we have only features in our data set. The objective is to understand the relationship between features. This can be formalised as follows. The set of M features $x_1, \ldots, x_M$, is generated by a joint density distribution function $P(x_1, \ldots, x_M)$. The goal is to understand such properties of the distribution function. In this case, there is no supervisor in the data set or loss function, which would assess how correctly the properties of the distribution function have been found.

Further, the objective of the model is to find the link between individual features rather than perform response analysis of part of the features to changes to the rest of the data set. Compared to supervised methods, the unsupervised machine learning algorithms face difficulties in assessing the power of the calibrated model. Thus heuristic methods are frequently used.

The unsupervised machine learning techniques can be easily solved for a very small number of dimensions as the joint probability function can be directly estimated. On the other hand, this is not possible in large dimensions, and various approximations are used. The favourite choices are for example variations to Gaussian mixtures. We note that the dimensionality of the feature vector is usually much larger than in the case of supervised machine learning problems. Further, researchers are trying to find patterns in high-dimensional data with various forms of clustering analysis, principal component analysis (PCA), independent component analysis, or self-organising maps. In this chapter, we focus in detail on another class of algorithms known as association rules. In particular, we discuss and implement the Apriori algorithm.

26.1 APRIORI ALGORITHM

The Apriori algorithm introduced by Agrawal et al. (1994) is one of the algorithms within the branch of association rules analysis. The association rules have been traditionally used for data mining to find frequent sets. The popular name for these methods is *market basket analysis*. The name comes from the following problem. Consider a store which sells M different items. For every customer at the counter, we create a record in the database. The entry in the database is an M-dimensional binary variable, $b_1, \ldots, b_M$, which indicates whether a given item has been purchased or not.

It is apparent that the joint probability distribution function $P(b_1, \ldots, b_M)$ cannot be written as $P(b_1) \cdot \cdots \cdot P(b_M)$. The customers tend to buy some goods together as it captures their habits. Being able to find regularity in the joint distribution function helps to improve sells by positioning goods in the store better and addressing the commercials more efficiently.

The association rules aim to work with subsets of $s_1, \ldots, s_L$, where s_l is a set of values $x_1, \ldots, x_M$ of any length. The objective of interest is such $P(s_l)$, which are in reality quite large. This means we do not aim to model every combination but rather the significant combinations in the data. If the number of items is large, the problem cannot be solved directly as a number of combinations grows above numerically reasonable limits.

In the Apriori algorithm, we first define all itemsets S_l. An itemset is any combination of items. It can contain the single variables x_i, or any combination of them. The cardinality of the set of all itemsets is huge, 2^M. The objective of the algorithm is to find all itemsets S_l such that given itemset in the data is frequent, exceeding a given threshold. The advantage of the Apriori algorithm is to find such itemsets without many iterations and being poisoned by the curse of dimensionality.

The frequency of the itemset is defined as the number of observations – rows of the database – when the given itemset is present – an itemset is a subset of the set of items present – divided by the size of the data set. The Apriori algorithm works as follows:

- *Initialisation:* Set a threshold on the frequency of itemsets in the data ϕ.
- *First iteration:* Calculate the frequency of all itemsets containing one item only. Keep those that exceed the frequency threshold of ϕ. Those which do not exceed the threshold ϕ are discarded.
  - It is important to realise that if a single item does not exceed the frequency threshold, then any combination of items which contains the low-frequency item cannot exceed the threshold.
- *Second iteration:* Form all itemsets containing 2 items. Consider only those single items that have passed the first iteration. Calculate the frequency of all such 2-item itemsets and consider those which exceed the threshold, then discard the rest.
- *Third iteration:* Form all itemsets containing 3 items. Consider only those 3-item itemsets which are composed of single items from the first iteration and where all 2 item subsets are present in the second step. Discard the rest.

- *General step of iteration:* Form all n-item steps, where every subset of the chosen n-item step passed the previous steps. Keep only those n-item steps whose frequency exceeds the threshold; discard the rest.
- *Stopping rule:* Stop when none of the n-item steps has exceeded the frequency threshold. Report all itemsets which exceeded the frequency threshold in any of the previous steps.

The algorithm itself resembles a technique of searching through the tree where all possible combinations have been expressed as a tree structure. Namely, the root node contains all zero itemsets, the first level of the tree contains all 1-item itemsets, the second level of the tree contains all 2-item itemsets, etc. Every node has assigned frequency. The algorithm seeks all the nodes with a frequency exceeding the threshold of ϕ.

The Apriori algorithm is the equivalent to a breadth-first search algorithm to search through the tree. The breadth-first algorithm is exploring the tree level by level and then rejects the entire sub-trees stemming from infrequent nodes.

The advantage of the algorithm is that it can report all relevant itemsets within a few iterations. Every iteration corresponds to a pass over data. Thus, the method can be used for very long data sets which cannot fit into memory and calculation has to be done sequentially. This will not be true if the threshold is very low. If we are facing a time budget, we can modify the algorithm to build several instances of the Apriori algorithm at once, each with a different threshold. When the time budget lapses, instances of the algorithm which finished can be reported for further analysis.

The algorithm itself is straightforward and intuitive. Still, it represents a powerful tool for data mining. In the next section, we implement the algorithm and illustrate it on a synthetic example. We encourage the reader to stretch the limits of the algorithm and investigate its performance on much bigger sets, preferably not using in-memory tables.

26.2 IMPLEMENTATION OF THE APRIORI ALGORITHM

In this section, we implement the Apriori algorithm as introduced before. First, for the sake of simplicity of the code, we impose the following constraint on the naming of the data: the first column, named `index`, of the data table is indexing observations and of the integer type. Then, columns with integer-valued features follow. The features are named as `a1`, `a2`, `a3`, …, i.e. the increasing sequence labels.

If the underlying features are not of integer type, or discrete, but rather float, we have to create bins. The binning mechanism is usually derived from the data. Let us illustrate a particular example, where we bin the array of float numbers into buckets according to a predefined scheme.

We create an array of floats as random numbers:

```
arrayOfFloats: 10?1.0;
arrayOfFloats
```

```
0.3348834 0.04512554 0.2390338 0.6859975 0.4762118 0.4516904 0.2570608
    ↪ 0.1200005 0.2444971 0.6768165
```

The scheme to create bins is defined as three split points:

```
binPoints: (0.1 0.2 0.3);
```

We can finally create buckets by using the `binr` verb:

```
binPoints binr arrayOfFloats
```

```
3j, 0j, 2j, 3j, 3j, 3j, 2j, 1j, 2j, 3j
```

The Apriori algorithm is then operating with the binned feature, and the underlying correct numerical values do not play any role for the algorithm itself.

We can now safely assume that our underlying features are of the integer type and the Apriori algorithm builds on the integer-valued features. We further convert each integer-valued feature into a list of dummies, where for every possible value of the feature there is a separate binary dummy variable. First, we need to create a function which goes over all possible values of a given feature and create a dictionary with dummies:

```
.quantQ.apriori.makeDictionary:{[x]
   / x -- list of discrete unique variables
   :x!x=/:x
};
```

The function works as follows:

```
.quantQ.apriori.makeDictionary[1 2 3]
```

```
(1j, 2j, 3j)!(100b;010b;001b)
```

We create a function which identifies in the underlying data table an *i*-th feature and creates another table with an additional set of dummy variables by using the function defined in the previous display. The function reads:

```
.quantQ.apriori.createDummies:{[largeTab;i]
   // largeTab -- table to convert
   // i -- index of variable to convert
   // get all variables except the first one
   listCols: 1_cols largeTab;
   // get unique values of selected variable
   distTMP: asc distinct largeTab[listCols[i]];
   // create dictionary
   dictTMP: .quantQ.apriori.makeDictionary[distTMP];
   // vector of values to convert
   tabTMP: largeTab[listCols[i]];
   // dummy variables
   :?[largeTab;();0b;(`$(raze string listCols[i],"_"),/:string til count
       ↪ distTMP)!flip (dictTMP tabTMP)];
};
```

Let us illustrate the function on a small table with one integer-valued feature `a1`:

```
tabTMP:([] index: til 10; a1: 10?3);
tabTMP
```

```
index a1
--------
0     2
1     1
2     1
3     0
4     0
5     1
6     1
7     1
8     0
9     2
```

```
.quantQ.apriori.createDummies[tabTMP;0]
```

```
a1_0 a1_1 a1_2
--------------
0    0    1
0    1    0
0    1    0
1    0    0
1    0    0
0    1    0
0    1    0
0    1    0
1    0    0
0    0    1
```

The index of the variable to be split into dummies is 0 as the function assumes that the first column is an index variable. The outcome of the function is just a list of dummy columns for the given feature, named using suffices `_0`, `_1`, ... for every possible value.

Thus, we can pre-process the table with an index and integer-valued features into dummy variables corresponding to every value of every variable. It is essential to admit that where the number of combinations of the features and its possible values is large, the wide table with dummies will be very wide, and thus memory-consuming. When data shows this type of behaviour, the Apriori algorithm may not be by its construction the best method to assess the pattern in the data.

Before we define the function corresponding to one iteration of the Apriori algorithm, we define a simple utility function checking whether one array is a subset of the other:

```
.quantQ.apriori.isIn:{[xOUT;xTEST]
   // xOUT -- unique list of values
   // xTEST -- unique list of values to be compared
   :count[xOUT]=sum sum xOUT=\:xTEST;
};
```

working as follows:

```
.quantQ.apriori.isIn[(1 2);(1 2 3)]
```

```
1b
```

```
.quantQ.apriori.isIn[(1 2 3 4);(1 2 3)]
```

```
0b
```

Finally, we define one step of the Apriori algorithm as a function which takes as an argument a dictionary with all important variables including the data itself in the wide dummy form, the outcome of the Apriori algorithm after a given iteration as well as temporary variables, and returns the same and updated dictionary.

```
.quantQ.apriori.aprioriOneRun:{[bParams]
   // bParams -- dictionary with all data and parameters
   // increase counter
   bParams[`step]+:1;
   // create set of all combinations -- distinguish first step
   $[bParams[`step]=1;zz:enlist each 1_cols bParams[`largeTabDummies]; zz:
       ↪ asc each t where
       bParams[`step]=count each t: distinct each distinct asc bParams[`
           ↪ colDummiesStepPrev] cross
       bParams[`colDummiesStep1]];
   // if step>1: test whether zz does not have subset from
       ↪ colDummiesStepALLX
   $[bParams[`step]>1;zz:first flip t where 1b=last each t:{[bParams;x] (x;
       ↪  not max
       .quantQ.apriori.isIn[;x] each bParams[`colDummiesStepALLX])}[bParams
           ↪ ;] each zz;];
   // numerical criteria
   yy: flip {[largeTabDummies;whr]
       :(whr;sum prd largeTabDummies[whr])
       }[bParams[`largeTabDummies];] each zz;
   // temporary column variables -- split zz into two sub-sets
   colDummiesStepTMP: asc each zz where bParams[`thresh]<(value first[yy]!
       ↪ last[yy])%
       count bParams[`largeTabDummies];
   colDummiesStepTMPX: asc each zz where not zz in colDummiesStepTMP;
   // define colDummiesStep1 in step 1
   $[bParams[`step]=1;bParams[`colDummiesStep1]:colDummiesStepTMP;];
   // populate bucket
   bParams[`colDummiesStepPrev]:distinct colDummiesStepTMP;
   bParams[`colDummiesStepALL]:distinct bParams[`colDummiesStepALL],
       ↪ distinct colDummiesStepTMP;
   bParams[`colDummiesStepPrevX]:distinct colDummiesStepTMPX;
   bParams[`colDummiesStepALLX]:distinct bParams[`colDummiesStepALLX],
       ↪ distinct colDummiesStepTMPX;
   // check if further improvement can be done
   $[0=count colDummiesStepTMP;bParams[`canImprove]:0b;bParams[`canImprove
       ↪ ]:1b];
   // return bucket
   :bParams;
};
```

The function reflects the description of the Apriori algorithm as introduced above. At every step, the local variable zz is created with all possible and allowed combinations of features to be explored at a given iteration. It explicitly checks whether the newly formed candidate does not contain sub-elements which have been previously rejected. The combinations are then tested to be frequent enough – above the threshold – and combinations which are frequent enough are preserved.

The entire algorithm is then run as a sequence of one-step functions. Let us illustrate the functioning of the algorithm on the set of artificial data. We first create the table with 1000 observations, which are already indexed and all features are appropriately named and being of the integer type.

```
largeTab:([] index: til 1000; a1: 1000?`a`b`c`d; a2: 1000?`e`f`g; a3:
    ↪ 1000?`k`l`m; a4: 1000?`p`q; a5: raze((20#`z);980?`x`y));
largeTab
```

```
index a1 a2 a3 a4 a5
--------------------
0     b  g  k  p  z
1     a  f  m  p  z
2     b  g  k  p  z
3     a  e  k  q  z
4     c  f  m  q  z
5     d  f  m  q  z
6     a  g  l  p  z
7     c  f  l  q  z
8     a  g  l  p  z
9     a  g  l  p  z
..
```

We need to transform the table into a wide table, where each feature is turned into a sequence of new dummy features corresponding to each value. Let us create the dummies using the `createDummies` function applied over every feature column of the `largeTab` table:

```
largeTabDummies: (select index from largeTab)(,')/(.quantQ.apriori.
    ↪ createDummies[largeTab;] each til count 1_cols largeTab)
```

Let us explore the structure of the wide table:

```
meta largeTabDummies
```

```
c    | t f a
-----| -----
index| j
a1_0 | b
a1_1 | b
a1_2 | b
a1_3 | b
a2_0 | b
a2_1 | b
a2_2 | b
a3_0 | b
a3_1 | b
```

```
a3_2 | b
a4_0 | b
a4_1 | b
a5_0 | b
a5_1 | b
a5_2 | b
```

It is worth visualising the wide structure. For that purpose, we need to offset each dummy variable by a certain amount such that we can clearly see when the values are non-zero, or `true`. We further choose offsets clustered around the underlying features. The transformation of the `largeTabDummies` table is thus performed as follows:

```
select index, 0.1*a1_0,0.2*a1_1,0.3*a1_2,0.4*a1_3,1.1*a2_0,1.2*a2_1,1.3*
    ↪ a2_2,2.1*a3_0,2.2*a3_1,2.3*a3_2,3.1*a4_0,3.2*a4_1,4.1*a5_0,4.2*a5_1
    ↪ ,4.3*a5_2 from largeTabDummies
```

Figure 26.1 depicts first 30 values of the transformed `largeTabDummies` table. There are four underlying features, which is visible by four clusters in y-values. For every cluster there is a unique point for every x value, thus the dummies for every feature are exclusive. We can visually identify the frequency of dummies and perform the Apriori algorithm manually. This will fall short once we would increase the number of observations.

Further, in order to run the `aprioriOneRun` function, we need to define the dictionary of variables. The following set of variables are needed for initialization of the bucket with variables:

```
// all accepted dummy variables and its combinations
colDummiesStepALL:();
colDummiesStepALLX:();
// all accepted dummy variables or its combinations in the previous step
colDummiesStepPrev:();
```

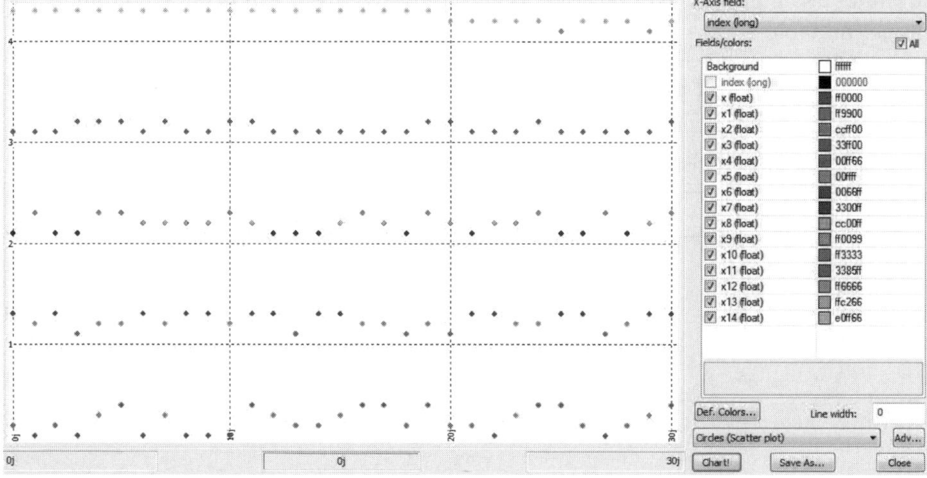

FIGURE 26.1 The visualisation of the `largeTabDummies` table in qPad, focus on 30 values

```
colDummiesStepPrevX:();
// counter of the steps within the iteration
step:0;
// candidate single dummy variables
colDummiesStep1:();
// control variable for improvement being possible
canImprove:1b;
```

Further, we explicitly define the global acceptance threshold of the Apriori algorithm. We choose 0.2 for initial example:

```
thresh:0.2;
```

We create the bucket which will be propagated through the iteration:

```
bucketParams:((`largeTabDummies`colDummiesStepALL`colDummiesStepALLX`
    ↪ colDummiesStepPrev`colDummiesStepPrevX`step`colDummiesStep1`
    ↪ canImprove`thresh)!(largeTabDummies;colDummiesStepALL;
    ↪ colDummiesStepALLX;colDummiesStepPrev;colDummiesStepPrevX;step;
    ↪ colDummiesStep1;canImprove;thresh));
```

Let us stress that the bucket contains also the data itself in its wide form. We run the iteration of the algorithm manually:

```
bucketParams:.quantQ.apriori.aprioriOneRun[bucketParams];
```

The set of accepted combinations contains after the first step only singlets, i.e. the algorithm has chosen individual values which are frequent enough:

```
bucketParams[`colDummiesStepALL]
```

```
(`s#enlist `a1_0;`s#enlist `a1_1;`s#enlist `a1_2;`s#enlist `a1_3;`s#enlist
    ↪ `a2_0;`s#enlist `a2_1;`s#enlist `a2_2;`s#enlist `a3_0;`s#enlist `
    ↪ a3_1;`s#enlist `a3_2;`s#enlist `a4_0;`s#enlist `a4_1;`s#enlist `a5_0
    ↪ ;`s#enlist `a5_1)
```

The algorithm performed the first step:

```
bucketParams[`step]
```

```
1j
```

and shows that after first iteration, it can run further and improve:

```
bucketParams[`canImprove]
```

```
1b
```

Let us run another step:

```
bucketParams:.quantQ.apriori.aprioriOneRun[bucketParams];
```

The set of accepted combinations contains, on top of the singlets, also pairs of frequent combinations:

```
bucketParams[`colDummiesStepALL]
```

```
(`s#enlist `a1_0;`s#enlist `a1_1;`s#enlist `a1_2;`s#enlist `a1_3;`s#enlist
    ↪ `a2_0;`s#enlist `a2_1;`s#enlist `a2_2;`s#enlist `a3_0;`s#enlist `
    ↪ a3_1;`s#enlist `a3_2;`s#enlist `a4_0;`s#enlist `a4_1;`s#enlist `a5_0
    ↪ ;`s#enlist `a5_1;`s#`a4_0`a5_0;`s#`a4_0`a5_1;`s#`a4_1`a5_0;`s#`a4_1`
    ↪ a5_1)
```

The algorithm shows that it is in the second iteration:

```
bucketParams[`step]
```

```
2j
```

and shows that it can run even further and check for combinations of three features:

```
bucketParams[`canImprove]
```

```
1b
```

The iteration continues further:

```
bucketParams:.quantQ.apriori.aprioriOneRun[bucketParams];
```

The set of accepted combinations is now the same as in the previous step, suggesting the algorithm was not able to identify new combinations:

```
bucketParams[`colDummiesStepALL]
```

```
(`s#enlist `a1_0;`s#enlist `a1_1;`s#enlist `a1_2;`s#enlist `a1_3;`s#enlist
    ↪ `a2_0;`s#enlist `a2_1;`s#enlist `a2_2;`s#enlist `a3_0;`s#enlist `
    ↪ a3_1;`s#enlist `a3_2;`s#enlist `a4_0;`s#enlist `a4_1;`s#enlist `a5_0
    ↪ ;`s#enlist `a5_1;`s#`a4_0`a5_0;`s#`a4_0`a5_1;`s#`a4_1`a5_0;`s#`a4_1`
    ↪ a5_1)
```

The third step thus seems to be the terminal one:

```
bucketParams[`step]
```

```
3j
```

as the `canImprove` variable confirms, the algorithm is not able to improve further:

```
bucketParams[`canImprove]
```

```
0b
```

We can achieve the same outcome by running the iterate function with the `canImprove` variable being the control for iterations to run:

```
bucketParamsOUT:(.quantQ.apriori.aprioriOneRun/)[{x[`canImprove]};
    ↪ bucketParams];
```

The output corresponds to the last step detailed above:

```
bucketParamsOUT[`colDummiesStepALL]
```

```
(`s#enlist `a1_0;`s#enlist `a1_1;`s#enlist `a1_2;`s#enlist `a1_3;`s#enlist
    ↪ `a2_0;`s#enlist `a2_1;`s#enlist `a2_2;`s#enlist `a3_0;`s#enlist `
    ↪ a3_1;`s#enlist `a3_2;`s#enlist `a4_0;`s#enlist `a4_1;`s#enlist `a5_0
    ↪ ;`s#enlist `a5_1;`s#`a4_0`a5_0;`s#`a4_0`a5_1;`s#`a4_1`a5_0;`s#`a4_1`
    ↪ a5_1)
```

```
bucketParamsOUT[`step]
```

```
3j
```

```
bucketParamsOUT[`canImprove]
```

```
0b
```

The global threshold parameter governs the acceptance of the possible combinations. Let us run two more exercises with decreased threshold. We expect that more and more combinations will be accepted, with possible formations of combinations from more than two features. First, let us set global acceptance threshold to 0.1:

```
thresh:0.1;
bucketParams2:((`largeTabDummies`colDummiesStepALL`colDummiesStepALLX`
    ↪ colDummiesStepPrev`colDummiesStepPrevX`step`colDummiesStep1`
    ↪ canImprove`thresh)!(largeTabDummies;colDummiesStepALL;
    ↪ colDummiesStepALLX;colDummiesStepPrev;colDummiesStepPrevX;step;
    ↪ colDummiesStep1;canImprove;thresh));
```

and we can run the new exercise with a bucket which was reset:

```
bucketParamsOUT:(.quantQ.apriori.aprioriOneRun/)[{x[`canImprove]};
    ↪ bucketParams2];
```

The outcome of the algorithm is indeed more associations. All associations are still composed of two features. The previous solution is a subset of the outcome with a lower threshold:

```
bucketParamsOUT[`colDummiesStepALL]
```

```
(`s#enlist `a1_0;`s#enlist `a1_1;`s#enlist `a1_2;`s#enlist `a1_3;`s#enlist
    ↪ `a2_0;`s#enlist `a2_1;`s#enlist `a2_2;`s#enlist `a3_0;`s#enlist `
    ↪ a3_1;`s#enlist `a3_2;`s#enlist `a4_0;`s#enlist `a4_1;`s#enlist `a5_0
    ↪ ;`s#enlist `a5_1;`s#`a1_0`a4_0;`s#`a1_0`a4_1;`s#`a1_0`a5_0;`s#`a1_0`
    ↪ a5_1;`s#`a1_1`a4_0;`s#`a1_1`a5_0;`s#`a1_1`a5_1;`s#`a1_2`a4_0;`s#`
    ↪ a1_2`a4_1;`s#`a1_2`a5_0;`s#`a1_2`a5_1;`s#`a1_3`a4_0;`s#`a1_3`a4_1;`s
    ↪ #`a1_3`a5_0;`s#`a1_3`a5_1;`s#`a2_0`a3_0;`s#`a2_0`a3_1;`s#`a2_0`a3_2
    ↪ ;`s#`a2_0`a4_0;`s#`a2_0`a4_1;`s#`a2_0`a5_0;`s#`a2_0`a5_1;`s#`a2_1`
    ↪ a3_0;`s#`a2_1`a3_2;`s#`a2_1`a4_0;`s#`a2_1`a4_1;`s#`a2_1`a5_0;`s#`
    ↪ a2_1`a5_1;`s#`a2_2`a3_0;`s#`a2_2`a3_1;`s#`a2_2`a4_0;`s#`a2_2`a4_1;`s
    ↪ #`a2_2`a5_0;`s#`a2_2`a5_1;`s#`a3_0`a4_0;`s#`a3_0`a4_1;`s#`a3_0`a5_0
    ↪ ;`s#`a3_0`a5_1;`s#`a3_1`a4_0;`s#`a3_1`a4_1;`s#`a3_1`a5_0;`s#`a3_1`
    ↪ a5_1;`s#`a3_2`a4_0;`s#`a3_2`a4_1;`s#`a3_2`a5_0;`s#`a3_2`a5_1;`s#`
    ↪ a4_0`a5_0;`s#`a4_0`a5_1;`s#`a4_1`a5_0;`s#`a4_1`a5_1)
```

The algorithm itself ends in the third iteration as before:

```
bucketParamsOUT[`step]
```

```
3j
```

We do omit the explicit check that the algorithm cannot improve further. Let us run the last exercise with the global acceptance threshold equal to 0.05:

```
thresh:0.05;
bucketParams3:((`largeTabDummies`colDummiesStepALL`colDummiesStepALLX`
    ↪ colDummiesStepPrev`colDummiesStepPrevX`step`colDummiesStep1`
    ↪ canImprove`thresh)!(largeTabDummies;colDummiesStepALL;
    ↪ colDummiesStepALLX;colDummiesStepPrev;colDummiesStepPrevX;step;
    ↪ colDummiesStep1;canImprove;thresh));
bucketParamsOUT:(.quantQ.apriori.aprioriOneRun/)[{x[`canImprove]};
    ↪ bucketParams3];
```

The solution contains even more associations between features with the presence of an association between three features. We can also see that the previous solution is a subset of the new one:

```
bucketParamsOUT[`colDummiesStepALL]
```

```
(`s#enlist `a1_0;`s#enlist `a1_1;`s#enlist `a1_2;`s#enlist `a1_3;`s#enlist
    ↪ `a2_0;`s#enlist `a2_1;`s#enlist `a2_2;`s#enlist `a3_0;`s#enlist `
    ↪ a3_1;`s#enlist `a3_2;`s#enlist `a4_0;`s#enlist `a4_1;`s#enlist `a5_0
    ↪ ;`s#enlist `a5_1;`s#`a1_0`a2_0;`s#`a1_0`a2_1;`s#`a1_0`a2_2;`s#`a1_0`
    ↪ a3_0;`s#`a1_0`a3_1;`s#`a1_0`a3_2;`s#`a1_0`a4_0;`s#`a1_0`a4_1;`s#`
    ↪ a1_0`a5_0;`s#`a1_0`a5_1;`s#`a1_1`a2_0;`s#`a1_1`a2_1;`s#`a1_1`a2_2;`s
    ↪ #`a1_1`a3_0;`s#`a1_1`a3_1;`s#`a1_1`a3_2;`s#`a1_1`a4_0;`s#`a1_1`a4_1
    ↪ ;`s#`a1_1`a5_0;`s#`a1_1`a5_1;`s#`a1_2`a2_0;`s#`a1_2`a2_1;`s#`a1_2`
    ↪ a2_2;`s#`a1_2`a3_0;`s#`a1_2`a3_1;`s#`a1_2`a3_2;`s#`a1_2`a4_0;`s#`
    ↪ a1_2`a4_1;`s#`a1_2`a5_0;`s#`a1_2`a5_1;`s#`a1_3`a2_0;`s#`a1_3`a2_1;`s
    ↪ #`a1_3`a2_2;`s#`a1_3`a3_0;`s#`a1_3`a3_1;`s#`a1_3`a3_2;`s#`a1_3`a4_0
    ↪ ;`s#`a1_3`a4_1;`s#`a1_3`a5_0;`s#`a1_3`a5_1;`s#`a2_0`a3_0;`s#`a2_0`
    ↪ a3_1;`s#`a2_0`a3_2;`s#`a2_0`a4_0;`s#`a2_0`a4_1;`s#`a2_0`a5_0;`s#`
    ↪ a2_0`a5_1;`s#`a2_1`a3_0;`s#`a2_1`a3_1;`s#`a2_1`a3_2;`s#`a2_1`a4_0;`s
    ↪ #`a2_1`a4_1;`s#`a2_1`a5_0;`s#`a2_1`a5_1;`s#`a2_2`a3_0;`s#`a2_2`a3_1
    ↪ ;`s#`a2_2`a3_2;`s#`a2_2`a4_0;`s#`a2_2`a4_1;`s#`a2_2`a5_0;`s#`a2_2`
    ↪ a5_1;`s#`a3_0`a4_0;`s#`a3_0`a4_1;`s#`a3_0`a5_0;`s#`a3_0`a5_1;`s#`
    ↪ a3_1`a4_0;`s#`a3_1`a4_1;`s#`a3_1`a5_0;`s#`a3_1`a5_1;`s#`a3_2`a4_0;`s
    ↪ #`a3_2`a4_1;`s#`a3_2`a5_0;`s#`a3_2`a5_1;`s#`a4_0`a5_0;`s#`a4_0`a5_1
    ↪ ;`s#`a4_1`a5_0;`s#`a4_1`a5_1;`s#`a1_0`a3_0`a4_0;`s#`a1_0`a4_0`a5_0;`
    ↪ s#`a1_0`a4_0`a5_1;`s#`a1_0`a4_1`a5_0;`s#`a1_0`a4_1`a5_1;`s#`a1_1`
    ↪ a2_2`a4_0;`s#`a1_1`a3_1`a4_0;`s#`a1_1`a4_0`a5_0;`s#`a1_1`a4_0`a5_1;`
    ↪ s#`a1_1`a4_1`a5_0;`s#`a1_2`a3_1`a4_1;`s#`a1_2`a3_1`a5_0;`s#`a1_2`
    ↪ a4_0`a5_0;`s#`a1_2`a4_0`a5_1;`s#`a1_2`a4_1`a5_0;`s#`a1_2`a4_1`a5_1;`
    ↪ s#`a1_3`a3_1`a5_0;`s#`a1_3`a3_2`a4_1;`s#`a1_3`a4_0`a5_0;`s#`a1_3`
    ↪ a4_0`a5_1;`s#`a1_3`a4_1`a5_0;`s#`a1_3`a4_1`a5_1;`s#`a2_0`a3_0`a4_0;`
    ↪ s#`a2_0`a3_0`a4_1;`s#`a2_0`a3_0`a5_0;`s#`a2_0`a3_0`a5_1;`s#`a2_0`
    ↪ a3_1`a4_0;`s#`a2_0`a3_1`a5_0;`s#`a2_0`a3_2`a4_0;`s#`a2_0`a3_2`a5_0;`
    ↪ s#`a2_0`a3_2`a5_1;`s#`a2_0`a4_0`a5_0;`s#`a2_0`a4_0`a5_1;`s#`a2_0`
    ↪ a4_1`a5_0;`s#`a2_0`a4_1`a5_1;`s#`a2_1`a3_0`a4_0;`s#`a2_1`a3_0`a4_1;`
    ↪ s#`a2_1`a3_0`a5_0;`s#`a2_1`a3_1`a4_0;`s#`a2_1`a3_1`a5_0;`s#`a2_1`
    ↪ a3_2`a4_0;`s#`a2_1`a3_2`a4_1;`s#`a2_1`a3_2`a5_0;`s#`a2_1`a3_2`a5_1;`
    ↪ s#`a2_1`a4_0`a5_0;`s#`a2_1`a4_0`a5_1;`s#`a2_1`a4_1`a5_0;`s#`a2_1`
    ↪ a4_1`a5_1;`s#`a2_2`a3_0`a4_0;`s#`a2_2`a3_0`a5_0;`s#`a2_2`a3_0`a5_1;`
    ↪ s#`a2_2`a3_1`a4_0;`s#`a2_2`a3_1`a4_1;`s#`a2_2`a3_1`a5_0;`s#`a2_2`
    ↪ a3_2`a4_0;`s#`a2_2`a3_2`a5_1;`s#`a2_2`a4_0`a5_0;`s#`a2_2`a4_0`a5_1;`
    ↪ s#`a2_2`a4_1`a5_0;`s#`a2_2`a4_1`a5_1;`s#`a3_0`a4_0`a5_0;`s#`a3_0`
    ↪ a4_0`a5_1;`s#`a3_0`a4_1`a5_0;`s#`a3_0`a4_1`a5_1;`s#`a3_1`a4_0`a5_0;`
    ↪ s#`a3_1`a4_0`a5_1;`s#`a3_1`a4_1`a5_0;`s#`a3_1`a4_1`a5_1;`s#`a3_2`
    ↪ a4_0`a5_0;`s#`a3_2`a4_0`a5_1;`s#`a3_2`a4_1`a5_0;`s#`a3_2`a4_1`a5_1)
```

The iteration took with the parameterisation one more step to finish:

```
bucketParamsOUT[`step]
```

```
4j
```

We leave a suggestion to readers to improve the algorithm in the following way. We have created in this presented version of the algorithm dummies for every value the feature can take. This is not necessary, as, for the simplest case of the binary feature, we create two new binary variables. We can assume a default dummy variable instead. This would mean changing the code slightly such that `_0` dummy variables would not be explicitly defined. As a reward, the outcome will be a more memory efficient algorithm.

CHAPTER 27

Processing Information

We have so far solely focused on numerical time series and devoted most of our time to analysing numbers. Recently, however, processing of non-numerical data, namely written text, has become an essential part of machine learning and data science. In this chapter, we introduce some concepts from the data processing field, which are motivated by how search engines assign importance to documents.

27.1 INFORMATION RETRIEVAL

The first method we review is from the information retrieval toolbox. The motivation is as follows. We have a set of basic building blocks, words, and a document composed of a subset of words. We want to assign a measure for the word given how important it is for a given document. Since some words are more frequent than others, the natural frequency of words within the entire corpus of all documents has to be taken into account, and the measure has to be corrected for it.

Imagine we have a document, and we want to understand whether its content is relevant for a reader or not. The relevancy means that it is not just "another" permutation of common words, but it contains unique words. Let us stress that we do base our analysis on the uniqueness of words themselves and not how they are structured within a sentence. Such an idea, if expressed using common words, cannot be captured with analytics we are building now and is beyond the aim of this book.

In this section, we first discuss the corpus we use for examples and then two approaches for information retrieval: intuitive frequency counting and tf-idf method.

27.1.1 Corpus: Leonardo da Vinci

In order to illustrate the concept of information retrieval, we need a sample text. We will use a text by Leonardo da Vinci called *Thoughts on Art and Life*, translated in 1906. We have accessed the text using Project Gutenberg; see daV. We focus on the third section titled "Thoughts on Science". We exclude side notes and page numbers. The text is stored on the local drive in a text file.

We filter the text as follows. First, we read the text into memory:

```
daVinci:"."vs" "sv read0`$"C:\\daVinciThoughtsOnArtAndLife_ChapterScience.
    ↪ txt"
```

and explore the content (we list only part of the output):

```
daVinci
```

```
("There is no human experience that can be termed true science unless it
    ↪ can be mathematically demonstrated";"  And if thou sayest that the
    ↪ sciences which begin and end in the mind are true, this cannot be
    ↪ conceded, but must be denied for many reasons, and firstly because
    ↪ in such mental discourses experience is eliminated, and without
    ↪ experience there can be no certainty";...
```

The sentences can contain symbols we do not need. In addition, we convert everything into lower case as the capitals do not make a difference for us. We clean the text as:

```
daVinci:lower{x where not x in ("\"";"?";"!";";";":";",";"'";"-";"(";")
    ↪ ";"[";"]")}'[daVinci]
```

Further, there are redundant spaces within sentences; we remove them as well:

```
daVinci:{x where not(x=" ") and (prev x)=" "}'[daVinci];
```

We can explore the content of the corpus after we have performed the cleaning of the text:

```
daVinci
```

```
("there is no human experience that can be termed true science unless it
    ↪ can be mathematically demonstrated";"and if thou sayest that the
    ↪ sciences which begin and end in the mind are true this cannot be
    ↪ conceded but must be denied for many reasons and firstly because in
    ↪ such mental discourses experience is eliminated and without
    ↪ experience there can be no certainty";...
```

The sentences are now standardised and ready to be analysed in terms of word frequency.

Further, the notion of a document is played by a single sentence. The corpus is then the set of all sentences within the sample text specified above. This approach does not require dealing with excessively large data, which would not be suitable for the pedagogical purpose of the book (but reasonable in practical circumstances while using q).

27.1.2 Frequency Counting

Our objective is to identify sentences – which play the role of documents – that carry the unique, informative content. Imagine we face a problem to choose a few sentences from the entire book (chapter in our case) which carry the most unique content. One possible way is to focus on sentences with different words. In addition, we extend the search question as follows. We are looking for a few sentences which contain a particular word or combination of words such that those sentences will tell us something unique about the word we search – yes, this sounds familiar; it is exactly what we want when we "google" some term.

The sentences we are looking for are those which contain unique content. The uniqueness of content within a sentence can be defined as "to contain as many unique words as possible". This can be mathematically expressed as having in a sentence frequently appearing words which are rare in the entire text.

For that purpose, we define a frequency, or count of occurence, for a given word, w, within the entire text as:

$$\phi_{\text{corpus}}(w) = \sum_{w' \in \text{corpus}} 1(w = w'), \tag{27.1}$$

and a frequency for a given word within the sentence:

$$\phi_{\text{sentence}}(w) = \sum_{w' \in \text{sentence}} 1(w = w'). \tag{27.2}$$

The measure of importance for a given word is then simply given as:

$$\Omega(w; \text{corpus}, \text{sentence}) = \frac{\phi_{\text{sentence}}}{\phi_{\text{corpus}}}, \tag{27.3}$$

where measure Ω is within $(0, 1]$. When the sentence contains all the instances of a given word within the entire corpus, the measure reaches 1 while for an appearance of a common word the measure will have value close to 0.

The measure Ω turns the sentence into a dictionary, where every different word in the sentence will have assigned numerical value. Let us implement the measure and illustrate it on our text sample. First, we define the global frequency for every word as:

```
.quantQ.infth.wordFrequency:{[corpus]
    // corpus -- corpus with cleaned text
    :count each group" "vs" "sv corpus;
 };
```

and use the function for our data set:

```
daVinciWordFrequency:.quantQ.infth.wordFrequency[daVinci];
```

The `daVinciWordFrequency` is a dictionary with word count throughout the corpus. In particular, the word "there" is present in the text 47 times, as can be seen:

```
daVinciWordFrequency["there"]
```

```
47j
```

The frequency within the sentence can be defined in the same way. We skip the step of creating the specific function for it and define directly a measure Ω, which will proceed sentence by sentence through the text and calculate the measure. Function `wordMeasure` takes two arguments: the document we want to analyse and the dictionary with word frequency, and returns the measure calculated sentence by sentence:

```
.quantQ.infth.wordMeasure:{[document;wordFrequency]
   // document -- text we want to analyse
   // wordFrequency -- dictionary with corpus word frequency
   // calculates word frequency measure
   :distinct {[x;y] tmp:count each group" "vs x;(tmp% y key tmp)}[;
       ↪ wordFrequency]each document;
};
```

In the provided function, the document to be analysed can be the entire corpus. Furthermore, the document has to be a subset of the corpus which was used to generate the dictionary. Recall that when a dictionary is called with a non-defined key, it returns the corresponding null value:

```
daVinciWordFrequency["xxx"]
```

```
0Nj
```

We encourage readers to correct the function such that the measure can cope with new words. This would add a Bayesian flavour to the procedure. It is important to keep in mind that when improperly done, the measure can exceed 1.0, which would be rather pathological.

Let us apply the measure on the `daVinci` sample:

```
daVinciSentenceAnalytics:.quantQ.infth.wordMeasure[daVinci;
    ↪ daVinciWordFrequency];
```

The outcome is an array of dictionaries, where every element of the array corresponds to one sentence decomposed by a measure.

```
first daVinciSentenceAnalytics
```

```
("there";"is";"no";"human";"experience";"that";"can";"be";"termed";"true";"
    ↪ science";"unless";"it";"mathematically";"demonstrated")!0.0212766
    ↪ 0.003278689 0.01923077 0.1428571 0.0625 0.006711409 0.05405405
    ↪ 0.01904762 0.2 0.08333333 0.06666667 0.1666667 0.004608295 1 1;
```

The word "there" has a measure 0.0212766, while "mathematically" has the measure 1. The former word is common across the corpus and thus does not have much value for us. On the other hand, the latter word is rather unique and adds value to the analysed sentence.

We add a function which adds two words to every sentence: one corresponding to the average measure per sentence, and one corresponding to the maximum value of a measure for a sentence. This will be a useful analytic tool to process the outcome:

```
.quantQ.infth.wordAddAnalytics:{[documentMeasure]
   // documentMeasure -- analysed document with defined measure
   // analyse sentence by sentence and add average and max measure
   :{tmpAvg: avg value x; tmpMax: max value x;  (raze (key x;enlist "
       ↪ AVERAGE";enlist "MAX"))!
       (raze (value x;enlist tmpAvg;enlist tmpMax))} each documentMeasure;
};
```

and apply it on the analytics we have so far calculated.

```
daVinciSentenceAnalyticsMeasure:.quantQ.infth.wordAddAnalytics[
    ↪ daVinciSentenceAnalytics];
```

The outcome is of the same form as the input, it just adds two more words. We can confirm it as follows looking on the first sentence:

```
first daVinciSentenceAnalyticsMeasure
```

```
("there";"is";"no";"human";"experience";"that";"can";"be";"termed";"true";"
    ↪ science";"unless";"it";"mathematically";"demonstrated";"AVERAGE";"
    ↪ MAX")
!0.0212766 0.003278689 0.01923077 0.1428571 0.0625 0.006711409 0.05405405
    ↪ 0.01904762 0.2 0.08333333 0.06666667 0.1666667 0.004608295 1 1
    ↪ 0.1900154 1
```

In particular, if we extract the two extra words we have just added:

```
(first daVinciSentenceAnalyticsMeasure) each ("AVERAGE";"MAX")
```

```
0.1900154 1
```

We are adding words into the sentences. Since we use upper case for the measures included, we are preventing any confusion with the original text.

The maximum measure reached within the sentence is 1. In fact, it was reached for two words `"mathematically"` and `"demonstrated"`. Our reference corpus is rather small; it is one chapter of a book written by a scientist and it is therefore likely that there is a number of unique words used in the text. Indeed:

```
sum {1=x["MAX"]} each daVinciSentenceAnalyticsMeasure
```

```
227
```

seeing 227 sentences with unique word while there are

```
count daVinciSentenceAnalyticsMeasure
```

```
260
```

altogether 260 sentences. The uniqueness of a word within a sentence is not of any value for our text.

The average measure per sentence is an alternative we have at hand. Let us take sentences which have an average measure above the threshold of 0.5 (we have chosen a value to be nicely rounded in the middle of the measure's range). The following reveals how many sentences we will obtain:

```
sum {0.5<x["AVERAGE"]} each daVinciSentenceAnalyticsMeasure
```

```
3
```

We chose three sentences we hope will give us a useful metric:

```
daVinciSentenceAnalyticsMeasure where {0.5<x["AVERAGE"]} each
    ↪ daVinciSentenceAnalyticsMeasure
```

```
(("syllogism";"to";"speak";"doubtfully";"AVERAGE";"MAX")!1 0.004 0.1666667
    ↪ 1 0.5426667 1;
("sophism";"to";"speak";"confusedly";"falsehood";"for";"truth";"AVERAGE";"
    ↪ MAX")!1 0.004 0.1666667 1 1 0.03225806 0.3333333 0.5051797 1;
("";"AVERAGE";"MAX")!1 1 1f)
```

The three sentences chosen have unique content. The last sentence is actually the result of our filtering method. The selected sentences are thus two. The dictionary above does not provide the full sentence, it is rather one decomposed into individual words. We thus recover the selected sentences:

```
daVinci  where {0.5<x["AVERAGE"]} each daVinciSentenceAnalyticsMeasure
```

```
("syllogism to speak doubtfully";"sophism to speak confusedly falsehood for
    ↪ truth";"")
```

The two sentences are indeed rather unique. They sound like quotes worth remembering. We let readers perform their own analysis of quotes by selected authors and establish a statistical validity to the hypothesis that quotes are likely to show increased average measure Ω relative to an average text sample.

27.1.3 tf-idf

In this section, we elaborate on the measure for word frequency and introduce properly defined metrics used in the information industry for information retrieval. The metric is called term frequency-inverse document frequency, or *tf-idf*. It is based on a similar foundation as the previous metric: it considers a document as a bag of words where the order of words does not play any role. It assigns importance to every word and then assesses the document based on the importance of individual words.

Let us stay with the notion of a bag of words. This means that two sentences "John killed Mary" and "Mary killed John" are considered as identical even though they carry a different meaning. In the end, a different person survived and a different one was killed. This immediately brings limitations to the provided method. If we would like to include the meaning of sentences, we would need to employ much more sophisticated models like deep neural networks.

The importance of a word within the document is composed of two components. First, it is proportional to the frequency of a word within the document. If we write a text about polar bears, the term "polar bear" should frequently appear across the text. This will make the text relevant to the polar bear term. On the other hand, the frequency itself has to be taken into context: How frequently is "polar bear" used throughout the entire corpus of all documents? If this is a term common and present in many documents, we require quite a few occurrences within a document to consider it relevant. On the other hand, for a term which is rare across the corpus, even one occurrence will make the document relevant.

The measure is in particular useful when we search a document based on several search queries. In such a case, the metrics are combined, and relevant document(s) is(are) chosen based on the combination of outcomes. Let us extend the polar bear example and imagine someone was looking for a combined query of "gargalesthesia" and "polar bear". The originator of the query could be an author of tales for children, who is writing a book about a ticklish polar bear and, for the sake of curiosity, wants to know if you can tickle a polar bear.

The two terms are very different in terms of frequency of appearance. Although probably everyone has heard of polar bears, it is likely that gargalesthesia, the sensation commonly associated with tickling, has never been heard of by a number of our readers. In October 2018, there were approximately 10,000 more pages found by `www.google.com` search engine for the term "polar bear" as opposed to "gargalesthesia". Thus, a document which has much fewer mentions of "polar bear" is not very relevant for the writer without "gargalesthesia" being contained in it. A text fully devoted to polar bears could provide some hints, where some physiological features of polar bears can be described and thus give hints about the original query. On the other hand, a document with only a few mentions of "gargalesthesia" can be relevant and offered as a feasible outcome of the search query even though "polar bear" is not contained in it.

This also provides hints on how to optimise the web pages to be found. If we write a text about a polar bear, mentioning it only once does not give us many chances to be found by algorithms described in the preceding paragraphs. Further, it is worth finding different synonyms for features described in the text. This gives a flavour of uniqueness into the text. If the reader wants to understand more how searches work, we encourage exploring resources of Google; goo, for example.

Let us start with a definition of the *tf-idf.* We recommend readers to explore Sparck Jones (1972), Manning et al. (2008), or Ricardo and Berthier (2011). As we have discussed above, the first component is a word frequency, or term *tf* in the definition. This corresponds to $\phi_{\text{sentence}}(w)$, where *sentence* is understood as a bag of words we want to classify. We can use the definition in eq. (27.2),

$$tf_{\text{sentence}}(w) = \phi_{\text{sentence}}(w), \tag{27.4}$$

or some alternative ones:

$$tf_{\text{sentence;boolean}}(w) = 1(w \in \text{sentence}), \tag{27.5}$$

or

$$tf_{\text{sentence;relative}}(w) = \frac{\sum_{w' \in \text{sentence}} 1(w = w')}{\sum_{w' \in \text{sentence}}}, \tag{27.6}$$

or

$$tf_{\text{sentence;log}}(w) = \log(1 + \phi_{\text{sentence}}(w)). \tag{27.7}$$

The *boolean* definition defines a binary indicator for the word frequency; it does not take into account the number of occurrences within the *sentence*. The *relative* definition normalises the word count by total number of words in the document. Finally, the *log* definition uses the log function to transform the rate of occurrence. The usage of log is popular among information analysts to scale the exponential laws out of the picture.

In terms of implementation, we can take previously implemented function `wordFrequency` and stick to the plain counting of words.

The second part of the *tf-idf* term corresponds to the inverse document frequency. The word count in the document has to be normalised by the overall frequency of the word across the corpus. In the previous section, we have used a word frequency extended across the entire corpus. This may be misleading, however. The corpus may contain texts, which can be overinflated with certain words. Such a phenomenon can occur, for instance, by mistake, where the frequency of a word can increase due to a technical error or the document in the corpus can originate in the automatically performed scan which failed. A more stable normalisation measure is the count number of documents in the corpus which contain a given word. This will represent a more stable measure of the overall word frequency chosen in this chapter.

We thus define the inverse document frequency (yes, we repeat the term again and again to increase the value of our document) within the corpus of all documents as (we use the term *document* interchangeably with *sentence*):

$$idf_{\text{corpus}}(w) = \log \frac{\sum_{\text{document}' \in \text{corpus}}}{\sum_{\text{document}' \in \text{corpus}} 1(w \in \text{document}')}, \tag{27.8}$$

where the numerator corresponds to the size of the corpus while denominator is number of documents within a corpus which contain a given word.

We implement the *idf* as the following function, which takes the entire corpus as a dictionary and returns a dictionary with *idf* defined for every word in the corpus. This definition is extensive enough such that it is supposed to execute only once. Subsequent queries should take the outcome from memory.

```
.quantQ.infth.idf:{[corpus]
   // corpus -- corpus with cleaned text
   uniqueWords: distinct " "vs" "sv corpus;
   // count of documents with a given word
   vals: {[corpus;word] sum { x in " "vs y}[word;] each corpus}[corpus;]
        ↪ each uniqueWords;
   // idf
   :log uniqueWords!(count corpus)%vals;
 };
```

The *idf* for a sample word `"there"` gives:

```
.quantQ.infth.idf[daVinci]["there"]
```

```
2.159484
```

Further, we combine the two measures, *tf* and *idf*, into single function. The function `tfidfSentence` calculates *tf-idf* measure. It accepts two arguments. The first one is a sentence and the second one is the *idf* evaluation for the corpus. The function returns *tf-idf* for every word in the sentence:

```
.quantQ.infth.tfidfSentence:{[sentence;idf]
   // sentence -- sentence of words to be analysed
   // idf -- idf calculated for the corpus
   // word frequency dictionary
   wordFrequency: .quantQ.infth.wordFrequency[enlist sentence];
   // tf-idf for every word
   :t!(value wordFrequency)*idf each t:key wordFrequency;
};
```

Let us calculate *tf-idf* for first sentence of the corpus:

```
.quantQ.infth.tfidfSentence[first daVinci;.quantQ.infth.idf[daVinci]]
```

```
("there";"is";"no";"human";"experience";"that";"can";"be";"termed";"true";"
    ↪ science";"unless";"it";"mathematically";"demonstrated")!2.159484
    ↪ 0.4792773 1.84711 3.614771 2.921624 0.9655618 4.52969 2.332465
    ↪ 4.462069 3.162786 3.075775 3.768922 0.7985077 5.560682 5.560682
```

The outcome is a dictionary, for every word of the sentence there is a corresponding numerical value, *tf-idf*. Let us illustrate the value for two words. The first one is very common:

```
tfidfA[enlist "is"]
```

```
enlist 0.4792773
```

and the second one is rather rare:

```
tfidfA[enlist "mathematically"]
```

```
enlist 5.560682
```

The values of *tf-idf* reflect the intuitive notion of being rare; the latter word has much higher score compared to the first one. The value itself, however, does not give much meaning. We thus slightly turn the problem and reformulate it as follows. We are provided with a word to search for and we should find a sentence which is the most relevant in terms of *tf-idf* metric. For that purpose, we define a function `findBestSentence` which takes as an input the entire corpus and the word we are searching for. It returns the sentence from the corpus which has for a given word the highest *tf-idf*:

```
.quantQ.infth.findBestSentence:{[corpus;word]
   // corpus -- corpus with cleaned text
   // word -- word to be searched for
   // subset of corpus with given word
   corpusSubset:corpus where { first x in " "vs y}[word;] each corpus;
   // return the sentence with the maximum tf-idf for a given word, if more
       ↪ then one, select randomly
   :first 1?corpusSubset where max[t]=t:{first x[y]}[;word] each
       .quantQ.infth.tfidfSentence[;.quantQ.infth.idf[corpus]] each
           ↪ corpusSubset;
};
```

Let us illustrate it on the following search:

```
.quantQ.infth.findBestSentence[daVinci;"there"]
```

```
"there can be no voice where there is no motion or percussion of the air
    ↪ there can be no percussion of the air where there is no instrument
    ↪ there can be no such thing as an immaterial instrument and this
    ↪ being so a spirit can have neither voice nor shape nor force and if
    ↪ it assumes a shape it can neither penetrate nor enter where the
    ↪ issues are closed"
```

The sentence found is the one with a large number of occurrences of `"there"`. The sentence does not have much meaning to find out more about the word itself. Since the test corpus is about science, we try to search for that word:

```
.quantQ.infth.findBestSentence[daVinci;"science"]
```

```
"science is that discourse of the mind which derives its origin from
    ↪ ultimate principles beyond which nothing in nature can be found
    ↪ which forms a part of that science as in the continued quantity that
    ↪  is to say the science of geometry which starting from the surfaces
    ↪ of bodies has its origin in the line which is the end of the
    ↪ superficies and we are not satisfied by this because we know that
    ↪ the line terminates in the point and the point is that which is the
    ↪ least of things"
```

Eureka! The sentence seems to explain the meaning of the word *science*. This is rather lucky, or a consequence of the fact that philosophers tend to construct long sentences which carry the compound message. In modern stylistics, the sentence would be likely cut into pieces, and this would not work. We would have to use at least a paragraph instead of a sentence to achieve the same outcome.

Finally, we check the behaviour of the function for words which are not in the corpus. Da Vinci's description of a computer from the provided text reads:

```
.quantQ.infth.findBestSentence[daVinci;"computer"]
```

```
()
```

There is no output of our search query. Da Vinci does not anticipate computers in his work – or at least in the provided manuscript.

27.2 INFORMATION AS FEATURES

In this section, we introduce another method which aims to work with non-numerical objects. In this case, we consider our problem as follows. We observe one feature and the corresponding dependent variable. The feature itself is not a numeric feature in a classical sense, nor is it ordinal/cardinal variable. Imagine the feature is a document. Further, we observe a number of observations. We want to establish formally how to work within such a framework, where we do not have features as we have been used to having.

The missing piece we have to establish is a way to compare two features. Imagine we have a corpus of paragraphs of a text. For every paragraph, we have a particular property, say, class. When we are provided with a new paragraph which is out-of-sample, our goal is to predict the class. In a simple case, the problem can be that we have one-half of all the paragraphs in English (class of a paragraph) and the second half of the paragraphs written in Latin. Then, the comparison of two paragraphs will be based on matching words and counting the number of matching words. We thus define a kernel of matching words and employ a method which can utilise kernels.

In the subsequent paragraphs, we introduce a sample data set and explain how we can use the kernel methods for classification. We implement the explained methods afterwards.

27.2.1 Sample: Simulated Proteins

We want to illustrate our method on the data. The nice and realistic subset for the algorithm we will introduce is a frequent problem in biomedicine, which is a comparison of proteins. For our exercise, the protein is characterised as a sequence of amino acids. We further consider the existence of 20 amino acids, which may contribute to the formation of any protein. Since the number of different amino acids is less than a number of characters in the alphabet, we represent each amino acid by an upper case letter, `A,B,C,...`. Protein can be naturally represented as a sequence of letters, where the ordering of the individual amino acids matters; i.e. `AB` and `BA` represent two simple and different proteins. Further, proteins main not have necessarily the same number of amino acids.

Let us illustrate the proteins in practice. We will use synthetic data and create our sample. The protein is an array of characters of a given length. The example of such a protein reads:

```
protein:"ABDLQEKBEQLE";
```

The advantage of this representation is that we can uniquely convert an array of characters into an array of integers using the ASCII table. Namely, we can cast between characters and ASCII representation as follows:

```
"i" $ "A"
```

```
65i
```

and back

```
"c" $ 65
```

```
"A"
```

We define two rather symbolic functions to achieve this:

```
.quantQ.infth.char2int:{[char]
   // char -- argument of type char
   // conversion from char to ASCII
   :"i" $ char;
};
```

and

```
.quantQ.infth.int2char:{[int]
   // int -- argument of type integer
   // conversion from ASCII to char
   :"c" $ int;
};
```

In order to create a random protein, we use random integer number generation and cast it between ASCII and characters. We will further consider the proteins of length ranging from 40 to 60 amino acids where we will allow for 20 different amino acids to be present in our laboratory. The function which creates such a protein is given in the following:

```
.quantQ.infth.getProtein:{[minLength;maxLength;nAcids]
   // minLength -- min length of the protein
   // maxLength -- max length of the protein
   // nAcids -- number of different amino acids, number should not exceed
       ↪ 26 to have alphabetic representation
   // capital "A" offset for ASCII
   offset:.quantQ.infth.char2int["A"];
   // choose the length of the protein
   proteinLength: first minLength+1?(1+maxLength-minLength);
   // create ASCII protein
   protein: offset+proteinLength?nAcids;
   // convert to chars and export
   :.quantQ.infth.int2char[protein];
};
```

Example of such a protein can be generated:

```
.quantQ.infth.getProtein[20;40;20]
```

```
"MLBAFRAAKRKTEODEIKGISTRMPKSCHCAFHOGASRR"
```

For two proteins, we want to be able to assess them and measure their difference. The suitable approach, as was already advertised, is to use kernels. The kernels should allow us to assess the proximity relationship between two proteins. Then, we can define a matrix with elements being pairwise kernels for corresponding pairs. The index of a row and a column of a proximity matrix corresponds to two proteins while the entry in the matrix is mutual proximity of those proteins. The kernels are the standard tool, and we can thus use methods we already know from literature dealing with numerical features. We will illustrate it in the nearest-neighbours method.

27.2.2 Kernels and Metrics for Proteins

We proceed with proteins and define the proximity between the two kernels. The proximity measure aims to capture the similarity between two proteins and to quantify the similarity of two proteins. We employ a measure based on the comparison of substrings of proteins; see Leslie et al. (2004). The motivation is as follows. The protein is represented as an ordered sequence of letters. We thus identify all substrings of a chosen length present in the protein and count their occurrence. The two proteins are then compared based on the matching substrings.

Decomposing a protein into substrings means that we form a space of all possible substrings as a new feature space and then represent a protein in the new feature space by counting the presence of substrings in the protein. If there are M building blocks of the protein (M letters) and we choose substrings of length N, the dimension of the feature space is M^N, which is for any practical considerations substantial. We thus do not aim to keep the new representation explicitly in memory but rather be able to calculate it on request.

Let us denote the set of all possible substrings as $L(M;N)$. Further, for the protein P we define a vector $l = \{l_i\}_{l_i \in L(M;N)}$, where l_i is a non-negative integer which denotes how many substrings of type i are contained within the protein P. The vector is M^N-dimensional object. Then, for a pair of proteins P_1 and P_2, we define the inner product using the two vectors as:

$$\langle P_1, P_2 \rangle = \langle l_1, l_2 \rangle, \tag{27.9}$$

where the inner product is calculated from the vectors l_i, which count occurrences of substrings.

The inner products themselves can be arranged into kernels. Methods like Support Vector Machines, among others, can directly work with such kernels. In the following, we derive the distance between two proteins using inner products defined as:

$$\|P_1 - P_2\|^2 = \langle P_1, P_1 \rangle + \langle P_2, P_2 \rangle - 2\langle P_1, P_2 \rangle. \tag{27.10}$$

Having such a measure at hand, we can employ the nearest-neighbour methods to make inference for proteins. In the following, we define a simplified version of the nearest-neighbour classifier using the inner product–based distance.

It is important to point out that our objective is not to calculate the full vector from $L(M;N)$. The dimensionality is so large that this task would be practically infeasible. More importantly, it is not necessary. We can effectively work with those substrings which are only present in the proteins at hand.

27.2.3 Implementation of Inner Products and Nearest Neighbours Principles

We implement the substring matching based on an inner product for proteins data. We start by creating a sample data set of 50 proteins. We assign a random binary class to every protein. This will be a proxy for the problem we may face in the laboratory, where the class is, for instance, the presence of a particular disease. The data are stored in the table proteinTab:

```
proteinTab: ([] protein: {.quantQ.infth.getProtein[20;40;20]} each til 50;
    ↪ classRisk:50?2);
proteinTab
```

```
protein                                        classRisk
----------------------------------------------------------
"CIFTPPMSINKQQMJHDFJI"                         1
"LRTHLFPRKDCLQRSLNASGBPEFBTFHCNGCH"            1
"LERTBHMJRTIBSPLJQBFEGQL"                      0
"IKSNGOLGQQHRIERTPHFRDNTSQSDKP"                0
"CFOLNAABTGSKIHHJLEAHPSTMALRFMHQINLJDLP"  1
"ERHSFONCBODHKPAILSTDNNOGQJBOIPORC"            1
"DHDGAMJCSESRDRFGGDJAMJ"                       1
"MPCQRGIJRKJAFGKEBPJLGPNGPPQRPEEJLEBAIL"  1
"EMMRHLMFIJKHAQGHFGELMFRILIBF"                 0
"PNTMETHJKFGGBPCFINQBILLFIQKOEHRB"             1
..
```

First, we define a function which extracts all substrings of length N from the provided protein. Let us remind the reader that protein is an ordered array of letters. The function returns an array of all substrings as are sequentially extracted from the array without any filtering:

```
.quantQ.infth.proteinGetSubstring:{[p;N]
   // p -- protein
   // N -- length of substring
   // return all substrings of length N
   :({[dict] dict[`strings]:dict[`strings],enlist 3#dict[`protein]; dict[`
       ↪ protein]:1_dict[`protein];dict }/)
       [{[x;N] N<=count x[`protein]}[;N];`strings`protein!(();p)][`strings
           ↪ ];
};
```

and apply it to the first entry of proteinTab table:

```
exec first protein from proteinTab
```

```
"CIFTPPMSINKQQMJHDFJI"
```

The decomposition reads:

```
.quantQ.infth.proteinGetSubstring[exec first protein from proteinTab;3]
```

```
("CIF";"IFT";"FTP";"TPP";"PPM";"PMS";"MSI";"SIN";"INK";"NKQ";"KQQ";"QQM";"
    ↪ QMJ";"MJH";"JHD";"HDF";"DFJ";"FJI")
```

The array of substrings itself can contain repeated patterns. We are further interested in knowing the number of occurrences for every unique substring. Thus, we create another rather simple function which groups the substrings and create a dictionary with values corresponding to their occurrence rate:

```
.quantQ.infth.proteinGetFeatureVector:{[substrings]
   // substrings -- outcome of .quantQ.infth.proteinGetSubstring function
   // returns the vector of features as dictionary of substrings and its
       ↪ occurrence
   :(#:)'[group substrings];
};
```

The function takes as an argument the outcome of `proteinGetSubstring` function:

```
.quantQ.infth.proteinGetFeatureVector[.quantQ.infth.proteinGetSubstring[
    ↪ exec first protein from proteinTab;3]]
```

```
("CIF";"IFT";"FTP";"TPP";"PPM";"PMS";"MSI";"SIN";"INK";"NKQ";"KQQ";"QQM";"
    ↪ QMJ";"MJH";"JHD";"HDF";"DFJ";"FJI")!1j, 1j, 1j, 1j, 1j, 1j, 1j, 1j,
    ↪ 1j, 1j, 1j, 1j, 1j, 1j, 1j, 1j, 1j, 1j
```

We can proceed with the definition of the inner product. The inner product will work with the substrings present in either of two proteins. We thus need significantly smaller subspace of $L(M;N)$, which makes the entire calculation numerically feasible.

```
.quantQ.infth.proteinInnerProduct:{[p1;p2;N]
   // p1 -- protein 1
   // p2 -- protein 2
   // N -- length of substring
   // calculate vector of features for both proteins
   d1:.quantQ.infth.proteinGetFeatureVector[.quantQ.infth.
       ↪ proteinGetSubstring[p1;3]];
   d2:.quantQ.infth.proteinGetFeatureVector[.quantQ.infth.
       ↪ proteinGetSubstring[p2;3]];
   // return inner product
   :exec (0f^d1)<-ALG71/>f^d2 from ([substring: key d1];value d1) uj ([
       ↪ substring: key d2];value d2);
};
```

and calculate the inner product between the first two rows of `proteinTab` table.

```
.quantQ.infth.proteinInnerProduct[exec first protein from proteinTab;exec
    ↪ first 1_protein from proteinTab;3]
```

```
0j
```

There is no overlap between the two proteins. This is likely as we have created completely random proteins and given that we use as a building block 20 letters of the alphabet.

Finally, we can define the measure of distance as defined in eq. (27.10). The measure employs the inner products as implemented in `proteinInnerProduct`.

The function returns the metrics of distance, which can be used to compare any two proteins:

```
.quantQ.infth.proteinDistance:{[p1;p2;N]
   // p1 -- protein 1
   // p2 -- protein 2
   // N -- length of substring
   // return measure
   :.quantQ.infth.proteinInnerProduct[p1;p1;N]+.quantQ.infth.
       ↪ proteinInnerProduct[p2;p2;N]-
      2.0*.quantQ.infth.proteinInnerProduct[p1;p2;N];
};
```

The distance for a previously mentioned pair of proteins from `proteinTab` table reads:

```
.quantQ.infth.proteinDistance[exec first protein from proteinTab;exec first
    ↪  1_protein from proteinTab;3]
```

```
49f
```

which can be compared to a distance measured between two identical proteins:

```
.quantQ.infth.proteinDistance[exec first protein from proteinTab;exec first
    ↪  protein from proteinTab;3]
```

```
0f
```

The illustration confirms the notion of measure: two identical proteins have zero distance between themselves while two distinct proteins have non-zero positive distance. Let us stress that this is just an illustration, though. We would need medical background to assess whether the distance has real medical sense as well.

Let us continue with our example and sketch the path of how to employ the nearest-neighbours algorithm to classify a new protein using the training sample. We start with defining an out-of-sample protein. Since we want to have one which is somehow close to the existing proteins in our training sample, `proteinTab`, we create the new protein by random re-shuffling of blocks of a selected protein from the training sample. Below, we create a simple query to perform an iterated switch of blocks for a protein:

```
pOut: ({ perm:first[1?floor 0.5*count[x]]; raze (neg[perm] # x; perm _ neg[
    ↪ perm]_x ;perm # x )  }/)[5;exec first protein from proteinTab];
```

where the new out-of-sample protein reads

```
"FJIMSITPPNKJHDQQMCIF"
```

We use the distance metric function and create a new column with the distance between the out-of-sample protein and the protein in a given row. We sort the table based on the distance measure in ascending order such that the first entry is the one the closest to the out-of-sample protein:

```
proteinTab: `distance xasc update distance: .quantQ.infth.proteinDistance[
    ↪ pOut;;3] each protein from proteinTab;
proteinTab
```

```
protein                        classRisk distance
-------------------------------------------------
"CIFTPPMSINKQQMJHDFJI"         1         24
"HPSMBMTMFPQFTLKDTNTR"         0         36
"SNDAQDCBJLHMSKDHSJQF"         1         36
"ODBRTPDNMIMBHDTBOFETG"        1         37
"EDBDCETGMAPHAHLMDMTMJ"        0         37
"MKTICDFDIIKSFCOPRBQDE"        0         37
"RRBACBNKFMDKLTMASISMBQ"       1         38
"LERTBHMJRTIBSPLJQBFEGQL"      0         39
"EJREJDHQPSSGINIRSONQPAB"      0         39
"DHDGAMJCSESRDRFGGDJAMJ"       1         40
..
```

Indeed, the closest protein is the one we used to derive the out-of-sample protein. The difference in distance between the first and second row and any other two consecutive rows is enormous. This further confirms that the notion of the distance we have defined using the inner products is reasonable and satisfies the intuitive requirements.

This concludes our investigation of the algorithms for non-numeric features. We aimed to provide guidance how to build such algorithms. Given we are equipped with distance, we can, for instance, employ the full suite of nearest-neighbour algorithms defined in Chapter 21.

27.2.4 Further Topics

In the previous sections, we have provided algorithms on how to treat the non-traditional data and perform statistical inference. The provided material is somewhat introductory and calls for further extensions. We encourage readers to implement the full pledge suite of algorithms dealing with protein-like data. It is an exciting path to strengthen the knowledge of machine learning algorithms outside of the usual time series comfort zone.

For instance, we have started the chapter with a hypothetical example of classifying the text into two languages based on a corpus of texts where we know the language. The proper metric is to find a distance between unknown text and all existing texts. We can proceed precisely in the same way as above with inner product being every word in the corpus. The presence/rate of occurrence of a specific word will be thus a new feature. The complete feature space will be huge; however, we do not need to work with words which are not relevant between two documents as we have not worked with substrings not observed in proteins. The rest is then nearly identical. We encourage readers to implement this exercise as a project especially if they are fluent in any other (non-programming) language.

CHAPTER 28

Towards AI – Monte Carlo Tree Search

In the previous chapters, we have been mainly working with traditional machine learning algorithms. The focus has been on methods which learn from experience. In this section, we take a step further and focus on elements of the machine learning literature leading to algorithms denoted as AI, or Artificial Intelligence. Each of the algorithms explored in this section aims to learn on the fly from its own experience, from its successes and mistakes, rather than from the provided data set.

The key concept for this chapter is the distinction between exploration and exploitation. The machine learning methods introduced so far have been constructed such that they exploit the knowledge learnt from the training data set. The exploration steps, on the other hand, stand for actions made by the algorithm, which explores new paths. The objective is to learn a profitable path and exploit it in the future. The outcome of the exploration step can be, however, a choice which is not optimal and which will be avoided in the following steps. The outcome of exploration steps is thus expected improvement in the future steps. Exploration helps the algorithms to deal in complex and/or changing environments and learn their characteristics. Exploitation then follows once the algorithm gains knowledge about the environment.

We start with a multi-armed bandit problem, which represents a textbook example of finding an optimal choice of slot machines in the casino without having prior knowledge about their performance. Then, we extend the introduced concepts and implement the Monte Carlo Tree Search algorithm, which is an algorithm behind many game engines. We implement a particular method for tic-tac-toe. Further, we discuss the extension of the Monte Carlo Tree Search leading to AlphaGo engine.

28.1 MULTI-ARMED BANDIT PROBLEM

Let us start with rather a classic example which illustrates the trade-off between exploration and exploitation. It is important to understand this concept as it is in the centre of most decision-making algorithms and AIs with learning ability. It also reflects the behaviour of living beings, which tend to explore unknown and risky options to maximise potential pay-out. For an overview of bandits see Bubeck et al. (2012) or Auer et al. (2002a).

The multi-armed bandit problem is defined as follows. Imagine that you are at a casino where are some slot machines. You can play one slot machine at time. You do not see the other players using the slot machines and their outcome. Each slot machine is different and may provide different pay-out. A question one has to answer is what is the optimal strategy to follow once you decide to play. You can play every game on a randomly chosen slot machine, or stick to one slot machine all the time. The question is whether there exists a more profitable strategy to follow.

Let us formalise the problem mathematically. Let us consider K distribution functions $P_1, P_2, \dots, P_K$ defined over real numbers. We identify the probability distribution functions with K random variables $X_1, X_2, \dots, X_K$. Each random variable X_i has a mean μ_i and is assumed to be σ^2-sub-Gaussian:

$$E[\exp(\lambda(X_i - \mu_i))] \leq \exp\left(\frac{\lambda^2\sigma^2}{2}\right), \tag{28.1}$$

for positive and real λ. The multi-armed bandit problem is an optimisation problem to find the index i which gives the maximum mean μ_i while evaluating the suboptimal choices as little as possible. The problem is by its nature iterative, where at time t, player chooses an index $I_t \in \{1, 2, \dots, K\}$ and then observes a reward $X_i(t)$. The reward is drawn independently from corresponding probability distribution P_i.

The multi-armed bandit problem is usually defined as minimisation of regret after n steps:

$$\arg\min_A \sum_{j=0}^{n} (\mu_{j*} - \mu_{A_j}), \tag{28.2}$$

where μ_{j*} is a mean of the optimal distribution, i.e. the distribution with the highest mean:

$$j^* = \arg\max_i \mu_i. \tag{28.3}$$

The strategy A is the ultimate goal of the problem and it represents the collection of indices chosen in each step. The indices may be chosen iteratively; i.e. in order to choose the j-th index, we know the pay-offs of all steps up to $j - 1$-st step. The regret function:

$$Reg_n = \sum_{j=0}^{n} (\mu_{j*} - \mu_{A_j}) \tag{28.4}$$

is a random quantity. The mathematical theory solving the multi-armed bandit problem seeks to estimate the bounds in expectations. For that purpose, one often defines the expected regret:

$$\bar{Reg}_n = E\left[\sum_{j=0}^{n} (\mu_{j*} - \mu_{A_j})\right]. \tag{28.5}$$

The solution sought by many numerical algorithms to the multi-armed bandit problem is thus the zero regret strategy. It is a strategy whose average regret per round tends to 0 as a number of steps taken grow to infinity, $n \to \infty$. The zero regret strategy converges to an optimal strategy for n large enough.

It is worth reviewing the existing approaches to solve the multi-armed bandit problem. Our objective is not to repeat the mathematical foundations and all the proofs but rather to understand the logic behind the various methods. This can give us many useful hints to follow in the numerical solutions for real problems we may face.

28.1.1 Analytic Solutions

First, let us mention a few theoretical achievements in this field. Lai and Robbins (1985) considered the reward to be generated from an exponential family of distributions with one parameter and showed the existence of policies with the fastest convergence rate to the optimal policy. Katehakis and Robbins (1995) studied the case of reward functions which are normally distributed. Further, literature focuses on the cases when reward functions have been affected by exogenous variables. Burnetas and Katehakis (1996) considered the case of reward function being driven by unknown variables and studied the strategies with maximum convergence rates towards optimal policies. This was further elaborated by Burnetas and Katehakis (1997), Tewari and Bartlett (2008), or Honda and Takemura (2011), among others.

Let us further focus on the details of some of the existing numerical algorithms to approach the multi-armed bandit problem. These algorithms provide approximate solutions. We focus primarily on the mechanics of algorithms and insight they can provide us.

28.1.2 Greedy Algorithms

The first group of algorithms are based on some form of a greedy search. They have been among first to be developed to solve the general multi-armed bandit problems; see Sutton et al. (1998) for an overview. The greedy algorithms split, in general, the strategy into two parts: exploration and exploitation. The exploration stage is randomly probing the options and assessing the profitability of such options while the exploitation stage is utilising the option which is at a given point in time perceived as the best. There are several possibilities for how to implement this greedy principle. In every algorithm, we aim to find a strategy to optimise the choice of n draws from K options.

Let us remark that there are two possible approaches to the exploitation stage. First, during the exploitation step, the algorithm opts for choice with the best-expected outcome. Once the choice is made and the outcome realised, the algorithm can learn from the outcome or not. The latter choice is simpler but it is less efficient and ignores the knowledge being acquired during the run of the algorithm. We thus consider in the subsequent parts the outcome of exploitation steps to improve our decision. The algorithm is thus able to leave the local minima which may be entered during the exploratory steps.

Exploration first greedy algorithm

The first algorithm works as follows. We split the actions into two parts based on the proportion ϵ. First, $\epsilon \cdot n$ draws – suitably rounded – is the exploration phase.

During this phase, the choice between available options is made randomly using the uniform distribution. At the end of the exploration phase, the outcome is evaluated and the choice with the best outcome is chosen. The moves in the exploratory phase are chosen based on the best average outcome. The option chosen in the exploratory phase may not be constant as the performance of the best option at the end of the exploratory phase may deteriorate during the exploration phase.

Random exploration greedy algorithm

The second algorithm extends the first one by placing the proportion of the exploratory choices randomly during the iteration. In particular, at every step, we make an exploratory step with probability ϵ, and an exploitation step otherwise. The exploratory step is as described above. Distributing the exploratory phase across the entire strategy improves the ability of the strategy to escape local maxima and it provides a check against heteroscedastic behaviour of the system, where choices are made.

Decreasing exploration greedy algorithm

The exploration in the greedy algorithms described in the preceding paragraphs represents learning. The rate ϵ can be understood as a learning rate of the algorithm to explore the possible options. It is thus intuitive to formulate an algorithm where the learning rate decreases over time. Such an algorithm will explore more during the initial stages, and the learning rate will decrease as the iterations progress. The exploration will be still preserved during the entire lifetime of the strategy to preserve the ability to escape the local maxima. The functional dependence of ϵ on the number of iterations passed is a matter of choice and object of study.

Adaptive exploration greedy strategy

The change of the learning rate during the progress of the strategy as introduced in the previous algorithm depends solely on the number of draws already taken. It may be optimal, though, to make it dependent on the outcome of the strategies as well. If the algorithm learns a stable solution, it may be a good idea to slow down the learning, i.e. less exploration, and exploit instead. The stable solution can be defined using the variability of the outcome so far realised. This is the basis of the VBDE algorithm in Tokic and Palm (2011).

28.1.3 Confidence-Based Algorithms

The popular group of algorithms to solve the multi-armed bandit problems are confidence-based algorithms with optimism. The idea can be outlined as follows. At a given point in time, we believe that the true mean μ_i of each arm i is within:

$$\mu_i \in [\hat{\mu}_i - \xi_i, \hat{\mu}_i + \xi_i], \tag{28.6}$$

where $\hat{\mu}_i$ is an estimator of the true mean and ξ_i denotes the confidence interval bounds. The width of the confidence interval decreases with time, i.e. $\xi_i \searrow$ as $t \nearrow$. Then, the value of arm i is optimistically $\hat{\mu}_i + \xi_i$. At time t, when we need to decide between arms, we choose the one with the highest optimistic value:

$$i = \arg\max_{i*} \hat{\mu}_{i*} + \xi_{i*}. \tag{28.7}$$

Auer et al. (2002a) elaborated the outlined approach and introduced the Upper Confidence Bound algorithm. In order to formulate Upper Confidence Bound algorithm and its convergence properties, we need to impose an assumption on the distribution of the individual arms: every distribution is σ^2-sub-Gaussian. Namely, we define the running average of the i-th arm at time t as:

$$\hat{\mu}_{i,t} = \frac{1}{\#(i,t)} \sum_{s \le t} X_{i,s}, \tag{28.8}$$

where $\#(i, t)$ stands for the number of instances when the strategy chosen has been i, and $X_{i,t}$ being the realisations of the random variable X_i in such cases.

The Upper Confidence Bound algorithms are based on the theorem which says that:

$$\mathbb{P}\left(\hat{\mu}_{i,t} \ge \mu_i + \sqrt{\frac{\sigma^2 \log \frac{1}{\delta}}{\#(i,t)}}\right) \le \delta \text{or } \mathbb{P}\left(\hat{\mu}_{i,t} \le \mu_i - \sqrt{\frac{\sigma^2 \log \frac{1}{\delta}}{\#(i,t)}}\right) \le \delta, \tag{28.9}$$

for positive real δ. Then, if the bandit is played sufficiently many times, the probability to choose the wrong one is going to zero. See Auer et al. (2002a) for proofs.

The algorithm then follows along these lines:

- Provide σ^2 and a sequence of probabilities $\delta_1, \delta_2, \delta_3, \ldots$.
- Initialise the algorithm by choosing every arm i once.
- Choose a strategy such that at every time t, the index i results from:

$$i = \arg\max_{i*} \hat{\mu}_{i*,t} + \sqrt{\frac{\sigma^2 \log \frac{1}{\delta_t}}{\#(i*,t)}}. \tag{28.10}$$

Practically, if the reward of each arm is within $[0, 1]$, the parameter $\sigma^2 = 1/4$ would be a suitable choice following Hoeffding's lemma. The convenient choice for the sequence of probabilities is:

$$\delta_t = \frac{1}{t^2}. \tag{28.11}$$

Such a choice of parameters provides an algorithm which optimises the Upper Confidence Bound and is adaptive enough to avoid some possible pathological cases which may occur – for instance, if one arm dominates other arms, then under certain circumstances the regret of the algorithm may be infinite. This will cause pathological behaviour as a difference between an optimal arm and any other arm will be infinite.

28.1.4 Bayesian Algorithms

Another class of algorithms to solve the multi-armed bandit problems are Bayesian algorithms. As the name suggests, the Bayesian strategies assume some prior knowledge about the bandits' distributions. This can be used to improve exploration strategies and work more accurately with information and regret.

In order to implement the strategy, we further assume that probability functions corresponding to bandits' arms are given as $P = \{P_\theta\}_{\theta \in \Theta}$ with Θ being parametric set. In the simple settings, it can correspond to a K-dimensional real vector. The prior distribution imposed on the parametric space is such that $\pi(\Theta)$. In order to solve the problem, we define the Bayesian regret as:

$$\bar{Reg}_n(A, \lambda, \pi) = E_\pi \left[\sum_{j=0}^{n} \lambda(A_j, \theta) - \lambda(A^*, \theta) \right], \tag{28.12}$$

where A^* is the minimiser of the loss function λ. We have denoted the expectations with index π in order to stress the dependence on the prior distribution.

The textbook example worth mentioning is the Bernoulli bandit problem, which nicely illustrates the meaning of the parametric set and choice of λ. The Bernoulli bandit problem is a setup where the probability functions modelling the reward of every arm i are given by Bernoulli distributions with parameter θ_i. The pay-off of the arm i is either 1, with probability θ_i, or 0 otherwise. To solve the Bernoulli multi-armed bandit problem means to find the arm with the highest θ_i. The loss function for the Bernoulli bandit can be suitably chosen as $\lambda(i, \theta) = -\theta_i$.

The schema for the Bayesian algorithm then follows along the following lines:

- Provide a prior distribution π for Θ, connected to probabilities $P = \{P_\theta\}_{\theta \in \Theta}$.
- At each step t, choose prior distribution π_t based on past realisations and corresponding losses. The step consists of:
  - Draw θ_t from the prior distribution π_t.
  - Choose an action which minimises the loss $\lambda(i, \theta_t)$ over a set of admissible strategies.
  - Obtain the outcome.

Thompson sampling

The simple implementation of the Bayesian algorithm is to follow Thompson (1933) and take prior distribution π_t equal to the posterior distribution of θ, conditional on the history of all observed pay-offs:

$$\pi_t(\theta) = \pi(\theta | \{A_0, X_0, \ldots, A_t, X_t\}). \tag{28.13}$$

The Thompson sampling procedure for the Bayesian algorithm at every time step t reads:

- Denote $\#(i, t, 1)$ the number of cases when arm i was chosen and it resulted in a pay-off 1, and analogously, $\#(i, t, 0)$ the number of cases when arm i was chosen and resulted in a pay-off 0.

- For each arm i, the parameter $\theta_{i,t}$ is drawn as: $\theta_{i,t} \sim \text{Beta}(1 + \#(i,t,1), 1 + \#(i,t,0))$.
- Choose an action i which solves $i = \arg\min_{i*} \lambda(i*, \theta_{i*,t})$.
- Observe the pay-off X_i at time t and update the information set for the next step.

The provided algorithm thus constitutes what is known as a Thompson algorithm. We have specified it for the Bernoulli bandit only. It can be elaborated for more general distributions, but it goes beyond the scope of this book.

28.1.5 Online Gradient Descent Algorithms

Finally, let us specify the algorithms using the online gradient descent approach to minimise the running regret or the loss function defined in the previous section. We assume that we can define a non-negative loss function for every action $\lambda(i,t)$. In order to use the online gradient descent method, we have to formulate the problem as an online convex optimisation problem, where we further know the gradient of the loss. Auer et al. (2002b) formulated the multi-armed bandit problem in a way the online gradient descent can be used. The resulting algorithm, known as *EXP*3, can be specified as follows:

- Define the step parameter Δ.
- Initialise the vector of probabilities $\omega_1 = \left(\frac{1}{K}, \dots, \frac{1}{K}\right)$.
- At time t, choose an action i proportional to probability $\omega_{t,i}$. Further, perform the following steps:
  - Observe reward for a chosen arm and interpret it as a non-negative loss $\lambda(i,t)$.
  - Define $\gamma_{t,j} = \delta_{i,j} \frac{\lambda(j,t)}{\omega_{t,j}}$ with $\delta_{i,j}$ being Kronecker delta.
  - For every arm i, update: $\omega_{t+1,i} = \frac{\omega_{t,i} \exp(-\Delta \gamma_{t,i})}{\sum_j \omega_{t,j} \exp(-\Delta \gamma_{t,j})}$.

The *EXP*3 algorithm is widespread in practice. The exploration mechanism comes from the probabilities ω, which ensures that all the arms can be explored. As some of the arms start to perform better, the probability assigned to them is more pronounced and they will be more likely chosen – exploitation comes into play.

This concludes the overview of the multi-armed bandit problem and various ways to construct algorithms to solve it. Our aim was not to provide an exhaustive account of all the options but rather introduce some insight into them which allows us to run numerical experiments. In practice, if a reader faces a problem which resembles multi-armed bandit setup, we strongly recommend studying various numerical techniques as every method has its merits, and one can achieve remarkable results with a suitable but still simple method. In the next subsection, we implement some of the algorithms outlined above and encourage readers to implement more of them on their own.

28.1.6 Implementation of Some Learning Algorithms

Let us implement an example of the multi-armed bandit problem and several algorithms to find the strategy which converges to the optimal one. We focus on a simple case of three-armed bandit and implement the three greedy algorithms presented above.

They provide intuitive grounds for readers to develop their algorithms which could be built upon the presented principles.

First, let us define the three-armed bandit as a collection of three uniform distributions P_1, P_2, P_3, each being given as $P_i \sim U[0, maxP_i]$. The set of three parameters – the upper bounds – fully defines the bandit and also the means of the bandit's arms. Without loss of generality, let us further consider $maxP_1 < maxP_2 < maxP_3$. The multi-armed bandit with uniform distributions is implemented as:

```
.quantQ.mcts.MAB:{[choice;mabSpec]
   // mabSpec -- vector of maxBoundK's
   // choice -- choice to be drawn
   :first 1?"f"$mabSpec[choice];
};
```

The MAB function has two arguments: the first one is the bandit chosen, and the second one is the specification of the bandit itself through mabSpec. The three-armed bandit is then defined by setting the mabSpec input variable to a three-dimensional array. The function returns a random draw for a given choice of the bandit's arm:

```
.quantQ.mcts.MAB[2;(1.0;2.0;3.0)]
```

```
1.178257
```

Let us further run a small numerical experiment: we choose each arm 100 times and return the average outcome for every arm:

```
{avg .quantQ.mcts.MAB[;(1.0;2.0;3.0)] each 100#x} each til 3
```

```
0.5238409 1.033051 1.608269
```

where each number is approximately half of the corresponding number in mabSpec.

Exploration of first greedy algorithm

Let us implement the greedy algorithm where all the exploration is done fully at the beginning of the iterative process followed by greedy exploitation afterwards. Let us summarise all the variables specifying our setup:

```
epsilon:0.1;
N:1000;
K:3;
```

where we consider 1000 steps to be performed by the algorithm.

Let us also introduce several further variables we need during the lifetime of the algorithm to be preserved across individual iterations: all the realised pay-offs, minimum bound for any pay-off in the situation when the bandit's arm has not been explored yet but is supposed to be exploited, the counter of iterations, time series of strategies taken, and finally the multi-armed bandit function itself:

```
payoffs:K#();
minBound:0.0;
counter:0;
strategy:();
mab:.quantQ.mcts.MAB[;(1.0;2.0;3.0)];
```

The function mabExplorationFirstGA takes as an input all the variables described above wrapped up into a single dictionary, performs one iteration, and updates the same dictionary:

```
.quantQ.mcts.mabExplorationFirstGA:{[bucket]
   // bucket -- the dictionary with all parameters
   $[bucket[`counter]<=bucket[`epsilon]*bucket[`N];
   // exploration
   [
       // decision randomly
       choice:first 1?bucket[`K];
       bucket[`strategy],:choice;
       payoffs:bucket[`payoffs];
       payoffs[choice],:bucket[`mab] choice;
       bucket[`payoffs]:payoffs
   ];
   // exploitation
   [
       // decision based on the best outcome
       avgReward:bucket[`minBound]^avg each bucket[`payoffs];
       choice: first where avgReward=max avgReward;
       bucket[`strategy],:choice;
       payoffs:bucket[`payoffs];
       payoffs[choice],:bucket[`mab] choice;
       bucket[`payoffs]:payoffs
   ]
   ];
   // increase counter
   bucket[`counter]+:1;
   // return bucket
   :bucket;
};
```

The algorithm has two phases: the exploration phase and the exploitation phase. It is important to repeat that we allow the algorithm to choose the most optimal option during the exploitation phase. An alternative would be to fix the decision at the end of the exploration stage and not allow any switch. This may lead to a sub-optimal solution for a small number of draws when suboptimal arm can be chosen during the exploration stage. We thus stick into this algorithm – and all the following algorithms – the option to choose the arm based on the most favourable expected outcome using all up-to-date information. The algorithm thus learns even during the exploitation stage.

Let us create the dictionary of variables needed to execute the iterations:

```
bucket:(`N`K`epsilon`mab`payoffs`strategy`counter`minBound!(N;K;epsilon;mab
   ↪ ;payoffs;strategy;counter;minBound));
```

The greedy algorithm itself is the repetitive application of the function bucket[`N] steps times. Since we are interested in the outcome presented in every step of the iteration, we use \ instead of /. The greedy algorithm is then applied as:

```
outcomeMAB1: (.quantQ.mcts.mabExplorationFirstGA\)[bucket[`N];bucket];
```

Let us extract from the table `outcomeMAB1` several important variables: the counter of steps, the chosen arm in a given step, the total average pay-off after given number of steps, and the average pay-offs for every arm after given number of steps:

```
select counter, strategy,payoff, p0: payoffs[;0], p1: payoffs[;1], p2:
    ↪ payoffs[;2] from select counter, {[bucket;x] bucket[`minBound]^x}[
    ↪ bucket;] each {avg each x} each payoffs, payoff:avg each raze each
    ↪ payoffs, last each strategy from outcomeMAB1 where i>0
```

```
counter strategy payoff    p0        p1        p2
-------------------------------------------------------
1       2        1.400526  0         0         1.400526
2       0        0.7903761 0.1802266 0         1.400526
3       1        0.6332032 0.1802266 0.3188573 1.400526
4       0        0.5796908 0.2996902 0.3188573 1.400526
5       0        0.5909738 0.4118288 0.3188573 1.400526
6       0        0.5994576 0.4693406 0.3188573 1.400526
7       2        0.6463291 0.4693406 0.3188573 1.164042
8       2        0.8340724 0.4693406 0.3188573 1.49212
9       0        0.8482637 0.5678313 0.3188573 1.49212
10      2        0.9136941 0.5678313 0.3188573 1.494732
11      2        1.023471  0.5678313 0.3188573 1.620034
12      2        1.177768  0.5678313 0.3188573 1.8292
13      1        1.138378  0.5678313 0.4922767 1.8292
14      1        1.163473  0.5678313 0.8247522 1.8292
15      0        1.145328  0.6217436 0.8247522 1.8292
16      2        1.131049  0.6217436 0.8247522 1.698867
17      1        1.18196   0.6217436 1.117699  1.698867
18      0        1.162579  0.651938  1.117699  1.698867
19      0        1.109707  0.5901974 1.117699  1.698867
20      1        1.075534  0.5901974 0.9794079 1.698867
..
```

In the last query, we have included condition `where i>0`. We leave for readers to answer why we apply this constraint.

Let us review the results visually. Figure 28.1 depicts a sequence of choices, `bucket[`strategy]`, as they have been chosen consecutively by running the algorithm. The picture confirms that the first 10% of the sample was an exploratory phase as demonstrated by switching the arms while the rest of the time the strategy has been exploiting the best option – the third arm.

Further, Figure 28.2 depicts a sequence of average pay-offs for choices taken. The figure shows the pay-offs as they have been revealed during the lifetime of the algorithm. The algorithm made at every step a decision based on the complete set of values available up to the given step. The figure shows the performance of the overall strategy – black line – and for each arm separately: arm number 1 (gray line), arm number 2 (light gray line), and arm number 3 (dark gray line), respectively. The pay-off during the exploratory phase at the beginning is rather volatile. The pay-off then stabilises during the exploitation phase where the total average pay-off averages towards the pay-off of the optimal choice, arm number 3.

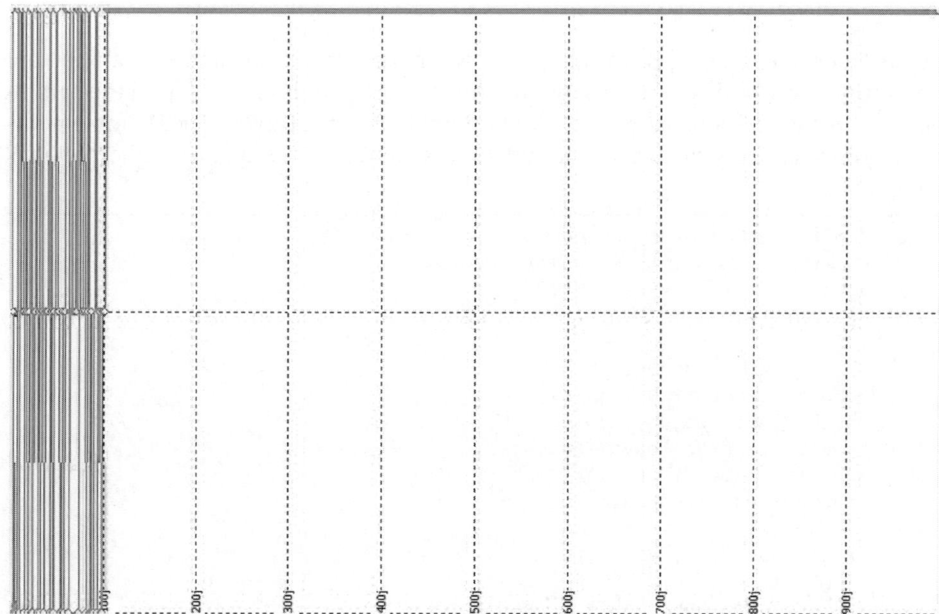

FIGURE 28.1 The sequence of choices done consecutively using the exploration first greedy algorithm

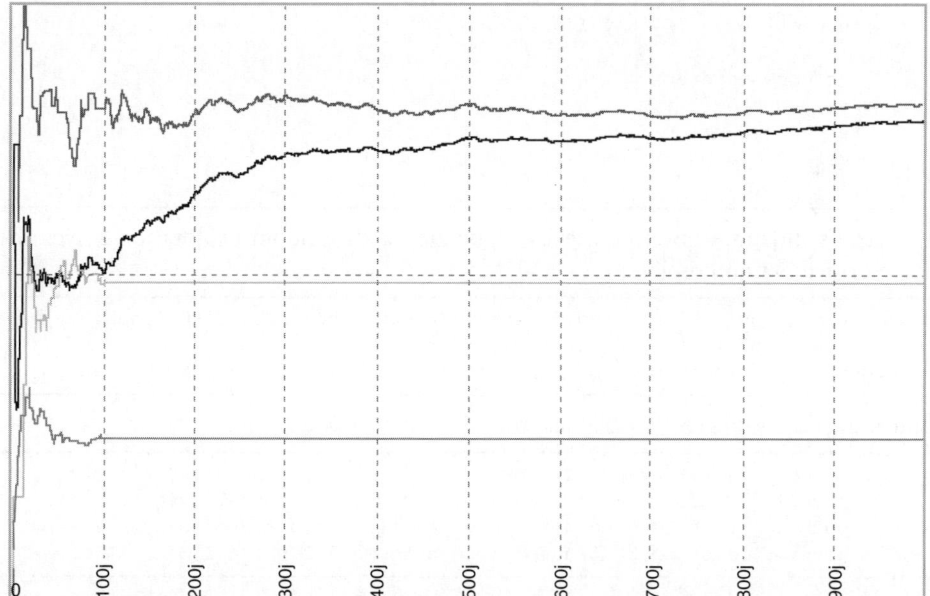

FIGURE 28.2 The sequence of average pay-offs for choices taken as perceived during the lifetime of the algorithm for the overall strategy (black), and for each arm separately – arm 1 (gray), arm 2 (light gray), arm 3 (dark gray) – using the exploration first greedy algorithm

Random exploration greedy algorithm

Let us focus now on the greedy algorithm, where the exploration and exploitation are proportionally mixed across the entire lifetime of the algorithm. We keep all the parameters as in the previous case. The function `mabExplorationRandomGA` implements the algorithm. The structure of the function is similar to the one from the previous paragraph:

```
.quantQ.mcts.mabExplorationRandomGA:{[bucket]
   // bucket -- the dictionary for algorithm
   $[bucket[`epsilon]>first 1?1.0;
   // exploration
   [
       // decision randomly
       choice:first 1?bucket[`K];
       bucket[`strategy],:choice;
       payoffs:bucket[`payoffs];
       payoffs[choice],:bucket[`mab] choice;
       bucket[`payoffs]:payoffs
   ];
   // exploitation
   [
       // decision based on the best outcome
       avgReward:bucket[`minBound]^avg each bucket[`payoffs];
       choice: first where avgReward=max avgReward;
       bucket[`strategy],:choice;
       payoffs:bucket[`payoffs];
       payoffs[choice],:bucket[`mab] choice;
       bucket[`payoffs]:payoffs
   ]];
   // increase counter
   bucket[`counter]+:1;
   // return bucket
   :bucket;
};
```

Let us illustrate how the greedy algorithm with random exploration solves the three-armed bandit problem:

```
bucket:(`N`K`epsilon`mab`payoffs`strategy`counter`minBound!(N;K;epsilon;mab
    ↪ ;payoffs;strategy;counter;minBound));
outcomeMAB2: (.quantQ.mcts.mabExplorationRandomGA\)[bucket[`N];bucket];
```

and extract the same set of variables from the `outcomeMAB2` table:

```
select counter, strategy,payoff, p0: payoffs[;0], p1: payoffs[;1], p2:
    ↪ payoffs[;2] from select counter, {[bucket;x] bucket[`minBound]^x}[
    ↪ bucket;] each {avg each x} each payoffs, payoff:avg each raze each
    ↪ payoffs, last each strategy from outcomeMAB2 where i>0
```

Figure 28.3 depicts a sequence of choices, `bucket[`strategy]`, as they have been chosen consecutively by the algorithm. Firstly, all the possible arms are chosen during the entire lifetime of the algorithm. Secondly, the algorithm starts using the optimal arm from the beginning. Further, Figure 28.4 depicts the sequence of average pay-offs

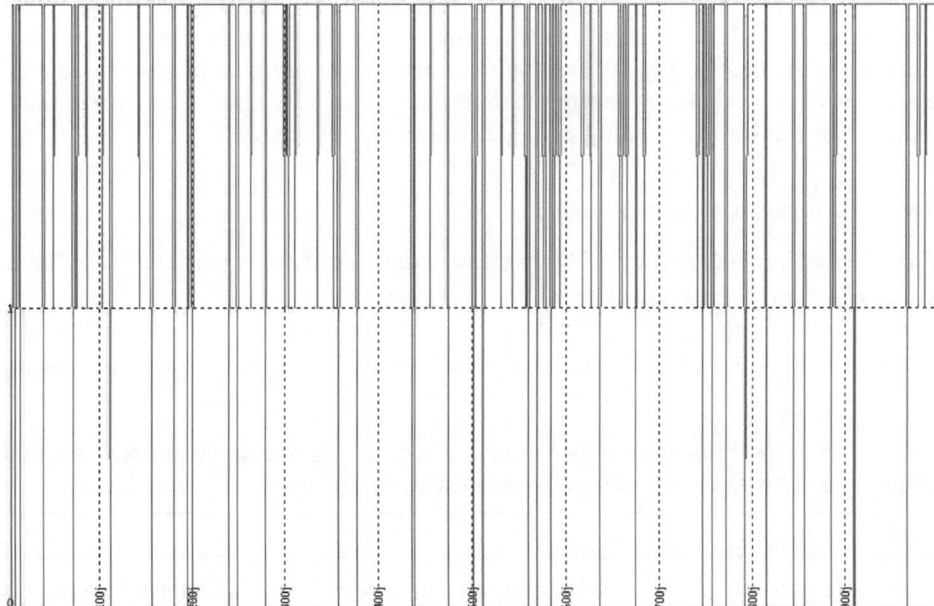

FIGURE 28.3 The sequence of choices done consecutively using the random exploration greedy algorithm

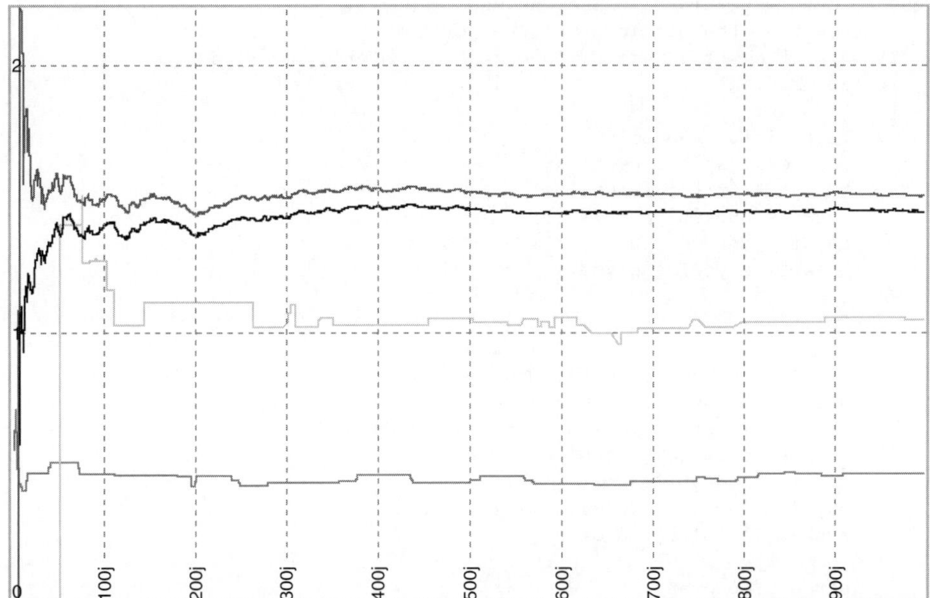

FIGURE 28.4 The sequence of average pay-offs for choices taken as perceived during the lifetime of the algorithm for the overall strategy (black), and for each arm separately – arm 1 (gray), arm 2 (light gray), arm 3 (dark gray) – using the random exploration greedy algorithm

for choices taken. The average pay-off of the overall strategy starts picking up towards the optimal choice much earlier relative to the exploration first algorithm with smaller volatility of the average pay-off. The figure shows the performance of the overall strategy – black line – and for each arm separately: arm number 1 (gray line), arm number 2 (light gray line), and arm number 3 (dark gray line), respectively.

Decreasing exploration greedy algorithm

Finally, let us implement the greedy algorithm where the learning rate decays over time. We consider the decay rate to follow the $\sqrt{n^{-1}}$ law:

$$\epsilon_n = \frac{\epsilon}{\sqrt{n}}, \tag{28.14}$$

where ϵ_n is the learning rate applied at n-th step of the algorithm. This choice is rather ad hoc and not meant to be optimal. Besides, we adjust the value of ϵ considered:

```
epsilon:1.0;
```

where a large value is chosen to amplify the learning process at the beginning while still keeping some learning process present towards the end. The other parameters are kept the same as in the previous cases. The function `mabExplorationDecreasingGA` captures the algorithm:

```
.quantQ.mcts.mabExplorationDecreasingGA:{[bucket]
   // bucket -- the dictionary for algorithm
   $[(bucket[`epsilon]%(sqrt 1.0+bucket[`counter]))>first 1?1.0;
   // exploration
   [
       // decision randomly
       choice:first 1?bucket[`K];
       bucket[`strategy],:choice;
       payoffs:bucket[`payoffs];
       payoffs[choice],:bucket[`mab] choice;
       bucket[`payoffs]:payoffs
   ];
   // exploitation
   [
       // decision based on the best outcome
       avgReward:bucket[`minBound]^avg each bucket[`payoffs];
       choice: first where avgReward=max avgReward;
       bucket[`strategy],:choice;
       payoffs:bucket[`payoffs];
       payoffs[choice],:bucket[`mab] choice;
       bucket[`payoffs]:payoffs
   ]];
   // increase counter
   bucket[`counter]+:1;
   // return bucket
   :bucket;
};
```

The algorithm can solve the three-armed bandit problem as follows:

```
bucket:(`N`K`epsilon`mab`payoffs`strategy`counter`minBound!(N;K;epsilon;mab
    ↪ ;payoffs;strategy;counter;minBound));
outcomeMAB3: (.quantQ.mcts.mabExplorationDecreasingGA\)[bucket[`N];bucket];
```

Let us continue in analysing the same set of variables:

```
select counter, strategy,payoff, p0: payoffs[;0], p1: payoffs[;1], p2:
    ↪ payoffs[;2] from select counter, {[bucket;x] bucket[`minBound]^x}[
    ↪ bucket;] each {avg each x} each payoffs, payoff:avg each raze each
    ↪ payoffs, last each strategy from outcomeMAB3 where i>0
```

Figure 28.5 depicts a sequence of choices, `bucket[`strategy]`, as they have been chosen consecutively by the algorithm. The algorithm frequently explores the options at the initial stage while it keeps using the optimal choice more frequently as the time progresses. The algorithm still shows a tendency to explore options throughout the running lifetime; however, spells with optimal choice are present longer. Figure 28.6 depicts a sequence of average pay-offs for choices taken. The average pay-off of the overall strategy picks up quickly towards the optimal one. The figure shows the performance of the overall strategy (black line) and for each arm separately: arm number 1 (gray line), arm number 2 (light gray line), and arm number 3 (dark gray line).

Finally, we compare the total outcomes across the three strategies. We capture the cumulative pay-off for the overall strategy in each of the three algorithms. We compare

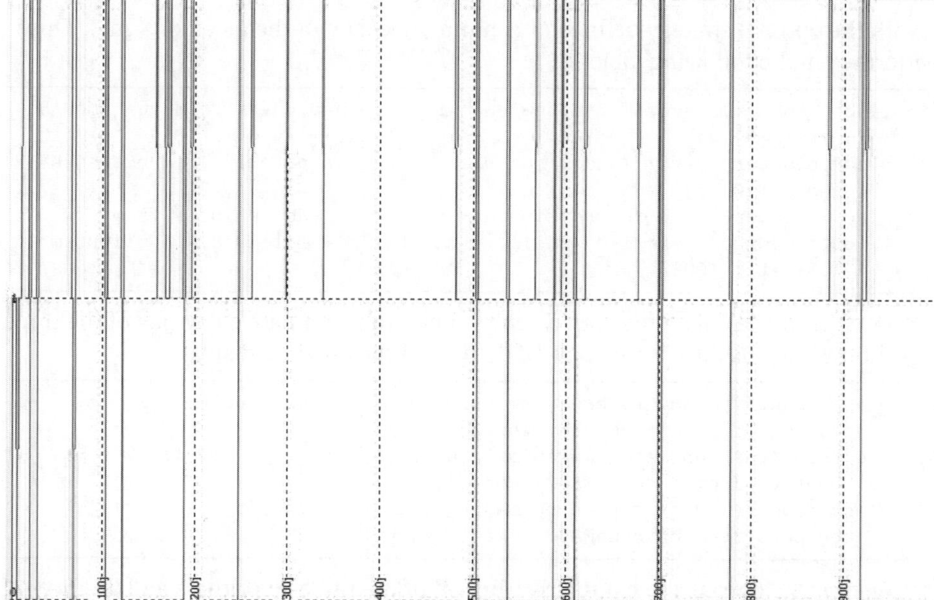

FIGURE 28.5 The sequence of choices done consecutively using the decreasing exploration greedy algorithm

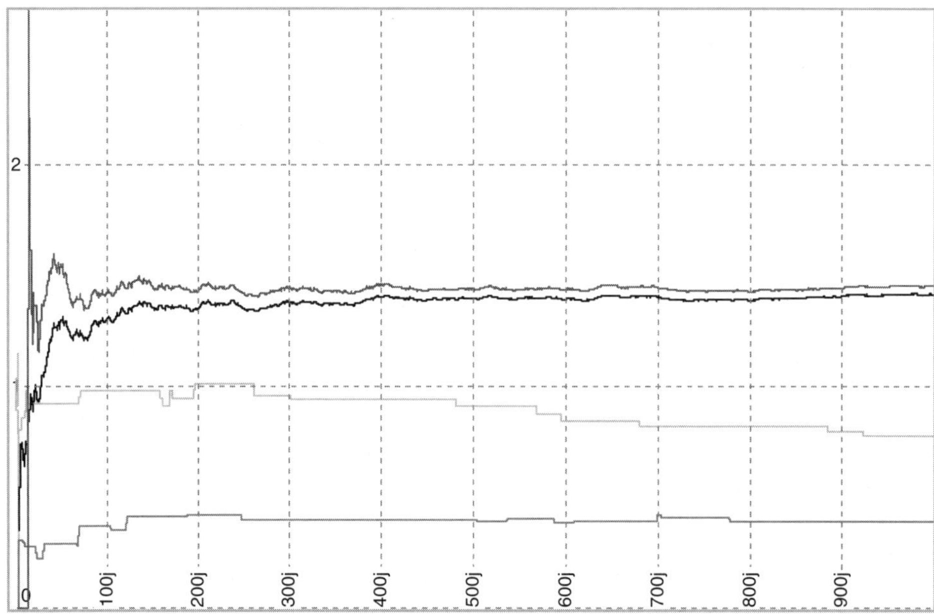

FIGURE 28.6 The sequence of average pay-offs for choices taken as perceived during the lifetime of the algorithm for the overall strategy (black), and for each arm separately – arm 1 (gray), arm 2 (light gray), arm 3 (dark gray) – using the decreasing exploration greedy algorithm

it with the optimal strategy defined as a cumulative sum of the mean of arm 3. This is performed in the following table:

```
(1!select counter, payoffFirst:sum each raze each payoffs from outcomeMAB1
    ↪ where i>0) uj
(1!select counter, payoffRandom:sum each raze each payoffs from outcomeMAB2
    ↪  where i>0) uj
(1!select counter, payoffDecreasing:sum each raze each payoffs from
    ↪ outcomeMAB3 where i>0) uj 1!([] counter: 1+ til 1000; payoffOptimal:
    ↪  1.5*1+til 1000)
```

Further, we calculate the convergence rate of the cumulative pay-offs of the three algorithms towards the optimal pay-off defined in the previous display:

```
(1!select counter, convergenceFirst:(sum each raze each payoffs)%(1.5*
    ↪ counter) from outcomeMAB1 where i>0) uj
(1!select counter, convergenceRandom:(sum each raze each payoffs)%(1.5*
    ↪ counter) from outcomeMAB2 where i>0) uj
(1!select counter, convergenceDecreasing:(sum each raze each payoffs)%(1.5*
    ↪ counter) from outcomeMAB3 where i>0)
```

Figure 28.7 depicts the cumulative pay-off of the three algorithms and the pay-off of the optimal strategy. The most optimal strategy seems to be the most straightforward

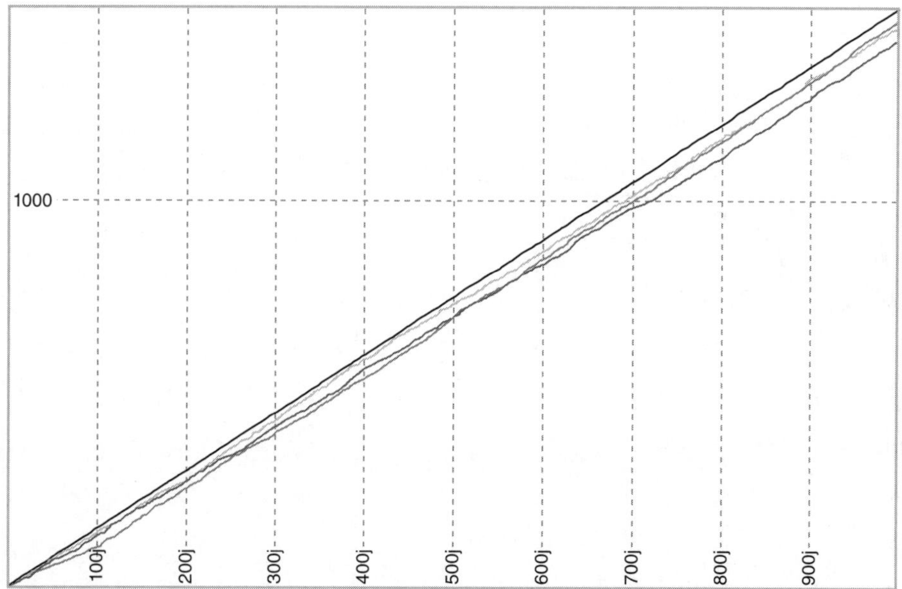

FIGURE 28.7 The cumulative pay-off of the three algorithms: the exploration first (gray line), the random exploration (light gray line), the decreasing exploration (dark gray line), and the optimal strategy (black line)

greedy algorithm with exploration first followed by pure exploitation. The figure presents the exploration first strategy (gray line), the random exploration strategy (light gray line), the decreasing exploration strategy (dark gray line), and the optimal strategy (black line).

Figure 28.8 depicts the convergence rate for the exploration first strategy (black line), the random exploration strategy (light gray line), and the decreasing exploration strategy (dark gray line), relative to the optimal strategy. Visually, the exploration first strategy shows the best convergence, where the line tends to be increasing towards one.

Let us finally remark on two points. First, the exploration first algorithm may perform the best as all the exploitation steps are taken on the best arm, which is fully revealed after the exploration. This is not true in the other two cases, where the algorithm may exploit even when not every option has been explored at least once. This can be mitigated by forcing the algorithm to explore each option at least once before engaging into further strategies. Second, the values of parameters, namely ϵ, are comparable for exploration first and random exploration algorithms, respectively, though the value for the decreasing exploration algorithm is not comparable, and thus the direct comparison is rather illustrative.

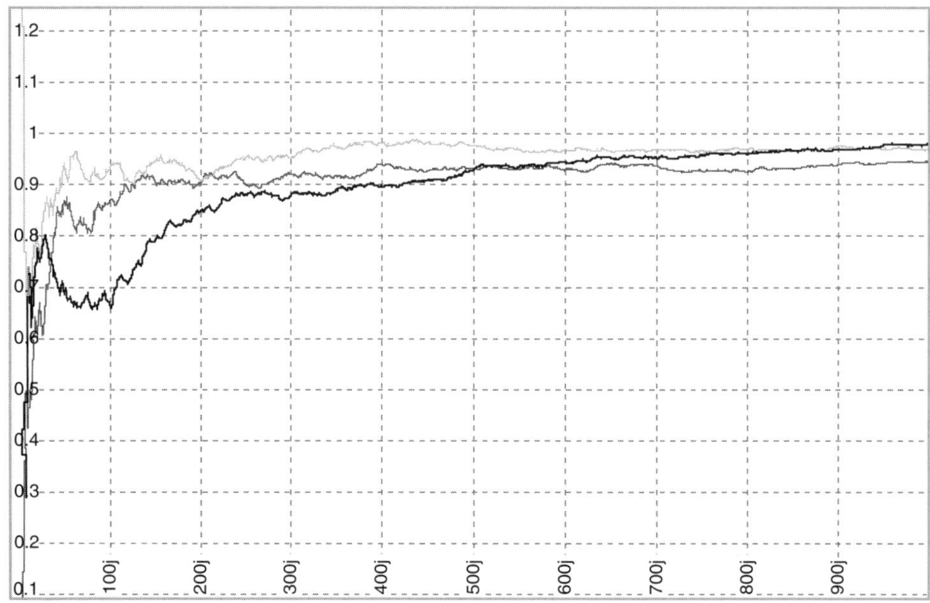

FIGURE 28.8 The convergence rate of the total pay-off of the three algorithms: the exploration first (black line), the random exploration (light gray line), and the decreasing exploration (dark gray line)

28.2 MONTE CARLO TREE SEARCH

We focus on the Monte Carlo Tree Search algorithm, which is a popular heuristic search algorithm for decision processes frequently used in AI engines. These engines are utilised in a variety of cases ranging from playing chess to driving cars to trading strategies. In a nutshell, the Monte Carlo Tree Search algorithm aims to find out at every point in time the most promising decision to be made by randomly expanding the tree of possible actions. In a game of chess, for example, this means that given the current state of the board the algorithm plays out various random continuations of the game and chooses the move which tends to result in a win with the highest likelihood. The first paper which proposed the *MCTS* as an engine for a game AI is Chaslot et al. (2008).

In this section, we explain the Monte Carlo Tree Search, or *MCTS*, algorithm using the examples from the gaming world. This is easy to understand and also easy to model on the desktop PC as opposed to testing the self-driving car or AI-driven execution algorithms. Ultimately, we implement the *MCTS* for the game of tic-tac-toe, which is interesting enough to specify it in a coherent code. Still, it is easy to extend towards the more complex games and situations.

Let us focus on perfect information games. These games are turn-based, and there is no hidden information among players. There is no random element in the game like drawing cards from the shuffled deck. Tic-tac-toe or chess are examples of such games.

The state of the game is determined by the position of stones on the board, which is visible to both players. We can, in theory, construct a game tree with all possible moves. Leaves of the tree are then the different ends of the game. Every node of the tree can be assigned a value which reflects the likelihood to end up in a winning leaf node. The straightforward strategy to solve such a game is the minimax algorithm.

The minimax algorithm is a strategy for decision-making which is based on selecting an option which minimises the possible loss in a maximum loss scenario. The maximin is an analogous formulation for gains. Since its development in the game theory for zero-sum games, it was extended to the situation with uncertainty and complex game rules. Mathematically, the minimax problem can be formulated as:

$$v_i^* = \min_{A_{-i}} \max_{A_i} v_i^*(A_i, A_{-i}), \tag{28.15}$$

where v_i is a value function for a player i, and A_i and A_{-i} denotes the action of the player i and the other player, respectively. In plain language, the player i wants to play the best action given the other player is doing the same. To be precise, the player $-i$, i.e. not i, wants to minimise the value of the game for player i.

The minimax algorithm is frequently used backwards from the end of the game. In each iterative step, player i wants to maximise the chance to win while player $-i$ is doing the opposite. The backward iteration can be, and thus it is frequently accompanied by some heuristic rules. The heuristic rules assign a value to every state of the game. The minimax algorithm thus does not have to run iteratively but rather serves as a decision on how to evolve from one state of the game to another.

The vanilla minimax algorithm as briefly outlined above fails when:

- The number of different states in the game is huge. In the case of go, it is $\sim 3^{19 \cdot 19}$.
- The game has high branching ratio, where at every given state of the game, there is a large number of possible actions.

The *MCTS* addresses the shortcomings of the minimax algorithm. Namely:

- *MCTS* does not need complex heuristics, i.e. to estimate the value of any given state of the game. This can be difficult to achieve in complex games like go.
- *MCTS* is very good for games with a large branching factor. The nature of the algorithm is such that it explores the more promising branches. The search mechanism is asymmetric; it does not need to devote time to branches which are likely to result in a loss.
- *MCTS* has a flexible running time. The heuristic-based algorithms need to go through the full tree with all the game options. This may take a large amount of time. On the other hand, *MCTS* can be run in a flexible way and stopped at any time. The bigger the time budget to run the more accurate the results of *MCTS*.

In order to introduce the *MCTS* algorithm, we need to elaborate more on the decision tree for a game. We consider a two-player game. The decision tree, or game tree, starts at the root node, which is a plain board. The next level of the tree is composed of child nodes of the root node, which contain all the possible moves by player 1. At the second level, the tree consists of all the moves of player 2 conditioned on the previous move of player 1. The third level, consecutively, captures the move of player 1 conditioned on the two previous moves. Switching the moves continues further down the tree by exploiting all the combinations. The leaf node of a game is such a game state where the game terminates and one of the players wins, or the game ends in a draw. In the game of go, the game ends when both players pass the move. Then, the player with the higher score wins, where the score is calculated based on the size of territory belonging to each player.

For a game of go, the root has $19 \cdot 19$ child nodes. At the second level, every node has $19 \cdot 19 - 1$ child nodes. This gives altogether at the second level $(19 \cdot 19) \cdot (19 \cdot 19 - 1)$ options. The branching ratio of the game is huge and suggests the infinite – in a numerical sense – dimension of all the possible states of the game. The tree is asymmetric as the difference in a number of moves between the longest and the shortest game can be huge.

When the game tree is not so huge, we can explore the full tree as we have explained in the minimax algorithm in the preceding paragraphs. Given the knowledge of the full tree, the move at every stage of the game can be optimised such that the chance to win is highest. This is not possible for complex games like go.

If we want to avoid the apparent curse of dimensionality, we have to abandon methods which rely on exploring the entire tree. The Monte Carlo comes at this point as an alternative method to full exploration. The basis for the *MCTS* method is to start at the current state of the game and play many games out of the current point. The idea is to build a game tree from the current state and explore many possible moves. Then, we can choose the best option from those explored. In order to build the tree, we face the problem which is in nature similar to the multi-armed bandit problem. The arms of the bandit are possible moves – stones to be played at a given state – and the pay-off is a likelihood to win when a given choice has been taken.

A naive approach would be to play a number of randomly simulated playouts. In every playout, the game would start at the current state. The progress of the game would be simulated by placing stones randomly player by player, starting with the player whose best turn we aim to find out. Among the set of allowed moves at a given turn, one move will be selected randomly. Every playout is then played until one of the players wins or there is a draw if allowed by rules. After the set of random playouts is finished, the next move is determined. The way to do it is to group the randomly simulated playouts by its first move. Then, for each group, the ratio of won games to all games played is calculated and the move with the highest ratio is chosen.

Playing random games is a highly inefficient approach as we have seen with the multi-armed bandit problem. Thus, the *MCTS* algorithm uses a more elaborate approach to find the optimal move. The *MCTS* is based on the iteration of the following four steps:

- Selection
- Expansion
- Simulation
- Back propagation

In the selection step, the existing tree is used to find the following child nodes down the leaf node. Then, in the expansion step, the existing tree is expanded by one child node. The tree is explicitly gaining a new node. In the simulation step, the game starts at the newly added node and is simulated until the end of the game, usually using random simulation. Finally, in the back propagation step, the information in the newly expanded tree is updated. The nodes which are on the selected path include the information of the outcome of the new game.

In the following section, we elaborate on all the steps in more detail. We assume that the game is at any state, i.e. it can be the empty board or the game can be close to the end. Without loss of generality, we assume that player 1 is to make a move. The four-step procedure already took place l-times, where l can also be 0.

Further, every node i of the tree is described by a pair of numbers (w_i, n_i) where:

- w_i – is the number of simulated games which contains the node i and resulted in a win of the player, who made a move.
- n_i – is the number of simulated games which contains the node i.

Every node is recorded from the perspective of the player who made a move. The nodes at the odd level of the tree correspond to the moves of player 1 while nodes at the even level of the tree correspond to the moves of player 2. The variable w_i is taken from such a perspective.

28.2.1 Selection Step

There is already a built-up tree. The selection process starts at the root of the tree, which is the current state of the game. Player 1 wants to find a suitable move to maximise her chances to win. Starting at the root node, the path through the tree is selected. The path ends at the node, where there is at least one move out of the possible moves which do not have an explored node. This corresponds to the case when some – or even all – of the possible options stemming from the node have not been explored yet.

What path to take? The objective is to combine exploration with exploitation. The mechanism to select the path should favour the promising nodes but still keep an option to exploit the paths which have been so far perceived as less favourable. The multi-armed bandit problem provides a way to resolve the dilemma. In particular, Kocsis and Szepesvári (2006) proposed the procedure to employ the Upper Confidence Bound algorithm frequently used to solve the multi-armed bandit problems to form the decision to select the path in the tree. When there is a decision to make, i.e. to choose among the child nodes which have been explored and thus each of them got assigned (w, n), the following quantity is calculated for every considered child node i:

$$UCT_i = \frac{w_i}{n_i} + C \cdot \sqrt{\frac{\log s_{parrent}}{s_i}}, \tag{28.16}$$

where $s_{parrent}$ is the number corresponding to the parent node at which the decision is being done, and constant C governs the balance between exploitation – the first term, and exploration – the second term. The value of C is a meta-parameter in the algorithm; the popular choice is $\sqrt{2}$.

The child node with the highest UCT_i is chosen in the selection step. If more than one node reaches the highest number, the node is chosen randomly with equal probability. The decision based on the formula in fact reflects the minimax algorithm. The meaning of w_i at a given point is recorded from the perspective of the player making a move. Thus, the formula makes the optimal decision for every player and thus player 1 is optimising her decision given player 2 is doing the same.

At the end of the selection step, the simulated game is at a node with at least one child node which has not been explored yet.

28.2.2 Expansion Step

The purpose of the expansion step is to extend the existing tree and include new nodes. The iteration process reaches at the end of the selection step a node which has at least one child which has not been selected before. Such a child node does not have an assigned pair (w_i, n_i). The iteration progresses from the node as follows:

- Among the child nodes which have not been visited yet, randomly choose one and extend the selection tree.

The new node is chosen uniformly as there is no preference among the unvisited nodes – or we assume a uniform prior. The new node is included in the selection tree. Using programming language, the (w_i, n_i) pair is initialised with 0s. This node will get assigned in last step its values (w_i, n_i).

The mechanism of the step is such that it explores new options and extends the knowledge structure – the decision tree – the algorithm is building up. Besides, the mechanism aims to expand every node fully. Namely, at a given node, there cannot be a situation where from any node there is a growing sub-tree and at the same time as there are unvisited nodes. If a specific node is promising – it is repeatedly chosen by the selection step – then all the options from the node are to be explored.

The full expansion of every node can have a disadvantage. In particular, if there is a large branching ratio, the tree will aim to progress too slowly. The selection tree being grown will be explored by moves which are deeply inferior and thus such a tree can be costly to grow. This is apparent for a game of go, for instance, where some moves are wasting of computational time. The reasonable component would be here some form of "value" function which would use heuristic rules and rule out some moves. Such an approach is taken in AlphaGo implementation of the *MCTS* using deep neural networks. Let us omit this at this stage and follow the expansion step as outlined.

We can expand by more than one node and provide faster building up of the game tree. Even though this is possible, we have to keep in mind that our objective is not to build the full/deep selection tree. The aim is to build a knowledge about the nearest neighbourhood of the game node we want to move from. The process of building a large tree would also carry a considerable storage cost; let us recall the dimensionality of the game tree for a go. It is thus feasible to stay at expansion by one node only.

Once the new node is added into the tree and the pair (w_i, n_i) is initialised, the game is played out.

28.2.3 Simulation Step

The purpose of the simulation step is to finish the game from the newly expanded node. The game is simulated randomly:

- Players are taking turns. In every turn, among all possible moves, one of the moves is chosen randomly with equal probability.

The simulation is played until the game ends. Let us assume that game is a zero-sum game, and one unit is awarded at the end:

$$\mathrm{Y}_1 + \mathrm{Y}_2 = 1, \tag{28.17}$$

where Y_i is the award assigned to player i. In the game with the binary end, the number can be 0 or 1. When there is a draw as an option at the end of the game, the value of 0.5 can be assigned to both players.

The critical feature of the simulation step is that the simulation itself is not stored. Once the simulation from the newly created node is finished, only Y_i are being remembered. This prevents the exhaustion of memory. During the simulation, we need to keep in memory the index of the player who makes a move and the state of the game, i.e. the arrangement of the board. As a result, the simulation step is memory efficient, and the simulation can be easily outsourced to some external resources without the need to transfer an additional amount of data. A possible option at this step is to simulate many independent games in parallel and then average Y_i's across simulations.

Once the simulation is finished, and the output of the simulated game is obtained, the iteration proceeds with the back propagation step.

28.2.4 Back Propagation Step

In the final step, the game tree is updated by the information obtained from the simulated playout. In particular, every node of the decision tree which has been chosen during the particular game is updated as follows:

$$n_i \rightarrow n_i + 1, \tag{28.18}$$

and w_i is updated based on which player was making a move:

$$w_i \rightarrow w_i + \mathrm{Y}_j, \tag{28.19}$$

where j corresponds to the index of the player who made a move. In particular, every odd-numbered level of the tree corresponds to $j = 1$, and every even-numbered level of the tree corresponds to $j = 2$, respectively.

This step concludes one iteration of the *MCTS*.

28.2.5 Finishing the Algorithm

The *MCTS* algorithm is composed of many iterations. Player 1 chooses such an action which corresponds to the node with highest w_i/n_i, where i corresponds to the index of nodes in the first level, i.e. child nodes of the root node. The decision rule at the end considers the best node as the one being chosen. The exploratory part is not employed when making a move; the move is pure exploitation.

The number of iterations is chosen based on available resources. The *MCTS* algorithm can be interrupted anytime, and the algorithm can have dynamically set the number of iterations. For instance, the game can contain a cap on the amount of time taken to decide the move. In such a case, the *MCTS* algorithm will try to run as many iterations as possible. Since simulated games can take a variable amount of time, such a numerical policy can be allocated resources efficiently as opposed to the fixed number of iterations. Similar policies can be adapted for variable numerical resources (CPUs or memory).

28.2.6 Remarks and Extensions

Let us make a couple of remarks about how to extend the *MCTS* presented above. First, for some games value of every move/stone can be independent of the stones already placed. In such a setup, we can cut the number of simulations needed tremendously. Gelly and Silver (2007) proposed an extension to the algorithm called Rapid Action Value Estimation, or RAVE. This assumes that the value of a stone is independent of the state of the game. Then, the backpropagation step is changed as follows. When we are supposed to update (w_i, n_i) for nodes contributing to the game, we update those moves across the entire game. Namely, if player 1 placed a stone at, say, a corner and the game where she did it resulted in a win, we identify all possible games in the game tree where player 1 places such a move and update the pair (w_i, n_i) in all of them. However, it is more convenient to keep updating in the same way as we have introduced above and preferably adjust the formula for *UCT* as we will see below.

This extension boosts the statistics gathered by the *MCTS*. The disadvantage of this approach is rather a strong assumption being made on the game. For the game of go, this assumption is highly unfeasible, given the game to be driven by various patterns. Further, players are introduced to the game through recognising patterns of varying complexity. The same holds for the game of chess. Since the usage of the *MCTS* goes well beyond the world of games, this is a possible extension. In order to mimic the absolute validity of the key assumption, the formula for *UCT* in the Selection step can be amended to provide some flexibility:

$$UCT_i = (1-\beta)\frac{w_i}{n_i} + \beta\frac{w_i'}{n_i'} + C \cdot \sqrt{\frac{\log s_{parent}}{s_i}}, \tag{28.20}$$

where w_i and n_i are defined and populated as in the original *MCTS* algorithm introduced above, w_i' and n_i' are the total numbers of wins and the total number of games containing the given move, i.e.

$$w_i' = \sum_{nodes} w_i \tag{28.21}$$

$$n_i' = \sum_{nodes} n_i, \tag{28.22}$$

with sum running over *nodes* of the tree which are the same.

Parameter β introduced above is meta-parameter of the method and has to be determined separately. The parameter is problem specific and can also be a function of n_i and n'_i, respectively. The reasonable logic to follow is to keep β large at the beginning of the simulation while slowly suppressing it towards zero as simulation progresses. This will allow us to improve statistical decisions in the initial stages of simulation while it will get marginal as more and more simulations have been run.

A further possible improvement to the *MCTS* algorithm relates to the use of heuristics, which affects the moves either in Selection or Expansion steps mentioned above. The motivation for such an improvement is to make the simulation more efficient and potentially to cut the simulation time. In Bayesian formulation, this means that some Bayesian priors can be introduced into the formula for *UCT*. Alternatively, we may modify the Expansion probability. It is essential to keep in mind that such an extension should be done in a way that still allows the *MCTS* algorithm as whole making moves, which are locally suboptimal. This is the way the algorithm can overcome the human player and find innovative game strategies.

We can roughly compare the *MCTS* to the way humans are thinking. The human player explores the viability of a move in the game similarly as the *MCTS*: playing forward several moves placing herself into a position of the other player and thus efficiently responding to her own moves. The best players can form strategies several stones ahead. The human brain, however, does not allow to keep in memory the full search tree and thus often only the best move in a given layer of the tree is kept in mind. The human thus builds a tree which is very narrow, not exploring all the options.

On the other hand, the human heavily relies on a heuristic. The ability of the *MCTS* to explore the suboptimal moves presents a significant improvement against human players. The heuristic is thus what stands between the human and the computer. Moreover, this is the element AlphaGo engine and its further extensions considered and closed the gap. The computer finally got better relative to human player – at least for the game of go.

28.3 MONTE CARLO TREE SEARCH IMPLEMENTATION – TIC-TAC-TOE

In this section, we illustrate the *MCTS* algorithm on the game tic-tac-toe. The game dates back to Roman Empire times. The rules of the tic-tac-toe are straightforward. The game is played by two players on the square board of 3×3. Players are taking turns, where each player places her stone on the board in every turn. We assume that Player 1 is placing `o` and Player 2 is placing `x`. The player who places three stones in a horizontal, vertical or diagonal row wins the game. The game allows for a draw, where none of the players achieves the criteria to win while all the places on the board are covered.

The game is rather trivial as the optimal strategy from both players results in a draw. The game is, however, suitable for explanation and is easy to programme. The detailed statistical account of the game as well various extensions can be found in Beck and Beck (2008). Let us review a few numbers characterising mathematical properties of the game. The game has 9! possible playouts, giving in total 362,880. This can be obtained because the first player has 9 possible places to place her stone, the second player only 8

TABLE 28.1 The number of possible games depending on their length

Win in	Number of games	Percentage
5 moves	1440	0.6%
6 moves	5328	2.1%
7 moves	47952	18.8%
8 moves	72576	28.4%
9 moves	81792	32.1%
Draws	46080	18.1%
Total	255168	100.0%

possible moves. Let us point out that we do not consider symmetries. If the symmetries would be considered, the number is much lower. Namely, when symmetries are taken into account for calculations, then there are three possible initial moves: the centre, the middle of a side and a corner.

In the 9! calculation, we assume that every game finishes when all 9 stones are placed. This is not true as the game may end earlier. The fastest game can end on the fifth move, assuming Player 2 is very weak. Table 28.1 captures the number of possible wins as a function of the total number of moves along with the number of draws. The table shows that there is altogether 255,168 number of moves.

Let us implement in the subsequent sections the *MCTS*. We first start with the game itself and random playouts. Then, we implement a version of the *MCTS*.

28.3.1 Random Games

Let us start with the implementation of random playouts of tic-tac-toe game. We define the tic-tac-toe game first. The definition is such that the game is inherently played on the 3×3 board. We encourage readers to change it into any dimension, but that would need the code change throughout the functions and definitions.

The game itself can be characterised as a sequence of available moves on the board, performed by two players making moves in turns. We do not need explicitly mark the players or make a dictionary between move and the type of the player. Instead, we assume that every odd move is made by Player 1 while every even move is made by Player 2. The game is thus a sequence of moves and the set of rules which determine the end of the game.

Let us start with the game itself and then add the stopping rule. We need to define a global variable `movesSpace` which captures all possible moves on the board. This is the set of elements from which the game tree will be built.

```
movesSpace:{x1:string first x;x2: string last x; `$x1,x2} each (`a`b`c)
    ↪ cross (`1`2`3);
```

Let us create a function, which will make the random move on the board. Namely, given the moves made and the moves available in `movesSpace`, the random move which has not been made yet is chosen and added into the game. To develop a game, we create a dictionary which will store the information about the game and update it during the game. The dictionary will contain two variables: `` `movesState``, which captures the sequence of moves made, and `` `isWinner``, which captures the status of the game. Such a dictionary looks like this:

```
bucket:(`movesState`isWinner)!(`a1`a2`b1;0j)
```

The `randomGameMove` function is then implemented as follows:

```
.quantQ.mcts.randomGameMove:{[bucket]
   // bucket -- information about the game
   // list of possible moves
   possibleMoves: movesSpace where not movesSpace in bucket[`movesState];
   // update movesState by a random move
   bucket[`movesState]: bucket[`movesState],1?possibleMoves;
   // return updated bucket
   :bucket;
};
```

The function finds available moves to make and appends one of them randomly chosen to the list of moves, i.e. it represents placing a stone on the board. Let us test the function:

```
.quantQ.mcts.randomGameMove[(`movesState`isWinner)!(`a1`a2`b1;0j)]
```

```
(`movesState`isWinner)!(`a1`a2`b1`b3;0j)
```

where the value under the index of `` `isWinner`` in the dictionary does not represent the truth as we have not checked whether the game ends or not.

The next element we have to implement is a check whether a given state of the game does not imply the end of the game. The check for the end is done after each turn and is implemented as a function which takes as an argument the dictionary with game content and returns the same dictionary, updated by check for the game:

```
.quantQ.mcts.checkGameWinner:{[bucket]
   // bucket -- information about the game
   // extract moves of two players
   player1: bucket[`movesState]{x where 0=mod[x;2]} til count bucket[`
       ↪ movesState];
   player2: bucket[`movesState]{x where 1=mod[x;2]} til count bucket[`
       ↪ movesState];
   // check the winners
   p1win:(sum[player1 in `a1`b2`c3]=3) or (sum[player1 in `a3`b2`c1]=3) or
       ↪ (0<sum 3=sum
       each player1 in/:{`$string[x] cross \:string[y]}[`a`b`c;`1`2`3]) or
           ↪ (0<sum 3=sum
       each player1 in/:{`${reverse each x} each string[y] cross \:string[x
           ↪ ]}[`a`b`c;`1`2`3]);
   p2win:(sum[player2 in `a1`b2`c3]=3) or (sum[player2 in `a3`b2`c1]=3) or
       ↪ (0<sum 3=sum
       each player2 in/:{`$string[x] cross \:string[y]}[`a`b`c;`1`2`3]) or
           ↪ (0<sum 3=sum
```

```
        each player2 in/:{`${reverse each x} each string[y] cross \:string[x
            ↪ ]}[`a`b`c;`1`2`3]);
    // update winner
    bucket[`isWinner]:$[0=count player1;0;p1win]+($[0=count player2;0;p2win
        ↪ ]*2)+$[((p1win=0)
        or (0=count player1)) and ($[0=count p2win;1;p2win=0] or (0=count
            ↪ player2)) and
        prd[bucket[`movesState][til 9] in movesSpace];1;0]*3;
    // output bucket
    :bucket;
};
```

The logic of the function is as follows. We extract the moves by each of the players. Then, we check if the stones belonging to each of the players do not form a winning strategy, i.e. three stones of the same type on a row/column, or lying on the diagonal. Further, the check for a draw takes place. The following logic for `` `isWinner `` applies:

- `0j` – the game continues,
- `1j` – the game is won by Player 1,
- `2j` – the game is won by Player 2,
- `3j` – the game ends as a draw.

The value `0j` is used for controlling the iteration of the game. The game terminates once `` `isWinner `` reaches value different from `0j`.

Further, the term `$[0=count p2win;1;p2win=0]` in the function protects the evaluation when we start with an empty board. If the board is empty, the first turn is a move by Player 1. Player 2's set of moves is empty and thus `p2win=0` is evaluated as `()=0`, which returns `()`.

Combining the two functions, we create a valid turn of the game. First, we place a new stone on the board, and then we check if the game ends. The two functions are inherently connected and we thus for convenience wrap them together into a function representing one turn of the game:

```
.quantQ.mcts.oneTurnRun:{[bucket]
    // bucket -- information about the game
    :.quantQ.mcts.checkGameWinner .quantQ.mcts.randomGameMove bucket;
};
```

It is playtime now! Let us run three instances of the random game. Each game starts with an empty board. To run such a game, we iterate the function `oneTurnRun` as long as the `` `isWinner `` control variable has zero value assigned. Every instance of a game is run with the same starting point: empty board:

```
(.quantQ.mcts.oneTurnRun/)[{0=x[`isWinner]};(`movesState`isWinner)!(`$();0)
    ↪ ]
```

The first run results in a draw:

```
(`movesState`isWinner)!(`b2`c3`a1`c1`a3`a2`c2`b1`b3;3j)
```

while the second run makes Player 2 to be a winner achieving the stones to be placed on diagonal:

```
(`movesState`isWinner)!(`a1`b2`a2`c1`b3`a3;2j)
```

and, finally, the last game ends up as follows:

```
(`movesState`isWinner)!(`a2`c2`b1`b3`c3`b2`c1`a3`a1;1j)
```

We leave it to the reader to interpret the result.

In addition, we can start the game with the board being pre-filled by stones. This is achieved by assigning some moves into `` `movesState`` variable. The game continues from the given starting point. Let us test it:

```
(.quantQ.mcts.oneTurnRun/)[{0=x[`isWinner]};(`movesState`isWinner)!(`a1`a2
    ↪ ;0)]
```

```
(`movesState`isWinner)!(`a1`a2`b2`c1`b3`c3`a3`c2;2j)
```

Let us use the provided functions to assess the probability of a win for two players. In particular, we run 100,000 random games, starting with an empty board. After each playout, we will record the `` `isWinner`` variable. In the end, we report the statistics.

Let us start with playouts:

```
isWinnerTS: {tmp: (.quantQ.mcts.oneTurnRun/)[{0=x[`isWinner]};(`movesState`
    ↪ isWinner)!(`$();0)]; tmp[`isWinner]} each til 100000;
```

and then count the cases by the type of the game end:

```
select count isWinnerTS by isWinnerTS from ( [] isWinnerTS)
```

```
isWinnerTS| isWinnerTS
----------| ----------
1         | 58605
2         | 28739
3         | 12656
```

In the random playouts, the probability to win for Player 1 is more than twice as much as for Player 2. Placing the first stone brings a considerable advantage in random games. The probability of a draw is approximately 13%, which underestimates the outcome of the statistical analysis.

Finally, it is convenient to provide some form of graphics interface to the game, at least to its output, and visualise the game as we are used to. The visualisation function aims to provide a convenient overview of the game from the console:

```
.quantQ.mcts.visualiseBoard:{[bucket]
   // bucket -- information about the game
   // player 1 moves
   player1: bucket[`movesState]{x where 0=mod[x;2]} til count bucket[`
       ↪ movesState];
```

```
    // player 2 moves
    player2: bucket[`movesState]{x where 1=mod[x;2]} til count bucket[`
        ↪ movesState];
    // visualise the board
    :3 3#{`$x} each ssr[;"0";"."] ssr[;"2";"x"] ssr[;"1";"o"] raze string (
        ↪ movesSpace in
        player1)+(2*movesSpace in player2);
};
```

First, let us play a random game and view the outcome:

```
bucket1:(.quantQ.mcts.oneTurnRun/)[{0=x[`isWinner]};(`movesState`isWinner)
    ↪ !(`$();0)]
bucket1
```

```
(`movesState`isWinner)!(`a3`a1`c2`c1`c3`a2`b3;1j)
```

The game was won by Player 1. The player won the game by placing the three stones in a vertical column. Let us view it:

```
.quantQ.mcts.visualiseBoard[bucket1]
```

In console, we obtain the following output:

```
x x o
. . o
x o o
```

This output nicely visualises the outcome. We may argue, though, that the game visualisation resembles the games from the early 1980s. That is partially true. The proper graphic interface is not the strength of `q` on its own. Let us instead return to the main topic of this chapter, which is the *MCTS* and implement it in the next section.

28.3.2 Towards the MCTS

In this section, we implement the *MCTS* algorithm. We will follow the steps outlined in the previous section and utilise the notion of `bucket`. We add more content into the dictionary when needed. The concept of the game as a sequence of moves or control variable for end games is preserved.

Let us start by defining the empty game tree, which we want to build during the *MCTS* iterations. The game tree is a table with three variables:

- `index` – variable indexing the iterations,
- `gameTree` – the list of nodes, which have been recorded for a given playout,
- `isWinner` – the status of the game at the end of the playout.

Let us further stress that `gameTree` is a list of nodes which are appended to the state of the board at which the game starts. Unless all the options have been played out, the last item of the list corresponds to the Expansion step. Such a node is newly explored. The information stored in the `gameTree` is used during every iteration of the *MCTS* algorithm when the Selection step takes place.

The empty game tree is thus defined as:

```
treeMCTS:([] index:"j"$();gameTree: `$(); isWinner:"j"$());
```

Further, we define the dictionary with all the variables needed to run the *MCTS*. The dictionary will be propagated through the *MCTS* algorithm and updated accordingly.

```
bucket:(`movesState`isWinner`numberOfRuns`treeMCTS`c)!(`$();0j;10j;treeMCTS
    ↪ ;sqrt 2);
```

where the dictionary corresponds to a game in the beginning when no stone has been placed yet and there is no information available how to proceed (no simulations done).

The meaning of the variables is as follows:

- movesState – starting position of the game, it can be empty,
- isWinner – control variable to run the MCTS,
- numberOfRuns – max number of trees to be run by the algorithm,
- treeMCTS – game tree built up so far,
- c – parameter of the *UCT* formula, chosen to be $\sqrt{2}$.

The key component of the *MCTS* algorithm is the formula for the Upper Confidence Bound, or *UCT*, defined in eq. (28.20). We implement it as a function `uct` with three input parameters. The first input parameter is a table with two columns: `gameTree` corresponding to the child nodes, and `isWinner` with the corresponding status of the game which contains a given node. The second input is a perspective, i.e. the player who makes a move, and, finally, the third input is the parameter *c* of the *UCT* formula. The function reads:

```
.quantQ.mcts.uct:{[tab;perspective;c]
   // tab -- table with history of data (gameTree and isWinner columns)
   // perspective -- player making move
   // c -- parameter of the UCT
   // adjust table by perspective -- isWinner
   tab: update w: ?[(isWinner=perspective) and isWinner<3;1;?[(not isWinner
       ↪ =perspective)
       and isWinner<3;0;0.5] ] from tab;
   // return choice based on UCT
   :first exec gameTree from `uct xdesc select gameTree, uct: (wSum%"f"
       ↪ $nSum)+c*sqrt
       log["f"$count[tab]]%nSum from select nSum: count w, wSum: sum w by
           ↪ gameTree from tab;
};
```

Let us create a provisional input for the `uct` function:

```
tab:([] gameTree:`a1`a2`a3`b1`b2`b3`c1`c2`c3`c3`c3`c3;isWinner:(1 2 3 2 2 3
    ↪ 1 2 1 1 1 1));
tab
```

```
gameTree isWinner
-----------------
a1       1
a2       2
a3       3
b1       2
b2       2
b3       3
c1       1
c2       2
c3       1
c3       1
c3       1
c3       1
```

Let us determine the best node based on *UCT*. First, from Player 1 perspective:

```
.quantQ.mcts.uct[tab;1;sqrt 2]
```

```
`a1
```

and, secondly, from Player 2 perspective:

```
.quantQ.mcts.uct[tab;2;sqrt 2]
```

```
`a2
```

The example illustrates well the trade-off made between exploration and exploitation. This is apparent as the node `c3 is winning node in four instances and still the *UCT* formula chooses `a2 instead. The pure exploitation algorithm would stick to `c3.

Let us implement a function which forms the *MCTS* algorithm. The function itself places a stone on the board, i.e. appends the move to the sequence of existing moves. The move is chosen according to the current state of the algorithm evolution, i.e. it can be the Expansion move driven by the *UCT* formula if there exists a populated game tree for all relevant nodes, or the Expansion step if a new node is explored, or even the Simulation step, when nodes are added randomly. The Backpropagation step is executed separately outside of this function. Function `oneMCTSTurnRun` takes as an input the dictionary with variables introduced previously, expanded for local variables :

- `indexInTree` – this variable defines what part of the game is stored into the persisting *MCTS* table (aka building the game tree).
- `treeDepthCounter` – counter of local iterations, to keep track when going through the existing game tree.
- `isWinner` – local meaning of `isWinner` controls the iteration of the *MCTS* algorithm, i.e., performing four steps.

The implementation reads:

```
.quantQ.mcts.oneMCTSTurnRun:{[bucket]
   // bucket -- information about the game
   availableMoves: asc movesSpace where not movesSpace in bucket[`
       ↪ movesState];
   // relevant trees, exception for first iteration
     relevantTrees: $[0=count bucket[`treeMCTS];bucket[`treeMCTS] ;select
         ↪ index, gameTree, isWinner from (update {[x;y] x~y}[bucket[`
         ↪ movesState]; ] each subTree from update subTree: gameTree[;til
         ↪ count bucket[`movesState]] from bucket[`treeMCTS]) where
         ↪ subTree=1];
   // all moves used in given level of tree, distinct and non-empty
   allExploredMoves:asc t where not null t:distinct {(x,())[y]}[;bucket[`
       ↪ treeDepthCounter]] each exec gameTree from relevantTrees;
   // decide what to do:
   $[(availableMoves~allExploredMoves);
       // use UCT rule, when we have explored all moves we can do
       [
           // decide who is on move -- affects the UCT rule below
           isOnMove:1+mod[count bucket[`movesState];2];
           // use UCT rule to find the best move
           bestMove: .quantQ.mcts.uct[select {(x,())[y]}[;bucket[`
               ↪ treeDepthCounter]] each gameTree,
               isWinner from bucket[`treeMCTS];isOnMove;bucket[`c]];
           movesStateTMP:bucket[`movesState];
           bucket[`movesState]:movesStateTMP,bestMove;
           // increase indexInTree when availableMoves>1
           indexTMP:bucket[`indexInTree];
           bucket[`indexInTree]:indexTMP+"j"$(1<count availableMoves);
       ];
       // use random non-explored node
       [
           movesStateTMP:bucket[`movesState];
           bucket[`movesState]:movesStateTMP,1?availableMoves where not
               ↪ availableMoves in
               allExploredMoves;
       ]
   ];
   // increase the treeDepthCounter by 1
   tmp: bucket[`treeDepthCounter];
   bucket[`treeDepthCounter]:tmp+1;
   // return the bucket with one turn and with updated game check
   :.quantQ.mcts.checkGameWinner bucket;
};
```

The table `bucket[`treeMCTS]` with the game tree built so far is in a format which needs some manipulation in order to be able to go through the game tree during the Selection and Expansion steps. For that purpose, we define a local subset of the table, called `relevantTrees`, which contains entries from `bucket[`treeMCTS]` relevant for a given iteration of the *MCTS* algorithm. The `relevantTrees` table is then used to extract allExploredMoves, a subset of moves which have been explored in the previous playouts.

This is then used in the body of the function, where the possible evaluations can take place based on the validity of the following condition: (availableMoves~allExploredMoves). If the condition is true, then all possible moves have been already tried. This means that we have a game tree which already explored every node of the tree spanning from the given node and we can thus use the *UCT* formula to select which child node to follow. On the other hand, if the condition is not satisfied, there exists at least one child node which has not been explored by the existing game tree. In such a case, the node is chosen randomly out of the set of all nodes which has not been explored yet.

Let us see how the function works. First, we reinitiate the bucket:

```
bucket:(`movesState`isWinner`numberOfRuns`treeMCTS`c)!(`symbol$();0j;10j;
    ↪ flip (`index`gameTree`isWinner)!(`long$();`symbol$();`long$())
    ↪ ;1.414214);
```

and update the bucket by adding three more variables into the dictionary:

```
bucket[`indexInTree]:0j;
bucket[`treeDepthCounter]:0j;
bucket[`isWinner]:0j;
```

We run the following code repeatedly until we reach the situation with `isWinner being different from 0:

```
bucket:.quantQ.mcts.oneMCTSTurnRun[bucket];
bucket
```

The first two runs give:

```
(`movesState`isWinner`numberOfRuns`treeMCTS`c`indexInTree`treeDepthCounter)
    ↪ !(enlist `a3;0j;10j;flip (`index`gameTree`isWinner)!(`long$();`
    ↪ symbol$();`long$());1.414214;0j;1j)
(`movesState`isWinner`numberOfRuns`treeMCTS`c`indexInTree`treeDepthCounter)
    ↪ !(`a3`b1;0j;10j;flip (`index`gameTree`isWinner)!(`long$();`symbol$()
    ↪ ;`long$());1.414214;0j;2j)
```

where we see that `movesState is being populated and `treeDepthCounter is increasing. After several repetitions of the code, we finally get:

```
(`movesState`isWinner`numberOfRuns`treeMCTS`c`indexInTree`treeDepthCounter)
    ↪ !(`a3`b1`c2`a2`c3`b3`a1`c1`b2;1j;10j;flip (`index`gameTree`isWinner)
    ↪ !(`long$();`symbol$();`long$());1.414214;0j;9j)
```

The game ends in the 9th move with Player 1 winning. This concludes one playout of the *MCTS* algorithm. Since there is no game tree available during the game, the playout is merely a random game.

The backpropagation step of the playout can be done at this step. This is done as a part of the runMCTS function, which wraps the oneMCTSTurnRun function and is responsible for building the game tree across iterations. The input of the function is the dictionary with variables. The three variables needed for oneMCTSTurnRun are added locally within a function:

```
.quantQ.mcts.runMCTS:{[bucket]
   // decide move first vs further
   $[0=count bucket[`treeMCTS];
       // randomly finish game
       [
       bucketTMP:(.quantQ.mcts.oneTurnRun/)[{0=x[`isWinner]};(`movesState`
           ↪ isWinner)!
           (bucket[`movesState];0)];
       tabTMP: bucket[`treeMCTS];
       bucket[`treeMCTS]:tabTMP,([] index:1; gameTree:enlist enlist
           ↪ bucketTMP[`movesState]
           [count bucket[`movesState]]; isWinner:bucketTMP[`isWinner])
       ];
       // continue building tree
       [
       // create local bucket and add features
       bucketTMP:bucket;
       // indexInTree defines what part of the game is stored into the
           ↪ persisitng MCTS table
       bucketTMP[`indexInTree]:0j;
       // treeDepthCounter counts local iterations, to keep track when
           ↪ going through the existing tree
       bucketTMP[`treeDepthCounter]:0j;
       // isWinner determines local winner
       bucketTMP[`isWinner]:0j;
       // run the MCTS game
       bucketTMP:(.quantQ.mcts.oneMCTSTurnRun/)[{0=x[`isWinner]};bucketTMP
           ↪ ];
       // extract variables for updated gameTree
       newGameTree:((count bucket[`movesState])_bucketTMP[`movesState])[til
           ↪  1+bucketTMP[`indexInTree]];
       newIsWinner:bucketTMP[`isWinner];
       newIndex: count[bucket[`treeMCTS]]+1;
       // update the existing game tree
       bucketTreeTMP: bucket[`treeMCTS];
       bucket[`treeMCTS]:bucketTreeTMP, ([] index: newIndex; gameTree:
           ↪ enlist
           newGameTree;isWinner:newIsWinner)
       ]
   ];
   // stop if the maximum number of trees have been reached
   if[(bucket[`numberOfRuns])<=count bucket[`treeMCTS];bucket[`isWinner]:1j
       ↪ ];
   // return bucket
   :bucket;
};
```

Let us stress several elements in the function. The first run of the *MCTS* algorithm is run explicitly as a random playout. Given there is no prior information available, the oneTurnRun is iterated until the end. Then, the `` `treeMCTS `` table is updated accordingly by appending the first row into the empty table. This approach allows us to start with a pre-trained table where this step would be omitted. For iterations beyond the first one, the oneMCTSTurnRun function is used. After the iteration of this function ends, the `treeMCTS table is updated by extracting newGameTree, newIsWinner, and newIndex variables, respectively. In order to append the values into the existing dictionary, we do that through the local temporary variables. Finally, the number of *MCTS* iterations is being checked against `numberOfRuns.

Let us run the runMCTS function. First, we reset the bucket:

```
bucket:(`movesState`isWinner`numberOfRuns`treeMCTS`c)!(`$();0j;10j;treeMCTS
    ↪ ;sqrt 2);
```

and run one *MCTS* iteration:

```
bucket:.quantQ.mcts.runMCTS[bucket];
bucket
```

```
(`movesState`isWinner`numberOfRuns`treeMCTS`c)!(`symbol$();0j;10j;flip (`
    ↪ index`gameTree`isWinner)!(enlist 1j;enlist enlist `b1;enlist 1j)
    ↪ ;1.414214)
```

where the `treeMCTS table is being populated. Let us see the output of three more *MCTS* iterations:

```
(`movesState`isWinner`numberOfRuns`treeMCTS`c)!(`symbol$();0j;10j;flip (`
    ↪ index`gameTree`isWinner)!(1j, 2j;(enlist `b1;enlist `a2);1j, 1j)
    ↪ ;1.414214)
(`movesState`isWinner`numberOfRuns`treeMCTS`c)!(`symbol$();0j;10j;flip (`
    ↪ index`gameTree`isWinner)!(1j, 2j, 3j;(enlist `b1;enlist `a2;enlist `
    ↪ b2);1j, 1j, 1j);1.414214)
(`movesState`isWinner`numberOfRuns`treeMCTS`c)!(`symbol$();0j;10j;flip (`
    ↪ index`gameTree`isWinner)!(1j, 2j, 3j, 4j;(enlist `b1;enlist `a2;
    ↪ enlist `b2;enlist `c2);1j, 1j, 1j, 2j);1.414214)
```

The game tree is being slowly built up. Let us skip output for further iterations and present the updated dictionary which will be achieved after 19 iterations:

```
(`movesState`isWinner`numberOfRuns`treeMCTS`c)!(`symbol$();1j;10j;flip (`
    ↪ index`gameTree`isWinner)!(1j, 2j, 3j, 4j, 5j, 6j, 7j, 8j, 9j, 10j,
    ↪ 11j, 12j, 13j, 14j, 15j, 16j, 17j, 18j, 19j;(enlist `b1;enlist `a2;
    ↪ enlist `b2;enlist `c2;enlist `b3;enlist `c3;enlist `c1;enlist `a1;
    ↪ enlist `a3;`a1`b1;`a2`a3;`a3`a2;`b1`a2;`b2`c3;`b3`a2;`c1`b3;`c3`b2;`
    ↪ a2`b2;`a3`b3);1j, 1j, 1j, 2j, 1j, 1j, 1j, 1j, 1j, 2j, 3j, 3j, 2j, 2j
    ↪ , 2j, 3j, 2j, 2j, 1j);1.414214)
```

Let us focus on the game tree:

```
bucket[`treeMCTS]
```

```
index gameTree isWinner
-----------------------
1     ,`b1     1
2     ,`a2     1
3     ,`b2     1
4     ,`c2     2
5     ,`b3     1
```

```
6       ,`c3      1
7       ,`c1      1
8       ,`a1      1
9       ,`a3      1
10      `a1`b1    2
11      `a2`a3    3
12      `a3`a2    3
13      `b1`a2    2
14      `b2`c3    2
15      `b3`a2    2
16      `c1`b3    3
17      `c3`b2    2
18      `a2`b2    2
19      `a3`b3    1
```

The first nine entries in the game tree correspond to games when child nodes have been expanded into a tree. From tenth entry onwards, the expansion is occurring on the second level of the tree. The column `gameTree` contains the history of each play-out, where stored are only the nodes already explored and the one newly expanded node. The values stored are sorted as the nodes have been reached. This allows us to collect all games which went through a certain sub-path starting at the root node. Until we explore the entire state space of all games, every row in this column will be unique.

We can run the *MCTS* simulation using the iterate function as the dictionary contains `isWinner` control variable to stop the run. Let us reset the dictionary again:

```
bucket:(`movesState`isWinner`numberOfRuns`treeMCTS`c)!(`$();0j;20j;treeMCTS
    ;sqrt 2);
```

where we have set 20 iterations to be run, then we run the iterations as:

```
bucket:(.quantQ.mcts.runMCTS/)[{0=x[`isWinner]};bucket];
bucket
```

```
(`movesState`isWinner`numberOfRuns`treeMCTS`c)!(`symbol$();1j;20j;flip (`
    index`gameTree`isWinner)!(1j, 2j, 3j, 4j, 5j, 6j, 7j, 8j, 9j, 10j,
    11j, 12j, 13j, 14j, 15j, 16j, 17j, 18j, 19j, 20j;(enlist `a3;enlist
    `b1;enlist `c2;enlist `b2;enlist `c3;enlist `a1;enlist `a2;enlist `
    b3;enlist `c1;`a1`a2;`a2`c2;`a3`b2;`b1`b2;`c1`a1;`c2`a2;`c3`a3;`a1`
    c3;`c1`c3;`a2`c3;`c3`a1);1j, 1j, 3j, 2j, 3j, 1j, 1j, 2j, 1j, 1j, 3j,
     2j, 2j, 1j, 3j, 1j, 3j, 2j, 2j, 1j);1.414214)
```

The variable of interest is the game tree, which we can again recover as:

```
bucket[`treeMCTS]
```

```
index gameTree isWinner
-----------------------
1       ,`a3      1
2       ,`b1      1
3       ,`c2      3
4       ,`b2      2
```

```
5       ,`c3     3
6       ,`a1     1
7       ,`a2     1
8       ,`b3     2
9       ,`c1     1
10      `a1`a2   1
11      `a2`c2   3
12      `a3`b2   2
13      `b1`b2   2
14      `c1`a1   1
15      `c2`a2   3
16      `c3`a3   1
17      `a1`c3   3
18      `c1`c3   2
19      `a2`c3   2
20      `c3`a1   1
```

At the end of the *MCTS* run, we have to decide which move is to be made. The move to be chosen is the child node of the root of the game tree built up. In order to choose the child node, we evaluate the average outcome for subtrees split by the child nodes. We choose the node which has the highest average outcome for the player who makes the turn. If there is more than one node with the highest score, we choose one randomly.

We implement the outcome of the game from Player 1's perspective. Thus, when we are going to decide which node to choose, we take the maximum average value if Player 1 is making the move, or the minimum average value when Player 2 is on the move: `$[isOnMove=1;...max[tab `w];...min[tab `w]]`. This ensures consistency for both players and utilises the game tree developed so far.

The function `evaluateMCTS` takes as input game tree and returns the node chosen for a player to make:

```
.quantQ.mcts.evaluateMCTS:{[tab]
    // tab -- table with `treeMCTS
    // decide who is on move -- it affects perspective
    isOnMove:1+mod[count bucket[`movesState];2];
    // convert isWinner to numerical value
    tab: update w: ?[(isWinner=1) and isWinner<3;1;?[(not isWinner=1) and
        ↪ isWinner<3;0;0.5] ] from tab;
    // evaluate each possible first move -- take the one with best average
        ↪ value
    tab: 0!select avg w by gameTree from select first each gameTree, w from
        ↪ tab;
    // return one of the best moves
    :first $[isOnMove=1;1?exec gameTree from (0!tab) where w=max[tab `w];1?
        ↪ exec gameTree
        from (0!tab) where w=min[tab `w]];
};
```

As an exercise, we encourage the reader to leave the Player 1 perspective and rather use `isWinner=isOnMove` comparison. This will need amendment of the rest of the function, though.

Let us evaluate outcome of the simulation we have just run and take the `` `treeMCTS `` feature from the `bucket`:

```
.quantQ.mcts.evaluateMCTS bucket[`treeMCTS]
```

```
`a1
```

The *MCTS* run recommends for Player 1 to start with move `` `a1 ``.

28.3.3 Case Study

We encourage the reader to utilise the provided functions and wrap them into a playing engine, where two algorithmic players will be playing with each other. It will be particularly appealing to let play the random player and the one using the *MCTS*. The statistical evaluation will be skewed towards the *MCTS*. This will also represent a step towards reinforcement learning and more practical applications.

28.4 MONTE CARLO TREE SEARCH – ADDITIONAL COMMENTS

Let us finally comment on the most famous extension of the *MCTS* in the context of games: AlphaGo. AlphaGo is a computer program developed by Alphabet's Google DeepMind team in London to play the game of go. AlphaGo achieved in October 2015 recognition by beating a human professional player on 19×19 board without any handicap. More importantly, in March 2016, it beat the 9-dan master Lee Sedol in a 5 game match. Honorary 9-dan was awarded to the program.

For our purpose, the most important is to review the architecture of AlphaGo, Silver et al. (2016). The foundation of AlphaGo is the *MCTS* algorithm we have explored above. However, it contains several important extensions which make it more powerful and suitable for the game of go. The three main components of AlphaGo are:

- Policy network,
- Value network,
- Reinforcement learning.

To be precise, the version AphaGo Zero was extended for the Reinforcement Learning; it was not part of AlphaGo itself.

Let us discuss in detail all three elements and how they extend the *MCTS* algorithm we have discussed so far.

28.4.1 Policy and Value Networks

The game of go has a large branching ratio and building the tree by using the four steps as outlined above is itself very costly. The game tree is built too wide and irrelevant nodes are emphasised. It also ignores the centuries of plays. The game when it is being taught heavily explores patterns and combinations. Notions like *fuseki* (opening), *tesuji* (tactics), life-and-death, or *ko* (repeated situations on the board), among others, are being well-documented and studied. Those concepts have been discovered through histories of games and are stemming from game principles, even though not always defined from first principles. The successful algorithm cannot ignore this knowledge, even if it should be used just for modelling the opponent's moves.

AlphaGo utilises this through a neural network, in particular, deep convolutional network with many layers. The network takes as an input the state s of the game and the history leading to the current board and provides two variables: probability distribution for the possible moves reachable from the current state, denoted as P, and the value of the current state v. The value is a scalar and reflects the probability for a current player to win given the state s. We can formally write the network as:

$$(P, v) = f_\theta(s), \tag{28.23}$$

where θ is a parameter set, and the probability of a given move a to be done can be extracted as:

$$P_a = P(s, a). \tag{28.24}$$

The model f_θ was estimated from the record of games played by professional players. AlphaGo combines the two networks in the following manner:

- The algorithm starts at a root node equipped with f_θ.
- The node has assigned prior probabilities for possible moves using $P(s_{root}, a)$, for all moves a, and every possible move gets assigned a counter of visits $N(s_{root}, a)$, initialised at 0.
- Each simulation starts at the root node and chooses a node a which maximises the analogue to the *UCT* formula:

$$a = \arg\max_{a'} Q(s_{root}, a') + U(s_{root}, a'), \tag{28.25}$$

where Q is an action-value and U corresponds to the exploration function. It is further utilised that:

$$U(s_{root}, a') \propto \frac{P(s_{root}, a')}{1 + N(s_{root}, a')}. \tag{28.26}$$

Since the value v is noisy, the action-value variable is defined for any state s as:

$$Q(s, a') = \frac{1}{N(s, a)} \sum_{s'} v(s'), \tag{28.27}$$

where sum runs over all end nodes s' reached in simulations running through s. This variable averages out the values achieved by all the games which have included move s.

- The eq. (28.55) is applied to traverse through the game tree until the leaf node is reached.
- The Expansion step takes place. The expansion is done by assigning (P, v) values, and initialising N for a given node. This makes the expansion *de facto* across all possible child nodes.
- The *MCTS* is played iteratively according to the available resources.

When enough simulations have been played, AlphaGo chooses the move to make. By its nature, the more valuable moves are explored more frequently by the algorithm and thus assessing the final value for deciding which move to make is done as:

$$\pi_a \propto N(s,a)^{1/\tau}. \tag{28.28}$$

The nodes with higher Q are visited more frequently. The probability for a node a to be chosen is proportional to the exponential of the number visits of the node during simulations, raised to the inverse power of temperature τ. With $\tau \to 1$, there is possible exploration when making a decision while for $\tau \to 0$ only the node with the highest count of visits is chosen. This concludes AlphaGo.

The role of the *MCTS* algorithm is the policy improvement operator. The initial values of P are prior probabilities in the Bayesian sense, and the *MCTS* algorithm is the posterior distribution, which is usually better than prior values themselves.

28.4.2 Reinforcement Learning

AlphaGo Zero goes one step beyond AlphaGo; see Silver et al. (2017). It uses Reinforcement Learning technique, which allows the algorithm to learn the policy and value networks f_θ without a need for any human input. The algorithm starts with the randomly initiated parameter set θ_0.

The neural network plays games with itself, in particular, with previous versions of itself. During the game, the neural network is re-trained based on the evolution of a game. The game thus starts as a random game where only the first principles, i.e. the rules of the game, are used. From the random moves, the neural network learns moves and values various board setups. The algorithm learns to use patterns on the fly. As the patterns are learnt, they are used, and thus the algorithm learns to explore the ways to beat the patterns learnt. This expresses the evolution learning cycle of the algorithm.

The algorithm does not need any human input. The role of the *MCTS* is exploring how to improve itself given the current knowledge. The reinforcement learning then assures that the algorithm learns from all past playouts. If by chance a good pattern is found out, the algorithm remembers it and learns to use it further. At the same time, it tries to find out how not to be beaten by the player using the very same pattern.

It is striking that starting with first principles, AlphaGo Zero has been able to learn all the patterns, tactics, and starting positions taught by the go masters. These patterns have been found out by the algorithm itself. Besides, new patterns have been explored and thus the AlphaGo Zero playouts have entered the go textbooks. It is not without surprise that it is time for human players to make their move and reinforce their understanding of the game and learn from AlphaGo Zero.

CHAPTER 29

Econophysics: The Agent-Based Computational Models

In this chapter, we step outside the main scope of this book and illustrate the usage of q for the analysis of models in the econophysics domain. This field is a fusion between theories developed in physics on the problems in social sciences and in particular in economics and financial economics. The emergence of econophysics dates back to the 1990s when some models from statistical physics were used to analyse data from stock markets. A very nice introduction of the methods from this period can be found in a seminal review by Mantegna and Stanley (1999). The main reason why the field itself appeared is likely due to the emergence of a large amount of financial data which required statistical methods to analyse them.

It is worth stressing that the influence of physics on finance appears before the 1990s. Among many achievements, we may recall the utility-based theory developed by Bernoulli (2011), the theory of gravity of international trade developed by a trained physicist and a first laureate in Nobel Prize in Economics Jan Tinbergen, Tinbergen and Hekscher (1962), or the apparent resemblance of the famous Black–Scholes equation and the heat equation used for a long time in physics to describe heat conductors. The trend in merging physics and finance was further shown by awarding the econophysicist Jean-Phillippe Bouchaud as Quant of the Year for 2016.

In terms of the equations, the most prominent trace of physics in economics and finance is the widespread use of the power-law behaviour, which tends to be closer to reality relative to the famous and easy-to-model exponential or Gaussian laws. The power-law stands for the relationship between two variables, where one variable is a function of the power of the other variable. Such a behaviour describes the distribution of many phenomena in biology or physics ranging from the activity patterns of neurons to the magnitude of earthquakes or solar flares. In finance, in particular, the power-law has been frequently used to model the distribution of magnitudes of price returns.

It is worth pointing out that in physics, the presence of the power-law behaviour in certain distributions is linked to phase transitions of the systems. The exponents of the power-law behaviour are referred to as critical exponents of the physical system. It was further shown that systems with similar critical exponents resemble the same dynamics. Besides, distribution-wise the power-law behaviour forms a set of different attractors for which the central limit theorem and law of large numbers may not hold. Let us now recall the requirements for finite mean and variance.

The power-law is mathematically given as:

$$f(x) = \alpha x^{-\beta}, \tag{29.1}$$

with β being the power of the power-law behaviour. Such a relationship is scale-invariant. When $\beta > 2$, the distribution has a finite mean, and when $\beta > 3$ it has a finite variance. A useful method to reveal the presence of power-law behaviour is the log-transform, which makes the relationship linear:

$$\log(f(x)) = \alpha' - \beta \log(x). \tag{29.2}$$

For the sake of completeness, the power-law behaviour is defined as:

```
.quantQ.ephys.powerLaw:{[alpha;beta;x]
   // alpha -- the coefficient
   // beta -- the power of the distribution
   // x -- the independent variable
   :alpha*(x xexp neg beta);
};
```

29.1 AGENT-BASED MODELLING

The power-law, however, is not the main scope of this chapter, even though it traditionally stands as a main selling point of physics in economics and finance. Econophysics has another significant contribution to economics and finance: the Agent-Based Computational Models, or ABMs. It is not entirely fair to attribute ABMs to physics, as its exact origin is instead the von Neuman machine, a cells-on-the-grid-based theoretical model of a machine which is supposed to reproduce itself.

The equation-driven approach to describe a particular system is to express its properties based on the macro-dynamics. This usually requires the presence of an equilibrium in the system. On the other hand, the agent-driven approach is based on describing the system as an explicit ensemble of interacting agents, or units, which follow some micro-driven rules. Such an approach may lead to a much more full range of phenomena going beyond the equilibrium. For instance, the agent-based approach may give rise to steady-states or phase transitions. Also, some problems are more naturally described through interacting agents rather than by the system dynamics.

29.1.1 Agent-Based Models in Society

Imagine you have the funds to make a movie based on a famous fantasy novel. The novel includes – besides other plots and stories – an epic final battle involving thousands of units ranging from desperate human villagers to a professional armada with shiny cavalry, to units riding elephants, to scary ogres and even dragons. To make the movie realistic and get your funds back, you need to employ state-of-the-art computer graphic to get all the animated objects into realistic scenes, but, more importantly, you have to solve the problem of how you want to drive the movement of units across the battlefield.

A naive approach would be to define and model the movement of every single unit explicitly from the first appearance on the horizon until its final breath or moments of glory. This approach is traditional and would likely be possible if a few units were involved. When we talk about an epic battle with a large number of units, such an approach is impractical.

Also, realistic battles require that units are organised in groups following their leader. Each type of unit responds to other types differently – humans hate ogres and have a fear of dragons, cavalry lead by heroic characters with spears could scare a dragon while horses panic when encountering elephants. These features nicely colour the storyline of a book and thus have to be seen over the battlefield. Furthermore, the units cannot be perfectly synchronous; they follow their orders but also what they see around them. Such rules inevitably lead to some chaotic behaviour and discordance. Enforcing straight rules on behaviour would not be realistic even in the fantasy genre.

The features revealed in the previous paragraphs naturally call for modelling the units on the battlefield following explicit rules. The agent-based models are a natural framework. The battlefield is then modelled as an ensemble of agents, where each agent represents a unit. Each unit has its type and characteristics. The agent can be a scared villager simply following others, prone to panic when seeing any inhuman creature, or a strategically thinking hero who knows their enemies and saves the day through their ingenuity and good luck. The agents are placed over some topology which affects their line of sight, and their movement is affected by the terrain they encounter. The battle is then just a step-by-step simulation of every agent. Since there is a randomness in the actions of agents, it should contain plenty of checkpoints to keep the overall simulation in check and in line with the main themes.

In the real world, epic battles in movies may or may not be an essential part of our life. An example which is more important for our daily lives is emergency evacuation planning for city buildings. Especially in the case of large and complex buildings where the exit cannot be in the line of sight, proper planning of escape routes is a vital safety measure. Modelling of safe routes through an equation-based approach is not trivial, as a flow of people cannot be easily described on a macroscopic level. On the other hand, we can formulate rules of human decision. We can even conduct targeted surveys or behavioural laboratory experiments to correctly understand the factors which drive a human decision in similar situations.

The rules can include factors like preferring usage of a route the agent already knows vs a new route; even though the sign may suggest that the exit is behind the corner, the agent may prefer to return to a more familiar route. Another rule is the tendency to follow a crowd, where fellow escapees change an agent's behaviour even though he has seen the exit sign. The factor of panic and chaotic behaviour should also be considered. The model of emergency evacuation plans and exit signs can be then back-tested by using an agent-based model with agents following the behavioural rules. Agents will be thus moving through the provided topological layout responding to their environment.

Simulations can be evaluated in a statistical manner and the environment and emergency signs can be modified such that the probability of survival for agents is maximized. This approach can be used to find the optimum emergency setup or the existing one can be tested. We can also stress-test the emergency setup such that some of the existing features may fail, or the behavioural rules may change. It is apparent that this approach is very versatile and provides an intuitive tool for architects to consider when designing buildings.

Let us now leave the epic battles and emergency evacuation plans and focus on finance.

29.1.2 Agent-Based Models in Finance

Finance and economics is another field where the agent-based models have been extensively used. For interested readers, we recommend Amman et al. (1996) as a first dive into the models in the field. The handbook shows models describing the dynamics of organisations, financial interactions, or social dynamics. It also illustrates how agent-based models can be used to model efficient markets or how to understand politics in society. The particular interest across the book is dedicated to learning and its effects on the evolving systems. The detailed overview of all possible models is beyond the scope of this chapter. The agent-based models are becoming more widespread across the significant economic and financial outlets.

As an illustration of a particular agent-based model in finance, let us mention Lavička et al. (2016), titled "Sand in the Wheels or Wheels in the Sand? Tobin Taxes and Market Crashes", where the authors focus on modelling the financial transaction tax – or Tobin tax – through the lenses of the agent-based models. Policymakers consider the financial transaction tax as a means to offset negative risk externalities. The academic research does not provide sufficient insights into the effects of financial transaction taxes on financial markets. The reason is that most of the theoretical and empirical research has been focused on Gaussian variance as a measure of volatility. In this paper, the authors argue that it is crucial to understand the relationship between price jumps, Gaussian variance, and financial transaction taxes.

Namely, Gaussian variance is not necessarily a problem per se; the non-normality of return distribution caused by price jumps not only affects the performance of many risk-hedging algorithms but directly influences the frequency of catastrophic market events. To study the relationship as mentioned above, the authors used an agent-based model of financial markets based on Raberto et al. (2003) and Mannaro et al. (2008). The model mimics the behaviour of artificial heterogeneous traders. Their market interaction leads to the price dynamics of financial assets satisfying the well-known stylised facts of clustering volatility, non-zero skewness, and higher kurtosis, or price jumps. There are four types of agents based on their behaviour: random traders, fundamentalist traders, momentum traders, and contrarian traders.

The results show that the relationship between FTTs and price jumps is intricate. This result implies that regulators may face a trade-off between overall variance and price jumps when designing optimal tax. The conclusion derived from the agent-based model cannot be described by an equation which in itself illustrates the power of the computational approach.

Since ABMs allow us to provide a much more general description of a system, one may ask why they have not replaced equation-driven systems. The answer is obvious: expensive numerical simulation is required to obtain a solution from an agent-based system. Thus, agent-based systems are usually thought of as "black box" and intractable. With ever increasing computational capabilities and the power of q, ABMs are proving their value and earning a position as a trusted method to model economic and financial systems.

In the following section, we focus on another model: the Ising model for financial markets. We implement the model in q and show that q can be easily used outside of the natural time series domain.

29.2 ISING AGENT-BASED MODEL FOR FINANCIAL MARKETS

The agent-based model based on the Ising model of ferromagnetism is the main scope of this chapter. We first review the Ising model in physics and then recast it into the model of interacting traders, who trade one or more assets and form the opinion on the price based on the mutual interaction.

29.2.1 Ising Model in Physics

The Ising model is a theoretical model of ferromagnetism in statistical mechanics and detailed by Brush (1967). It describes the interaction of a system with a finite number of states. The very first version of the model can be dated back to 1924, when Ernst Ising, a German physicist, published his thesis in which he solved the one-dimensional model of the interacting magnetic dipole moments of atomic spins, which are in two discrete states denoted as ± 1. The one-dimensional formulation does not allow for phase transitions, which appear in higher-dimensions only.

The Ising model can be described as follows. Let us consider a d-dimensional lattice – or a graph – where each node of the lattice carries a spin, $\sigma = \pm 1$. The configuration of all spins for every lattice node determines the macroscopic properties of the lattice. Besides, the lattice nodes are interacting with neighbourhood nodes through an interaction term, and at the same time the entire lattice is under the influence of the external field.

29.2.2 Ising Model of Interacting Agents

Let us follow the formalism of Takaishi (2015), which is a multivariate generalisation of a standard Ising model for one asset as proposed by Bornholdt (2001). The model demonstrated the ability to mimic the basic stylised facts of price time series as observed in the markets; see, e.g. Yamano (2002), Kaizoji et al. (2002), and Krause and Bornholdt (2011).

The Ising model is defined as follows. Let us consider a set of $N = n \times n$ agents – traders in this case – placed on a square lattice, who trade K stocks. Each trader, i, forms a view about each asset, where the trader can be either bullish about asset k, the spin takes value $\sigma_i^{(k)} = +1$, or bearish about asset k, the spin takes value $\sigma_i^{(k)} = -1$. The spin reflects the desire of a trader to either buy or sell the asset. The opinion of a trader to be bullish/bearish is formed by the local field, an analogy to the local energy in the ferromagnetic material, given as:

$$\eta_i^{(k)}(t) = \sum_j^N I_{i,j}\sigma_i^{(k)}(t)\sigma_j^{(k)}(t) - \alpha\sigma_i^{(k)}(t)\left|\Pi^{(k)}(t)\right| + \sum_{l=1}^K \rho_{lk}\Pi^{(l)}(t), \tag{29.3}$$

where $I_{i,j}$ is a term describing an interaction of a trader i with its neighbourhood, the term α is anti-polarization of trader to the prevailing opinion, and ρ_{lk} is perceived correlation between asset k and other assets.

The interaction term is further assumed to have a zero diagonal while for non-diagonal terms it reflects the reach of interaction between traders. The nearest neighbour interaction can be described by the lower and upper diagonal being non-zero, usually equal to one, while the rest is zero. The correlation of the perceived relationship between assets is a free parameter of the model and can be set accordingly, with diagonal terms being equal to zero.

On that account, Bornholdt proposed the following updating procedure:

- At time t, the trader i is randomly chosen.
- The spin of the trader i is updated using the following updating procedure:

$$\sigma_i^{(k)}(t+1) = +1 \text{ with probability } p = \frac{1}{1+\exp\left(-2\beta\eta_i^{(k)}(t)\right)}, \tag{29.4}$$

$$\sigma_i^{(k)}(t+1) = -1 \text{ with probability } 1-p. \tag{29.5}$$

- Set time to $t \to t+1$.
- Calculate the market imbalance between buy and sell orders:

$$\Pi^{(k)}(t+1) = \sum_{j=1}^{N} \sigma_j^{(k)}(t+1). \tag{29.6}$$

- Continue the iteration.

The market imbalance reflects the price of the asset and serves as a proxy for the price. The price process can be further enhanced by considering a certain number of assets to be traded per agent as well as some market clearing mechanisms. In our approach, we stick to the basic model with the price process being equal to market imbalance.

29.2.3 Numerical Implementation

We now implement the Ising model as outlined in the previous section. Let us start with the simple case of $K = 1$. Every agent is described by the 2-dimensional integer coordinates (x, y). For the sake of simplicity, we build the one-dimensional Ising model. We consider an economy where agents live on a square lattice of the size 10×10:

```
nGrid:10j;
```

with the number of agents equal to 100:

```
nOfAgents:nGrid*nGrid;
```

The main grid is defined as a key table. Let us suggestively name it `wallStreet` as this table consists of the artificial traders in the market following the Ising model.

The reader is reminded that a keyed table in q is simply a map (i.e. dictionary) whose key and value are both tables. The cross function is handy here to create a nested column of coordinates:

```
wallStreet:([]agentNo:til nGrid*nGrid)!([]coord:{ x cross x}til nGrid);
```

Each trader has a view about the asset which is either bullish (spin equal to one) or bearish (spin equal to minus one). In the beginning, we randomly distribute the view about the asset according to the uniform distribution. We follow the literature and denote the view as spin:

```
wallStreet: update spin:(nGrid*nGrid)?(-1 1j) from wallStreet;
```

We can depict the initial distribution of the market sentiment using qPad and a trick we have used several times before. We select a subset from the table with a specific property, in this case, positive spine, and depict the coordinates of the selected traders using the scatter plot:

```
select x:coord[;0],y:coord[;1] from wallStreet where spin=1
```

The initial distribution of the bullish traders is depicted in Figure 29.1. The size of the grid used in the simulation is small, and the distribution of the bullish traders does not show any spatial pattern. The initial conditions represent a homogeneous dispersion of traders with a given market view.

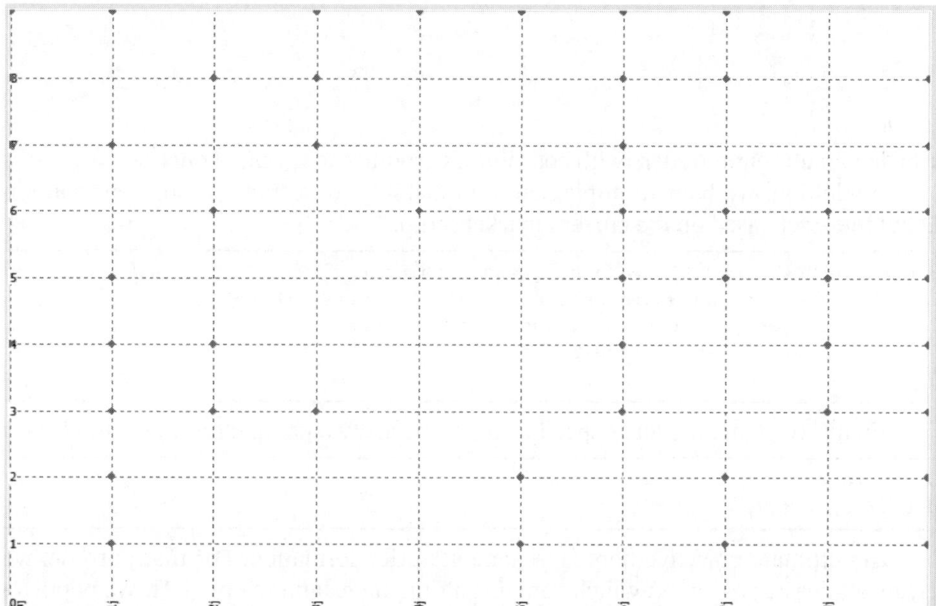

FIGURE 29.1 The initial distribution of the bullish traders in the Ising model

In addition, we consider a local interaction such that for every i, the $I_{i,j} = 1$ for every j which lies in the surrounding eight squares around trader i and zero otherwise. For that purpose, we utilise the two-dimensional coordinate grid as defined in the wallStreet table. In order to incorporate the function $I_{i,j}$, we define a function which selects for every specified point a set of eight neighbourhood coordinates. In addition, we consider the cyclic boundary conditions to mimic the infinite economy. The function is defined as:

```
.quantQ.ephys.getSquareAround:{[nGrid;coord]
   // nGrid -- the overall size of the grid for cyclic conditions
   // coord -- 2-dimensional coordinate
   grid:(cross).{((y+-1 0 1)mod x)}[nGrid]each coord;
   // exclude the point itself
   :grid except enlist coord;
};
```

We can illustrate the functionality of getSquareAround by selecting a subset of the table wallStreet around point (0;1):

```
select from wallStreet where coord in .quantQ.ephys.getSquareAround[nGrid
    ↪ ;(0;1)]
```

```
agentNo| coord spin
-------| ----------
0      | 0 0   -1
2      | 0 2   -1
10     | 1 0   -1
11     | 1 1   1
12     | 1 2   1
90     | 9 0   -1
91     | 9 1   -1
92     | 9 2   1
```

which contains eight traders with coordinates around the specified one.

In addition, we have to implement a probability for a trader to form an opinion about the asset based on the current market setup:

```
.quantQ.ephys.probPositiveSpin:{[beta;localEnergy]
   // beta -- the paratemer proportional to inverse temperature
   // localEnergy -- the local energy of a trader
   :1.0%(1+ exp[-2*beta*localEnergy]);
};
```

Finally, the Ising model as specified above needs two parameters *alpha* and *beta*:

```
alpha:10.0;
beta:2.0;
```

The ultimate objective here is to generate price formation. For that purpose, we create a table priceIsing which contains a time index and the price Π. We populate it with an initial randomly generated value.

```
priceIsing:([] t:0,();price:(sum exec spin from wallStreet));
```

Thus, we have fully specified the main objects for the Ising model. We create a dictionary of input parameters in order to be able to use the convergence function:

```
isingModel:
((`nGrid`nOfAgents`alpha`beta`getSquareAround`wallStreet`probPositiveSpin`
    ↪ priceIsing)!(nGrid;nOfAgents;alpha;beta;.quantQ.ephys.
    ↪ getSquareAround;wallStreet;.quantQ.ephys.probPositiveSpin;priceIsing
    ↪ ));
```

We are now equipped with all we need to define the main function, which performs one step of the iteration in the Ising model. In this one step, one trader is randomly chosen and her sentiment is updated according to the dynamics described in the previous section. Once the sentiment is updated, a new price is generated. The function `oneRunIsing` takes as an argument the dictionary from the previous code snippet, updates it, and returns the same object. The function reads:

```
.quantQ.ephys.oneRunIsing:{[isingModel]
    // isingModel -- object with all data
    // randomly choose one candidate to update
    pivot:2?isingModel[`nGrid];
    // recover price
    price:last isingModel[`priceIsing][`price];
    t:last isingModel[`priceIsing][`t];
    // calculate local energy
    term1: (first exec spin from isingModel[`wallStreet] where coord in
        ↪ enlist pivot)*sum
        exec spin from isingModel[`wallStreet] where coord in isingModel[`
            ↪ getSquareAround][isingModel[`nGrid];pivot];
    term2:isingModel[`alpha]*abs[price]*first exec spin from isingModel[`
        ↪ wallStreet]
        where coord in enlist pivot;
    localEnergy:term1-term2;
    // probability for positive spin
    pPos:isingModel[`probPositiveSpin][isingModel[`beta];localEnergy];
    // set the new spin
    newSpin:$[(first 1?1.0)<=pPos;1;-1];
    isingModel[`wallStreet]:update spin:newSpin from isingModel[`wallStreet]
        where coord in enlist pivot;
    // update price and time in the priceIsing table
    isingModel[`priceIsing]:isingModel[`priceIsing] upsert (t+1;sum exec
        ↪ spin from
        isingModel[`wallStreet]);
    :isingModel;
};
```

One run of the Ising model iteration can be performed as:

```
.quantQ.ephys.oneRunIsing[isingModel]
```

We restrained from publishing the output as it is a dictionary. We are interested in running a large number of steps, for which we use the converge operator / and save the output into a new object:

```
isingModelResult:.quantQ.ephys.oneRunIsing/[1000;isingModel];
```

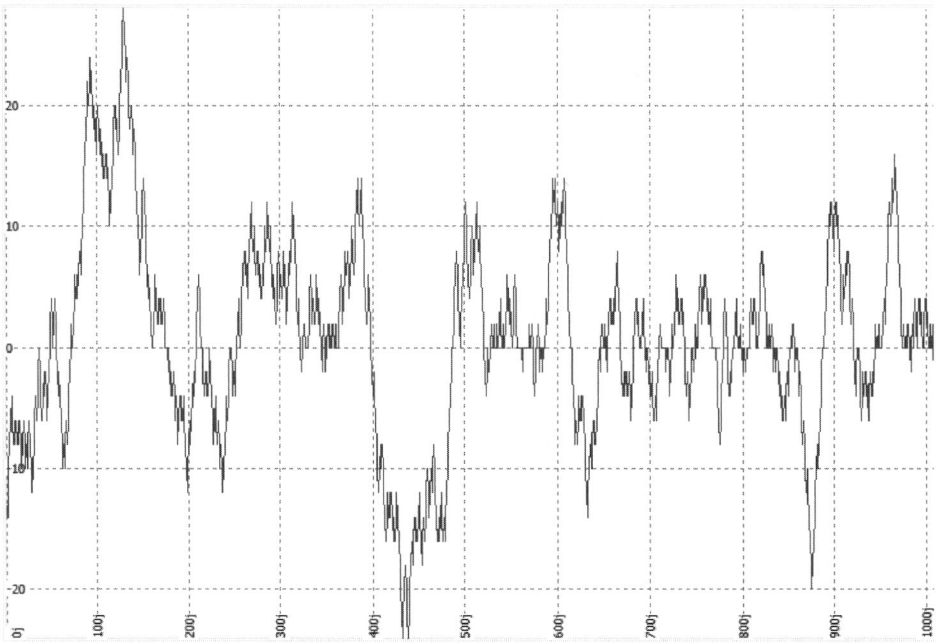

FIGURE 29.2 The price process of the Ising model

The result of interest is the price process, which can be viewed by selecting the `priceIsing` table from the `isingModel` object:

```
isingModelResult[`priceIsing]
```

Figure 29.2 contains the price process of the Ising model as evaluated above. Visual inspection reveals that the price driven by the simulated Ising model undergoes sudden drops, as can be seen around the index time 400. To confirm the stylised facts, however, one would have to perform proper statistical analysis on a large number of simulations and confirm stylised facts, for example, fat tails of returns, serial correlation and long memory of volatility.

29.3 CONCLUSION

We can thus conclude that q is flexible enough to create and simulate agent-based computational models. The model presented in this section is straightforward and simple. It lacks any object-oriented approach, which is so popular among the agent-based modelling community. Typically, the agents are objects as are the links between agents. See for example a C++ based library Zarja zar, which defines agents and links between agents as objects, whose properties can be defined in a modular way.

In our approach, we have instead aimed for a demonstration of the possibility to approach the agent-based models in addition to time series analysis connected to q.

The model presented in this section can still answer many interesting questions, namely those related to the emergence of critical phenomena in the system. The presented model can be extended by including more than one asset and analysing the correlation of prices through correlation of agents' interest.

The ability of the model to capture the stylised facts of the financial time series gives another use for the presented model: a generator of random financial time series for testing of models/analytics. This is particularly useful when one needs some synthetic data to develop for instance an analytic suite and test its performance under realistic data. Besides, the model can be set up as a data generator which is captured by a ticker plant and stored into the database – another potential use of the data.

We encourage the reader to run his or her simulation and consider the following research questions, among others, to be investigated numerically:

- What if the interaction is random? Do a random interaction on every turn.
- What if the traders can interact with more traders? Extend the neighbourhood around each trader. Make the number of traders to interact with random.
- What if the traders can trade more than one asset? Extend the number of assets.
- What if the traders can trade more than one unit? Extend the model for the non-uniform amount to be traded.
- What if the system is vast? Extend the model to include thousands of traders.
- What are the stylised facts assumed for the price process of traded assets? Confirm whether it is satisfied by the price time series generated by the model described in this section.

CHAPTER 30

Epilogue: Art

Data science and machine learning are frequently presented as an art rather than an exact science given their complex nature and lack of universal recipes. Certain meta-parameters do not always allow for simple formulas and construction of the most suitable models is often the result of experience and a certain form of craftsmanship. In that spirit, we would like to conclude this book with a bit of pure art.

The motivation for this chapter is the work of Czech artist Zdenek Sykora. Sykora is well known for his black-and-white geometric paintings, the Structure. His art was also affected by the collaboration with mathematician Jaroslav Blazek which resulted in computer-assisted art pieces, where the artist combined various abstract elements and deterministic rules. What was unique to Sykora was the usage of mathematical rules and the emphasis he put on them. This led to the author's "line" era, where he worked with clusters of curved lines, whose properties – like thickness, position, colour or curvature – were solely driven by mathematical expressions. A famous piece from this era is *Lines No 24*.

We look at the early stage of Sykora's paintings and use q to produce some black-and-white geometric art which follows the artist's philosophy: the combination of geometric patterns and randomness driven by formulas. To depict the drawings themselves, we use qPad. The objective is not to provide correctly rendered graphics but rather give an artistic taster.

We begin with the definition of our canvas:

```
dimensionOfCanvas:1000;
canvasEmpty: update x: first each coord, y: last each coord from ([] coord:
    ↪ t cross t:(til 1000));
```

The canvas is a table with coordinates. We have chosen a square canvas with dimension 1000×1000.

Further, we add a colour feature. We consider a black-and-white picture, and thus a value 1 for black and -1 for white. We use a negative value for white as the operation of changing the colour will be mathematically represented by multiplying the colour feature by -1 (or changing the byte).

We add the colour feature and set to black as:

```
canvasEmpty: update colour: 1 from canvasEmpty;
```

At this point, the empty canvas is ready and we may start creating geometrical pictures. We will create the following pattern.

We place a geometrical object on the canvas. The area covered by the object will change the colour and every pixel will be changed independently. In other words, we place the object and identify all the points within the object. Every point will then get its colour feature multiplied by −1, which will invert the colour.

We start with circles and define a function of two arguments: the diameter of a circle and the canvas. The function will return the canvas where a circle of a given diameter has been placed and all the points within the circle have their colour inverted.

```
.quantQ.art.placeCircle: {[diameter; canvas]
   // diameter -- diameter of the circle in units
   // canvas -- table with canvas to be modified
   // random position
   position: (first 1?1+exec max x from canvas;first 1?1+exec max y from
       ↪ canvas);
   // find a circle around the position and invert colour
   :update colour:colour*neg[1] from canvas where
       diameter>=sqrt[xexp[x-position[0];2]+xexp[y-position[1];2]];
};
```

We also create a similar function which will randomly place a square:

```
.quantQ.art.placeSquare: {[side; canvas]
   // diameter -- length of side of a square
   // canvas -- table with canvas to be modified
   // random position
   position: (first 1?1+exec max x from canvas;first 1?1+exec max y from
       ↪ canvas);
   // find a circle around the position and invert colour
   :update colour:colour*neg[1] from canvas where
       (x-position[0])<=0.5*side,
       (x-position[0])>=-0.5*side,
       (y-position[1])<=0.5*side,
       (y-position[1])>=-0.5*side;
};
```

To plot the canvas using qPad, we convert the canvas into a slightly different table, where each colour will have its variable – column. Such a construction will allow us to choose a different colour in the editor for each different value. We use `uj` to join the two colours by the value of the `x` coordinate. This will produce cases where one of the variables for colour will be empty while the other colour will be populated. If we want to plot such a table, the missing values will take a numeric value of $-\infty$ and spoil the graphic. For that reason, we replace the missing values by −1, which will create a buffer with the `y` coordinate equal to −1, where all those points will be "stored".

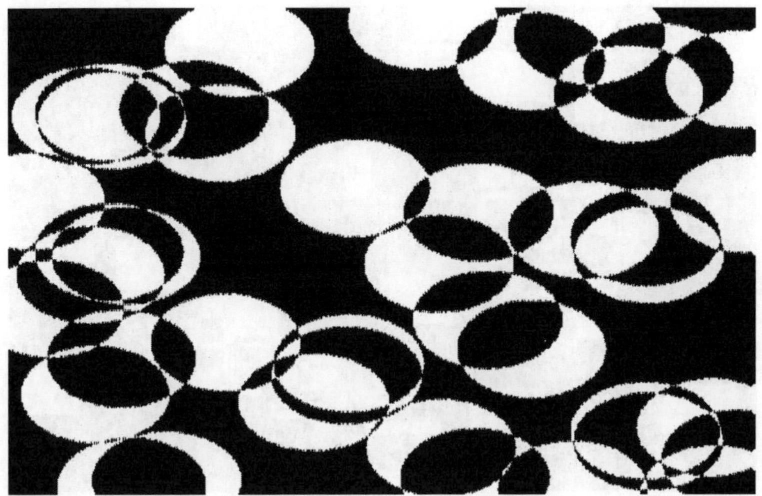

FIGURE 30.1 Circles

```
// convert into table
.quantQ.art.pivotColours:{[canvas]
   // canvas -- table with canvas and patterns
   :update (-1)^colour1, (-1)^colour2 from
       (select x, colour1:y from canvas where colour=1) uj
       (select x, colour2:y from canvas where colour=-1);
};
```

Let us produce two canvases, one with circles and one with squares. In each picture, we place 42 objects. First, we produce a random circle pattern:

```
canvas1: canvasEmpty;
canvas1: ( .quantQ.art.placeCircle[100;]/)[42;canvas1];
canvas1: .quantQ.art.pivotColours[canvas1];
```

and then a random square pattern:

```
canvas2: canvasEmpty;
canvas2: ( .quantQ.art.placeSquare[100;]/)[42;canvas2];
canvas2: .quantQ.art.pivotColours[canvas2];
```

Figure 30.1 depicts `canvas1` and we call it Circles. Figure 30.2 depicts `canvas2`, which we will refer to as Squares. The rendering is far from that of a professional artist, but the idea behind the pictures should be visible. The interplay of geometric objects and randomness follow Sykora's spirit.

Let us add one more step beyond pure randomness and put some mathematical order into our art. Instead of the uniform random placement, we use a more advanced rule to place the objects. In particular, we increase the likelihood of setting an object towards the upper-right direction using the quadratic transform $\propto x^2$.

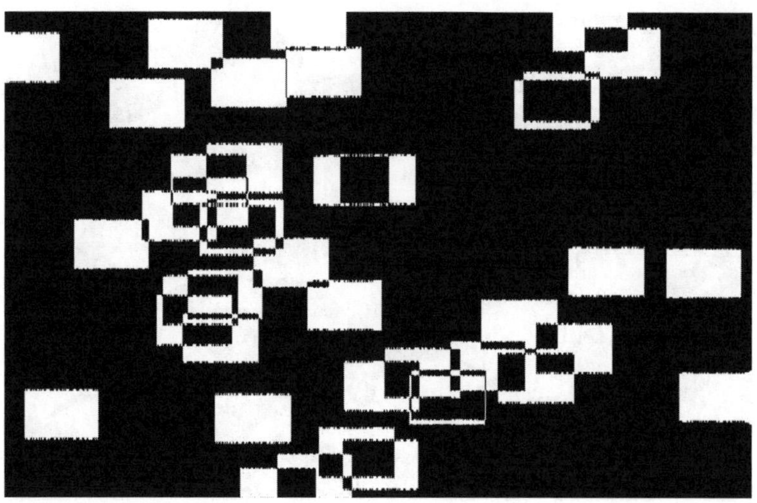

FIGURE 30.2 Squares

```
.quantQ.art.placeCircleGradient: {[diameter; canvas]
    // diameter -- diamater of the circle in units
    // canvas -- table with canvas to be modified
    // random position, position is float
    position: (sqrt first 1? t*t:1+exec max x from canvas;sqrt first 1?t*t
        ↪ :1+exec max y from canvas);
    // find a circle around the position and invert the colour
    :update colour:colour*neg[1] from canvas where
        diameter>=sqrt[xexp[x-position[0];2]+xexp[y-position[1];2]];
};
```

FIGURE 30.3 Gradient Circles

Let us produce another canvas with a new quadratic rule:

```
canvas3: canvasEmpty;
canvas3: ( .quantQ.art.placeCircleGradient[100;]/)[42;canvas3];
canvas3: .quantQ.art.pivotColours[canvas3];
```

Figure 30.3 depicts canvas3 and we call it Gradient Circles. The difference is apparent; there is an order in the random objects.

The presented art taster produced by q and qPad aims to encourage readers to step outside of the data science box. We can easily employ different mathematical rules to place the objects and combine their shape and properties. The readers can provide their ideas and share them with us. We have to keep in mind that there is no such thing as a bad picture; the only bad picture is no picture.

Bibliography

Thoughts on art and life by da vinci leonardo, project gutenberg. https://www.gutenberg.org/ebooks/29904. Accessed: 2018-09-30.

Google search. https://www.google.com/intl/en_uk/search/howsearchworks/. Accessed: 2018-09-30.

Fisher's iris dataset. https://archive.ics.uci.edu/ml/datasets/iris. Accessed: 2018-09-30.

Jupyter notebook. http://jupyter.org/. Accessed: 2018-09-30.

Jupyterq. https://github.com/KxSystems/jupyterq, a. Accessed: 2018-09-30.

Q insight pad. http://www.qinsightpad.com/, b. Accessed: 2018-09-30.

Qstudio. http://www.timestored.com/qstudio/download. Accessed: 2018-09-30.

How many tic-tac-toe (noughts and crosses) games are possible? http://www.se16.info/hgb/tictactoe.htm. Accessed: 2018-08-31.

vim editor. https://www.vim.org/. Accessed: 2018-09-30.

Zarja. https://sourceforge.net/projects/zarja/. Accessed: 2018-08-31.

Ravi P Agarwal, Kanishka Perera, and Sandra Pinelas. *An introduction to complex analysis*. Springer Science & Business Media, 2011.

C. C. Aggarwal, *Neural Networks and Deep Learning: A Textbook*, Springer, 2018.

Rakesh Agrawal, Ramakrishnan Srikant, et al. Fast algorithms for mining association rules. In *Proc. 20th int. conf. very large data bases, VLDB*, volume 1215, pages 487–499, 1994.

Hirotugu Akaike. A new look at the statistical model identification. *IEEE transactions on automatic control*, 19(6):716–723, 1974.

Hans M Amman, Leigh Tesfatsion, David A Kendrick, Kenneth L Judd, and John Rust. *Handbook of computational economics*, volume 2. Elsevier, 1996.

Torben G Andersen, Dobrislav Dobrev, and Ernst Schaumburg. Jump-robust volatility estimation using nearest neighbor truncation. *Journal of Econometrics*, 169(1):75–93, 2012.

Stevan Apter. Treetable: a case-study in q. *Vector*, 24(4):42, 2010.

George Arfken. Discrete orthogonality–discrete fourier transform. *Mathematical Methods for Physicists*, 3:787–792, 1985.

Peter Auer, Nicolo Cesa-Bianchi, and Paul Fischer. Finite-time analysis of the multiarmed bandit problem. *Machine learning*, 47(2-3):235–256, 2002a.

Peter Auer, Nicolo Cesa-Bianchi, Yoav Freund, and Robert E Schapire. The nonstochastic multiarmed bandit problem. *SIAM journal on computing*, 32(1):48–77, 2002b.

József Beck and József Beck. *Combinatorial games: tic-tac-toe theory*, volume 114. Cambridge University Press, 2008.

Michele Bergamelli, Jan Novotnỳ, and Giovanni Urga. Maximum non-extensive entropy block bootstrap for non-stationary processes. *L'Actualité économique*, 91(1-2):115–139, 2015.

Daniel Bernoulli. Exposition of a new theory on the measurement of risk. In *The Kelly Capital Growth Investment Criterion: Theory and Practice*, pages 11–24. World Scientific, 2011.

Stefan Bornholdt. Expectation bubbles in a spin model of markets: Intermittency from frustration across scales. *International Journal of Modern Physics C*, 12(05):667–674, 2001.

Jeffry A. Borror. *q for Mortals Version 3: An Introduction to q Programming*. q4m LLC, 3 edition, 2015.

Ronald Newbold Bracewell and Ronald N Bracewell. *The Fourier transform and its applications*, volume 31999. McGraw-Hill New York, 1986.

Leo Breiman. Bagging predictors. *Machine learning*, 24(2):123–140, 1996.

Leo Breiman. Random forests. *Machine learning*, 45(1):5–32, 2001.

Markus M Breunig, Hans-Peter Kriegel, Raymond T Ng, and Jörg Sander. Lof: identifying density-based local outliers. In *ACM sigmod record*, volume 29, pages 93–104. ACM, 2000.

L Brieman, JH Friedman, RA Olshen, and CJ Stone. Classification and regression trees. wadsworth. *Inc, Pacific Grove, CA*, 1984.

Stephen G Brush. History of the lenz-ising model. *Reviews of modern physics*, 39(4):883, 1967.

Sébastien Bubeck, Nicolo Cesa-Bianchi, et al. Regret analysis of stochastic and nonstochastic multi-armed bandit problems. *Foundations and Trends® in Machine Learning*, 5(1):1–122, 2012.

Michael Bulmer. *Francis Galton: pioneer of heredity and biometry*. JHU Press, 2003.

Apostolos N Burnetas and Michael N Katehakis. Optimal adaptive policies for sequential allocation problems. *Advances in Applied Mathematics*, 17(2):122–142, 1996.

Apostolos N Burnetas and Michael N Katehakis. Optimal adaptive policies for markov decision processes. *Mathematics of Operations Research*, 22(1):222–255, 1997.

Ricardo JGB Campello, Davoud Moulavi, Arthur Zimek, and Jörg Sander. Hierarchical density estimates for data clustering, visualization, and outlier detection. *ACM Transactions on Knowledge Discovery from Data (TKDD)*, 10(1):5, 2015.

Guillaume Chaslot, Sander Bakkes, Istvan Szita, and Pieter Spronck. Monte-carlo tree search: A new framework for game ai. In *AIIDE*, 2008.

Alonzo Church. *The Calculi of Lambda-Conversion*. Annals of Mathematical Studies. Princeton University Press, 1941.

Olive Jean Dunn. Estimation of the means of dependent variables. *The Annals of Mathematical Statistics*, pages 1095–1111, 1958.

Bradley Efron. Bootstrap methods: another look at the jackknife. In *Breakthroughs in statistics*, pages 569–593. Springer, 1992.

Bradley Efron, Trevor Hastie, Iain Johnstone, Robert Tibshirani, et al. Least angle regression. *The Annals of statistics*, 32(2):407–499, 2004.

Bjørn Eraker. Do stock prices and volatility jump? reconciling evidence from spot and option prices. *The Journal of Finance*, 59(3):1367–1403, 2004.

Brian P Flannery, Saul A Teukolsky, William H Press, and William T Vetterling. *Numerical recipes in C: The art of scientific computing*, volume 2. Cambridge university press, 1988.

Yoav Freund and Robert E Schapire. A decision-theoretic generalization of on-line learning and an application to boosting. *Journal of computer and system sciences*, 55(1):119–139, 1997.

Jerome H Friedman. Multivariate adaptive regression splines. *The annals of statistics*, pages 1–67, 1991.

Francis Galton. Regression towards mediocrity in hereditary stature. *The Journal of the Anthropological Institute of Great Britain and Ireland*, 15:246–263, 1886.

Sylvain Gelly and David Silver. Combining online and offline knowledge in uct. In *Proceedings of the 24th international conference on Machine learning*, pages 273–280. ACM, 2007.

Leo A Goodman and William H Kruskal. Measures of association for cross classifications. *Journal of the American statistical association*, 49(268):732–764, 1954.

Loukas Grafakos. *Classical fourier analysis*, volume 2. Springer, 2008.

HL Gray, RW Thompson, and GV McWilliams. A new approximation for the chi-square integral. *Mathematics of Computation*, 23(105):85–89, 1969.

Simon Hawkins, Hongxing He, Graham Williams, and Rohan Baxter. Outlier detection using replicator neural networks. In *International Conference on Data Warehousing and Knowledge Discovery*, pages 170–180. Springer, 2002.

Lütkepohl Helmut. *New introduction to multiple time series analysis*. Springer Berlin Heidelberg, 2005.

Sture Holm. A simple sequentially rejective multiple test procedure. *Scandinavian journal of statistics*, pages 65–70, 1979.

Junya Honda and Akimichi Takemura. An asymptotically optimal policy for finite support models in the multiarmed bandit problem. *Machine Learning*, 85(3):361–391, 2011.

Roger Hui. The TAO of J. http://code.jsoftware.com/wiki/Essays/The_TAO_of_J, January 2006.

Roger K. W. Hui. *An Implementation of J*. Iverson Software Inc., 1992.

Roger K. W. Hui. Rank and uniformity. In *APL 95 Conference Proceedings*, June 1995.

Kenneth Eugene Iverson. *A Programming Language*. Wiley, 1962.

Kenneth Eugene Iverson. Notation as a tool of thought (Turing award lecture). http://www.eecg.toronto.edu/~jzhu/csc326/readings/iverson.pdf, 1979.

Taisei Kaizoji, Stefan Bornholdt, and Yoshi Fujiwara. Dynamics of price and trading volume in a spin model of stock markets with heterogeneous agents. *Physica A: Statistical Mechanics and its Applications*, 316(1-4):441–452, 2002.

Michael N Katehakis and Herbert Robbins. Sequential choice from several populations. *Proceedings of the National Academy of Sciences of the United States of America*, 92(19):8584, 1995.

Edwin M Knorr, Raymond T Ng, and Vladimir Tucakov. Distance-based outliers: algorithms and applications. *The VLDB Journal – The International Journal on Very Large Data Bases*, 8(3–4):237–253, 2000.

Levente Kocsis and Csaba Szepesvári. Bandit based monte-carlo planning. In *European conference on machine learning*, pages 282–293. Springer, 2006.

Sebastian M Krause and Stefan Bornholdt. Spin models as microfoundation of macroscopic financial market models. *arXiv preprint arXiv:1103.5345*, 2011.

Hans-Peter Kriegel, Peer Kroger, Erich Schubert, and Arthur Zimek. Outlier detection in arbitrarily oriented subspaces. In *Data Mining (ICDM), 2012 IEEE 12th International Conference on*, pages 379–388. IEEE, 2012.

Jack B Kuipers et al. *Quaternions and rotation sequences*, volume 66. Princeton university press Princeton, 1999.

Tze Leung Lai and Herbert Robbins. Asymptotically efficient adaptive allocation rules. *Advances in applied mathematics*, 6(1):4–22, 1985.

Hynek Lavička, Tomáš Lichard, and Jan Novotný. Sand in the wheels or wheels in the sand? tobin taxes and market crashes. *International Review of Financial Analysis*, 47:328–342, 2016.

Aleksandar Lazarevic and Vipin Kumar. Feature bagging for outlier detection. In *Proceedings of the eleventh ACM SIGKDD international conference on Knowledge discovery in data mining*, pages 157–166. ACM, 2005.

Suzanne S Lee. Jumps and information flow in financial markets. *The Review of Financial Studies*, 25(2):439–479, 2011.

Christina S Leslie, Eleazar Eskin, Adiel Cohen, Jason Weston, and William Stafford Noble. Mismatch string kernels for discriminative protein classification. *Bioinformatics*, 20(4):467–476, 2004.

Wei-Yin Loh. Classification and regression trees. *Wiley Interdisciplinary Reviews: Data Mining and Knowledge Discovery*, 1(1):14–23, 2011.

James G MacKinnon. Numerical distribution functions for unit root and cointegration tests. *Journal of applied econometrics*, 11(6):601–618, 1996.

Benoit B Mandelbrot. *The fractal geometry of nature*, volume 1. WH freeman New York, 1982.

Katiuscia Mannaro, Michele Marchesi, and Alessio Setzu. Using an artificial financial market for assessing the impact of tobin-like transaction taxes. *Journal of Economic Behavior & Organization*, 67(2):445–462, 2008.

Christopher D Manning, Prabhakar Raghavan, and Hinrich Schütze. Scoring, term weighting and the vector space model. *Introduction to information retrieval*, 100:2–4, 2008.

Rosario N Mantegna and H Eugene Stanley. *Introduction to econophysics: correlations and complexity in finance*. Cambridge university press, 1999.

Michael S. Montalbano. A personal history of APL. http://ed-thelen.org/comp-hist/APL-hist.html, October 1982.

Douglas C Montgomery, Elizabeth A Peck, and G Geoffrey Vining. *Introduction to linear regression analysis*, volume 821. John Wiley & Sons, 2012.

James N Morgan and John A Sonquist. Problems in the analysis of survey data, and a proposal. *Journal of the American statistical association*, 58(302):415–434, 1963.

Amir Navot, Lavi Shpigelman, Naftali Tishby, and Eilon Vaadia. Nearest neighbor based feature selection for regression and its application to neural activity. In *Advances in Neural Information Processing Systems*, pages 996–1002, 2006.

Jan Novotny and Giovanni Urga. Testing for co-jumps in financial markets. *Journal of Financial Econometrics*, 16(1):118–128, 2017.

Karl Pearson. Liii. on lines and planes of closest fit to systems of points in space. *The London, Edinburgh, and Dublin Philosophical Magazine and Journal of Science*, 2(11):559–572, 1901.

Nick Psaris. *Q Tips: Fast, Scalable and Maintainable Kdb+*. Vector Sigma, 2015.

J Ross Quinlan. *C4. 5: programs for machine learning*. Elsevier, 2014.

Marco Raberto, Silvano Cincotti, Sergio M Focardi, and Michele Marchesi. Traders' long-run wealth in an artificial financial market. *Computational Economics*, 22(2-3):255–272, 2003.

BY Ricardo and RN Berthier. Modern information retrieval: the concepts and technology behind search second edition. *Addision Wesley*, 84(2), 2011.

Herbert Robbins and Sutton Monro. A stochastic approximation method. In *Herbert Robbins Selected Papers*, pages 102–109. Springer, 1985.

BA Rosenfeld. The history of non-euclidean geometry: Evolution of the concept of a geometrical space (trans: Shenitzer, a.), 1988.

David E Rumelhart, Geoffrey E Hinton, and Ronald J Williams. Learning representations by back-propagating errors. *nature*, 323(6088):533, 1986.

Bernhard Schölkopf, John C Platt, John Shawe-Taylor, Alex J Smola, and Robert C Williamson. Estimating the support of a high-dimensional distribution. *Neural computation*, 13(7):1443–1471, 2001.

Zbyněk Šidák. Rectangular confidence regions for the means of multivariate normal distributions. *Journal of the American Statistical Association*, 62(318):626–633, 1967.

David Silver, Aja Huang, Chris J Maddison, Arthur Guez, Laurent Sifre, George Van Den Driessche, Julian Schrittwieser, Ioannis Antonoglou, Veda Panneershelvam, Marc Lanctot, et al. Mastering the game of go with deep neural networks and tree search. *nature*, 529(7587):484, 2016.

David Silver, Julian Schrittwieser, Karen Simonyan, Ioannis Antonoglou, Aja Huang, Arthur Guez, Thomas Hubert, Lucas Baker, Matthew Lai, Adrian Bolton, et al. Mastering the game of go without human knowledge. *Nature*, 550(7676):354, 2017.

Robert H Somers. A new asymmetric measure of association for ordinal variables. *American sociological review*, pages 799–811, 1962.

Karen Sparck Jones. A statistical interpretation of term specificity and its application in retrieval. *Journal of documentation*, 28(1):11–21, 1972.

Nitish Srivastava, Geoffrey Hinton, Alex Krizhevsky, Ilya Sutskever, and Ruslan Salakhutdinov. Dropout: a simple way to prevent neural networks from overfitting. *The Journal of Machine Learning Research*, 15(1):1929–1958, 2014.

Richard S Sutton, Andrew G Barto, et al. *Reinforcement learning: An introduction*. MIT press, 1998.

Tetsuya Takaishi. Multiple time series ising model for financial market simulations. In *Journal of Physics: Conference Series*, volume 574, page 012149. IOP Publishing, 2015.

Ambuj Tewari and Peter L Bartlett. Optimistic linear programming gives logarithmic regret for irreducible mdps. In *Advances in Neural Information Processing Systems*, pages 1505–1512, 2008.

William R Thompson. On the likelihood that one unknown probability exceeds another in view of the evidence of two samples. *Biometrika*, 25(3/4):285–294, 1933.

Jan Tinbergen and A Hekscher. *Shaping the World Economy. Suggestions for an International Economic Policy.[With Forew. Bf A. Hekscher]*. Twentieth Century Fund, 1962.

Michel Tokic and Günther Palm. Value-difference based exploration: adaptive control between epsilon-greedy and softmax. In *Annual Conference on Artificial Intelligence*, pages 335–346. Springer, 2011.

Martinus Veltman et al. *Diagrammatica: the path to Feynman diagrams*. Number 4. Cambridge University Press, 1994.

John von Neumann. First draft of a report on edvac. Technical report, Moore School of Electrical Engineering, University of Pennsylvania, 1945.

Frank Wilcoxon. Some rapid approximate statistical procedures. *Annals of the New York Academy of Sciences*, 52(1):808–814, 1950.

Takuya Yamano. Bornholdt's spin model of a market dynamics in high dimensions. *International Journal of Modern Physics C*, 13(01):89–96, 2002.

Index

N

O

P